MICHIGAN

Yesterday and Today

By Ferris E. Lewis

HENRY FORD
COMMUNITY COLLEGE
DEARBORN, MICHIGAN

HILLSDALE EDUCATIONAL PUBLISHERS, INC.

HILLSDALE, MICHIGAN

PREFACE

MICHIGAN YESTERDAY AND TODAY was first published in 1956. Since that date it has been used in many of the schools and libraries throughout Michigan. In order to keep a book of this type up-to-date, because it contains much current information regarding recent changes that have taken place in the state, it becomes necessary to revise the material as often as possible. This is the fifth edition. All of the type has been reset. Some of the older material has been eliminated. Much new material has been added to make the content more interesting and explanatory. Many new pictures appear in this fifth edition in place of others that appeared in the earlier editions.

Again I wish to express my thanks to the many people and companies for their help and cooperation in supplying information and pictures for this new and enlarged fifth edition. Each individual and company has been credited for the picture, or pictures, that have been so obligingly supplied.

FERRIS E. LEWIS
September, 1965

TABLE OF CONTENTS

1. How Michigan Was Formed 1

2. The General Geography of Michigan 42

3. The Indians of Early Michigan 56

4. France Wins and Loses the Great Lakes Area (1608-1760) .. 76

5. Early Years of English Rule (1760-1775) 115

6. Revolution and Change (1775-1796) 127

7. The First Years of American Rule (1796-1815) 143

8. The Settlement of Southern Michigan 165

9. Pioneer Life in Southern Michigan 194

10. Early Cultural Development (1815-1875) 224

11. The Early Development of Water Transportation
    on the Great Lakes 244

12. The Sawmill Comes to Michigan 252

13. Early Beginnings in the Upper Peninsula 266

14. The Lumber Story (1860-1910) 291

15. The Great Lakes Carriers and Their Cargoes 327

16. More Industries Develop in Michigan 364

17. Agricultural Development Since 1860 407

18. Cultural and Political Growth Since 1875 443

19. The Upper Peninsula Today 464

20. The Northern Part of the Lower Peninsula 497

21. The Southern Part of the Lower Peninsula 527

22. Michigan's Southeastern Industrial Triangle 549

CHAPTER ONE

How Michigan Was Formed

MICHIGAN's interesting history began when the Great Lakes Basin was first beginning to form. This was some five, or more, billion years ago when the continent of North America was first beginning to develop. By that time according to geologists, and our modern Geiger counters, our slowly forming earth had solidified enough so that an outer crust of hard rock material, called granite, had formed. This granite had hardened from materials that had once been so hot that it was in liquid form. Such a rock is called igneous rock, for igneous rock is rock that has cooled from a molten state.

Beneath the granite layer a thick layer of still heavier rock, called basalt, also formed. Still farther toward the center of the earth, under the basalt layer were the hot, heavier materials that still make up the center of the earth. In these original rock masses, that lay near the surface of the earth, were locked most of the elements from which many of the earth's rocks and minerals were later formed. Slowly during the long ages of time that have passed since that early period, some of these elements have been gradually released from their original rock to give us the minerals that are so valuable to us today.

ARCHEOZOIC ERA

The forming of the earth's granite crust begins one of the earliest periods in Michigan's geologic history. Geologists call this era the Archeozoic Era. The Archeozoic Era lasted some three billion years or more. It is the longest and least known of all the periods in the history of our earth. Much of the thin granite layer of the earth spread down under vast oceans, just as it does today; but some of it, as the earth slowly cooled and shrank, was pushed upward above the surface of the water, on some parts of the earth, to form the first known land masses. One of the earliest granite land masses that formed during the first days of our cooling earth, is now called the Canadian Shield, or the Laurentian Upland. You will find this large rock area shown on any physical map of Canada, or of North America. As you look at the location of the Canadian Shield on a map, you will notice that it forms a large U that swings from the Arctic Ocean, on the north,

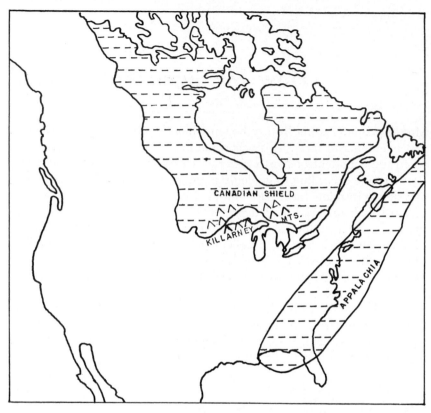

southward around Hudson Bay, and then east and northeast to the present rocky wastes of Labrador. Today, the Canadian Shield spreads across two million square miles and forms about half of all the land area of Canada. It is some of the oldest, exposed land area in the world. In the Canadian Shield, uranium, iron ore, copper, nickel, and gold are now being mined and hundreds of other valuable mineral deposits have also been located.

The Canadian Shield came as far south as northern Minnesota, northern Wisconsin, and the western half of the Upper Peninsula. Some of the present northern shore of Lake Superior is formed from the same granite rock that hardened into the Canadian Shield when the earth's crust was formed some five billion years ago.

Another land mass, known as Appalachia, was uplifted along with what is now the eastern coast of the United States. All the rest of what is now the continent of North America was still under an ancient ocean.

In many sections of the Trans-Canada Highway north of Lake Superior, the roadbed is cut through sheer rock of the ancient pre-Cambrian formation of the Canadian Shield. This section of the highway near Cavers, Ontario, is typical of the engineering achievement in opening this rugged wilderness area to motorists.

Very, very slowly the crust of the earth went on cooling and shrinking. Sometime during the long Archeozoic Era, the granite mass of the Canadian Shield was slowly forced upward along its center to form huge mountain ranges which are now called the Laurentian Mountains. These huge mountain ranges followed the same U shape from the Arctic to Labrador. As the granite rocks were pushed upward, under tremendous pressure, they sometimes weakened and cracked. Into these weak spots, hot, molten magma from the lower basalt layer pushed up from far below the surface of the land. Volcanoes were formed. In other places huge cracks, or fissures, in the earth's crust developed. From the volcanoes and fissures in the rock, hot lava, forced upward by tremendous pressures from below, spewed out across the rocky land to cover the original granite layer with basalt rock in some areas. The remains of many of these ancient volcanoes and lava flows can still be found in the area of the Canadian

Courtesy National Film Board of Canada

The Trans-Canada Highway curves along the shoreline of Nipigon Bay on the north side of Lake Superior. The rugged wilderness in this area was inaccessible to motorists until the Trans-Canada Highway went through in 1960.

Courtesy National Film Board of Canada

Lake Superior Beach, near Old Man River, Mile 131 of the Trans-Canada Highway, Ontario, Canada.

Shield. These Archeozoic rocks are so old and weathered that it is not known just how many mountain ranges were formed or how high they were in comparison with later mountains that have been formed from sedimentary rock.

As time passed, the lava flows became less and less active as the Canadian Shield slowly cooled. Later, much of the hard old granite of the Shield, and the basalt of the later lava flows, were slowly eroded away during the long Huronian Age that followed this early period of mountain building. Heat, cold, wind, sunshine, running water, chemical action, and the other weathering agents of our earth were constantly at work wearing away the exposed rocks of the Canadian Shield just as they are now doing in our time.

After three billion years or more, the long Archeozoic Era came to an end. It was a longer era than any single geologic era has been since that ancient time. The new era that followed is called the Proterozoic Era.

THE PROTEROZOIC OR ALGONKIN ERA

The word Proterozoic comes from the Greek and means former plus life. Although geologists start a new division here and give this new era a new name, one must be very careful to remember that there was no violent change in nature or in nature's way of doing things. Nature went on much as it had for long ages past. The difference lies in this: sometime during the Archeozoic Era, life had begun on our Earth. Traces of this early life can now be found in carbon, microscopic algae, and in imprints of segmented worms that are now found in the rocks that were formed during this early age.

The Proterozoic Era is divided into two main periods of time, the Huronian Period and the Keweenawan Period. The first, or Huronian Period, was a long period of erosion during which time vast sedimentary deposits were laid down on the bottoms of the seas that then bordered the Canadian Shield. Such sedimentary layers are called "strata." The second period, the Keweenawan, was again a period of extensive uplift and vulcanism when new mountain ranges were formed as the sedimentary layers, formed in the earlier Huronian Period, were folded upward in some areas as the earth's crust slowly shrank and buckled.

The Huronian Period

During this long period, vast deposits of eroded rock and mineral were slowly deposited in the seas that bordered the Canadian Shield. When the rains, or snows, fell on the Laurentian Mountains the run-off water, flowing back to the oceans, carried little pieces of rock or mineral that had been eroded from the larger masses, or freed by chemical action, with it to the oceans that then bordered the Canadian Shield, just as streams carry sediment and minerals into the oceans and lakes today. These little pieces of rock and mineral carried by the rivers, or blown by the wind settled onto the ocean floor. The heavier pieces were dropped near the mouths of the rivers. The finer particles along with minerals in solution were spread by waves and ocean currents farther out across the ocean floor. These little pieces of rock and mineral gradually settled to the ocean bottom where they later formed thick layers of sedimentary rock. These clastic sediments of pre-existing rock, or mineral, were sorted by wave action or ocean currents to become beds of sand, silt, clay, sand-silt-clay, or mineral composition. Later these particles were cemented together by materials that were deposited by running water. Other rocky debris settled in the valleys between the mountain peaks where it also slowly hardened into sedimentary rock.

Gradually, during long, long periods, these little pieces of rock and minerals that settled on the ocean floor became deeper and deeper until, by their own weight, they pressed the lower sediments together as the lighter water was squeezed out, or as they became dry land and thus dried out to form a kind of rock which is known today as sedimentary rock. The materials in these early sedimentary rock layers were carried into the seas, bordering the Canadian Shield, which at different times covered the area as the earth's crust slowly rose, or sank, over long periods of time. Some of these Paleozoic sedimentary rocks, because of heat, pressure, or chemical action, later became very hard. Sedimentary rocks, so changed, are known as metamorphic rocks. Sometimes it is difficult to tell metamorphic rocks from igneous ones.

It is by studying these layers of ancient sea deposits, that later became layers of sedimentary rock as the ages passed, that geologists have learned so much about how our earth has changed since its earliest beginning and also some things about the type of life that lived on the earth during each succeeding geologic period. These sedimentary rock layers are, as it were, the later pages of nature's history book as Nature has recorded the past in the rocks. By reading the story of our earth from each of the many rock layers, starting from the bottom, or oldest layer, and working upward, geologists have been able to learn much about what happened long ago. To geologists

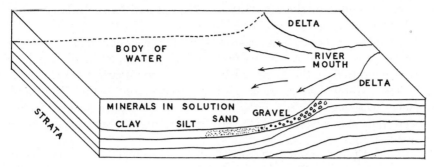

ROCK STRATA ARE MADE OF MATERIALS THAT WERE
DEPOSITED IN THE ANCIENT SEAS

time is measured not so much by years as it is by what materials and fossils are found in each of the underlying sedimentary rock layers.

The Huronian Period is known to us today as "the iron forming period," for it was during the Huronian Period, in our earth's history, that the vast iron ore deposits on the earth were formed on the bottoms of ancient seas in many places on the earth. This Huronian Period is of special interest to people studying Michigan's past for it was during this period that Michigan's iron deposits, like those of Minnesota, and Ungava, in Canada, were first formed.

The type of sediment, or mineral, carried down to the ocean depends on the kind of rock through which the cutting streams are traveling and also their rate of flow.

In the early part of the Huronian Period the bottom of the ancient sea, that lay in the Michigan Basin, was covered with what today is called common beach sand, or silica, that had been carried from the mountains.

Over this sandy bottom layer, the ancient rivers next spread a second layer of sediment in which there were small iron particles. This ancient sea, like others in other parts of the world at that time, was different from the seas, or oceans, as we know them today, in that it was rich in soluble iron and silica. This iron and silica may have been released from iron rich volcanic rocks as they slowly disintegrated and released their minerals.

As this iron and silica settled to the sea bottom, over many centuries of time, thick beds of sediment, several hundred feet in thickness, were deposited. The iron particles in this second layer seem to have been concentrated by chemical action and microscopic algae that took the iron minerals from the solution and deposited them along with the silica and other minerals as a rust-like deposit in the deeper troughs on the sea bottom. This second layer became what is known today as the mother lode.

Later, as ages of time passed, the area changed again and the sea became shallower. The rivers then brought in clay and silt which were deposited as the third layer over the iron-bearing beds.

These three layers are sometimes spoken of as the "iron-sandwich." In some areas this order of sedimentary deposit seems to have been repeated several times, thus giving rise to several layers of stratified rock.

Ages later, through pressure and the slowly rising of the land, these layers were compacted into hard sedimentary rock layers, or strata. The beach sands, on the bottom hardened into a sedimentary rock now called quartzite.

The second layer of iron and silica deposits formed a very hard sedimentary rock now known as "taconite" in Minnesota and "jasper" in Michigan. This layer contains about 20 to 35 per cent iron ore. Later the iron mineral oxidized, or rusted, to form brown limonite and red or blue hematite. The iron bearing layer, formed during the Huronian Period, is called the "mother lode." It has been the source of all the iron ore that has been carried down the Great Lakes by our fleet of ore carriers during the last one hundred years. What is more, this same sedimentary layer will be the source of nearly all of our domestic iron ore in the years to come, as you will learn when

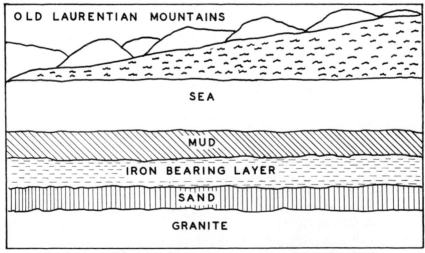

DURING THE HURONIAN PERIOD AN IRON BEARING
SEDIMENTARY LAYER WAS FORMED

you read about the latest methods of taking the iron ore from the "taconite," or "jasper" by the new beneficiation processes.

Above the second, or iron layer, the third layer of clay and silt changed into shale and in some places metamorphosed into slate.

In some parts of the ancient Huronian seas during this period, layers of limestone, or dolomite, were also laid down in areas where less sediment was being carried into the seas. Microscopic algae found in the Kona Dolomite, formed during this period and now being quarried near Marquette, gives us one of our first evidences of earliest life in the Great Lakes Basin.

The Keweenawan Period

During the later part of the Proterozoic Era, in the period known as the Keweenawan Period, new changes in the land formation came to what is now the western part of the Upper Peninsula and the surrounding area. Slowly, the sedimentary layers of the "iron sandwich" which had been deposited on the bottoms of ancient seas during the Huronian Period were pressed together and slowly forced upward in large ridges to form a new mountain chain, which geologists now call the Killarney Mountains. This upward folding and bending in the earth's changing crust may have been as little as an inch or so during a century. But, slowly the ancient sedimentary layers of the "iron sandwich" were bent upward in vast ridges of twisted rock to form a new mountain range which was once probably as high as some mountains that are now found in the western United States. This newly formed mountain range ran across what is now northern Minnesota, Wisconsin, and then northeast across what is Lake Superior and on into Canada. It covered an area about one hundred miles wide and about seven hundred miles long. Like all large mountain ranges that have been formed since the early Archeozoic Era, when they were formed of solid igneous or basalt rock, the Killarney Mountains developed where thick sedimentary layers had first accumulated. In this location they were the sediments from the older Laurentian Mountains of the Archeozoic Era. Part of these mountains crossed the western end of the Upper Peninsula and thus this ancient range of mountains is part of Michigan's early story.

The constant, ceaseless pressure that forced the Killarney Mountains to slowly rise caused weaknesses to develop in the earth's crust along the sharply bent ridges of the mountain folds. Hot basalt magma, forced upward by pressures far below, pushed its way through these weak spots to form new volcanoes that spewed hot basalt lava out onto the rising land. This lava covered the lower folds of bent sedimentary rock over vast areas of the mountain range. We know this because vast remains of these old lava flows can still be found in the area that was once the ancient Killarney Mountains. The Killarney lava flows covered many square miles around what is now Lake Superior. In some areas these lava flows seem to have been as thick in depth as four or five miles. In the Keweenaw Peninsula, the sharply tilted lava beds rest upon the edges of earlier Keweenawan sediments. In the Lake Superior area, there are some five hundred early lava flows that are known to us. Many extinct volcano cones have been found in the Keweenaw Peninsula. In fact, what later became some of Michigan's best copper mines were located in old volcanic conduits where copper was later deposited in the open spaces in the frothy amygdaloid ancient lava flow that cooled in the old volcanic conduits of the Killarney Mountains.

About this time in the Earth's history the first of our five Great Lakes seems to have been formed. This lake is now called Lake Superior. One basic difference in this lake from the other four Great Lakes is that it lies almost entirely within the Canadian Shield. The story of Lake Superior's formation is different from that of the other four Great Lakes and its bottom, unlike the others, is formed of granite and deep deposits of upper Keweenawan sedimentary rocks. Of the way in which Lake Superior was formed, geologists can only deduct from the evidences that nature left for us from so long ago. Around what is now Lake Superior, as has just been said, there were many ancient volcanoes in the Killarney Mountains that spewed hot lava from their fiery cones. As this magma, hot igneous fluid rock and gases, pressed upward in such vast amounts, it may have created a weak spot under the earth's crust and as the eruptions subsided the overlaying heavy crusts seems to have faulted and sank into the weakened under layers during the late Keweenawan age thus causing a huge depression in the surface of the earth. Today, a long fault line runs northeast from Duluth, Minnesota. This fault line forms the northwestern shore of Lake Superior.

In the summer of 1961, further geological explorations were carried on in hopes of learning more about the beginning and early history of Lake Superior. Extensive depth soundings indicated an earlier granite lake bed far below the present lake bottom. Deep valleys in the lower granite bottom were also clearly indicated by the soundings. The origin and nature of these deep troughs in the original lake bottom remains unsolved. Some troughs on the Minnesota shore are more than 1,000 feet below present sea level. These deep, early valleys in the granite were long ago filled with Keweenawan sediments. The early bottom of Lake Superior was much farther below our present sea level than is its bottom at the present time. A new and deeper spot, than any known before on the present lake bottom of 1,333 feet, was located in Lake Superior just north of Grand Island on the United States side of the lake. Core drillings were also taken from the lake bottom between Isle Royale and the Keweenaw Peninsula. By studying these cores, it is hoped that more will be learned about the early formation and development of Lake Superior.

For hundreds of thousands of years, the Killarney Mountains raised their rugged peaks across the face of the ancient land. At one time, the Killarney Mountains formed a rocky shore line, along the northeastern shore of a sea that filled the Michigan Basin, just west of present-day Munising and Escanaba, as can easily be seen on any physical map of Michigan. This mountainous shore line continued on south into what is now Wisconsin. All the rest of the Michigan Basin, south and east of this old shore line was still covered with water by ancient seas.

Little by little, as long periods of time passed, the agents of erosion, the constant levelers of the land, worked upon the Killarney Mountains, just as they are still slowly wearing away the roots of those old mountains today. At first, as the rocks of the Killarney Mountains wore away, swift, angry rivers, running through steep mountain valleys, again carried much of the same little pieces of rock and mineral, that had long before been deposited in the Huronian seas, into the sea for the second time. Out across the sea bottom of the Michigan Basin these little pieces of rock were deposited to form a new layer of sedimentary rock now called Cambrian Sandstone. The formation and nature of this layer of sedimentary rock will be discussed later under the Cambrian Period.

Two things of importance to Michigan, and the United States, took place during the Keweenawan Period, for it was during this period that our iron ore deposits were further concentrated and our copper deposits formed. As the upper part of the sedimentary folds of the Killarney Mountains slowly eroded away, the raw, broken edges of the upturned iron layer of sedimentary rock became exposed. Running water, no longer blocked by the upper slate layer, seeped into the exposed edges of the iron layer. It seems that much of this water must have been hot, like the hot springs and geysers found in

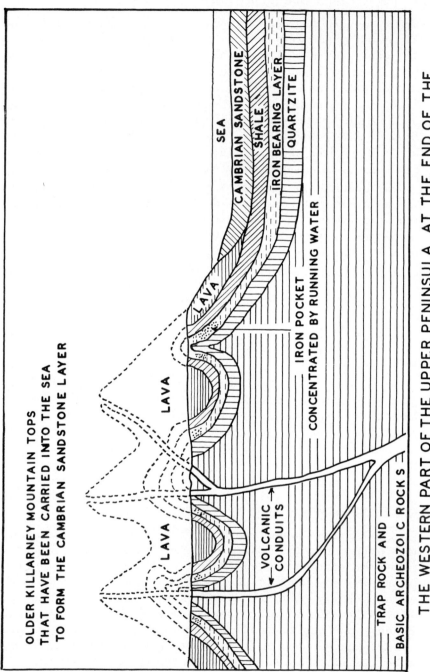

OLDER KILLARNEY MOUNTAIN TOPS
THAT HAVE BEEN CARRIED INTO THE SEA
TO FORM THE CAMBRIAN SANDSTONE LAYER

SEA

CAMBRIAN SANDSTONE

SHALE

IRON BEARING LAYER

QUARTZITE

LAVA

LAVA

LAVA

IRON POCKET

CONCENTRATED BY RUNNING WATER

VOLCANIC
CONDUITS

TRAP ROCK AND
BASIC ARCHEOZOIC ROCKS

THE WESTERN PART OF THE UPPER PENINSULA AT THE END OF THE
CAMBRIAN PERIOD

Yellowstone National Park today. In some areas of Ontario and Quebec, in Canada, and in Wisconsin, Michigan, and especially in Minnesota, this hot water, where conditions were favorable, slowly dissolved the silica as it filtered through the iron layer and carried away with it much of the silica and unwanted minerals that had been deposited in the iron layer. Where most of the silica was removed, there was left behind a high grade concentrate of iron ore (hematite Fe_2O_3) that could be used directly in making iron and steel without further processing. Thus, soft pockets of hematite, or iron ore, were concentrated in the Lake Superior region and in the Ungava region of Quebec, Canada. In other places only part of the silica was removed. In other places the iron deposits seem to have been concentrated by water action. The rich Marquette range seems to have been formed by huge sedimentary deposits.

In eastern Minnesota a large intrusive, upward movement of hot magma heated much of the iron ore just west of Lake Superior. This heating of the iron ore caused it to become magnetic. Such iron ore is called magnetite. Only a small percentage of Michigan's ore is magnetite.

It is these naturally-formed iron ore pockets, concentrated by water slowly seeping through the mother lode during the Keweenawan Period, that were later to become our open pit and shaft iron ore mines. For the last hundred years most of the iron ore used in the United States has come from these naturally formed concentrates that were then formed in the Lake Superior region. But now, the known deposits of good natural iron ore concentrate have become nearly exhausted and steel companies are having to import iron ore from foreign lands or to concentrate the lower grade iron ore that is found in the iron bearing layer of the Huronian rocks, that were not concentrated by nature during the Keweenawan Period.

This iron ore pocket later became the Fortune Lake open pit mine near Crystal Falls. This mine is now filled with water. Photo 1955.

Our unusual deposits of native copper were also formed during the Keweenawan Period. Most of Michigan's copper is called "native copper" and was formed in a pure state. It does not have to be refined, or purified.

Michigan's native copper deposits were also formed in the old Killarney Mountain Range on the Keweenaw Peninsula and on Isle Royale in Lake Superior. These two areas have a similar forma-

The main iron ore mining areas in Michigan

tion, for the same rock that forms the Keweenaw Peninsula dips down under Lake Superior in a large trough to rise again on Isle Royale and in Minnesota. The Keweenaw Peninsula copper bearing rock lies in a strip about eight miles wide and one hundred miles long. Some native copper is also found east of Sault Ste. Marie in Canada in the area of the old Killarney Mountains.

Some Killarney volcanoes spewed from their cones a froth like basaltic lava that later hardened into a porous igneous rock. When this igneous rock, formed from volcano lava froth, filled with water vapor and gas bubbles, cooled in the conduits of the volcanic cones it had holes in it similar to those found in a sponge. Such a rock is called scoria. The holes were often almond shaped and thus we get the Greek word amygdaloid for this type of rock. Sometimes, the amygdaloid holes were as small as the head of a common straight pin. At other times the amygdaloid holes were as large as a big room. In

Centennial Copper Mine at Calumet (1952)

other places cracks, or fissures, developed in the Killarney rocks. As time passed, copper was slowly deposited in the holes in the amygdaloid rock and also in the open fissures by water moving through the porous rock. A cross section of amygdaloid rock with its copper filled pockets would thus look like a large cake that has raisins in it. The solid copper masses that formed in the cracks were known as veins of mass copper. Sometimes these solid copper masses that formed in the fissures were a foot or two across, several hundred feet in length. Copper was also deposited in the porous spaces in the interbedded sandstones and conglomerates. Such copper bearing rock is known as conglomerate. In the flat lying beds of shale, such as the Nonesuch shale, in the siltstone small grains of copper as well as copper sulphide (chalcocite) were also deposited.

From Ontonagon to Copper Harbor, and on Isle Royale, one can still find pieces of pure copper lying on the ground. Such pieces of copper are called "float copper" because they were often picked up and carried along by the glaciers. Except for the present White Pine Mine, which will be discussed later, only the richest native copper deposits, found in the old lava flows, faults, and in the sedimentary conglomerates of the area, have been mined. Many of the low-grade copper deposits in the area still remain unworked.

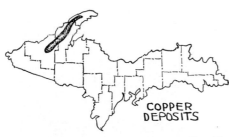

COPPER DEPOSITS

The copper mining area in the Keweenaw Peninsula

A small amount of silver was also deposited along with the copper and the two were often found together in the same mine. Such a combination is called a "half-breed."

East of Sault Ste. Marie, at Sudbury, Ontario, the largest known nickel deposit on earth was formed during the time of the Killarney Mountains. Here a large magma flow left a very rich deposit of nickel, so rich in fact that the mines there still produce about 90 per cent of of the world's annual nickel output. Some copper and platinum, as well as other metals, are also found in the Sudbury deposit.

There are definite evidences left for us that show that during the Proterozoic Era, the entire area of the Michigan Basin was at least once covered by a huge glacier. Other evidences here also show, as in later periods of time, that most of the Killarney Mountain area was

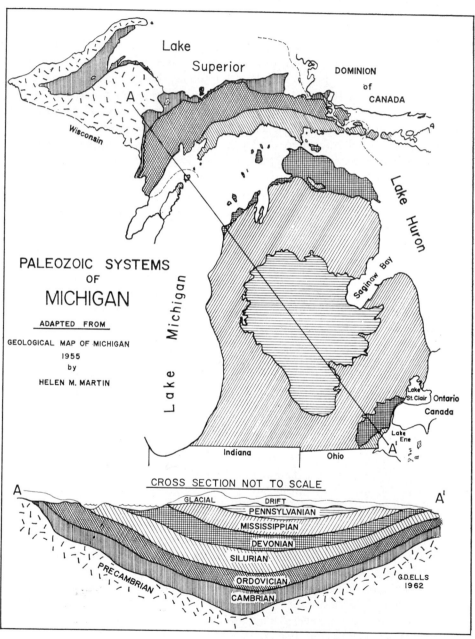

PALEOZOIC SYSTEMS
OF
MICHIGAN

ADAPTED FROM

GEOLOGICAL MAP OF MICHIGAN
1955
by
HELEN M. MARTIN

CROSS SECTION NOT TO SCALE

GLACIAL DRIFT
PENNSYLVANIAN
MISSISSIPPIAN
DEVONIAN
SILURIAN
PRECAMBRIAN
ORDOVICIAN
CAMBRIAN

G.D.ELLS
1962

Courtesy Department of Conservation

also submerged below sea level at different times. The late Proterozoic Era provides us with some fossils of early life. Similar types found in the late Cambrian Period show a much more advanced stage of development.

If you were to drive through the western part of the Upper Peninsula today, you would hardly realize that you were driving through an area that once was very mountainous. Little remains, today, in Michigan of the Killarney Mountains except the weathered, worn roots of those once rugged mountains. These roots can still be seen in the Huron Mountains, the Keweenaw Peninsula, and in the Porcupine Mountains. However, if you were to dig down through the shallow glacial till, that lies over most of the area, you would soon strike the basic rocks of the ancient Killarney Mountains.

THE PALEOZOIC ERA

Up to this time, life on this earth seems to have been only of the simplest forms. However, the sedimentary layers which were deposited during this later era are now found to contain the fossil remains of several more complicated forms of life. That is why geologists start a new era and call it the Paleozoic Era. The word Paleozoic comes from two Greek words and mean old plus life. Because this age shows several major geologic changes, as well as several changes in the forms of life during the era, geologists divide this major era, like they do the other eras, into smaller periods.

The Cambrian Period

The first period of the Paleozoic Era is called the Cambrian Period. During the Cambrian Period most of the land area that is now Michigan, except for the western part of the Upper Peninsula, was still under water, as large arms of ancient seas spread inland and covered what is now land. On the bottom of these ancient seas vast layers of debris were laid down. Later this material formed layers of rock. It is by studying these different sedimentary deposits that now fill the Michigan Basin, which were laid down upon the bottoms of ancient seas, that geologists have been able to learn much about what took place in Michigan during the long Paleozoic Era. Today, these Paleozoic sedimentary rocks, near the center of the Lower Peninsula, are some 16,000 feet thick.

As ocean followed ocean, layer upon layer of various kinds of debris was slowly laid down as each layer was later covered by still another layer. Today, these former ocean bottoms, that lie under much of

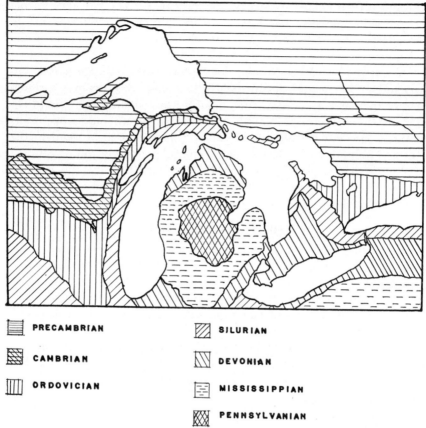

▦ PRECAMBRIAN	▨ SILURIAN
▧ CAMBRIAN	▨ DEVONIAN
▥ ORDOVICIAN	▤ MISSISSIPPIAN
	▨ PENNSYLVANIAN

Michigan and parts of Ontario, Ohio, Indiana, Illinois, and Wisconsin, are shaped like a huge nest of shallow bowls, each one lying on top of the one below it. Each sedimentary layer is a little smaller in area and its center a little nearer to the surface of the land than the lower one upon which it rests. All of them, in general, slope very gradually from their outer edge toward the deeper center of the Michigan Basin. Each layer, or stratum, was formed from the debris brought into the ocean by ancient rivers during the time the stratum was form-ing, just as debris is carried by rivers to their deltas today. The layers were made up of rocky particles or other minerals such as lime, gyp-sum, anhydrite, or salt that were precipitated from the water, or by millions and millions of small sea plants and animals that lived in the ocean and left their remains in the limey ooze that covered the bottom of those ancient seas.

The first and deepest of the underlying saucers which lie under all of Michigan, except the western part of the Upper Peninsula, rests upon an unconformity of earlier eroded rocks and sediments from the Proterozoic Era. This layer of rock, now known as the Cambrian Sandstone, was formed from crushed and eroded rocks and minerals that were carried into the Michigan Basin by rivers as the Killarney Mountains slowly eroded away during the early part of the Proterozoic Era. This Cambrian Sandstone layer has a reddish-brown color because of the iron that eroded from the mother lode and was carried along with other small pieces of rock by the rivers that then ran down from the Killarney Mountains. Gradually this debris was spread by waves and ocean currents far out across the ocean floor. Later this eroded material changed to a reddish-brown sandstone.

Today, the Cambrian formation comes to the surface (outcrops) on the west side of the Keweenaw Peninsula, and along the edge of Keweenaw Bay. The Cambrian sandstone makes some of Michigan's beautiful waterfalls, such as Miner's Falls and Tahquamenon Falls, as the run-off water of some of the rivers in the Upper Peninsula, on their way to Lake Superior, spill over the edge of the Cambrian layer. Sunlight, passing through the falling water, reflects the iron color in the rocks and gives the falling water a reddish-brown coloring.

Upper Tahquamenon Falls (1950)

Grand Island, near Munising, and the other islands near it in Lake Superior are formed from Cambrian sandstone. The beautiful Pictured Rocks, which stretch along the southern shore of Lake Superior from Munising toward Grand Marais, are formed of this same Cambrian sandstone. Wave action and the tremendous ice pressures on Lake Superior, chewing at the northern edge of the exposed Cambrian formation at the Pictured Rocks, have developed cliffs, some fifty to eighty feet in height, in the sandstone where it outcrops along the southern shore of Lake Superior.

It is this Cambrian formation that also causes the rapids in the St. Mary's River, at Sault Ste. Marie, as the run-off water of Lake Superior spills over into the St. Mary's River. When the first lock

of the Saint Mary's Falls Canal was built at Sault Ste. Marie, a little
over one hundred years ago, it was into this Cambrian sandstone
layer that the canal workers had to cut.

A part of the Pictured Rocks on the
south shore of Lake Superior, east of
Munising. This rock is Cambrian sandstone. Photo 1963.

From the Cambrian out-
crop that runs north, from
west of Escanaba to Muni-
sing and then east across the
upper part of the eastern end
of the Upper Peninsula, the
Cambrian rock layer dips
gradually down and under
Lake Michigan, the Straits of
Mackinac, the Lower Peninsula, Lake Huron, eastern
Ontario, and into northern Ohio, Indiana, and Illinois. In the central
part of the ancient Michigan Basin the Cambrian layer lies far below
the present surface of the ground.

The Cambrian Period in Michigan covers the time in the earth's
history when the sedimentary deposits that were laid down were
made mostly of the weathered rock that was being carried from the
Killarney Mountains into the seas.

By the time of the late Cambrian Period there had developed, not
only plant life, but an abundance and rather large variety of marine
life. These organisms were far more complex than earlier forms of
life, even though they had not as yet developed backbones. Among

One of the lower Tahquamenon Falls.
It is spilling over Cambrian sandstone.
Photo 1963.

this early marine life one can
now find jelly-fish, sponges or
coral, brachiopods, gastropods, trilobites, and tracks and
borings of worms. The cause
and manner of these early
changes to more complex organisms presents an intriguing
mystery to students of this
early time. The changes in life
forms no doubt took place
over a long period of time, but
it is difficult for geologists to
find out more about life at that early age because of the tremendous

pressures, the chemical actions, and the long period of time that has passed since this rock was formed, that may have greatly altered the original structure and texture of the Cambrian sandstone deposits.

The Ordovician Period

Considerable physiological and biological changes had come in the Michigan Basin by the time the Cambrian Period had come to its close. By the end of the Cambrian Period the Killarney Mountains had become much lower and the rivers that then flowed from them had become less swift and turbulent. Less and less rocky sediment was carried into the sea until it almost stopped. Because of this change in sedimentation, the new layers that lie upon the lower Cambrian sandstone were formed from other types of debris that gradually settled to the ocean floor.

Major changes in marine life also took place during the Ordovician Period. No one can explain why, but many new forms of still more advanced and complex life began to abound in the Ordovician seas that spread across the Michigan Basin, just as they were also developing in the earth's oceans on other parts of the earth. Among the sea life can now be found fossils of more advanced trilobites, brachiopods, and cephalopods. The first fish that we know of are found in the ordovician sedimentary layers. Also, among the more advanced forms of life that can be found in these rock layers are starfish, giant nautiloids, and several varieties of coral. Some early life forms, no doubt, were soft and nothing of them is left but imprints, or holes, in the rocks that were made by them. Other forms developed shells, such as clams and oysters have today. When these marine organisms died they left their little shells in the slimy ooze that was slowly forming on the ocean floor. Here, these shells or bony structures, or their imprints, have remained for eons of time undisturbed by all the forces of erosion such as winds, waves, or ocean currents, except chemical action, in perhaps one of the most motionless and quietest of all the places on this earth, the deep, dark ocean floor. There the remains of these early organisms were slowly covered with the lime that slowly settled onto the bottoms of those ancient seas.

Evaporation during this period, and several of the periods that followed, caused lime mud to be precipitated from the water. Slowly this accumulation of lime mud sank to the bottom and became soft ocean ooze that covered the coral reefs and the hard shells of the little animals that had lived in those ancient seas. Other limey particles came out of solution as the result of the life processes of the marine organisms, while other limey particles were formed by the disintegration of shells and other organisms.

Today, one often finds the fossil remains of these early forms of

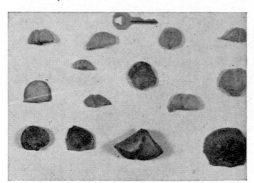

Brachiopods. Millions of these little sea animals, similar to present day oysters, lived in the Silurian and Divonian seas. Their size can be seen by comparing them with the key.

sea life between limestone layers when they are cracked apart. These shells, or imprints of them, are called fossils from the Latin word "fossilis" which means dug up. It is from these fossil remains, or imprints of them, that we learn something about what life was like so long ago. From these early fossils, and those that were later laid in the upper layers, we learn that many forms of life have existed on this earth in ages past that are no longer here today.

Today, the Ordovician Saucer rim outcrops along the western side of Green Bay, then swings across the Upper Peninsula just south of the Cambrian Sandstone outcrop. In Ontario, Canada, it runs along the north side of the Manitoulin Islands, then south of a line drawn from a little north of the south end of Georgian Bay to the source of the St. Lawrence River where the water spills out of Lake Ontario.

It is in the underlying Trenton-Black River formations of this period that oil pools have recently been discovered in the area from Albion to Jonesville.

The Silurian Period

About five hundred million years ago, the next period of the Paleozoic Era began. This interesting period is called the Silurian Period because of the extensive beds of salt that were formed at different times. Sometimes the seas were warm and much sea life, such as trilobites, squids, brachiopods, and cephalopods, lived in the seas along with starfish, fish, and various types of coral. When these forms of life died, they left their harder body parts, such as shells and coral, or the imprints of them, in the limey bed at the bottoms of the seas.

Today, the outer edge of the Silurian saucer begins on the western

Silurian Limestone Cliffs at Fayette, on the Garden Peninsula. Photo 1956.

shore of Lake Erie north of Monroe, goes south into and across northern Ohio, Indiana, and Illinois. It then swings northward past Chicago and follows along the western shore of Lake Michigan. From here its north-facing bluffs can easily be followed all the way from Wisconsin to New York State. In northern Wisconsin, the edge of the Silurian saucer forms the Door Peninsula on the eastern side of Green Bay. It then crosses into Michigan to form the Garden Peninsula. Then, the edge of the Silurian outcrop swings east across the southern side of the Upper Peninsula and the Manitoulin Islands. Continuing its circle, it then forms the basic rock formation in the Bruce Peninsula. From there it crosses south across Ontario, Canada, to the western end of Lake Ontario. At this point, the edge of the old Silurian seas swings east-ward between Lake Erie and Lake Ontario and continues across the northern part of New York State. Along this line, where it crosses what is now the Niagara River, it forms a sharp drop on its northern edge, known as the Niagara Escarpment. Water in the Niagara River falling over this escarpment now forms Niagara Falls. Below the falls, the swiftly swirling water has cut a deep gorge into the old Silurian layers.

We know that the Silurian seas were often warm, like those in the tropics today, because several kinds of coral then grew in the shallow waters all along the edges of the ancient Silurian seas. Pieces of various kinds of coral, as well as the fossil remains of many kinds of sea life, can be found in the limestone deposits that are now being quarried in many places round the edges of the Silurian outcrop that was described above.

In Michigan, several coral reefs were formed during the Silurian Period. In the Detroit River area, near Lake Erie, the Silurian and Devonian limestone layers come very close to the surface. Because the upper edges of these limestone layers come so near to the surface the Detroit River is very wide and shallow for a few miles before it enters Lake Erie. In order for our large lake boats, and ocean ships, to pass up and down the Detroit River it has been necessary to blast a channel,

Organ Pipe coral

now called the Livingstone Channel, through the limestone sedimentary layers at the lower end of the Detriot River. Coral stems as well as other fossils can be found in the limestone that was blasted from the bottom of the Detroit River when the Livingstone Channel was made.

The Silurian Period is also known for the extensive deposits of salt (halite) (NaCl) that were laid down in the Michigan Basin during this period. During portions of the Silurian Period, the inland seas must have been large salt seas at different times.

During part of the Silurian Period the Michigan Basin seems to have been cut off from the ocean by only a narrow bar of land. This bar of land must have been low enough to allow water from the ocean to have been repeatedly forced over it and into the Basin. Once trapped in the Basin

Organ Pipe coral found near the shore of Lake Charlevoix in 1957. This coral grew during the Silurian Period. Note how the limestone has been deposited between the coral stems. Some of it has been eroded away so that the stems begin to stand out from the mass.

the water evaporated and left behind the salt and other sediments that the water had been carrying. During this long period of time the Basin seems to have sunk lower and lower. In some areas the Silurian salt deposits are over one-third of a mile thick.

Changes in the earth's crust and climate caused other materials, at later times, to be deposited over the salt layers in the Basin. Thus, layers of anhydrite, limestone, dolomite, and a bluish-black shale were deposited over the salt layer. Layers of gypsum were also laid down during this period. Altogether, the alternate layers of salt, gypsum, anhydrite, and limestone that were laid down during the Silurian Period are several hundred feet in thickness. As the salt forming periods of the Silurian Period came to an end layers of clay spread over the vast salt layers. Later this clay turned to shale. This shale prevented water from entering the lower salt beds and dissolving the salt when other later seas again covered the Michigan Basin during the Devonian and later periods.

The salt layers that were laid down during the Silurian Period reach from St. Ignace and Muskegon south and eastward under Lake Huron and Lake Erie all the way to northern Pennsylvania and southeastern New York State. Because these salt layers are dry and hard, they can actually be mined. Salt from these layers is mined at Goderich and Windsor in Ontario, Canada. It is also mined in northern Ohio and in New York State. It is from these

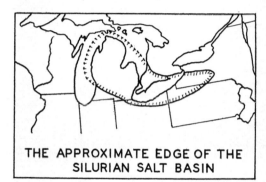

THE APPROXIMATE EDGE OF THE
SILURIAN SALT BASIN

Silurian salt deposits, which underlie Detroit, that salt miners now secure rock salt from the Detroit salt mine. This salt is used in large quantities to keep our highways free from ice and snow during the winter time and in many of our industries to help make hundreds of chemical products that we use every day.

The shaft for the Detroit salt mine was started in 1906 and not completed until 1910. From the very beginning the workmen ran into trouble. The first hundred feet was through glacial drift. Some of this was quicksand and was highly impregnated with hydrogen sulfide gas. Below this the workmen had to go through 600 feet of sandstone and limestone. After one year's work, they had gone down only 190 feet. At this point they were flooded out by water pouring into the shaft at about two million gallons each minute. But in spite of financial losses the work was pushed on until they had reached a depth of 1,060 feet. Later the shaft was extended downward about 100 feet more where a better grade of salt was formed.

During the Silurian Period traces of land vegetation began to appear. The first known air-breathing animals also developed during this period.

Limestone, from outcrops of the Silurian layer, has been quarried at several places in the Upper Peninsula. Today, large limestone quarries are located at Port Inland near Manistique, at Cedarville, and on

Main haulway in the International Salt Company's Detroit Mine. Huge electrically powered bottom-dumping trucks carry 20-ton loads of Sterling Rock Salt from the mine face to the primary crusher several thousand yards away. Note the alternate layers of salt (halite—white color—NaCl) and Anhydrite (dark color—$CaSO_4$). (1961)

Drummond Island that provided millions of tons of limestone that is used in making cement and in refining iron ore into steel. Thus, the limestone deposited during the Silurian Period, and the Devonian Period that followed, provides Michigan and the Great Lakes Area with one of its major natural resources — limestone.

The Devonian Period

The Silurian Period was followed by the Devonian Period, which began about four hundred millions years ago. By the time of the Devonian Period, the size of the Michigan Basin had become very much smaller and shallower. Today, the Devonian layer comes near the surface along the western side of the Leelanau Peninsula. From there it crosses Grand Traverse Bay, just north of Old Mission Peninsula, and then swings across the upper part of the Lower Peninsula to near Harrisville. At this point, the outer rim has been scraped away by the glaciers, but the edge of the basin lies under Lake Huron. It comes near the surface on the west side of the Detroit River and along the western side of Lake Erie. It then swings west across northern Ohio and northern Indiana. Its western rim was scraped away when the glaciers gouged out the basin of Lake Michigan.

During this period, which lasted some fifty million years, the sea trilobites became fewer in number and the cephalopods became smaller in size. New forms of life came into the seas during the Devonian Period. Several new kinds of fish began to appear. Fossil remains of Devonian fish can now be found, especially in the area near Alpena, in the limestone layers that were deposited during this period.

The front end, or face, of a trilobite. It is about as wide as a twenty-five cent piece.

During the Devonian Period, primitive evergreen trees, called seed ferns, grew on the land that was then above the water. These evergreen trees formed the first known forests. In what is now Monroe County, a deposit of pure white sand (quartz) was deposited in the sand dunes that then formed along the eastern edge of the ancient Devonian seas. Today, this pure white sand is quarried near Rockwood and is used for making optical glass, plate glass, and table glassware. Some oil and gas were also formed during this period.

The Devonian layers contain layers of limestone, shale, dolomite, gypsum and sandstone. Because the Devonian limestone outcrops near the shore of the Great Lakes, in the upper part of the Lower Peninsula and in the Detroit area, it provides one of Michigan's major sources for supplying high grade limestone for making cement and smelting iron ore. At Calcite, near Rogers City, is located the largest limestone quarry in the world. This quarry is operated by Michigan Limestone, a division of United States Steel Corporation. Much of the limestone quarried at Calcite is used as a flux for smelting iron ore. At Alpena is located the largest cement plant in the world. Cement is also made at

Courtesy Michigan Limestone Division United States Steel Corporation

In the quarry at Rogers City the huge 20-cubic yard electric shovel loads stone in the cars for the trip to the crusher house. Capacity of the cars ranges from 50 to 60 cubic yards.

Petoskey. From both Alpena and Petoskey cement is shipped as a bulk cargo in lake boats to ports on the lower lakes. Near Detroit, where the Devonian layer comes near the surface, can still be seen the old Sibley Quarry near Wyandotte. Although this quarry is no longer worked it produced limestone for many years which was used in smelting iron ore and in making many chemical products. A new cement plant has recently been opened at Dundee, near Monroe. This new plant is one of the largest and best equipped cement plants in the state. In northern Ohio,

Near Alabaster and National City gypsum is quarried. This picture shows how the glacial till has been removed so that the gypsum can be secured.

other quarries produce limestone from this same Devonian layer. This limestone is also used in industry and in the making of cement. The Devonian limestone layer is the source of much of the cement that is now used in the Great Lakes area for making buildings, walks, bridges, water and sewer pipe, and for paving the many miles of new highways that are being built across the area of the old Michigan Basin where the limestone was first formed so many million years ago on the bottoms of ancient seas.

Gypsum for the making of plaster and plaster board is quarried near Alabaster. It is also mined at Grand Rapids.

Other coral reefs were formed during the Devonian Period. They swung in a large circle around the Lower Peninsula. Fossil coral, from this Devonian reef, can be found in the Petoskey area, at Rainy River Falls, at Ocqueoc Falls, in the limestone quarries in the lower part of the Lower Peninsula, and in northern Ohio and Indiana. One variety of coral that can easily be picked up at quarries, outcrops, or along the shore of Lake Michigan or Lake Huron in the northern part of the Lower Peninsula is called "Petoskey Stone" after the city of Petoskey. Because this coral reef later formed a porous rock, natural gas is often found in the early coral formations where it has been trapped. One of these coral reef pockets has recently been located near Port Huron.

The Mississippian Period

The Devonian Period was followed by the Mississippian Period. During this period some change in the earth's surface caused eroded materials to again be brought into the seas. Several alternate layers of shale and sandstone were deposited on the bottoms of the smaller seas within the center of the Michigan Basin. On top of these lower layers of shale and sandstone, limestone layers were again deposited. This upper limestone layer is known as the Bay Port layer.

Marshall Sandstone quarry at Napoleon. Photo Aug. 1962.

The sedimentary layers laid down during the Mississippian Period provide Michigan with several natural resources. The lower layers provide some

natural gas and petroleum. One of the middle layers is known as the
Marshall Sandstone layer. It is a rather porous layer of sedimentary
rock and in between the particles of sand which make up the rock
is found fresh water and also a very valuable salt brine. It is this brine
from the Mississippian layer that the Dow Chemical Company at
Midland, and the Morton Salt Company, at Manistee, use to make
their many products. The Marshall Formation outcrops at Jackson,
Marshall, and at the top of the Thumb in Huron County. It is the
second layer of this Marshall Sandstone that was quarried at Grindstone City for a little over a hundred years and used there to make
whetstones and grindstones. At Napoleon the reddish sandstone of
this period is still quarried. Some of it is still used for building
material, but most of it is used for patios and garden walks.

Courtesy the Detroit News

**Michigan shore line near Port Austin. Here the Marshall Sand-
stone outcrops along the shore of Lake Huron.**

During the Mississippian Period, life was much the same as it
had been during the Devonian Period, but fewer fossils are found in
the Mississippian layers that were formed during this period. The
trilobites became still fewer in number. More and more fish seem to
have lived in these ancient seas.

The Pennsylvanian Period

This is the period when vast coal deposits were formed on many parts of the earth's surface. As time passed by, the area that had been the Michigan Basin gradually filled in or rose to a higher level and the earlier seas that had left their thick deposits of limestone and sandstone slowly retreated from the basin. All of the Michigan Basin, except the central part of the Lower Peninsula, was by this time probably above water. The central part of the Lower Peninsula had not as yet entirely filled in with sedimentary materials nor had it risen high enough to completely drain its shallow water away to the ocean. The central area of the Lower Peninsula during the Pennsylvanian Period formed a vast, shallow, swampy, forested area in which grew primitive fern-like trees.

In the shallow, muddy pools of this vast swamp land lived some of the earliest reptiles. Some of these reptiles looked much like our present day salamanders. In the air above the swamp were large flying insects that made their homes in the dense, fern-like trees that then grew in the shallow water. Large bugs, like our present cockroaches, only larger, also lived in this ancient forest. Many reptiles, like our present alligators, crawled about in the shallow, swampy water and over the fallen, decaying vegetation.

We know what the ancient trees and ferns of this period looked like, for they often left their imprint, or cast, in the soft material into which they fell. When they died, or were blown down, they were often covered by the shallow, stagnant water of the swamps. Thus the trees; ground pines, horsetail rushes, and ferns that lived in the central part of the Lower Peninsula at least two hundred and fifty million years ago, gradually formed a layer of organic matter that slowly changed to peat and then to soft coal. The remains of this organic layer now forms a bed of soft coal that lies under the glacial till from Saginaw to Jackson. For about one hundred years, Michigan coal was mined and used. But, because of its poor quality in comparison with soft coal found in other nearby areas, it has not been commercially mined since about 1950.

During this period more sandstone and shale layers were also laid down. From the shale, face brick and tile are now being made. Some natural gas is found in the Parma Sandstone layer.

The Permian Period

This is the last period of the Paleozoic Era. What had been a swampy waste in the central part of the Lower Peninsula for many thousands of years at last became dry land area like the rest of the state as the land rose higher and the swamps slowly filled in. All of Michigan, except the western end of the Upper Peninsula, was by then a low, flat, featureless plain. Salamanders and insects could no longer live here, but other larger animals, common to that period, no doubt lived on the land as the Paleozoic Era came to an end.

Whereas, from the Proterozoic Era came our iron and copper metals, from the later Paleozoic periods that followed the Cambrian Period have come many non-metalic resources that have been and still are very valuable in making Michigan an industrial state; such as, coal, natural gas, petroleum, dolomite, limestone, salt brine, gypsum, sandstone and shale.

THE MESOZOIC ERA

With the coming of the land animals, the geologists begin the next division of time. This next division geologists call the Mesozoic Era.

By this time, the Michigan Basin had all risen above the level of the oceans then surrounding North America and it has remained dry land ever since that time. Because of this, no marine deposits that would record the happenings in this era were laid down. There were no rivers large enough to leave their story in their deltas. Because of this, geologists know very little about what happened in the Michigan Basin during the next one hundred million years. The sedimentary rocks laid down at this time in other areas of the world are all missing from the old Michigan Basin because the land here was then above water.

The climate during this era seems to have been warm and much plant and animal life no doubt existed here, just as it did in other parts of the world. Much erosion probably took place on the time-worn Killarney Mountains and along the exposed edges of the limestone, shale and sandstone saucers; but, just what happened in this area during the long Mesozoic Era is hard to learn because the surface remains of this long period of time were destroyed when the glaciers came scrubbing over the surface of the land during the most recent period of glaciation.

THE CENOZOIC ERA

The Mesozoic Era was followed by what geologists call the Cenozoic Era. The remains of the early periods of this era have also been destroyed by the glaciers that passed over the Michigan Basin during the Pleistocene Period during the later part of the Cenozoic Era.

The Glacial Age (Pleistocene)

To many people, one of the most interesting periods in Michigan's past is the last glacial period. Michigan had been covered by glaciers at other times in the ancient past, but it was the last glacial age that did so much to give Michigan, and the Great Lakes area, its present surface features and prepare the area for its recent economical development.

A glacier is a huge mass of ice, a mile or more in depth, like the vast ice sheet that covers Greenland today. Glaciers form slowly over long periods of time as the weather gradually grows a little cooler. Each winter a little more snow falls than is melted during the following summer. In this way huge masses of snow gradually accumulate. Because of the increasing weight, the snow on the bottom very slowly turns to ice. As the slowly accumulating ice mass increases in depth and weight it pushes heavily downward. This downward force causes the lower layers of ice to be pressed outward, thus forcing the outer rim of the icy mass to move ever outward. In Greenland, at the present time, the huge ice mass pushes ever outward from the central land area until huge chunks of it break off along its outer edge to form large icebergs that drift slowly southward with the cold Labrador Current.

During the last glacial age, similar ice masses developed in what is now Labrador and in the area of Hudson Bay. Slowly, per-

Porcupine Mountains at Lake of the Clouds

haps only a few inches a year, these huge ice masses pushed steadily outward in all directions from their massive centers. We know the directions of the movements of these huge ice masses because of the rock scratches, called glacial grooves, that were scraped into the surface of the bed rocks over which the glaciers, or their glacial lobes passed. The glacial grooves are natural historical records showing us the general directions of the outward movements of the vast ice masses as they pressed slowly outward from their pressure centers.

So heavy were these enormous masses of ice, that gradually accumulated over many, many centuries, that they seem to have pressed the earth's hard crust downward because of their tremendous weight. Even as late as our time, the land area north of a line from Alpena to Duluth, Minnesota, is slowly rising as the earth's crust is gradually coming back to near the original position as it was before it was pressed downward by the tremendous weight of the last masses of ice.

As these large ice masses pushed out from Canada they pressed heavily upon the underlying surface of the ancient land. Fragments of rock were broken off and together with the sand and gravel, then lying on the surface of the land, were frozen into the accumulating ice masses. As the glaciers constantly pushed outward, this rough, rocky debris on the bottom of the glaciers acted like a continuous huge sheet of coarse sandpaper that scoured, scraped, and gouged the underlying rock surfaces over which the glaciers slowly passed. Stones, boulders, and other general surface debris were thus picked up and carried along as the huge ice masses pushed outward in all directions. Thus the ancient Canadian Shield was swept clean of whatever soil that had formed there during the long eras before the last glacial age,

Lake of the Clouds. Part of the Porcupine Mountains can be seen in the background. These are part of the old Killarney Mountains.

as the glaciers pushed ever outward across the ancient, weathered, granite rock. Old mountain tops were scraped away and valleys were scoured wider and deeper to form a vast peneplain where long before the rugged Laurentian Mountains and Killarney Mountains had once stood. Like a slowly but continuously moving giant conveyor belt, the slowly moving glaciers constantly carried this eroded and fractured material out in all directions to their outer rims. Here, in our study of Michigan, we are concerned only with the southern side of the glaciers as they moved down from Canada across Michigan.

As the glacial masses pushed south over the ancient Killarney Mountains, the icy masses pressed heavily downward against the already old and weathered mountain tops. Much of the weathered upper materials were scraped away and slowly carried southward. As the tops of the ancient Killarney Mountains were scraped away, the ragged edges of the upturned "iron sandwich" became exposed on the surface of the land. Thus, some of the softer iron ore pockets that had concentrated during the Keweenawan Period were left near the surface of the land where mineral prospectors looking for iron ore deposits were later to find them. The same is true of the copper deposits in the Keweenaw Peninsula and on Isle Royale. The scraping of the glaciers as they passed over the area ripped away some of the overlying rock and brought the copper deposits closer to the surface of the land. As the glaciers pushed over this area, they picked up pieces of iron and copper and carried them along with them as they moved southward. Pieces of native copper, carried southward by the glaciers, have been found as far south as the Ohio River. Such fragments of copper that are now found on or near the surface of the land where the glaciers dropped them are known as pieces of "float copper."

Some of the last glacial lobes pushed as far south as the Missouri and Ohio Rivers. There the warmer air melted the glacial fronts as rapidly as the glaciers pushed southward. As the ice melted along the glacial fronts, just as ice melts on glacial fronts in mountains today, it ran away as clear, cold, icy water. The melting ice, running away as melt-water from the glaciers formed the Missouri and Ohio Rivers and thus developed much of the present upper Mississippi River system. In this way the glaciers helped to form two large river systems that were later to play such an important part in the early westward movement of settlers across the United States.

Gradually, as the air again grew a little warmer over long periods of time, the glacial fronts receded farther and farther back toward the north. Sometimes the glaciers held their own for a time against the slowly warming weather. Then, the debris being carried outward by the glaciers would be pushed upward at their melting ends, thus forming moraines, or, as they are commonly called in Michigan, hills. When the last glacial front retreated back, these last ridges of rocky debris were thus left behind. In this way our hills were formed. Since the last retreat of the glaciers, some eleven or twelve thousand years ago, these hills have been slowly eroded downward and have become more rounded on their tops. Some of the finer materials have been carried by the wind and streams and deposited in the lakes, but much of it was carried into the valleys between the hills to form what is known as outwash plains.

Another massive work that the glaciers accomplished was to gouge out the basins for hundreds of inland lakes and for four of our present Great Lakes over which now passes the largest inland waterway traffic in the world. The story of the formation and development of these glacial lakes is a long and interesting story but only a small part of it can be told here.*

As the glaciers scoured over the Canadian Shield, they cut many of the ancient mountain valleys wider and deeper, thus making basins for holding water. Today the number of these pretty, rock-shored lakes lying in the Canadian Shield, in Canada, run into several thousand. Some are several miles in length and have many branching arms. The same is true of the area in northern Minnesota. These hundreds of lakes and their connecting streams, together with the cold winters found in the area around Lake Superior, provided the natural environment for the fur trade that brought the Frenchmen and the English into the Great Lakes area.

As the glaciers pushed southward they found the ancient rim of the Ordovician limestone deposits relatively soft and gouged deeply into them. Thus, Green Bay, Georgian Bay, and Lake Ontario were gouged out of the softer Ordovician layers by the glaciers as they pushed over the Michigan Basin. The Silurian limestone rim was more resistant to the scrubbing, pushing action of the glaciers and one can, as has been shown, easily trace this saucer rim, as it swings from west to east.

Into the sedimentary layers above the Silurian, the glaciers gouged out the basins for what later became Lake Michigan, Lake Huron, and Lake Erie. Thus, the four lower Great Lakes, as well as Georgian Bay

---

*See Hough, Jack L. *Geology of the Great Lakes* Urbana. University of Illinois Press. 1958.

and Green Bay, were formed by the advancing ice lobes as they pushed southward along what may have been ancient river valleys. When the last of the four recent glaciers, the Wisconsin glacier, retreated north, it left these huge depressions that had been gouged out by the glaciers filled with fresh water.

What is now Lake Erie, because of its southernmost location, is the oldest of the present post-glacial Great Lakes. Since the time of the last glacier it has passed through many stages. As the ice mass receded northward, the Lake Erie basin was the first to fill with water. Carbon tests indicate that it is about 9,000 years old. The basin of Lake Erie at that time was much larger than it is today. It covered much of what is now Wayne, Monroe, and Macomb counties. Water from the earlier larger lakes that followed each

Lake Superior shore line at the Pictured Rocks

other in the present Lake Erie basin at first drained south into the developing Mississippi River system. Thus, many kinds of fish that by then had adapted themselves to fresh river water, entered the Great Lakes. One of these early varieties was the whitefish that can still be found in the waters of the Mississippi River. Along the old watershed from the Lake Erie basin to the Mississippi now flow the Maumee and Wabash Rivers. These two rivers later formed one of the main water routes used by the French and English as they crossed from Lake Erie to the Mississippi River when going between Quebec and New Orleans. Later along this route was built the Wabash and Erie Canal.

At a later time, when the glacial front still kept the water of Lake Erie from running out the St. Lawrence Valley, Lake Erie drained eastward across New York State from Buffalo to north of Albany. Here the run-off waters turned south and flowed down what is now the Hudson River. It was along this old water route, that the Erie Canal was dug at the beginning of the past century. Thus, the glacial age helped to prepare the way for the migration of settlers into Michigan and the Great Lakes area. Even today, our fast trains running between Chicago, Detroit, and New York follow along this early water route. When the last glacier retreated farther northward, the run-off waters from Lake Erie developed a new outlet by way of the Niagara River, Lake Ontario, and the St. Lawrence River. This change in direction brought into being Niagara Falls as the water from Lake Erie began spilling over the northern confining rim of the Silurian limestone layer, now known as the Niagaran cuesta.

The St. Lawrence River outlet, down which the run-off waters of the five Great Lakes now drain, had a principal part in the early exploration and settlement of North America. It is the only large river that leads deep into the heart of the North American continent from its east side. Westward up it went the first French fur traders and the early Jesuit missionaries. At the present time this river, together with the Great Lakes, forms the largest inland waterway in the world. Each year more and more foreign ships pass along the new Saint Lawrence Seaway that now makes it possible for all of the cities along the water-way to become ocean ports for sending and receiving world commerce during the warmer months, when the seaway is open.

Lake Ontario and the lower end of Lake Michigan were the next post glacial lakes to be formed. Geologists estimate that these two bodies of water were clear of ice about 6,000 years ago. It was many years after this before all of Lake Michigan and Lake Huron were free from ice. As the glacier retreated northward, the water from the lower Lake Michigan ran out its southern end and into the Mississippi River. It was along this old river course that the French and English fur traders portaged from Lake Michigan to a stream flowing into the Mississippi system. Later the Illinois and Michigan Canal was dug along this same route. Today, a vast quantity of Lake Michigan water is taken from Lake Michigan, used by Chicago, and then discharged into the Mississippi system.

Post-glacial Lake Superior, because of its location farther north, was the last one of the present Great Lakes to be freed from its icy overburden. Geologists estimate that this was about 4,000 years ago. Present indications of former shore lines show that at one time, during the glacial age when ice blocked the eastern outlet, the Lake Superior shore line was 530 feet higher than the present shore line of the lake.

At one time, the run-off waters from the Upper Great Lakes found an outlet across Ontario along what today is the French River, Lake Nippising, the Mattawa River, the Ottawa River, and the St. Lawrence River to the sea. This early waterway later became the route that was followed by the French fur traders and missionaries as they first pushed into the Lake Region along this old water course with their

Indian friends. Later, this route became the main highway for the French fur trade that was to make Montreal the main fur trading center of North America for many years.

In all the world there is no area similar to the Great Lakes area. In no other continent is there such a heavy concentration of people in the interior such as that found in the area bordering our Great Lakes. This has been made possible because of the climate, soil, transportation routes, and natural resources found in this area.

Large masses of glacial ice, pressing deep into the glacial till left massive depressions when the ice melted away. These depressions, together with natural dams, form most of our inland lakes in the eastern part of the Upper Peninsula and in the Lower Peninsula of Michigan today. Slowly, over the last few thousand years, many of these depressions, or lakes, have been gradually filled in as the wind and streams dropped their debris into the water. Today, what once were lakes, are now swamps, marshes, muck lands, marl beds, or peat bogs.

So vast are these lake basins, left by the glaciers, together with the ones scoured out in the Canadian Shield that the area from Lake Winnipeg to the city of Quebec in Canada now contains about half of all the fresh water in the world. This fresh water, found in hundreds of lakes and streams, together with the forests of the area, provide us with one of our most valuable resources, a vast recreation area. Today the tourist industry is one of Michigan's major industries. Not only is this fresh water a recreational asset, but it has tremendous potential for boosting Michigan's industrial growth as well. Modern industries demand vast amounts of fresh water. This can be found only in limited amounts in most areas of the world. Because of this great need for fresh water, more and more industries will develop in the Great Lakes area where water can be had for both industries and expanding urban centers that will accompany their growth.

Of all the Great Lakes that the glaciers formed, Lake Agassiz was the largest in North America. All that is left of this once huge lake, today, is now known as Lake Winnipeg. As the retreating ice sheet held the waters back from flowing north into Hudson Bay, the waters of Lake Agassiz spread across an area around modern Lake Winnipeg that was larger than all the present five Great Lakes put together. For long periods of time, as the ice masses kept the water from this huge lake from flowing north to Hudson Bay, the water from it drained south and flowed down the Mississippi River. Sediment spreading across the bottom of this huge lake was later to form vast plains when the waters finally drained away. Today, this Red River Valley land is used by Canadians to grow wheat.

As the last glacier retreated north the Great Lakes region once more was exposed as a water and land area. Then the vast work that the glaciers had been doing could be seen. Five Great Lakes lay sparkling under the warmer sun. West of the old shore line of the Killarney Mountains, from Munising to Ecanaba, the ancient Killarney Mountains had been rubbed and scrubbed and the mountain tops in many places had been carried away. Vast quantities of crushed rock called glacial till, or glacial drift, had been carried southward and deposited on top of the ancient Killarney Mountains and the sedimentary rock bowls in the eastern end of the Upper Peninsula, all over the Lower Peninsula of Michigan, and also much of Ohio, Illinois, and Indiana. This glacial overburden varies in the thickness, from nothing to as much as 1,000 feet. It is the deepest in the "High Plains Area" in the upper part of the Lower Peninsula. Less high deposits are found in the Irish Hills and in the hilly area of Oakland County. This glacial till was made up of boulders, stones, sand, gravel, pebbles, and clay. Some of this debris was igneous, some metamorphic, and some sedimentary depending on where the glacier picked it up or broke it loose from the massive rock in which it had formed. Today these fragmnts are again slowly forming into new conglomerate rock called "crag" as nature is slowing cementing the rocky particles together.

Michigan's glacial debris is one of her most valuable assets. In many places large gravel pits can be found where the crushed glacial till is dug up, screened and sized. Such material is used for railroad beds, gravel roads, and in all kinds of cement work such as in buildings and our spreading highways. In some places, such as Wayne County, running water deposited beds of clay on old lake bottoms. This clay is used for making brick or tile.

Hundreds of small inland lakes could be seen. Across the areas where the glacial till had been deposited spread many low moraines that we now call hills. In the north around Lake Superior lay the exposed copper and iron deposits. By means of large boats on the Great Lakes, cheap transportation for these ores was later provided so that the iron ore could be taken to the coal fields south of Lake Michigan and Lake Erie and the copper could also be brought to market. Because of these deposits of natural mineral resources, and the easy water transportation provided by bulk transportation on the Great Lakes, large cities would later rise at favorable locations and vast industries would develop along the shores of these glacial scoured lakes. In this way, the glaciers did much to shape Michigan's history and present economic pattern.

As the last glacier melted, the glacial debris that it had been carrying was left exposed on the surface of the land. No trees, bushes, mosses, grasses, or other plant life lived on this barren waste land. It was a land of broken rocks, gravel, sand, and clay particles. When the sun shone on it, it sometimes formed hard, flat masses. When it rained there was no vegetation, or vegetable matter, to act as a blotter to hold the water. It sank into the till or ran off in streams that carried the finer particles to a lake or outwash plain. No life as we know it could live on this barren waste land.

As the weather grew warmer, other changes came to the land. Gradually by exposure to the weather, rocks and minerals were slowly changed by chemical action and fell apart to become soil. Slowly lichens and mosses took root and grew on the barren soil. This helped to hold water. As those simple forms of plant life died they helped to enrich the soil by providing humus. As the humus deepened, grasses grew on the developing soil. These in turn added more humus. At last enough soil had developed to sustain trees and these in turn provided more humus. Hardy Arctic plants came first; next came willows, birches, pines and such other trees as grow in the colder parts of the temperate climate. Then came the harder woods such as oak, elm, hickory, walnut, and maple to take over the better soils.

Growing plants began to provide food for animals that came north as the last glacier retreated from the area. Thus, Michigan became the homeland of the musk ox and the mastodon. Over one hundred fifty authentic records of these large elephant-type animals, called mastodons, have been recorded here in Michigan. A splendid specimen of a mastodon skeleton, formed near Owosso, may be seen in the Museum of Natural Science at the University of Michigan at Ann Arbor.

As the land lifted after the glaciers melted away, many of the old water outlets, that once carried the Great Lakes waters to the sea, were abandoned as our present drainage system developed. About two thousand years ago, the waters of Lake Superior began draining out its eastern end in place of the western end. Thus the St. Mary's River was born. We know this is a young river, for it has not yet cut deeply into the Cambrian Sandstone layer that forms the rapids at Sault Ste. Marie. The Detroit River, too, is a young river, for it has not cut deeply into the limestone layers at its mouth.

CHAPTER TWO

The General Geography of Michigan

MOST of the state of Michigan lies in the center of the Great Lakes region which forms the upper St. Lawrence River drainage basin. For that reason much of Michigan's history has been closely connected with the development of the St. Lawrence River system.

The St. Lawrence River system is one of the three large river systems that drain much of the North American continent. Beginning in the hundreds of small streams that flow into the Great Lakes, the water of this river system flows in a general northeast direction to the Atlantic Ocean. As it nears the ocean, the river valley narrows. Only a few people live in this area. On the north side of the valley the Canadian Shield forms a barren wasteland of weathered rock, while on the south side of the river the upper end of the Appalachian Mountain system presses in to help form the narrow valley.

Courtesy Victor Lemmer
Gabbro Falls on the Black River near Bessemer. Photo 1964.

The St. Lawrence system is fed by several smaller rivers. Near the mouth of the St. Lawrence River can be found the Saguenay that flows from the Canadian Shield. Because it is the first large stream entering the valley, it became one of the first streams to interest the earliest Frenchmen who entered the valley to trade with the Indians for furs. At the mouth of the Saguenay a little Indian village called Tadoussac was located.

Farther up the St. Lawrence Valley the Richelieu River, carrying the run-off waters of Lake Champlain, flows northward into the St. Lawrence. This river valley became of interest to the French traders

42

as soon as they founded their settlement at Quebec. Up this waterway Champlain went in 1609, to fight the Iroquois Indians. Later, during the colonial period, the Richelieu River together with the Hudson River formed the main highway between the English settlements and the French at Quebec.

Montreal, in Canada, now stands at the junction of the Ottawa and St. Lawrence rivers. This place was also of interest to the early Frenchmen. Here the St. Lawrence River has a rapids that stopped their little ships from going farther up the St. Lawrence River. Here, too, a large stream, now called the Ottawa, enticed them farther to the west. Paddling up its rugged course the early Frenchmen made their way on exploring expeditions farther into North America.

Not far westward from Montreal lies the Great Lakes region from which the St. Lawrence river draws most of its water. The Great Lakes form the largest fresh-water lake system to be found in any part of the world. Michigan is situated in the very center of the Great Lakes Basin and touches four of the Great Lakes: Lake Superior, Lake Michigan, Lake Huron, and Lake Erie. From the earliest French explorers to our modern ore carriers, and the recently developed St. Lawrence Waterway, Michigan's history has been closely associated with this water relationship.

Michigan has a lake shoreline of 3,251 miles. This is 62 per cent of the total United States Great Lakes shoreline. Tides are not large enough on the Great Lakes to be noticeable. Sometimes, however, where the air is unstable, as in thunderstorms and sudden rises and falls in the barometric pressure, the water level in one of the lakes suddenly rises. Such a sudden rise is called a seiche. Seiches sometimes raise the lake level as much as six feet. In June, 1954, eight people were drowned when a seiche came in upon the Chicago area.

The Great Lakes form the major part of the St. Lawrence drainage basin. All the rivers of northern Ohio, northern Indiana, northeastern Illinois, eastern Wisconsin, northeastern Minnesota, many of Ontario's rivers, and all of Michigan's rivers except a few in the western part of the Upper Peninsula spill their run-off waters into the Great Lakes or connecting waters. From Lake Ontario this run-off water passes down to the Atlantic Ocean by way of the St. Lawrence River.

The Great Lakes and St. Lawrence river, today, form one of our nation's most important waterways. During the shipping season, when the lakes are free from ice, large freighters carry iron ore, coal, limestone, cement, and wheat from one port to another while many ships flying flags of foreign nations enter the Great Lakes to discharge or receive cargo.

Near Montreal the St. Lawrence valley expands outward as it pushes farther west. Today, in this expanded valley, can be found the Canadian-Ottawa Region, comprising southern Ontario, and the United States Great Lakes drainage area. These two regions, though separated politically, form one geographic region.

The Ontario region is now the most heavily populated area of Canada. Over sixty per cent of Canada's people live in the area north of Lake Ontario and Lake Erie. This area is now the center of a large part of Canada's agriculture and industry. Here, too, can be found Canada's largest cities.

Courtesy Massey-Ferguson, Inc.

MF 35 Special Tractor and MF 66 Moldboard Plow. (1961)

The United States Great Lakes drainage area is one of the most important drainage areas in this country. It contains the land of northern Ohio, northern Indiana, and northern Illinois, together with parts of Wisconsin and Minnesota, as well as nearly all of Michigan. It is one of the major industrial and agricultural regions of the United States. Many people live in the area, and many large cities are to be found here, such as Cleveland, Toledo, Detroit, Flint, Grand Rapids, and Chicago. The Saint Lawrence Waterway has now made many cities on the Great Lakes ocean ports to which foreign ships can bring cargo or pick up cargo for foreign ports. No other continent has a similar concentration of people, cities, agriculture, and industry in its heartland as does North America.

The St. Lawrence system, even from the earliest days of settlement, has shaped in many ways the pattern of historical development in the Lake region. Its course leads directly to the markets of Europe, and even today, in our age of air transportation, the shortest route from Detroit to London lies along the St. Lawrence River valley. Many planes follow this general course in going from the United States to Europe.

Then, too, the river provides the only direct route leading into the heart of North America from the eastern seacoast. What is more, the river provides easy access to other water systems. Only a short portage took the early explorers from the St. Lawrence system to the Hudson River Valley, to the rivers of the Ohio and Mississippi watershed, and to many streams that flow north to Hudson Bay.

There are, however, many disadvantages to the St. Lawrence River system. During the winter the water freezes and shipping has to stop until spring comes again. The Lachine Rapids at Montreal as well as other rapids in the St. Lawrence River, between Montreal and Lake Ontario, made it impossible to use the river for boats larger than canoes until a system of canals was developed. Niagara Falls was also a hindrance to commerce to and from the West until the Welland Canal was opened in 1827. The rapids in the St. Mary's River stopped any real shipping between Lake Huron and Lake Superior until the Saint Mary's Falls Canal was opened in 1855.

Then, too, since the American Revolution, economic and international barriers stretching from Lake Superior to Montreal along the Great Lakes and St. Lawrence River have hindered the valley's growth and kept in force, until recently, the rivalry for commerce between the St. Lawrence and the Hudson River systems.

Michigan has a land area of 57,980 square miles. This figure does not include the water area of Lake Erie, Lake Michigan, Lake Superior, and Lake Huron that is commonly shown on maps as belonging to Michigan. If this water area were added to Michigan's size, it would make Michigan the largest state east of the Mississippi River.

The land area of Michigan is formed by two large peninsulas and several small islands. The two peninsulas are separated from each other by the Straits of Mackinac. Some of Michigan's larger and better known islands are Belle Isle, and Grosse Ile, in the Detroit River; Bois Blanc Island and Mackinac Island, in the Straits of Mackinac;

Drummond Island and Sugar Island, between the Upper Peninsula and Canada; Beaver Island, the Manitou Islands, and the Fox Islands in Lake Michigan; and Grand Island and Isle Royale, in Lake Superior.

The land surface of Michigan is mostly gently rolling glacial drift. In the western part of the Upper Peninsula the land is the rocky remains of what was once the Killarney Mountains. In Marquette, Iron, Baraga, and Gogebic counties the land pushes upward to 1,600 feet

MICHIGAN'S LAND TYPES

Department of Conservation

Information & Education

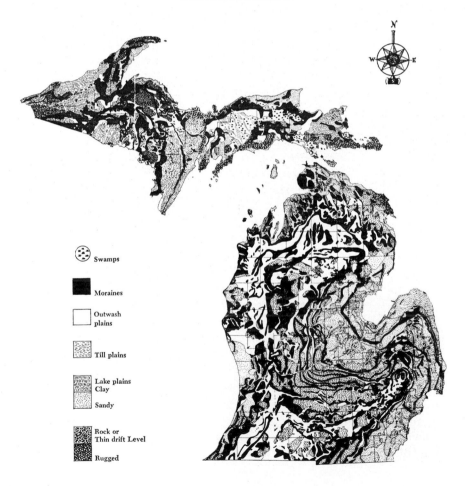

Swamps

Moraines

Outwash plains

Till plains

Lake plains
Clay

Sandy

Rock or
Thin drift Level

Rugged

and more. For many years, Michigan's highest elevation was thought to be in the Porcupine Mountains, in Ontonagon County, but more recent surveys, made by the United States Geological Survey, show several Huron Mountain peaks in Arvon township, in Baraga County, to be over 1,500 feet high. One of these peaks is the highest in the state.

Courtesy Modern Portrait Studio, Ironwood

Presque Isle Falls on the Big Presque Isle River north of Wakefield. Many pretty waterfalls like this one are found in the western part of the Upper Peninsula in the area that was once part of the Killarney Mountains. The Upper Peninsula was the homeland of the Chippewa Indians. Photo 1963.

It is an unnamed prominence located in the northwest one fourth of the southeast one fourth of section two, township fifty north, range thirty-one west in the northeast part of Baraga County. It has an elevation of 1,978 feet.

The eastern part of the Upper Peninsula, east of a line from Escanaba to Munising, is gently rolling land like that found in the Lower Peninsula. It is a land of swamps and sandy plains.

In the Lower Peninsula the highest part is the area roughly bounded by Cadillac, Wolverine, and West Branch. Here a deeper layer of glacial till was deposited. This elevation is known as the "High Plains Area." The soil is sandy and porous and easily absorbs the rainfall. Because of its elevation the growing season is short. In Oakland County and Hillsdale County the hills reach up to 1,200 feet above sea level.

The average annual temperature in Michigan varies from forty-nine degrees in the southern part of the state to thirty-nine degrees in the northern part. The average growing season varies from one hundred eighty days in the southwestern part of the Lower Peninsula to only ninety days in Iron County and Crawford County. Michigan's summers are not as warm, nor are her winters as cold, as they are in the states lying west of Lake Michigan. Water warms and cools more slowly than does land, and therefore the Great Lakes have a cooling effect on Michigan during the summertime and a warming effect during the wintertime.

Michigan receives an average rainfall of thirty-one inches. The heaviest rainfall is in the extreme south central and southwestern parts of the state along the Michigan-Indiana boundary line. In this area the rainfall averages thirty-six inches a year. In the Thumb area the average rainfall is only twenty-eight inches a year.

The surface area of Michigan is nearly all composed of transported materials that were pushed, or carried, down from north of Lake Superior and dropped as the glaciers melted away. Therefore, every acre of Michigan soil is the result of ice work and running water. Large piles of glacial debris, called moraines and more commonly known as hills, stand today just where they were dropped as the last glacier melted away. These moraines cover some thirty to forty per cent of the state. They are not as large, or high, as they were when they were dropped as the last glacier melted, for as the running water ran away it carried some of the smaller pieces of crushed rock with it. As the running water slowed down, part of this load was dropped, and thus outwash plains at the sides of the moraines were formed. Some-

At this plant near Oxford, sand and gravel are screened and graded. Sand and gravel are used in all kinds of construction work.

times this material was fine, and clay soils were thus formed. At other times sand and gravel were carried and deposited in valleys and in old lake bottoms. Sometimes the run-off waters from the glaciers left gravel deposits. These gravel deposits are often used today for material with which to build roads.

At almost any place in the state one may find large chunks of granite that have been rounded on the corners as they were scrubbed along by the glaciers. These boulders, which have now been removed with great effort from some farm lands, have sometimes been used in building foundations for houses, outside walls of houses, and fireplaces in homes and cottages.

Michigan has over eleven thousand inland lakes. These lakes vary in size from very small ones to the largest one, Houghton Lake in Roscommon County. The size and location of Michigan's ten largest lakes is shown in the following table:

Lake	Acreages	County
Houghton	20,044	Roscommon
Torch	18,700	Antrim-Kalkaska
Charlevoix	17,000	Charlevoix
Burt	16,700	Cheboygan
Mullet	16,630	Cheboygan
Gogebic	14,781	Gogebic-Ontonagon
Manistique	10,130	Luce-Mackinac
Black	10,130	Cheboygan-Presque Isle
Crystal	9,711	Benzie
Higgins	9,600	Roscommon

Most of Michigan's inland lakes have sand and gravel bottoms, but sometimes mud and soft ooze are found. Many of Michigan's lakes have sandy, shallow shores and beautiful wood-lined borders. During the summer these lakes sparkle in the sunshine and reflect the passing clouds and the green, wooded shores. Thousands of wild ducks and geese settle on the lakes' surfaces as they pass north each spring and south each fall, going to and from their nesting grounds

Courtesy Mrs. J. T. Braun

Marshall sandstone outcrop on Lake Huron near Grindstone City at the top of the Thumb. Photo 1961.

far to the north near Hudson Bay. In Michigan's lakes may be found many kinds of fish, plant, and animal life. During periods of heavy rainfall the lakes act as reservoirs which catch the run-off water and then let it flow slowly into the many streams.

From these lakes usually flow outlet streams which wind through farm or forest lands as the water runs to the Great Lakes. Once these lakes and streams were the source of furs, for on these streams beavers built their dams and lodges and reared their young. Here the muskrats built their homes. To the lakes came the animals of the forest to quench their thirst and swim in the pure, cool water. Later, many of these streams were used to float pine logs to Michigan's many sawmills. Today, Michigan's forests, lakes, and rivers, together with her long shore line, help to make Michigan one of the most visited tourist states in the Union.

Most of Michigan's rivers are not very long. Because most of them flow over sand and gravel areas and because they are fed by

Upper Ocqueoc Falls. (1961)   **Lower Ocqueoc Falls. (1961)**

lakes and springs, their rate of flow remains about the same throughout the year. In general they flow through long, shallow valleys. Because most of them flow through areas of glacial drift, there are some rapids but few waterfalls.

In the Lower Peninsula there are only two natural waterfalls, Ocqueoc and Rainy River Falls, which are both found in the area east and north of Onaway. In the Upper Peninsula, however, many of the streams flowing into Lake Superior flow over rocks and many waterfalls are found, especially in the old Killarney Mountain area.

Rainy River Falls. Photo (1961.)

The St. Joseph River is one of Michigan's largest rivers. It starts in Hillsdale County and drains the southwestern part of Michigan. In the early Indian and French days the St. Joseph River was used as a part of one of the main river highways leading into the Mississippi Valley.

North of the St. Joseph River lies the Kalamazoo River. Rising in Jackson County, the Kalamazoo River runs through Calhoun, Kalamazoo, and Allegan counties. During the later part of the glacial age, both the St. Joseph River and the Kalamazoo River, as well as the Grand River, carried much more water than they carry today.

Still farther to the north in Michigan flows the Grand River. In some places this river flows over bedrock. At Grand Rapids the Grand River has a fall of sixteen feet in one mile. This drop formed a rapids which gave the city of Grand Rapids its name. The Grand River empties into Lake Michigan at Grand Haven.

North of the Grand River flows the Muskegon River. This river has its beginning at Higgins Lake. It is one of the longest rivers in Michigan. During the lumbering days, many pine logs were floated on this river to the busy sawmills at Muskegon. Today, dams across the Muskegon River furnish water power for generating electricity.

There are no large rivers in southeastern Michigan except the Detroit and St. Clair rivers which run along Michigan's southeastern border. The run-off waters from Lake Huron pass first into the St. Clair River, which carries the water to Lake St. Clair. From Lake St. Clair the Detroit River carries the water into Lake Erie. Several small streams drain the area. The Raisin River empties into Lake Erie. The Huron River drains parts of Oakland, Livingston, Washtenaw, and Wayne counties. The Clinton River flows into Lake St. Clair at Mount Clemens. The Black River flows into the St. Clair River at Port Huron.

The Saginaw River flows into Saginaw Bay. Many well-known streams empty into the Saginaw River. They are the Cass, the Flint, the Shiawassee, the Bad, and the Tittabawassee.

In the upper part of the Lower Peninsula may be found the Manistee, Sturgeon, Black, Thunder Bay, Au Sable, and Rifle rivers. All of these rivers, as well as the Muskegon River, have their beginnings on the High Plains Area and flow from there to the Great Lakes. During the lumbering days these rapidly flowing streams carried thousands of pine logs to the sawmills at their mouths. Today, these same rivers attract thousands of people who come to Michigan each summer to spend a few weeks in cabins along the rivers' banks and to swim and fish in the clear water. Small power dams have been built on several of these rivers. These dams are used to generate electricity.

Most of the rivers of the Upper Peninsula are rather small. The Menominee, which forms part of the boundary between Michigan and Wisconsin, runs through wild, rocky country and has many rapids and waterfalls. The Manistique River runs through a large swampy area in the central part of the Upper Peninsula. It empties into Lake Michigan at Manistique. Many other rivers such as the Black, Presque

Isle, Ontonagon, Sturgeon, and Tahquamenon empty their waters into Lake Superior. Because these rivers pass over rocks, beautiful waterfalls are often found on them. The largest waterfall in Michigan is on the Tahquamenon River, a short distance east of Emerson on White Fish Bay. The Saint Mary's River carries the overflow from Lake Superior to Lake Huron. Today, the Saint Mary's River is one of the busiest waterways in the world.

No community in Michigan is more than 85 miles from one of the Great Lakes or more than 6 miles from a lake or stream.

Before the white man came, nearly all of Michigan was covered with forests. For countless centuries the trees of Michigan had grown almost untouched by man. From Copper Harbor, at the tip of the Keweenaw Peninsula, to the southern boundary of the state stretched one vast forest broken only here and there by lakes, rivers, little grassy plains, or prairies that were sometimes called "oak openings." Of Michigan's 37 million acres, 25 million were once covered with hardwood, pine, or swamp forests.

Many kinds of trees were found in Michigan. In general, the trees can be classed into two main groups, softwoods, and hardwoods. In the Lower Peninsula most of the softwoods grew north of a line drawn between Bay City and Muskegon. Most of the hardwoods grew south of this line. In the Upper Peninsula the area east of Munising and Escanaba was largely occupied by pine and swamp forests, while in the area west of these two cities hardwood forests predominated. Where the various kinds of trees grew depended largely upon the kind of soil that the glaciers had left and the amount of moisture to be found in the area.

In general the pine trees grew on the lighter, sandier soils. On the very best of the lighter soil grew the white pine. On the medium soil grew the red, or Norway, pine. On the poorest of the sandy soil grew the little jack pines.

The whole upper part of the Lower Peninsula and the eastern part of the Upper Peninsula formed one vast pine forest broken only here and there by small areas of swamps or lakes, or by small stands of hardwoods which had driven the pine trees from the better land. The lower part of the Lower Peninsula and the western half of the Upper Peninsula were once covered with hardwoods.

The pine forests were made up of three kinds of pine trees. The most numerous trees were the Norway, or red, pines. You can easily tell a red pine because it always has two long needles in every sheath and when you bend a needle it breaks with a snap. Another type of pine, the one that the lumbermen wanted the most, was the white pine. You can tell this tree when you see it because it has five needles in every sheath. Thus you can remember that there are just as many needles in each sheath as there are letters in the word "white" or as

you have fingers and thumb on one hand. The third type of pine that was found in Michigan was the jack pine. It was a smaller tree and lived on the poorest soil in the state. Because of its slow growth and stunted size it has been of little commercial value.

Pine trees at the Hartwick State Park, Grayling, Michigan. Photo 1947.

A Jack pine near Grayling. These scraggly trees grow on the poor sandy soil. Photo 1948.

The hardwood forests were made up of the trees that had broad, flat leaves. In the hardwood forests one could find such trees as beech, maple, ash, elm, white oak, and hickory.

Michigan's swamp forests grew in the moist soil found in swampy areas or near lakes or streams. In the swamp forests grew such trees as the tamarack, spruce, cedar, balsam, and birch.

Today, about 53 per cent of Michigan's land area is still classed as forest land.

In Michigan's forests there were small areas in which the trees would not grow. Near Grayling these areas were called "plains." In the southern part of the state these areas were spoken of by the early settlers as "oak openings." Oak openings were found mostly in Oakland County and, in the southwestern part of the state, in Berrien, Cass, and Van Buren counties.

Until the settlers cleared the land, much of Michigan was what is known today as a "biological desert." Because large areas of the state were covered with vast forests which shut out the sunlight, small plants, on which animals could feed, did not grow on the deeply shaded forest floor. The animals that did live in Michigan lived in the swampy areas or near the rivers and lakes where sunshine could find its way to the ground and small plants could grow. Along the

Replanting of red pine as it looked at Higgins Lake, 1948. It is too dark for anything to grow under a thick pine forest. This lack of food greatly limited animal life in vast areas of the state.

streams could be found such animals as beavers, muskrats, minks, martins, and otters. In the woods and swamps could be found deer, elk, wolves, and occasionally a moose or a buffalo.

Many minerals are found in Michigan. Most of these were discussed in the last chapter on geology. Many of them, such as salt, copper, iron ore, gypsum, and limestone, have had an important part in the industrial development of the state.

In many of the streams a fish known as the grayling could be found. Many birds such as geese, ducks, wild turkeys, passenger pigeons, and numerous varieties of small song birds came to Michigan each year. The grayling and the passenger pigeon are both now extinct.

CHAPTER THREE

The Indians of Early Michigan

EXACTLY when the American Indians came to live in North and South America no one knows, for there are no records of their ancestors' ancient wanderings. Students of history now think that the first American Indians came from Asia, by way of Alaska, and slowly worked their way downward across both North and South America. Evidence seems to show that early man came to live in southern Michigan between 8,000 and 4,000 B.C., following the retreat of the last glacier. Artifacts show that these early people used argillite, which is a kind of slate, to form their projectile points. Sometimes in the upper part of the state quartzite was used.

When the early mineral prospectors began looking for deposits of copper in the Lake Superior Region, between 1845 and 1850, they soon discovered that earlier miners had worked copper mines throughout the area hundreds of years before them. In fact, the prospectors soon learned to look for ancient copper workings as a clue for locating copper-bearing rock.

The people who worked these prehistoric copper mines are now referred to as the prehistoric copper miners of the Lake Superior region. Whoever they were, they were Michigan's oldest known human inhabitants. The identity of these early copper miners now presents us with one of the most interesting archeological problems in all North America. Who these early miners were we do not know. Neither do we know at what period in the history of North America they did their extensive copper mining. Some tests made on pieces of charcoal, found on the bottoms of some of their ancient pits, indicate that these prehistoric people must have worked the copper pits at least 3,500 or 4,000 years ago.

On Isle Royale and in the Keweenaw Peninsula and also along the eastern shore of Lake Superior, north of Sault Ste. Marie, Ontario, many pits and trenches, made in the rocky surface of the land by these early copper miners, have been found. None of the pits contain any glacial debris. This clearly shows that the pits were made after the last glacial retreat. Some 5,000 early copper mining pits have been located and identified as the work of these early copper miners.

Most pits are but a single hole sunk into the trap rock. In some areas single open pits extend in an almost continuous line for as far as thirty miles or more along the top of a copper vein. In other places wide-open trenches are found that show where the ancient miners broke the hard rock in which the copper deposits lay. Most of the pits are about 20 to 30 feet deep. Some pits, however, reach down to a depth of about 60 feet. This was about as deep as these early miners could go and still keep the water bailed from the pit by humans using wooden or birch bark buckets. The practice of pit mining was probably used so that the rock between the pits would act as a dam to keep the water from coming into the pit being worked.

As the early mineral prospectors searched the copper area they also learned that the early copper miners had been very thorough in their search for copper deposits. Nearly all of the main native copper deposits had been located and worked. How they located the deposits presents another mystery, for many of the copper deposits were hidden under a layer of glacial drift that had to be removed before the copper deposits could be found.

These early copper miners worked with only the most primitive mining techniques. First, fire was used by the miners to heat the solid rock and cause it to expand. Then, when the rock had become hot, the fire was pushed aside and cold water was dashed onto the heated rock. This quickly cooled the rock and caused it to contract and crack. By this method chunks of rock, containing pieces of pure copper were broken from the parent mass. These smaller pieces of rock were then pounded with a stone hammer to make them release the chunks of native copper from the rock.

The mauls used by these early miners tell us more about how these early miners worked. These mauls were really beach stones, glacial drift and local beach worn rock, that were used as hammers to beat the rock. These were, in general, about 8 or 10 inches in diameter. On Isle Royale the mauls are nearly all of a different type rock formation from that of the rock which forms the island. Most of the mauls found on Isle Royale are usually fine-grained, dark gabbro, showing plainly their igneous origin. All of them show the weathering action of having been rolled by waves and thus rounded and smoothed like stones found along any beach today. They seem to have been picked up along the northern shore of Lake Superior, in what is now Canada, and from there they must have been taken to the island. That means that nearly all of these mauls must have been transported for at least seventy-five miles. One can but wonder what kind of boats these early miners used to carry these black stones across treacherous Lake Superior to the island and how they docked the boats, or canoes, on the rocky island shore. Hundreds of tons of these stone hammers were thus transported across the Lake to Isle Royale.

Courtesy Judge Charles Willman

A collection of "Rock Hammers" which were found near Rockland by Judge Willman in November 1958. These hammers were used until broken and then discarded by the ancient miners.

These stone mauls in general weighed between 7 and 10 pounds. Nearly all of the mauls are broken or chipped on one end or on both ends. This plainly shows that they were used to pound against other rocks.

Another interesting thing about these prehistoric stone hammers is that only a few of those which have been found on Isle Royale have grooves on them while those that have been found on the Keweenaw Peninsula are nearly always grooved. Some, in fact, on the Keweenaw Peninsula have two grooves on them. These grooves seem to have been chipped entirely around each stone by hammering another stone against it. The groove was then smoothed by drawing a buckskin thong, to which an abrasive was applied, back and forth along the groove. These grooves made it possible to fasten a wooden handle onto the hammer with a wythe. Whereas the stone hammers used on the Keweenaw Peninsula seem to have been swung with the aid of a wooden handle it seems that those used on Isle Royale were merely held in the worker's hands while pounding. One can but wonder if these two different types of stone mauls, so unlike in workmanship and location, might not denote two different cultural eras of aboriginal stone age copper miners. If this could be true, then the copper mines on Isle Royale may be older and had been worked out before the copper mines were later developed on the Keweenaw Peninsula. Research on the work of these early miners seems to show that the work on these early copper pits extended over a period of perhaps 4,000 years. Much copper seems to have been mined even before the mound builders came to live in the area.

To the best of our knowledge, these early stone age men, although they used fire to heat the mass rock, never learned to smelt the native copper ore or to mix any alloy with it. Although copper melts at a relatively low point, about 2,500 degrees, this was still hotter than their wood fires could, without blowing air into them, have been made. For this reason they seem to have sought only the smaller pieces of copper that they could pound into the object, or shape, which they desired to make. They learned that by pounding the copper it was hardened. This pounding changed the internal structure of the copper by an annealing technique.

In some of their anscient workings, like the later Minesota Mine, large masses of copper, weighing several tons, have been found that had been freed from the parent rock. Such huge masses, however, were of little value to those early miners for they had no way of cutting them up or of smelting them. All the large copper masses that have been found showed definite evidences of repeated hammering. All the projections that could have been used had been pounded off, thus, leaving a fairly smooth unusable copper mass that was left in the pit.

The copper that these early miners found was pure native copper and not copper sulphide or copper oxide that forms most of the world's copper resources and needs refining. The Lake Superior region is the only place in the world where this native pure copper has been found in any large quantity. Some native copper has been found in the southwestern part of the United States, and in the early 1920's some was also found in Bolivia. But the source of all of the copper that the Indians had must have been the Lake Superior region.

Once a piece of copper had been freed from the mother rock these early workmen pounded it with a stone to beat it into a useful product. This they could do as the pieces of native copper were pure and malleable. Selecting a piece of copper of the size that could be used, they beat out between stones many things: such as, axes, knives, chisels, spear points, daggers, arrow-heads, awls, needles, bracelets, amulets, and pendants. All of these artifacts have been found in Indian graves and burial mounds from Lake Superior to Central America and from Pennsylvania to Arizona.

As one looks at these old mining pits, carved into the rock with so much human toil, one can but wonder who these ancient miners were. From where did they come? Did they mine only during the summer months when the weather was warm? How did they get their food? Both Isle Royale and the Keweenaw Peninsula are very limited hunting areas. Many fish could have been used along with grain they could have brought from farther south. Careful estimates made about these ancient pits show that there must have been several hundred men working over a period of several hundred years to move such a huge amount of rock and the copper they took from the area. On the basis of later mining operations, which has shown the approximate percentage of copper to the parent rock, it has been estimated that these ancient miners carried away with them between 500,000 and 1,000,000 pounds of pure copper from their ancient pits. We know something about where this copper went but we know little about how it was carried away or the routes over which it went or how the miners traveled to or from the mining area.

All that has been found in the area are the pits, mauls, and a very few artifacts. Little evidence of permanent villages has been found to give us a clue as to the identity of such an intelligent and industrious people. Unfortunately, too, for students of this early era, many of the artifacts that were found by the early prospectors and residents of the area were carelessly destroyed or lost. Then, too, accurate and careful records of their findings were not made.

So old are the pits that the miners left that by the time the white man came into the area most of them were filled with debris that had fallen into them. For nature to do this on Isle Royale and the Keweenaw Peninsula must have taken a long, long time, for both are isolated areas where the winds carry little debris.

Articles made from this copper and an occasional stone maul, similar to those used in mining, have been found in the Indian burial

Courtesy Henry C. Lang

Burnt Bluff Indian paintings on the Garden Peninsula. These paintings, on the Silurian limestone, are the only known original Indian paintings in Michigan.

mounds all the way from Wisconsin to the mouth of the Mississippi River and from Pennsylvania to the mountains in the western part of the United States. Early European explorers, coasting along the shores of North America often reported seeing Indians with copper knives, earrings, and other articles. The conquerors of Mexico reported much copper among the Aztecs. But from where did the Aztecs get copper at so late a date as 1500 A.D.?

It seems reasonable to think that the early stone age miners were Indians from the Ohio Valley area that came north each summer to work the copper-bearing pits. Each year they carried the copper back south with them. From their homelands it was traded with other Indian tribes or captured by them. But why did the miners stop coming? Why were their tools left in the pits as if they had expected to return to work the next morning? What is still more mysterious to us is: why was this most ancient of all North American industries, copper mining, completely forgotten and unknown by the later Indians who lived in the Great Lakes area? When the white men came to the Great Lakes area the Indians living here at that time knew nothing about the ancient copper mines, either the nature of the pits or the manner in which they had been worked. What is more, the Indians

Indian mound near Grand Rapids. Photo 1963.

had no legends that dealt with this ancient mining industry. Such copper as the Indians had, when the white man came, were pieces of copper that they had found along the beach or buried in the glacial drift. To these strange masses of copper metal, because of their difference from common rocks, the Indians often gave a special religious reverence.

Another group, or perhaps the same group, of ancient Indians, that we know very little about, are now called the mound builders. These Indians lived in southern Michigan, Ohio, Indiana, Illinois, and Iowa. In Michigan over six hundred Indian mounds have been located and recorded. Nearly all of the Michigan mounds lie south of a line drawn west from Saginaw Bay. These mounds were made for burial places by heaping soil into a pile on the ground. Michigan's mounds were merely dome shaped piles of earth but some of the mounds in Ohio and Wisconsin were made in the shape of animals. One of the best known is the serpent mound in Ohio. In the Indian mounds have been found human bones, clay dishes, tools made of copper, stone, or bone, arrowheads, and crude pieces of jewelry made from animal claws, shells, and small pieces of copper. All these artifacts tell us much about this ancient culture, but who the people were, or why their culture declined still remains a mystery. Some of the burial mounds still remain but most of them have been destroyed by the white settlers that moved into the area.

Besides the mounds the early Indians left circular and irregular open spaces that seem to have been enclosed by banks of earth. These open spaces are known as "forts" and may have been used as such by the early Indians. Holes in the ground, known as "pot holes," present to students of this period another mystery. Were they used as root cellars for storing food, as places for cooking, or for fighting, as "fox holes" are used by soldiers today? In some places low earth ridges have been found. These are known as "garden beds." Garden beds were of several shapes, but the most common shape was that of the spokes and rim of a wheel. Unfortunately for those who wish to learn more about Indian culture nearly all the mounds, pot holes, and garden beds in Michigan have now been destroyed.

Not all the Indians of North America were living in the same stage of cultural development when the first white men came here from Europe. There were many levels of Indian culture. Each group of Indians had developed its own culture or way of life that was adapted to the geography of the area in which it lived. Some tribes on the Great Plains of the West lived in tepees and made their living by follow-

Courtesy Museum of Anthropology, U. of M.
Central burial pit Mound "C" of the Norton Mound Group. Grand Rapids. 1963. The individual on the left is a male. The conch shell dippers are from the Gulf Coast. Crushed pottery can be seen in the upper right hand corner.

ing the buffalo herds as these large animals roamed across the broad plains in search of food. Other tribes in the southwestern part of the United States lived in large houses made of clay and were farmers who made their living by raising food on irrigated land. Many other Indian tribes were forest dwellers. The Indians who were living in Michigan when the Frenchmen found them were a forest people living in a land of lakes, streams, and trees. Their way of life was one they had developed to best meet the needs of a people living in a forest land.

Fortunately for us the writings of the French missionaries tell us much about the culture of the Indians that lived in the Great Lakes area. Then, too, the early Indians have left behind many interesting artifacts in their burial mounds and refuse pits. These remains of early Indian life have been carefully studied by people who have been interested in the cultures of the various Indian tribes that once made the Great Lakes area their homeland. From these two sources we have learned much about what Indian life was like in this land of lakes, streams, and forests.

The Indians that lived in the Great Lakes area when the French and English first came to America were divided into two large groups. The basis for these groups is the Indian language that was spoken. One group is known as the Iroquois. The other group is known as the Algonquin.

Although Iroquois war parties came as far west as Michigan their homeland was the region of Ontario above Lake Erie and Lake Ontario, in Canada, and in New York State. The Iroquois that lived in Ontario, Canada, were known as Hurons or Wyandottes (Wendat). They lived north of Lake Erie in the area of Lake Simcoe and around the south end of Georgian Bay. By the time the French came to their homeland the Hurons, although Iroquois by language and culture, were already at war with the other Iroquois nations that lived south of Lake Ontario, in New York State.

The Iroquois seem to have come from farther to the south and to have brought with them more of an agricultural way of life than was practiced by their neighbors, the Algonquins. The Iroquois lived in long houses which were covered with elm bark and often had a palisade, made of tall poles, around their permanent villages. Several families lived in each long house. The Iroquois Indians were divided into several smaller groups, or nations; such as, the Hurons, the Senecas, and the Mohawks.

The Algonquin Indians were also made up of several groups such as the Ottawa, Chippewa, Menominee, and Pottawattomie. They completely surrounded the Iroquois nations. They depended less on agriculture than did the Iroquois. They were less warlike, but in general, their culture was not as far advanced as that of the Iroquois. Of the many Algonquin tribes that lived around the Iroquois we are concerned with only the tribes that lived in the Great Lakes area.

As the French moved westward they made friends with the Algonquin tribes and with the Hurons. One of the first Indian tribes that the Frenchmen met as they pushed west was the Ottawa that then lived along the Ottawa River. The French called them the "Odohwah" meaning traders, because they began acting as traders, or middlemen, between the Indians farther to the west and the French at Quebec.

When the Frenchmen came to live with the Indians, they found the Algonquins living in what we now call the Neolithic or New Stone Age. They knew how to make a fire and to chip flint to make arrowheads and tools, such as awls and scraping knives. They had also taken the first steps in writing their language. They had not yet discovered the wheel and had tamed only one animal, the dog, which they used for hunting, for guarding the village, and sometimes for food. Some plants, such as corn, squash, tobacco, and pumpkins, they had already domesticated. Socially they had begun to develop a home and family life. They practiced some farming, but most of their food was still secured by hunting.

Among the Indians there was a division of work just as there is among our people. The Indian men were known as braves. Most of their time was spent in hunting and fishing. To the Indians, hunting and fishing were not sports as they are for us today. Hunting was their chief means of getting food and failure meant hunger and sometimes starvation for all.

For hunting and in war Indian braves used bows and arrows and stone war clubs. An Indian bow was large and strong and carefully made from one of the hardwoods, such as the ash. The ends of the strong, springy bow were bent toward each other and held there by a strong bowstring made from a tough piece of animal sinew or hide. Arrows were made from light, straight sticks, called shafts. Each shaft was tipped at one end with a pointed, chipped, flat piece of flint called an arrowhead. On the opposite end of the shaft, feathers were skillfully fastened so that the arrow would fly straight to its mark.

Nearly all of the Indian braves' time was spent in hunting and fishing. Quietly they made their way through the forests in search of game. Here they found animals such as squirrels, muskrats, beaver, deer, elk, moose, bear, and sometimes a buffalo. These animals they killed with arrows or clubs. Sometimes they caught them in pitfalls, or carefully made deadfalls, or drove them into the water where other Indians in canoes clubbed them to death.

During the spring, summer, and early autumn the braves hunted waterfowl such as ducks and geese. In the lakes and streams the braves caught fish. Sometimes the fish were driven into shallow places and there they were grabbed by the hands of the hunters. Others were caught on bone or copper hooks to which was attached some animal sinew for lines. Others were shot with arrows or caught on spears having a stone or copper point. Still others were caught in crude nets. The Indians killed all this game so that they and their families might live.

Because of this endless search for game the Indians of Michigan lived in easily moved homes that they called "wigwams." These dome-shaped wigwams were made by covering bent trees, or poles, with pieces of bark or animal skins. These quickly made, and easily moved, shelters kept out some of the cold, rain, and snow. Near the center of a wigwam a small fire gave out some heat for warming the wigwam and for doing what little cooking the Indian family did. Most of the smoke from the fire passed out through an opening which had been left at the top of the wigwam. The Indians lived outside most of the time, but on rainy or cold days the family often gathered inside. Here they sat around the fire on animal skins or reed mats that had been placed upon the ground.

Among the Indians one could find skilled workers just as we can among the people living in Michigan today. In some places the remains of Indian workshops have been found. At these places broken stones and stone chips show that arrowheads, chisels, gouges, drills, and flint knives were once made there by very skilled Indian craftsmen.

Indian braves spent much time making traps and weapons. Spear handles were made from hickory or ash. Knives were formed from shells, antlers, teeth, or pieces of flint. Pipes of many descriptions were made. Some pipes were made of clay, others of wood, and still others from a soft stone called "pipe stone." No two pipes were alike. Some were made to look like birds, while others were shaped like turtles or other animals. With crude, handmade stone tools the Indians felled small trees, peeled bark from birch trees, or elm trees, to make their canoes, made bows and arrows, formed snowshoes, skinned and cut up animals, sewed their buckskin clothing, and cared for their little garden plots.

There was little of what we call government among the Indians. Their constant wanderings gave them little chance to collect things or to develop village life as we know it today. Outside of their tribal customs each person was allowed to do much as he pleased unless he harmed other members of the tribe. There were no chiefs who received their titles from their fathers. The tribal leaders, known as chiefs, won their positions by being heroes and leaders in battle or around the council fire.

The Indians' ideas as to property values were far different from those we have today. Private property was almost unknown to them in their way of life. The Indians thought of most things as being owned by the tribe. The hunting grounds belonged to the tribe and were open to all for hunting and fishing. There were only a few small things that they thought of as personal property, such as birch bark dishes, bows and arrows, and jewelry. This lack of governmental development and private ownership made it difficult for the Indians to understand the white man and his ways when he came to America.

This circle of trees, known as the Indian Council Trees, stands on Greensky Hill, northeast of Charlevoix. Photo 1957.

Because the Indians fought the white settlers who were taking their homelands away from them, the white men came to look upon the Indians as fearful warriors. It seems, however, that before the white men

Each of the council trees has been bent outward from the center. This is one of the best Indian relics in the state. Photo 1957.

began pressing in upon the Indian hunting grounds the Indians often spent long periods of time living in peace. But, like the white man, they sometimes went to war because of wrongs done to their tribe or to gain new and better hunting grounds. When on the warpath, braves were cunning, vengeful, and ruthless. All men, women, children, and even the aged then felt the brutality of the enraged warriors. Captive warriors were sometimes cruelly tortured, but captured women and children were often adopted into the winning tribe.

The Indian women were known as squaws. To the Indians the word squaw meant the same as our word mother. They stayed at home and did most of the work around the village and in the wigwam. When the braves killed a deer or bear, it was the women who dragged it home, dressed it, and prepared it for food for the family. Sometimes extra venison was cut up into small pieces about an inch square and strung on bark strings. This meat was then smoked and dried to cure it. This was called "jerked venison." These preserved pieces of dried meat were eaten when game could not be found. The women tanned deer skins to make buckskin for clothing. Tanning was a long, tiresome task. One squaw could tan only a few deer skins a year. A skin was first carefully scraped with a stone knife to get off all the flesh and hair. Then it was treated with tanning materials and buried in the ground for some time. Later the skins were dug up, treated again, and then buried again. When finished, doeskin and buckskin became a soft, pliable material for making Indian clothing.

It was the women who gathered fallen wood from the forest to keep their little fires burning. They carried water for the family in birch bark pails from a nearby stream, spring, or lake. They gathered nuts, berries, and herbs. Now and then they found the eggs of some water fowl. Water for cooking meat, as well as maple sap for making maple syrup, was boiled by means of placing stones on the bottom of a bark trough onto which hot stones were dropped into the liquid to make the water boil.

From birch bark the women made pails, dishes, and boxes. These they used for carrying water or nuts and berries and also for containers in which to keep various articles. Sometimes these birch bark boxes were decorated with brightly colored porcupine quills that had been tinted with dyes which were made from the juice of berries or plants. Sometimes they wove mats from reeds that they had gathered from marshy places. These mats were placed on the earth floors of the wigwams.

Michigan Indian women were also good basket makers. Long strips of clean, white wood were secured from black ash. First a log was soaked in a lake or river for several weeks. Then the water-soaked log was pounded for hours with a heavy pole to loosen the long fibrous strips. These strips were then cut to the desired widths by using a sharp stone. With these wet strips of wood, the Indian women wove baskets of many sizes and shapes. Sometimes the wooden strips were dyed bright colors so that the baskets would have bright designs. Sweet grass was often worked into the weaving of baskets or sewn onto birch bark boxes so that the boxes and baskets would carry the pleasing aroma.

It was the women, too, who packed the family belongings and carried them to the canoes each time the Indians moved to another camping place. If they moved overland, the Indian braves, to guard the group, walked ahead of the women, carrying only their bows and arrows. Each woman followed behind in Indian file, carrying all her belongings and perhaps a papoose on her weary back.

The Indian women were also Michigan's first farmers, for they were the ones who planted the little clearings and cared for the gardens. In this land of forests the Indians found it difficult to prepare the land for planting. Their stone axes were too crude to clear away the larger trees. The Indians did, however, sometimes cut the bark all the way around some trees and thus caused them to die. This let more sunlight fall upon their little gardens, which often were planted

Courtesy Thomas E. Mackie, River Rouge, Mich.

Michigan barbed axes. Most of them have been found in Kent and Ionia counties. No other county shows more than one or two specimens. Few are found outside the state. No artifact is more representative of Michigan.

among the dead trees if no cleared ground could be found. Sometimes these dead trees, which had been girdled, were later burned and thus small clearings were made. In the southwestern part of the state and in Oakland County the Indians used the open spaces called "oak openings" for making their gardens.

Most of the seeds which the squaws planted were such as could be planted by merely pushing a hole into the ground with a sharp stick. They planted beans, squash, melons, pumpkins, sunflowers, tobacco, and Indian corn, which they called maize. These plants, being either tall or of the running vine type, could thus seek out their own sunshine.

During the summer the women, girls, and a few of the old men hoed their gardens with little hoes made from flat stones, clam shells, or the shoulder blade of an animal. In the fall the women gathered the corn and stored it in baskets for the coming winter. The best Indian farmers in early Michigan were the Pottawattomies who lived in the southwestern part of the state.

In the fall the Indians who lived near Menominee gathered the wild rice that grew in the marsh lands near by. In the spring the Indians caught the sweet sap of the sugar maple trees in little birch bark cups. From this sweet sap the squaws made maple syrup and maple sugar for their families. This sweet syrup and, now and then, some wild honey were the nearest things to candy that Indian children ever had.

Women now spend much of their time doing the laundry and washing the dishes. Neither of these tasks was expected of the Indian women. Indians did not know about soap. Birch bark or wooden dishes were used again and again without washing. Clothing was never washed as it is today, and no doubt it was as full of vermin as were the heads of the people who wore it.

Indian women usually wore their hair braided or wound on wood chips and pinned to the backs of their heads. In cold weather they wore animal skins to keep them warm. Loads were carried by means of a wide "carrying strap" that passed from one's back across the forehead and then again to the back. These straps were used for carrying papooses or other loads.

During the summer months the Indians wore little clothing. Bear grease was smeared on their bodies to help keep away black flies, mosquitoes, and other pests. Sometimes they painted their bodies with dyes made from berries and roots. Soot was used for black to paint on their bodies and faces. For red they used red hemitite iron ore. During the wintertime they wore warm clothing made from the skins of animals such as the beaver. Large garments, like shirts and trousers, were made from buckskin. Soft-soled shoes, known as moccasins, were made from tanned skins. Often skirts, jackets, and leggings were decorated on their edges with dyed quills, or fringed with shells, stones, or animal teeth.

The lives of the Indians were filled with toil and hardships. They had few of the things that we call comforts today. By the time most of the women were thirty-five, or forty years old, they were already old women.

The real highways of the Indians of the Great Lakes region were the many lakes and their connecting river systems. This was a land of lakes and rivers, and traveling on them was much easier than tramping through forests and swamps. Indian canoes were well adapted for travel, and the Indians used them with both grace and speed.

Courtesy Newell E. Collins, Algonac, Michigan

Eagle Pipe

Indian braves made canoes by putting green skins over wooden frames and letting them dry until the skins became taut, or by covering the wooden frames with birch bark or elm bark. Although similar in shape, each Indian group usually had its own variation in the shape of the two canoe ends and one could usually tell by looking at a canoe the tribe to which it belonged. These Indian canoes should not be compared with the small pleasure canoes of today, for Indian canoes were usually much larger. Records left by the early missionaries and explorers tell us that the bark canoes of that time were usually large enough to carry an Indian family of five or six and all the possessions of the family such as bows, arrows, skins, and dishes for cooking.

In thinking of these early Indian canoes we must remember that we do not really know just how they looked before the Frenchmen came with better tools to make them. The Indians' tools were crude, and their canoes must have been rather roughly made because they had no saws, planes, glue, nails, shellac, or varnish with which to work. Whatever their shapes, they were used for hunting, fishing, and carrying the family and its supplies.

Bark canoes had several good points. Materials from which to make them and keep them in repair could be found in the forest. They were light and could be carried with ease by one or two men across any of the many portages between the headwaters of streams, or where falls or rapids made it necessary to travel by land. They did not sink far into the water but rather floated lightly upon it. Because of this, it was possible to paddle canoes far up the smaller streams where larger boats, sinking deeper into the water, could not have gone. This made it possible to greatly shorten the distance required in making portages from one river to another.

Although canoes had these very good qualities, they also had several faults that caused their users much trouble. Since they were made of bark and had light frames, they were often very short-lived. During the cold winter weather the bark often shrank and split open. Then too, the bark would often become brittle and peel. To keep canoes from shrinking and peeling they were sometimes buried in the moist sand beside a river or lake.

If you look closely at a large map of North America which shows the lakes and rivers, you will notice that the St. Lawrence River system and the Mississippi River system almost touch in a number of places. By going up these streams and from one river to another the Indians, and later the Frenchmen, could make their way far into the continent.

In cold weather, when the winter snow lay deep on the marshlands, frozen lakes, and forest floors, the Indians, while hunting or on the trail, used snowshoes to keep their feet from sinking into the soft, white, fluffy drifts.

A few trails, or traces as they were called, the age of which nobody knows, ran through the ancient forest. No one could tell how they came to be. We can only surmise about their beginnings, but we do know that animals roamed the forests before man made his home here.

Buffalo, in their wanderings, pushed back the brush and trampled down small trees and, by some instinct known only to creatures of the wilds, marked with their pounding feet the easiest paths throughout the wilderness. Years later government surveyors, seeking the best places to run new roads across the land, found that the best routes often led along the same traces that the animals had made across the ancient land. No one knew all the turnings of these silent, mysterious paths where danger might lurk around any bend or an enemy spring from behind some nearby tree or stump.

Sometimes the trees were small and the trails led through leafy walls on either side. At other times the trails ran through forests where the ground was always damp and musty and where, in the summertime, tall trees held aloft their canopied tops and all was open underneath. Then one walked as if in a great cathedral.

Along lake shores and rivers and across swampy areas the flora often grew thick and dense and the traveler had to push his way through branches and undergrowth which blocked his path. Swamps, especially, were a problem to foot travelers. Often the soft, water-filled, boggy land would hardly support the weight of the traveler. Cattail marshes and long swamp grass gave little footing. Long black snakes and timber moccasins wriggled through the water and the long marsh grass. Here the smell of spruce and cedar blended with the stench of swamp muck and decaying grass and leaves.

At other times the traces ran across "oak openings" or open grassy plains among the jack pines. Here the traces were dry and firm. In the summertime the sun beat down and the June grass turned yellow along the trace. In the grass grew wild strawberries, deep red in color. So thick were these strawberries that they often stained the moccasins of Indians and the hoofs of animals.

Twisting and turning through shaded, silent woodlands, across oak openings and jack pine plains, past quiet blue lakes, up hill, down hill, across streams at fords, where the water ran wide and swift, went the traces or ancient forest paths. They were of little value even for the Indians because it was often very hard to push oneself through the forest, even without a pack on one's back.

One of these trails, now US 112, was known as the Great Sauk Trail. It ran across Lower Michigan from Detroit to the southern end of Lake Michigan. Another ran from Toledo, Ohio, to Kalamazoo, through Grand Rapids, and on to Mackinaw City. Another ran from Detroit to Saginaw and then to Mackinaw City by following the western shore of Lake Huron. Another ran from Saginaw to a spot near Higgins Lake. There it divided; one trail led to the Traverse City region while the other followed the present line of the railroad through Grayling and Gaylord to Cheboygan and Mackinaw City. Other trails ran across the Upper Peninsula. One ran from Sault Ste. Marie to St. Ignace and then on west to Escanaba. Others went north through the forests to Lake Superior.

During the warm summer months the Indians of Michigan often gathered in small villages at places where hunting and fishing could support the people. The same tribe did not always occupy the same place. During the wintertime the Indians usually divided into smaller bands and went to winter hunting grounds so that the need for food would not be more than the region could supply. In all, before the white man came, there were not more than fifteen or twenty thousand Indians living in Michigan.

When the Frenchmen first started coming to Michigan after 1660 they found several Indian tribes living in the area. In the western part of the Upper Peninsula lived the remnant of the Huron tribe that you will read about in the next chapter. Their real name was Wendat, now called Wyandottes and they formerly lived east of Lake Huron in what is now Ontario, Canada. During the early days of New France this area was known as Huronia. They were really Iroquois by language though they had broken away from the Iroquois tribes living south of Lake Ontario.

In the area around Menominee lived a tribe called the Pottawattomies. In the rest of the Upper Peninsula lived the Chippewas who were also called Ojibwas. In the area around Saginaw Bay lived the Sauk and Fox Indians. LaSalle tells us that the Miami Indians were living in southwestern Michigan when he built his little fort on the Miami River (St. Joseph River) in 1679. No tribe occupied southeastern Michigan as it was too close to the Iroquois and was often raided by them.

By 1750 some changes had been made in the tribal locations. Around 1700 the Miami seemed to have moved eastward and settled in northern Ohio around the western and southern shore of Lake Erie. The Pottawattomies moved into the area vacated by the Miami in the St. Joseph and Kalamazoo River valleys. The Ottawas, driven from their homeland along the Ottawa River by the Iroquois, occupied the Grand River Valley and the area of the northeastern part of the Lower Peninsula from Mackinaw City to Little Traverse Bay. When the Pottawattomies left the area around Menominee the Menominee Indians, from farther west, moved into the area. About the time the Miami moved to the Maumee River area in northern Ohio the Sauk and Fox moved from Michigan to Wisconsin. The Ottawa and Chippewa still continued to live in the eastern part of the Upper Peninsula. Some Hurons, or Wyandottes settled near Detroit after the settlement was started.

Although the Indians no longer possess the Lake Region, they have left many names to remind us of them. Many of our familiar names of Michigan places and rivers are of Indian origin, such as: Michigan, Michilimackinac, Cheboygan, Owosso, Petoskey, Munising, Ishpeming, Negaunee, Calumet, Tahquamenon, Wyandotte, Tecumseh, Tekonsha, Tittabawasse, Saugatuck, Muskegon, Escanaba, Menominee, and Pontiac. Many other words that we commonly use are also of Indian origin, such as: tobacco, succotash, hickory, toboggan, moccasins, moose, caucus, squash, tomato, and potato. We use these words when talking or writing about Michigan, but seldom stop to think of their Indian origin, much less their meaning.

During the French and English periods the Indians remained in possession of their ancient tribal homelands but with the coming of the Americans the land was gradually taken from them. Between 1796 and 1842 all the land of Michigan was ceded to the United States through a series of Indian treaties.

Today there are four small Indian communities or reservations in Michigan. The largest of these is the L'Anse Reservation in Baraga County. Here some 800 Indians live on a 15,000-acre tract of land. A small community in Menominee County, of some twenty-three families, live on a 3,400-acre tract known as the Hannahville Indian Community. At Bay Mills, west of Sault Ste. Marie, is another small settlement of about thirty-five families living on 2,200 acres of restricted land. The fourth Indian Community is in Isabella County east of Mt. Pleasant. Here a small group of Indians live on about 450 acres of restricted land. In all there are about 25,000 acres of such restricted land in Michigan which is under the protection of the Bureau of Indian Affairs, Great Lakes Agency, Ashland, Wisconsin.

Besides these semi-reservations there are a few small communities that contain small groups of Indians such as Cross Village and Good Hart, in Emmet County, and at Peshwabestown, in the Leelanau Peninsula, on Grand Traverse Bay.

Very few Indians today are farmers. Many are skilled in the various types of woods work and find employment in Michigan's growing forests. Many have moved to the growing cities and have found employment in the expanding industries. Since June 2, 1924, all American Indians have been citizens of the United States and as such are entitled to vote. In Michigan all Indian children attend public or private schools. Because of the Indians' long association with European culture little of their original culture now remains among them. Some have married European stocks and many people living in Michigan today can name one or more Indians as one of their ancestors.

CHAPTER FOUR

France Wins and Loses the Great Lakes Area (1608–1760)

WHEN Frenchmen first began coming to North America we do not know. It is known that Frenchmen were among the first fishermen who came to North America to fish for cod, on the Grand Banks east of Newfoundland, for as early as 1506 French fishermen were fishing off Cape Breton Island and they had already given this name to that island.

French fishermen coming to the Grand Banks to fish soon learned that they could get valuable furs from the Indians in trade for things made in Europe. So before leaving to carry their salted fish to Europe, the fishermen tried to find Indians with whom they could trade. Furs thus became a side cargo that was carried to Europe by the early fishing fleets.

As the years passed the French learned that there were huge profits to be made in the fur trade. In 1603 Champlain visited the St. Lawrence River area looking for a place to set up a fur-trading post. Because of the bitterness of the winters there, Champlain decided to locate his trading post a little farther to the south. The following year, 1604, Champlain with a few other Frenchmen came to the St. Croix River, in present-day New Brunswick, and built a little post on an island not far from the river's mouth. The following year the post was moved to Port Royal, and this settlement thus became the first permanent French settlement in North America.

Champlain searched the area for rivers leading into North America, but found none like the huge St. Lawrence farther to the north. As the local supply of furs was not large enough to meet the demand, Champlain decided to start a new post on the St. Lawrence. In the spring of 1608 he sailed from France to start a new settlement. The spot he chose was on the St. Lawrence River where the city of Quebec now stands.

The first winter at Quebec was a trying one for the French traders but in June, 1609, more men and supplies arrived from France. In

that same month there also came to the little settlement a band of
Huron and Ottawa Indians. These Indians were planning an attack
upon their enemy, the Iroquois. The Indians asked Champlain and
his men to bring their strange guns and join their war party against
the Iroquois.

As Champlain wanted to explore the region farther up the St.
Lawrence River, and also desired to make friends with the native
Indians, he agreed to go with the warriors and to take eleven French-
men with him. This pleased the Indians very much and, after looking

Courtesy National Film Board of Canada

**The City of Quebec. From 1608 to 1760 the central government of New
France was located here. On the right side of the picture can be seen Cape
Diamond and the St. Lawrence River.**

at the strange guns and armor of the white men, they made ready
for the raid on the Iroquois by dancing the war dance and eating
the battle feast.

Champlain and the Indians went up the St. Lawrence River to
the mouth of the Richelieu River. There the Indians began to quarrel
among themselves. About three-fourths of them left the party and

returned to their homes. In spite of this action on the part of his Indian allies Champlain did not turn back. With the few Indians that remained, the party went up the Richelieu River in twenty-four canoes and a small French sailboat. Later the sailboat and nine of the Frenchmen were sent back to Quebec.

On July 4, 1609, Champlain and his party came to a large lake of clear, blue water lying among beautiful green mountains. Since the lake had never before been seen by any white man, Champlain named it Lake Champlain in honor of himself. Although Champlain and his Indians tried to hide their movements, they were finally discovered and on July 30 a band of Iroquois attacked them.

The Iroquois were strong, brave Indians and were always ready and willing to fight their old foes. However, just as they were getting ready to let fly their first shower of arrows, the loud report of a musket rang out through the woods. Champlain had fired upon the Iroquois. Three Iroquois warriors suddenly fell forward. One was badly wounded and two were dying. Never before had the Iroquois heard the report of a musket. Yet, true Indian warriors, they held their ground and let fly a flight of arrows at their enemy. Again a loud noise was heard as Champlain again fired his musket at the Iroquois. This strange weapon belching smoke and fire was too much for the Iroquois, and they fled in panic.

This little battle, if it can be called even that, fought on the shore of Lake Champlain, was one of the main turning points in the history of New France.

It was not a large battle in which several men were killed. Yet it bound the Algonquin and Huron Indians in friendship to the French and made the Iroquois ever afterward their bitter enemy. Champlain had unknowingly made an enemy of one of the strongest and fiercest Indian tribes then living in all North America. The story of this defeat was handed down by the Iroquois from father to son. Several times, during the years that followed the Iroquois attacked the little French settlements along the St. Lawrence and killed many of the French settlers who had come there to live.

It is one of the strange happenings of history that a Dutch sailing vessel sailed up the Hudson River just a few months after Champlain's battle with the Iroquois. It was the "Half Moon," the ship of Henry Hudson, an English sea captain then sailing for the Dutch. The "Half Moon" was soon followed by other Dutch trading vessels and a strong friendship grew up between the Dutch traders, who came up the Hudson River, and the Iroquois, for the Dutch traders gave the Iroquois firearms in exchange for furs. This coming of traders into the Hudson Valley made it possible for the Iroquois to again meet their old enemies as equals in battle.

Tales of the coming of the Dutch traders soon were heard at Quebec, and the French quickly learned that if they were to push farther into the wilderness of the West they must do so by going up the Ottawa River, thus keeping away from the Iroquois.

The silent, mysterious lands to the west of Quebec, where no white man's foot had ever trod, enticed the Frenchmen to go up the St. Lawrence and Ottawa Rivers and search out the secrets that lay hidden in the vast forest domain of their Indian friends. Might there be another Indian empire like the ones the Spaniards had found in Mexico and Peru? From what kind of a land did the massive waters of the St. Lawrence River come? What kind of people lived along its banks? Might its source lie near the Pacific Ocean? Could the land be crossed and the way to the fabled East be found at last?

In order to find out about the Indians, their languages, their manner of life, and the nature of the lands in which they lived, Champlain sent young men into the wilderness to live with the Indians. One of these young men was Etienne Brulé, and some historians think that he was the first white man to reach the area now known as Michigan.

When only eighteen years old, Brulé may have journeyed with a party of Indians through the Sault Ste. Marie waterway. On his return to Quebec he startled the other Frenchmen there by showing them a nugget of copper he had secured in the Lake Region and by telling them of a large sea that lay to the west. Other returning traders and explorers brought other stories of a large sea that lay far to the west of Quebec. Stories of this new discovery made Champlain eager to see the sea for himself, so, in 1615, he made his way up the Ottawa River and crossed by way of Lake Nipissing to Georgian Bay, where he saw what is known today as Lake Huron. The lake was named the Lake of the Hurons after the Huron Indians who then lived on its eastern shore.

Because the Iroquois Indians lived near the upper St. Lawrence River, the Frenchmen did not dare to venture up that river. Instead, they turned more directly westward and following the Ottawa River pushed into the homeland of their Indian friends, the Hurons and Ottawas. From them they learned how to turn from the Ottawa up the little Mattawa and then to cross over to Lake Nipissing and by using the French River to reach Georgian Bay on Lake Huron. It was

at the mouth of the French River that the Frenchmen got their first view of the Great Lakes of North America. This water route into the wilderness was soon to become the main highway for the fur traders and missionaries of New France.

Rapids in Ottawa River at Ottawa, Ontario (1950)

Not many years after the founding of Quebec, Catholic missionaries were asked to come to Canada. The first that came were Recollects, a branch of the Order of St. Francis. Four of these begging friars came to Quebec in 1614. One of them was Father Le Caron, who without delay went west to the Huron Indians, then living in Huronia between the southern end of Georgian Bay and Lake Ontario. There he began missionary work among the Huron Indians at what is now Midland, Ontario. But the order was poor and small while the mission field was large and many missionaries were needed. To meet this need members of the larger and more powerful order of Jesuits arrived in New France and were soon at work among the Indians. Thus, Quebec became a missionary center as well as a fur trading post. At first some Protestants had been allowed to come to Canada, but before many years had passed only Roman Catholics were permitted to come to New France and thus the entire missionary field was reserved to the Roman Catholic fathers. Leaving the little post at Quebec they went into the wilderness to seek converts among the Indians. Each year they wrote a report of what they had done. These reports, now called the *Relations,* give us much information about Indian life in New France as well as the labors of the Jesuits. Catholic nuns also came to New France where they founded at Quebec the Convent of the Uruslines, a school for girls, and the Hotel Dieu, a hospital.

One of the first Jesuits to go westward was Father Brébeuf. He spent some time among the Hurons in 1626. In 1634, the Hurons agreed to let the Jesuits come to their homeland and establish a permanent mission. Father Brébeuf and two other Jesuits soon set up the first permanent mission among the Hurons.

Of all the Jesuit missions the one among the Hurons was the most successful. Near the mouth of the River Wye, at the south end of Georgian Bay near present-day Midland, Ontario, the Jesuits founded a mission which they named Sainte Marie. Here they built a little enclosure, of logs and masonry, and a little church. In the Huron Indian villages they founded other stations like the two they called St. Ignace and St. Louis. Cattle, pigs, and chickens were brought to the missions. Daily the Jesuits labored among the Hurons, with fair success, to change the savages from their cruel ways and get them to accept the Christian faith in place of their ancient magic and cruel savage ways.

In 1634, a young Frenchman named Jean Nicolet was sent out by Champlain to further explore the West. He followed the westward route until he came to Lake Huron. Nicolet perhaps went up the St. Mary's River to the place where the city of Sault Ste. Marie now stands. Returning south and west Nicolet discovered what is now the Straits of Mackinac. From here he went on westward across Lake Michigan to Green Bay. Just how far west Nicolet went is not known. He had no way of telling us, for as yet the lakes and rivers had no names. Some historians think he went almost as far west as the Mississippi River. Soon after Nicolet's return, Champlain, the founder of New France, died on Christmas Day, 1635.

In 1641 two Jesuit missionaries, Fathers Raymbault and Jogues, left the Jesuit missions on Georgian Bay and went up the St. Mary's River, which they named after their mission in Huronia. Paddling up the river they came to the St. Mary's Rapids, which they called the "Sault." Here at the rapids they found an Indian settlement of about two thousand people who greeted the Jesuits with kindness and asked them to stay in their village. This the missionaries could not do, so after learning from the Indians of another large lake (Lake Superior), the two Jesuits returned to their mission on Georgian Bay.

After the journey of Fathers Raymbault and Jogues to the Sault, almost twenty years passed before the Frenchmen again came to Michigan. Cruel Indian wars raged between the Algonquins and the Iroquois, and traveling into the West was dangerous for both traders and missionaries.

At first the French had been able to secure furs from the nearby areas. Not only that, but the Indians usually brought their furs to the ships, or posts, along the St. Lawrence River. In this way the Indians not only paid the cost of transportation but also took the risks of having their furs stolen or captured. But, as time passed, the local supply of fur-bearing animals grew fewer and fewer in number while the demand for more and more furs grew. As the local supply of furs in the St. Lawrence Valley and the Hudson River Valley grew smaller, both the Hurons and the Iroquois wanted to act as middlemen between the tribes living farther to the west and the Europeans living in their own regions. This rivalry for the fur trade increased the old hatred between the Iroquois and the Hurons.

If the Iroquois could drive out the Hurons, they could then control both the St. Lawrence and the Ottawa rivers and carry the fur trade down the Hudson River to their friends the Dutch and, later the English. Thus, the commercial ambitions of the Iroquois doomed the Jesuit missions in Huronia. Armed with guns they had bought from the Dutch traders, the Iroquois attacked the French settlements and the villages of their Indian allies, the Hurons, with a savage fierceness springing from years of bitter hatred and the new rivalry that had developed in the clash for the position of middleman in the expanding fur trade.

At first they struck the fringes of the Huron country but in 1648 the Iroquois made a deeper thrust. Going up the Ottawa River, the Iroquois fell upon the newly converted Hurons and the Jesuit missions. St. Joseph was taken. The Hurons were no match for the fierce Iroquois who burned their homes, killed and captured many, and drove the rest into the wilderness. Father Daniel was killed along with many Hurons. During the winter of 1648-49 hundreds of Iroquois warriors made their way to the Huron country. In March of 1649, the Iroquois attacked and destroyed the Indian villages of St. Ignace and St. Louis. Father Brébeuf and Father Lalemant were captured and killed by cruel torture. Only the mission of Ste. Marie, with its stronger walls, remained. But it too had to be given up. An attempt was made to set up a new mission on nearby St. Joseph's Island, but after much suffering this also was abandoned and the Jesuit missionaries who had been fortunate enough to escape the Iroquois raids, went back to Quebec.

The French living along the lower St. Lawrence could give little aid to the Huron Indians because of the distance between them. Then, too, they were busy defending themselves from the Iroquois who were also attacking their little settlements. Some of the Hurons followed the Jesuits to Quebec there to seek protection under the French guns. Others fled north and northwest into the wilderness along the southern shore of western Lake Superior.

By 1650, all of New France was in a state of siege and Frenchmen had to keep very close to their forts and villages. The Iroquois, having destroyed the Hurons, then fell upon the Tobacco and Neutral Indians who lived in western Ontario, north of Lake Erie and either massacred them or drove them away. The Iroquois thus gained control of both the St. Lawrence and the Ottawa River routes.

No longer did the Hurons come down the Ottawa at springtime with canoes heavily loaded with fine furs. The trade in pelts, for the French, declined to a mere trickle and then stopped altogether.

Pushing west from their homeland, the Iroquois fell upon the Eries and Andastes that lived south of Lake Erie, but they found these tribes to be more powerful. In 1653 a strong Iroquois war party was destroyed west of Lake Michigan. This defeat somewhat checked the war spirit of the Iroquois for a time and they arranged a truce with the French which lasted until 1658.

The fur trade of the French could not be carried on while the Indian war lasted, but illegal traders, known as *coureur de bois,* were usually ready to risk capture for the large profits that could be gained from the fur trade. How many illegal traders went into the woods during this period no one can say, but it is known that two men, Radisson and Groseilliers, set out for the West in the year 1654. In the spring of 1656 they avoided the Iroquois and came back to Quebec with their canoes, and those of their Indian friends, heavily loaded with furs from the Far West. They also told of visiting some of the Huron Indians whom they had found living in the northern wilderness near the western end of Lake Superior where they had fled to escape from their enemies, the Iroquois.

In 1658 Radisson and Groseilliers again went to the West in search of furs. They followed the southern shore of Lake Superior and went as far west as eastern Minnesota. How much farther they went we do not know, but there is little doubt that they pushed even farther. Some records seem to show that they went as far as Hudson Bay. In 1660 these two men and their Indian friends returned to Quebec in sixty large canoes bearing many thousands of dollars worth of furs. Again they told about the Huron Indians who were then living in the wilderness on the western shore of Lake Superior.

The Jesuits were eager to again take up their missionary work among the Huron Indians, so in 1660 they chose one of their group, Father Rene Mesnard, to go west with the Indians who had come to Montreal with Radisson and Groseilliers, and search for the Hurons.

Passing up the St. Mary's River with the returning Indians, Father Mesnard then followed the southern shore of Lake Superior to Keweenaw Bay. There he set up a mission, the first in the Old Northwest. The Ottawas near his mission were not very friendly to him and cared little for the Christian religion, so when spring came he set out again to continue his search for the Huron Indians. He became lost from his party, and what became of him is not known.

Radisson and Groseilliers made still another trip to the West, but when they returned in 1663, the governor of New France took most of their furs from them because they had been trading with the Indians without a license.

At last the mother country, France, came to the aid of her American colony. In 1665 the Marquis de Tracy arrived in Canada with over one thousand French soldiers. In 1666 this army, with some six hundred Canadians and their Indian allies, attacked and destroyed the villages and crops of the Mohawk Indians. Though not defeated, the war spirit of the Iroquois was weakened, and they were now willing to make an uneasy peace. New France at last could again push her trade and missionary work among the Indians to the west.

Marker to Father Allouez at Niles, Michigan. Photo 1956.

Father Claud Allouez was chosen by the Jesuits to take up the work of Father Rene Mesnard. In 1666, he joined a band of some five hundred Indians who had come to Montreal to sell their furs and with them journeyed up the Ottawa River. Passing up the St. Mary's River, Allouez entered Lake Superior, which he named Lac Tracy. Following its southern shore, Allouez went westward as far as La Pointe, Wisconsin. There, on Madeline Island in what is now the Apostle group of Chequamegon Bay, he founded a mission called La Pointe and built a little bark chapel. This church was the first to be built in what later became the Old Northwest.

Allouez returned to Quebec in the fall of 1667 to report on his missionary work and to ask for more Jesuits to help him. The Jesuits were pleased to hear his report and learn of the work that could be done in the region of Lake Superior among the Hurons who had escaped the attacks of the Iroquois. Others at Quebec who were not so interested in missions were very interested in the pieces of copper that Allouez had brought back with him and in his stories of a great river, the Mississippi, that lay still farther to the west.

To find out more about the copper and to further explore the region, Jean Pere was sent westward in 1668. In 1669 a supporting expedition was sent west under the leadership of Adrien Joliet. Joliet and Pere spent the entire summer of 1669 searching the shores of Lake Superior for copper but they found only a few small pieces which could easily be carried back to Quebec in their bark canoes. Their interest, however, was aroused by stories of another large river that led to an unknown sea which lay to the southwest.

While at Sault Ste. Marie, Joliet rescued an Iroquois prisoner who was about to be burned at the stake by his Indian captors. In return for this the grateful Iroquois promised to take Joliet on a more southerly route when he went back to the French settlements on the St. Lawrence. Joliet's party, with the Iroquois as their guide, followed the western shore of Lake Huron southward, and at last entered what is now called the St. Clair River. Passing over Lake St. Clair they entered upon the Detroit River and followed it to Lake Erie. Turning east they followed the northern shore of Lake Erie almost to its eastern end. Then, fearing that the Iroquois Indians might attack them, Joliet and his men turned north and passed overland near the place where Hamilton, Ontario, now stands, and thus came to Lake Ontario. Joliet was thus the first white man to follow the southern route from Sault Ste. Marie to Montreal and Quebec. Because he turned north too quickly, he did not discover the Niagara River and Niagara Falls.

Just who was first to explore the Detroit River area is not known but a map printed in Paris in 1656 has a fairly accurate map of the water route from Lake Huron to Lake Erie. All of Lake Erie is shown as well as the Niagara River and Lake Ontario. Only a little of Lake Michigan and Lake Superior are shown.

In response to Allouez's request for aid, two Jesuits, Father James Marquette and Father Claude Dablon, were sent into the region of the Upper Lakes to help him with his missionary work. Father Allouez returned to LaPointe while Father Marquette and Father Dablon started a mission at Sault Ste. Marie. Later this mission at Sault Ste. Marie became a French settlement. Thus Sault Ste. Marie was the first settlement in Michigan* and the first west of the Allegheny Mountains, except for the older Spanish settlements in the southwestern part of the United States.

In the fall of 1669 Allouez left LaPointe and went to Green Bay, Wisconsin. Here he founded a mission in response to a request from the Pottawattomie Indians. Part of his work was to try to keep the French traders from cheating the Indians. Marquette took Allouez's place at LaPointe while Dablon continued to work at the mission at Sault Ste. Marie.

Soon after Marquette took up Allouez's work at LaPointe, the Sioux, whom Marquette called "the Iroquois of the West," attacked the Ottawas and Hurons who lived near the mission. Many Hurons and Ottawas were killed, and those who remained fled into the wilderness for safety. Most of the Ottawa Indians took refuge on the Manitoulin Islands. The Hurons set out for Quebec and the protection of the French, but when they reached the southern part of the Upper Peninsula, near the Straits of Mackinac, they began again to fear the cruel Iroquois so they went no farther.

When Father Marquette learned that the Hurons had gathered at Michilimackinac, he left his mission at LaPointe and started a new mission, which he named St. Ignace, on the Straits of Mackinac in 1671. This little mission was well located for carrying on missionary work among the Indians of northern Michigan.

Sixty years had passed since the first French settlement had been founded at Quebec. They had been years of hardship for the little French settlements along the St. Lawrence, but now, at last, the time had come when it was fairly safe to travel into the West. Both the fur traders and the Jesuits followed the Ottawa waterway into the strange unknown wilderness of the Lake Region. One came seeking furs and wealth; the other came to carry the message of Christianity to the Indians.

But though New France had opened the way to the furs of the

---

*It was abandoned in 1679 and remained without a resident for 80 years.

West by way of the St. Lawrence-Ottawa route, she soon found this valuable trade endangered by the English who began sailing into Hudson Bay. For the next ninety years the two nations were rivals for the furs from north of Lake Superior and west of Hudson Bay.

Hudson Bay had been discovered by an English sea captain named Henry Hudson who had, just a few years before that time, discovered the Hudson River for the Dutch. England paid little attention to Hudson's discovery of the bay until the possibilities of the fur trade in that area were made known to the English by the two French traders, Radisson and Groseilliers. When the French authorities in New France had taken three-fifths of their furs, in 1663, because they had traded with the Indians without having a license, the two Frenchmen deserted to the English. They told the English of the profit that could be made by carrying on the fur trade along the shores of Hudson Bay where they had been.

King Charles II of England became interested in the story that the two French traders were telling. In 1669 ships were sent to the bay to trade with the Indians in that region. The ships came back loaded with furs. In the following year King Charles II granted a charter to "The Merchants of England trading into Hudson's Bay." This company, now known as Hudson's Bay Company, was to be the only fur trader permitted on the bay. The company was also given the ownership of all lands drained by the rivers flowing into the bay. This huge area of land around Hudson Bay became known as Prince Rupert's Land.

The formation of this trading company by the English was a threat to the growing western fur trade of New France, for furs could more easily be taken to Hudson Bay by the Indians than they could be carried to the French settlements along the St. Lawrence. What is more, English ships could carry goods to the trading posts on the bay much more cheaply than Frenchmen in canoes could carry them to the French trading posts in the West. England was now threatening France's fur trade from Hudson Bay as well as from the Hudson River area.

The French, kept from the lower lakes by the Iroquois, became very much interested in the Upper Lake Region which was then being opened and explored by fur traders and Jesuit missionaries. So far had the work of discovery progressed that by 1669 a fairly accurate map of the region had been made by two Jesuits. The French were eager to seize upon the friendship that was offered them by the Ottawas and other Indians of the region, and therefore made plans to take formal possession of the Upper Lake Region and thus to challenge the English who had started the Hudson's Bay Company, in 1670, to carry on the fur trade from Hudson Bay.

The task of carrying out this formal ceremony of taking possession of the western lands fell to Simon Francois Daumont. With fifteen companions, Daumont made his way to Sault Ste. Marie where he arrived in May, 1671. An invitation had been sent to the Indian tribes of the region asking them to come to the meeting, or council, which was going to be held. Fourteen Indian tribes sent members of their tribes to represent them. Indians, French officers representing the King of France, and the black-robed Jesuit priests all gathered for the ceremony. Father Allouez acted as the interpreter so that the Indians would know what the Frenchmen were saying. A large cross was erected and also a huge post upon which had been placed the arms of France. After the formal ceremony, Allouez told the Indians of the French king, whom he called "the greatest king in the world" and a "chief of chiefs." Thus France, in 1671, took formal possession of the Upper Lakes Region and warned the English, who had begun trading from Hudson Bay, that the whole Northwest belonged to the King of France.

But, for all its boasting, New France was still a weak colony. Only some 6,705 people lived in New France at the time. It was really but three small settlements — Quebec, Three Rivers, and Montreal — which were strung along the St. Lawrence River. But it was growing in population and fast becoming one long struggling village spread along the St. Lawrence River's edge. What is more, there came to the colony in 1672 a new governor, Governor Frontenac. He was soon to prove himself to be the greatest of all the governors of New France.

The year after his arrival in the colony, Governor Frontenac sent Louis Joliet on an expedition to the West to search for the large river about which the French had so often been told. At the request of Joliet, Father Marquette, then at Michilimackinac, joined the expedition going to explore the West.

The two, Marquette and Joliet, went westward from the mission at St. Ignace, crossed the northern part of Lake Michigan, entered Green Bay, and then made their way up the Fox River. From this river they portaged to the Wisconsin River. Down this river they paddled until they came to the Mississippi River on June 17, 1673.

Pushing their bark canoes out upon the mighty river they began drifting slowly southward during the long pleasant summer days. On the way Marquette stopped to visit the Illinois Indians to keep a promise he had made to some of their tribe who had once visited him at his mission at LaPointe. He found them friendly but, although they desired that he stay with them, he and Joliet pushed on down the Mississippi as far as the Arkansas River. As they drifted along, their disappointment grew, for the Mississippi River ran steadily southward toward Spanish territory. Afraid to enter Spanish territory, they started the long journey northward back to the little mission in the wilderness at Green Bay.

When they reached the Illinois River they followed it northward and then passed over onto Lake Michigan. Following Lake Michigan's western edge, the party again came to the Jesuit mission at Green Bay. There Marquette and Joliet parted.

Joliet set out for Quebec to report his discoveries to Governor Frontenac. While going down the St. Lawrence River his canoe was upset at the foot of the Lachine Rapids, near Montreal. Two of the canoemen were drowned and everything in the canoe, including Joliet's records and charts, was lost in the water. Thus most of our knowledge of this expedition down the Mississippi comes from Marquette's journal which he wrote while staying with Allouez at Green Bay the following winter.

When fall came again, Marquette set out to return to the Illinois Indians whom he had visited the year before. He followed the shore of Lake Michigan to its southern end. Here misfortune beset him and he became ill. His Indian friends deserted him. However, Jacques and Pierre, his French companions, stayed with him. Unable to go farther, the little group passed the winter of 1674-1675 near the place where Chicago, Illinois, now stands.

When spring came at last, the feeble Marquette again took up his journey to the land of the Illinois Indians. They received him with kindness and listened to him when he told them about the Christian religion. They asked him to stay with them, but Marquette was ill and wished to return to Quebec. He promised them that he would return or send another missionary.

Thinking that it might be a shorter way to reach Michilimackinac, the party followed the eastern shore of Lake Michigan. As they went northward along the shore of the lake, Marquette's strength failed him. He was carried ashore by members of his party and then, after saying Mass, he died alone on May 18, 1675.

Marker to Father Marquette at St. Ignace, Michigan. Photo 1958.

In a shallow grave near Ludington, Marquette was laid to rest in the vast wilderness that he had made his home. Two years later, friendly Indians brought his bones to the little mission of St. Ignace. There, where he had labored among the Indians, his bones were buried beneath the floor of the mission chapel.

Soon after the death of Marquette, another Frenchman, LaSalle, began his work of exploration. This man was then called a dreamer, but we today know that he really had good plans for New France. Although much of his work lay outside of Michigan, no history of this region can keep from telling something of LaSalle and his plans and work.

He dreamed of winning this vast area for New France. He would build ships to sail upon the Great Lakes and thus aid the fur trade and hold the English and Iroquois in check. He would enter the forests to the south and west and build forts upon the banks of the streams and thus hold the western land for France.

LaSalle was not only a dreamer; he was also a hard worker. He tried to keep the Iroquois nations at peace. He had material for a sailboat, which he planned to build on Lake Erie, sent across Lake Ontario to the Niagara River. The materials for the boat were then carried across the twelve miles from Lake Ontario to Lake Erie, and there, on the shore of Lake Erie, the "Griffin," the first sailboat upon the Upper Lakes, was built. In the spring of 1679 the little vessel set

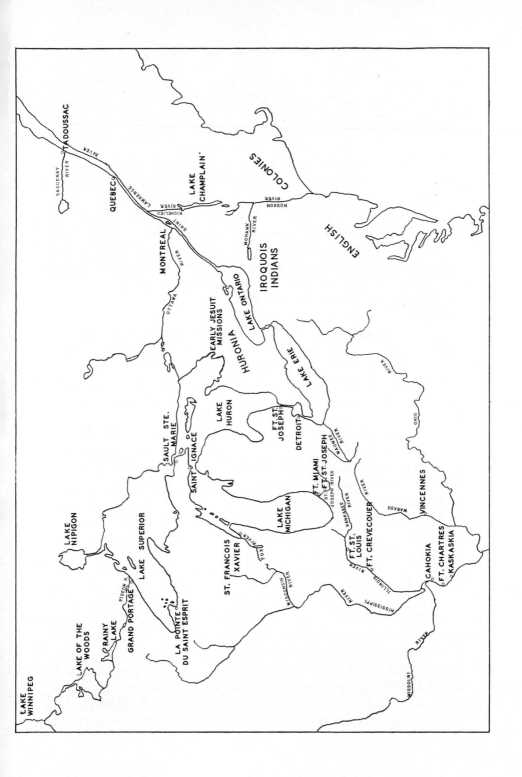

sail upon the clear, blue water of Lake Erie. Westward she sailed across the lake. Turning to the north the Griffin passed up the Detroit River and on north into Lake Huron. At last, after a stormy voyage, she reached Michilimackinac, where she was welcomed by the Jesuits and fur traders at the little mission of St. Ignace.

From there LaSalle sailed the Griffin to Green Bay, where the little boat was loaded with a cargo of furs. The Griffin was to return to Niagara Falls. After leaving her cargo there, her captain was to sail her back to the lower end of Lake Michigan, near the St. Joseph River, where LaSalle and his men would meet her.

After the Griffin had sailed east toward Niagara Falls, LaSalle and his men made their way down Lake Michigan to the St. Joseph River, where they built a little log fort which they named Fort Miami after the Miami Indians living in the region at that time. There La-Salle waited for the coming of Tonty, who was one of his helpers, and the return of the Griffin. After some weeks Tonty and his men appeared. Eagerly the Frenchmen watched the blue water of Lake Michigan for the white sails of the little Griffin.

Loaded with furs, the little boat had headed east across Lake Michigan for the Straits of Mackinac. Unlucky was the first voyage of the Griffin, for she was never seen again.

Giving up hope for the Griffin's return and faced with the problem of getting ready for winter, LaSalle left Tonty at Fort Miami with a few men. With the rest he went south into the land of the Illinois Indians. There he stayed during the winter at another fort which he built and named Fort Crevecoeur.

When spring came he sent some of his party on an exploration trip up the Mississippi. Then he and four men of his party made their way on foot across lower Michigan to the Detroit River and then to Quebec in quest of news of the Griffin and her crew. This is the first record of any white man crossing the Lower Peninsula of Michigan.

Three times LaSalle passed through Michigan. He was always dreaming of the great empire he would build in the wilderness. Later he started a settlement near the mouth of the Mississippi River. He tried to go from this settlement to Quebec, but he had not gone far inland when he was killed by one of his own men. Thus ended the life of LaSalle, the great empire builder of New France.

Other explorers, too, joined the long list of Frenchmen who journeyed into the Great Lakes region to help hold it for New France.

In 1684, DuLhut pushed as far north as Lake Nipigon. In 1686, he was the leader of a party of Frenchmen who built a fort on the western shore of the St. Clair River where Port Huron now stands. This new post, called St. Joseph, was built to guard the St. Clair River and thus keep the English fur traders and Iroquois from entering the French trading grounds from the south. DuLhut and his men stayed there during the following winter. The post was abandoned the following spring, however, when DuLhut and his men were called east with their Indian allies to help fight the Iroquois.

In 1689, Jacques de Noyon went as far west as the Lake of the Woods. Farther and farther the Frenchmen ventured into the wilderness to win the friendship of the Indian tribes. In this way the Frenchmen hoped to keep the Indians from taking their furs to the English on Hudson Bay. Soon a highway of lakes and rivers which carried them to the Lake of the Woods area was known to the French. There, on the thousands of lakes and streams, west and north of Lake Superior, lived the little animals whose skins the French wanted for the fur trade. Now French trading canoes were bringing the valuable furs along the waterway each spring to the post at Michilimackinac. From Michilimackinac (St. Ignace) they were then carried in canoes to Montreal and Quebec.

The vast forest became the fur trader's home as truly as it was the home of his Indian brother. The land the French had discovered seemed to be too big for them. A few small groups settled here and there, but so vast was the spreading wilderness that their little posts seemed to have been lost in the silent depths of the forests which lay all about them. The Frenchmen were rovers, not settlers. They adopted both the Indian's homeland and his way of life. The fleur-de-lis flew above the little posts as a sign of possession and not of conquest or settlement.

Each spring the French traders gathered as many Indians with their furs as they could at the western posts. Then, in canoes loaded down with bundles of furs, Indians and traders set out for the French settlements along the St. Lawrence. Thus the Indians not only caught the furs but often had to deliver them all the way to Montreal, some one thousand miles away. Sometimes this spring flotilla numbered as high as four hundred canoes. Often it was midsummer before the Indians and the *voyageurs* arrived at Montreal and set up their huts on the river bank for the annual fair. Day after day more canoes laden with furs joined the others already on the river bank. Everywhere there was feasting and happiness. Naked savages from the western forests, *voyageurs,* French merchants, and French nobility all joined in making the annual fair the one leading event of the year in New France.

The fair usually lasted from ten to fourteen days. Amid the drinking and carousing the merchants bartered their goods, which had just arrived in the ships from France, for the valuable furs of the Indians. Usually the Frenchmen got by far the better of the bargain. The Indians often gave valuable furs for a little brandy which increased their always-present weakness for a few cheap, bright-colored trinkets.

For some time the post at Michilimackinac, on the Straits of Mackinac, was the leading fur trading center in the Lake Region. Other posts which spread farther into the wilderness helped to gather the furs that were carried to Michilimackinac and then to Montreal. One was built at Green Bay, Wisconsin. Another was on the St. Joseph River in the southwestern part of Michigan. Sault Ste. Marie also had its post. Others were started on the far western and northern shores of Lake Superior. They were all little log forts in a vast wilderness. The forts were made by standing logs upright in the ground. Each log was pointed at the top. These wooden walls around the fort were known as a palisade. Usually there was a priest or two at each post who conducted Christian services for the French settlers and tried to teach the Indians about Christianity.

The Jesuit missionaries and fur traders were often opposed to one another over the brandy trade. While the Jesuits gave their lives to help the Indians, the fur traders sold them guns and brandy. Brandy was the most wanted article in the fur trade. Often Indians would spend their entire winter getting furs and then get little more for them than enough brandy to allow the trader to cheat them out of the rest. Brandy often turned the Indians into raving madmen who did cruel things which they would not have done if it had not been for the brandy that was sold to them by the Frenchmen.

But once the brandy trade had been started, it could not easily be stopped. When Indians had tasted it they wanted more, and if they could not get brandy from the Frenchmen they could get rum from the English. What is more, the Jesuits feared that their Indian converts might pick up the Christian teachings of the English who were not Catholics.

By 1690, the fur trade had greatly changed. The area near the French settlements no longer produced the furs as it had during the first years of French settlement. Furs had always to be brought from farther and farther to the west. Local traders gave way to large trading companies with offices in Montreal or Quebec. These trading companies had many men who worked for them in the woods as traders. The fur companies now had to risk the dangers of transportation and had to pay for having the furs brought from the far west. Because the Iroquois were never friendly to the French, these trading companies never built ships on the Upper Lakes as LaSalle had tried to do. They continued to use the old route along the Ottawa River as their main highway.

Only individuals, or fur trading companies, were given a government permit called a *congé* as a license to carry on the fur trade. These individuals, or fur trading companies, then hired men to paddle the canoes and carry on the fur trade with the Indians. The Frenchmen who paddled the canoes and carried the merchandise over the many portages were called *voyageurs*. They were a colorful, carefree group of men who found adventure and toil in the wilderness more enjoyable than the monotonous life of the French *habitant*. Other men, usually with a little education, were stationed at the western posts to actually carry on the trade with the Indians and to keep the company records. Because the profits from the fur trade were high, and trading permits were hard to secure, illegal fur traders called *coureur de bois* (forest runners) sometimes went into the woods and traded without a permit from the government. These illegally gotten furs were later traded to the English or smuggled on a ship bound for France, for no Frenchman was permitted to remain in the woods for even twenty-four hours without a license to trade. The penalty for trading with the Indians without a license was death and sometimes coureur de bois were hanged at Quebec.

The French voyageurs were a vigorous, daring, strong-limbed group of men. Because of the limited space in the canoes these men were seldom more than five feet six inches in height and rarely weighed more than 150 pounds. Each wore moccasins topped by high leather leggings, trousers, a shirt belted with a gaudy colored sash, and a red cap into which he had stuck a feather. He also carried with him a pouch for his pipe and tobacco, and a blue hooded cloak. By the age of forty he was usually an old man with rheumatism, arthritis, hernia, and torn ligaments as the result of exposure and toil in the wilderness.

At the French settlements along the St. Lawrence River the voyageurs, working for a fur company, loaded their bark canoes with articles that had been brought in the ships from France, such as brandy

Courtesy Minnesota Historical Society

Scuba divers examine some of the axes, musket balls and gunflints found below a rapid on the Basswood River, Minnesota.

Courtesy Minnesota Historical Society

From left, Curt Anderson, Don Franklin, and Dennis Dalen, scuba divers who found the collection of 36 wrought iron axes and 24 assorted ice chisels and spears on the Basswood River, Minnesota, in July, 1961. All the items were trade goods lost in an accident in the rapids.

blankets, beads, guns, gunpowder, tomahawks, iron arrowheads, and knives, which the fur companies knew the Indians would like to get in trade. Then, after attending Mass at the local church, they bade their family and friends good-by and set out with their French companions and Indian friends, on the long hard journey to the French trading posts in the West.

During the last few years many of these early French and English trade articles have been recovered by scuba divers from the river bottoms at several places along the old voyageurs' highway where trade canoes were wrecked in rapids or at waterfalls and the heavy articles sank to the bottom of the stream, or falls, where the traders could not get them. Wrought-iron axe heads, iron arrow points, ice chisels, brass kettles, and rusty flintlock muskets have all been found.*

*The two pictures of scuba divers are from the Minnesota Historical Society. The Quetico-Superior Underwater Research Project is jointly undertaken by the Minnesota Historical Society and the Royal Ontario Museum. The National Geographic Society is also a principal sponsor of the project. More research along the voyageurs Highway is planned for the summer of 1965.

From Montreal the fur traders followed the Ottawa westward. When they reached what is now the little village of Mattawa, in the Province of Ontario, the traders turned westward up the little Mattawa River, which took them to Lake Talon. Paddling up these two rivers was hard work, for not only were their currents rapid but also the streams often came dashing and spilling between rocky banks and over rough, jagged rocks which could easily have pierced the bottom of a bark canoe. It was necessary when going up, or down, the old waterway to have to portage around many rapids, falls, and other dangerous places. In all, there were thirty-five portages that had to be made between Montreal and Georgian Bay. This meant that everything, including the canoes, had to be carried overland to a place on the river bank where the current was less swift and dangerous. These toilsome portages, where everything had to be carried on the backs of the voyageurs, delayed the travelers and tired them

The Mattawa River flowing east from the portage at the outlet of Lake Talon. Between its high rocky walls passed the French and Indians as they traveled to and from the Lake Region. Photo 1956.

Courtesy National Film Board of Canada
Scenic view along the French River, Ontario. Note the rocky shore formed by the rock of the Canadian Shield. This is part of the "Voyageurs Highway."

as they toiled to get their canoes, trading goods, or furs along the many portages. So slow, and toilsome, was this river travel that it usually took several weeks to go from Montreal to Michilimackinac.

After crossing Lake Talon the French travelers then paddled westward up a little stream that flowed eastward from Trout Lake. After crossing this lake to its western end the voyageurs came to a height of land that acts as a water divide. From Trout Lake the water flows eastward to the Ottawa and St. Lawrence Rivers. West of the divide the

water flows westward from Lake Nipissing to Georgian Bay, on Lake Huron. All goods and canoes had to be portaged three times in making this portage called Varles Portage between Trout Lake and Lake Nipissing. Paddling across Lake Nipissing the voyagers then glided down the fast flowing French River to Georgian Bay. Because the French River flows

The French River flowing west from Lake Nipissing. Westward along this rapidly flowing river came the French and Indians to Georgian Bay and the Lake Region. Photo 1956.

very fast, when going east the Frenchmen used the Key River, which had a much slower current, and then portaged to Lake Nipissing.

Paresseux Falls near Lake Talon, Ontario. At each waterfall it was necessary to portage all merchandise and furs.

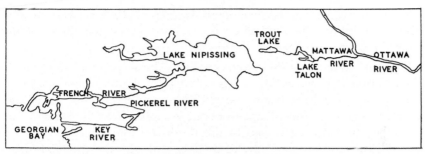

THE VOYAGEURS' HIGHWAY INTO THE UPPER GREAT LAKES AREA

Once on Georgian Bay the entire lake system, with its many rivers, lay before the travelers. They could go south to the old Huron settlements at the south end of Georgian Bay or paddle down Lake Huron toward Detroit. The main trade route, however, lay along the north shore of Lake Huron to Sault Ste. Marie, or Michilimackinac. Usually the French followed the North Channel between the Manitoulin Islands and the north shore of Lake Huron. Traders going to Michilimackinac could then push on west to the many rivers that flowed into Lake Michigan. Several of these rivers led to portages that took the Frenchmen to streams that flowed into the Mississippi River system. This was the main highway to the French settlements of Kaskaskia and Cahokia and to New Orleans at the mouth of the Mississippi River. From Lake Erie travelers went up the Maumee River and then portaged to the Wabash River. On this river the French made their little settlement of Vincennes to guard the water route.

But the main fur trade highway of New France led up the Saint Mary's River to Lake Superior and the colder, rich fur-bearing lands to the north and west of the lakes. When they reached the rapids in the St. Mary's River everything had to be portaged around it to Lake Superior. This portage was about one mile in length. When the canoes were again loaded the Frenchmen set out along the south shore of Lake Superior. Sometimes they followed the northern, rocky shore of Lake Superior but here the shore was more dangerous and the waves were usually higher because of the prevailing westerly winds. Because traveling on Lake Superior was dangerous, the Frenchmen usually followed its southern shore where there was more protection from the wind and waves. West of Grand Marais, in the area we now call the Pictured Rocks, the shore line was rocky and there was little chance to beach the canoes if a storm arose. Lake Superior is cold and deep. Storms, especially in the spring and fall, sometimes even now, wreck our large modern freighters. Canoes were tossed about like little chips of wood on the mighty waves that came rolling from the west when a storm stirred up the icy water.

Farther to the west the traders came to Huron Bay and Keweenaw Bay. Huron Bay was easily crossed, but often bad weather on Keweenaw Bay forced the traders to paddle many extra miles along the shore. When they came to a point about ten miles from the head of the bay, they turned their canoes to the northwest and paddled eight or ten miles across the open water of the bay to the Keweenaw Peninsula, which juts out some fifty miles into Lake Superior. To paddle around this peninsula meant a hundred-and-ten-mile detour out into the lake. This detour was dangerous too, for the shore was often rocky and provided few places where the canoes could be beached without the risk of smashing them on the rocks.

To avoid this long, dangerous trip around the Keweenaw Peninsula, fur traders and missionaries followed the old Indian route now known as the Keweena Portage. This name was taken from the Chippewa Indian language and means a place where one walks across a point of land. From Keweenaw Bay to Lake Superior by way of the Keweena Portage was about twenty-five miles, and most of this distance could be traveled by canoe. After going up the Portage River for about six miles, the *voyageurs* entered Portage Lake. The next twelve miles of the way were across Portage Lake. At the northwestern end of the lake a small stream took the traders still farther across the peninsula.

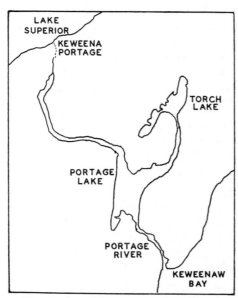

The Keween Portage Route across the Keweenaw Peninsula

This little stream was so small, narrow, and crooked that canoes could pass along it only with great difficulty. Paddles were usually put aside and poles were used to push the canoes along the narrow, winding river. So narrow was the stream that marsh grass often brushed the canoes on both sides. So winding was the stream that the canoes could hardly make the turns in it as it meandered through the swampy land. When the *voyageurs* were within a mile and a half of Lake Superior, it became necessary to walk the rest of the way. The first half mile of the portage was across a swampy bog where the men, carrying their heavy burdens, tramped knee deep, and often belt deep, in the water and muck of the marsh. Then the trail reached firmer ground, and the portage path, for the last mile, wound through a pine forest to a little sandy slope on the western shore of the Keweenaw Peninsula.

The Keweena Portage, like the one at Sault Ste. Marie, was one of Michigan's most used portages. Nearly all early travelers, going along the south shore of Lake Superior, used it to keep from having to go around the Keweenaw Peninsula. Pierre Esprit Radisson crossed the portage in 1658-59. As late as 1820 Governor Cass and Schoolcraft passed along it on their way to the West. No doubt hundreds of unknown *voyageurs* used the same portage and waterway to take supplies to the West and bring the furs back to Michilimackinac and Montreal.

After the Keweena Portage had been crossed, the Frenchmen continued west along the south shore of the lake past the Apostle Islands, in Northern Wisconsin. When they reached the western end of Lake Superior, where Duluth, Minnesota, now stands,

Shallow Rapids in the Pigeon River in Minnesota. The Grand Portage went around these obstacles in the river. Photo August, 1963.

they followed the rocky northwestern shore of Lake Superior to the present village of Grand Portage, Minnesota. Just a little farther on, along the lake shore was the mouth of the Pigeon River that ran into

Lake Superior from the west. Near its mouth the Pigeon River becomes a series of falls and rapids as it descends the old fault line
along the northwestern shore of Lake Superior. Because of waterfalls and rocky rapids, it was necessary to portage all goods from
the lake shore overland some nine miles, or more, to the Pigeon
River. Because this was the longest of all the portages, it became
known as the Grand Portage. A voyageur would carry two packs
of merchandise, each weighing 90 pounds, from the lake shore
to the Pigeon River and then return with two packs of pelts each
weighing 90 pounds to the lake in six hours time.

The many portage paths along the voyageur's highway, whether
they ran along the side of some stream where an obstacle stopped
the passage of a canoe, or whether they led from one river system to
another were not made by the French fur traders. The portage paths
were already ages old before friendly Indians first showed them to the
Frenchmen. By the time that the Frenchmen began to use them they
were already well beaten paths that had been formed by animals and
men that had lived in the area since the last glacial period. Most of
the portage paths from Mattawa to far off Lake Athabasca, and even
farther toward the north, still remain and are still used by people taking
canoe trips and by the Indians now living in those vast areas of Canada
where canoes, snowshoes, and dog sleds are still the only means of
land transportation.

All of the goods of the traders, merchandise or furs, as well as the
canoes, had to be carried over the portages. This was hard work for
the *voyageurs* and required the hardiest kind of men for the task. All
merchandise and furs were wrapped in bundles weighing about
ninety pounds. When portaging, a *voyageur* would carry two of these
bundles on his back as he picked his way over fallen logs or along
the rocky path of the portage trail. Bundles of furs and freight were
carried by means of a tump-line that passed over the forehead and
then back over the shoulders to the weight on the trader's back. Bending forward, because of the weight on his back, the *voyageur* walked
along the portage trail. Sometimes the trail was firm and ran over
rocks and sand. At other times it ran through swampy places. Whatever its course, the trader, bending forward against a broad moose-
hide band—a tump-line—stretched across his forehead, his hands up-
raised and grasping the tump-line on each side of his lowered head,

between ear and shoulder, he pushed on, around stumps, over fallen logs, under low-hanging limbs, across slippery rocks, or through swampy areas from one resting place to another.

One unaccustomed to portaging found the task painful and exhausting. It usually required several years of experience to accustom men to the difficulties of the portage path and the strategy of handling a canoe in rocky rapids or the rolling waves of the lakes.

Several trips along the portage trail were usually required before all the goods and the canoes had been carried across the land. Sometimes traders took their merchandise and canoes the entire length of a portage at one time. At other times, however, when the portage was a longer one, they would divide the distance into one or more places of deposit. All goods and canoes were brought to one deposit before the traders moved on to the next one. Because of this practice, portage distances were often spoken of as so many "poses" or deposits in length.

From the Pigeon River, the voyagers passed on to Lac La Croix and Rainy Lake. From here they went down Rainy River to the

Courtesy National Film Board of Canada
Falls on the Pigeon River west of Grand Portage, Minnesota

Lake of the Woods. In going from Grand Portage, on Lake Superior, to Rainy Lake, it was necessary to make thirty-six more portages. If the voyagers pushed on to Lake Winnipeg, they had to portage twenty-six more times. Thus, if furs were taken from Lake Winnipeg to Montreal, the voyagers had to carry the furs and their canoes ninety-seven times.

Canoes used in the fur trade were known by two general names, "Montreal canoes" or "Canot de Maitre" and "canoes of the North." The Montreal canoes weighed about 600 pounds, were larger, and were used on the trip from western Lake Superior to Montreal. These canoes were about thirty feet in length, six feet in width at the widest part, and could carry thirty men, or a cargo of sixty or seventy bundles of fur weighing ninety pounds each equal to three tons, as well as the crew of fourteen and their provisions, which usually weighed about one thousand pounds. The total weight carried by one canoe has been estimated at about four tons.

When going farther to the west, the Montreal canoes were exchanged for the smaller *canots du nord*, which were better adapted to the smaller streams and the winding portages of the rocky wilderness land northwest of Lake Superior. A *canot du nord* weighed about 300 pounds, was usually about twenty-five feet in length, and was paddled by six to ten men. It was light enough to be carried by one or, at most, two men when the party was making a portage in the wilderness.

When the fur trade was at its height, and the fur trade was being carried on by the North West Company during the English period, the Montreal merchants used two sets of canoes. Each spring the Montreal canoes carried the merchandise to Grand Portage, or Fort William, or sometimes even to the fort at Rainy Lake. Here the *mangeurs de lard* (pork eaters or greenhorns among the *voyageurs*) met the Athabasca men who had left their distant quarters early that spring to bring their furs to Lake Superior. Each group exchanged loads. The canoemen returned to Montreal with the furs. In this way the fur companies were able to transport their furs and goods some 6,000 miles between the spring thaw and fall freeze when all lakes and streams became impassible to canoe travel.

The French forest rovers became expert woodsmen and paddled their canoes as well and as far as could the Indians themselves. One man, known as the *avant*, stood or sat in the bow, or front, of the canoe. Behind the *avant* came the regular *voyageurs* who paddled the canoe. In the back, or stern, of the canoe sat the steerman, known as the *gouvernail*. It was his task to guide the canoe, as it sped along on the surface of the water, by using a paddle having a long handle. In the *gouvernail's* hands this paddle guided the canoe across lakes, down swirling streams, through boiling rapids, and past dangerous rocks which might easily have torn into the fragile bottom of the canoe.

If you had visited this region during the French period, you would not have been at all surprised to have seen a flotilla of forty or fifty canoes come up to the beach in front of you, for in such large groups the French *voyageurs* and Indians often journeyed through the wilderness. These brigades often traveled forty or fifty miles in a day. Distance at that time was not measured in miles but rather in "smokes" or "pipes." If you were to inquire the distance to any point, you would be told that it was so many "pipes" or "smokes" away. This custom came from the practice of resting every two or three miles for three or four minutes. During these brief rest periods, every man lighted his pipe and smoked. Such brief rests were greatly needed, for the French *voyageurs* and Indians paddled their big canoes in earnest. Often they paddled at the rate of forty strokes a minute. To the smooth, even motion of their paddles they often sang together the popular tunes of the day. As they paddled away down the river, their singing grew fainter and fainter as the canoes got farther and farther away.

Sometimes the *voyageurs* were gone for months, and often they did not return for a year or two, or even three. They had little education, and often what little culture they did have was changed because their constant life with the Indian savages caused them slowly to adopt many of the Indian ways of life. Sometimes they almost forgot the ways of their French fathers. Some took Indian squaws for their wives, and it was not at all uncommon to see one of these traders surrounded by a group of half-breed children who came to be known as *bois brulés* (burnt wood).

Furs were the most important article sent from New France to the mother country. The Land of the Lakes, with its thousands of lakes, its streams, wet prairies, swamps, and cold winters, made an excellent homeland for wild fur-bearing animals, especially the much-sought-after beaver. Each winter, when the skins were most valuable, the Indians shot, trapped, snared, and clubbed hundreds of the smaller animals in order that they might get furs to trade to the French, or English, for the goods they were beginning to find necessary for their new way of life.

Of all the furs that of the beaver was the most desired. This was because the beaver hair, which has small barbs along the side, made an excellent material for the making of a high grade felt. This felt was used for making hats of all shapes and sizes. Thus, the beaver skin became the most prized pelt in the American fur trade. Otter, martin, mink, muskrat, and weasel were also killed for their furs but these pelts were not as valuable in the fur trade as was that of the beaver. Some moose and buffalo skins were taken to Montreal but they were bulky and of much less value.

When the French came to North America, the Indians were living a simple life and using only such things as they could find, or make, in their own little community. Seldom did they venture far from their tribal lands. The coming of the Europeans, however, suddenly changed the Indians from a stone age culture to that of the age of iron, and they became more and more dependent upon the white man's goods in their way of life. Birch bark buckets were replaced by copper and iron pots. Blankets were soon used in place of skins to provide warmth. Bows and arrows were quickly discarded for the crude muskets of that day. Steel hatchets, knives, and needles became not luxuries but necessities of the everyday life of the Indians. To get guns, gunpowder, lead, brandy, and blankets the Indians had to trap animals, not to get food as they had in the past, but to secure more and more furs for the French or English fur traders. This hunting for more and more furs soon exhausted the local supply of animals and did much to break up the old tribal locations and to break down the Indian way of life. They became greater rovers than they had been and were often found far from their native hunting grounds. Even though the Indian standard of life was raised by these material things, other aspects of European culture brought havoc to the Indian tribes. Brandy, rum, and strange new diseases of the white man, like smallpox, tuberculosis, diphtheria, and measles, brought sickness and sorrow into many a native Indian wigwam.

The French government knew that if New France was to become a permanent colony it would be necessary to send settlers who would found homes and turn the wilderness into good farms. At different times the French government offered to aid settlers from France if they would come to America and live. Yet, because of the political troubles at home and a poor system of colonization in America, French settlers did not come to New France in very large numbers. However, more and more French settlements gradually grew up along the St. Lawrence River and at a few scattered spots in the wilderness.

Their farms would seem very strange to you today. You are in the habit of seeing farms laid out in squares. The French farms differed greatly from this. They were long, narrow strips of land which ran straight back from the river, or lake. Usually they were not more than three or four hundred feet wide, if that, yet they sometimes ran back into the land a distance of two or three miles. To go from one end of a farm to the other required much time. When a man died, these small strips of land were often divided among his children and thus the strips became smaller and smaller.

Along the river not far from the bank stood a row of French farmhouses. They were little cabins made of any materials which the French settlers could easily get. Usually they were plastered on the inside and out with a kind of mortar which was made by mixing mud and straw. Sometimes they were whitewashed, but seldom, if ever, were they painted. The roofs were made of bark and were often covered with moss. Few, if any, nails were used in building these homes, which were sometimes made from rough lumber produced in the settlement. Each house usually had around it a picket fence. Behind the houses, on still higher ground, ran a road which followed the river.

All the baking was done in a general community oven. A churn, a small number of wooden or leather buckets, and copper pots were the few household articles which were usually carried into the wilderness. When washday came, the women took the soiled clothes down to the river and washed them there.

Usually the farms were located near the forts. The forts gave the farmers protection and in a way provided a small market for the farmers' crops. Near these forts or villages there was often a strip of common land called "the commons" which was used for pasturing the stock of the settlement. Sometimes the field was large and sometimes it was small, depending upon the size of the community.

Farming was hard work. The land had to be cleared. Homes had to be built. The ground had to be tilled and the crops cared for. When a farmer finished his year's work he often had little to show for it because there was no place to sell most of his goods. Therefore he often wished to leave the farm and go into the woods and trade for furs.

However, this he was forbidden to do by very strict laws, for the fur trade was a large monopoly and its huge profits usually went to only a few favored people who were friends of the king.

As the years passed, the small posts in the Great Lakes region came to be more and more important. The constant demand for more and more furs caused the Indians and Frenchmen to push farther and farther west in their quest for new regions where game was more plentiful. Gradually better fortified posts were built by the French government to hold the region for France and to keep the Indians in check.

Of all the posts in Michigan, the one at Michilimackinac became the most important. There, at what is now Saint Ignace, a fort named Fort Du Buade was built soon after 1671. It was surrounded by the usual wooden palisades for protection from the Indians, and it was sometimes garrisoned by as many as two hundred French soldiers. French settlers gathered there too. They lived in about sixty small wooden houses that were built along a single narrow street. The Huron Indians lived near the fort in houses which they had built.

In 1689 the first of four wars between England and France began. French raiding parties, made up of Frenchmen from New France and Indians from her western lands, went south and attacked the English settlements in New England. The French were fearful of losing the friendship of their western Indians and so sent soldiers under Cadillac to St. Ignace to be stationed at Fort Du Buade.

Their time in Michigan was short-lived, however, for in 1697 King Louis XIV of France, at the request of the Jesuits, ordered all the traders, except those stationed in the Mississippi Valley, to leave the West. The Jesuits were to be the only people who could go into the West to teach and trade with the Indians. So the following year Cadillac and all the legal traders and soldiers in the West left their little posts and went eastward to the French settlements along the St. Lawrence.

But, though Cadillac left the area, he was soon to return. While at Michilimackinac, as commander of the troops stationed there, he had learned all that he could about a large river far to the south which is now called the Detroit River. Like LaSalle before him, Cadillac was a man of vision. A post on the Detroit River, somewhere near Lake Erie, would act as a block and keep the English from coming north into the lands of the French, with their rum and better-made English goods, to trade with the Indians.

From New France, Cadillac crossed the ocean to lay his plans before the king of France. In the court of the king, Cadillac found friends who listened to his plan and helped him to get permission from Louis XIV to start a little colony on the Detroit River.

The English, too, had a similar idea about building a fort in the same area. Thinking that it would be wise, for reasons of trade, to build a fort upon the Detroit River, they entered into an agreement with the Iroquois Indians, who claimed the land, for permission to build a fort on the river. The Iroquois thereupon, deeded the land to the English on July 14, 1701. The English, however, had acted too slowly.

Cadillac had already been given permission from the French government to found his new settlement and he was then on his way from Montreal by way of the Ottawa route. When they left Lake Huron they passed the place, at present day Port Huron, where Du Luth had made his settlement in 1686. On July 23, 1701 Cadillac and his followers made their way across Lake St. Clair and entered the Detroit River. As they paddled down the broad river, they scanned its banks for a good place to found the new settlement. They continued on down the river to Grosse Ile at the mouth of the river. South of them lay the waters of Lake Erie. Cadillac and his party spent the night on the island. Although this seemed to be a good place to build the new fort, the location was rejected because of the many islands, the width of the river, and the difficulty of seeing any English or Indians that might go up or down the river.

On the following day, July 24, 1701, Cadillac and his party came back up the river and chose the spot where Detroit now stands as the best place to build the fort. At that point the river is the narrowest and a small stream, the Savoyard, running into the Detroit River provided a point of land protected by water on three sides. Drawing their canoes upon the shore where the Veterans Memorial Building now stands, Cadillac and his men climbed the steep riverbank and selected the spot now crossed by West Jefferson Avenue as the best place to build the new fort, which they named Fort Pontchartrain in honor of Cadillac's friend at the French Court. Fifty soldiers, fifty traders and artisans, and two priests formed the white population of Cadillac's little settlement. Before long Indians—Hurons, Miamis, and Ojibways— began to gather at the fort on the Detroit River. They came seeking protection from the Iroquois.

Although Cadillac had named his little post Fort Pontchartrain, in time it came to be called the Village of the Straits (ville de troit).

Later the word for village was dropped and the name became Detroit and means "of the straits."

It was Cadillac's plan to make his little post on the Detroit River a French settlement and not just a western fur trading post. Cadillac's wife and Madam de Tonty, together with one of Cadillac's sons, James, came to Detroit from Quebec by way of Lake Erie. One of Cadillac's other sons had come with his father when Cadillac had come to start the settlement. These two French women, Madam Cadillac and Madam de Tonty, were the first French women to come to Michigan. Their coming meant that French family life was to be a part of Cadillac's new settlement.

Only a little farming was done in the area during the years that France held the Great Lakes Region. The French were more interested in their missions and the fur trade than they were in developing agriculture in New France. What is more, France tried to set up a feudal system in New France. Land was not given, or sold, to settlers like it was in the English colonies, but rather it became the property of local lords, called seigneurs. Frenchmen wishing to farm had to get the right to farm the land from some seigneur. Then, too, the Great Lakes area was far from any good market, and canoe transportation was too slow and costly to permit carrying farm products to the French settlements back east along the St. Lawrence River.

After 1701 a few French farmers were to be found in Michigan but they grew crops only for their own use or the very limited local market. They found the soil rich and easily able to supply food for their families. Their farms were small strips of land about a block wide that ran back into the country from the Detroit River. Usually they were cleared only a little way back from the settler's cabin, for the Frenchmen saw little use in the hard work of clearing land if it was not needed for immediate use. The French farmers had a few cows and some horses which were really only ponies. These ponies they hitched to little two-wheeled carts. These little carts and canoes were the Frenchmen's only means of transportation. Near each French farmer's house there was usually a garden. Near the garden was often an orchard in which grew peach trees and apple trees. These trees furnished fresh fruit that was then considered of little value, but the juices were made into brandy for the Indian trade.

Although Cadillac had good plans for his little settlement on the Detroit River ill fortune followed him from the start. The fur trade had been given to him as part of his grant, but he had no sooner left

France than the French king gave the same grant to a group of men known as the Company of Canada. To try to straighten out his trading rights and to try to get settlers to come west to his new settlement, Cadillac spent much of the next ten years at Quebec.

Unfortunately for Cadillac's small settlement, war again came between France and England in 1702. This war was called Queen Anne's War and lasted until 1713. The king of France was now too busy to be interested in Cadillac's little settlement on the Detroit River. In 1710, the king appointed Cadillac as governor of Louisiana. He served there as governor until 1715 when he returned to France.

In 1711 after Cadillac had left, a band of Sauk and Fox Indians attacked Detroit. They had been told by their friends, the Iroquois, that France and England were at war and they thought that it would be a good time to destroy Detroit and open trade with the English for their cheaper goods. Fortunately for the French at Detroit, although there were no soldiers in the fort at the time, the French traders were able to keep the Sauk and Fox Indians away until a band of friendly Pottawattomie Indians came to the rescue of the settlement.

When Queen Anne's War came to an end, in 1713, England gained in the peace treaty the control of Hudson Bay, Newfoundland, and Nova Scotia. France was slowly losing her American possessions to the English, but France still continued to hold onto her posts in the Great Lakes area and some new posts were built.

For a few years after Cadillac settled Detroit, the post at St. Ignace became less and less important until it was almost abandoned. However, after Cadillac left for Louisiana, to become governor there, the post at Michilimackinac again became the main trading post in the Great Lakes area. The old abandoned post of Fort du Buade, at St. Ignace, was not restored but a new one was made, about 1715, on the south side of the straits at what is now Mackinaw City. Its site is just west of the new Mackinac Bridge.

The little post at St. Joseph (Niles), on the St. Joseph River, which had been established in 1691, was restored. In 1721, when Charlevoix visited the St. Joseph area, he reported that a commandant and a small garrison of soldiers were there. Because of the "oak openings," good hunting, and fishing, and fertile land, this area seems to have been well liked by both the Indians and Frenchmen. A mission seems to have been maintained there by the Jesuits during most of the period when France controlled the lakes.

Another fort was also built about this same time to strengthen

France's hold on the West. In 1720, Major Pierre Boisbriant came up the Mississippi River with one hundred men and built Fort de Chartres between Kaskaskia and Cahokia. At first the fort was a wooden one but later, in 1756, during the French and Indian War, much of the fort was rebuilt with stone at great expense to the French government. Although large for its time, the garrison stationed there was always small. At most it rarely numbered three hundred men. For a short time it was the center of French culture in the Illinois area. Later, about 1772, the Mississippi River undercut part of the fort and it was then abandoned.

Just south of Fort de Chartres was the French settlement of Kaskaskia which was settled in 1721. North of it was the French settlement of Cahokia, founded in 1699. Nearby were also the little French settlements of St. Philippe and Prairie du Rocher. Farther to the east, on the Wabash River, the French also founded, in 1734, a little settlement known as Vincennes. In these villages lived mostly French hunters and traders who had married Indian women. Like the Indians before them they found the country more open and abounding in game such as buffalo, elk, bear, and deer. The soil was also more fertile for growing their few crops.

But France's control of New France was soon to come to an end. Aggressive fur traders from the English colonies soon began crossing the mountains with pack horse trains to trade with the Indians in the Ohio country for furs. Soon they were going as far west as the Wabash and Illinois Rivers. What is more, English settlers were soon to spill across the mountains and begin to settle in the West.

Another war, King George's War, was fought between England and France from 1744 to 1748. Although Michigan was too far to the west to take part in these wars, Indians from the Great Lakes area often went eastward to aid the French armies and to help defend the French settlements or to help attack those of the English. In 1748 the French seemed to sense their weakness in the growing rivalry between the French and the English in America. In that year the French government tried to encourage settlers to come to Detroit by offering to provide them with a spade, an ax, a plow, a large wagon, a small wagon, a cow, a pig, and other grants. As a result of this offer some Frenchmen came from France to settle at Detroit the following year. About this time the first farms were started across from Detroit in what is now Windsor, Ontario. However, France had waited too long to develop her settlements and agricultural resources in New France.

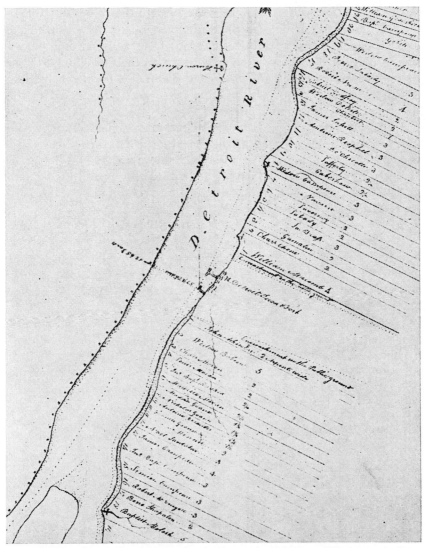

A small section of a map made by Patrick McNiff showing the location of the town, fort, and ribbon farms along the north bank of the Detroit River as of 1796.

English settlers were now becoming eager to push into the Ohio Valley. In the same year that King George's War came to an end the Ohio Company was formed. When New France learned of this threat, from the English colonies against land she claimed in the Ohio Valley,

Pierre Celoron, Sieur de Blainville was sent into the valley the following year, 1749, to put up lead plates announcing France's title to the land. These lead plates were fastened to trees at important places, such as places where large streams flowed into the Ohio River. Other plates were buried in the ground. When Blainville's party reached the Miami River they turned north. From this river they crossed to the Maumee and by this route came to Detroit.

In 1756 war again came between France and England. Indians and Frenchmen from Detroit and Michilimackinac again hurried eastward to help New France. Some of these men took part in the defeat of General Braddock. The lake posts were still too far away to enter into the actual struggle, but men from this area took part in most of the campaigns of the French and Indian War.

In 1759 General Wolfe's army scaled the heights at Quebec and, on the Plains of Abraham on top of Cape Diamond, they defeated the French general, Montcalm. Quebec, the key to New France, thus fell into the hands of the English. The following year English armies marched upon Montreal. The French surrendered and New France then passed to the English.

Like the Indians before them, the French explorers and settlers gave names to many places in Michigan. Here are a few of them: Presque Isle, "almost an island"; Belle Isle, "beautiful island"; Les Cheneaux, "the channels"; Sault Ste. Marie, "falls, or rapids, of the St. Mary's"; Bois Blanc, "white woods"; Grosse Pointe, "large point"; and Grosse Ile, "large island."

CHAPTER FIVE

Early Years of English Rule (1760–1775)

To AN ENGLISH forest ranger, Major Robert T. Rogers, fell the task of reaching the distant French posts on the Great Lakes and telling the French soldiers that Canada had been captured by the English. With a small party of Englishmen and Indians, Major Rogers came westward along the south shore of Lake Erie and reached the outpost of Detroit late in the fall of 1760.

The French commandant at Detroit had not yet heard of the surrender of Canada by the French, but when he was shown the official papers which Major Rogers had with him, he gave up the fort to the English. He and his French soldiers were then sent as prisoners of war to Philadelphia.

In spite of the lateness of the season, Major Rogers planned to go on to the post of Michilimackinac, but because of the bitterness of the fall weather he changed his plans and remained at Detroit during the following winter. The other posts in the area were not occupied until the following year.

While Major Rogers was spending the winter at Detroit, things were happening at Michilimackinac. From that post a French settler and trader named Charles Langlade had gone east to the war at the head of a party of Indians from the region of Michilimackinac. It was he, in company with other Frenchmen, who led the French and Indians in the battle against Braddock near Fort Duquesne.

At the close of the war Charles Langlade and his Indians were at Montreal. The French commander, knowing that he must soon give up to the English and not wishing the Indians to be there, sent Langlade and his Indians back to Fort Michilimackinac. They had not gone very far when a messenger overtook them and told Langlade that Canada had passed to British control. Langlade continued homeward and upon reaching Michilimackinac, told of the passing of Canada to the British.

When Langlade reported the news to the French commander, Beaujeu, the commander, dismantled the little fort at what is now

"Shooting the Rapids." A painting by Mrs. F. A. Hopkins.

Mackinaw City. He and his soldiers then started for the French fort of Chartres, which was located on the Mississippi River in what is now the state of Illinois.

Beaujeu and his men found the weather against them just as it was against Major Rogers. The Frenchmen were unable to reach Fort Chartres before the rivers froze over. Being unable to continue their journey, they were forced to spend the winter among the Indians. The following year Beaujeu and his soldiers arrived at Fort Chartres, where they remained for the next four years until the fort was abandoned in 1765.

The English fur traders were eager to get the profits that the French had been making from the trade in furs. Perhaps they were too eager. It was not long, therefore, before English fur traders began to appear in the Land of the Lakes. If a peace had been signed in Montreal in 1760 things might have been different, but the war continued in Europe and it was not until 1763 that peace was finally made between England and France. It is no wonder then that the English soldiers and fur traders who had taken the lake posts soon became the victims of a French plan to regain the region for France.

Many causes have been given for the Indian uprising against the English which is known as Pontiac's Conspiracy. The English had failed to push into the Mississippi region and take over the French forts located there. Frenchmen at these posts supplied the Indians with guns and ammunition and set afloat many rumors that aroused the war spirit of the Indians. Before the defeat of the French both the French and English had tried to keep the friendship of their Indian allies so that the Indians would not join the enemy. Now that the French had been defeated, the English did not feel that they had to try to win the Indians' good will. What is more, England needed all her powder and supplies to continue the Seven Year's War which she was still fighting in Europe.

By 1763 it was plain to the Indians that Englishmen were different people from Frenchmen. They seldom married Indian women. They treated Indians as if they were not as good as Englishmen. Moreover, the rivers did not flow with rum as the Indians had been told they would. In fact, it became hard for the Indians to get even the necessary supplies such as gunpowder and blankets upon which they had come to depend. They grew dissatisfied and willingly listened to the tales of the French who were still at Fort Chartres, their half-breed brothers, and the *coureur de bois* who were still eager for the profits of the fur trade. Rumors aroused hatreds. Hatreds bred plots. At last the well-planned Indian conspiracy of Pontiac was born.

Early in the spring of the year 1763 an Indian called Chief Pontiac, who lived on Peche Island near Belle Isle in the Detroit River, held an Indian council on the Ecorse River near Detroit. To the council came many Indians and also several Frenchmen. The council reached its height with the speech of Chief Pontiac. Using all his force of words and character Pontiac clearly pictured to his Indian listeners how they were being mistreated by the English who had come into their homeland. Then he aroused in their minds a glowing memory of the many kindnesses of their French brothers with whom they had lived for years. Gradually, as a skillful speaker can, he excited the Indians by telling them of the ways in which the English had neglected their brothers, how they had driven the French fur traders from the country, and how they were only waiting for some excuse in order to drive the Indians from their ancient tribal hunting grounds.

Pontiac then held up a belt of wampum which he told his listeners had been sent to him by the great French king from far across the sea. He said that the long sleep into which the French king had fallen was now at its end and that soon his large war canoes would be coming up the Mississippi and the St. Lawrence rivers to win Canada back for France.

Under the leadership of Pontiac the Indians planned to return to their homes and then, when a certain time arrived, each group would attack the English post nearest them. Thus, each of the English forts was to be attacked at about the same time so that the English soldiers could not help one another. When the forts were taken, all the English-men would be killed and thus the land would be rid of the hated English.

Of the forts located in the upper lake area the one at Michilimack-inac was the largest and best garrisoned. It was at that time under the command of Captain Etherington. Ninety-two English soldiers made up the garrison stationed there.

Although Captain Etherington had been warned by friendly French and Indians of the danger of an Indian attack, he paid little atten-tion to the Indians when they began to gather about the fort, for they acted in a manner very friendly to him and his men.

On one of the first days in June, 1763, the Indians invited the English soldiers to see a game of lacrosse that was going to be played between two rival Indian tribes. As it was the king's birthday, the soldiers were already in a holiday mood. Carelessly they straggled out of the palisade which surrounded the fort and sat down in the shade to watch the Indians as they tossed the ball back and forth from one side to the other.

Courtesy Mackinac Island State Park Commission

Front gate of the restored Fort Michilimackinac at Mackinaw City. It was here that the Indians during Pontiac's Conspiracy entered the fort to massacre the English garrison. Photo 1964.

For some time the game of lacrosse continued. Back and forth flew the ball as each group of braves tried to win for their tribe. Meanwhile many squaws, one after another, passed into and out of the fort through the open gate. None of the English soldiers noted their careless but well-planned actions. About noon one of the players threw the ball high into the air so that it would fall well within the pickets of cedar which surrounded the fort.

This was the signal for the Indians to attack the post. As if still in friendly play, the Indian braves dashed in through the open gateway of the fort in one mad rush as though they were all eager to get the ball. Once inside, the Indian warriors raised the war whoop and were quickly given tomahawks which the squaws had carried into the fort well hidden beneath the heavy folds of their blankets.

Where all had been peace and friendly play, all was now excitement. Tomahawks flew and most of the Englishmen were killed. Captain Etherington and about fourteen soldiers and traders were taken prisoners. After weeks of cruel suffering, they were finally freed.

Thus fell the fort at Michilimackinac (Mackinaw City) before the crafty Indian attack. The Indians then wandered through the fort and took whatever they wanted. Then they burned the fort.

Fort St. Joseph, at present-day Niles, was attacked by a band of Pottawattomies on May 25. The small garrison there was wiped out except for Ensign Schlosser and three men. These four were later taken to Detroit where they were exchanged for Indian prisoners then held by the English.

The attack on the fort at Detroit was led by Chief Pontiac. The crafty chief with a band of his trusted Indian followers planned to hold a council with Major Gladwin who was then in command of the post. On May 7, 1763, Pontiac and sixty of his warriors entered the fort and were greeted in a friendly but stern manner by the English commander who had his soldiers on duty and ready for quick action.

For some time the Indians talked with the English officers. At last Pontiac rose to make a speech. The Indians had planned that, as their chieftan talked, he was to present a belt of wampum and at this signal the Indians were to take their sawed-off guns from under their blankets and make an attack on the officers while their brothers were to attack the fort and the soldiers stationed there.

It looked for a time as if the Indians' plans would succeed. The guns, whose barrels had been sawed off, were actually there, hidden

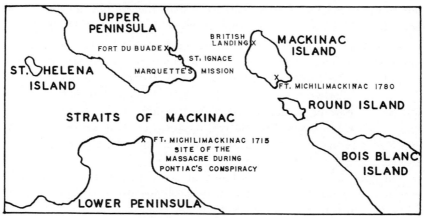

UPPER PENINSULA

FORT DU BUADE X

BRITISH LANDING X

MACKINAC ISLAND

X ST. IGNACE

MARQUETTE'S MISSION

ST. HELENA ISLAND

X FT. MICHILIMACKINAC 1780

ROUND ISLAND

STRAITS OF MACKINAC

X FT. MICHILIMACKINAC 1715
SITE OF THE
MASSACRE DURING
PONTIAC'S CONSPIRACY

BOIS BLANC ISLAND

LOWER PENINSULA

Michilimackinac is a general name that applies to all of the general area around the Straits of Mackinac. The French started a little post at St. Ignace in 1671, when Father Marquette built a little mission there. Later a fort named Fort du Buade was built there by the French. Just where this fort stood is not certain but it was on the little stream that flows into East Moron Bay. The fort was abandoned when Cadillac was called to Quebec with the French soldiers in 1697. From 1701 to 1715, Fort Pontchartrain, at Detroit, was the main western post of the French but about 1715 the French again built a post at the straits area. This new post was located at what is now Macknaw City on the south side of the straits. The English occupied this post in 1761. It was this post that was taken, in 1673, by the Indians during Pontiac's Conspiracy. A new and better fort was built on Mackinac Island by the English during the Revolutionary War to protect the area from the threatened invasion of George Rogers Clark. This new fort on Mackinac Island was occupied by the English in 1780. In 1796 this fort was turned over to the Americans. During the War of 1812 it was this fort on the island that was captured by the English. It was returned to the Americans in 1815. Both the fort on the island and the older one at Mackinaw City are now being restored.

beneath the blankets of the warriors. But a strange thing happened just as Pontiac was about to present the wampum belt. Drums rolled, a door opened, and there stood a group of English soldiers ready for the Indian attack should the braves try to carry out their plan. Then one of the Englishmen stepped forward and pulled back the blanket of an Indian and uncovered his hidden gun.

The Indians were taken by surprise. They now understood why the English soldiers had all been at their posts when they entered. Someone had told the English that the Indians were planning to capture the post.

Pontiac finished his speech very quickly but he did not present the wampum belt. When he had finished, Major Gladwin arose and spoke to the Indians. He told them the English would be friends to the Indians as long as they were peaceful, but if they took the war path they would soon feel the mighty power of the English king.

How had the English at Detroit learned of the Indians' plans? Many stories have tried to explain the mystery. One story tells that women saw the Indians filing off their gun barrels. Still another tells that Major Gladwin was warned by an Indian maiden who came to sell him a pair of Indian moccasins. A study of the records shows that there were many Frenchmen who were loyal to the English, and it was probably they who gave the warning of the coming Indian attack.

On May 9 Pontiac and a band of warriors again tried to gain entrance into the fort in order, they said, to smoke the peace pipe with the commander. Major Gladwin told Pontiac that he and a few of the Indian chieftans might enter but the rest of the Indians must stay outside the stockade.

This action on the part of Major Gladwin angered the Indians, and they no longer tried to keep the false face of peace. They set up a war whoop and fell upon the luckless Englishmen who happened to be outside the palisade of the fort. Not far away lived an old lady and her two sons. These the Indians killed and scalped. Going to Belle Isle, they attacked Mr. Fisher and his family who were living there. Mr. and Mrs. Fisher were killed and their two children were carried away.

English traders were no longer safe in the woods. Everywhere they were in danger of being robbed and murdered by the Indians. More than a hundred English traders were killed by the Indians during the summer of 1763.

On May 10 Pontiac and his Indians moved their camp across the river to what is now the American side near the Belle Isle Bridge. Then began the Indian siege of Detroit. It is one of the few sieges to be found in all Indian history. English sentries had ever to be on their guard lest they expose themselves to the gunfire of one of the Indians who lay hidden just outside the walls of the palisade.

As the days passed, the English soldiers learned, little by little, the fate of the English soldiers who had been stationed at the other frontier posts. Nearly always the story was the same: cruel treachery, murder, and the smoldering remains of what had once been a British post. Such news was disheartening, and gloom settled over the little post on the banks of the Detroit River.

But help would surely come. In fact, they were expecting supplies from Fort Niagara to arrive at Detroit about the last of the month. Could Major Gladwin and his soldiers hold out that long against the Indians? Eagerly the English sentries watched the river for the coming of the canoes that would bring aid to the imprisoned garrison. On May 30 a shout of joy ran through the fort. A fleet of canoes could be seen coming up the river from Lake Erie. All rushed to the pickets and watched anxiously to see what would happen. Would the Indians attack the canoes? Did the soldiers in the canoes know that the Indians were attacking the fort?

Steadily the canoes came on up the river. Why did the Englishmen not return the salute from the fort? Why did they keep to the far side of the river? Suddenly the war whoop of the Indians rent the air and the little garrison at the fort knew what had happened to the supply expedition. Their friends were prisoners of the Indians. The Indians had captured them while they were camped on the north shore of Lake Erie. Now the Indians were forcing the Englishmen to paddle the canoes for them. A few of the Englishmen tried to break away and reach the fort. Two did reach it, but most of those who tried were killed by the Indians. Up past the fort the flotilla of canoes went, twenty-three canoes filled with provisions and powder for the fort.

At the Indian camp the party landed. Then began one of the most cruel happenings ever to take place in Michigan. For the pleasure of the squaws and children the English prisoners were put to cruel Indian torture and death.

On July 29, two hundred and eighty men with supplies did reach Detroit. Captain Dalyell had made his way up the Detroit River under cover of a heavy fog. The arrival of more men and supplies brought new hope to the soldiers in the little fort, but hope lingered for only a short while.

Captain Dalyell was not a seasoned Indian fighter like Major Gladwin. Captain Dalyell thought that the Indians could easily be defeated if their camp were attacked by surprise. Unwillingly, Major Gladwin finally gave permission to Captain Dalyell to make an attack on the Indian camp.

On July 31, at two-thirty in the morning the English soldiers marched quietly out of the gate of the little fort beside the river. Up the River Road (now East Jefferson Avenue) they marched toward Lake St. Clair. On their right flowed the Detroit River. On its surface came two boats, the "Michigan" and the "Huron," armed with guns. It was hoped that the boats with their guns could aid the soldiers, or that they could at least help to cover a retreat should the men be driven back toward the fort.

Silently the English soldiers marched in the darkness of the early morning hours. French farmhouse after farmhouse was passed. On they went until they had gone about two miles from the fort. Then they came to a bridge where the River Road ran over Parent's Creek* just before the stream entered the Detroit River.

Bloody Run in Elmwood Cemetery in Detroit. Near here the Indians under Pontiac defeated the English soldiers led by Captain Dalyell. (1961)

As the leading soldiers of the English column reached the bridge, the Indian war whoop and heavy musket fire came from the Indians who had been waiting in the darkness for the English soldiers to arrive. All quickly became confusion in the darkness of the early morning. Then the English began their retreat to the fort. Back along the road from French farmhouse to French farmhouse the fight went on as the retreat continued. Slowly the English soldiers gave ground before the Indians' attack. Several soldiers were killed as they tried to save their wounded comrades from the Indians. Captain Dalyell

---

*Also called Bloody Run.

was thus killed while trying to save an English sergeant. By eight o'clock that morning the English soldiers who were left had struggled, weary and beaten, into the shelter of the fort.

The siege of Detroit lasted from May until October. During this time the garrison had little touch with the outside world. Fortunately there were two sailboats, the "Huron" and the "Michigan," which were stationed just outside the fort. These boats aided the garrison in many ways. Their gunfire helped to protect the side of the fort next to the river. Then too, they sailed down the Detroit River and across Lake Erie and brought back supplies from Fort Niagara.

The Indians tried may times to destroy these boats. At one time they made large rafts, loaded them with material that would easily burn, and sent them floating down the river in hopes that the flaming rafts would pass near enough to the fort to burn the boats.

As the summer passed, the Indians' hopes, patience, and ammunition grew smaller and smaller. Some wandered off into the forest in search of winter hunting grounds. Yet Pontiac held on even though his warriors grew fewer and fewer in number. In late October Pontiac received a letter from the commandant at Fort Chartres telling him that he could no longer expect aid from the French in Illinois.

Pontiac began to understand that he had been made the tool of crafty planners. No war canoes from France were to come up the Mississippi or the St. Lawrence River. Defeated and humiliated, he left Detroit. At first he planned to return again the following summer and take up the siege. This, however, he did not do. When he did return, he asked for peace.

In the same year, 1763, that the Indians of the West had tried to drive the English from the West, France, which had now been fighting England for seven years, gave up the war and accepted defeat. In the peace, signed in 1763, England gained most of France's colonies throughout the world. Canada and all of New France east of the Mississippi River were given to England by the treaty. France was allowed to keep only two very small islands near Newfoundland, St. Pierre and Miquelon, to serve as a base for her fishing fleet. These islands France still holds today.

England thus claimed, after 1763, all the land from her West Indies Islands north to the top of Hudson Bay and east of the Mississippi River. This vast colonial possession in America brought with it many new problems of government for England.

What should be done with the new unsettled land to the west of the Atlantic colonies was one of the major problems. Many of the colonial charters had stated that the colonial grants ran from sea to sea. Thus each colony would have to deal independently with the Indian problem. The English government, however, disregarded the wishes of the colonies in regard to the western land and passed what is now known as the Proclamation of 1763 in an attempt to settle the Western Indian problem for a time. This act forbade the colonial governments to grant land to settlers west of the head waters of rivers flowing into the Atlantic Ocean, and ordered any settlers already west of this line to return to the East. It was hoped that such an act would help the Indians to give up their war-like practices against the English and that the fur trade of the Lake Region would be kept for English traders.

This act of the English home government greatly angered the colonists and, though unable to get title to the land, they began pushing into the Upper Ohio Valley. Wheeling and Pittsburgh soon became permanent settlements. Other settlers, in 1768, began settling the upper Tennessee Valley. In 1774 they began coming into the center of Kentucky, and in the following year, when the Revolution began, Daniel Boone and others cut a road from the Cumberland Gap to Boonesboro. Englishmen thus began their expansion into the West, and the Indians soon were beginning to see their hunting grounds taken from them and turned into farm lands.

In 1774 England passed an act that angered many of the people living in the colonies. It was known as the Quebec Act. By this act the colony of Quebec was to extend west to the Mississippi River and south to the Ohio River. This large area took in lands that the colonies claimed at theirs. The Quebec Act said that all Frenchmen living in the area must swear allegiance to the English king but that they could keep their religion, language, and way of life. This act did much to help the French people in Canada keep their French customs.

CHAPTER SIX

Revolution and Change
(1775-1796)

IN 1775, THIRTEEN of England's American colonies began a war against their mother country. England's other colonies in the West Indies and Canada remained loyal to her. The thirteen colonies tried to win the good will of the Indians from the English, for each side knew that the Indians would be useful allies. However, the colonies failed to lure the Indians away, and most of them remained loyal to England during the Revolutionary War.

The Quebec Act of 1774 had made the Lake Region a part of the colony of Quebec. Under provision of this act, four local governors were sent into the area of the lakes and the Illinois country. Col. Henry Hamilton was appointed lieutenant-governor at Detroit and Captain Patrick Sinclair was appointed to the post at Michilimackinac.

When Colonel Hamilton arrived at Detroit on November 9, 1775, the Revolutionary War had already begun and the task of keeping the Indians loyal to the English became an important one.

At that time Detroit had only a little over 1,300 people, not including the soldiers stationed at the fort. The little fort, that sat by the river where Cadillac had built his Fort Pontchartrain, was in a bad state of repair, so Colonel Hamilton set to work immediately to replace the pickets of the stockade so that it would be in a better condition to hold out against a colonial army and the Indians, should they try to attack the post. At best, it would hardly be called a fort because it had no earthworks or cannon. But, small as it was and located in the vast expanse of forests, lakes, and rivers, it was the headquarters for the English Indian Department in the West and for the fur traders and rangers operating in the Great Lakes Region.

Michilimackinac, now Mackinaw City, was only a small settlement of some four hundred people. The stockade there was still just about the same as it had been when it had been captured by the Indians in 1763. Sault Ste. Marie was very small and so was the little post of St. Joseph. The old French fort, Fort Chartres, on the Mississippi, had been undercut by the Mississippi River and had been abandoned. On the Wabash River was the French settlement of Vincennes, while on the Mississippi River were the settlements of Cahokia and Kaskaskia and the new post of St. Louis that had been started, in 1764, in Spanish territory.

To keep the friendship of the Indians, the English gave them many presents such as kettles, tobacco, vermilion, knives, tomahawks, guns, gunpowder, and blankets. Thus Detroit and Michilimackinac became centers of war activity far behind the fighting along the Atlantic Seaboard.

Plans were soon under way to use Indians and rangers to strike at the colonies from the West. This the English felt would weaken the colonial armies because they would have to send soldiers to aid the western settlers against the Indians and rangers. Before long, raiding parties made up of whites and Indians were leaving Detroit to go on raids against the frontier settlements in New York, Pennsylvania, West Virginia, and Kentucky. Other war parties left Michilimackinac and went to Montreal to aid the English armies stationed there.

Going south from Detroit through the vast wilderness of Ohio and Kentucky, these raiding parties of English and Indians fell upon the backwoods settlements. Such havoc was done in these raids in the year 1777 that the American settlers came to call that year "the year of the three bloody sevens." Just how many of these raids there were, or where the raiding parties struck, no one will ever know, for many times no one was left to tell of the war whoop that came so suddenly from a silent, midnight forest or of the death and destruction that lay behind as the raiders vanished into the gloomy wilderness. We do know, however, that these English war parties, often led by white men like Simon Girty, covered vast areas and brought fear and death to many of the early settlers on the frontier.

Mutilated bodies with scalps gone, smoldering ashes of what had once been cabins on the frontier, tales of horror and massacre — these were the signs that marked the bloody trail of the Indian raiders. Many settlers and their families thus perished from the guns, tomahawks, and scalping knives of the Indian war parties.

Sometimes the settlers' women and children were spared by the Indians and brought as captives to Detroit. Only a few men were that fortunate, although Daniel Boone and some of the other frontier Indian fighters whom the Indians admired for their cunning and bravery were brought to Detroit.

Little mercy was shown to the Indians' prisoners as they made their way to Michigan with the returning rangers and Indians. Should one of the prisoners become ill, or too tired to continue the journey, he was often speedily put to death with the tomahawk, or a club, and only the scalp continued the journey.

When a returning war party reached Detroit, the people turned out to greet it. With a savage pride, supported by an inner feeling of justice in fighting for their homeland, the Indians showed their prisoners and the strings of scalps which they had taken from their enemy, the Kentucky "Long Knives." To them, scalps were badges of bravery and signs of loyalty to show to their English brothers.

But what of the women and children who had been forced to come with their Indian captors to Detroit? Sometimes they were forced to become members of an Indian tribe. Many small children thus learned to live like Indians and lived out their lives as brothers of the red men. Sometimes the women and children were bought from the Indians by the settlers living at Detroit. To arouse the feeling of the settlers for the white captives, and thus increase their willingness to pay, the Indians often tortured their captives as they paraded them around the streets of the little town.

But the year 1777 was not all bad for the colonies. In the fall of that year General Burgoyne, with his Indian allies, was defeated as he pushed down the Lake Champlain-Hudson River water route. Then too, in that year France joined the colonies in their fight against England. This move on the part of France, together with letters to the French living in the Northwest, made many of the French settlers willing to quietly side with the colonists against the English.

In order to check the raids on the frontier, the government of Virginia planned a military campaign that would strike at the French settlements in the Illinois country and at Detroit. Such a campaign would carry the war into the Indian country from which the raiders were coming.

George Rogers Clark, a frontiersman, was granted permission to raise a band of volunteers for this campaign. With a war party of only about one hundred seventy-five men, dressed in their frontier coonskin caps, buckskin shirts with fringed edges, leather leggings, and moccasins, he floated down the Ohio River to a point about sixty miles from its mouth. From this point on the Ohio River he marched with his men overland to Kaskaskia. That little French post, and

Cahokia, then held by the English, gave up to the Americans without a fight. Vincennes, on the Wabash, also surrendered to Clark's men without a struggle.

News of Clark's raid on the Illinois settlements soon reached Lieutenant-governor Hamilton at Detroit. Hamilton, with a few troops and some Indians set out for Vincennes by way of Lake Erie, the Maumee River, and the Wabash River. More Indians joined the war party on the way.

Vincennes was easily taken because it was guarded by only a captain and one soldier. Then Hamilton settled down to spend the rest of the winter at Vincennes before moving further against Clark and his men.

But Clark had no desire to wait with his little band until spring came and Hamilton would be able to rally the Indians to help him. So in mid-February, 1779, Clark and his men set out to cross the flooded prairies that lay between them and Hamilton at Vincennes. Hamilton had not suspected such a bold move by Clark and so was caught unprepared and was forced to surrender.

Though it had been Clark's plan to move north against Detroit, he never had the men, or supplies, that would have been necessary for such a military campaign. But small as his force was, it was still large enough to keep the English and Indians from driving him from the area he had already taken.

The year 1778 was a busy one at Detroit. Not only had it seen Hamilton's party off to Vincennes, but also several raiding parties, with which a number of Frenchmen were "ordered to go," had left the post to attack the frontier. In that summer also the Indians captured Daniel Boone and Simon Kenton and brought them with other prisoners to Detroit. Simon Kenton escaped while at Detroit and made his way back to Kentucky. Although a large reward was offered for Daniel Boone, the Indians would not release him to the English. He was taken back south to Chillicothe, Ohio, where, upon learning that the Indians planned an attack upon Boonesboro, he escaped and reached it in time to warn the settlers.

Hamilton had no sooner left for Vincennes than Captain Lernoult, then in command at Detroit, began the building of a new fort on the spot where the Federal Building now stands. The old palisade by the river was much in need of repair, and if Clark and his frontier fighters had reached Detroit and placed even a small cannon on the higher ground overlooking the old palisade, there would have been no way for the English to defend the town. For this reason, settlers, soldiers, and prisoners were all put to work to build a new fort and to dig a moat which was to surround the fort on all sides.

When finished, the fort occupied the higher ground and a picket fence or palisade, somewhat like a large V, ran down from it to the water's edge and enclosed the old village of Detroit, the cemetery, the parade ground, and the gardens of the garrison.

On May 8, 1779, Spain joined France and the colonies in their war against England. At Detroit work was still being pushed on the building of Fort Lernoult. On October 4, 1779, Patrick Sinclair, after much delay, arrived at Michilimackinac to take up his post as lieutenant-governor in that area. The English post at that time was still on the south side of the straits where a new palisade had been built to replace the one destroyed by the Indians in 1763. As it had no cannons, its only defenses were small arms and a vast, spreading wilderness, in which lived savage Indians and which any raiding party of Americans must cross before reaching the fort.

Sinclair, therefore, during the same fall in which he arrived at Michilimackinac, began work upon a new and better fort on Mackinac Island. To build a fort so far back in the wilderness was no small task. Laborers were always scarce, and skilled workmen were even harder to find. But Sinclair kept his men building the fort all through the year of 1780. In the summer of 1781 the Indians deeded Mackinac Island to the English for $12,500. The old post at Mackinaw City was abandoned and the garrison was moved over to the new fort on Mackinac Island. The fort was to be known as Fort Mackinac, but the post was still to be known as Michilimackinac. This name it kept until the Americans occupied the island in 1796, and then both the fort and the post became known as Mackinac.

On January 1, 1781, a small party of Spanish and French with some Indian allies made their way across what is now Illinois and Indiana to the little fort at St. Joseph (now Niles, Michigan). This advance was made through country that was inhabited by Indians who had been loyal to England but whose loyalty had weakened after Clark had captured the French settlements in Illinois. The little post of St. Joseph quickly fell to the raiders. The Spanish flag flew from the fort for a few hours. Then the post was looted and burned by the raiders. After spending a few days at the post, the Spanish raiders went back to St. Louis carrying with them the captured English flag. The little post at St. Joseph was not rebuilt.

Courtesy Mackinac Island State Park Commission
East Blockhouse. Fort Mackinac on Mackinac Island. Photo 1964.

Indian raids continued through 1781 and 1782 and border fighting took place in what is now Ohio and Kentucky, but the Revolutionary War was coming to a close. The colonies, together with their European allies, were winning the long struggle.

In March, 1781, when the Articles of Confederation went into effect, the colonies which had claims to western land gave up their claims and turned the entire land area over to the new confederation government. Thus, the vast area lying between the Appalachian Mountains and the Mississippi River became the possession of the new Continental Congress. From it new states were to be formed that later would join the union of states then fighting against England.

In Ohio at this time there lived a tribe of Delaware Indians. These

Indians are known to us today as the Moravian Indians* because of the work Moravian missionaries had done to convert them to Christianity. When the war began, these Indians, because of their Christian teaching, did not wish to take either side in the struggle. Unfortunately for them their homeland lay along the path of the raiding parties from Detroit. Both sides began to mistrust these Indians and wish them out of the way.

In 1782, a group of Virginians cruelly killed several of these Indians after taking their arms away from them and promising to take them to safety. The rest fled to Detroit and the protection of the English. Until the war was over these Moravian Indians lived on the banks of the Clinton River near Mt. Clemens. Here they built the first Protestant church in Michigan. When the war was over, some of these Indians returned to their homeland in Ohio. Others, still fearing the Kentucky "Long Knives," crossed over to Canada and founded the settlement of Fairfield on the banks of the River Thames. Later, in 1792, more Delaware Indians from the eastern part of the Northwest Territory also moved to Fairfield on the Thames River. Many of their descendants still live in that area today.

In 1783, peace was made between England and the thirteen American colonies. Power politics soon entered the peace negotiations and England tried to keep some friendship with her colonies even if it meant being indifferent to her Canadian colony which had no representative at the conference. At first the American delegates asked for all of Canada to the Arctic Ocean but later two northern boundaries were considered in earnest. One proposed boundary was to begin at the St. Croix River and run to the height of land and then west along the forty-fifth parallel to the Mississippi River. The second was to follow a middle line through the Great Lakes and connecting waters to the Lake of the Woods, and then west to the Mississippi River. This later line was accepted but many years were to pass before a definite boundary line was settled between Canada and the United States.

In accepting this line much of what had been New France was lost to the St. Lawrence settlements. England seems to have forgotten that just a few years before, in the Quebec Act, she had given the land north of the Ohio River and east of the Mississippi to Canada and that Canada needed this area for her economic development. Also England seems to have forgotten that Canada had been loyal to her during the

---

*Also called United Bretheren.

war. In so doing, England hampered the Montreal fur trade and also abandoned the Indians in the West that had fought for both England and their homeland during the war. Detroit and Mackinac had not been conquered by the Americans. These factors became obvious soon after the peace was signed and a few years were still to pass before England finally gave up her control of the Northwest Territory.

Although England still had her soldiers stationed in the Northwest, the Continental Congress went ahead with plans for the sale of the land and the settlement of the area.

In order to give each settler who moved into the Northwest Territory a clear title to his land, the Continental Congress in 1785 passed the Grayson Land Ordinance. This Ordinance made a plan for a general land survey of the entire area. According to it, all the Northwest Territory was to be divided into congressional townships each six miles square. This would make a map of the area look somewhat like a huge checkerboard. In Michigan these squares, called congres-

Map Showing Congressional Townships

sional, or geographical, townships, were to be measured east and west from a Prime Meridian that runs north and south through the state at 84 degrees, 22 minutes, and 24 seconds west longitude. They were to be numbered north and south of a Base Line that now forms the

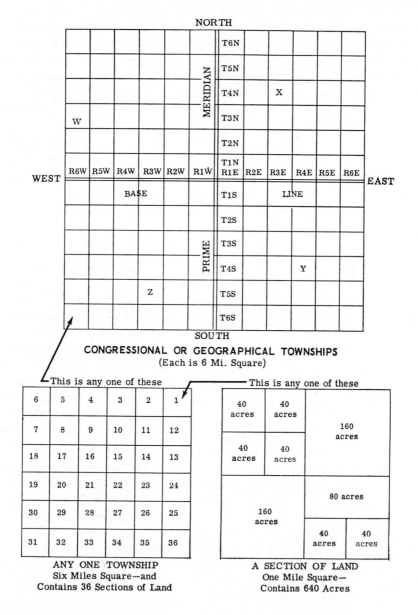

CONGRESSIONAL OR GEOGRAPHICAL TOWNSHIPS
(Each is 6 Mi. Square)

This is any one of these

This is any one of these

ANY ONE TOWNSHIP
Six Miles Square—and
Contains 36 Sections of Land

A SECTION OF LAND
One Mile Square—
Contains 640 Acres

Eight Mile Road, or the northern boundary of Wayne County, and is located at 42 degrees, 26 minutes, and 30 seconds north latitude. If you look at a map of Michigan you will see that this line forms the northern boundary of the second row of counties.

If a farmer settled on land in township W his title would be described as being in Township 3 North, Range 6 West. No other township in the state can have this same description. Township X would be described as, Township 4 North, Range 3 East. Y would be described as Township 4 South, Range 4 East. Z would be described as Township 5 South, Range 3 West. In this manner every congressional township in the state can be described in its relationship to the Base Line and Prime Meridian.

To locate a township was well but a township six miles square in size contains 36 square miles and many acres of land—23,040 in all. The early settler in the West grew farm produce and usually forty or eighty acres of land was all that a man could work with the agricultural tools then to be had.

In order to locate more specifically these smaller pieces of land each township was again divided into thirty-six smaller parts called sections.

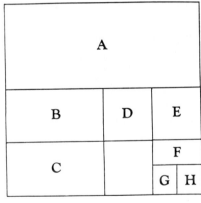

Thus the entire Northwest Territory was divided into areas of one mile square. Each of these square mile blocks is called a section. It takes thirty-six of these sections to make one township such as W, X, Y, and Z, or any other township in the state. Each of these sections contains 640 acres of land, and can be divided in the following manner to locate smaller pieces of land.

A is described as N. ½ of Section (1, 2, 10, 36) or any other section of a definite township and contains 320 acres more or less.

B is described as N. ½ of the SW. ¼ (80 acres more or less).

C is described as S. ½ of the SW. ¼ (80 acres more or less).

D is described as NW. ¼ of the SE. ¼ (40 acres more or less).

E is described as NE. ¼ of the SE. ¼ (40 acres more or less).

F is described as N. ½ of the SE. ¼ of the SE. ¼ (20 acres more or less).

G is described as SW. ¼ of the SE. ¼ of the SE. ¼ (10 acres more or less).

H is described as SE. ¼ of the SE. ¼ of the SE. ¼ (10 acres more or less).

Let us suppose that this section drawn is section 21 of Township 4 North, Range 5 West. The title to the 320 acres marked A would read: north ½ of section 21, township 4 North, Range 5 West and contains 320 acres more or less.

The North ½	Section 21	Twp. 4 North Range 5 West
(This part tells the location in the section)	(This part tells which section it is in the township)	(This part tells in which township it is located)

This method of surveying land would give a settler who chose that area a definite title to his land that could not be duplicated by any other settler coming into the region. The system of land survey, provided by the Grayson Land Ordinance of 1785, was much better than the one then in use in the East, for it made it possible to exactly locate land anywhere in the area if measured from a definite point.

According to this ordinance the land was to be sold for one dollar an acre, but the purchaser must buy at least one square mile of land or six hundred forty acres. Few settlers had the six hundred forty dollars in cash to spend for western land. If they possessed that amount of money there was little need in their having to find a new home for themselves in the wilderness. Speculators thus became the principal land buyers. They bought the best land in large amounts and after the price had advanced resold it in smaller parcels to the incoming settlers.

Although this was the general system of land survey and title granting, some areas of the state were already claimed by the older practice of "meets and bounds." Such areas as those that had been granted by the French and English before the Americans came were not granted under the land survey system, but rather described by natural markers such as a river, a tree, a large stone or other objects.

Then, too, some of the early traders had secured titles to lands from Indian chiefs and friendly tribes. Many of these titles were written deeds bearing the totems of the Indians then living in the area. These private claims did much in early days to confuse treaty making and the granting of land to new purchasers.

In 1787 the Continental Congress, in one of its last acts, passed what has since come to be known as the "Ordinance of 1787" to provide a government for the area north of the Ohio and east of the Mississippi

Courtesy Department of Conservation

An old Witness Tree as it looks today to a modern surveyor (1953)

River. Under the ordinance, the government of the territory was to be carried on by a governor, a secretary, and three judges. Later the area was to be divided into states and the people were to be allowed to carry on their own government. The Ordinance of 1787 contained six very important articles. They provided for the area: (1) freedom of worship; (2) a bill of rights; (3) "religion, morality, and knowledge being necessary to good government and the happiness of mankind, schools and the means of education shall forever be encouraged"; (4) all states formed from the area were to remain in the union as part of the United States; (5) not less than three states nor more than five were to be made from the area; and (6) slavery and involuntary servitude were not to be allowed in the territory or any of the states made from it except as a punishment for crime.

Courtesy Burton Historical Collection

Detroit—July 24, 1794

Settlers were soon coming over the mountains to Wheeling, West Virginia, and from there floating down the Ohio on flatboats to take up new homesteads in the Northwest Territory. Soon the Ohio Valley and the valleys of the streams flowing into the Ohio River had many settlements. However, northern Ohio and Michigan had few settlers because there was no good way for settlers to reach the area or to send their goods to market. Then, too, the Indians of the area were not friendly at that time, and their lands had not yet been taken from them by treaty.

Until after the Revolutionary War, the little settlements in Michigan were still small French communities with a controlling English governing group at their head. But after the end of the war loyalists began settling along the Detroit River. Two of these early settlers were Captain McKee and Captain Elliott. They settled on land just east of Bois Blanc Island at what is now Amhurstburg, Ontario. Others followed and settled in the area east of the Detroit River.

After the Revolutionary War, when American settlers began pushing west in the United States, similar changes were taking place in Canada. During the war, many Loyalists had found refuge in Nova Scotia. When the war was over, hundreds of them came west to what is now Ontario. Here they were joined by many other Loyalists that left the new United States to start new farms in Ontario where they would still be under the English government. Thus, the land north of Lake Ontario and Lake Erie began to be settled by people who were still loyal to the King of England. The story of this settlement was similar to the story of the settlement of Ohio and Michigan. Forests were cleared from the land to make little farms. Crude log cabins were built by the settlers for homes. Roads were cleared through the forests. Children got an elementary education in little log schoolhouses. Churches were built at the cross roads. Gradually, the area changed into settled communities as the people prospered on the land which they found to be very good for farming.

One of the new military highways in this area of Ontario was cut from Toronto, through the forest for thirty-three miles, to Lake Simcoe. This new road led to the abandonment of the old Ottawa-Mattawa-French River fur trading route between Michilimackinac and Quebec. Trading goods could now be brought up the St. Lawrence River in batteaux, although they still had to be portaged at several places along the river. By sailboat, they were then taken across Lake Ontario to Toronto. From Toronto they were taken to Lake Simcoe. From there they were taken by water to Georgian Bay and then by boat to Fort Michilimackinac. This new road saved the fur companies some fifty dollars a ton on freight taken into, or from, the West. This new route was used only between 1797 and 1821 when the North West Company was absorbed by the Hudson's Bay Company that could more cheaply transport trading to the West from Hudson Bay.

Another military road ran west from Toronto to Burlington at the western end of Lake Ontario. From there, it was cut on through to the Thames River where by water Lake St. Clair could be reached. Detroit and Michigan were still too far west to be much touched by this settlement of English Loyalists. But the area was made into the District of Hesse in 1788. This district included all the area west, northwest, and southwest of Long Point on Lake Erie. In 1792 Detroit had its first popular election and chose representatives to the Parliament of Upper Canada.

The English settlers who came to Canada, after the Revolutionary War, had a different culture from that of the French of Lower Canada. What is more the French Canadians could see that they would become a minority group if the English still continued to settle in the vast western areas. Governmental disputes soon arose between the two groups. Because of the political and cultural differences between the two groups, England passed the Canadian Constitutional Act of 1791 and divided the old Province of Quebec into two parts divided by the Ottawa River. This separated the older French settlers along the St. Lawrence River from the new English Loyalists who were moving into the area north of Lake Erie and Lake Ontario. Lower Canada, still known as Quebec, contained the major part of the French settlers, while Upper Canada, called Ontario, contained the English Loyalists.

Meanwhile the new constitution of the United States of America had come into being and George Washington had become president in 1789. This new and better government was interested in its claims to the western lands, and campaigns against the Indians living in Ohio were soon under way. General Harmar and St. Clair both led unsuccessful military expeditions into the Ohio country. Then the command was given to General Anthony Wayne. After careful preparation, Wayne pushed into northern Ohio and, in 1794, defeated the Indians under Little Turtle in the battle of Fallen Timbers in the Maumee Valley not far from Toledo, Ohio. Although this battle was fought in Ohio, it was so near the boundary line and had so much effect on the later development of Michigan that one can almost call it a Michigan battle.

In 1795 a treaty, called the Treaty of Greenville, was signed by the Indians which gave the Americans a claim to the post at Detroit, together with a strip of land six miles in width, from Lake Erie on the south to Lake St. Clair on the north; Mackinac Island; a small tract of land at the northern tip of the Lower Peninsula; and the country about St. Ignace in the Upper Peninsula. This was the first land in what is now Michigan to be ceded by the Indians to the United States Government.

CHAPTER SEVEN

The First Years of American Rule (1796–1815)

In November, 1794, John Jay completed a treaty in London between England and the United States. This treaty, now known as Jay's Treaty, was ratified by the United States government in June, 1795. Among the other provisions the treaty specified that England was to surrender its military posts in the Northwest Territory by June 1796.

In the summer of 1796 the Americans sent troops to occupy the Northwest Territory and take over the military posts. On reaching Michigan the troops stopped first at Monroe (Frenchtown). Here the American flag was raised over Michigan for the first time. The following day, July 11, 1796, two boats carrying sixty-five United States soldiers under Captain Moses Porter docked at the foot of what is now Griswold Street in Detroit. The American soldiers then marched up to Fort Lernoult and replaced the English garrison. Two days later Colonel John Francis Hamtramck came with some five hundred more soldiers. The following month General Wayne also arrived in Detroit.

With the surrender of Fort Lernoult the English had to construct a new fort. For the location of their new fort the English chose a spot on the Canadian side near the mouth of the Detroit River just north of Amhurstburg. When the English moved from Detroit to Amhurstburg very little had been done to provide buildings and a fortification. The fort was to have five sides, bastions, a dry moat, and a naval yard. Part of the buildings were made at Detroit and then, in sections, floated down the Detroit River to the new site. The Indian stores were also moved to this place. Soon Malden became the center of the English relations with the Indians in the area. To it the Indians came each year to hold council meetings and to receive their presents from the English. In 1797, the town of Amhurstburg was platted with about fifty lots. It soon became the leading town on the eastern side of the Detroit River.

For some time there was a friendly feeling between the two forts. Sometimes the commanders even loaned supplies to each other. Both

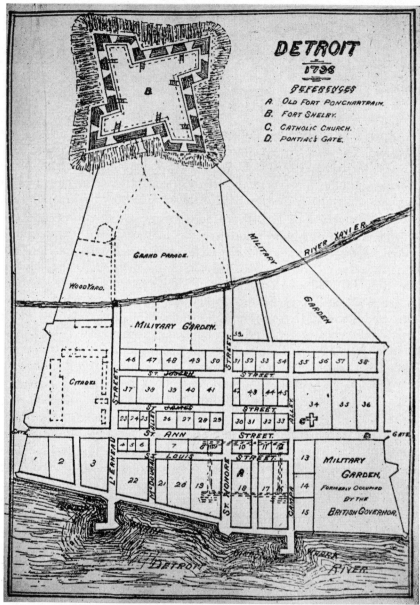

Courtesy Burton Historical Collection

the English and Americans tried to win the friendship of the Indians who made social calls at both forts to collect the free gifts of each government.

Although the posts were surrendered, the treaty also contained other provisions that were to cause much trouble in the Northwest Territory for several years. All people living in the area could remain, with all their possessions, if they desired to. They had one year in which to declare that they wished to retain their English citizenship. If they did they could still reside in the area. If they did not so declare by the end of the year, they would then be considered as United States citizens.

Model of Fort Malden

The treaty also said, "The merchants and others of each of the two nations, residing in the domains of the other, shall have the privilege of remaining and continuing their trade, so long as they behave peaceably, and commit no offense against the laws." If they did they were to have twelve months to remove their possessions from the area. The Mississippi River was to be open to both parties.

The fur trade was still the major occupation of the area and was still in the control of the merchants and traders working out of Montreal. North and west of Lake Superior the old French fur trade was carried on by the North West Company. During these years it spread as far westward as the Pacific Ocean. With the transfer of Grand Portage, Minnesota, to the Americans the company established a new post at Fort William a little farther to the north in English territory.

South and west of Lake Superior the fur trade was carried on by other companies and independent traders. The main one, which went by different names, was the South West Company. Using the Fox-Wisconsin waterway the traders entered the Upper Mississippi River and the Missouri River areas where they came into conflict with the American fur traders after 1803 when Louisiana was bought from France.

Mackinac Island, although in American hands, was the main rendezvous for the English fur traders working the area south of the Canadian border. To it came the merchandise passing westward to the Indians and the furs from the West on their way to markets in the East. Goods came from both Montreal and the United States to supply the merchants. If they came through the United States, the fur traders were to pay the usual United States customs duties. English fur traders thus still controlled the Indians living west of Michigan. When the War of 1812 came it was easy for them, as friendly traders, to rally the Indians to the English side against the Americans who were pressing into the area and taking their lands from them. Thus, this English fur trade did much to influence the War of 1812 in the West.

At that time Mackinac Island was the main rendezvous for the North West Company, trading for furs north of the United States-Canadian border, and the Michilimackinac Company trading south of the border. The name of this company was later changed to the South West Company. John J. Astor, who was later to control the fur trade in this area, was already a partner in the South West Company.

Up to the year 1796, the Detroit area on both sides of the Detroit River had always been one single community but when the Americans occupied the Northwest Territory the Detroit River became an international boundary line. Although some settlers lived across the Detroit River, in what is now Canada, there was no village there. But with the coming of the Americans to Detroit two new towns, Sandwich across from Detroit, and Amhurstburg across from Bois Blanc Island, soon developed. Lots in the new village of Sandwich were drawn by interested persons, in a lottery, on July 7, 1797. Several English merchants moved from Detroit across the river to the new village of Sandwich. The English courts and jail were also moved across the river to the new village. Some of the settlers also moved across the river so that they could still live under the government of England.

In 1796, the year that the Americans came to Detroit, Detroit was still a small French frontier village. Most of the people living there were descendants of the early trappers and settlers. The little log houses were now old and weathered. Men and animals still walked in the muddy, narrow streets that had been laid out by Cadillac nearly one hundred years before. To the north, on the second rise of ground, stood Fort Lernoult which the English had built during the Revolutionary War. This fort and its garrison were the main features of the little frontier post. A wooden picket palisade ran down from the fort like a large V spreading out from the fort to enclose two sides of the village. Another palisade ran along the waterfront just below West Jefferson Avenue. Several gates opened into the palisades. Most of the business of trading and shipping was done near the river in the old French village. French farmhouses sat along both sides of the river. The little ribbon farms behind the houses pushed back only a short way from the river. Just beyond the farm land, the spreading forest began. No roads ran into the heavy stands of hickory and white oak. Only Indian trails led into the vast forest that reached out in all directions. Indians could always be seen in the village or encamped in the nearby forest.

The fort on Mackinac Island was occupied by Americans in the same year as the fort at Detroit. Michilimackinac at this time had a population of about five hundred people. They were mostly Canadian French and half-breeds who fished, farmed, and traded with the Indians. The English occupation had had very little effect upon the people living there. When the English left the fort on Mackinac Island, they built a new one on St. Joseph's Island in the Saint Mary's River.

With the coming of the Americans the English moved their fur warehouses across the Saint Mary's River to the Canadian side of the rapids and began to use the canoe route along the north shore of Lake Superior. This route was less satisfactory because of the waves produced by the prevailing westerly winds, the rocky shore, and the many islands and peninsulas. The trading center at Grand Portage was abandoned by the English and new centers opened at Fort William and Port Arthur.

One of the first tasks of the Americans was to start a new government for the area. On August 15, 1796, Wayne County was formed. The county included all the area of what is now Michigan and parts of Wisconsin, Illinois, Indiana, and Ohio. Soon a court system was organized.

In December, 1798, the people of Detroit elected three men to represent Wayne County in the Legislative Assembly of the Northwest Territory which at that time was meeting in Cincinnati, Ohio.

In 1800 the Northwest Territory was divided into two parts by a line which ran between what is now Ohio and Indiana and which continued northward through Michigan. The Lower Peninsula was thus cut in half. The eastern part remained as a part of the Northwest Territory but the western half and nearly all the Upper Peninsula went to the newly created Territory of Indiana. This change had little effect on the people living in Michigan at the time as most of them lived in the Detroit area. In 1802 the Legislative Assembly for the Northwest Territory passed an act making Detroit a town. This act gave to the people of Detroit the right to choose a board of five trustees and other town officials to regulate local affairs.

This building was the territorial capitol at Vincennes when Michigan was part of Indiana Territory. Photo 1963.

During these years many settlers came into the Ohio Valley to start new farms and villages. Soon there were enough people living in what is now the state of Ohio to let the area qualify for statehood, so in 1803 the state of Ohio was formed. Unfortunately, Ohio's northern boundary was not settled at this time, and later Michigan and Ohio were to have a dispute as to just where this boundary line was to be. When Ohio was made a state, all of Michigan was placed under the Territory of Indiana.

The people of Michigan did not like this. The new capital was at Vincennes, and it placed them once again back under the rule of a governor and judges. What is more, Vincennes was far away to the southwest and was difficult to reach in a time of canoe and snowshoe travel.

Fortunately for the people of Michigan, Congress created a new territory called Michigan Territory in 1805. The southern boundary of the new territory was to be an east-west line starting at the most southerly point of Lake Michigan and running due east to Lake Erie. All of the Lower Peninsula and the eastern part of the Upper Peninsula were included in the new territory. Detroit became the capital on

July 1, 1805. Gen. William Hull was chosen to be the first governor of the new Michigan Territory. He reached Detroit in July, 1805, and found the little town in ashes.

The old town of Detroit had disappeared in one day. The day of June 11, 1805, was a tragic one for Detroit. It was one of those windy June mornings in late spring. A baker named John Harvey needed to get some flour from the grist mill on May's Creek, located near the place where the New York Central depot now stands. Going to his stable, he hitched his little French pony to a small two-wheeled cart. Before climbing upon the seat he stopped to knock the ashes from his pipe because the wind was blowing sparks from it into his face. As the lighted tobacco dropped from the pipe, it was caught by the strong wind and blown through the open doorway and into the barn. There it was scattered among some dry hay which it quickly caught on fire. Before Harvey could put the fire out, the whole pile of hay was a roaring blaze. The cry of "fire, fire" rang through the town. Men and boys seized buckets and axes to stop the fire but it kept on spreading before the strong wind. The century-old timbers of the the early French settlement were too dry to be saved.

By three o'clock in the afternoon, what had once been houses was but smoldering remains with gaunt, smoke-blackened chimneys standing among the glowing embers. Here and there a mother could be seen gathering her children about her and watching sadly over what few household things they had been able to snatch from their little cabin before it was burned by the advancing fire. Fortunately the homes of the settlers along the river had not caught fire. Many of the homeless people from Detroit soon found shelter there among their friends or relatives. Not only their homes but also their food had perished. Father Gabriel Richard, then pastor of Ste. Anne's Church, was quick to see the need of the people. Under his leadership canoes were sent up and down the river to call on the farmers for supplies such as corn meal, eggs, and milk.

Old Detroit with its little cabins had vanished. Some of the people left and went south to Ohio. The land there was good and the fear of Indians in that region was now almost gone. Yet, hardly had the fire ceased before people were talking of a new city to be built upon the charred ruins of the old. Judge Woodward drew up a plan for the new city. He made his plan similar to that of the city of Washington, D. C., which was then being built as the nation's capital. The city was to be laid out in a manner which was to be a combination of a checker-

board and a spider web. After the lots of the new city had been surveyed by Thomas Smith, they were given out by lot to those who had
owned property in the old town.

Before settlers could come into Michigan to start new homes more
land had to be secured from the Indians. In November, 1807, Governor Hull held a meeting at Detroit with chiefs and warriors of the Pottawattomies, Wyandottes, Chippewas, and Ottawas. At this meeting
a treaty known as the Treaty of Detroit, was signed with the Indians.
In it the Indians agreed to give up more land in southeastern Michigan.
A western line was run due north from a point about twenty miles
west of the western end of Lake Erie to the southern end of Lake
Huron. From this point the line ran northeast to White Rock on Lake
Huron. For this land the Indians were to receive ten thousand dollars
cash and two thousand four hundred dollars each year thereafter.

Not many years after this, Detroit and Michigan became once
again the center of military activity. Europe was being torn by the
wars of Napoleon. For years the new United States had remained
out of the European struggle, but at last it was drawn into the war on
the side of France against England.

To the aid of the English cause in America came a famous Indian
warrior and chieftan named Tecumseh. Tecumseh was a chief of
the Shawnee Indians and lived not far from where Springfield, Ohio,
now stands. Tecumseh was glad to aid the English against the United
States. He looked upon the English as the friends of the Indians, for
they had not taken the hunting grounds from his Indian people. To
him the Americans, as the people of the United States now began to
be called, were enemies. It was they who were ever pushing farther
and farther into the West and taking the land from the Indians and
driving away the game.

Tecumseh, like Pontiac before him, was a good speaker and a great
leader of his Indian people. In reply to his messengers, bands of
Indians came to his wigwam to talk with him and make plans against
the Americans. Some of these bands also visited Fort Malden on
the Detroit River. The British gave the Indians many presents and
encouraged the Indians to strike against the Americans. The hatreds
born in the last war were not yet dead and the fact that the Astor
Fur Company, which had been started in 1809 and was using Mackinac
Island as its center of trade, was taking much business from the
English fur companies, kept alive the feeling of bitterness.

Gradually the Indian menace in the West grew stronger and

stronger. Large bands of hostile Indians began to gather around the frontier posts as they had done under the leadership of Pontiac. The people of the West became fearful of an Indian plot and asked Congress to come to their aid by sending more soldiers to protect them.

In reply to this request General Harrison advanced with Federal troops into the region and on November 7, 1811 defeated the Indians at Prophetstown in the battle of Tippecanoe. Many of the Indians fled to Amherstburg, Ontario, to seek protection from their English friends at Fort Malden. They set up camp on Bois Blanc Island in the Detroit River and were given provisions by the English during the following winter. Although Tecumseh was not present at the battle at Tippecanoe, his spirit was aroused to still greater bitterness against the Americans when he returned from the South where he had been seeking allies to join his confederation. The following year, when the war of 1812 began, the Indians in the Great Lakes Area joined themselves to the English cause.

General Hull was still governor of Michigan Territory. Fearing a united English and Indian attack upon the western posts, he went to Washington to secure more military aid for the territory. This was granted to him, and on June 1, 1812, with about twelve hundred soldiers, he began the long march through the wilderness from Dayton, Ohio, to Detroit.

There was no road from Ohio to Detroit at that time, so a road across the Black Swamp of northern Ohio, around where Toledo, Ohio, now stands, had to be made. As they came north the roadway had to be cleared and bridges had to be built across many streams and swampy areas.

When General Hull and his army reached the mouth of the Maumee River, near the place where Toledo now stands, some of their supplies and papers were put on a little schooner named the "Cuyahoga" which, with another small vessel, was sent on ahead to the fort at Detroit. When the little vessels came into the channel of the Detroit River, opposite Fort Malden, they were stopped by the British and taken as prizes of war along with Hull's supplies and papers which were on board. This was the first capture of an American vessel in the War of 1812.

Meanwhile Hull, who had learned by special dispatch from Philadelphia that war had been declared, pushed on to the Raisin River. While building a bridge so that his army might cross the river, General Hull learned of the fate of his boats and supplies.

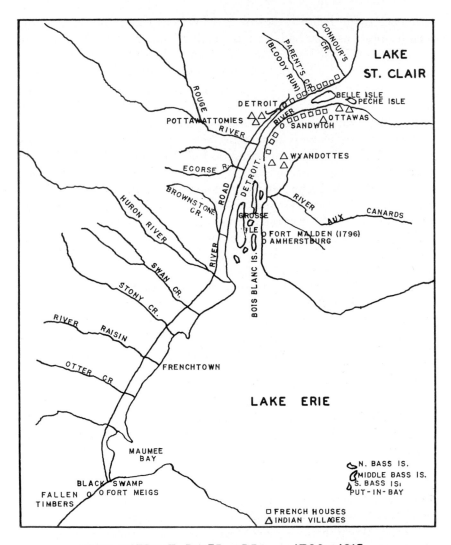

THE DETROIT RIVER AREA   1760–1815

Though the English and Indians in the Detroit area knew, by a dispatch from the English Fort on St. Joseph's Island in Upper Lake Huron, that war had been declared and that Hull was advancing on Detroit with soldiers, they did not attack him. When the American soldiers reached Detroit they urged General Hull to cross the river and attack Fort Malden and recapture the boats and supplies. General Hull, however, feared to make such an attack. At last, on July 12, in response to repeated urging, he sent a large force of men across the river to the Canadian side as though an attack on Fort Malden were to be made.

Had Hull made a strong attack on Fort Malden, the fort would probably have fallen because there were then few men there to defend it. Hull, however, hesitated. He sent out a scouting party, which went as far as the Canard River Marsh, south of present-day Windsor, Ontario. Here the first blood of the War of 1812 was shed when the Americans were stopped at the Canard River. The scouting party was soon called back to the fort at Detroit.

Hull then received word that Captain Henry Brush was on the way to Detroit with two hundred and thirty men, one hundred head of cattle, and other needed supplies, and that he was being attacked near the Raisin River by Tecumseh and his Indian allies. Col. Thomas Van Horne was sent with a force of two hundred men to Brush's aid. While going down the river road,* two of his scouts were surprised and scalped near Trenton. A little farther on, the whole relief party walked into an ambush at Brownstown. Van Horne slowly retreated toward the fort. Although he asked for aid, none was sent to him.

While General Hull dallied at Detroit, the British and Indians were active. Because Michilimackinac, then held by the United States, was a direct threat to the English fur trade, because of its nearness to the main route of canoe travel between Montreal and the West, both General Brock and the Canadian Government were anxious for its early capture. News of the declaration of war was sent to Captain Charles Roberts, the English commander of the fort on St. Joseph's Island and he was ordered to attack the fort on Mackinac Island. Captain Roberts at once gathered together a large force of English soldiers, Indians, and French voyageurs and set out to attack the fort on Mackinac Island.

Lieut. Porter Hanks was at that time the American commander of the fort. Hanks and his men did not yet know that war between England and the United States had been declared. They awoke at sunrise on July 17, 1812, to the sharp report of a cannon being fired. The startled American garrison was taken by surprise. During the night the English had landed on the north side of Mackinac Island at a place since known as "British Landing," and had placed their guns on the north side of the fort so they could shoot down into it. All was

---

*Now West Jefferson Avenue.

now in readiness for their attack upon the fort, but no attack was made. Hanks, so greatly outnumbered, was forced to surrender. Thus, the post on Mackinac Island again passed into the hands of the English.

At Detroit things changed little. Six hundred fifty French Canadians joined Hull against the English but still no attack was made, for Hull imagined the English and Indians to be far stronger than they were. A party was at last sent from the fort to the aid of Brush and his men. At Brownstown they defeated a party of English militia and a band of Indians under Tecumseh.

Although General Hull had by far the larger force, he still delayed attacking Fort Malden. Meanwhile General Brock had made his way from Fort Niagara to Fort Malden with three hundred militiamen and thirty English soldiers.

General Brock, then 42 years of age, was a much younger man than General Hull. The year before he had visited the Detroit River Area to acquaint himself with the situation in the West, for he felt that war would soon come between England and the United States. From Fort Malden Brock had come up the river to Sandwich and inspected the English battery there. Then he crossed the river and visited the fort at Detroit.

When war came General Brock decided that the best military strategy was for him to take the defensive along the Niagara frontier and to quickly strike an offensive blow in the West where he felt the American immigrants in Western Canada could not be too well trusted in case of an invasion by the Americans. The fall of Detroit and Michilimackinac were part of his western plan of attack.

On the evening of the day that General Brock arrived at Fort Malden he called the English officers and Indian leaders into council. They advised General Brock against attacking Detroit, but General Brock disregarded their advice and decided to attack the fort although his forces were much smaller than those under the command of General Hull.

The next morning after his arrival General Brock advanced with his troops and Indian allies up the Canadian side of the river to Sandwich, across the river from Detroit. Here he made his headquarters in Mr. Baby's house that had been used by General Hull only a few days before.

In the morning of the following day the English crossed the river and began to advance upon Detroit. Halting outside, Brock sent a messenger to General Hull demanding Detroit's surrender.

Although General Hull had more men than the English, and sufficient military equipment in the fort, he ordered his outposts to retreat into the fort. Without asking advice from anyone, Hull ordered the American flag lowered and a white tablecloth raised as the sign of the fort's surrender. The soldiers, the people, and the French allies were all very angry with this sudden action of General Hull.

Part of the surrender agreement was that the Indians would not attack or molest the soldiers or the American citizens. Yet in spite of the English promise of protection it is to the credit of Tecumseh and the other Indian leaders that they did not fall upon the garrison because many of the men under Hull's command were the 4th regiment and it was this same regiment that had attacked Tecumseh's village of Prophetstown the year before at the battle of Tippecanoe.

The next morning, after Detroit's surrender, General Brock left Colonel Proctor in command of the western front and started back east to prepare to meet the expected American attack at Niagara. Two months later, on October 13, 1812, Brock was killed at the battle of Queenston Heights by an Ohio scout.

General Hull was later tried at Albany. Although he was declared innocent of treason, the court found him guilty of other charges that were placed against him and General Hull was sentenced to be shot. This order, however, was not carried out, for he was later pardoned by the President because of his services during the Revolutionary War.

Where the city of Chicago now stands there then stood a little fort named Fort Dearborn. General Hull ordered Captain Heald to abandon the post and to go with other Americans to Fort Wayne, Indiana. When hostile Indians began gathering around the post, Captain Heald told them that he was going to leave and that the Indians could have everything in the fort. The night before he left the post, Captain Heald had the powder of the fort emptied into the creek and the liquor poured into the well. The Pottawattomie Indians discovered this trickery of Captain Heald when they went to the river the next morning. They, however, kept their anger to themselves.

Captain Heald with the soldiers and settlers then set out on the road to Fort Wayne. They had gone only a little way along the lake shore when they were attacked by the enraged Pottawattomies led by Shavehead and other chiefs. Nearly all the Americans were killed and scalped. Thus the Great Lakes region again passed into the hands of the English.

No sooner had the Americans lost the Lake Region than they began preparing for its recapture. Men from Kentucky and Ohio joined General Harrison. When spring came in 1813, General Harrison was at Sandusky, Ohio, ready to advance into the region of Michigan.

In January, General Harrison sent Colonels Lewis and Allen with five hundred men to Frenchtown (Monroe) to give protection to the people living there. These men advanced upon Frenchtown on the ice that covered the swamps south of it. When they reached the stockade, they drove the British from it and took over the town. Soon Lewis and Allen were joined by General Winchester and two hundred fifty other men.

At that time the Detroit River was frozen over and English soldiers from Fort Malden with their Indian allies could easily cross on the ice and make an attack upon Frenchtown. General Winchester was warned that the English were crossing on the ice and soon would attack the Americans, but General Winchester paid no attention to the friendly warning of his French friends.

The night of January 23, 1813, was bitter cold. The American sentries at Frenchtown grew lax and gathered around their fires to warm themselves and sleep. When morning came the British, who had worked through the wintry night, were ready for action. Their guns had been placed within three hundred yards of the American position. General Winchester was aroused from his sleep in the Navarre home. He hurried, half-dressed, to the fort and fell an easy prisoner to the English and Indians. Two Kentucky Indian fighters, Graves and Madison, in spite of General Winchester's surrender, continued to hold their ground against the surprise attack of the English and Indians. They surrendered only when Colonel Proctor promised that there would be no massacre or violence from the Indians.

The able-bodied prisoners were then lined up and made ready for the march across the frozen river to Fort Malden. The wounded were to be left behind in the town. A few of them were taken into private homes. The rest were lodged in two large buildings which were used for storing furs.

Soon after the English and Indians left Frenchtown with their prisoners they came to Stony Creek. There Colonel Proctor kept the promise he had made to his Indian allies. A barrel of rum was smashed open. Most of the Indians stayed behind and started drinking. As the fiery rum in the barrel grew less and less, the Indians' spirit for bloodshed rose. A few Indians followed the English across the ice and quickly killed and scalped any of the American prisoners who fell behind the main party.

Most of the Indians returned to Frenchtown. In spite of angry words from some of their leaders, who tried to guard the wounded Americans, they began their bloody work since known in American history as the Massacre at the River Raisin.

A few of the less seriously wounded Americans had left the warehouses. These were seized, killed, and scalped. In their eagerness for American scalps the Indians set fire to the buildings to drive out the wounded Americans. Driven out by the increasing heat, the wounded men made their way through the door only to be killed and scalped and to have their bodies thrown back into the flames.

Meanwhile the English with their prisoners arrived at Fort Malden. There the Americans were turned into the open stockade of the fort and left to suffer in the bitter January weather.

News of the terrible happenings at Frenchtown soon reached Detroit. Everyone was shocked to learn of the cruel neglect on the part of Colonel Proctor. Fearing the prisoners at Fort Malden would be turned over to the Indians, a party from Detroit made its way to Fort Malden and asked if the prisoners could be ransomed from their captors. Thirty prisoners were brought out by the Indians and four were quickly killed to increase the bidding. The rest of the prisoners' lives were spared when money and presents were given to the Indians.

Other battles were fought in northern Ohio and more prisoners were brought to Detroit by the Indians. To save them from cruel torture, the people bought them from the Indians, usually paying between ten dollars and eighty dollars for each. Before long, some of the people at Detroit had spent all they possessed. However, they still tried to save the lives of the wretched prisoners by offering to the Indians blankets and other articles from their homes. This action on the part of the people of Detroit angered Colonel Proctor and he had some of the leading persons driven from the country.

The Massacre at the River Raisin aroused the Americans to a greater war spirit. "Remember the Raisin" became their battle cry. Frontiersmen flocked to General Harrison to help rid the land of the Indians and their savage ways. But the Americans could not hope to win the lake region again as long as Lake Erie was controlled by British boats. They knew that American boats must be built and a naval battle won on Lake Erie. This would allow the Americans to better transport supplies and to weaken England's strength in the region.

Where Erie, Pennsylvania, now stands, the Americans began the building of some boats in the spring of 1813. The work was pushed as rapidly as possible. Commodore Oliver Hazard Perry, of Rhode Island, was sent to take command of the little fleet which had been quickly made from unseasoned timbers. Getting sailors to sail the ships was a problem. To supply the need raw frontiersmen from Kentucky, that had never been on a boat, were used for part of the crew. When the English, who had been watching Perry's work from their boats, sailed back to Fort Malden, Perry got his new ships over the sand bar and out into the lake. First the little fleet sailed to Fort Malden so that Perry could see if an attack could be made against the English. Because of the narrow channel of the river in front of the fort, and because of the danger from the guns in the fort, Perry sailed south across the lake to Put-in-Bay where he waited for the English to come and meet him on the lake. Because the English would have to get supplies he knew that they would have to face the new American fleet or retreat from Fort Malden.

On the morning of September 10, 1813, the English boats under Captain Barclay sailed away from Fort Malden and down across Lake Erie to attack the new American fleet commanded by Commodore Perry. Tecumseh and other Indians, as well as Englishmen from the area that were interested in the success of the English fleet, followed the English boats along the Canadian shore as far as they could until they reached the mouth of the Detroit River. There they stood and watched the little boats of the English sail slowly south upon the surface of the lake until even the tops of the sails finally disappeared from sight. In the early afternoon the roar

Courtesy Pennsylvania History Commission
The "Niagara"

of guns could be heard from across the water. Anxiously Tecumseh and the others waited, watched, and hoped as they stood there on the shore. Would the English fleet return or would the Americans win the victory?

The coming of the English fleet was reported to Commodore Perry by an American lookout. Everything was in readiness, so Commodore Perry sailed out to give battle to the English squadron. The boats moved slowly toward each other, for there was little wind on Lake Erie that day. For some time the two fleets sat watching each other just out of gunshot. A little after twelve o'clock the American boats came within the longer range of the English guns. Soon the battle was on in earnest.

About two-thirty that afternoon Commodore Perry left his flagship, the "Lawrence," which had been badly damaged, and was rowed in a small open boat to the "Niagara," which up until that time had taken little part in the battle. A slight change of wind favored the Americans and the boats closed in for final action. Although the English guns were of longer range, the American guns were heavier and so, as the boats came closer together, the American guns raked the English boats with heavy fire. The English were forced to surrender. Commodore Perry then sent a message to General Harrison which said, "We have met the enemy and they are ours; two ships, two brigs, one schooner, and one sloop."

As the day closed, hope dropped in the hearts of Tecumseh and the others who were still watching from the Canadian shore. The distant roar of the guns had ceased but no boats came sailing back from out upon the lake. Each knew what had happened without having to be told. The Americans had become the masters of the Upper Lakes.

Now that the Americans controlled Lake Erie, Colonel Proctor knew he could no longer hold Fort Malden. Therefore, he quickly abandoned it and set out by land for Fort Niagara. This action on the part of Colonel Proctor angered Tecumseh and he upbraided Colonel Proctor saying that he could at least have left the arms and supplies for the Indians if he did not have the courage to stay and fight for his Indian allies.

Tecumseh Stone at Fort Malden. Tecumseh is said to have stood on this stone when he spoke to the English and Indians and tried to convince the English to hold the fort against the Americans. Photo 1961.

General Harrison made use of his opportunity. The little fleet carried the Americans to the Canadian side on September 27. They advanced upon Fort Malden, but no battle took place. The Americans found the English fort deserted and partly burned. Proctor had left.

General Harrison then advanced up the Canadian side of the Detroit River. The next day General McArthur was sent across the river to occupy Detroit. The English had set fire to the fort at Detroit before they left but the people at Detroit had put out the fire before it had done much damage. Once again the American flag floated above the fort. The fort was now renamed Fort Shelby in honor of Isaac Shelby, Governor of Kentucky, who had led mounted Kentucky volunteers to Detroit against the English forces.

Joined by new troops, General Harrison pushed on into Canada after Colonel Proctor and his retreating forces. The two forces met at Moraviantown in what is known as the Battle of the Thames which was fought in October, 1813. Colonel Proctor was not a wise and daring leader like General Brock and by this time even the English under him had lost confidence in him. Only the Indians tried to hold

Part of the old moat at Fort Malden. 1929

Marker at Sault Ste. Marie, Ontario, to the American raid on the Sault area in 1814. Photo 1963.

Part of the early Canadian Lock built at Sault Ste. Marie, Ontario, in 1796, for canoes and small boats. Photo August, 1963.

their ground during the Americans' attack. During the battle Tecumseh was killed. This was a major blow to the Indians, for Tecumseh was one of their greatest chiefs and was in many ways a remarkable man even when measured by our present standards of thinking. For his poor conduct at Moraviantown Colonel Proctor was court-martialed, condemned, and suspended from command for six months.

In the summer of 1814 American troops, under Lieutenant Croghan, raided the English fur storage houses at what is now Sault Ste. Marie, Ontario. The buildings were burned along with a boat and the little locks that had been made for canoes in 1796 were also destroyed. Then the troops raided on the other side of the river and destroyed the Johnson home and buildings. From there they went to Mackinac Island to recapture the fort but the attack was not successful and the British retained control of the fort until the end of the war when it was returned to the Americans in the spring of 1815.

When the War of 1812 was over major changes came in the fur trade. On April 29, 1816, the United States congress passed a law which barred foreigners from the Indian trade within the United States. They could, however, use Mackinac Island as a base of operations providing they paid the regular duties on goods passing through the United States. Faced with the law, the South West Company sold out their remaining shares to one of their partners, John J. Astor, in March 1817. This meant that Astor now had much of the fur trade between the Ohio River and the Upper Mississippi. The new company was given the name of the American Fur Company. This company had been chartered in 1808 by the State of New York.

Because the Americans did not know the Indians and the many details of the fur trade, it was necessary for the American fur Company to hire English clerks, traders, winterers, and French Canadian voyagers. This tended to prolong the English influence among the Indians south of the border but gradually Americans were trained for the fur trade.

Mr. Astor never visited the area in which the fur trade was carried on. He cautiously provided the capital for the enterprise and left the work in the field for others. For general field manager he chose Ramsay Crooks. Crooks was a young man who had crossed the continent to Astoria and back in Astor's disastrous attempt to found a fur post on the Pacific side of the continent. Mackinac Island was still the central distributing and receiving point for the fur trade below the Canadian border. At this busy trading center was stationed Robert Stuart. There Mr. Astor sent bookkeepers and traders to carry on his business. In the Astor House, on Mackinac Island, the merchandise for the trade was packed into standard bundles for the winterers and to it came the furs the brigades of the company brought in from the West. Here they were graded and packed for the trade. The Astor House has now been restored so that visitors going to Mackinac Island can see how the fur trade of the company was carried on.

Gradually through constant pressure the small independent traders and trading companies were driven out of business and partnerships were formed with other companies trading up the Mississippi River from St. Louis. Although whiskey was forbidden in the Indian trade, much of it still found its way into the Western area. One reason given for the smuggling of whiskey was to meet competition from the strong Canadian traders just north of the border where in 1821 the old North West Company and the Hudson Bay Company had combined into one company to abolish the rivalry between them.

The new Erie Canal, that was being built across New York, and the coming of steamboats on the upper lakes made it easier to bring in supplies and send out the furs, but the days of the fur trade in Michigan were coming to an end.

By 1834, Astor was an old man. He had made some of his fortune in the fur trade but most of it he had made in New York real estate and the growing China trade. So, in that year, he sold his company to Crooks and others but the hatters no longer wanted beaver and muskrat furs as they had in the past. Silk and other fabrics were taking the place of felt. Farmers were soon to occupy the area and thus deplete the area of its fur bearing animals. In 1842, Crooks' company went quietly out of business and the busy, rowdy fur trading days of the fur business on Mackinac Island came to an end.

CHAPTER EIGHT

The Settlement of Southern Michigan

AFTER the War of 1812, Lewis Cass was made governor of Michigan Territory. Lewis Cass had come to Michigan with General Hull's army just before the War of 1812. Cass was among the main political leaders in American history of that time, and his leadership did much in developing the new territory. He not only aided in exploring the territory but also made several treaties with the Indians for their land. For eighteen years Lewis Cass was territorial governor. He then became Secretary of War in President Andrew Jackson's cabinet. Later Cass served in another President's cabinet, spent twelve years as a United States senator, was our minister to France, and ran for President of the United States in 1848.

It was during the early years of Cass's term as territorial governor that settlers began coming to Michigan in large numbers. After the War of 1812 many people from the eastern states began to go west to take up new lands in the wilderness. For many years the Ohio River had been the main road to the West. Enough settlers had pushed down the Ohio River and settled in southern Ohio to enable Ohio to become a state in the year 1803. Enough settlers had taken lands in southern Indiana to allow Indiana to become a state in the year 1816. Illinois followed and became a state in 1818. But the area around the Great Lakes was too far off the path of westward advance, down the Ohio River, to interest settlers. There was still no easy way to reach the land or to send crops from it.

Because of this lack of transportation, Michigan was not settled as soon as the area along the Ohio River. Only a few places had little settlements by 1825. As early as 1780, some French traders had set up a trading post near the mouth of the Raisin River. Later other Frenchmen came to this area and Frenchtown grew up on the north side of the Raisin River. It was here that the massacre of the War of 1812 had taken place. Later, Americans settled on the south side of the river and the name for both places was changed to Monroe, after President Monroe who visited Michigan soon after the War of 1812. French settlers laid out ribbon farms along the Rouge River just west of Detroit, but no village was begun in that area. About

1785, French settlers had begun a little village at St. Clair on the St. Clair River. In 1809, a trading post had been set up, which later became Ypsilanti, so that trade could be carried on with the Indians living farther up the Huron River.

Hull's treaty of 1807 with the Indians had opened the land of southeastern Michigan to settlement but, as the land had not yet been surveyed, title to it could not be given to settlers. In 1815, Mr. Edward Tiffin was hired by the government to survey a small area of land near Detroit. This was the first survey of land that was made in Michigan. The report of the survey stated that Michigan land was not suited for farming because it was swampy and sandy and had scarcely one acre in a thousand fit for cultivation. No doubt this report of Mr. Tiffin kept many settlers from coming to Michigan during the next ten years.

Life in Michigan at that time was crude and hard. There were no grist mills in the area, and grain had to be ground by hand in crude grinders which were made by burning a hole in one end of a log and then setting it upright. In these grinders, corn was crushed by pounders that were attached to spring poles thirty or forty feet in length.

Fish was a principal item of food, and the mouth of the Detroit River was one of the favorite fishing spots for miles around. To it the Indians, with their families, came to catch fish, which they dried for their winter food supply. One writer of the time, in speaking of this area, said, "This river afforded more fish and in greater varieties than any other river of fresh water in America, and perhaps in the world. The most numerous and valuable were the wall-eyed pike, the muskallonge, catfish, bass, and many other kinds, amounting to thirty or more varieties. The fishing was done with hooks, spears, and dip nets. The fish were so numerous, it was quite common for Indians to spear from one to three at one stroke, at some stages of the water, particularly when roily."

To reach this wilderness land at that time one had to come across Canada, by boat across Lake Erie, or come up from Ohio along the road that led through the Black Swamp south of where Toledo, Ohio, now stands. Those who came by way of Lake Erie faced the dangers of storm and shipwreck, and those who came by way of the Black Swamp were often obliged to wade through water, mud, and ice, and to provide their own quarters for the night. It is no wonder that settlers preferred to drift leisurely down the Ohio and leave the Lake

Lands to the Indians and French who were more at home in its forest area.

Even the shores of the lakes and rivers, with the exception of the old French settlements, were still as wooded as nature had made them. The islands in the Detriot River, too, were still all heavily timbered and untouched by the settler's or woodsman's ax.

The little Canadian settlement near Fort Malden was a small wilderness village where a fort with a breastworks, barracks, and warehouse was still maintained by the English. Each year the Indians gathered at the fort for their annual gift of presents.

On sailing up the Detroit River in 1817, one passed through pretty, heavily timbered lands where the mighty forests stretching to the water's edge were broken only by the French farm houses which, being whitewashed, contrasted markedly with the dense woodlands' heavy green of summer or golden brown of fall. Here and there on prominent points where the breeze was strong stood little windmills which were the only markers for sailors since there were then no lighthouses or buoys along the inland waterways.

Indian canoes still glided across the blue water of the river. French bateaux passed by. Now and then a sail on one of the few lake boats billowed out with the wind. As yet, the lakes knew no steam-powered boats; however, even then one was being built near Buffalo. The following year, 1818, its paddle wheels began to churn the waters of the river and its wood smoke commenced to drift over the forest land beside the river.

Such was Southeastern Michigan in the year 1817. But all was soon to change, for back east in New York state Judge Rutherford, on July 4, 1817, turned the first shovel of earth on the new Erie Canal at Rome, New York. This new canal was soon to place the Upper Great Lakes area on the best direct highway to New York and the East.

At this time about the best way to explore the lands around Detroit was still to use the rivers. People began pushing up the Clinton River and, in 1816, started a little settlement at Rochester. Pontiac began just two years later, in 1818, when some men from Detroit purchased two square miles in that area. Mt. Clemens was also started in that same year. Settlers pushing up the little rivers around Detroit usually looked for a place where a dam could be placed across the river so that water power could be had to run a little gristmill or sawmill.

French settlers were still farming the little ribbon farms along the Detroit, Rouge, and Huron rivers, but as yet no farm land was offered for sale. This was perhaps the main reason why settlers did not come into the area. However, in 1818, some of the land that had been surveyed three years earlier was put up for sale and auctioned off to the highest bidder. Some of it, near Wyandotte, sold for as much as forty dollars an acre.

A new land law, passed in 1820, made it possible for a person to buy eighty acres of land at $1.25 an acre in cash. Thus, for one hundred dollars a man could become the owner of an eighty-acre farm. Today, an eighty-acre farm seems small, but in those days of hand tools and hand farming eighty acres was a large farm.

In 1818, the same year that public land was put up for sale in Michigan, the first steamboat on Lake Erie docked at Detroit on her first trip from Buffalo. At Black Rock, on the Niagara River, the "Walk-in-the-Water" had been built for use on Lake Erie. This new boat was called the "Walk-in-the-Water" after what one Indian had said about Fulton's "Clermont": "She-walks-in-the-water." As it was the only steamboat on the lakes at that time, it was usually called "The Steamboat" by the white men, and the white man's "Big Canoe" by the Indians.

The "Walk-in-the-Water" was modeled after the clipper ships which were then being built on the Atlantic coast. She was made of white oak which was cut on the land where Buffalo, New York, now stands. She was one hundred thirty-five feet long, thirty-two feet wide, and eight feet six inches deep. On each side of the boat, at its center, was a large paddle wheel which was turned by a steam engine. A wood fire was used to make steam in the boiler. Bass wood, pine, or hemlock, split fine and well seasoned, were, the firemen soon found, the best wood to burn. Their quick fire made a hot blaze that kept up the steam in the boiler. From her funnel came the smoke of the burning wood, and sometimes flying sparks.

You would think the "Walk-in-the-Water" a strange steamship if you could now see her. Her funnel, or stack, was like a large stovepipe. There was no pilothouse. The paddle wheel on each side was in plain view. To aid the steam engine, two masts were erected on the "Walk-in-the-Water." One mast was in the bow and the other in the stern. Upon these masts the usual sails were rigged and used whenever the wind was favorable. As the current in the Niagara River was very swift, the little steamer could not force her way against it. Twenty oxen were therefore used to tow the vessel up into the still waters of Lake Erie. These oxen were jokingly spoken of by the people of that time as the "horned breeze."

The "Walk-in-the-Water" began making regular runs from Buffalo to Detroit. On the way she stopped at Erie, Pennsylvania, and Cleveland and Sandusky, Ohio. Sometimes, if the weather was fair, the vessel ran in close to the shore and, as there were few docks, the passengers and freight were often carried to the land on the backs of sailors who waded to shore through the water. During stormy weather the vessel stopped in deeper water or not at all. On board was a small brass cannon. It was fired to announce that the vessel would leave in half an hour, or on nearing a port to announce her arrival.

At Detroit a new dock was built at the foot of Bates Street for the steamboat. To go from Buffalo to Detroit and back took about two weeks, for lack of steam, shortage of fuel, and bad weather often delayed the little vessel. The fare from Buffalo to Detroit was eighteen dollars in the cabin and seven dollars if one traveled steerage.

The life of the "Walk-in-the-Water" was a short one, for on October 30, 1821, she ran aground, near Buffalo, during a storm.

Although the "Walk-in-the-Water" thus came to an early end, it nevertheless began a new age in lake travel. More steamboats were soon built. The engine and boiler of the "Walk-in-the-Water" were used to drive two other boats before they were finally scrapped. A path was cleared through the forest from the wreck and the machinery was brought overland and placed in a new vessel called the "Superior." In 1835, when the "Superior" was turned into a sailing vessel, the old engine was again placed in a new boat called the "Charles Townsend."

The second steamboat was the "Superior." She left for Detroit on her maiden voyage April 23, 1822. Two years later, in 1824, another steamer was built and named the "Henry Clay." Still another early boat was the "Pioneer."

By 1818 the horrors of the War of 1812 were being forgotten and life in Detroit was getting back to normal. The Indians were again at peace. In order to keep the Indians satisfied, Governor Cass thought it best to get a new and larger land grant from the native owners of the land. This was a real task. The Indians were still friendly to the English who had not threatened to take the Indians' land from them as the Americans were now doing. Nevertheless, Governor Cass thought that the time had come for action, and in 1819 he went to Saginaw to make a treaty with the Indians for more of their land.

Arrangements for the treaty-making council, to be held at what is now Saginaw, were made by Louis Campeau, a French settler then living there and running a trading post.

Governor Cass sent his brother, Captain C. L. Cass, by boat to Saginaw with a company of soldiers, three thousand dollars in silver, and such trinkets as they thought the Indians would like. Governor Cass then set out overland to the meeting place.

The Indians met with Governor Cass in the council house. Governor Cass then proposed to them that they should give up their land and all leave Michigan and settle beyond the Mississippi River. His message was then repeated by the Indian interpreters to the tribes. Of course this plan was not pleasing to them, and some of them left the council in disgust.

Then the usual means was used to bring the Indians to terms. They were given liquor to drink. At last it was agreed that the Indians would give up about six million acres of land for the three thousand shiny silver dollars lying on the table and five barrels of rum. The tribes were also to be paid one thousand dollars in silver coin every year thereafter.

Five barrels of rum were then opened. This Governor Cass knew would be a safe amount for two thousand Indians. Louis Campeau, however, had not been pleased with the deal that had been made because the Indians owed him much money. He therefore went to his own warehouse and brought out ten barrels of his own whiskey which he gave to the Indians. Soon the Indians were nearly out of control, and General Cass and his troops were almost scalped. Peace was then made with Campeau and he quieted the Indians.

This treaty gave the Americans, for three thousand dollars and five barrels of rum, the land east of a line drawn roughly from Kalamazoo, in Kalamozoo County, to Lewiston, in Montmorency County.

In August, 1821, Governor Cass and Solomon Sibley, acting for the United States, and fifty-five chiefs and leaders of the Pottawattomies signed another treaty at Chicago. This treaty gave the Americans a large section of land in southwestern Michigan.

What Michigan lacked was a better system of communication with the older settlements back East. There was still no good route for settlers to use in coming to Michigan from the East. Moreover, once crops were raised in the Great Lakes area there was no way to send them to the markets in the East. If New York City was to get any of the growing western commerce, she must provide a route to the

West that would compete with the National Road and the Ohio River. To expand her western trade and open the western part of New York State, the state of New York began the building of a canal reaching across the state of New York from Albany to Buffalo along the route followed by the old Genesee Road.

"Clinton's Ditch," people jokingly called the new canal, as men and mules began to excavate the three hundred and sixty mile canal from Albany toward Buffalo on Lake Erie. There were then no large, powerful machines, as there are today, to do the work. It was man power, horse power, and mule power which dug the canal steadily toward the West and the Great Lakes. Many men died from swamp fever, from accidents, and from exposure, but the project went steadily on.

The Erie Canal had been started in 1817. Soon it was opened from Rome to Albany. By 1819 it was opened to Utica. Smoke hung over Lake Erie as the steamer "Walk-in-the-Water" ran from Buffalo to Detroit. A new era was coming to shipping on the Great Lakes.

Courtesy Onondagua Historical Association, Syracuse, N.Y.

Junction of the Erie Canal and the Oswego Canal at Syracuse, N.Y. Horses going along the Erie Canal used the over-pass while those going along the Oswego Canal went under the bridge.

During the the years 1820, 1821, and 1822 the canal lengthened. Straining men, mules, and oxen moved wheelbarrows and wagons. More men with axes cleared a sixty-foot-wide path farther and farther into the forest toward the West. New machines brought from Europe ripped the tree stumps from the earth. Newly designed plows with sharp edges cut through the trailing roots ahead of the lengthening canal. Four feet deep, forty feet wide at the top, and twenty-eight feet wide at the bottom, the workmen made the water highway for the settlers and goods that were soon to move along the canal.

All through 1823 and 1824 the men and horses worked on. With pick, shovel, and black blasting powder the canal was cut farther and farther toward Lake Erie. Then, in 1825, the Erie Canal was completed.

The Erie Canal had been built in eight years. Now it lay like a long, narrow ribbon stretching some three hundred and sixty miles across New York State from Buffalo, on Lake Erie, to Albany, on the Hudson River. Seventy-two locks carried the Erie Canal waters up and down. One of America's most important early highways of commerce had been built at a cost of about eight million dollars. This all-water route from the Great Lakes to New York City was soon to change the course of westward expansion. No longer would freight have to be dragged along muddy roads at excessive cost. Freight rates from Buffalo to New York dropped from $100 a ton to $15 a ton, and the time for the trip between these two cities was cut from twenty days to only eight days.

In the West, thirty-cent wheat rocketed to one dollar a bushel. The golden grain, harvested from the rich lands of the Great Lakes area, was soon being carried eastward along the canal. More and more land was cleared along the southern shore of Lake Erie in northern Ohio. Land values in northern Ohio shot rapidly upward. Boom times hit the Lake Erie region. Towns along the Erie Canal grew rapidly. New York City doubled its population by 1830, thus passing Philadelphia in size and becoming America's largest city and seaport. Buffalo, Cleveland, Toledo, Detroit, and even far-away Chicago all soon felt the effects of the Erie Canal.

Boats which did not sink into the water more than four feet could now easily be pulled along the canal. Later the canal was made seven feet deep and canal boats carrying two hundred and forty tons could pass along it. The canal brought the Great Lakes region to the very front door of New York City and the Atlantic Ocean, and it served as the main highway to and from the Great Lakes until the coming of the railroads some twenty-five or thirty years later.

The canal made possible good dependable transportation from early spring until it froze over in late fall. Farm crops and lumber from the Great Lakes area could now be economically shipped to the markets of the East and to the markets of the world. Soon provisions in large quantities began to be shipped east along the lake route and the Erie Canal.

Captain Samuel Ward sailed a small schooner from Detroit to Buffalo. There he lowered the schooner's masts so the little boat could clear the bridges of the canal. He then had the boat towed along the canal to Albany. At Albany he again raised the schooner's masts and sailed it down the Hudson River to New York City, thus making the first voyage from the Great Lakes to the Atlantic Ocean. Before long as many as twenty thousand canal boats were passing along the canal in a summer season.

Up to this time freight moving across New York State had been hauled in Conestoga wagons. The new canal soon put an end to the wagons as freight carriers. Although many people used canal boats in going east or west, the canal did little harm to the stage coach business because the canal was open only about seven months of the year. Stage coaches ran even in the winter and were usually subsidized by year-around government mail contracts. What is more, stage coaches often made as high as six or eight miles an hour while canal travel usually averaged only about four miles an hour.

The price of farm products dropped sharply in the East. Farmers living on the poor stony lands in New England could not receive enough for their crops to pay their expenses. The value of their farms went down. Farming the worn-out lands of New England was no longer profitable. Therefore many farmers began to seek work in the new factories then beginning in New England. Others set out with their families for the West to begin farming on more productive land.

In 1826, the general survey of Michigan lands began. Later, this land survey became a geological survey as well. As the surveyors staked out the land, they collected samples of minerals and rocks and sent them to Washington with their papers. A land office had been established at Detroit in 1804. Another was established at Monroe in 1823. Until 1824, only 61,919 acres of land had been sold and it was nearly all in the Detroit area.

The system of land survey used by the United States Government affected the system of farming in Michigan in two ways: First, Michigan farms were laid out in definite lines running north and south along the lines of survey. These section survey lines also later became roads and thus in many parts of Michigan these roads cross each other every mile and thus form square blocks of land one square mile in area. This is why so many of Michigan's roads run straight north and south and east and west. Second, as the land passed from government ownership to individuals, settlers set up the practice of each family living on its own farm. In Europe, China and India, the peasants often live in little villages and go out to their farms each day. The French farmers had lived in little houses that sat in one long line on each side of the St. Lawrence and Detroit rivers. As each settler who came to Michigan built his cabin on his own land he was often a quarter of a mile, or even more, from his nearest neighbor. Usually a settler built his house not far from the section line that was to be used as the road. Thus today our farmers live in houses scattered here and there along the roads that spread across Michigan.

Michigan now needed better roads so that people coming west by way of the Erie Canal could reach their claims in the vast wilderness. The French and English had made no effort to make roads in this undeveloped wilderness. Thus, when the Americans began to come only the Indian trails led across the state.

The problem of building roads near Detroit was a difficult one. The region around Detroit for about twenty miles in any direction is old lake bottom. The land surface is mostly clay of a very sticky kind. Moreover, the whole region was covered with forests, bushes, oak openings, and marshes. The water drained away slowly and seeped into the clay, making it a heavy paste. The bogs and marshes could be crossed only with great difficulty.

One of the first roads in Michigan was what is now called East Jefferson Avenue in Detroit. It was made during the French period and was merely a muddy path running behind the row of French farmhouses that sat along the river bank.

When General Hull came north from Dayton, Ohio, just before the War of 1812, his men cleared a road from Dayton to Detroit. This road, however, was poorly located and poorly built and passed through the Black Swamp near where Toledo, Ohio, now stands.

One early settler at Ann Arbor says, "Soon after I came to Detroit I made a contract to carry the mail from Detroit to Ann Arbor for four years, and all that time I forded all the streams, never once crossing a bridge, for there were none to cross. During the winter of 1825 and 1826 my son Lucius and I carried the mail on horseback, and often in fording streams and rivers in high water we were obliged to secure the mail bag on the top of the saddle, grasp the horse's mane, and swim him over.

"On the first day of March, 1826, I began to cut a road from Ann Arbor to Detroit, on the Indian trail running by my present residence. I got all the help I could, and in sixty days completed a wagon road through from Ann Arbor to Plymouth. On the first day of May, 1826, I took a light two-horse wagon and three Indian ponies, and went to Detroit one day and back the next. This was a great wonder in those days."

Before settlers could come into the newly ceded lands, better roads than this had to be built. Soldiers stationed at Fort Shelby were put to work improving the road to Toledo. About this time, too, a company was hired to cut and corduroy a road north of Detroit. This road has since become Woodward Avenue in Detroit. The company was to receive $1,000 a mile for building the road. The area, past the six-mile road, was found to be too swampy for a highway. Later a road was constructed there with great difficulty. Most of the way to Royal Oak the road had to be cribbed and corduroyed.

In 1824 Father Richard was elected to Congress from Michigan Territory. As a representative he became active in getting Congress to grant money for road construction in Michigan. By 1825, it was enacted, for military purposes, that several roads leading into the state from Detroit should be built. One of these roads was to follow the old Sauk, or Pottawattomie trail, and run from Detroit to Chicago. At first Congress granted only three thousand dollars for building the road, but two years later it added twenty thousand dollars to the original grant. This road, for many years called the Chicago Road, was under construction for ten years. When finished, it was a typical turnpike of the time. From Detroit the road ran west through what are now Wayne, Ypsilanti, Saline, Clinton, Jonesville, Quincy, Coldwater, Sturgis, and White Pigeon. This old Chicago Road is now known as U.S. Highway 112. Another road was put through the second tier of counties and was known as the Territorial Road.

Further grants by Congress provided for a road from Detroit to Saginaw Bay, and from Detroit to Fort Gratiot (Port Huron). A later grant was made for road construction from Detroit to the mouth of the Grand River.

These new trunk roads led in a fan-shape into and from Detroit. Bridges were soon built over the streams and rivers, making the roads, in a way, reasonably passable. To the forest the settlers turned for a better road and from it they cut thousands of poles to make corduroy roads. By 1836, the first twelve miles toward Pontiac had been corduroyed. These roads gave wagons and stagecoaches a bumpy motion that made riding very uncomfortable. Yet, these humble beginnings were the forerunners of our modern roads and wide expressways that now spread across all of the state.

As early as 1827, a stagecoach line was opened between Detroit and Toledo. A stagecoach ran three times each week between the two places. Another coach line soon began to run between Detroit and Romeo. When the Chicago road was opened, still another stage began running three times a week between Detroit and Chicago.

Behind the four, or six, horses came the coach bouncing the tired passengers up and down and from side to side. During dry weather the ride was hot and dusty. During wet weather the coach had to be actually dragged through the mud. So poor were these early roads that often only fifteen or twenty miles could be covered in a day. Traveling was done mostly during the daylight hours, for the traveler on the highway at night was always in danger of being robbed.

Because of the many delays in travel, inns or taverns sprang up at short intervals along the road. Often these inns were the beginnings of some of our modern villages and cities such as Dearborn, Wayne, Ypsilanti, and Ann Arbor. Where the stage stopped there was trade and people began to settle.

When the stage arrived at an inn, there was much excitement. If the coach were to continue, the tired horses were changed for fresh ones. The mail, as well as the wants of the passengers, had to be cared for. If the coach stopped for the night, the passengers made themselves at home in the inn. Some stayed in their room, if they were lucky enough to get one; others sat in the living room and talked of their journey with their traveling companions or with the owner of the inn and his family. The passengers were served their meals from the inn's kitchen where the food was cooked in a huge fireplace.

Most of the early settlers took up farm lands in or near Wayne County. Gradually the old flat lake bottom around Detroit was cleared and drained. Fields of grain appeared where only a few years before had stood dense forests of virgin hardwood. With the opening of the Erie Canal this grain began to move eastward to feed the new industrial centers that were then growing in the East. This large increase in the grain supply caused the price of grain to fall in the East.

The growing number of settlers wanting to come west caused lake traffic to boom even more than it had previously. In 1825, the year the canal was opened, there were seven side-wheelers (steamboats) running to Detroit from Buffalo. In 1827, the first steamboat steamed down Lake Michigan to Chicago. By 1833, there were eleven steamboats on the lakes. In 1845, there were two hundred and seventeen sailing vessels and forty-five steamboats.

During the long, warm summer days, when the canal and lakes were free from ice, the busy steamers and sailing vessels left the bustling, crowded port of Buffalo carrying hundreds of settlers and their families westward across Lake Erie to Toledo, Detroit, and as far west as Wisconsin, and Chicago in northern Illinois.

The great surge of people to the new West by way of the lakes was on. Ann Arbor was founded in 1824, Adrian in 1825, Niles, Jackson, and Kalamazoo in 1829, Battle Creek and Grand Rapids in 1831, and Coldwater in 1832. In the year 1830, two thousand four hundred immigrants arrived at Detroit in one week. In that same year also the first steam ferry boat started to run between Detroit and Windsor, Ontario. In July, 1831, settlers were passing through the booming port of Buffalo at the rate of one thousand a day. As many as two thousand landed at Detroit in one week. In 1833, after the cholera scare in 1832, twenty thousand arrived at Chicago. In 1834, nine hundred arrived in one day at Detroit. In 1836, ninety boats arrived at Detroit during the month of May and docked at the wharves along the Detroit waterfront.

The steamers grew in numbers and spread their smoke along the horizon where it contrasted with the ever-growing number of white sails as steamers and sailboats hurried back and forth across Lake Erie to carry the ever-swelling numbers of settlers to the western lands.

The little frontier village of Detroit was now a busy place during the summer shipping season. From the crowded decks of the steamers and sailing boats came an almost endless flow of Yankees who were going west to start life anew in the lands which the Indians had so recently ceded to the Americans.

By the 1830's, a new Detroit, built after the fire of 1805, stood on the site of the old French settlement. Many of the new buildings that had been built by the French gave the little village an odd look to the Yankees coming from the more settled parts of New York and New England. Among these buildings of the older French settlers

Courtesy Detroit Historical Museum

The Detroit River—1838

stood others of more recent and different designs that had been built by the immigrants from back East. These new houses stood out from the older French ones and gave notice that a new group of people was already at work in making the area American.

Jefferson Avenue was then the main street. East of Woodward, the the muddy road ran along the river behind the houses of the French farmers, then meandered on along the river and up along the shore of Lake St. Clair. West of Woodward it ran as far as Cass Avenue, where the old Cass house then stood on a high bank overlooking the Detroit River. One settler coming to Detroit, in 1834, had this to say about Jefferson Avenue: "I went up Jefferson Avenue; found some brick buildings, barber poles, wooden clocks or large watches, big hats and boots, a brass ball, etc. I returned to the hotel, satisfied that Detroit was actually a city, for the things I had seen were, in my mind, sufficient to make it one."

There were at that time some six or more blocks of brick buildings, but there were no large buildings of any kind. The streets were muddy and gave the whole town a primitive appearance. But the slippery, impassable mud of the streets did not seem to stop the steady stream of ox teams and wagons that passed along them.

Four hotels and a few small inns cared for the steady stream of settlers if the newcomers had any money to spend. Of these hotels, the most fashionable was the Mansion House which was followed by the Steamboat Hotel, the Eagle Hotel, and the United States Hotel.

The capitol of the territory stood far out on the commons and away from the other buildings on a spot in present-day Detroit now called Capital Park at Griswold and State streets. Where the Federal Building now stands stood the remains of old Fort Shelby which General Hull had surrendered to the British during the War of 1812. On the southeast corner of Jefferson and Woodward avenues stood a one-story wooden building in which was a saloon. Across the street stood a market place. One block below, toward the river, was a dry goods store.

Many of the people were still French, and the soft French language was often heard along with the noisy English of the Yankees. Many Indians and half-breeds mixed with the French and Americans. Some were still clothed in their native dress. With mixed feelings they watched the Yankees pour into the city on their way west to take up farms in areas that up to then had been their hunting grounds.

Courtesy Henry Ford Museum, Dearborn, Michigan

Clinton Inn now at Greenfield Village. For many years this inn stood at Clinton, Michigan.

The ring of axes increased in the forests. Huge trees, centuries old, came crashing to the ground. Little log cabins and log barns nestled in small clearings amid the forested area. Villages were platted on drawing boards. Village lots, where as yet no man had stood, often sold and resold for fancy prices, but no surveys were ever made of them while other unplanned villages were mushrooming in the wilderness. Marine City began in 1831, and Port Huron, which had been a lumbering center since 1827, was laid out in 1835.

Along the new roads leading from Detroit in an ever-widening circle, little frontier villages were springing up. In 1834 lumbering operations began on the Saginaw River at Saginaw. In that same year a little stock of goods was offered for sale at Jonesville. This was the first store west of Tecumseh.

By 1836 a change had already taken place in the huge fan shape of settlement around Detroit. The frontier was already passing from the area near Detroit, and culture from the East was coming in. Land values had already skyrocketed, and farm land along the Chicago Road was now selling for $20 an acre.

New land offices were established in order to take care of the increasing demands of the settlers for lands. One was located at White Pigeon in 1831, another at Kalamazoo in 1834, and another at Grand Rapids in 1836. In 1836, 1,475,725 acres of land were sold in the Detroit district alone while in the territory as a whole about four million acres passed from the government to the settlers.

Settlers following the Chicago Road began settlements at Saline, Clinton, Jonesville, Coldwater, Sturgis, and Mottville. Others taking the Territorial Road that ran west through the second tier of counties, settled Lima, Grass Lake, Jacksonburg, Sandstone, Marshall, Battle Creek, Comstock, Kalamazoo, and St. Joseph.

The area of southwestern Michigan had been of interest to trappers and missionaries since the time of La Salle, and a settlement at Niles had been in existence since the time of Father Allouez. Now this area was to attract a new type of men, the American settlers. Here in southwestern Michigan were to be found what were then known as prairies or "oak openings." These small plains were open spots, some being as large as five miles across. They were, as it were, meadows in a forest land. Heavy grass and thick sod spread across them. In the springtime they were bright with flowers. Wild strawberries grew among the grass and flowers, and their red juice stained bright red the feet of deer, ox, or man that wandered across the prairies.

The Pottawattomies had found the open prairies good for farming and had for many years made their gardens in the fertile prairie soil. The land did not have to be cleared and was better for farming than the acid soil of the forest lands.

The Treaty of Chicago, signed by Cass and Sibley in 1821, had promised the Pottawattomie Indians that a mission worker would be sent among them. In response to this promise to the Indians, Rev. Isaac McCoy came by wagon from Fort Wayne, Indiana, in 1822 to the south bank of the St. Joseph River, not far from present-day Niles, and there set up a mission for the Indians. Several acres of land were cleared, some buildings were built, and a school for the Indians was started. For a short time the mission, known as the Carey Mission, was successful, but disease, whiskey, and the coming of white settlers to the area forced the mission to close in September, 1830.

As early as 1823 a family by the name of Thompson settled in Berrien County. The Putnum family settled in Cass County in 1825, and in 1829 the Morris family came to live in Van Buren County. Most of the early settlers in southwestern Michigan came over the route from Fort Wayne, Indiana, and were southerners from Ohio and Indiana. At first there was no link that joined them to the settlements growing near Detroit, but with the coming of the Chicago Road about 1834, the western settlements of southwestern Michigan were more closely joined to the expanding eastern settlements. Soon easterners from New England were coming west along the Chicago Road to join the settlers coming north from Fort Wayne. In 1840 a new road was cut from Hastings to Battle Creek and thus new areas were opened for settlement.

The settlers pushing into southwestern Michigan were thus beginning to settle upon the tribal lands of the remnant of the only strong tribe in southern Michigan, for at this time the Pottawattomies were still living there and in northern Illinois. In their earlier days they had been a strong war-like nation. They joined Pontiac in hopes of driving the English from the land. They helped defeat General Harmar and General St. Clair. Their chief, Topinabee, was one of the signers of the Treaty of Greenville after the battle of Fallen Timbers. At this treaty the Pottawattomies gave up, for the first time, lands claimed by the tribe. They, too, signed the Treaty of 1807 that ceded southeastern Michigan to the Americans. Topinabee and his warriors were in the defeat at Tippecanoe. When Tecumseh led his warriors in the War of 1812, the Pottawattomies were part of the band. They took part in the massacres at both River Raisin and Fort Dearborn (Chicago). Pottawattomies, too, were fighting along with Tecumseh in the Battle of the Thames. Each June from 1812 to 1834 both the Ottawas and the pottawattomies went to Fort Malden, over the Indian trail that led eastward to Detroit, to receive their annual gift of presents as payment for their services to the English.

Topinabee had been their chief for over forty years and had led them on many of their war parties. Two other leaders of this tribe should be mentioned, Shavehead and Pokagon. Shavehead was the older of the two and no doubt got his name from the manner in which he wore his hair, for it was his habit to draw his hair upward and then tie it on top of his head with a string. Into this top lock he usually thrust a feather or two. He was a sullen man and had a great hatred of the white men who were coming into his tribal lands. Tradition says of him that he had ninety-nine white men's tongues strung on a strip of bark and that he wanted one more to make it an even hundred. He played a leading part in the massacre at both River Raisin and Fort Dearborn, and his scalp locks showed that he spared not even women or children. By the time settlers began to move into the area he was an old Indian living on Shavehead Prairie in what is now Cass County. Time, war, and whiskey had made him a poor, despised old man. Like Tecumseh, with whom he fought, his death is hidden in several conflicting stories.

Pokagon was far different from either Topinabee or Shavehead. He, too, was at the massacre at Fort Dearborn but by now had become a friend of the white men. He signed the Treaty of Chicago in 1821. He was a man of high intelligence and understanding, and though he had little education himself, his son became one of the best-educated Indians of his time. Pokagon was a man of temperance and tried to get the other Indians to follow his example but he had little success. Furs were growing more and more scarce and, as they did so, whiskey flowed more and more freely as the competition between traders grew. This competition for the fur trade, plus the fact that many Pottawattomies had died in the cholera plague of 1832 and in the smallpox epidemic of 1837, no doubt helped to reduce the once powerful Pottawattomies to a miserable little band and led to the failure of Reverend McCoy's Mission.

With sad hearts the Pottawattomies watched the settlers push into their tribal lands. With each passing year, more prairie sod was ripped open by the white men's plows and more trees fell from their swinging axes. Most of the Pottawattomies who still remained were living on a little reservation on Prairie Nottawa Seepe in northern St. Joseph County. Once they had been a powerful nation of warriors. Now they were reduced to a little band. But even this little area of land was soon to be taken from them, although they had been granted it by the Treaty of Chicago. Why this should happen the Indians could not understand. As one chief in council said, "You have more lands than you can use, so why do you want more? You have much; we have little; why do you want our little?"

But the white man did want even the little. That it had been the land where these Indian people had played as children, where they had sat by the council fire, or danced the war dance with braves that never returned from battle made no difference to the settlers. Even the graves of the Indians had little meaning for them. The land would be better without the Indians around.

By another treaty signed in 1833, the Pottawattomies agreed to give up all of their remaining lands and to move west of the Mississippi River as General Cass had wanted them to do in 1819. Governor Cass was then Secretary of War in the President's cabinet. He sent Reverend McCoy with Chief Noonday, of the Ottawas, and five other Indians west to find a place where the Pottawattomies would be less under the influence of the whites.

The Pottawattomie Indians were called together in 1838 so that they could be taken to new reservations west of the Mississippi. Bands from the north, Ottawas and Chippewas under military escort, joined the saddened Pottawattomies. Escorted by federal soldiers and military wagons carrying supplies, the unfortunate, helpless Indians began their westward journey to strange lands beyond the Mississippi. The soldiers had little regard or respect for these old warriors and their families that had fought them in years past and so had little sympathy for their sufferings and hardships. There was much malaria that year, and many of the Indians who started never finished the westward journey. A few Indians escaped to the woods along the way, but most of these and other stragglers were rounded up the following year and sent westward to join the band. At first they were settled in Missouri. Two years later they were moved to Iowa. From there the few that remained were taken to Kansas and then to Indian Territory (Oklahoma). Only Pokagon, the friend of the whites, and a few of his Christian followers remained of the once proud war-like Pottawattomies.

Michigan had hardly begun making roads when a new and better means of transportation began in the state. Railroad building began in Michigan even before Michigan became a state. In fact, the first railroads and locomotives in the Old Northwest were in Michigan. The first railroad to be chartered within the limits of the Old Northwest was the Detroit and Pontiac Railroad. This road was chartered on July 31, 1830. By this charter a group of men was granted permission to build a railroad from Detroit to Pontiac. This first company, however, laid no track.

Among the first railroads to receive a charter in this area was the Erie and Kalamazoo. The charter for this road was granted in 1833. According to the charter the company was to build a railroad between Toledo and Adrian. Although this charter was granted after the Detroit and Pontiac Railroad Charter, the Erie and Kalamazoo was the first railroad to begin active service. The line opened on November 2, 1836. The Erie and Kalamazoo Railroad is still in existence and is now part of the New York Central System under terms of a perpetual lease.

Courtesy Henry Ford Museum, Dearborn, Michigan
An early train

At first the cars on this road were pulled by horses which ran along ahead of the cars on a path between the rails. The horses were changed every four miles. Horses, however, were not used very long, for in January, 1837, the first steam locomotive to be used in Michigan arrived at Toledo and began pulling cars behind it.

The early railroads were far different from the ones that may pass near your home today. The tracks upon which the trains ran were at first made of wooden rails. Long timbers, about one foot thick, were laid lengthwise of the track on top of ties that had been hewn flat on three sides. On the long stringers were later placed long iron strips upon which the wheels of the engine and cars ran. Sometimes, with the changes in temperature, these iron strips broke. When the trains passed over them they suddenly curled upward. This would cause the next wheel to run under the iron strip instead of on top of it. This forced it upward and forward, thus breaking it off. Sometimes these bent strips tore a hole through the bottom of a car and injured the passengers. Occasionally passengers were killed by these "snake heads" as the bent rails were then called.

The engines were small and usually had only one pair of driving wheels. Behind the engine came a car that looked like a wagon. On

this car was piled four-foot wood which the fireman used to heat the water in the boiler of the engine to make steam. It also carried barrels of water for use in the boiler. To aid the fire, these early engines had a large smokestack. Sometimes these smokestacks were almost as large as the boilers. With each puff of the little engine, huge glowing sparks from the fire went flying up the stack

Courtesy Henry Ford Museum

This train is like the one from which Thomas Edison was put off with his experimental equipment. Note the wooden coaches and the wood for burning in the engine to make steam.

much to the dislike of the passengers and the people living along the railway. Fires were often started by these flying sparks. To stop this, laws were passed requiring that wire screens be placed over the tops of the engine stacks to keep the burning wood from flying out.

Behind the engine came the little cars. They were not much more than stagecoaches put upon the rails. Sometimes the seats ran lengthwise of the coach while in other coaches they ran crosswise. Often half

Courtesy Michigan R.R. Association

Early engine on the Flint and Pere Marquette Railroad. This line is now part of the Chesapeake and Ohio system.

of the passengers rode backwards in these seats. The freight cars and
passenger cars had only four wheels each. For springs on these early
cars white ash wood was used. The wheels on the engines and coaches
were the same distance apart as were the wagon wheels of that day.
That distance became known as "standard gauge" (four feet eight and
one-half inches), and even today our railroad rails are laid the same
distance from each other.

In 1834 permission was granted to another group of men to build
the Detroit and Pontiac Railroad. In April, 1836, work on this railroad
was started. Building this road proved to be a real task, for when
the workers reached the Six Mile Road, just a short distance out of
Detroit, they came upon a boggy region which was then called a
"quaking prairie." The ground, although it had the appearance of
being solid, would not hold up the weight of even the lightweight
trains of that day. Trees were cut, dirt was hauled, and at last, after
great delay and expense, the line reached to Royal Oak. Train service
between Detroit and Royal Oak began in 1838. Later the road was
built to Birmingham and service to Birmingham was started on August
16, 1839. In 1843 the little line was pushed north as far as Pontiac.

At first the trains, or cars, of this railroad were pulled by horses, but
in the summer of 1839 the "Sherman Stevens," the second railroad
engine to arrive in Michigan, was put to work pulling the little cars
on the Detroit and Pontiac Railroad. In 1858, the name of this engine
was changed to "Pontiac," and it was then used to haul cars on the
Port Huron and Owosso Railroad.

For a time the Detroit and Pontiac Railroad ran its line into Detroit
on what is now Gratiot Avenue. The depot for the road was then
located on the southwest corner of Woodward and State Streets in
Detroit. People living along the tracks soon complained that the trains
made too much noise, frightened their horses, and set fire to their
houses. A group of angry citizens twice tore up the downtown tracks
of the Detroit and Pontiac Railroad. Then the depot was changed to
a new location.

Still another early railroad was the Detroit and St. Joseph Railroad. Plans were made as early as 1830 for this road which was to
run from Detroit to St. Joseph on Lake Michigan. In 1832 a charter
for the road was granted. Because of the military advantages of the
new line across the state, the War Department aided its building by
surveying the route to be followed. By 1836 the line was graded as
far as Ypsilanti.

When Michigan became a state in 1837, she was very railroad-minded, and the new state legislature soon voted fifteen million dollars for building railroads that were to be owned by the state. It was then planned that three roads should be built at state expense: the Michigan Northern, the Michigan Central, and the Michigan Southern.

The Michigan Northern was to run across the state from Port Huron to Grand Haven on Lake Michigan. The Michigan Central was to run across the state from Detroit to St. Joseph. This line had already been chartered and was being built as a private line under the name of the Detroit and St. Joseph Railroad. The road was bought by the state and renamed the Michigan Central. By January, 1838, the line was opened for service from Detroit to Dearborn. The following month it was opened to Ypsilanti. In 1838 it reached Ann Arbor; in 1844, Albion; in 1845, Marshall and Battle Creek; and in 1846, Kalamazoo. At that time the tracks of this railroad ran down Michigan Avenue in Detroit, and the depot for the road was located where the old Detroit City Hall used to stand on the corner of Woodward Avenue and Michigan Avenue.

The Michigan Southern was to run from Monroe to New Buffalo on Lake Michigan. All of these roads were to be built and operated by the state. The fact that the state had little money at that time seems to have made little, if any, difference. It was felt that the money could easily be borrowed on the state's credit.

The bonds were printed and delivered to the Morris Canal and Banking Company of New Jersey. Part of the money was received, but before it was all paid to the state that company and its bank went bankrupt and Michigan found herself with a few miles of poorly built railroads, some worthless paper money, and a debt of $5,000,000. Michigan's railroad building program was part of the wild speculation in western development that helped to bring about the Panic of 1837.

In addition to the railroad building program Michigan had extensive plans for building canals. The success of the Erie Canal had interested other states as well as Michigan. Canals were built in Pennsylvania, Ohio, and in Indiana. The Erie and Ohio canal, in Ohio, ran from Cleveland to Portsmouth, Ohio, by way of the Scioto, Muskingum, and Cuyahoga rivers. It was opened in 1833 and connected Lake Erie with the Ohio River. Another canal, running from Toledo to Cincinnati, was being built. It was later opened in 1845.

Michigan, too, had canal building plans. One canal, that you will later learn more about, was to be built at Sault Ste. Marie, beside the rapids in the St. Mary's River, so that lake boats could pass from Lake Huron to Lake Superior. Other canals were to be dug so that rivers flowing into Lake Michigan and Lake Huron or Lake St. Clair could

Remains of the Clinton-Kalamazoo Canal at Utica. Photo Fall, 1958.

Where the Clinton-Kalamazoo Canal crossed the Clinton River near Rochester. Water can be seen spilling from a break in the canal wall. Photo 1958.

be joined. This would let canal traffic pass across the Lower Peninsula and thus aid its economic development and settlement.

One of these canals was called the Bad River Canal, or the Saginaw and Northern Canal. It was to have a cut on only about 20 miles. This canal was to go up the Saginaw River, the Bad River cross over to the Maple River and then enter the Grand River. Some work was done on this canal. Traces of it can still be seen near Brant. Another was to go up the Clinton River and then cross over to the Kalamazoo River. It was called the Clinton-Kalamazoo Canal. Work on this canal extended from Mt. Clemens to Rochester. Sections of the Clinton-Kalamazoo Canal can still be seen in the Utica-Rochester area.

But Michigan had entered the canal building program too late. The Panic of 1837, and the coming of the railroads put an end to Michigan's canal program before it had hardly begun. Unable to carry out her huge program because of financial troubles, the state abandoned the idea of constructing canals. This was just as well, for the days of canal transportation were already passing. Railroads were to become the new means of transportation for reaching the interior parts of the state. Not only did the building of more railroads affect the success of the canals but they soon affected stagecoach lines as well. By 1850, stagecoaches were being driven out of business except for lines that ran in out-of-the-way areas.

In 1846 Michigan was ready to sell her interests in the state-owned railroads. Accordingly, the Michigan Southern, which had been built from Monroe to Hillsdale, and the Michigan Central, which then ran from Detroit to Kalamazoo, were offered for sale. The Michigan Northern had been graded for some distance west of Port Huron but, because no tracks had been laid, the road was abandoned.

Buyers were found and the railroads then passed into private ownership. The Michigan Central was sold to the Michigan Central Railroad Company with the understanding that the new company would extend the line to Lake Michigan as rapidly as possible. This they did, and the Michigan Central reached Lake Michigan.

The road did not go to St. Joseph as had been originally planned but went to New Buffalo on Lake Michigan. From New Buffalo the Michigan Central Railroad began to run passenger and freight boats across Lake Michigan to Chicago. Also, by 1849 the old strap-iron rails of the road had been replaced by T rails made of iron.

Under private control the Michigan Southern, like the Michigan Central, soon began to pay its owners a profit. In 1849 it leased the

Erie and Kalamazoo Railroad and began to push rapidly west toward Lake Michigan. Great rivalry developed between the two railroads as to which would be the first to reach Lake Michigan and then Chicago. Both wanted the traffic of that rapidly growing city.

When the two rival roads wanted to extend their lines through northern Indiana and Illinois, they found their plans blocked by the legislatures of those two states which had railroad plans of their own. By agreements with roads in those states the two railroads finally reached Chicago. The Michigan Central made an agreement with the Illinois Central, and even today the two roads use the same station in Chicago.

Both the Michigan Central and Michigan Southern reached Chicago in 1852, and so great was the rivalry between the two companies that the Michigan Southern reached Chicago only one day after the Michigan Central.

As the years passed, settlers from Europe joined those of New England in the Michigan wilderness. After the revolutions of 1830 and 1848, many Germans left the Old World and came to the United States to live. Some of these immigrants settled here in Michigan. Today the children of these German immigrants form a large part of our rural population.

Many Irishmen, too, found their way here from Ireland during this period. The potato famines of Ireland caused poverty and starvation among the Irish people. By the hundreds they came to America. Few of them had any money left after they arrived in New York City, and so they sought work in the growing number of factories in the East. A few came west and worked as laborers or started farming on new and better lands than they had had at home.

Among the settlers who came to Michigan from Europe were many people from Holland. These people in many ways were very similar to the earlier Pilgrims who came to America in 1620. The Pilgrims came here to escape religious persecution, and so did the Hollanders, or Dutch, from Holland. Both were people from the middle classes that were suffering from political and economic conditions unfavorable to them.

The Holland government had set up a state church which some ministers like Rev. Van Raalte and Rev. Vander Meulen and their followers did not like. The same potato blight that brought suffering to the Irish had also caused poverty and starvation among many of the middle-class people of Holland. Because of high taxes, famines, and religious persecution, many people left Holland and came to America and settled in Michigan, Iowa, Wisconsin, and Minnesota.

The first group of these Dutch settlers in Michigan came here under the leadership of their pastor, Rev. Van Raalte. On October 2, 1846, Rev. Van Raalte, his wife, and their five children, together with fifty-seven other men, women, and children, left Rotterdam and sailed for New York. In November the party reached New York, where they met others who had sailed from Holland on other ships. From New York the immigrants went to Albany and then to Detroit.

Rev. Van Raalte had planned to take the group to Wisconsin to settle, but, since the freezing of the lakes had closed the season of navigation, the party was forced to stay in Detroit for the winter. A large warehouse then sheltered many of them during the winter that followed. Many of the men found work at Detroit while others found work in the St. Clair shipyards.

Rev. Van Raalte, not yet fully decided as to the best place to settle, studied maps of Michigan and the Great Lakes area and discussed his plans with several people. He and a few of his friends went to Kalamazoo and that winter they set out from there by dog sled to explore the area in Allegan County near the shore of Lake Michigan. Day after day in snow and cold Van Raalte and his party explored the forest-covered wilderness until he was sure that the area would make a good homeland for his followers and their children. Then, kneeling in the snowy cold of the silent forest, he thanked God for leading him to this fertile area.

This area he had selected because it had not yet been settled and because there was room enough for farms for all of his followers and they would not have to mix with the other settlers. This would keep their church strong and also let them help one another. Because of Lake Michigan the area would be good for growing fruit. The open lake also would provide fisheries and good transportation to the eastern markets. Black Lake* could become a fine harbor from which boats could sail not only to Lake Huron and Lake Erie but also to the growing number of Wisconsin ports and to Chicago, Illinois.

Several thousand acres of this wilderness land were then purchased for the settlement. Early in February, 1847, Rev. Van Raalte and a small group of his followers came to the spot they had chosen near the mouth of the Black River and began cutting trees and making

---

*Now called Lake Macatawa.

cabins. Soon the others followed from Allegan, Detroit, St. Clair, and New York. Thus, the city of Holland was settled by the Hollanders under the leadership of Rev. Van Raalte. Another group of Hollanders, seeking a place to settle, came up from New Orleans and joined the group already at work making the new settlement.

Still another group, four hundred and fifty in all, under the leadership of Rev. C. Vander Meulen came from Zeeland, Holland, and founded a Michigan settlement called Zeeland in 1847. Another group settled at Vriesland in August, 1847. Still other groups settled south of Black Lake, at Kalamazoo, and at Drenthe.

Sickness struck the group during the first summer and many died. The first fall was beautiful, and the first winter was rather mild. By the time winter came again, the thrifty Dutch settlers were better prepared for it. Heavy rains in 1851 together with rodents, which attacked what little crops there were, again brought misery to the settlers. In 1856 dysentery struck the settlement. Some families lost two or three children. In one school district forty-five of the one hundred and twenty-three children died during the summer.

Like the Pilgrims before them, these settlers were a stern, religious people. They read their Bibles daily and carefully taught their faith to their children. Their little log meeting houses were filled each Sunday by a happy people who had found freedom to worship as they chose in the wilderness of Michigan.

Today the descendants of these settlers from Holland form the largest group of people of Dutch descent to be found in America. Their farms cover some five thousand square miles of some of the best farming land to be found in Michigan.

By 1860 the southern part of the Lower Peninsula had become a settled area. Thus, in just thirty years, the spreading wave of settlers had turned Michigan from a wilderness to a land where one could find homes, churches, schools, railroads, highways, and farmlands.

CHAPTER NINE

Pioneer Life in Southern Michigan

SETTLERS coming to Michigan from the East could choose one of three routes. Some of them drove their teams from Buffalo, New York, across Ontario to Windsor and then crossed the Detroit River to Detroit. Others came south of Lake Erie along its southern side. Most of the settlers, if they could afford it, came westward along the Erie Canal to Buffalo. Those who could not ride on the canal, boats, or stagecoaches, drove their teams, or walked, along the Genesee Road across New York to Buffalo on Lake Erie. From Buffalo they took a sailboat or steamboat to Detroit.

Each summer during the 1830's and 1840's canalboats on the Erie Canal moved endlessly back and forth from Buffalo to Albany, New York. Straining, sweating horses and mules, followed by drivers with whip in hand, wore a deep groove in the towpath along the side of the busy canal. Freight boats, with wagons and supplies, and packet boats, crowded with tired passengers, came westward in a never-ending line on the narrow blue ribbon of water.

On warm summer days, some of the passengers sat lazily in deck chairs on the flat roofs of the canalboats. They passed the little cabins of the lock-keepers, the farmhouses of the settlers in the wilderness of western New York State, straining horses pulling wagons along the Genesee Road, new and growing cities fed by the growing commerce of the busy canal, and the green foliage of the forest wilderness. Heads all bent low as the canal boats passed under every bridge.

Other canalboats coming east from Buffalo were always passing by. These boats carried goods from the growing West. Some were filled with wheat; others carried corn; still others carried barrels of cider, salt pork, bags of corn meal or flour that had been ground in the little gristmills on western streams, crates of eggs, hams and bacon from farm smokehouses, hogs grunting and squealing; others carried cattle; and others were loaded with lumber. What could have been more amusing to travelers than to pass a canalboat going east loaded with crates of turkeys, ducks, and chickens? All were passing eastward to markets along the busy canal.

All day the canalboats moved slowly along. Regular packet lines that carried passengers had horses stationed every few miles. At these stations the tired horses rested while others took up the task of keeping the packet boats moving. Some lines carried extra horses on each boat. One team would pull while the other rested as it rode along.

When night came, the passengers went into the cabin. Tables and chairs were pushed aside and beds for the passengers were dragged from storage closets. Women slept up in front, while the men slept in the room at the rear of the canalboat. No curtains gave personal privacy. Beds were narrow and hard, and usually the passengers had to furnish their own bedding. Some boats docked for the night; others moved steadily along. When morning came, all the passengers were aroused. The berths were put away for the day, chairs and tables appeared, and the pleasing aroma of breakfast drifted through the packet boat.

So the immigrants came westward into the Land of the Lakes—single men, young couples, middle-aged men with their wives and children, and elderly ladies and men who could not be left behind. All followed the canal as the boats moved westward toward Buffalo.

At Buffalo the settlers changed to lake steamers, or schooners that would carry them westward across Lake Erie. The fare for the passage from Buffalo to Detroit was about five dollars and there were special rates for families. Those with money could get cabins while the others had to fare the best they could. All streamed aboard. Wagons were driven on deck. There the wheels were taken off and tied securely to the boat so that they could not roll around and cause damage if the boat should run into a storm. The wagon boxes, still sitting on their axles, were placed on deck, and families often lived in them during the voyage westward across the lake.

All summer long little passenger steamers and schooners plied back and forth across Lake Erie on a somewhat regular schedule. The brightly burning fires of the steamers always called for more and more wood. Whenever they stopped along the northern shore of Ohio, cords of firewood, later called "propeller wood," were hastily thrown aboard so that the boilers could be kept hot. Farmers then settling in northern Ohio hauled the wood to the docks in their wagons and got cash for it so that they could buy such things as sugar, flour, salt, guns and gunpowder, axes, and other tools.

Steaming across Lake Erie was far different from crossing it today. There were no weather warnings, no lighthouses, no buoys or charts to guide the boats. Sometimes the steam pressure got too high for a boiler, and then it blew up, killing many passengers. At other times storms blew across the lake and many settlers found this part of the journey the most difficult of all. Some were drowned and others became seasick and were sure that the little boat was going to sink.

But hour after hour the little boats pushed westward across Lake Erie, and the turning paddle wheels left a foaming track in the blue water behind. Sparks flew upward from the smokestacks and hot ashes drifted down upon the deck and passengers, but the steamers moved steadily on to the new lands of hope along the shores of the Great Lakes.

As the boats left the broad expanse of Lake Erie and steamed up the wide mouth of the Detroit River, past Fort Malden and Grosse Ile, on their second or third day out of Buffalo, the passengers gazed in wonderment at the green-forested shores on either side as the boats slipped quietly along on the pure, blue water of the silent, steadily flowing river. To the majesty of the forest was added the quaintness of the Indian villages on the western shore, the white-washed French cabins, and the spreading wings of the French wind-mills that stood out so plainly along the river bank.

When the boats docked at Detroit the horses, mules, and oxen were led ashore. People, boxes, and bundles all spilled from the holds of the boats along with babies, older children, axes, shovels, and pieces of cherished furniture, and cooking utensils.

Among the confusion along the waterfront where settlers were getting their families, teams, and wagons ashore were criers who called out the name of one of the local hotels, or inns, for which they were drumming up business. Cries of "American," "Mansion House," "Eagle Hotel," and others were heard as the drummers tried to get some of the settlers to seek rest in one of the frontier inns where roughly dressed men sat around in small groups passing the time of day in talking, drinking, and squirting brown streams of tobacco juice on ground, floor, stove, or any other handy target.

When the wagons were assembled, and fixed at the local smithy if needed, and all the family was loaded amidst the assortment of luggage, the settlers were ready to continue their journey into the wilderness. Leaving the busy docks at the foot of Woodward Avenue, the straining teams of horses, or oxen, hauled the wagons up the hill to the place where Jefferson Avenue and Woodward Avenue cross and where stood the town market of that day. Then dipping downward the wagons crossed the little Savoyard River and passed on out through the town. Mothers, not used to the roughness of a frontier town, clutched their little ones close to them and urged their sons and husbands to hurry on their way.

Long black-snake whips cracked with snapping stings that stung the backs of horses and oxen. Men shouted at their straining teams. Slowly the lumbering wheels of the mud-stained and weathered Conestoga wagons turned in the oozing mud as the straining horses or oxen dragged the wagons out of Detroit along one of the main roads leading into the forest-covered land. Indians standing along the way watched the newcomers move into their old homelands.

Immigrant wagons were of various kinds, sizes, and construction. Usually they were drawn by one, two, or three teams of oxen. The more prosperous settlers drove teams of horses, but horses were not then considered as good for frontier work as oxen. Most of the wagons had open boxes, but a few were covered with crude canvas tops of unsimilar designs.

Wagons, wagons, wagons—one for every five minutes from daylight until dark during the summer of 1836 left Detroit for points north or west. Most of them went west out Michigan Avenue and followed the road toward Chicago or branched off to the Territorial Road that ran west in the second row of counties. All were loaded with boxes of precious household goods and supplies. The larger boxes were usually placed on the bottoms of the wagons. Onto these were piled smaller ones with the smallest ones on top. The rest of the settler's belongings, not easily lending themselves to box transportation, were often fastened here and there where best they could hang on the sides of the wagons.

In the front of the wagons on the only seat rode the settler and his wife. However, the men often walked along beside the oxen. Among the various boxes, crates of chickens, ducks, and a small pig or two could be seen the curly heads of children covered

Courtesy Henry Ford Museum, Dearborn, Michigan
A conestoga wagon. These wagons were the freight trains of their day.

with caps or sunbonnets. Behind, tied securely to the wagon by a piece of old rope, came "Old Crumplehorn," the family cow. Other stock, such as pigs or sheep, were often driven along by boys of all ages. Many settlers brought a cat or two to catch rats, field mice, and squirrels. Under the wagon box, in the shade, often ran a lean, panting hound or two. Now and then the hound ran off into the forest, hot on the trail of some animal that had chanced to cross the road a short time before.

Thus, the settlers left Detroit and followed the new turnpikes to new farmlands deep inside Michigan. Back east, far across Lake Erie, lay their former homes and loved ones. To many of the settlers it seemed as if they were still going away from home and not getting closer to one.

Soon the little village of Detroit lay behind and all about them were trees, for all of Wayne County was then heavily timbered. Trees, trees were everywhere—elm, ash, oak, hickory, black walnut, and maple. So thick were these hardwood forests, especially in Oakland County, that the trees often reached upward to a height of one hundred fifty feet.

Overhead, a huge green summer canopy of broad leaves shut out the bright sunlight, thus leaving a dark and dusky gloom beneath the trees where the road lay. Huge tree trunks, standing clear of underbrush, closed any distant view except in places where clearings had been made by settlers.

This was truly a forest area. It lay like a great, deeply napped green carpet stretching on and on across the gently rolling hills of Michigan. Through this forest the slowly moving settlers struggled along the little turnpikes like a column of tiny ants wriggling and straining through tall grass.

From Detroit the flat and often swampy land stretched away in all directions for a distance of twenty miles or more. Long ago this area had been a part of the bottom of a large lake that has shrunk in size to present-day Lake Erie. This old lake bottom is mostly heavy clay soil. Scarcely a stone of any kind is to be found in the area.

Crossing this area was for the settlers often one of their greatest problems, especially in wet weather. There were days when a steady drizzle fell for hours. Then the trees, bushes, and roads became soaked with water. Horses and oxen became wet, as they plodded faithfully along. Little streams of water ran off their backs and down their legs. Men covered themselves with oiled leather jackets and splashed along beside the teams through the slippery mud.

Sometimes all sought shelter in the covered wagons or in little temporary camps that the settlers set up along the road. Clothing and bedding picked up the moisture and grew clammy, soggy, and cold. Dry wood for their fires was hard to find in the wet, dripping forest. Little pools of water gathered in the wagon tracks, in the ditches along the way, and in the low, swampy places in the woods. Streams rose and flooded marsh lands, thus making both the marshes and streams harder to cross.

The wet clay was churned and mixed by the feet of horses, oxen, men, and the slowly turning wheels of the pioneers' wagons as they moved along. It oozed up through the cloven feet of oxen, sheep, and swine and was sucked downward with a sticky sound as men or horses raised their feet from the slippery paste. It stuck to the slowly turning wheels and sometimes filled the spaces between the spokes until the wheels looked almost solid.

At times the weary travelers wondered where the water was the deepest and the ground most firm: in the center of the crisscrossed mass of wagon tracks or in the watery ditches along the side of the road? Wagons mired, horses and oxen strained forward as they tried to pull, only to slip in the clay. Men secured poles from the forest and helped the teams by pushing or prying the wagons.

If unable to go on, the settlers and their families waited until others coming along the road came to them. New friendships, that often lasted many years, began at many of the mud holes along the roads to the West. Teams were then doubled, or even tripled, and the little wagons rolled on.

During the summer season mosquitoes, in dense clouds, buzzed in the air and in the evening settled in black masses on humans and animals alike. Deer flies bit with a nasty sting.

When the hot days of summer came and the rains fell less often, the clay roads began to dry. The yellow paste became thicker and thicker until at last it was baked into solid ridges and ruts by the summer sun. Old water holes stood empty and dry, and where once had been wagon tracks filled with dirty, muddy water, there stood huge ridges of baked clay. Horses and oxen picked their way across the pattern of ridges and holes. Wagons and stagecoaches rattled, bumped, and shook along behind.

Travelers pushing west on the Chicago Road found on the bank of the River Rouge Ten Ecyk's inn that he had built to care for weary travelers after a hard day's journey from Detroit. Just past the inn, in what was soon to be the center of Dearborn, they came to the Detroit Arsenal which the Federal Government had started to build in 1833

The rear view of the commandant's quarters as seen from inside the United States Arsenal. Photo about 1860.

to care for troops and supplies needed in the Detroit area. At Eloise there were two cabins covered with one roof and named the Black

Interior construction of the commandant's headquarters of the Detroit Arsenal. Note the manner in which the wooden joints were made and how they were held in place by wooden pegs. Photo 1963.

Horse Tavern. At Wayne, then known to travelers as Derby's Corners, stood another inn that had been built by Mr. Stephen G. Simmons in 1825. At Clinton stood the Clinton Inn which was built in 1832 and which has now been reconstructed in Greenfield Village in Dearborn.

Now and then as the settlers pushed out on the roads from Detroit they passed little clearings in the forest where sat tiny log cabins from which smoke sometimes wafted gracefully upward until it drifted off among the forest trees and disappeared in the blue sky far above. Around the cabins, amid "girdled" trees, grew little patches of wheat or potatoes half lost in the debris that

littered the half-cleared ground. Now and then a settler's dog barked
at the passing wagons, some settler waved a hand, or children's voices
called out to the newcomers as they passed along the road.

When the straining teams had pulled the wagons about twenty or
thirty miles from Detroit and the rolling hilly land was reached, the
clay often changed to sand. During rainy weather these roads were
fairly good, but warm dry weather dried out the golden sand until it
slid from the sharp angle of the turning rims of the wheels and fell
back in a steady flow.

Steep hills were hard to climb. When going down them the loaded
wagons often pressed hard upon the teams. Men sometimes stopped
their rapid descent by tying a log to the back of the wagon or pushing
a stick into the spokes of a back wheel, thus keeping it from turning.

Rivers were a never-ending source of trouble for the westward
pushing pioneers. Sometimes the settlers were fortunate enough to
find a "ford" where the water was shallow and the river bed firm
enough to allow the team and wagon to cross. Sometimes, during
flood seasons, settlers often had to wait for days before they could
get across. Some rivers could not be crossed at all in this manner,
so bridges had to be built. From the forest the travelers cut piles,
braces, and girders for the bridges. Over these wooden spans they
placed logs or planks hewn from the forest near by.

Scattered here and there along the way were poles and rails that
had been cut from the forest to use as pries by men when their wagons
had mired. Old wagon wheels, broken wagon tongues, and broken-
down wagons that could go no farther were strewn here and there
along the way telling of the troubles encountered by others who had
gone on before. These pieces of equipment had often been searched
for spare parts to repair the wagons that had followed, for there was
no chance to get new parts to replace the broken ones. Everything
was used as long as it could be, and then when it no longer was of
value it was abandoned by the wayside. Like the dead ashes of the
campfires, the discarded articles told the story of a people who were
then coming into the wilderness.

Thus day after day the settlers toiled along the muddy or dusty
roads. Some, with money to spend, stayed at the new log-cabin inns
that were built in the shadow of the forests along the way. Others,
closely saving the little money they still possessed, slept in their wagons
or on the ground around little campfires beside the road. Fires glowed
along the road at evening time, and their flickering lights cast weird

shadows on the trees along the way. In battered and dented kettles and pans the settlers' wives cooked the evening meal.

The timid deer on their nightly forage stopped and looked from their forest cover, with big soft eyes, at the curious invaders who were coming in ever-increasing numbers to their ancient land. The slinking bobcat, attracted by strange new odors arising from the cooking kettles, crawled, with belly pressed close down, to sniff again the odors that came drifting down wind on the evening air. Distant howls

Pioneer graves on the bank of the Huron River near New Boston

of wolves broke the starry silence of the summer night. The howls grew closer and closer until at last shining eyes glowed in the bushes along the road and the rattle of dry leaves not far distant in the forest told of their presence. Horses or oxen pawed the ground and pulled at their tethers. The settlers threw another stick of wood upon their fires.

But the settler was a realist, and along with his troubles he found pleasures as well. In the inns and along the road he found friends and swapped stories far into the night. He discovered that the land was far from being the great swamp which had been pictured a few years before. The vast forests, the many streams, the "oak openings," the hills, the prairies, and the bright blue, sparkling lakes along the way added charm and variety as they slowly passed by. But best of all, somewhere—not now too far ahead—lay a new farm that would be their own.

Many of the new settlers could not afford wagons and had to depend upon their own feet for transportation. Often these foot travelers walked five or six hundred miles before they selected their land and purchased it at the land office. Then they walked back east to get their family. In later years they jokingly told of how they came to Michigan on the "Foot and Walker Line." As the wagons rolled along, these less fortunates walked along with the slowly moving wagons. Most of them had little but a dream and, in their pockets or in a bag slung over their shoulder on a stick, what few worldly possessions they had carried all the way. Journey's end found nearly all very weary and almost, if not, penniless.

The sick, suffering, and dying struggled along as best they could, and when the rigors of the journey proved to be more than their health would stand, their fellow travelers, relatives, and friends, in simple frontier fashion, lowered them into shallow lonely graves along the wayside.

Thus the settlers, spreading outward in the shape of a growing fan, kept pushing into the wilderness out past the latest settlements. The spreading frontier lay just a mile or so from the traveled roads. As the settlers neared their journey's end their problems of transportation often increased because there had been fewer people ahead of them. Often, as they came near the place where they were to settle, they had to make the first road through the forest. Trees had to be cut, "down timber" had to be pushed aside, and bridges had to be built. But the turning wheels moved slowly on.

At last, after many trials and hardships, the long journey from the East came to an end. Weary children no longer asked how much farther they had to go. The tired oxen were perhaps as happy as the family that the journey had at last come to its end. Where the settler and his family stood probably no white man had ever stood before. The sound of strange English voices, foreign to the ancient land, re-echoed from the trees. Their feet now trod ground that had known no other footprints than those of soft-padded feet, the split hoofs of animals, or the soft press of an occasional moccasin as an Indian had chanced to pass by while hunting. The nearest settler's cabin might be close or it might be miles away.

Few of Michigan's early settlers had a home to come to. When they arrived on the spot that they had chosen for their home, most of them found themselves in the midst of the ancient wilderness. Sometimes a family continued to live in the wagon, while others built crude shelters in which to stay for the first few weeks. A few of the more fortunate ones were able to stay with neighbors.

Once the spot had been selected and the proper title to it had been granted by the nearest land office, the settler and his family began the task of building a little log cabin that they would soon call their home.

A good supply of pure water for the family and stock was a necessity, so if possible the settler chose as the site of his cabin a place near a spring or stream. Then, taking his ax, he began the task of felling the trees to make his cabin. The larger trees were of no use to him because they were too heavy to be handled by men or oxen. Logs for the cabin must be about a foot in thickness. So for days the settler worked, cutting and trimming logs. When enough logs had been made ready, he set out to tell the neighbors that he was ready to put up his cabin, or log house, as it was called. On the day set the men from all around, perhaps as far away as ten or fifteen miles, came to the "house raising bee," as the frontier people called it. If any had oxen, they brought them along to "snake" the logs from the forest to the place where the cabin was to be built. Sometimes even Indians came to make, as they said, the white man's wigwam.

The earlier French cabins in Michigan had been built by placing logs upright in the ground. This method was not followed by the early English settlers of Michigan. Their cabins were made by laying the logs parallel with the ground. Four logs were thus placed on the ground on the spot where the little cabin was to stand. Upon these the others were placed with their rough ends sticking out to form the corners. Men known as "corner men" skillfully notched each log where it overlapped at the ends. The first few logs were not hard to put up, but as the little building grew in height, it became more of a task to raise the heavy logs. Slanting poles were then placed from the top log to the ground, and up these slanting poles the logs for the cabin were rolled. Sometimes oxen were used to pull chains that passed over the building and rolled the logs upward into their places. If oxen were not to be used, men used long poles called "hand spikes" or poles having a crotched end called "moleys" to pry and push the logs up the slanting poles into place on the wall.

Pioneer cabins were usually very small, only about twenty feet square in size. When the logs had reached the height of about seven feet, the workmen began to make the roof. The two ends of the cabin were "cubbed" or "cobbed" up. That is, each log was cut shorter and

This is perhaps the oldest log house remaining in Michigan. It is located on the Old River Road at Gibralter. 1961.

Corner construction on an early log cabin

shorter until it came to a point at each end of the cabin. From point to point of the cubbed-up ends, a pole, called the "ridge pole," was placed. Onto this roof rafters, other small poles, were placed. More poles were placed lengthwise of the cabin on these rafters. These poles were held in place by pegs or tied into place with strips of the inner bark of a tree, called "withes," which held the poles to the roof. Onto these poles were placed marsh grass or hand-split shingles called "shakes." Long poles, held in place by pegs or withes, held the shakes in place. Although these roofs kept out the rain and most of the snow, they also let out most of the heat. During the storms of the winter, the wind often blew small flakes of snow through the cracks between the shakes. These flakes settled down onto everything in the room.

A door was cut into one side. Usually there were no windows. A fireplace was cut into one end of the cabin and built up on the outside with smaller sticks to form the fire box and chimney. The inside of the fire box and chimney were then plastered with a mixture of sand and clay to keep the wood from catching on fire. Each night before going to bed, the settler would have to look up the chimney, after the fire had burned low and been banked for the night, to see if the chimney had caught on fire as it often did when the clay coating cracked open.

At best the cabin was only a secondary house for the settler. Like the Indians, he kept his body warm by wearing warm clothing day and night during the long, cold winter.

At first the settlers used oak shakes for shingles. These were followed by oak shingles. Still later pine or cedar shingles were used.

At first there were no floors in the little cabins. Later oak logs were cut in half and hewn smooth on one side. These pieces, laid round side down into the dirt, served as flooring. Later, when sawmills came, lumber could be used for floors and building material. Each cabin door swung on wooden hinges. It had a wooden latch with a string which could be pulled inside to serve as a lock. Usually, however, the latch string hung on the outside as a sign of welcome to any who might chance to come that way. Not a nail or piece of iron was used in building these early pioneer log cabins.

Between the logs the pioneers drove grass, mud and chips called "chinkers." These helped to keep the wind and rain from coming in between the logs. To keep the cracks filled required repairs from time to time as the mud fell out and the chinkers then came loose.

If a settler had oxen or horses, a little log barn similar to his log house was built to protect the animals from the cold storms of winter as well as from the wolves and bears that came prowling around the buildings during the night.

At first there was little furniture in these tiny cabins. Now and then a few choice pieces had been brought from back East, but wagon transportation greatly limited the carrying space. The article most commonly brought was the spinning wheel, and this was more of a necessity than a piece of furniture. At first blocks of wood served as chairs. Beds were built into one corner of the room by using small poles and wooden pegs. As almost every settler had an auger, he soon began making chairs with legs. Where boards could be secured, other and better pieces of furniture were often made. Clothing was sometimes stored in trunks that the settlers brought with them as they came west.

The years of settlement were the years of the age of wood. From wood the settlers made pitchforks, shovels, ax handles, carts, wagons, houses, barns, machine parts, dishes, bowls, ladles, boxes, barrels, roads, bridges, pails, furniture, spinning wheels, and looms. Moreover, it was the fuel with which they cooked their food and heated their cabins.

To the new settler, the spreading forest about him had little value. There was too much of it. He had come to farm and not to lumber. Every one, except those settling on the oak openings, had timber or could take what he needed from nearby lands still belonging to the government. So the next big job for the settler's family was to clear the land.

Most people today, third or fourth generation descendants from these early settlers, or children from more recent immigrations, are used to seeing open farmlands and well-paved and ordered streets with trees selected and arranged in orderly fashion. Unless one has been in the woods where trees are being cut, it is difficult for one to realize the extent of debris and toil that went into clearing a forest land to make it into farming land suitable for even a single plow and swinging scythe.

Only a few of the early settlers had good tools with which to work. Good grades of steel were scarce and tools were easily broken. An ax was the most common and useful tool. Its constant thud, thud, thud was the battle sound of the struggle between the forests to remain in possession of their age-old lands and the new settlers to claim it for themselves and their children. Axes, swung by muscles that had grown strong from daily toil, bit through the rough outer bark of the trees and then with each stroke sank deeper and deeper into the moist, clean, sappy wood beneath. White, damp chips snapped out with each swing of the ax and fell among the dead leaves and decaying twigs around the foot of the trees. Clearing the land was a task that took long hard days of toil, and fortunate was the settler who, at the close of the year, had the trees down on as much as five acres of land with the stumps still left standing.

To cut these huge trees with merely an ax was a huge task and one that could not be done in a single season. Yet food had to be planted so the family could live through the following winter. But food could not grow in such heavy shade as the forests made. To let the sunlight in, settlers often "girdled" trees by cutting a wide band in their bark. Then the uprunning sap, checked in its rise, oozed out and went running back onto the ground from whence it had come. The green leaves, high overhead, curled up, shriveled, turned brown, and finally came drifting gently downward to the ground, finding their places of rest before their time.

Even when the trees were down the settler's clearing problems were far from over. A felled tree was one thing; cleared land was yet another. Hours of toil were often required to cut the branches from the fallen trunk. Some of the branches were cut into firewood for the coming winter. The rest were gathered into piles, and when they had lain long enough to dry a little, they were burned. The stumps and trunks still remained to be cleared.

To get rid of the huge tree trunks was a seemingly endless task, often requiring more strength than a single settler could provide. At first the tree trunks had to be chopped into logs, but later with the coming of cross-cut saws the trunks could more easily be cut. Once a tree trunk was cut into logs it was still far from being destroyed. If a settler were fairly prosperous, he might have the help of a team of oxen or horses, but many settlers had no such luxury.

Because the large logs were too heavy for one man to handle alone, the settlers often helped each other in getting rid of the logs. When a settler had felled his trees and cut them up into logs, his neighbors came to his farm to help him. These gatherings were known as "logging bees." If a settler had a team of horses or oxen, he brought them along to help drag the logs close together so they could be burned. With pries, made from small poles, the men rolled the logs into piles three or four high. Over these log piles dry branches were placed and then the whole was set on fire. It is safe to say that the clearing fires of the settlers destroyed as much good timber as ever came from the sawmills of Michigan as lumber.

Hardwood stumps rot out in a few years, and so they were sometimes left to slowly decay. To chop and dig them out was hard, tiring work that gave little sign of the hours of toil which a settler spent upon them. Besides his ax, the settler had another force to put against the stumps and that was fire. When the stumps had dried out and the oozing sap no longer came from the ground, the settler tried to burn them. With his spade he dug a hole under the dried roots. Into the hole he pushed dried twigs and chips. These he then set on fire. The little flames grew and crept upward. Brush was piled on.

Shocked corn. Farmers used to cut their corn and stand it in shocks to cure. Later in the fall the ears would be pulled from the stalks. The ears were then husked. The stalks were used for cattle feed. Photo Fall, 1963.

Then the stump caught fire and burned for a time. Sometimes a settler had to do this several times before the entire stump was burned.

So the early settler farmed as best he could around the stumps. If he had a plow, he ran his furrows in curves around the stumps and across his half-cleared land. If he had no plow, he dug up the fresh earth with his spade and planted his crops for food for the coming winter.

Other settlers came and soon the thud of more axes sounded just beyond the settler's line. Curling smoke, rising skyward, showed plainly that another family had arrived and was busy changing woodland into open farmland where a good man could with a plow run a true straight furrow from one side of his field to the other. The sound of voices broke the silence of the wilderness: voices of men at work, voices of mothers calling for their children, voices of children at play. Strange new smells, too, blended with those of the flowers and trees. The greasy smell of frying bacon, the warm, pleasing aroma of fresh baking bread or biscuits, the dark smoke drifting lazily from the smokehouse where bacon and hams were being cured—all mingled with the smoke from the smoldering clearing fires as the forest land changed to farmlands.

The blue, hazy smoke, like a soft, misty vapor, rose from the ever-increasing number of clearing fires, where roots, logs, stumps, and rot-ing debris of the forest were burned to clear the land. Dry brush and limbs burned quickly with an intense flash that sent the crackling flames high into the air. Rotten logs and old stumps burned slowly. Sometimes they smoldered on for days, or even weeks, before they were consumed. Blue smoke drifted upward among the tree tops, or hung like a thin blue haze in the valleys between the higher green ridges. The clean, fresh air of the forest took on a new odor, the odor of burn-ing wood.

The hardwood lands yielded easily to the plow once the trees were down and the stumps and roots removed, but the prairie land was hard to break on the first plowing. Prairie land did not have to be cleared, but the sod was so tough that it usually took from two to six teams of oxen pulling together to "break" the land. A large plow called a "bull plow," made entirely of wood except for the "share" and "coulter," was used for the first plowing of prairie land. The standard price for plowing the tough prairie land was five dollars an acre.

Fences were a problem for the early settlers too, but the fields had to be strongly fenced to keep horses, cattle, and pigs from wandering off into the woods where they would be caught by the wolves. To fence their fields, settlers split fence rails from the forest trees. In fact,

Left: A rail fence near Ann Arbor. 1961. Right: Pine stump fence near Cadillac. Photo 1947.

rail splitting became a regular employment for some men. By means of a large wooden hammer, called a "beetle," and wedges and gluts, smaller oak logs were cracked lengthwise into fence rails. A good workman could make about one hundred fence rails a day.

A few of the settlers who lived near the Great Lakes were able to sell some of their timber as cordwood for the early steamships. Others who happened to have farms along the early railroads drew the cordwood to a "wooding station" along the tracks, where they sold it for sixty-five cents a cord. To cut this cordwood was hard work, but it did give some early settlers a little cash money with which to buy a few things like salt, flour, and gunpowder.

Getting and keeping a fire was always a problem to a pioneer family, for they had no matches as we have today. Sometimes live coals were brought from a neighbor's fire. At other times "punk" (a soft, rotten wood from maple trees), a flint stone, and a piece of steel were used to start a fire. By striking the flint stone with the steel, a spark could be thrown against the dry punk. Careful blowing would cause the spark of fire to spread. Fine, dry "whittlings" were then placed on top. Before he went to bed, a settler carefully banked his fire for the night by covering it with ashes. In the morning the ashes were carefully removed, and by means of a "bellows" which blew air onto the coals, the fire was again started.

As the settlers prospered, the old wooden fireplaces gave way to better ones made of stones or bricks. Until the coming of stoves, the fireplace was still used for doing all the cooking. Potatoes were baked in the glowing coals. Fresh corn from the fields was roasted.

Sometimes "bake ovens" or bake kettles" were placed over a bed of coals and thus biscuits, bread, and johnny cake were made. Large frying pans, called "spiders" in Michigan, standing on three or four legs could be placed over a bed of coals and used to fry bacon or pancakes. From the side of the brick, or stone fireplaces, later hung a swinging iron bar called a "crane." The bar could be pulled out in front of the fireplace or pushed back in over the fire. Onto this bar were fastened "pot hooks" which held the iron "pots" or kettles" in which the foods were stewed or boiled. Other mechanical devices called "spits" allowed an iron bar to be pushed through a roast of meat or fowl and then turned slowly so that the meat would be evenly cooked on all sides. Some spits were turned by hand, others had a clock arrangement with a weight that kept the spit slowly turning. Some later fireplaces had a brick oven built in at one side of the fireplace opening. These were slow to heat, but once hot, they stayed warm for a long time and were used for much of the baking that was done by the family.

When bread was baked, some of the dough called "emptins" was saved for starting the next batch of dough. There was no way to buy yeast and thus some dough was always saved to start the next batch of bread. Cider was used to make homemade vinegar. Into the fresh cider the settler's wife placed some "mother" from old vinegar. This would cause the cider to ferment and turn to cider vinegar.

The fireplace was the center of family life, especially during the wintertime when the family gathered indoors. On cold days a bright fire in the little fireplace bade welcome to strangers and the cheer and comfort of home to father and boys as they came in from doing the chores or from the hunt. In the evening the glowing coals lit up the family circle. Before it mother and the girls sat and knit, or patched the family clothing, while father and the boys cared for their guns, shoes, and other outdoor equipment. All lived together before the open fire and thought mostly of one thing—how could they make a living in the wilderness?

Almost everything the pioneers ate came from their own farms or the nearby woods. The first year or two, until the crops were harvested, were often hungry years for many settlers and their families. But food could be had if the settler had a gun. Wild turkeys, bears, deer, ducks, passenger pigeons, geese, and rabbits could be found in the forests and marshes. Wild berries too could be gathered. Fish were then plentiful in the lakes and streams. Wild honey was found in bee trees and used for a table sweet. When a settled found a bee tree, he chipped it with a mark or put his initials on the tree, thus marking it as his property. No Indians or other white men would then touch it.

There was very little fruit other than wild berries to be had by the early settlers, but from their farms soon came wheat, corn, potatoes and many kinds of vegetables.

Because hogs multiply quite rapidly, the early settlers depended upon them for much of their meat supply to replace the diminishing game of the forest. Hogs were often allowed to run in the woods so that they could feed on the mast beneath the trees. In about one year they had usually eaten all the rattlesnakes for miles around the cabin. Fencing in hogs was a problem because they could usually root under any pioneer fence. The early varieties of hogs were usually of poor quality. Moreover they were lean and tough from much wandering.

A flock of sheep. Photo 1956.

Sheep furnished wool for clothing and food for the table. Chickens, ducks, and geese were raised by every settler. Cows became common and milk could be found on most tables. Oxen provided draft animals and also meat. Bears and wolves often raided the farmer's stock and killed pigs, sheep, calves and chickens. Poultry was hard to keep because of the foxes and hawks that carried off the birds. Because tea, coffee, and butter were costly, they were rarely seen on the settlers' tables. Sometimes substitutes for coffee, such as crust coffee, or coffee made from browned grains, were served. Tea leaves were saved and used again and again in order that young folks could have their fortunes told. Baked and boiled potatoes were common, as were johnny cake and milk gravy, which was made of milk, flour, salt, and bacon grease. Salt was scarce and costly for many years.

Though the food was plain, there was usually much of it from the fertile lands and people ate heartily. Many developed what was jokingly called the "Michigan appetite," and as one settler said, there was "nothing but the dishes left after the meal."

Maple syrup and maple sugar furnished the settler his only sweet except wild honey. The art of gathering maple sap and making maple syrup and sugar had been learned from the Indians. Early each spring, just as the snow was leaving the ground, the settlers gathered maple sap and boiled it. "Sugaring off" as they called it was a jolly time when candies and sweets made up part of the social occasion.

Clothing such as we know it today was scarce in the early settlements. Children sometimes went barefooted all winter. Some buckskin jacket like the Indians had were worn by the men, but wool was the most-used item. This the settlers got from their sheep. The women carefully cleaned, carded, and spun the wool into yarn on the spinning wheel that could be found in nearly every home. Often the skeins of yarn were dyed with colors made from nuts, berries, or roots. Pioneer women spent much of their time knitting. They knitted sweaters, socks, mittens, and shawls. The yarn was also made into cloth called "homespun" and then made into suits or dresses. There was little store clothing before 1880.

Courtesy Henry Ford Museum, Dearborn, Michigan

Looms like this one were used for making cloth. This loom has a flying shuttle. One of the boxes into which the shuttle flies can be seen just to the left of the warp threads. The shuttle is thrown back and forth by the ropes which this boy holds in his left hand. His right hand is on the beater.

Hooked rugs fashioned from discarded cloth, or clothing, were made to cover the floors. By 1840, carpets could be found in some of the settlers' homes.

Bedding was important to the early pioneers, for their houses were cold at night after the fire had been banked. There were no springs on their beds. Rope crossed at right angles served in place of springs. Onto this was usually placed a tick filled with straw or marsh hay. In the wintertime a feather tick was placed over the straw tick. A feather tick was a big bag made of "ticking" just the size of the bed and filled with goose "down" that had been plucked from the live geese. Feather ticks were soft and warm.

Over them the settlers put "comforters" or large quilts. Making quilts took long hours of work for the women and girls. They were made by placing a thickness of cotton or wool between two layers of cloth. The wool or cotton in the center was held in place by threads which passed from top to bottom every few inches. Putting these threads and knots in a quilt was called "tying it." Quilts were carefully made and skillfully stitched by hand. Sometimes the stitches were spaced almost as evenly as they are now done by machines.

The women and girls made all the soap used by the family. All the ashes from the fires were carefully saved. Water was then allowed to drip through the ashes. This water then contained lye. To it were added old fats that had been saved from day to day. After boiling the fats and lye together, the liquid was allowed to jell. Thus soap was made.

Doing the family washing was a hard task for the women and girls. Water had to be heated and poured into wooden wash tubs. Then each article to be washed had to be scrubbed by hand. It took long hours of tiring work.

As the cows increased in number, butter was more often seen on the settlers' tables. Fresh milk was placed in pans and left to stand overnight so that the cream would rise to the top. This rich, yellow cream was then skimmed off and placed in an upright churn. The churn was usually a tall crockery one, or one made of wood that looked like a tall wooden pail. On top there was a cover with a hole in the center. Through this hole went a round stick like a broom handle. To the lower end of the stick was fastened a round, flat piece of wood or two crossed sticks that splashed in the cream as the handle was raised or lowered. Up and down, up and down, up and down went mother's arms each time the ladle splashed in the churn. At last the golden butter came to the top of the liquid in the churn. Skimming it off with a wooden "butter ladle," she put the freshly churned butter into a wooden bowl and then worked it with the ladle into a yellow lump. The liquid that remained in the churn was called "buttermilk." Sometimes this was drunk by the family. If there was more than the family wanted, it was added to the skimmed milk, milk from which the cream had been taken, and fed to the pigs.

Candle-making was another household task. Tallow was carefully saved and then melted and poured into candle molds through which a piece of string had been stretched. These candles, Betty lamps, and the fire in the fireplace were the only sources of light during the hours of darkness. Tallow candles, however, were not so good as our candles today. They burned rather quickly and gave off a black, greasy smoke.

Courtesy Henry Ford Museum

Using antique molds to show the manner in which early candles were made

Brooms were made by hand, as were ox yokes, sleighs, carts, and many of the farm tools.

At first many of the settlers' cabins had no windows, but before long small pieces of window glass began to be put into little window frames. This made the cabins lighter and better, and, since the danger of Indians looking into the open windows was past, the settlers were glad to have the glass windows.

Sickness was a dreaded thing to the early settlers, for many of them were ill much of the time. Malaria, or the "fever and ague" or "ager" as they called it, was common among them. One of the first questions they often asked a newcomer among them was, "Have you had the fever and ague yet?" If he said, "No," they knew that he had not lived in Michigan very long. This dreaded disease, carried by mosquitoes that lived in the swampy lands, caused the early settlers much suffering and loss of work. One day they would be burning with fever and the next day cold and shaking all over even if the weather was warm and bright. Gradually, as the land was drained and the breeding places of the mosquitoes were made much smaller, the cases of fever and ague became fewer and fewer.

Cholera, a type of dysentery, was another disease that visited the settlements almost every summer. Many people, especially children, died after having it only a few hours because of the dehydration of their bodies. Sometimes whole families died in two or three days. Typhoid, pneumonia, diphtheria, and smallpox were other diseases dreaded by every family. Though there were often many children in these early pioneer families, many times only a few lived to become men and women.

Doctors were few and often miles away. Sometimes before the doctor could be brought to the house, the sick were already dead. The women did the best they could to care for the sick. Every summer they gathered herbs and dried them for medicines. Sassafras was used for boils, boneset for fevers, lobelia for measles, sage for worms, and elder blossom tea, or catnip tea, for upset stomach.

Barn raisings, house raisings, and logging bees furnished occasions for mutual help and community gatherings. Then there were dances, too. A violin or two, and sometimes an accordion, provided music for the dances. Square dances were popular at that time, and all present entered into the fun and spirit of the gay occasion. The pioneers found pleasure also at the corn husking bees. When fall came they gathered for the husking. What fun there was when someone found a red ear of corn! The lucky finder had the right to kiss any girl at the bee—that is, if he could catch her.

Harvest time was a busy time for the early settlers. The sun shone and the little fields of grain ripened. Men and women looked and were glad. There would be bread next winter and feed for the chickens and the stock. There would be some to sell, too, and that would bring money for salt, gunpowder, and a few things from the local stores that were beginning to appear at the crossroads.

But the grain had yet to be gathered. At first little sickles were used, and gathering grain was a very slow, hard task. Later scythes were used, and the grain could be cut faster. Scythes and sickles were carefully sharpened, because the harvesting had to be done by human muscle power.

At harvest time dawn found the farmers starting across their fields with scythes well sharpened on a hand whetstone. With a swinging rhythm, developed by days of toil, the long blades of the settlers' scythes mowed through the standing grain, and the golden blades of the wheat fell back into the cradles. The filling cradles swung back and forth with the scythes as they were carried by muscles as strong as steel.

Each cradle full was carefully bound and stacked. Every now and then the working men stopped to whet their scythe blades with a whetstone that they carried in their hip pockets.

The sun rose higher. The day grew warm. Sweat broke out upon the men as they moved slowly across their golden fields. Shirts grew dark with perspiration. Great beads of water rolled down cheeks, necks, and brows and dripped from noses and chins. Sweating arms and moist shirts gathered the flying dust and chaff.

Across the fields came children carrying jugs filled with water— clear, cool water from the spring—for their fathers. Sometimes a beaten egg, ginger, salt, and pepper were added to the water. The toiling

Shocked grain. Each shock is made up of several sheaves. In this way the grain was left to cure and dry before being threshed. Photo August, 1963.

men paused. Taking one of the jugs, they tossed it up into the air and brought it to rest upon the elbow of their bent arm. The cool water ran gurgling from the brown jug into thirsty dry mouths.

At last the grain was cut and gathered in. Then it was "flailed," or "tromped," and "winnowed" and hauled by wagons to the nearest railroad or port, where it began its journey eastward to the markets of a hungry world. The great golden stream of wheat had begun its flow from the West to the East along the busy Erie Canal. At first it was only a small trickle started forward by tired human arms gathering it from dawn to dusk, for as late as 1830 the entire grain supply of the world was still being gathered by hand with no better tools than the sickle, scythe and cradle.

At first it was hard to get grain ground for home use. Sometimes the settlers had to grind it by hand. As the settlements increased, small gristmills, run by water power, appeared on several of the streams in the southern part of the state wherever enough water fall could be made in the streams to turn a water wheel. Mills run by water power were few in number, however, because most of the rivers did not permit enough fall to turn a water wheel.

To these early mills the settlers took their wheat and corn to be ground. From the bins above, the wheat or corn ran down into the center of two burr stone grinding wheels. One stone, the bottom one, was held firmly in place while the upper one turned

Courtesy Henry Ford Museum

These men are grinding grain at the Loranger Gristmill at Greenfield Village. The grain passes through the hopper and is ground into flour between the two burr stones.

slowly upon it. As the grain passed outward from the center of the stone it was crushed between the two stones into flour or meal. Then the ground material was sifted, or "bolted," through a "bolting cloth."

This bolting process removed the outer husk of the grain which could not pass through the cloth. These early flours did not keep as long as our present-day flours because they retained the heart, or germ, of the grain and all the materials nature had stored in the wheat.

The gristmills also ground corn, rye, and buckwheat for both human use and animal feed. Corn was commonly used among the Michigan pioneers as a food. From corn meal they made corn meal mush, spoon breads, and johnny cake. Corn meal mush was eaten as a cereal with milk or cream and a little syrup. Johnny cake was eaten with maple syrup. Later some butter was also used. Buckwheat flour was used for making buckwheat pancakes.

Later, steam-driven gristmills were built in places where water power could not be found. With the coming of the large flour mills in the West, during the latter part of the nineteenth century, most of the little gristmills in Michigan stopped running. However, a few throughout the state are still grinding grain just as it was ground over a hundred years ago. One of these early gristmills is now in operation at Greenfield Village in Dearborn. Today at the Village you can see grains being ground just as they were in the days when the settlers took their grain to the gristmill to be ground into meal or flour.

To keep his other crops such as carrots, potatoes, and turnips from freezing during the winter, the settler often stored them carefully away in a place called a root cellar. This was usually a cave dug into the side of a hill and packed with straw to keep the food from freezing.

Not only did the settler have to put away supplies for himself and his family, but he had to put away hay and grain for his livestock as well. Often hay was stacked in the open barnyard.

Up to 1850, ox teams were used more than horses. Although they were slow, the settlers liked them better to use in clearing the land and plowing up the tough sod. Then, too, their meat could be used to supply food for the family table. Wagons pulled by oxen provided the main means of transportation on the farms and from the farm to the village. A man with a team of oxen was regarded as being well off, for many early settlers had to do all their own work and carry provisions from town on their backs.

Work on these early farms was all hard toil. Farmers and their sons worked long hours, from dawn to dusk. The ground, at springtime, was turned by a spade or a crude heavy wooden plow. A tree branch often served as a drag to break the earth into fine pieces. Sometimes it was pulled by oxen but in many families the father, mother or sons dragged the tree branch over the ground. Sowing was done by hand. During the summer, crops such as potatoes, corn, and vegetables had to be hoed. In the fall all the grain had to be cut by hand. Sickles and scythes were used. Grain was threshed with a flail and winnowed in the open air. Often the tools with which they worked, such as rakes, hoes, spades, plows, and pitchforks, were made of wood by the farmer who used them. All the milking was done by the farmer's family.

At first Michigan's farms were all general farms. The farmers raised a variety of crops like they had on the New England farms from which they had come. But before long, some of them closer to the routes of transportation, like the Erie canal and the expanding railroads that led to markets, began raising cash crops. One of these early cash crops was wheat. The heavy clay soil of southeastern Michigan was well suited to wheat growing. So new and rich was the land that many bushels of wheat could be produced to the acre. Wheat kept well, could be easily shipped to market on the new railroads and the Erie Canal where it could be sold in the growing cities of the East or in Europe. Wheat from Michigan and from the area around and west of Chicago formed the first bulk shipments of freight on the Great Lakes. It has been estimated that, even with the crude methods of production, about one million bushels of wheat were produced in Michigan in 1837. By 1840, it had increased to about two million bushels and by 1850 it had reached about five million bushels. Other farm produce such as chickens, pigs, and cattle were also sent east to help feed the rapidly growing cities where the people were coming to depend more and more upon the western farmers for food for their tables.

Though transportation by rail and water had grown better, local transportation was still very poor. Some main roads leading out from Detroit had been built, but these roads were not well made. Often they were little more than lanes cut through the forest. They were poorly graded and drained. In wet weather they became muddy and slippery. During dry weather they were hard and bumpy.

In 1844, a charter was granted for the building of the first plank road in Michigan. It was to run from Detroit to Port Huron. In 1848, the state legislature passed an act known as the Plank Road Act. Plank roads were to be eight feet wide and three inches thick. These roads were made possible because of the improvements in sawing lumber and because of the vast amount of hardwood that was near at hand. A plank road was built between Detroit and Pontiac. Another ran from Detroit to Howell. One was also built from Flint to Saginaw. Anyone who used a plank road had to pay for its use. A two-horse wagon paid two cents a mile. A one-horse wagon paid one cent a mile. To take twenty cattle one mile cost two cents. Plank roads were never very successful. The planks rotted rapidly and wore away with use as hoofs and wheels passed over them. When new planks were put in to replace the old ones, they were higher than the worn ones and thus made the road bumpy. Some boards warped out of shape. Horses often got slivers in their feet.

Until about 1880, the only roads in Michigan besides the toll roads were township roads. These highways were supposed to be cared for by the people living along the road. Each taxpayer was expected to work out part of his tax by working so many days on the road or paying cash for his share of the tax. People who were not taxpayers were to give one day's work or pay a man's wages for one day's work. But the roads were poorly kept. This lack of good highways hindered cultural and economic development.

By 1860, the southern part of the state could be called a settled community. The early pioneer farms had changed to cleared farms more like our farms today. Better houses and barns made of lumber began to replace the earlier log cabins and many of them were built between the period of 1860 and 1900 when lumber was plentiful and cheap.

Before 1860, the slow hand methods of planting and harvesting greatly limited the amount of food that could be produced on the farms. Farm produce, produced over and above the many other tasks of each day, was largely limited to only enough to supply the farmer's family. Farming methods were crude and production was low. There was no system of crop rotation as we know it today. The same crops were grown in the same fields year after year. Manure was considered a nuisance and was hauled away and not spread on the land for fertilizer.

There was little iron in that day and most of the farmer's tools, such as rakes and pitchforks, were still made of wood. The standard farm tools from 1800 to 1840 were an ax, a broad ax, a heavy iron hoe, a wooden pitchfork with wooden tines, a flail for threshing grain, a wooden rake, a sickle, a home made harrow or just the top of a tree that was used as a drag, a roller made from part of a tree trunk, a two-wheeled cart or a wagon if it could be afforded, and a sled.

The old bull plow had a wooden moldboard and a piece of iron fastened onto it for a plow share. Sometimes old pieces of iron from saws were fastened to the moldboard to keep it from wearing too fast. To pull this heavy plow, it often took three yoke of oxen. Two men and one boy were needed to use it. The boy broke up the clods of earth with a hoe, or club, as they were turned up by the plow. All three working together could plow only about one acre a day.

Courtesy Henry Ford Museum, Dearborn, Michigan

Plows like this one were brought to Michigan by the early settlers.

But changes were coming in farming just as they were in other occupations. In 1819, Jethro Wood patented a plow that could be considered the first of our modern plows. It was made of standard iron parts bolted together. This made it possible to replace a broken part. In 1837, the year that Michigan became a state, John Deere made his first steel plow from an old saw blade. Steel plows were, however, thought to poison the ground. Yet by 1850 steel plows were replacing the earlier wooden ones. With the new steel plow one man working alone with a team of horses could plow one and one half acres a day. This saved labor and increased each farmer's production.

Up to about 1815, all grain was still cut with a sickle. A man held some of the stalks of grain in one hand and then cut it with the sickle he held in the other hand. In one day he could cut about one acre of grain. As all the grain ripens at once, this method of cutting greatly limited the amount that any one farmer could grow and harvest. After the Civil War the sickle was replaced by the scythe and cradle. With the coming of the scythe and cradle one man could cut about three or four acres of grain in a day. The grain was bound into bundles called sheaves. These were then put into little piles called shocks where the grain was allowed to dry and harden. The scythe was a big improvement over the little sickle, but still other and more important changes were soon to come in the manner of cutting grain.

As early as 1814, and from that time on, men were experimenting with reaping machines to cut their grain. In June 1833, Cyrus McCormick, of Virginia, patented his reaper. In July, 1833, the same year, Obid Hussey, of Cincinnati, Ohio, successfully used his new reaping machine. By 1860, better machines were commonly used to cut both hay and grain, but the grain still had to be bound by hand into sheaves and put into shocks in the field to dry.

By 1860, or soon thereafter, steel plows had, in general, replaced the earlier wooden plows. Horse drawn rakes had begun to replace the earlier wooden hand rakes. Mowing machines were widely used to cut hay for the horses. Threshing machines, run by horse power, were beginning to replace the flail for threshing. These threshing machines also saved much labor because they not only threshed the grain but winnowed it as well. Some steam powered threshing outfits were also being tried. Two horse, straddle-row, steel-toothed cultivators were beginning to be used in place of the old heavy hand hoes. Seeders, or drills, were being used in place of the earlier method of hand sowing. These drills not only saved much grain but also planted it better as well. Corn planters and potato planters were also beginning to be used. All of these did much to reduce the labor required in farming as well as to greatly increase the amount of crops that one farmer could produce.

CHAPTER TEN

Early Cultural Development
(1815–1875)

MOST of Michigan's early settlers came from New England, New York, Pennsylvania, or from Ohio and Indiana. Most of them were poor. Often they lived far apart. Most of them were Protestants. At first there were no Protestant churches in the settlements. Occasionally an itinerant preacher stopped for a day or two, preached a sermon, said a few words over the grave of one of the settlers who had been buried by the family, and then passed on to another settlement. But within a few years little churches were being built in the wilderness.

To care for the spiritual needs of the settlers living in the Detroit area, the first continuing Protestant organization built a little log church, in the spring of 1818, on the banks of the Rouge River just west of where the Ford Rouge Plant stands in Dearborn. At that time there were just ten people who were members of this little congregation. This was the beginning of the First Methodist church in Detroit and Dearborn.

During the years from 1820 to 1830 other little log churches began to appear in the Michigan wilderness. These early log buildings were later replaced by buildings made of lumber. To these little churches the early settlers went on Sunday mornings. Those who lived close by often walked to church. Others who lived farther away came in buggies, or wagons, that were drawn by horses or even by oxen. At first the horses were tied to trees near the church while the church service was being held. Later, back of most churches there was a long wooden shed where horses could be sheltered from storms, or sun, as they waited during the time of the service.

The church played an important part in the settlers' lives. The weekly church meetings not only cared for their spiritual needs, but also gave them a chance to meet their neighbors and friends. At the church they met and visited with their neighbors and often invited them home for Sunday dinner. Picnics, too, were common on Sunday afternoons after church when the weather was warm. Huge tables, spread with all the best cooking of the women for miles around, drew young and old.

A Presbyterian church was started at Monroe in 1820, at Pontiac in 1824, at Farmington in 1825, and at Ann Arbor in 1826. A Mormon church, more correctly called a church of the Latter-day Saints, was started in Pontiac in 1834. Many of the settlers were Methodists, and soon several Methodist churches could be found in southern Michigan. In 1855 people of the Seventh-day Adventist faith began settling in the area near Battle Creek. Lutherans who came from Germany and the Scandinavian countries started Lutheran churches in their communities. A few Quakers came to Michigan from Pennsylvania. About the time Michigan was settled, there was a religious awakening in America. The rapid spread of churches across the southern part of the state was a part of this general movement that spread

Marker erected at Dearborn in 1954 on the site of the oldest continuing Protestant church in Michigan.

across America in the years before the Civil War.

As the population of Michigan grew larger, there began to be a need for banks. In 1819 the first bank in Michigan was started. It was known as the Bank of Michigan and was located in Detroit. Two more banks were started in 1827. One of these banks was the Farmer and Mechanics Bank of Detroit. The other new one was the Bank of Monroe. In 1834, banks in Michigan were allowed to set up branch banks. Branch banks appeared in that same year at Kalamazoo and St. Joseph. During the next three years these banks were kept very busy because of the land speculation which was going on at that time. A new law, passed in 1837, made it easier to establish banks. Many new banks quickly sprang up. Most of these new banks had little capital and some of them were in places that were hard for the bank examiners to find or to visit even after they once found out where they were located. These banks are usually written about in your history as "wildcat banks." Many of them had little cash. Some of them had only land as security, and sometimes the land was just swamp. When the Panic of 1837 came, several of these early banks failed and many of Michigan's early settlers lost all their money. This panic and the failure of these banks hurt the early economic advancement of Michigan. Later better banking laws were passed and safer banks were started.

As early as 1817 there was a feeling among many of the people then living in Michigan that the state should have a university. In that year the governor and the judges of the territory passed an act founding a university. It was called the University of Michigamia. There were to be thirteen professorships in the new university. This means that thirteen men were to be appointed as heads of the thirteen departments. When the excitement died away and the search for these thirteen men began, they were not to be found in the territory. Rev. John Monteith, the Presbyterian minister at Detroit, was made president of the new university and given seven professorships. The remaining six, as well as the vice-presidency, were given to Father Gabriel Richard. Thus Michigan's first university began in Detroit on what is now Bates Street, between Larned and Congress. This little university was not very successful. The main reason for its failure was that there were few qualified students to enter it at that time. What Michigan needed was a system of public schools that would prepare students to enter a university. Such a system was started a little later because the settlers felt strongly the need for their children to have a chance to get an education.

The Ordinance of 1787 had stated that "religion, morality, and knowledge being necessary to good government and the happiness of mankind, schools and the means of education shall forever be encouraged." But such high phrases did not pay the bills for educating the settlers' children. The settlers were busy clearing land and trying to raise enough crops to feed their families. What is more, children were needed around the farm to do what work they could. Although many of the settlers realized the need for schools, they did not feel that they could afford the expense such schools would require.

As early as March 26, 1804, the Congress of the United States had started a long-time plan to aid education in the United States. According to the act passed on that date, section sixteen of every congressional township was to be set aside as the school section and the funds received from the sale of the school sections were to be used for education. During the years before Michigan became a state, this money was often spent by local school districts to pay teachers. Some districts received more money than did others because of this grant.

Some section sixteens were good land and were sold at a good price, but other section sixteens were poor, or even swamp land, and therefore brought in little or no money. Because of this, all districts did not share alike in the amount of money each received from the sale of these public lands.

In 1827, Michigan territory passed a law that made each township responsible for the schools in its area. Most townships, however, had little money to spend on education, and most of them sent out what were known as rate bills to parents who had children in school. Besides these early schools there were some private schools and academies. The first fully organized school district in Michigan seems to have been started near the present village of Maybee, on the Raisin River in 1828.

In 1829 further funds were raised for education by placing a tax on property belonging to people who did not live on it. A law of that same year divided the townships into smaller primary school districts that were nearer to the homes of the children going to school. As yet Michigan had no organized school system.

When the settlers began to come into Michigan in greater numbers, there developed a demand for newspapers. The first newspaper ever printed in Michigan was published at Detroit by Father Gabriel Richard and was known as the *Michigan Essay* or *Impartial Observer.* It was a four-page paper that was printed once a week. Most of it was printed in English, but usually a page or so was printed in French so that the French-speaking people in Detroit could read the news.

The *Detroit Gazette* was started in Detroit in 1817. At first, part of this paper was also printed in French, but this practice was soon discontinued. This little weekly, that now gives us much information about early Detroit, came to an end in 1830.

Another paper, the *Michigan Sentinel,* was started at Monroe in 1825. In 1829 the *Northwestern Journal* appeared at Detroit and the *Western Immigrant* began publication at Ann Arbor. In 1830 the *Detroit Courier* appeared in Detroit and the *Oakland Chronicle* in Pontiac. In 1831 there appeared at Detroit the *Democratic Free Press* and *Michigan Intelligencer.* This paper, known today as the *Detroit Free Press,* is Michigan's oldest newspaper that is still being printed. In 1833 another paper appeared at White Pigeon. This paper was moved to Kalamazoo in 1837, and the name was then changed to the *Kalamazoo Gazette.* In 1840 still another paper, the *Monroe Advocate,* was started. This paper is also still published and is known today as the *Monroe News.*

These early newspapers, though small and often very political, were the first of many to be published later throughout Michigan.

Replica of the little mission built on Old Mission Peninsula in 1839. The bell is the original mission bell. Photo 1956.

During their first years they usually were printed only weekly, but after 1840 some of them began to be printed as daily papers. As there were no means of rapid communication then as there are today, most of the news was of a local nature. Any outside news that was printed was usually several days old before it appeared in any of the local papers. As settlers pushed farther and farther across the state, many other papers were started. For many years these newspapers did much to mold the way people thought about public issues.

Soon after the abandonment of Fort Shelby, in 1827, plans were made for the building of an arsenal near Detroit. This need for a handy supply of guns and powder was shown in the fear that swept across southern Michigan at the time of the Black Hawk War. The site chosen for the new Detroit Arsenal was about ten miles west of Detroit at Dearbornville. This arsenal consisted of eleven buildings located along the outer edge of a square some four city blocks in size. A wall twelve feet high and three feet thick ran around the entire square. Two other buildings, the powder magazine and the hospital, were located outside the wall. All the brick used in building the Detroit Arsenal were handmade brick from the area. The timbers were hand-hewn or hand-sawed. Two of these buildings are still standing and are now used as historical museums in Dearborn. These buildings, with their pegged beams, wrought ironwork, and original fireplaces, are good examples of pioneer skill and industry.

When Governor Lewis Cass was appointed Secretary of War in Andrew Jackson's cabinet in 1831, General John T. Mason, then Secretary of Michigan Territory, became the new governor. The office passed to his son, Stevens T. Mason, that same year. As Stevens T. Mason was not yet twenty-one years of age, he is usually called the "boy governor." It was under Mason's leadership that Michigan became a state.

The population of Michigan had grown rapidly during the twenty years from 1815 to 1835. In 1835 the people of Michigan Territory made ready for the admission of Michigan into the Union as a state. On April 4, 1835, delegates were chosen by the voters of Michigan Territory to draw up a constitution for the new state that was to be presented to Congress along with a request that Michigan be admitted as a state. The delegates to the Constitutional Convention met at Detroit on the second Monday in May. A constitution for the state was then drawn up and later submitted to the people for their approval. On the first Monday in October, 1835, the people of the state accepted the new constitution and at the same time elected their first state officers. Stevens T. Mason was chosen as the first governor. In November, 1835, the newly elected legislature met and chose two senators to represent Michigan in the Congress of the United States. Thus, Michigan made ready to be admitted as a state into the United States. Michigan, however, was not to be admitted as a state for two more years.

As Michigan began making plans for admission into the Union, a dispute arose between the state of Ohio and Michigan Territory over the location of the boundary line between the two. When Ohio had become a state, in 1803, the northern boundary of Ohio had not been definitely fixed. Now both the state of Ohio and Michigan Territory claimed the twenty-mile strip of land that lies just south of Michigan's present southern boundary.

Michigan claimed, under the Ordinance of 1787, all the land north of a line drawn east from the southernmost bend of Lake Michigan to near where Port Clinton, Ohio, is now located. This strip of land included some good farm land and also the growing city of Toledo, Ohio. What is more, Ohio had built a canal from Toledo to Cincinnati by going up the Maumee River and then down the Miami River. If the territory around Toledo should go to the new state of Michigan, it would mean that the northern end of the canal would run through Michigan territory for a few miles near Toledo. The people of Ohio, therefore, felt that Michigan might hinder commerce over the new Ohio Canal. Michigan's claims to this land aroused the people of Ohio, and in 1835 Governor Lucas of that state laid claim to the strip, and the Ohio state legislature then organized it into the county of Lucas.

Governor Mason of Michigan Territory was also active and sent the Territorial militia to Toledo to keep Ohio from seizing the strip of land. Although a few shots were fired, no one was harmed. The battle over the Ohio strip was mostly one of words.

Because there would soon be a presidential election, a compromise favorable to Ohio was proposed to Michigan. This was done so that Ohio's electoral votes would not be lost in the coming election. According to the compromise, the southern boundary of Michigan was to be drawn where it is at present. In return for the loss of this strip of land, Michigan was to be given the western part of the Upper Peninsula. Many people then living in Michigan thought of the Upper Peninsula as a land of swamps. What did Michigan want with the Upper Peninsula? What good was it, anyhow? Nevertheless, a convention held at Ann Arbor in December, 1836, voted to accept the terms of the compromise. This convention was called the "frostbitten" convention. Congress accepted its work, and on January 26, 1837, Michigan became the twenty-sixth state to enter the Union.

Detroit was to be the capital of the new state. The state capitol building was then located in Capital Park, which is now but a little, busy, bus-loading station in downtown Detroit. This location, however, was to be only a temporary one, for the new state constitution stated that the state legislature should give the state capitol a permanent location by the year 1847.

At that time there were two well-educated men who lived in Marshall. As early as 1834 they saw the need for better education for Michigan's children. On many summer afternoons these two men, Rev. John Davis Pierce and Isaac Edwin Crary, discussed the future of education in Michigan as they sat in the shade of an old oak tree that has since become known as the "educational oak"

When Michigan became a state, the new state constitution accepted public education as a state duty. The general plan of state education suggested by Crary and Pierce was adopted. The state legislature was to provide a school system that would be open to all children for at least three months each year. The cost of paying for these public schools, however, was still to be paid by the local school districts. The state at the same time changed the method of collecting and spending the money derived from the sale of public land in the school sections. Now all the money received from the sale of such land was to be kept by the state. The money thus secured was to be known as the Primary School Fund. This money was spent by the state for other purposes. The state was to pay interest to the school districts each year on the money the state had borrowed.

Each year since that time, up to 1964, the state paid interest to the school districts on the Primary School Fund Money that it then borrowed. The state did not pay back any of the Primary money. The annual interest paid by the state to the school districts was known as the Primary Interest Fund. To this amount was added other moneys such as taxes on railroad companies, telegraph and telephone companies, interest on money that escheated back to the state from unclaimed estates, and part of the money received by the state from inheritance taxes. This Primary Interest Fund money was divided among the school districts in proportion to number of children enrolled in each school district. In 1964, the state legislature abolished the Primary School Fund and the Primary Interest Fund. Utility taxes and other taxes that were formerly placed in the Primary Interest Fund are now deposited in the state's General Fund from which the school aid money is drawn.

When Michigan became a state, the new state constitution provided for a State Superintendent of Public Instruction whose duty would be to develop a public school system for Michigan. In 1838 Governor Stevens T. Mason appointed John D. Pierce, of Marshall, to this new state office. Under the leadership of John D. Pierce the beginnings of our public school system were started. Under the plan of public education which Mr. Pierce set up, a system of state schools was to be organized whereby a child could progress upward through the primary grades, the grammar school, the high school, and then enter the state university at Ann Arbor. However, it was several years before this plan was actually put into practice in the entire state.

When we think of schools in Michigan as they were before the Civil War, we should not think of them as large brick buildings such as they are in the state today. Schools in those days were usually little log cabins. Often they had just one room about eighteen feet by twenty feet in size. Some of them were better than others, but at best they were far from modern standards. These little log schoolhouses usually were built on one of the four corners where two roads crossed. Thus children could walk to them from any one of four directions. At other times the little schoolhouse sat proudly beside the road on the brow of a hill.

At first, these one-room buildings often had no windows. Sometimes, as in homes, scraped deerskin was used to let in some light.

Later glass windows were used. At best, these little log schools were small, dark, and often cold and drafty in the wintertime. Chinking between the logs kept out some of the cold and snow in the winter and some of the flies and bugs in the summer. The schoolhouse door and the floor were usually made of rough planks. Later some schools were lined on the inside with boards. In the first schoolhouses small fireplaces gave out the only heat. Later, when stoves were made, a large heavy iron stove usually sat in the center of every rural school-house. Although twenty to thirty children often met in these little schoolhouses, there was plenty of fresh air for all, as usually there was plenty of it blowing in through the cracks between the logs. Screens were unknown, so flies and mosquitoes often made life miserable for everyone.

In these schools there were no desks or other school furniture such as we are familiar with today. Long planks that served as one long desk were sometimes pegged into two sides of the room. In front of these long desks the students usually sat, facing the wall, on a long bench that ran the entire length of the room on each side. No one then ever thought of playgrounds. Children got plenty of activity walking to and from school and doing the chores around the farms each night and morning. Though they had no special play-grounds, the children did have fun in the fields and woods that stood near their little schoolhouses. The teacher and some of the older children did the work done by janitors today. Either the teacher or one of the older boys came early on winter mornings and built a fire so that the schoolroom would be warm when the little ones arrived. Wood for the fire was often furnished by one of the parents as all or part of the cost of teaching his children.

Teachers were often not well prepared, and received only a small amount of pay. Men got as much as fifteen dollars a month, but women often were paid not more than five dollars a month. Both men and women were expected to be able to thrash any of their students should such treatment be needed. Sometimes the students were older and larger than the young ladies who taught them. Teachers usually boarded around at the homes of the children. They would spend a few days at the home of one child and then move on to live for days at the home of another.

To these schools the pioneers' children went when possible, but during the winter there was deep snow, in the spring there was plant-ing to do, during the summer the crops had to be cared for, and in the fall came the work of the harvest. Thus there was often little time left for school. The winter months were not so busy and then the children were sometimes sent to school. However, there was no law which made them go. Because the settlers were usually scattered, small children often had to walk long distances from their homes to the little log schoolhouses. This was hard for them when the snow was deep and the weather cold.

As theirs was not a complex society such as ours is today, the children were taught only such subjects as reading, writing, arithmetic, and spelling. Sometimes geography and grammar were also taught. Because there were few, if any, books, lessons were sometimes learned orally. All the children repeated the lessons at once. For this reason these early schools are sometimes called "blab schools." Long hours were spent in teaching the alphabet. Spelling was a favorite subject. Most of it, because of the lack of materials, was oral spelling. Spell-downs were a part of everyday school life. In fact, so popular were spelling bees that our pioneer forefathers often held them at picnics, especially on the 4th of July, and at evening parties, just for the fun they gave to people.

Paper was often too expensive for school children to use, but most scholars had a slate on which they wrote and figured. Pencils and steel pens were unheard of at that time. For writing on slates, school children used slate pencils. If paper was used, people of that time wrote on it with a quill pen and homemade ink. One of the tasks of the teacher was to sharpen the quill pens of the students. Penmanship was stressed, and children spent long hours learning to make the letters like they were in the copybook. To own a textbook, or reader, was to possess a rare prize. There were few books then, but the few that did exist were read and reread again and again and then passed on to younger children. In those days students measured their progress by the reader they were using. When a student had mastered one reader he passed on to the next harder reader.

There were few colleges in Michigan before the Civil War. Many of the early colleges such as St. Philip's College, at Detroit; Marshall College, at Marshall; and St. Mark's College, at Grand Rapids, did not last long. In 1829, Kalamazoo College was started by the Baptists at Kalamazoo. This college was granted a charter by the state in 1831, and is, therefore, the oldest continuing college in Michigan.

Albion College is a Methodist college that was founded in 1836. It was started so that men could be educated as ministers for the

Methodist Church. At first classes were held in the local Methodist church, but in 1844 the college moved into the first of its new buildings. According to its early history this college accepted "gentlemen, Indians, ladies." At first there was a school for men and a school for women. These two colleges were combined in 1861.

The following year, 1837, when Michigan became a state, the present University of Michigan was started by the new state government. This university was to be the successor of the earlier university that had been started in Detroit in 1817. The site of the new university was to be at Ann Arbor rather than Detroit. Because it was hard, in those days, for the students to reach Ann Arbor and as there were

Indian Agency, Sault Ste. Marie, Michigan. Photo 1963.

still no high schools, the university established preparatory schools in Detroit, Kalamazoo, Monroe, Niles, Pontiac, Tecumseh, and White Pigeon. In these preparatory schools young people were prepared to enter the university. At that time there was only the College of Literature, Science and Arts. The first class consisted of six students. There were two professors on the faculty. By 1844 the teaching staff had been increased to three professors and three assistants, while the number of students had increased to fifty-three. About 1850 many of the old classical college subjects, that had been taught in universities up to that time, were dropped and the student body soon became larger. In 1850 the university started a Medical School. The Law School was started in 1859. By 1860 there were five hundred nineteen students enrolled at the university. Since that time the University of Michigan has grown to be one of the largest and best known in the country. However, at the time the university was founded, there was much discussion as to whether higher education should be controlled by the churches or by the state. Some people at that time favored the university, while others gave their support to the church colleges which were then being built.

The charter for Adrian College was granted in 1839. At first the college was located at Marshall, but from there it was moved to Lenoi, in 1845, and was then known as the Lenoi Theological Institute. In 1859 it was moved to Adrian. This time it was chartered as Adrian College. This early college, also supported by the Methodists, became coeducational in 1861.

The public schools of Detroit were made into a separate school district in 1842, and the city was allowed to lay a tax of not more than one dollar a child for the support of the city schools. By 1842 over one-third of the school districts still had no school at all. There was not yet any law saying that children must go to school. However, the district was to receive no money from the state if it did not keep school for at least three months. The main question facing the schools of the time was who should pay for the cost of education. As yet people had not accepted the idea that education is a public duty and that the public in general, rather than only the parents of children going to school, should pay for the schools.

In 1843, were started what we today call graded schools. Children were to pass upward by grades rather than by readers. From the primary grades they were to pass to the middle school. This took them through what is now our eighth grade. That is as far as tax-supported schools went in those days. This left a four-year gap between the eighth grade and college. Private schools filled this gap if one wished to go on to college. When the University of Michigan was first formed, it found it necessary to start a few high schools as feeder schools to supply the University with students. The University soon found this too expensive, and the feeder schools were dropped one by one.

In 1844, Michigan Central College was started by the Baptists at Spring Arbor, in Jackson County. This college was the first coeducational college in Michigan. In 1853 the college was moved to Hillsdale and the name was changed to Hillsdale College. In 1844 the Congregationalists started a college at Olivet called the Olivet Institute. In 1859 the name of this college was changed to Olivet College.

St. Mary's Academy was founded at Monroe in 1845. This college was the first to be founded in Michigan to provide for the higher education of women. This college later became St. Mary's College. In 1927 the college was moved to the corner of McNichols Road and Wyoming in Detroit and was renamed Marygrove College. Marygrove College is a girls' college and is taught by a group of Catholic sisters.

Unfortunately for the plans of Michigan's early state-supported schools, they did not progress as well as some people had hoped they would. The same year that Michigan became a state, the Panic of 1837 upset the economic life of the people. Banks failed, farmers could not sell their crops and thus they could not pay for their farms, prices fell, and land went down in value. It was hard for the settlers to provide for their families, and there was little or no money left during the panic years for schools. But in 1845 the state took another step in bringing better education to Michigan's children. In that year the state placed a tax of one mill on each dollar's worth of property evaluation. This money was to be used to support public education. The law further stated that schools, if they were to get their primary money, were now to remain open five months a year instead of three.

As the time drew near for choosing a permanent location for the state capital, a struggle developed between several cities and villages. The people of Detroit wanted the capital to remain in their city. Others, outstate, however, objected to this. They said that Detroit was too near Canada and English power. It would be too easy to disturb the officers and records in case of another war with Canada. Then, too, Detroit was too far from the center of the state. They reasoned that the state capital should be nearer the center of the state so that it could be more easily reached by all the people of the state.

Nearly all the cities of any size tried to influence the state legislature to locate the capital in their locality: Ann Arbor, Albion, Battle Creek, Charlotte, Dexter, Eaton Rapids, Flint, Marshall, Owosso, and other places tried to get the capital located there. All of these places received some votes but not enough to bring the capital to them.

At last section sixteen, the school section, in the township of Lansing, in Ingham County, was selected as the location for the new state capital. In the fall of 1847 men began clearing away the forest for the building of a new city which was to be called Michigan. Enough land had been cleared to permit the building of the new capitol building by December of that year. This first capitol building was made of wood. In 1854 this first wooden building was replaced by a new one made of brick. The name Michigan, however, did not last long, for the legislature changed it back to Lansing the following year. Although Lansing is perhaps well located now for the state capital, it nevertheless was difficult to reach at that time. There were no railroads, and its only link with the rest of the state was by means of poor, muddy, swampy roads.

The first state constitution that had been adopted in 1835 was not long-lived, for in 1849 the people voted in favor of a new convention to draw up another constitution for the state. The delegates to this convention met at Lansing on the first Monday in June, 1850, and drew up a new constitution which was adopted by the voters in November of that year. Many democratic advances were made in this new constitution, but one amendment—to give Negroes then living in Michigan the right to vote—was defeated by a vote of almost three to one.

The year Michigan became a state, the people living in Canada, across the Detroit River, had a political uprising known as the "Patriot War" or rebellion. There was some unrest along the border, and there were a few clashes between Americans and Canadians. Because of this feeling between the two countries, people felt that Detroit should

The Johnson House, Sault Ste. Marie. Photo August 1963.

again be fortified against any attack that might come from Canada. The Detroit Arsenal at Dearbornville was not a fortification. It was only a place for repairing and storing arms and other military supplies. Thus, in 1840, plans were made by the United States government to build fourteen forts along the Canadian border. One of these forts was to be built at Detroit. The following year the Congress of the United States provided the needed money, and a new fort was started in 1843. The site chosen for the new fort was in Springwells township, on the southward bend of the Detroit River about three miles west of Detroit. This new fort at Detroit was completed in 1849 and named Fort Wayne after General Wayne. No troops, however, were stationed there until 1861. Fort Wayne, though a good fort for its time, was never really armed or used as a fort. During the Civil War, troops going south to join the Union Army used it as a meeting and drilling place. It was also used as an induction center during World War II and is still used for that purpose. In 1949, just one hundred years after it was completed, part of Fort Wayne was turned over to the city of Detroit for use as a historical museum.

In order to prepare teachers for Michigan's new growing educational system a college for training teachers was founded at Ypsilanti in 1849. This college, known for years as Ypsilanti Normal College, is the oldest of Michigan's teacher training institutions. At the time it was founded it was the first normal school west of Albany, New York. For over one hundred years students have been prepared by this college to teach in Michigan's public schools. Today it is known as Eastern Michigan University.

As a further aid to public education the Congress of the United States granted 5,838,775 acres of land to the State of Michigan in the year 1850. The money received from the sale of this land was added to the Primary Fund. Interest at the rate of five per cent on this money was to be paid by the state each year. This money was added to the Primary Interest Fund. Another step toward better education for all was taken, in 1854, when a school for the blind and deaf was started in Flint. Later, in 1880, the students of this school were divided, and a new school for the blind was started at Lansing.

The Dutch people who settled at Holland were eager to have their children have the benefits of a college education. In 1851 they began the "Pioneer School." In 1866 this school became Hope College. This college is partially supported by the Dutch Reformed Church. Hope College is one of the largest of the denominational colleges in the state.

The first teacher's association in Michigan was formed in 1852 and met that same year at Ypsilanti. This association of teachers was known as the Michigan State Teachers Association. Since that time the name has been changed to the Michigan Education Association. This new association made a strong effort, in 1858, to have the rate bills abolished and the schools put on a better financial footing. In 1859 at least two-thirds of the public school districts were still charging parents tuition for their children. Yet progress was being made toward public support of education, and in that year the state legislature passed a law allowing school districts to tax for the support of high schools as well as grammar schools. Finally rate bills were done away with by an act of the state legislature in 1869. People were gradually coming to believe that education is a state responsibility and that state and local taxes should pay for public education. In that same year the legislature also made a law saying that in school districts where there were more than eight hundred children, school would have to remain open nine months of the year. In districts of thirty to eight hundred children, school must be kept open for five months. In all other districts of thirty or less children, there must be at least three months of school.

The early settlers of Michigan realized the need for training in agriculture. In 1855 the state legislature established a State Agricultural College. This same legislature also provided $40,000 and set aside twenty-two sections of land for the building of the new agricultural college. This new agricultural college, one of the first of its kind in the nation, opened in 1857 in what is now the city of East Lansing. At that time the new brick buildings of the college were surrounded by stumps and forest. To reach the college, students had to travel over muddy roads and across long stretches of marsh land.

By the time settlers began coming to Michigan, the North and the South were already becoming divided over the question of slavery. As many of Michigan's early settlers were from New England and New York, they brought to Michigan the anti-slavery feelings of the North. Some settlers in the old Northwest were Quakers, and this group especially was against slavery. Before many years had passed, several people developed an organization, known as the underground railroad, so that they could help slaves reach the northern states where they could have their freedom. Many escaping slaves were even taken to Canada, where they no longer needed to fear the men from the South that came into the northern states looking for runaway slaves.

Once an escaping slave reached one of the stations on the underground railway, he received much help on his journey to the North. Stations were usually people's homes where the runaway slaves were hidden until they could be passed along to the next station. Negroes were hidden in the woods, in barns, under hay, in attics, and in cellars during the daytime. When night came, farmers or townsmen hitched up their horses, hid the negro, or negroes, under straw, blankets, or bales of hay, and drove him to the next station on his way north. Sometimes the white friend and the negro merely walked north along back fence rows or through a woods to the next station. From this station his new friend passed the escaping slave along to still another. At last the escaping negro crossed into Michigan or even into Canada. As the years passed, regular routes, called lines, developed on the underground railroad. Slaves were passed along from the Ohio River through Ohio, Indiana, and Illinois to Michigan or western New York State. Battle Creek became a central station for the lines coming north from Indiana and Illinois. From Battle Creek, slaves were passed along to Detroit or to Port Huron, and from there they often were taken to Canada. Many of the present villages and cities in southern Michigan were once stations on the underground railroad.

Several times trouble arose between men from the South, who were looking for slaves, and the people living in Michigan. One of the best known of these cases took place at Marshall, Michigan, in 1847. An escaped negro family by the name of Crosswhite was living at Marshall at that time. There were six in the family, Mr. and Mrs. Crosswhite and their four children. There were also other free negroes and escaped slaves living in Marshall. Mr. Crosswhite feared that men from the South might come at any time and try to take his family back into slavery. It was agreed between Mr. Crosswhite and his neighbors that should Southerners come to take him and his family back into slavery, Mr. Crosswhite was to fire a gun as a signal to his friends. When men from Kentucky did come to his house, Mr. Crosswhite gave the signal that they had agreed upon. Soon a group of friendly people, both black and white, gathered around the Crosswhite home. The Kentuckians were arrested by the sheriff for breaking into Mr. Crosswhite's house. Meanwhile the Crosswhite family was quickly taken to Canada. The case entered the courts, and after many months the court ruled that the people of Marshall were to pay for the escape of Mr. Crosswhite and his family. This case aroused much attention at that time and helped to raise the public feeling that resulted in the passing of Henry Clay's Fugitive Slave Law in 1850, by the Congress of the United States.

In the years immediately following the Crosswhite case, the anti-slavery feeling grew in the Michigan area and in the adjoining states. While the Congress of the United States compromised with slavery and the courts of the nation upheld the property rights of the southern slave owners, there grew up a feeling in the area around Michigan that there could be no more compromise with slavery. Old political party lines broke down as more and more people came to feel strongly against slavery and its further extension into more of the new territories of the West. A meeting of anti-slavery people was held at Ripon, Wisconsin, in February, 1854. This meeting was followed by another at Jackson, Michigan, on July 6, 1854. Many leading men in Michigan business and politics were at this meeting in Jackson. They were in favor of federal aid for internal improvements and at that time wanted the federal government to dredge the mouth of the St. Clair River so that larger boats could be used on the Great Lakes.

So large was the crowd of people which gathered there on that date that their meeting had to be held out in a park at the edge of Jackson. There, "under the oaks," men pledged themselves to drop their old political parties and join the new Republican party that would devote itself to the stopping of the further extension of slavery in the United States, and spend federal funds for internal improvements. Many farmers in Michigan and the other nearby states soon joined the new Republican party. Protestant ministers also lent their support to the new moral crusade. Abraham Lincoln once came to Michigan and addressed a meeting of this new party at Kalamazoo on August 27, 1856. Because of the rising feeling against slavery in the North, the Republican party grew rapidly. The movement was also strengthened because of the Dred Scott decision handed down by the Supreme Court of the United States in 1857.

When President Lincoln issued his call for troops for the Civil War, many men from Michigan joined the Union Army. The state legislature met and voted $1,000,000 for raising and equipping an army. They also voted $15 a month for the support of families who were left dependent because of husbands or fathers going to war. From the farms, the colleges, and the high schools men came to join the units preparing to leave for the fighting front. Units were formed at several places in the state, such as Grand Rapids, Kalamazoo, and Detroit. Some of these men trained at Fort Wayne near Detroit, while others trained at other places in the state. Michigan men took part in almost every major campaign of the Civil War. It was the 4th Michigan Cavalry that captured Jefferson Davis at the end of the war.

During the Civil War, President Lincoln signed what is known as the Land Grant College Act. Under this act a state legislature in any state having an agricultural and mechanical college could accept a land grant from the United States for the support of such a college. To any state applying, thirty thousand acres of land were to be given for each senator and representative it then had in Congress. Under this Morrill Act of 1864, Michigan State College added engineering to its program, in 1865, and thus received 24,000 acres of government-owned land for its support. Because this act was passed during the war years, military training was offered all male students attending colleges that accepted government land under the act. That is why military training has been offered to all male students attending Michigan State University.

Another bill of this same year, 1862, was the Homestead Act. This law, passed by Congress, gave a quarter section of public land, 160 acres, free to any man twenty-one years or older who was a citizen of the United States or to any alien if he had taken out his first papers. All one had to do to receive title to the land was to live on it for five years and show that he was improving the property. Many acres of land in northern Michigan were homesteaded by farmers who claimed land under the Homestead Act.

After the Civil War the population of Michigan grew rapidly. In fact, between 1860 and 1880 Michigan doubled her population. Many new railroads were built. Many foreign immigrants came to Michigan and found work in the woods, mines, and new industries. Better homes in both the country and city were being built. Horse-drawn streetcars were appearing on the city streets. Eighteen sixty-eight saw the beginning of what later became the Detroit College of Medicine and Surgery.

In 1871, Michigan passed her first compulsory school attendance law. This law required that all children between the ages of eight and fourteen must attend school at least three months each year. In 1873, the time was increased to four months. Slowly people were accepting the idea of tax-supported public schools. There were still some, however, who felt that people who did not have children should not be taxed to help pay for the education of other people's children. In 1872 there appeared in the Michigan courts the now famous "Kalamazoo Case." Action was brought against tax-collecting officers to stop them from collecting the state tax for the support of high schools. The case was taken to the State Supreme Court, and that court upheld the tax. This was a great victory for public-supported education and in the twenty years that followed high schools and high-school attendance both grew rapidly in numbers.

Michigan's third capitol building, the present state capitol building in Lansing, was begun in 1873. Unfortunately for Michigan planners, their plans were again upset by another depression. The Depression of 1873 caused many of Michigan's banks to fail. The market for lumber dropped, and hundreds of woods and mill workers were unable to work. Railroad building was slowed down. Many of the iron furnaces and mines shut down or worked only a few days a week. But work continued on the new capitol building. The new state capitol building, made of Ohio sandstone, was finished in 1879. This building is the present capitol building in Lansing.

CHAPTER ELEVEN

The Early Development of Water Transportation on the Great Lakes

SAILBOATS appeared on Lake Ontario soon after the French settled in the St. Lawrence valley but none reached the Upper Lakes until LaSalle built the "Griffin." Only a few sailboats were built during the French period, and only the "Griffin" was used on the Upper Lakes.

When the English took over the region, they built two small sailboats at Niagara on Lake Erie. The boats were called the "Huron" and the "Michigan." The "Michigan" seems to have also carried the name of Beaver. These two boats did much to aid the English at Detroit during the siege by Pontiac because they were able to go to Niagara for supplies. Between 1764 and 1796, while England controlled the lakes, some twenty-four more sailboats were built. Some were built at Niagara, some were built at Detroit, others were built at Michilimackinac and in Saginaw Bay. About this time sailboats also began to appear on Lake Superior. The building of sailing vessels on the Great Lakes was prohibited unless they belonged to the king or were sailed by naval officers. Thus, the English tried to limit the trade in furs and discourage illegal trade and settlement.

In 1796, the first American boat appeared on Lake Erie. It was a war vessel named the "Detroit." The following year it was wrecked near Erie, Pennsylvania. Between 1800 and 1805, more schooners and sloops were built.

The early settlement of Michigan is closely tied to the opening of the Erie Canal and the development of shipping on the Great Lakes. Up to the War of 1812 there were only a few boats on the Great Lakes. During that war, the Americans hastily built a few small boats with unseasoned lumber. With these, Perry won his victory over the English on Lake Erie. These were the last of the fighting craft to appear on the Great Lakes, for in the Treaty of Ghent, signed in 1815 at the close of the War of 1812, and in the Rush-Bagot agreement, signed two years later, both England and the United States agreed not to build fighting boats on the Great Lakes. What is more, they agreed that the long border stretching west between the two countries of Canada and the United States should never be fortified. For that reason the story of lake shipping after the War of 1812 is the story of freight and passenger boats.

The push of settlers into the area after the War of 1812 caused an increase in shipping on Lake Erie. By 1820 there were some thirty small sailing boats, averaging in weight about thirty tons, sailing on Lake Erie. Both sailboats and the newly developed steamboats competed for the growing commerce of the lake trade.

Abundant supplies of white oak and pine made boat-building Michigan's first major industry. The increasing carrying trade demanded more and more sailboats. Because they were of a very small size,

An early steamboat

shipyards for building them were not necessary. Later, the building of larger steamers required shipyards, and such yards were built at Marine City, Detroit, and at other ports on the lower lakes where materials and skilled workmen were available.

In the early sailboat days, however, lake captains often built and sailed their own boats. Some of these lake captains like Samuel Ward and E. B. Ward soon owned several boats and became wealthy from the early carrying trade. The Wards began their boat-building at Marine City, on the St. Clair River, where white oak lumber could be cut for the holds of the boats and pine for masts could be brought down from the area near what is now Port Huron.

Others wishing to build sailboats chose a good launching place along the Detroit, St. Clair, or Saginaw River and then began the building of a vessel. Ship carpenters and their helpers sawed out by hand the timbers and planks to be used in building the sailboat. Sometimes beams, or square timbers, were hewed by using a broad ax. Making lumber in this manner was cheaper than buying it from the little sawmills. This hand-sawed, or hewed lumber, was then left to cure in the open air. Large braces, called "knees," were cut out with axes and allowed to dry with the lumber. Other pieces of oak, called "ribs," were also carefully cut and dried. When the oak had properly seasoned, the little sailboat was then built.

To a large oak beam, call the "keel," the ribs were fastened. Onto the ribs the oak planking was fastened to form the sides of the vessel. Then the masts were put in place and the deck built. No nails were used. All the pieces were held together by making joints and fastening them together with wooden pins driven into holes which had been bored with an auger.

Courtesy Ralph Price

Schooners in Round Lake, Charlevoix, drying sails after a rain

Native white oak was the cheapest and best material for boat construction, and was used until about 1870 when the supply of oak trees became scarce and lumber more expensive. Oak was replaced first by iron. When steel became abundant, it replaced iron for boat construction.

The War of 1812 had shown the superior maneuverability of the schooner, and although many other craft were still sailing the lakes, by 1846, over eighty per cent of the sailing vessels on the lakes were schooners.

Wouldn't you like to have gone sailing on one of these early sailboats? Overhead was a clear, blue sky, while beneath was the cold, blue, sparkling water. Against your cheek would come the wind that filled the white billowing sails above your head. In the hold of the boat you would have carried furs, grain, lumber, or perhaps passengers. The Great Lakes, with their spreading waters, appealed to the youth of that day, and many boys and men took up the life of a sailor on the inland waterways.

Sailing had its bitter side as well as its pleasant one. At times severe storms suddenly swept across the lakes. Then the wind whistled through the sailboat's rigging. The waves grew high. Then the sailors reefed their sails and rode before the storm, hoping that their staunch craft would ride out the fury of the gale. Many times their boats were broken by the storms or driven upon the rocks along the shore, and then crew and boats were lost. The stories of the lakes tell of deeds just as heroic as those that happen on the high seas.

Sailing on the Great Lakes in those days was much different from today. There were few harbors where boats could take refuge when a storm struck. After 1831, the Federal Government began to improve shipping conditions on the Great Lakes. A few lighthouses, with lights that burned whale oil, were built at dangerous points along the water's edge. Harbors and channels were deepened in a few places. But there were no buoys or beacon lights to warn sailors of the sand bars and shoals or to guide them through the narrow channels that connected the lakes. Most of the entire coast line of the lakes was still a wilderness where the forests crept down to the water's edge. There were no lifesaving stations. In fact, there was often no one upon the shore, and sailors had to depend upon their own resources. Failure meant shipwreck and often death.

Fur trading companies built small schooners to carry the furs across Lake Superior. The "Discovery," "Recovery," "Invincible," "Mink," and "Otter" had all ended their days of sailing on Lake Superior by 1830. Four had gone to the bottom of Lake Superior. The "Recovery" had been sent through the rapids of the St. Mary's River and was by that date sailing in the carrying trade on Lake Erie.

In 1835, boats larger than canoes again came to Lake Superior when the "John Jacob Astor" was launched. Soon several boats from the Lower Lakes were hauled around the St. Mary's rapids in the wintertime and began their part in the carrying trade of Lake Superior.

At only a few places along the lakes were there docks for these early boats. Sand bars often kept the boats from entering the harbors at the rivers' mouths, and it was many years before these bars were removed so that boats could go into the harbors. Freight and passengers were often carried to and from land in small boats. Horses and cattle were pushed overboard and allowed to swim to land. Such loading and unloading not only was unhandy but also caused much delay, for often the water was too rough for small boats to leave the shore.

With the increase of western traffic, sailing vessels soon became too slow for people who were eager to hurry westward to start life anew. The new steamboats answered this demand. Soon several steamers were running across Lake Erie each summer on a somewhat regular schedule. By the time the Erie Canal opened, there were four steamboats on Lake Erie and soon others were added.

Traffic on the Great Lakes grew very rapidly. From the East came an increasingly steady stream of passengers, while from the West began to flow a steady stream of furs in even greater volume than ever before. In 1833-1834 the number of skins shipped out ran into the thousands. With this fur trade there began to appear shipments of what was then called "Ohio fur." Ohio fur was white oak barrel staves and barrel heads that were then used to make flour barrels and pork barrels. To these items were soon added such others as wheat, corn, flour, whiskey, salt-pork, dried fruits, cider, and jerked beef.

Courtesy Ralph Price

The Rosabelle on Lake Charlevoix about 1900. This boat sank with all hands in a Lake Michigan storm on October 30, 1921.

At first freight rates were high. Passenger rates ran something like this: It cost six dollars to go from Buffalo to Cleveland. From Buffalo to Detroit the fare was eight dollars. Twelve dollars was charged to go from Buffalo to Mackinac Island or to Sault Ste. Marie. The fare was twenty dollars from Buffalo to Green Bay or Chicago. Of course, these fares are only general, as they varied from boat to boat and also with the type of room and service.

In 1835, a boom in land prices swept the East, and many people, as we have seen, came westward seeking new homes. In that year there was much cheap money in use, and everyone seemed to be getting rich. Many people thought they saw good opportunities in the Great Lakes carrying trade, and in 1835 and 1836 several new boats were built and others were being built when the Panic of 1837 hit the country.

With the coming of the steamboats on the Great Lakes there arose a demand for more and more firewood. Fuel was needed to fire the boilers of these boats to make steam. Thus all the early steamboats became markets for wood. Until about 1850, wood for the roaring fires was plentiful, cheap, and easy to secure. Farmers living near the fueling points could thus get ready cash for wood that other farmers, living farther inland, just burned in their clearing fires. The supplying of fuel for steamboats became a regular business for many people. Because wood is bulky, each steamer usually wooded up at every stop. The roaring boiler fires called endlessly for more and more wood. The run from Buffalo to Chicago usually took about one hundred fifty cords of wood. Many wooding stations sprang up along the northern shores of Lake Huron and Lake Michigan. For this wood the steamboat lines usually paid from a dollar and a half to two dollars a cord. On long trips the boats' wood bunkers were filled and sometimes huge piles of cordwood were even stacked above deck. This bulky fuel cut into the cargo space of the early steamers unless wood could be easily picked up from time to time as the steamboats made their way along the lake shore.

As the near supplies of fuel along the lake shore were cut, wood had to be brought from farther and farther inland. The supplying of this fuel wood for steamers running on the lakes became a regular business for many men and helped in the settling of many new areas. Frenchmen living along the Detroit and St. Clair rivers began to run what were known as "wooding scows" as well as wooding docks. These scows, loaded with firewood which later came to be called "propeller wood," met steamers passing up or down the two rivers and "wooded" them up as the steamers went along on their way. This practice of using wooding scows saved time for the passing steamers. When the scows were empty, they returned to dock where they were again loaded with firewood and thus made ready to meet the next passing steamer.

By 1839 there was regular passenger traffic between Buffalo and Chicago. Eight steamers were making this their regular run. This meant that many of the goods that had been transhipped at Detroit for Chicago were now taken directly to Chicago. At that time there was not as yet a harbor at Chicago. Vessels arriving there were not able to find a harbor until after 1854, when a twelve-foot channel was cut through the sand bar at the river's mouth. Up to that time all boats had to anchor outside on the lake and send passengers and freight ashore in small boats. In the long run, however, this passenger traffic to Chicago was to aid Michigan, for the settlers pushing out onto the western plains were soon to demand more and more lumber from Michigan to build their homes.

By 1840, there were more steamboats on the lakes than were needed to carry the passenger traffic. Soon some began to reduce their rates in order to secure the passengers of the other boats. At that time it was not at all uncommon to see two steamers racing into port, each trying to get there first so that she could get the passengers before the other boat arrived.

In 1841, a new type of boat appeared on the lakes: the screw propeller. Before this time all the steamboats had been driven by paddle wheels on their sides. The screw propeller was a new development and was turned by a shaft which jutted out from the stern of the boat just below the surface of the water. This new method of driving a steamboat has now come to be used on all the boats on the inland lakes except one old railroad car ferry operating between Detroit and Windsor.

By 1850, the mineral resources of the Upper Peninsula began to be developed. This new traffic called for better transportation than sailboats could supply. In 1845, a group of mine owners bought a little propeller steamship, called the "Independence," for use in transporting ore on Lake Superior. To get the new boat to Lake Superior was a difficult task. They sailed her up the St. Mary's River as far as she could go and then they hauled her around the portage and across the snow on rollers. It took seven weeks to get her around the rapids. In 1846, the "Julia Palmer," a side-wheeler, was also hauled around the rapids.

There were three lines running ships between Buffalo and Chicago by 1845, and as many as 200,000 people crossed the lakes westward bound in that one year. Even though steamboats had gotten well under way, the great bulk of the freight was still being carried by sailboats.

In 1847 the Michigan Central Railroad tried to gain more traffic for its line by running steamships to Buffalo, at the western end of the Erie Canal. In 1849, the year that the railroad reached Lake

Michigan, the Michigan Central launched the "Mayflower" for passenger service across Lake Erie. This was one of the finest passenger boats ever to steam across our inland lakes. Eighty-five staterooms cared for the people traveling on her. So large was she that three hundred steerage and three hundred cabin passengers could be carried.

By 1850, it was becoming harder for the Michigan Central to get business. To increase its traffic, the Michigan Central in 1853-1854 built two new steamers called the "Western World" and the "Plymouth Rock." Fine steamers were these, both in size and in comfort, but the age of passenger traffic on the lakes had already begun to pass. In 1857, the two new boats were kept in port, tied up at Detroit. Soon they were sold and taken apart.

Courtesy Henry Ford Museum, Dearborn, Michigan

The "Western World," built by the Michigan Central Railroad in 1853-54. Note the walking beam in the upper part of the center of the boat and also the long wooden arch that gave support to the wooden boat.

At first the railroads aided shipping on the Great Lakes as the railroads were short and brought freight to the lake shores but by 1850 the railroads were becoming linked together and through railroad traffic was possible all the year around. In 1852, a railroad was built across northern Ohio from Cleveland to Toledo. This new line, together with the New York Central, made a through route from New York to Chicago. Running along the southern shore of Lake Erie these combined railroads began to get much freight and passenger traffic that had before gone by boat across the lake. Even the new liners of the Michigan Central Railroad were no match for this through, all year around, traffic on the new railroads.

Although the days of heavy passenger traffic on the lakes was fast passing, the best days of lake shipping still lay ahead. With the development of the farms, the iron and copper mines, the opening of the "Soo" Canal, and the rise of the steel industry, most owners of lake boats turned to carrying vast cargoes of lumber, wheat, iron ore, limestone, and coal in place of passengers and package freight.

CHAPTER TWELVE

The Sawmill Comes to Michigan

As THE YEARS PASSED, the crude little pioneer log cabins of the settlers were replaced by better and warmer houses. Up to the time of the Civil War, lumber was still a luxury in Michigan and only a few people could afford to build homes or barns with such expensive material.

Some of the settlers, however, had broad axes and with these they began to hew round logs into square timbers. These hand-hewn beams, or square timbers, were used in making the houses, barns, and boats of that time. Even today in many old houses and barns the skillful ax work of those early craftsmen can still be seen and admired.

In hewing a log the worker first snapped a chalk line along the length of the log to show where the cut was to be made. Then taking a regular ax, a "square timber" man, as he was then called, stepped up onto the log. With the common ax he "score-hacked" away the largest part of the curving part of the log, thus removing most of the unwanted material. Then as he neared the chalk line with his ax, he changed to a "broad ax." This tool was similar to a regular ax but had a broader face, or cutting edge, and

Courtesy Henry Ford Museum, Dearborn, Michigan

A broad axe. These axes were used to make square timbers or to hew planks.

the handle was off-set about two inches. With swings of this ax a good "broad ax" man could hew well to the line leaving a flat cut on the side of a log. Having thus "faced" one side of a log, it was rolled over onto the flat face and the same manner of cutting was repeated until all four sides were faced and the square timber was finished and ready for use. A good "square timber" man was as proud of his straight line and flat-hewn surface as any craftsman could be.

Soon whole cabins were being built of these hand-squared timbers. They were called "block houses." By placing one square timber on

252

top of another, the amount of space between the logs was made smaller and thus the houses were made much warmer. The ends of the square timbers were cut flat with the corner and thus a square corner was made on the house. A few log cabins of this block house type can still be found in Michigan today. As lumber became more abundant and cheaper, the block houses were replaced by houses made from mill-cut lumber.

As early as 1749, during the French period, Michigan's first sawmill was built on the St. Clair River to cut pine boards from the logs coming from a pinery near Lake Huron. Little is known of this early mill except that from it came clear pine and cedar lumber for the little French homes at Detroit and along the river. This little mill was probably driven by animal or windmill power, and its output was very small. After the fire of 1805 hewn timbers from this same pinery, as well as hand-sawed boards, were floated down the Detroit River for the rebuilding of Detroit.

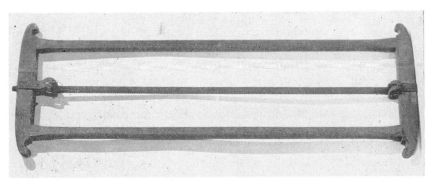

Courtesy Henry Ford Museum, Dearborn, Michigan

A Whip-saw. Saws like this one were used to make lumber. They were used by two men. Note the two handles on each end where the men held the saw. This saw is also called a pit-saw.

As more and more people came to settle in Michigan and on the plains of the West, the demand for lumber grew. Settlers needed window sashes, doors, wagons, buggies, roof boards, barrels, churns, wooden pails, and furniture. At first boards and barrel staves were made by hand. Lumber was supplied by human labor in a process called "pit sawing" that was centuries old. To cut lumber in this manner a log was placed on a rack over a pit, or raised upon a strong wooden frame. A line was marked along the top of the log where the cut of the saw was to be made. One man called the "sawyer" stood on top of the log and pulled the saw up and guided the cut along the line on the downward stroke. Another man, called the "pitman," stood under the log in the pit and pulled the saw on its downward stroke.

Gate saw (left) and wooden gears on an early saw. Spoffard Mill, Greenfield Village.

The saw that was used was called a "whip saw" or "pit saw" and was often stretched tight in the center of a wooden frame or "gate." These saws usually measured from five to seven and one-half feet in length and were usually tapered from the back, or upper end, to the point. The teeth were hooked and set for ripping with the grain on the downward cut. As it was pulled downward, all the sawdust came with it, and much of it fell on the man standing in the pit. Because such sawing was hard work, only the softer woods such as pine, cedar, whitewood, and basswood were cut into lumber. The hardwoods that spread across the settlers' lands were then considered useless for lumber and so were usually destroyed by burning.

Pit sawing was not only slow, hard work but expensive as well. Yet as slow, hard, and tedious as this labor was, many an early house and sturdy sailboat was built from lumber cut in this manner.

Pit sawing in the early colonial days in the East had been followed by little sawmills that were run by water power. The first sawmill in the United States had been built at Pistoga on the line between Maine and New Hampshire as early as 1634 and began cutting logs from the large pine forests of Maine. Two hundred years later, mills of this same type were built in Michigan. Both overshot and undershot water wheels were set up at places along Michigan's streams where waterfalls offered such power. In 1817 a little sawmill was set up on the Black River near present-day Port Huron. Another was built on the middle branch of the Clinton River some thirty miles from Detroit. Others were later built at Ann Arbor, Ypsilanti, Tecumseh, Sharron Hollow, and at other places where enough water power could be had to turn a water wheel.

Such early mills were at best, by modern standards, crude affairs. The slowly turning water wheel turned a set of gears made by placing wooden pegs in a wheel. These gears in turn worked on an arm, called a "pitman," which slowly raised and lowered the saw. The saw then used had an upright blade, similar to the whipsaw, held in position by a heavy wooden frame, called a "gate," from which was derived the name of "gate saw." As the gate raised and lowered it brought the saw blade up and down and held it firm for the downward cut as the gate dropped with the pitman. Thus water power had taken over the work of human muscles, but the method and rate of sawing remained about the same.

A feed of the ratchet variety edged the log along as the saw rose in the cut. The carriage crept slowly forward on a track made of wooden ribbons. The "gig wheel," the "shafts," and the "cogs" were all made from wood. The "head blocks," which held the head of the log securely in position, were heavy oak blocks fitted with the old-fashioned "brail dogs."

The saw was not allowed to cut the entire length of the log, but was stopped about four inches before the cut was finished to keep the saw from running into the iron "brail dogs" at the rear end of the log. The uncut end was called the "stubshot." After sawing, the stubshot had to be removed by an ax or adze. Because of the remaining stubshot, it became customary in those days to cut all logs three or four inches longer than the desired length of the finished board.

From daylight until dark the heavy gates and the crude saws went up and down. Men pulled, pried, and strained to move the heavy logs. The earth shook as the gate came down and the teeth of the saw bit farther into the log. For a hard day's toil such a mill produced a cut of only about two thousand feet of lumber, but crude as were these early mills they were better for making lumber than was hand sawing in the pit.

The heavy gate saw was replaced by the lighter "muley." The muley saw was an upright saw like the gate saw, except that the heavy frame which had been drawn up and down to carry the older gate saw was taken off. The muley was fastened at the bottom while the upper part slid up and down in a groove. The blade was still

Muley saw in the Tripp Sawmill at Greenfield Village. Picture taken about 1940. Note that the saw does not cut all the way through the log.

the same upright saw and cut as it made the downward stroke. A muley saw was about six feet long and ten inches wide. It took a two-foot stroke and cut a one-fourth-inch kerf, thus wasting much good timber. The teeth marks that the saw left on the lumber were still the vertical marks instead of the curved ones soon to be made by the newer whining circular saws. The carriage upon which the log rested was still pinched along with a pry as the log was pushed into the saw.

A raceway and sawmill were built at Fort Brady at Sault Ste. Marie as early as 1822. This mill burned in the summer of 1826 but was soon rebuilt and continued in operation for over thirty years.

In 1826 a little mill was erected at Schwartsburg, Nankin township in Wayne County, on the bank of the River Rouge. On the Thread River at Grand Blanc a mill was built in 1828-1829. There appears to have been a mill at Waterford at the time, but twenty miles was too far to haul lumber over the roads of that day. The Grand Blanc mill, however, proved a failure because of its poor construction and the lack of a good pinery from which to get logs, and was soon

Muley saw in the Tripp Sawmill in Greenfield Village, Dearborn, Michigan.
Note the large teeth and the up-and-down stroke of this early saw.

abandoned. Another mill built about the same time and four or five miles north of the site of the other sent downstream the first raft of lumber ever floated on a tributary of the Saginaw River.

The year 1832 saw still more mills come into operation. In that year a little sawmill was built near Jonesville and still another appeared there in 1835. In 1832 a mill was also built across the river from Menominee on the Wisconsin side. Another mill was built at Grand Rapids on what is now called Indian Creek. Here an undershot water-power-driven wheel furnished power to run a saw that cut about two thousand feet of lumber a day. In this same year a mill was built on the Black River at Port Huron. Still another was built at Detroit on a strip of river frontage at the foot of Hastings Street. The builder of this mill in Detroit was Harvey Williams who was a prominent blacksmith and steam engine builder of the time.

In 1834, this same Harvey Williams built a steam sawmill at Saginaw. To run this first steam-driven sawmill Mr. Williams used the old engine that had once been used to drive the "Walk-in-the-Water." Though steam power had been applied, the little mill produced only about the same amount of lumber as one driven by water power. In 1836, a little mill was built at Portsmouth. This was the second sawmill to be built in the Saginaw Valley. In 1836 and 1837, Mr. Williams built a second sawmill, called the Emerson Mill, at Saginaw.

By this time the newly developing steam engines were being put to many uses. Steam power was being used to drive boats, railroad engines, and to run the machinery in factories. Crude as these early engines were they were also soon being used to drive the new circular saws and band saws that greatly increased the rate of cutting. No longer was water power needed to run the saw or saws. Wherever water and fuel could be secured it became possible to start a sawmill near the source of timber supply. Soon many little steam-driven saw-mills were being built at the river mouths along the northern shore of Lake Michigan and Lake Huron where good pine logs could be floated down the rivers from the pineries located farther up the river.

At Greenfield Village, in Dearborn, now stands the Tripp Sawmill which was built in Franklin township, Lenawee County, in 1835.

About three or four miles from the present city of Holland, a little village, called Superior, was platted on the shore of Lake Macatawa in 1835. Industry followed the founding. A tannery was built and a shipyard started. A sawmill was set up in 1836. Disaster threatened from the very first. The harbor was blocked with sand, and boats could not get in or out. The village was abandoned. When the Dutch arrived they bought what remained and built the first post office and hotel at Holland from the old buildings at Superior.

Lumbermen soon found ideal places for sawmills on the western side of the state along the shore of Lake Michigan. One of the first sawmill towns to develop was Muskegon, which derived its name from a Chippewa word "Muskego," meaning marshes or river of marshes. In 1837 the first sawmill on Muskegon Lake was built. In 1841 this mill burned, and the machinery was later moved to Grand Rapids. By 1840, there were three mills cutting lumber at Muskegon, but all together they could cut only about 13,000 feet of lumber a day.

Like many other western Lake Michigan cities, Muskegon is located by a large lake at the mouth of a river. The far-reaching Muskegon River, with vast pineries scattered up its meandering valley for some two hundred miles to Houghton and Higgins lakes and with Muskegon Lake at its mouth, made Muskegon an ideal location for a busy sawmill town.

In the spring of 1839 the first attempt was made at running logs down the Muskegon River. The river drivers found that many old logs, stumps, and fallen tree tops had to be removed from the river bed to let the logs come down the river, but the drive did reach the mills. This little drive was but a beginning of the many that were to follow it, for it is said that before Muskegon's lumbering days were ended, the Muskegon River floated more pine logs to the sawmills than any other river in the world.

Another mill was built at Menominee in 1841 and still another in 1854. Escanaba had its first mill in 1841 and Ontonagon in 1852. All of these early mills cut timber from the nearby forest to supply the needs of a local market, but as early as 1838 Charles Mears bought a sailboat called the "Ranger" and began shipping lumber to Chicago. By 1849 larger mills had appeared which turned out quantity production. By 1854 there were sixty sawmills in the state. These mills were cutting about 108,000,000 board feet a year. As early as 1858 a bandsaw was first used at Bay City, but the attempt was unsuccessful as the right tension on the saw could not be maintained.

By this time sawmills had also improved in other ways. The driving machinery was usually located on the ground floor while the upper floor was reserved for the mill proper. A sloping incline called a "jack ladder" was used to bring logs up into the mill. At first logs were pulled up the incline on a carriage. Later a wheel called the "bull wheel," because it was at first powered by a bull, was placed at the top to drive an endless chain, called a "bull chain," that ran in a slot up the bottom of the jack ladder. Logs placed in this slot

were grabbed by spiked teeth projecting upward from the bull chain and thus carried upward into the mill.

Even greater changes were soon to appear. A new circular saw came into use around 1850 and soon its shrill whine, as it gathered speed for its next cut into a log, could be heard in many places throughout the state.

An early circular saw. Note the hammer marks left by the saw filer where he hammered the saw to make it run true.

The circular saw's invention is credited to Benjamin Cummins. He is said to have made the first circular saw at Bentonville, New York, in 1814, with the crude tools found in a local blacksmith's shop. Mr. Cummins died in 1843 and is now buried in a rural plot in Kalamazoo County.

Circular sawmill, Greenfield Village

At first the use of the circular saw was limited and there was much trouble with the teeth breaking off. A few years later the circular saw was greatly improved by the invention of individual teeth that could be easily replaced if damaged. Then the circular saw, driven by the new steam engine, really began to bite into the timber of Michigan.

As the number of sawmills in Michigan increased, they demanded more and more logs. The timber around the mills was soon cut and men had to push farther and farther up the waterways in search of more and more timber.

A new type of speculator then began coming to Michigan. He was the lumberman. Soon whole tracts of land were being sold, not to settlers, but to those men who looked upon land not as a place to build homes but rather as a place from which to cut logs.

Beginning in the 1830's "timber cruisers," sent out by eastern firms, began coming west along the Erie Canal. They did not come here to clear the land, burn the trees, and make little farms. They came looking for the choice stands of pine that could be felled and cut into lumber. To the settler it was the land under the trees that was considered of value. To the lumbermen the land was of little, if any, value. It was the pine trees that stood on it which had value to them. These men knew what they were after because they came from a long line of lumbermen who had had two hundred years of training. When they came here they brought this knowledge of lumbering with them.

Timber cruisers usually did their work in the winter when the forests were more open from underbrush, mosquitoes and flies were gone, and swamps were frozen. Sometimes cruisers used dog teams to carry in their supplies, but usually they carried their few supplies on their backs. Leaving the settlements these men pushed into the forests where perhaps government surveyors were the only white men who had ever been there. Among the forest lands they searched for the best stands of white pine to be found close by the river banks.

Because pine logs floated, and as there were no roads or railroads, the rivers of Michigan became the first carriers of saw logs. Logs were a heavy commodity, and as such they could not be easily hauled for any distance as long as men had to depend upon muscle power as the source of energy. Back east in Maine lumber men had been floating pine logs downstream to the mills for many years. When these men came to Michigan they used the same methods here.

When a cruiser located a fine stand of pine near a river he then went about estimating its size. Five hundred paces equalled about eighty rods. Two thousand paces equalled about one mile. Here and there around the stand he would choose an acre of trees about the average of the stand. These trees he would count and scale. By doing this he could estimate the amount of lumber that the trees in the stand would cut.

He would then make pencil recordings in his little notebook. These recordings were of the size, quality, and location of the stand. Then if he were sure that this would be a good pinery he would look up a government survey stake and from there pace off its location and carefully record it in his notebook. Sometimes a cruiser would locate several tracts on one cruise trip. Then he or some member of the lumber company would go to the government land office and purchase the land if it had not already been sold. Cruisers were sometimes paid in cash for their work, but often they received title to part of the timber lands they had found. This method of payment made them interested in searching for the best stands.

Up to the time of the Civil War only crude little sawmills were to be found in this country. But small as they were, by 1860 they had cut nearly all the good timber in the East. First the good pine of Maine had been cut. Then, as the supply of pine there grew smaller and smaller, the lumbermen pushed west into New York and Pennsylvania. Even here the supply of pine trees was not endless, and as early as 1830-1840 timber men were looking with interest at the fine pine timberlands in the Great Lakes area and buying large tracts from the government.

Each year more and more lumber was needed to build the rapidly growing cities back East and to build barns and houses for the settlers pushing westward out onto the treeless plains of the Middle West. Large quantities of timber were also needed for building plank roads, railroads, bridges, ships, and as braces in the mines.

When one spoke of lumber in those days one usually referred to pine lumber. Some lumber such as cherry, maple, oak, and walnut was used in making furniture, wagons, and buggies, but by far the largest amount of lumber used was pine lumber. Pine was used because it could be sawed more easily, was more easily planed by hand, and could be more easily worked into the shapes desired than could hardwoods.

In the United States there are thirty-four species of pine trees. Only three of these are native trees to Michigan. These three are the jack pine, the red or Norway pine, and the white pine. Of these three the white pine was by far the most valuable for making lumber. In general white pine trees reached to a height of about eighty feet, although in good soil they often grew to a height of one hundred to one hundred fifty feet. The bole, or trunk, of the white pine often measured from four to seven feet in diameter. The wood of the white pine is soft, straight-grained, light brown in color and easily worked. If protected from the weather, it is very durable.

The red pine, or Norway, was very common in northern Michigan, but it was not so well liked for timber to make lumber. Red pine trees are usually smaller than white pines, being only two to three feet in diameter at the bottom of the bole and fifty to seventy-five feet in height. In the lumbering days the red pine was usually spoken of as Norway pine. Norway pine seems to have taken its name from the little town of Norway in the state of Maine. Today, these trees are usually called red pine because of the reddish color in their bark and in their inner heartwood.

The third native pine of Michigan is the jack pine or, as it is sometimes called, the scrub pine. Jack pines are small scrubby trees that grow only to a height of about twenty or thirty feet. They grow only on the poorest sandy soils. Jack pine trees were very common from Clare County northward, but they also appeared as far south as Grand Haven and Port Austin. These trees were not cut by the lumbermen.

From eastern Ontario westward across northern Michigan, northern Wisconsin, and northern Minnesota stood vast forests of pine trees which, up to 1860, had hardly been touched by an ax. Until the opening of the Erie Canal and the coming of the railroads these vast stands of pine were of little, if any, value as there was no way to get the lumber to the market once it had been cut. With the increased demands for lumber, the rise of better transportation, and the coming of the steam sawmill, lumbermen soon began to see the money that could be made by cutting the pine forests in the Great Lakes area.

Much of the finest of these spreading stands of white pine once stood in Michigan. By 1860, the hardwoods of the southern part of the state had been mostly cut and burned. Beginning at a line drawn from Muskegon east to Bay City and Saginaw the whole upper half of the Lower Peninsula and the eastern half of the Upper Peninsula were, until about a hundred years ago, a vast forest made up mostly of cone-bearing trees. Among the pine trees stood strips of hardwood trees such as beech, ash, and maple that were of little interest to the early lumbermen. They were hard to saw. In general the hardwoods would not float, and thus there was no way to get them to the mills.

Before the Civil War, Michigan's first lumber camps had already come into being. They were small and crude compared with the later camps that were built after the Civil War by the big lumber companies, but they were camps nevertheless. The men working in them had begun the rich harvest of Michigan's timber lands.

These early logging camps were built much like the frontier cabins of the settlers. They were made of logs and chinked with mud and chips. The building where the men slept was called the "bunkhouse." Many of the earlier bunkhouses did not have any windows.

In these earlier bunkhouses there was usually an open place in the center of the room where a fire could be made. It was really a sand box six or eight feet long by six or eight feet wide. Upon this sand a fire was built to warm the bunkhouse and cook the food. The smoke from the fire passed out through a large hole in the center of the roof. Sometimes a wooden chimney the same size as the hole carried the smoke above the roof. On this open fireplace, called a "caboose," the "shanty boys," as lumberjacks were then called, would place large logs five or six feet long. These logs were brought in from outside by three or four men. Two men would place a stick crosswise under the front end of a log and carry the front end of the log across the fire while two others carried the back end of the log by means of another stick which supported it. Thus, they could place good-sized pieces of wood upon the fire.

This crude fireplace furnished the only means of heating the bunkhouse. It was often the only source of light during the long, dreary, winter evenings. The only other light in those days came from a candle or two placed at one end of the bunkhouse. Most of the heat from the fire went up the large open chimney. If the fire did not furnish much heat for the men, at least it can be said that it did provide plenty of smoke as each wintry gust of wind blew down the smoke hole. The early shanty men who spent long winter nights in the bunkhouse often had sore eyes because of this primitive condition.

On the inside of the bunkhouse along the walls were rows of upper and lower bunks. Sometimes shanty boys got into these bunks from the end. These bunks were called "muzzle loaders." Others called "side loaders" were gotten into from the side. These lumber camp bunks could hardly be what one would today call comfortable beds. They were usually boxes in which sawdust, pine needles, or cedar boughs had been placed for the men to lie upon. For bedding, the shanty boys used a few blankets which were often not washed from one fall to the next. The best that can be said for lumber camp bunkhouses in the early days is that they were dark, smoke-filled places in which the men spent the winter nights.

Men seldom washed their clothing, and body lice, called "gray-backs," were very plentiful. Graybacks, flies, bedbugs, gnats, and mosquitoes were all part of the shanty boy's life.

Another log building served as a barn. There the oxen were stabled during the cold winter nights. Often another building housed the camp supplies of food, such as barrels of flour, salt-pork, corned beef, dried apples, beans, and potatoes. From these supplies the cook prepared the meals for his crew. Butter, cream, milk, and eggs were seldom used in cooking.

All trees were cut by using only axes. Once the trees were down, the whole trunk, or bole, was usually dragged by ox teams to the river. There on the river bank the trunk was chopped into logs.

In this way the early lumbermen began to cut Michigan's pine forests and to provide lumber for a growing nation.

CHAPTER THIRTEEN

Early Beginnings in the Upper Peninsula

FOR MANY YEARS Michigan's Upper Peninsula has been the source of raw materials. To it the French came seeking furs and along its northern shore ran the voyageurs highway to the vast fur lands to the west and north. Great as were the profits from the fur trade they were small in comparison with the vast wealth that was later to be taken from this area in copper, iron ore, and timber.

Copper and Lake Superior had been thought of together since the earliest French missionaries and traders had visited the area. Just where the metal could be found the French never discovered although some searched for the source of the metal. Not even the friendly Chippewas, then living in the Upper Peninsula, knew from where the metal came and their legends contained none of the knowledge of the early Indians that had once mined vast amounts of the ore on Isle Royale and in the Keweenaw Peninsula. The only copper known to the French and Indians were pieces of "float" copper that they found lying on the ground among the leaves and glacial drift of the ages past. We today call such pieces of copper "float" copper because it had been carried away by the glaciers from the place where it was formed. Pieces of float copper have been found as far south as Illinois and Indiana.

In 1765, Alexander Henry, an English fur trader, who had been fortunate enough to survive the massacre at Fort Michilimackinac two years earlier, discovered a large mass of pure copper lying in the bed of the Ontonagon River a few miles up stream from Lake Superior. For years this strange copper mass, now known as the "Ontonagon boulder," had been regarded as an object of worship by the Indians but in spite of this they allowed Mr. Henry to cut from the copper mass about one hundred pounds of copper. Mr. Henry also discovered an outcrop of copper along the river bank.

Mr. Henry organized an English copper mining company and in 1771 sent miners and supplies to the outcrop on the Ontonagon River

to start a copper mine. During the following winter the miners dug
an adit some forty feet into the frozen soil and rock of the river bank
and did secure some pieces of pure copper. When spring came the
ground thawed and the adit collapsed. Supplies for the miners were
sent to them that same spring but the miners had put in one winter
on the Ontonagon and they had had enough of copper mining in
Michigan's cold Upper Peninsula. Leaving their caved-in mine behind
the miners returned to Sault Ste. Marie on the supply boat. Nearly
seventy-five more years passed before other men again tried to mine
copper on the south shore of Lake Superior. During this time the
area passed from English control to that of the United States.

The area was far north of the westward routes that settlers were
then using in going west to new farmlands. The American Fur Company still had its post on Mackinac Island, and traders and trappers
were still using the Keweena Portage in going to and from the fur
lands of the West but sailboats were beginning to be used on Lake
Superior to carry the merchandise from Sault Ste. Marie to Grand
Portage and Fort William and bring the furs from the West to Sault
Ste. Marie. Other boats were carrying merchandise from the lower
lakes to Sault Ste. Marie and bringing the furs down the lakes. This
together with the Erie Canal made it easier to carry on the Indian trade.

Governor Cass passed along the old Keweena Portage in 1820.
Others like Henry R. Schoolcraft, the Indian Agent at Sault Ste. Marie,
used the portage also. But though few traders and Indians ever
ventured into the interior of the land, stories of copper still intrigued
the people. But what good was copper when it was so far from even
the small market of that day? Few but fur traders, missionaries, and
government agents showed any real interest in the land lying south
of the huge, cold lake that separates northern Michigan from Canada.
French, English, and American fur traders had followed the old
voyageurs highway for over one hundred and fifty years, but they
knew little or nothing about what secrets lay hidden in the dense
wilderness a few feet back from the wooded shore.

When Michigan received the Upper Peninsula in return for the
disputed Toledo strip of land, most people then living in Michigan
thought that the new state had received the bad end of a very poor
bargain. They looked upon the Upper Peninsula as being a land of
little value to the new state of Michigan. Michigan had given up
some 470 square miles of its best farm lands to Ohio, but she had
received in the Upper Peninsula some 15,600 square miles for the

470 she had given up. But what good, thought the people, who really knew little about the Upper Peninsula, were all those cold, worthless acres? People wanted farms and more farms, and the Upper Peninsula seemed to them a poor place to start farming. In truth, very little was known about the Upper Peninsula.

It remained for a young man named Dr. Douglass Houghton to really tell the people of Michigan about the good bargain they had received in having the Upper Peninsula added to the newly formed state. Soon after Michigan became a state, in 1837, the state legislature provided money for a geological survey of the Upper Peninsula. The state legislature chose Dr. Douglass Houghton to do this work. Thus Dr. Douglass Houghton became Michigan's first state geologist and soon began making a geological survey of the Upper Peninsula. The area was not entirely new to Houghton, as he had gone with Lewis Cass and Henry R. Schoolcraft as their medical doctor when they made their trip in 1820. From the time he was appointed to find out about the geology of the Upper Peninsula until his death, in 1845, Dr. Houghton did much to let the people of Michigan know about the mineral resources of the Upper Peninsula.

In 1841 Dr. Houghton made his first report. The report stated that copper and iron ore were both to be found in the Upper Peninsula, but as yet they had not been found in large enough quantities to pay for mining. Dr. Houghton had worded his report very carefully, for he feared that prospectors would rush into the area and at that time the land still belonged to the Indians.

In 1842 the United States Government made a treaty with the Chippewa Indians for their remaining land in the Upper Peninsula.

In spite of Dr. Houghton's care in making his geological report, the words copper and iron seemed to be magic ones that stirred men's imaginations. Facts grew larger with each telling and quickly mixed with gossip and idle fancy. Whole mountains of copper were said to reflect the setting sun and turn Lake Superior to a brilliant copper color.

In the summer of 1843 another event occurred that helped to arouse people's interest in Michigan's Upper Peninsula and the copper that was thought to be there. On October 11 of that year a Mr. James Eldred unloaded from a boat at Detroit the Ontonagon boulder that Mr. Henry had discovered in 1765. Soon he was charging twenty-five cents for each person to see it. There seems to be much dispute as to just who raised the boulder from the Ontonagon River, hauled it to the mouth of the river, placed it on a boat, and portaged it around the rapids at Sault Ste. Marie. But there it was at Detroit — a huge block of pure copper from the Upper Peninsula.

For some reason the Federal Government purchased the boulder from Mr. Eldred. It was shipped to Washington, D.C., by way of the Erie Canal, the Hudson River, the Atlantic Ocean, and the Potomac River. At Washington the boulder was placed in the yard of the War Department. It then seems to have been forgotten for some time. In 1881 the boulder was moved to the Smithsonian Institute. There, today, rests what remains of the huge mass of copper that once lay in the Ontonagon River and interested so many passersby. It is four feet six inches long, four feet wide, and seventeen inches thick.

Stories about copper spread from person to person. Copper was the magic word on many people's lips. But where were the mines to be found? Soon the first big mineral rush in the United States was on. People began going across the portage at Sault Ste. Marie and then passing on west to the mineral lands in the Keweenaw Peninsula that Dr. Houghton had told of in his report. The few boats that were then on Lake Superior were soon crowded with prospectors and their supplies. Many copper seekers could not get passage on the boats and were forced to continue their journey from Sault Ste. Marie with French *voyageurs* who took prospectors and their supplies to the Keweenaw Peninsula in canoes.

Few, if any, in this wild rush of speculators in 1843 were miners. One thing they had in common: they were all sure that their fortunes would be made just as soon as they reached the "copper lands." Teachers, doctors pharmacists, and many others all braved stormy Lake Superior to reach the land where copper metal was said to be found, the copper that was soon going to make all of them rich. Just how this was going to be, they did not stop to  COPPER DEPOSITS think, for in those days there was really little use for copper. Some of it was used to make pots and pans, buttons, and ornaments. Most of it was used to put on the bottoms of ocean ships. The copper bottoms helped to keep the barnacles from forming on the ships' bottoms. But ocean ships were far away and copper was a heavy metal to carry for any distance.

Filled with the idea that they would strike it rich, the prospectors, during the summer months, roamed across the Keweenaw Peninsula in search of copper deposits. Here and there among the decaying vegetation they found a piece of float copper lying on the ground. They walked over deposits of copper worth millions. They climbed into and out of old Indian copper pit mines, little dreaming as they did so what these holes were or what lay buried underneath the rotting leaves and trees that by then lay in the ancient mining pits. With shovels and picks they dug among the leaves. They chipped off pieces of hard rock. But where was the copper?

Copper outcrops were hard to find, for nearly ninety-five per cent of the Keweenaw Peninsula is covered with glacial till. What is more, nearly all the land is covered by dense forests of cedar, spruce, and tamarack. During the summer the black flies and huge mosquitoes made the lives of the prospectors very uncomfortable. But all that summer of 1843 and for several summers that followed, the search for copper went on. Men wandered through the forests and waded across the swamps. They dug a little here and picked into this rocky face and that. There must be copper here somewhere, for from time to time they picked up pieces of float copper that lay here and there upon the ground. But from where had these pieces of copper come?

Nearly all the prospectors left the area when fall came. One could not search for copper under the deep drifts of snow that settled on this forest land. Winters on the Keweenaw Peninsula are long and cold. Even the huge cold lake across which they had come grows colder until at last its shores are frozen fast. When ice closed the shipping season on Lake Superior, there was no way to get out of the Keweenaw Peninsula unless one walked on snowshoes two hundred miles overland to the south. Winter in the Upper Peninsula in those days meant being shut off for four or five months from all friends and relatives "down below." Each fall, during the following few years, most of the prospectors left the area. Often they took with them a piece or two of the copper metal they had found lying on the ground.

Three mining boom towns sprang up during these early years of prospecting: Copper Harbor, Eagle Harbor, and Ontonagon. Each summer, for the next few years, tents spread along the lake shore at each of these places. Soon these boom towns were experiencing the typical rowdy life that develops in a frontier mining community.

Pieces of copper were not the only reason for people becoming interested in the Upper Peninsula. Fort Wilkins, at the tip of the Keweenaw Peninsula, had been built in 1844 and was garrisoned by a small detachment of United States troops. The Federal Government, too, was interested in the area and was pushing ahead its land survey so that title to the land could be given to prospectors and settlers in order to do away with the need for mineral land permits.

Eagle Harbor on the Keweenaw Peninsula. This little harbor was once the site of one of the first mineral rushes in the United States. Photo 1957.

In the year 1844 Mr. William Burt and his party of government surveyors were pushing their linear and geological survey near the present site of Negaunee. Burt's party of surveyors were doing two jobs at once. They not only were surveying the section lines, but also were making notes in their survey reports of the geological nature of the land as they went along. On September 19, 1844, Mr. Burt and his surveyors were working on the west line of township forty-seven north, range twenty-seven west when they began to have trouble with their survey work because of the strange behavior of their compass needle. It did not act properly. Instead of pointing steadily north, the compass needle moved crazily in all directions.

Those in charge of the survey thought that minerals in the ground might be the cause of the compass needle's strange actions. Leaving their work, the surveyors set out in search of the cause of their trouble. Before long the mystery was solved, for pieces of magnetic iron ore were discovered near the place where they had been working. Thus, by this mere chance, the first of the huge iron ore deposits of northern Michigan was discovered.

Shortly after Mr. Burt's find of iron ore, the first deposit of copper was located. In the fall of 1844 a soldier at Fort Wilkins led a party of prospectors to the first copper find just back of the fort. In December of that year the first copper mine in the Upper Peninsula was opened at Copper Harbor. But this mine, although it caused much excitement at the time, did not last long. It was only a small sample of what was to follow. Fifteen feet down, the copper pocket gave out entirely. But copper had at last been really mined on the Keweenaw Peninsula.

The year following the opening of the first copper mine at Copper Harbor the same company started working at another place about twenty-five miles down the peninsula and south of Eagle Harbor. Here, at what later became the Cliff Mine, the first large deposit of native copper ever discovered in the world was found in 1845. Soon huge masses of bright, pure copper were coming from the ground. A real strike had at last been made, and the Cliff Mine became the first mine to pay dividends to its stockholders. In the years that followed, much copper was taken from this mine. Before the Cliff Mine closed down, it had produced some forty million pounds of pure copper. Most of it, about two-thirds in fact, was made up of huge masses of solid copper that lay buried in an old lava flow.

The years 1845 and 1846 were busy years of anxious prospecting and speculation. While hundreds of men wandered across the Keweenaw Peninsula looking for copper or iron deposits, Mr. Burt and Dr. Houghton went on with their survey work. Mr. Burt, although the first to really locate iron ore, was a surveyor at heart and never took advantage of his great discovery. Dr. Houghton, too, left prospecting to others and went on with his geological survey until he drowned in Lake Superior near Eagle River on October 13, 1845.

During these early years, hundreds of copper and iron mining companies were formed. One of these companies was formed by Philo M. Everett at Jackson, Michigan. It was known as the Jackson Mining Company. In July, 1845, Mr. Everett, with two other members

IRON DISTRICTS

of the new company, set out for the Upper Peninsula to look for copper. They went by train to Marshall, by stage coach from there to Grand Rapids, by wagon from there to Mackinaw City, by canoe to Mackinac Island, then by steamer to Sault Ste. Marie. At Sault Ste. Marie they bought a Mackinaw boat and had it hauled around the rapids. In this boat they coasted along the south shore of Lake Superior to the place where the city of Marquette now stands. Thus to go from

Jackson to Marquette, in the year 1845, took Mr. Everett and his friends twenty-one days of travel.

Mr. Everett and the other members of his company had come to the Upper Peninsula looking for copper but on their way up had become interested in the iron ore deposit that Mr. Burt had discovered the year before. At what is now Marquette the party was kindly received by an Indian who was living there. His name was Marji-Gesick. The following day this friendly Indian took Mr. Everett and his friends up the hill to the south of Marquette and showed them where iron ore lay hidden under the roots of a big pine tree. That day the Jackson Mining Company changed from a copper mining company to an iron mining company.

Mr. Everett took home some samples of the iron ore to show his partners in Jackson. The next year, 1846, members of the Jackson Mining Company again visited the area and again took home more

Courtesy Oliver Iron Mining Co.
Monument marking the place where iron ore was first discovered. This monument, erected in 1904, contains a piece of every kind of rock, ore, and mineral found in the iron country.

samples of the iron ore. The company began mining iron ore in 1847 at the Jackson Mine, located near the Carp River and not far from the present city of Negaunee. Here on the Carp River a forge was built and the first iron smelted. Iron production, as well as copper production, had now begun in Michigan. Later, furnaces were erected near the mine. Smelting iron ore in those days was a difficult task. There was no coal supply, and charcoal had to be used for fuel. Large areas of hardwood forests were cut to make charcoal for fuel to run the furnaces that melted the iron ore. Yet the task once begun was carried on, and in 1850 the Jackson Mine made its first shipment of five tons of iron bars.

The second big strike in copper was found in the year 1847. In that year Mr. Samuel Knapp was prospecting for copper near where Rockland is now located. He was looking far to the south of the earlier finds, at the top of the Keweenaw Peninsula. He did not know it then, but he was coming into the copper range from its southern end. One day a line of slight depressions in the ground caught his eye. Were these holes pits of earlier Indian diggings? With a pick and shovel he cleaned out one of the pits. Along with decayed trees and the wind-blown and fallen debris that almost filled the pit, Mr. Knapp found many Indian hammers—in fact, many truck loads of them—that had been used by the Indians long ago when they had been toiling in the pits. Eighteen feet down Mr. Knapp came upon a mass of pure copper ten feet long, three feet wide, and two feet thick. There can be no doubt that the Indians had once tried to raise this huge mass of copper from where it lay in the pit, for the

Old wooden ore bucket now at Fort Wilkins at Copper Harbor. This bucket was once used to lift rock and copper ore from the Cliff mine.

whole mass was still resting upon oak timbers just as the Indians had left it centuries before Mr. Knapp again opened the mine. Thus Mr. Knapp uncovered one of the old Indian mines and brought into being the Minesota Mine. The following year, 1848, the Minesota Mine sent ten tons of copper down the Ontonagon River to Ontonagon. In the years that followed, the Minesota Mine paid more profits to its stockholders than all the rest of the Ontonagon copper mines put together. At first the ore was sent down the Ontonagon River, but in 1859 a plank road was built from Rockland to Ontonagon. Another plank road was built to Greenland in 1874.

In 1849 the Cliff Mine paid the first dividend in copper history. The Minesota Mine paid $30,000 in dividends in 1852. Thus Michigan, by 1852, had two good paying copper mines. Several other mines were started and a good many companies formed, but most of the mines were shallow and soon gave out. Others failed almost before they had begun. Both the Cliff and Minesota mines were mines in which copper was found in large masses. It came in chunks, or masses, and was found in the old fissures and volcanic conduits of the Killarney Mountains. Some of the pieces were small, but others weighed five or six hundred tons.

In 1848 copper deposits were discovered midway between the two ends of the range, and the Quincy Mine and Pewabic Mine were started near Hancock. For many years the Quincy Mine was one of the largest and best known copper mines in Michigan. Its number two shaft went down into the ground at an angle for some 9,400 feet, and was at one time the deepest mine shaft to be found in North America. If this shaft were straight down, it would be a shaft some 6,400 feet in depth. The Quincy and Pewabic had hardly started to produce when mining began just south across Portage Lake at Houghton. Here, at Houghton, the Isle Royale Lode was discovered in 1852 and the Huron in 1853. In 1854, John Slawson found an ancient Indian pit east of Eagle River. This discovery became the Central Mine.

Eagle Harbor, Copper Harbor, Eagle River, and Ontonagon all became copper ports from which copper was sent from the Keweenaw Peninsula. For some time the copper that came from the mines at Houghton and Hancock had to be taken to the mouth of the Portage River and there loaded onto boats. During the early days of copper mining much of the copper ore was sent to Detroit and Cleveland to be smelted, but before long the copper was being smelted near the mines and sent down the lakes as copper bars.

During the early days of copper and iron mining many mining companies were organized. Nearly all of them failed. Some of the companies were pure swindles. Many of the mining companies never worked a mine. Some locations were poorly chosen and the deposit

Courtesy Cleveland-Cliffs Iron Co.

Open cut at Jackson Mine near where ore was first discovered in 1845. (Picture taken about 1860.)

was soon exhausted. Starting a mine even in those days cost much money to get in supplies. There were no railroads in the area. Lake shipping was undependable and costly. There were few docks. No roads led into the wilderness. Often all the tools and supplies had to be carried into the mining location on men's backs. Moreover, it was costly to get the copper, once it had been produced, down to Lake Superior. In the early days much of it was sledded out in the winter time when it was easier to move the heavy metal and rock. Unless there was a good deposit to pay later dividends the capital was often exhausted in the early part of the venture. Many of these mines produced some copper but never enough to cover the original expenses. Some paid a small profit in dividends. A few paid their lucky owners many millions in dividends during the years that the mines were worked. Many of the small mines that had failed to pay dividends to the original investors were run for years, not by the mine owners, but by independent miners under a system called tributing where they continued to mine at their own risk and expense and paid the mine owners one-eighth of what they produced in copper.

By July, 1846, over 104 iron mining companies had been formed. But the iron mining companies found even greater difficulty in getting started than did the copper companies and so most of these early companies also failed.

Samples of iron ore which were sent to the smelters proved to be too high in quality for the furnaces, for the smelters then were still using bog iron ore. Furnace men had to learn how to smelt the new ore. What is more, there was at that time no good way to ship iron ore to the smelting centers south of Lake Erie.

The first shipment of iron ore down the lakes was made on July 7, 1852. It was six barrels filled with iron ore that was being sent to the furnaces "down below." This was not much of a shipment but it marked the beginning for hundreds of thousands of tons of iron ore that were to follow during the next hundred years. But shipping ore in barrels did not prove to be the proper method. Some better means had to be developed. Why not smelt the iron ore right at the mine?

The mining companies, therefore, turned to smelting the iron ore and making it into iron bars, or "blooms," as they were called, near where the ore was mined. These blooms were two feet long and four inches square. These blooms were easier to handle and to ship. They were hauled to Marquette on sleighs during the wintertime.

Several furnaces were built at several places in the Upper Peninsula and later in the upper part of the Lower Peninsula.

To heat these early furnaces and smelt the ore, charcoal was used the same as it had been in England and the United States. Fortunately for these early mining companies vast stands of hardwood trees were close by. Into these hardwoods went the French Canadians to cut up the trees to be made into charcoal in large beehive charcoal ovens. The year 1896 marks the high peak of charcoal production in the United States and in that year Michigan produced one-third of the total. Some of these charcoal furnaces operated as late as 1922 when the supply of hardwood for charcoal became exhausted. The early mining companies, however, soon found that blooming was not the best way to get their ore to market and therefore they began to look for a better way to ship their iron ore direct to the smelters south of Lake Erie.

Soon boats began to carry the red ore on their decks but the boat owners did not like to dirty their boat decks with the red, dusty iron ore. Then, too, once the ore reached Sault Ste. Marie it had to be wheeled in wheelbarrows from the boat, taken along the portage path in a wagon, and again wheeled onto the deck of another boat

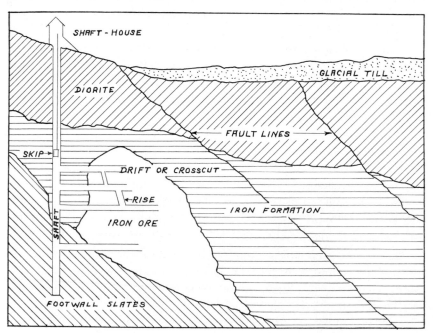

to continue its journey down the lakes. This excessive handling added much to the cost of shipping and this in turn reduced the profits.

During the summer the mines at Ishpeming and Negaunee mined the red, hard ore. When winter came, the ore was moved by sleigh to the little dock at Marquette. Horses pulled the sleighs, and about one thousand tons of iron ore could thus be taken to Marquette in a winter season. It took many horses and mules to haul the iron ore to the dock. Hay was costing the mining companies about fifty dollars a ton, and money was then worth much more than it is today. There was no one raising hay in the Upper Peninsula, and hay was a bulky load to haul all the way around the portage at Sault Ste. Marie and across Lake Superior. Using horses was an expensive way to move iron ore but at first there was no other means of getting the ore from the mines to Marquette.

The mine owners saw great possibilities in mining iron ore if it could be more easily transported to the lake cities along the southern shore of Lake Erie. Soon they began to propose the building of a canal around the rapids in the St. Mary's River so that boats could go from Lake Superior to Lake Huron. Yet to build a canal so far away in the wilderness seemed to many people like wasting money.

If you look at a map of the St. Mary's River, you will see that the St. Mary's River connects Lake Superior to Lake Huron. The length of the river is about sixty-three miles. The river has a drop of twenty-two feet from Lake Superior to Lake Huron. Most of this drop is made at one place about forty-nine miles up the river. There, in a distance of a little over half a mile, the river drops about eighteen feet in the form of a rapids as the water spills over the Cambrian sandstone. This rapids is known as the Sault.

Because of this rapids in the St. Mary's River, boats could not pass between Lake Huron and Lake Superior. From the days of the French traders to 1855 everything passing this point had to be portaged around the rapids.

In 1797-1798, the North West Fur Company built, on the Canadian side of the river, the first canal and lock at the Sault. The canal and lock were to aid in getting canoes and other small boats of that day around the rapids. The lock was very small, only thirty-nine feet long and eight feet wide. Much of this early work was later destroyed by American troops during the War of 1812.

As soon as Michigan became a state, people began to talk about making a canal at Sault Ste. Marie. In 1837 the state legislature made plans for building a canal, and granted $25,000 for the purpose. The following year $25,000 more was provided, and, when surveys had been made, a contractor was hired to build the canal. When the contractor reached the Sault, he found that the canal was to pass over land that then belonged to the United States Government. When he commenced work, he and his men were driven away by United States soldiers.

In 1840 the United States was asked to aid the state in building the canal. Iron ore and copper had as yet not been found in the Upper Peninsula, and most people could see little value in building a canal so far from where people lived. Henry Clay, who was in the United States Senate, strongly opposed Federal aid, and Congress could not see the spending of money on a canal which was then thought to be too far back in the woods to ever be used.

The developing iron and copper mines called people's attention to the need of a canal at the Sault. In 1852 Congress did awaken to the need of a canal at the Sault, and offered for sale three quarters of a million acres of government land to raise the funds.

Following this Federal grant, the State Canal, 5,674 feet long, was built in 1853-1855. The canal was provided with two locks, one leading into the other. At first it had been planned to make the locks just 250 feet in length. People laughed at Mr. Harvey when he said that the locks should be larger. But Mr. Harvey, who was put in charge of the work of building the canal, won the state legislature to his plan, and the locks were built as he had suggested. Each was 350 feet long and 70 feet wide. Their sides were lined with limestone blocks that were quarried on Drummond Island. These locks allowed the passage of boats which did not sink more than twelve feet into the water. Each lock had a lift of nine feet. At the time these locks were made, they were the largest in the country.

The building of the "Soo" canal was a large undertaking for that day. All of the canal had to be cut into the Cambrian formation. To cut away the rock with the tools of that time was a slow, hard task. Immigrants were secured to do much of the labor, and real labor it was, especially in the wintertime when the ground was frozen and the temperature remained below zero for days at a time. There were no railroads to bring in the needed supplies. Supplies had to be brought to the Sault by boats. During the winter the lakes were frozen, and then the boats stopped running. To send a letter to New York and receive a reply took about six weeks.

To help pay for the cost of building the canal and locks, tolls were charged on each ton of freight that passed through the locks. At first the rate was six and one-half cents per ton. Then later it was done away with and boats were allowed to use the canal free.

Courtesy *Steelways*, published by American Iron and Steel Institute

The brig "Columbia." This brig brought the first load of iron ore through the "Soo" locks.

The new canal was ready for use on June 18, 1855. The first boat up-bound was the "Illinois." The first down-bound boat was the "Baltimore." Two months later the little schooner "Columbia" passed through the locks carrying on her deck a shipment of iron ore. It was 120 tons of the red metal going from Marquette to Cleveland, Ohio. Four days after the "Columbia" passed through the locks, the schooner "George Washington" passed downward bound with 332 tons of iron ore on her deck. That first season 1,447 tons of iron ore passed through the locks of the new canal. A new day in shipping had come to the Great Lakes.

While the canal was being built, the mine owners began to improve the manner of getting iron ore from the mines to Marquette. In 1855, the year the canal opened, a plank road was built from the mines to Marquette. In that year only 1,447 tons of ore were hauled, but the next year, 1856, when the new plank road had been finished, the tonnage increased to 11,297 tons. Each team still made only one round trip a day, but as much as four tons of ore could now be hauled at one time. The plank road was not used for long because, in 1857, the Iron Mountain Railroad Company opened its line from the mines to Marquette. Soon whole trains of ore cars filled with red ore were coming from the mines to the dock at Marquette. The days of horse-drawn sleighs and wagons for hauling iron ore were past. The mines had horses and mules for sale.

Soon after the opening of the "Soo" canal, the Civil War drew the states into a bloody conflict. In 1861, copper was selling for seventeen cents a pound, but by 1864 the price had gone up to fifty-five cents a pound. Copper and iron mines that otherwise would not have been self-supporting began to pay a profit as armies demanded more and more iron and copper.

Iron was needed for cannons, horseshoes, and other war supplies as well as for the expanding Northern railroads. Copper was needed to make canteens, as well as to make the brass buttons for the soldiers' uniforms.

In August, 1863, the Union Army approved a new gun for the Union soldiers. This gun used what could be called the first modern cartridge. It could fire seven balls in half a minute. The cartridges were placed in a magazine in the stock of the gun. From there they were automatically injected into the chamber of the gun. To make these new cartridges required much Michigan copper.

The high prices that the North was willing to pay for copper and iron ore during the Civil War helped the iron and copper mines to get started. Fortunately for the North, the canal at Sault Ste. Marie was in operation and these minerals could be more easily shipped to the Northern industries. The increasing supply of copper and iron, together with the "Soo" canal, aided the North in winning the Civil War.

The North, during the war years, was afraid that men from the South, or friends of the South, might destroy the locks at the "Soo" and thus cut the North off from its supplies of iron and copper. Because of this the United States government had a railroad built, in 1864, from the Marquette range south to Escanaba. This railroad would keep the North supplied with iron ore even if the canal was destroyed so that boats could not go into Lake Superior.

In 1863 President Lincoln ordered that a road be built from Fort Howard, on Green Bay, Wisconsin, to Fort Wilkins at Copper Harbor on the northern tip of the Keweenaw Peninsula. This road, now called the Military Highway, followed along an old Indian trail. Still another road was opened from Saginaw to the Straits of Mackinac.

By the time of the Civil War, several mines were producing copper. The Cliff Mine had been worked since 1844. The Minesota had been producing since 1848, and the Quincy and Pewabic had been putting out ore since 1848. In all, over three thousand copper mining companies had been formed between 1845 and 1864. However, only thirty were mining copper by 1865.

In 1860 the waterway leading into Portage Lake from Lake Superior was deepened so larger boats could come into Portage Lake from Lake Superior. This work was started in 1859 by several mining companies located near Houghton and Hancock so that supplies

could more easily be gotten into the mines on Portage Lake. Before
that time all supplies had to be unloaded at the mouth of the Portage
River, hauled overland, and then again put on boats on Portage Lake
and taken to Houghton and Hancock. In 1861, some 230 boats used
the new channel and entered Portage Lake. The new waterway made
Houghton and Hancock important shipping centers, and their importance increased when copper was discovered at Calumet in the area
just north of Portage Lake.

The Calumet Lode was discovered, in 1856, by Edwin J. Hulbert.
In 1855, while making a survey for a new road that was to run between
Ontonagon and Copper Harbor, Mr. Hulbert located a copper deposit
where Calumet now stands. This new mine, however, was not opened
until 1864. It has since proven to be one of the richest of Michigan's
copper mines. In the years that followed, the Calumet Mine was
driven down to a depth of 9,600 feet. The Tamarack number five shaft
went straight down into the rock for over a mile.

Michigan's early copper mines were developed in a long, narrow
corridor of ore-bearing rock that stretches some one hundred miles
south through the Keweenaw Peninsula from Copper Harbor to south
of Ontonagon. The width of this copper-bearing rock varies from
two to eight miles and extends down into the earth to an unknown
depth. In some places the veins widen out as they go deeper into
the ground. In other places they give out altogether. In general, the
deeper the vein, the less copper was found in each ton of rock that
was removed.

All of the early copper mines worked deposits of pure native
copper. In the mass mines where the copper formed in large fissures,
the copper often appeared in huge masses. These huge masses of
copper were hard for the early miners to cut up because of their
poor mining equipment. One huge mass in the Minesota Mine weighed
572 tons, and it took twenty men fifteen months to cut it up and bring
it to the surface. The amygdaloid deposits were found in the old
volcanic conduits. In these mines the copper was usually found in
smaller masses. In some mines, like the Calumet Mine, the rock
formation was called conglomerate. In these deposits the copper was
mixed with sand, gravel, and pebbles, and in this type of formation
the copper often came in strings and was very hard to free from the
hard rock with which it was mixed.

Silver was also found in many of the copper mines. This was
especially true of the Minesota Mine. From that mine, kegs filled

with the precious metal were shipped south. Most of the silver was usually deposited near the surface. Often these pieces of precious metal found their way into the miners' pockets. There seems to have developed an unwritten law that said copper was for the company but silver could be taken by the miner lucky enough to find it.

Mining copper was far harder and more costly than the early prospectors had imagined it would be. All of Michigan's copper was buried in hard rock. In those days all drilling had to be done by hard labor. One man held and turned the drill as it slowly cut into the lava flow or the sedimentary rock. Two, or three, other men with sledge hammers pounded the drill as it went down, sideways, or even up into the rock overhead. This type of drilling was very slow, hard work. When enough holes had been drilled, the holes were filled with black blasting powder. This was the only blasting force known at that time. When the powder was exploded, the rock containing the copper was shattered. In this manner shafts were sunk into the ground. As the shafts went downward, drifts and crosscuts ran outward from the main shaft. The various levels grew in size and length as the miners cut farther and farther away from the main shaft.

All the fallen rock had to be shoveled or lifted by hand into little cars and then pushed to the shaft. Then the ore was hoisted to the surface. At first the copper and rock were raised by horsepower. A crude lifting device known as a "horse-whim" had a large round drum on which the cable was wound as one or more horses walked round and round, turning the drum beside them. As the cable was wound up a bucket filled with rock or ore was raised to the top of the mine.

When the rock was out of the mine, the work of freeing the copper from the rock was far from finished. The rock had to be further crushed before it would let go of the copper. During the early days of copper mining, the ore-bearing rock had to be crushed by hand. Strong men pounded the rock with heavy sledge hammers to crush it and thus free it from the copper masses. But in this crude manner of crushing the hard rock only a part of the copper was freed from the rock. Thus, much copper, perhaps one-fourth of it, was thrown out with the discarded rock. Later very expensive crushing mills were developed to crush the rock into much smaller pieces and thus free more of the copper.

For a few years the rock was taken from the mines to the crushing mills on wagons. Because the roads were so poor, only a small amount of rock could be carried on any one load. As in the iron mines, this type of transportation was slow and expensive. When the copper had been freed from the rock, it was then melted into bars for shipment down the lakes. These heavy bars were taken from the mines to one of the copper ports on sleighs in the wintertime.

For several years all the iron mines were worked as open pit mines, but the copper mines began as shaft mines almost from the very start. Down, down, far into the stumps of the old Killarney Mountains went the copper miners as they pounded on their steel

Courtesy State Department of Conservation

The Tionesta docked beside a dock full of copper ingots at Houghton. The Tionesta was launched in 1903. She was a combined passenger and freight steamer that ran between Duluth and Buffalo until 1934. Picture taken about 1910-1915.

drills. Black powder blasted and shattered the rock until tunnels, drifts, and crosscuts grew far longer than the length of the streets of the little mining towns which sat near the top of the shafts.

The copper mines developed three rather definite mining areas. In the area south of Ontonagon many mines were developed. Some of them were the Nonesuch, White Pine, Minesota, Mass, Victoria, and the Adventure. In this area grew up the villages of Ontonagon, Bergland, Rockland, and Mass.

The second district grew up around the old Keweena Portage. Here could be found the Quincy, Atlantic, Superior, Baltic, Champion, Huron, and Isle Royale mines. These mines centered around the twin cities of Houghton and Hancock.

North of the Keweena Portage area many other mines developed along the copper range. In this third area could be found the Calumet, Allouez, Ahmeek, Seneca, Ojibway, Cliff, Phoenix, and Central mines, as well as several others. The communities of Calumet, Laurium, Eagle Harbor, Eagle River, and Copper Harbor grew up in this area.

Today nearly all of these copper mines, which were busy places one hundred years ago, have been abandoned. The mines are filled with water. The houses where people once lived have burned or have been torn down. Often only site markers now tell the modern tourists where the villages and mines used to be.

The first group of men to work in the new copper and iron mines were Cornishmen. These men came from a long line of men who had worked as miners in the Duchy of Cornwall in England. They knew mining as well as a sailor knows the sea or a farmer knows his land, and they loved it just as much. As the years passed by and newer immigrants came to work in the mines they were usually put to work under a Cornish mine captain.

During the Civil War years many Swedes, Finns, Danes, and Norwegians came to the United States. Many of these people found their way to the Upper Peninsula of Michigan to work in their newly adopted country. In many ways the Upper Peninsula reminded these immigrants of the lands from which they had come. It was a pine country filled with many pretty lakes. Even the winters were long and cold like the winters were in their native lands. Many Canadian French also came, but mining had no attraction for these men who had spent their lives in the forests. Why work in the dark, damp underground when one could work in the open woods amid the fresh air and sunshine? These French Canadians usually supplied the wood that was used to make charcoal for the iron mines. During the war years many of these newcomers left their jobs and joined the Northern army.

Each of these groups has left its mark on northern Michigan. Towns like Bergland, Rockland, and Greenland remind us today of the people who came here from Scandinavia to start life anew in the little houses not far from the shafts of copper or iron mines.

Many Finnish farmers now living in the Upper Peninsula can tell you tales about the early days when their grandfathers, or great-grandfathers, came into the area when it was still a rough wilderness. One cannot visit these mining districts even today without becoming aware of the Cornish pasty that comes fresh from the baker's ovens every day. Mining was hard work, and a miner needed plenty of good, solid food for his noonday meal. This the Cornishman's wife fixed for him in his daily "pasty" which he took into the mine each morning. A pasty was made from vegetables and meat all folded nicely into a wrapper of pie dough. The whole was then baked to a golden brown in the family oven. At noon a miner placed his pasty on his shovel and held the shovel over a candle until the pasty was thoroughly heated. Thus he had a well-balanced, warm meal, though he was eating it deep underground in a mine.

Men working in the copper and iron mines always faced hazards that often took their lives. Sometimes the black powder did not explode as it should have done. These unexploded packings of powder the miners called "sleepers." While the broken rock was being shoveled into the cars, these sleepers sometimes exploded and killed some of the miners. Falling rock was also a constant danger. To brace up the rock ceilings huge timbers like telephone poles were placed in the mines. These sometimes caught on fire. Such fires filled the mines with smoke and fumes. Sometimes these timbers burned for days before the fire could be put out. In the early mines, in the days before fans were developed, the air was often foul and the "wet damp" from blasting spread throughout the mines. Water seeping into the mines was a problem from the start, but pumps were soon used to bring the water out of the mines.

At first miners used only candles for light. These candles were fastened to the front of their hats. As you know, candles give very little light, so mines in those early days were very poorly lighted. Because the winter days are short in the Upper Peninsula, the miners saw very little sunlight except in the summertime. A few years later candles were replaced by carbide lights that were worn on miners' hats just as the candles had been worn.

By the time of the Civil War, mining had become one of Michigan's major industries. Around each mine shaft, houses were built of fresh-cut lumber, and new towns, several with Indian names, came into being. To these towns came Cornishmen, Swedes, Norwegians, Finns, and French Canadians. Stores were built, schools were begun, and churches were built for both Catholics and Protestants. Over the mine shafts, shaft houses were built, and smelters were built in which the copper was freed from the crushed rock and melted into bright, pretty copper bars. Each summer, boats carried these shiny bars away from the copper ports.

But the mining towns a hundred years ago, in those days of poor transportation, were still very far from the other towns of Michigan "down below." During the summer when the boats came sailing westward across the cold, blue waters of Lake Superior, the mining people felt a little nearer to other people. But when ice formed on the lake and the black smoke of the steamers, or the white sails of the sailboats, could no longer be seen coming across the water, the people of the mining towns felt as if they were living far, far away from their friends and relatives.

Winter with its cold, snow, and ice blocked the water highway for nearly five months of the year. Between the mining towns and their closest neighbor, Green Bay, Wisconsin, lay two hundred miles or more of snow-covered forest land that could be crossed only by walking on snowshoes. Little in the way of food could be brought in through the snow-covered forests, for there was not even a road through the forest land. All food and supplies had to be brought in during the summer shipping season. Sometimes, when the last boats could not come because of ice and storms, the people in the early mining towns had few supplies to last them through the winter. Mail for the area had to be brought in from Green Bay by dog sleigh in the wintertime. This method was used at Ontonagon until 1864.

When spring came, the ice in Lake Superior turned to water, the green leaves again grew on the hardwood trees, the birds came back to their nesting grounds, and the boats again came westward from Sault Ste. Marie to carry away the copper and iron ore that had been mined during the winter.

Up to about 1875, there was only one iron mining region in Michigan, and all the iron ore was shipped from Marquette or Escanaba. This range, known as the Marquette Range, reached some thirty-five miles, from Ishpeming and Negaunee almost to L'Anse. Besides the Jackson Mine at Negaunee and the Cleveland Mine at Ishpeming, some fifty or so mines, by 1878, spread across the range, giving rise to many iron mining towns such as Champion, Michigamme, and Republic.

Iron is a very heavy commodity, and a hundred years ago, in the early days of iron mining, there were none of the huge machines to handle the ore that there are today. The red, heavy ore had to be shoveled into cars in the mines. Horses, or mules, pulled the cars to the skip where the loaded cars were raised to the top of the mine and the ore dumped into a bin. From there the ore ran down into railroad cars. The cars were then taken to Marquette or Escanaba

Courtesy Republic Steel Corp.

Iron ore may be taken aboard through as many as eight or more hatches at a single time. When the ore pockets in the dock are emptied, the boat is moved either forward or backward to permit a new set of ore chutes to be lowered into place and the pockets emptied. (Escanaba, Michigan)

where the ore was dropped through the bottom of the cars into a huge ore dock. From the bin the iron ore ran down into an ore carrier. In the holds of the new ore boats that were being built for the ore trade, men called "trimmers" shoveled and pushed the ore around as it came from the chute into the hold of the boat so that the boat would not list to one side. This was hot dirty work on a warm summer day.

Unloading an ore boat was also much work. Men had to go into the hold of the boat and shovel the ore into a bucket. This work on a hot summer day when the sun was beating down upon the boat, especially one of the metal ones that were beginning to be used to carry iron ore, was a task almost beyond human endurance. The bucket was then pulled upward by horses or oxen. The ore was then dumped into a wheelbarrow and a man had to wheel it off the deck of the boat. By this method it sometimes took three or four days to unload an ore boat.

Later, powerful machines came into the mines to do much of the work, huge loading docks were built to load the boats, and huge bucket scoops were developed to do the hard work of unloading. Such machines as we have today, to handle our vast shipments of iron ore, were beyond the imagination of the men who worked in the iron mining industry in the earlier days.

CHAPTER FOURTEEN

The Lumber Story
(1860–1910)

As THE SETTLERS pushed west across the United States and the cities grew larger, several demands for more and more timber products came into being. Builders of boats needed beams, planking, and masts. Settlers moving onto the plains land of the West, needed fence posts and lumber to build their houses, barns, and sheds. Thousands of railroad ties were needed for the new railroad tracks that were spreading across the nation. Hundreds of poles were needed for the new telephone and electric lines. Lumber was also needed back east to build homes, stores, churches, and schools in the rapidly growing cities in an area in which most of the timber had been cut into lumber. As these demands for forest products increased, so did the ring of the woodmen's axes and the high-pitched whine of the better saws in the lumber mills of Michigan.

Lumbermen went up the streams in the upper part of the Lower Peninsula, and in the Upper Peninsula, seeking out the better stands of pine that stood near some stream. Others built steam-driven sawmills at the mouths of the rivers where the logs could be cut into lumber and other products such as bed slats, lath, and pickets for fences.

Many men came to Michigan to help in the timber harvest. Among this group were many immigrants from Europe. Poles, Finns, Swedes, and Norwegians came to work in the forests and the lumber mills. Also many sons of the earlier settlers, who were Civil War veterans, went north to find work in the mills and woods.

Up to about 1870, the timber supply for the sawmills had been cut near the sawmills, but as the nearby forests were quickly destroyed, lumbermen had to go farther and farther up the rivers to get logs for their mills.

Soon after the Civil War thousands of pine logs began coming down the Au Sable, the Rifle, the Black, the Jordan, the Boardman, the Manistee, the Pere Marquette, the Manistique, the Menominee, and many other smaller streams every spring to add their numbers to those already coming down the Saginaw and Muskegon rivers. It seems that any stream large enough to float a pine log, if it flowed through pine country, was used, during this period of logging, to carry pine logs to the busy sawmills.

It became the usual custom during those years of logging in Michigan for a man preparing to log his land to first cut a road through the forest to the place where the lumber camp was to be built. Over this road all supplies for the camp for the coming winter had to be taken to camp by tote team. Sometimes this distance was twenty or thirty miles.

As soon as this road was finished a crew of men went into the forest area where the winter's cutting was to be done. These men usually went into the woods in the early fall. The first thing they did when they reached the site of the lumber camp was to clear a road from the "cuttings" to a high bank on the nearest river. Over this road the logs, which the men would cut during the coming winter, would be hauled to the river bank. Then the men built the lumber camp itself. In the fall after it was finished the logging crew arrived to begin their winter's work in the woods.

In the lumber camps of that time there were usually several buildings. One of the buildings, called the "bunkhouse," was the building in which the men slept. Then there was usually another building used as the "cook shack" and dining room. Still another building was used as a barn for the horses. Other buildings were used for storing supplies and for the camp office and "van." The van was a small store where the men working in the camp could buy such items as socks, mittens, shirts, and tobacco. Usually the camp foreman and scaler had their living and sleeping quarters in the van.

By 1880, logging in Michigan had become big business as eastern capital came west with the lumbermen. More and more of the big lumber companies at that time began operating so many lumber camps that their camps were often referred to by number.

The old "bunkhouse" of the earlier logging days had, by 1880, given way to a newer and better one. The bunkhouse in these later camps was usually a long, narrow building. Whereas in earlier days the bunkhouse had been built of logs, most of the bunkhouses of this period were built of lumber and then covered with tar-paper. Logs were becoming too valuable to be wasted in building camp buildings. What is more, a building made of boards and covered with tar-paper could be more easily heated than one made from logs. When a camp was no longer needed, the buildings were often torn down and the lumber used to build another camp at some other place in the forest. The old "caboose," in the center of the building, had by now been replaced by a large iron stove. Sometimes these stoves were as long as eight feet. A stovepipe ran upward from the stove and then divided and ran the entire length of the building where it entered a smokestack at each end of the bunkhouse. By running the stovepipe lengthwise of the bunkhouse, heat was spread over the entire room. The old wooden bunks were slowly replaced by beds, or bunks, made of iron. These beds ran along both sides of the bunkhouse. Usually they were double-deckers and had some type of wire springs. The bunks were double; that is, two men slept below and two above. In front of the bunks on each side of the bunkhouse were benches called the "deacon seat," which ran the entire length of the room. These deacon seats were the only places, besides the edge of the beds, where a "shanty boy" could sit. A long wire, running on each side of the room between the stove pipe and the bunks, was used by the shanty boys as a clothesline on which to dry their wet clothing.

Loggers, up to about 1890, were known as shanty boys or shanty men. This term no doubt came west with the lumbermen and got its origin in the East where the loggers lived in buildings in the woods which were known as Maine shanties. After about 1890 timber cutters began to be called lumberjacks. Today such workers in the forests are called loggers.

The cook shack, or cook house as it was called, was another long building. It was usually divided by a board partition into two rooms. In the smaller room, called the kitchen, the cook and his "cookee" helpers prepared the meals on one or two large iron cook stoves, then called "wood ranges." The meals were served to the shanty boys in the larger room at the other end of the building. Long, heavy tables and benches were the usual dining room furniture. Kerosene lamps and lanterns furnished the only light.

The barn was usually large so as to care for the many teams of horses that worked in the woods. The barn, like the bunkhouse, was built of lumber, but whereas the bunkhouse had rough plank floors made from two-inch unplaned pine, there often was no floor in the barn. By 1880, horses had, with few exceptions, replaced the slower oxen that had been used in the woods in the earlier lumbering days.

Logging horses were medium-sized horses weighing about fifteen hundred pounds. They were known as woods horses, and after a winter or two of working in the woods they, like the shanty boys, became skilled in solving the problems of getting the logs from the forests. A man known as the "barn boss" had general charge of the barn and the horses. He was usually an old teamster who knew much about horses. The horses were kept well shod, well fed, and well groomed. Every teamster took pride in his team and often he would spend many hours in the barn currying them and seeing that his horses were well cared for. Sometimes, in the smaller camps, farmers who came to work in the woods during the winter brought their teams with them. Often their teams earned more money for the farmer than he could earn for himself.

The larger camps had a blacksmith shop. In this building the blacksmith shod the horses, repaired the logging chains and helped to build the huge bobsleighs and fasten on their large iron runners. A blacksmith was one of the most important men in the camp. Usually he received more pay than did the regular lumberjacks. The larger camps also employed a wood worker. He was called a "tinker" or "wood butcher." He, with the blacksmith, built the large bob-sleds that hauled the logs from the woods. He also helped keep the tools in repair and did such carpentry jobs as were needed in a large lumber camp.

After a hearty breakfast the shanty boys picked up their axes, swung their saws over their shoulders, and started walking down the road behind the bobsleighs, teams, and teamsters to the "cutting ground." On the cutting ground new changes had also taken place since the earlier days in lumbering. Whereas before the Civil War trees were felled by chopping them, the shanty boys of this period now began using cross-cut saws. These new saws cut much faster and also saved much good timber. A "feller" would determine the direction a tree should be felled, then with his ax he would chop into that side of the tree. When he had finished chopping, two men called "sawyers," using a six-foot cross-cut saw, started to saw the tree from the opposite side. As the saw neared the chopped place, the huge pine tree started to fall toward the ground. As the large crown of the falling tree began its long arc earthward, the sawyers cried out "TIMBER-R-R-R" to warn other nearby workmen that the tree was coming down. Then the sawyers quickly stepped away from the falling tree so that if the butt of the tree should bounce they would not be hurt. This method of felling trees with cross-cut saws saved two or three more feet of the valuable trunk of the tree in the lower and larger part near the ground. Later, as lumber became more and more valuable, sawyers began to saw the trunks of the trees closer to the ground so the stumps would have as little good wood left as possible.

When the huge pine was down, other men, called "limbers" or "axmen," came up to the fallen tree and began chopping off the branches. When the huge trunk, or bole, lay stripped of its branches, other men called "buckers" began to saw the bole of the tree into saw-logs of 12, 14, 16, 18, or 20 feet in length. Buckers also used the new cross-cut saw, and two men working together would usually "buck" about one hundred saw-logs in a day. Just when it became the practice to cut the tree trunk into logs in the woods we do not know, but whole trunks were now seldom taken to the "landings" in one long piece as they had been in the earlier days of logging. The distance which the timber now had to be hauled was too far to log in that way. This new custom of cutting the tree trunks into logs while the tree still lay in the forest was called the "Canadian way."

After a tree had been cut into saw-logs, a teamster, following a path that had been cut by men called "swampers," brought his team of horses up to the newly cut logs. Behind the team, on the ground, dragged a pair of "skidding tongs" that were really a pair of large pincers having a barb like a fish hook has at each end. These tongs were then fastened into the small end of a log. Then the log was dragged, or "snaked," from the woods to a nearby spot known as a "cross-haul." At the cross-haul the logs were loaded onto bobsleighs. The men usually worked in groups, or gangs, and there was usually much serious rivalry between the groups as to how many logs they could cut and get to the rollway, and this rivalry was encouraged by the foremen, for it meant more logs from his camp. A typical gang consisted of two choppers, two sawyers, two buckers, one limber, one swamper, and one teamster.

By this time the lumbering sleigh, or "bobsleigh," had been developed into the major vehicle for carrying saw-logs from the forests to the landings beside the rivers. A bobsleigh was made with two pairs of large runners. The runners were six or eight inches wide and about six or eight feet long. They were fastened together by cross chains so that the back runners would follow in the path of the front runners. Above each pair of runners was fastened, by means of a

"kingbolt," a large wooden cross beam known as a "bunk." The kingbolt would let the runners turn freely under the bunk. Bunks were
usually about nine feet or ten feet wide, although some bunks were
as wide as fifteen or sixteen feet.

A sleigh load of logs arrives at a banking ground on the Manistee River
in 1895. This sleigh had nine-foot bunks. The runners were five and one half
feet long. This size was typical of the sleighs used to haul the logs from
the woods.

Onto these bunks the logs were rolled at the cross-haul. At first
the logs were rolled onto the bobsleigh up inclined skids by a team
of horses pulling a chain which ran at a right angle to the bobsleigh.
Thus the loading place was called a cross-haul because the team
pulled at a right angle to the road. Later, lifting devices known as
"jammers" raised the logs onto bobsleighs or railroad cars. When
the logs were loaded and securely fastened by a "binding chain" or
toggle chain, as it was called, the teamster started his horses on the
road to the banking ground, or landing, beside the river.

During most of the pine logging period in Michigan's history,
logging roads and rivers were the important lanes of log transportation. Roads were built from the cuttings to the riverbank. Over
these roads, during the winter days, the logs were hauled to the river's
edge. In winters of good snowfall logging roads were quite easily
kept in good hauling condition. However, some winters the snowfall
was light, and then snow had to be hauled and dumped onto the
road. This the shanty boys jokingly called a "Swedish snowstorm."

This was costly for the logging companies, in a day when the snow all had to be shoveled by hand, but there was no other way to get the huge pine logs moved from the cuttings to the river bank. To make the roads firmer and more slippery they were sometimes iced during a cold winter night. Many camps had what was known as a sprinkler or "icer." The icer was a sleigh with a watertank on it. While the rest of the men slept, the icing crew filled the water tank at a pump or stream. A small fire under the tank kept the water from freezing. Then as the horses pulled the icer over the road, the water was sprinkled along the sled tracks. When it froze it made a good hard surface for the large bobsleighs. A team of horses could pull a huge load on these well-iced roads. It cost the logging companies much money to cut, grade, and keep up these logging roads, but they were one of the necessary expenses of running a lumber camp.

In every camp one or more men, called "road monkeys," cared for the roads. Sleighs must move easily but not too fast. If they did they overran the horses and often killed them. If the road became too slippery, the road monkey sprinkled sand on it to slow down the huge loads of logs as they came down the hills from the forest. All horses working in the woods were kept "sharp shod." That is, they were shod with shoes that had sharp points, or spikes, on them. The sharp points kept the horses from slipping and also helped the horses' feet to catch into the ice so that they could move the huge loads of logs.

A shanty boy's work day was a long one. Usually he worked at least twelve hours in the cold and snow in the woods. At noon the cook brought the noonday meal to the place where the men were working. This noonday meal, or dinner served in the woods, was called "flaggin's." Taking his plate of hot food from the lunch wagon, the shanty boy would find a log or stump on which to sit and there in the forest eat his warm noonday meal. While the men were eating their food, the horses ate their noonday meal of oats from nosebags. Then when the meal was over, the men and horses went back to their work in the woods.

When the long day's work was done and the darkness fell over the snow-covered forests, the weary men and teams left the cuttings and took the road to camp. One by one as the men reached camp they filed into the bunkhouse. The teamsters drove their tired teams into the barn. Often by lantern light, amid the sound of crunching oats and hay, the teamsters slid the harnesses from the backs of the tired horses and hung them on the wooden pegs behind the stalls. Then they too went into the bunkhouse.

Wet clothing was changed for dry. Hands and faces were washed. Pipes were lit. Gradually the deacon seat was filled with men eager for their supper after a hard day's work in the fresh, cold air. Then

came the call for supper. Sometimes the cook beat on an old dishpan; sometimes he struck a triangle bar with an iron bar. Some cooks blew a horn, but whatever the source of the noise it meant the same to all tired, hungry shanty boys: "Come and get it." The cook was ready and so were they. Quietly they filed out of the bunkhouse and into the cook shanty.

Lumber companies of this period saw to it that the men were well fed. The cook was one of the most important and best paid men in a lumber camp. Failure to have a good cook meant discontent among the men, and often they went to work for other lumber companies. Most of the cooks were men, but sometimes women did the cooking. All the meals, even breakfast, were hearty ones for the shanty boys. Beans, ham, thick

Dinner gong found in Midland County about 1930. It was used to call the men to come to the cook shack.

bacon, dried-apple pie and raisin pie, fried potatoes, hash, prunes, and buckwheat pancakes all found their way to the breakfast table. Even the tables had changed by this time. On most of the camp tables there now began to appear the new oilcloth that was then being manufactured. Some of the lumber companies even began to give their men coffee and tea. Canned goods, which were then beginning to appear on the market, also found their way onto the lumber camp tables. By 1890, most of the lumber camps were well built, clean, and well provisioned.

While eating their meals shanty boys never talked to each other, except to ask to have something passed to them. That was usually not necessary for the cookees saw to it that there was plenty within easy reach of every man. The evening meal was called supper. Though it was a hearty meal and though each man ate much, the time spent in the cook shack was usually not very long. Shanty boys ate quietly and quickly.

After supper the men went back to the bunkhouse. There the red-hot stove kept the men warm and comfortable. As the cold winter night settled down upon the camp, the kerosene lamps and lanterns that had replaced the earlier candles and light from the fire in the "caboose" gave a feeble light that cast long, dim shadows about the room. Small groups of men sat around on the deacon seats, smoked, and swapped stories. A few of the men played cards with ragged, dirty, worn cards. The thick, heavy tobacco smoke from their pipes soon filled the bunkhouse. This was mixed with fumes from the drying socks, clothing, and the fumes from kerosene lamps. There was usually no fresh air in the bunkhouse, and before long it had an odor which was all its own. For some unknown reason shanty boys took their fresh air only in the daytime. As bedtime neared, teamsters sauntered out to the barn to make one last check on their horses. Some men went to bed early, and by nine it was "lights out" for all.

The day's work was finished. Heavy snores filled the bunkhouse as the tired men rested from their work. As they slept, their clothing slowly dried by the dying fire.

The wood fire in the bunkhouse stove died down to a bed of red coals, then turned to a pile of warm, soft, gray ash. The air in the bunkhouse slowly took on a wintry chill. The sleeping men pulled their blankets closer around them. Then, as the cooling chill of the night settled on the camp, the boards of the bunkhouse, like the logs in the settler's cabin, snapped with a loud crack like the shot of a rifle. Outside in the moonlight from across the hills could now and again be heard the howl of timber wolves.

Sometimes during the night a wintry storm would roar and cover the camp and roads with a new layer of downy whiteness. The snow, driven in gusty whirls, was piled against the bunkhouse and the other buildings, around stumps, and against fallen logs or trees. When morning came, new sights and strange shapes greeted the men. Strange mounds of white snow appeared where sleighs, stumps, barrels or bushes had stood the night before.

The first one up at camp in the morning was the "chore boy." He was usually not a boy at all but an old shanty boy who could no longer stand the hard work in the woods. Usually he was up by four in the morning. Building fires in the cook shack and the bunkhouse was his first task. Then he called the cook, the cookees, and the teamsters. While the rest of the shanty boys still slept, the cook and the cookees started gettting breakfast. Meanwhile the teamsters went to the barn to feed their horses. The fire in the stove in the cook shack melted the ice in the water pails. With some of this water to prime the pump, one of the men, properly clad against the cold, went out to get fresh water. Sometimes there was no pump and water had to be carried from a spring or a brook. Often the man sent for the water had to cut a hole in the ice before he could get any water. But the water was brought and soon coffee was being made on the huge wood range. The pleasant smell of coffee, frying bacon, and pancakes soon filled the cook shack.

About four-thirty in the morning one of the cookees, called the "Gabriel blower," blew the "Gabriel," a long tin horn. This aroused the sleeping men and then someone called out, "Get up, you lazy lumberjacks; it's daylight in the swamp." Aroused from their deep sleep the men would roll from their bunks. Pairs of legs, clad in long, bright-red underwear, would swing down from the edges of the bunk beds. Rough, calloused hands rubbed eyes yet sleepy from the night and pushed back mussed-up hair. From the wire strung along between the stove pipe and the bunks each shanty boy pulled his heavy wool socks, which by then were dry. Quickly, over his long underwear, he put on one or two pair of heavy wool socks, heavy woolen pants, a pair of heavy shoes, and one or two heavy woolen shirts. Pants were held up by wide bright-colored suspenders. Most shirts were bright plaids.

At one end of the bunkhouse was a bench that ran across the room. Upon this bench there were usually several tin wash basins. To these wash basins the men went to wash before breakfast. Dipping the basins into one of the water barrels, which had been filled by the chore boy, the shanty boys washed for breakfast. One by one they used the basins and then threw the wash water out the bunkhouse door. There the water gradually froze into a pile of ice which often did not disappear until the coming of spring. All the men, as a usual thing, used towels that were furnished by the company. No one thought of such a thing as sanitation or very much about cleanliness. Why should a man refuse to use a towel? Was he any better than the fifteen or so men who had used it ahead of him?

About five o'clock came the call for breakfast. Soon the men were helping themselves to huge chunks of sausage and large thick pancakes and plenty of blackstrap molasses. Within a few minutes all had been fed and quietly, one by one, they left the cook shack. The teamsters went to the stable and finished harnessing their horses. Soon they were on their way to the cutting grounds for another day's work.

Cold was no excuse for not working. With good woolen socks on their feet, with warm mittens on their hands, and often with a short-stemmed pipe, called a "nose warmer" and smelling ages old, the shanty boys did another day's work in the woods. Often when they had reached the cutting grounds where the winds could not hit them, they became so warm from working that they had to take off part of their heavy clothing.

On Sundays no work was done. The meals were served at the usual hours, but the rest of the time the men were free to do as they wished. Sunday was known as "boil up day" because many of the men used part of the day to do their washing. Boiling their clothes not only freed the dirt from the clothing but also killed the lice and bedbugs in them. Only a few of the men could write. Some-times these men wrote home to their families or to the families of other men who could not write. These letters went to town with the "tote teamster" the following week when he went to town for supplies. Sunday was a good day to play jokes on "greenhorns" who had just come into camp. Some men played cards in the bunk house. Others spent hours sharpening their axes on the grindstone. This was a slow, tiring job, but a sharp ax was a shanty boy's best tool. For hours they turned the slow-cutting grindstone as the axes were sharpened for the coming week. A few of the men read papers and magazines which were often weeks or months old. Some rested in their bunks. Others sat outside, if the day was warm enough, and whittled on pieces of clean fresh pine.

In many of the camps there were men who were natural enter-tainers. Some were good singers, others played violins, guitars, mouth-organs, accordions, or dulcimers. Sometimes they would entertain the others with music and song. Most of the songs they sang were ballads that told some story of woods life. Many of these ballads were originally written in Maine and brought to the Michigan woods by the lumbermen as they came west.

Usually the lumbermen cut only the timber that was on the land the company had purchased. However, some companies lumbered what were called "round forties." They would purchase a piece of

Banking grounds on the Manistee River, 1895. Picture taken in Crawford County.

land and then cut all the area around it, thus stealing government or privately owned timber. Nothing much was ever done about this practice during the lumbering days, but in 1903, after most of the timber was gone, the state legislature finally passed an act making it illegal to cut timber on state-owned land.

Every day, all winter long, teams of horses, or oxen, were busy hauling logs from the cuttings to the landing on the river bank. By early spring huge piles of brown pine logs lay "decked" along the banks of many of Michigan's rivers. The places where the logs were piled, or decked, were called "landings," "decking grounds" or "rollways." The rollways were usually on a high bank along the deep side of a stream. Even today these old rollways can often be located by the scars that the logs left on the river bank as they were rolled into the water.

Carefully the woodsmen watched the river. Too little water in the upper branches meant that the logs would ground on the river bottom. Too much water meant the flooding of the stream, and then valuable saw logs would be carried from the main course of the river and pushed into swamplands or marshes where they would be left by the river. To get these "stranded" logs back into the stream often took much time and hard work.

At last, when the spring rains and the melting snows had raised the river high enough, the river drive began. The decks of logs were rolled over the bank and into the river. "Breaking the rollways," as this was called, was dangerous work, for the rolling logs sometimes hit a shanty boy and killed or injured him. With a rumble the logs went rolling over the bank and splashed into the river. Water splashed high into the air as the first rolling logs hit the running river. Up and down the logs bobbed and churned as others rolled in

Ford operations at Iron Mountain 1948. By using a log scale, a man called a scaler could determine about how many board feet of lumber could be cut from a log. In this way a lumber camp could know about how much lumber the men were cutting.

on top of them. Slowly they began to move downstream with the running water. If the river was high and running free, the first logs soon began to disappear around the first bend of the river. Thus the logs began the second part of their journey from forest to sawmill.

In rain, snow, sleet, and spring sunshine, the river drivers, called "river jacks," "river hogs," "river pigs," or "white-water men," worked at the task of getting the winter's cut of logs into the river. Logs piled farther back from the river bank had to be rolled by a peavey to the water's edge. This "tailing down" was hard work but required no great skill. In a few days' time all the winter's cut had been rolled into the stream. The winter's work in the woods was finished. Most of the men packed their belongings in their "turkey" and started for town or home. Only a few river drivers remained behind to bring the logs down the river. When the men reached the nearest town, some of them spent all their winter's hard-earned money in one wild "spree" that lasted only a few days. Others carefully guarded their earnings and took the first train, or boat, and went back to their families and to a summer's work on their farms.

Sometimes so many logs floated on the water that the surface of the river looked brown. The river drivers could walk about on the bobbing pine logs wherever they pleased. Not all shanty boys could be white-water men. River drivers had to have a good sense of balance, a quick step, and a good eye to judge logs and sudden movements of the river.

Many of the early river drivers were French Canadians and forest workers who had come to Michigan from Pennsylvania or Maine. They had a costume as gay and typical as any in American history. They dressed in red, blue, or yellow plaid mackinaws. Their trousers were also of heavy woolen material like their mackinaws. Usually they wore two or three pairs of socks which came up above their shoepacks. Sometimes their trousers were "stagged off" short with an ax in order to keep from catching their "spikes" in them. At other times their trousers were tucked into the tops of their socks. Around their belts they often wore sashes made of very bright colored yarns. Their "mits" were often tucked in behind their sashes. Tobacco pouches hung from strings around their necks.

The river drivers, carrying their peaveys with them, stepped from the river's edge onto the bobbing logs and began their ride from the camp to the town at the river's mouth. Sharp "calks" on the bottom of their shoes jabbed into the bark of the logs and kept their feet from slipping on the wet and slippery logs as they turned and slid in the cold running water. Riding the logs was fun as well as hard work for the river drivers. Most of the time the logs usually floated along with the current, but at other times they were caught by stumps, dead logs, or old trees which were lying in the bed of the stream. Stepping from log to log, or riding the one that they were on, the river drivers kept the logs floating downstream toward the sawmills.

But all the logs did not go easily downstream. Some logs called "sackers" drifted, or were pushed, into swampy places where the river had flooded the lowlands. Others grounded on sand bars in the bed of the stream. Often as much as one third of the drive would get "hung up" as they called it. Each of these logs had to be worked back into the running stream. This was hard, wet, cold work for the "sacking crew" or "rear enders" who came along behind the drive to clear up the stray logs. They had to splash about in the mud and cold water as they heaved and pulled on their peaveys to get the stranded logs back into the river.

Behind the sackers came the "wanagan." The wanagan was usually a raft on which had been built a small shed to carry the "chuck" and extra supplies such as tools and clothing that were needed by the men working on the drive. When night came, the river men walked back to the wanagan ready for a "real feed" before they rolled up in their blankets to spend the night on the bank along the river. Somehow, in spite of moving, rain, snow, or other misfortunes that overtook the wanagan, the cook always managed to have good meals ready for the tired, hungry river drivers. After they had eaten, the river drivers lay down to a carefree rest, for was it not true, as they believed, that logs always ran free at night, especially in the full of the moon?

When morning came again the river drivers were up early. After breakfast in the wanagan they began walking along the path beside the river or stepping out onto the logs to keep them on their way down to the sawmill. Sometimes the river men sat idly by on the river's bank watching the large, brown logs drift quietly by. But always they were watching to see that the logs did not start a "jam."

Beside the river ran a path through the brush. Usually it was an old animal path that the lumbermen had taken over. Along these paths they walked back and forth as the brown logs ran free with the moving current. From the path they could nearly always see the moving surface of the river. Sometimes this path ran along firm sandy ground beneath pine trees. At other times it dropped to the low marshy ground along the river's edge. Up hill and down, across sandy plains and through soggy bunch grass, ran the path beside the river that was now torn free and soft by calks on heavy shoes. Along these paths, among trees and bushes still leafless and bare in the early spring, walked the rivermen as they watched the logs drift downstream toward the sawmills. The last such river drive was on the Menominee River in 1910.

In a week or two after leaving camp the saw logs began arriving at the booms at the river's mouth where there were sawmills waiting to cut the logs into lumber. On the faster-floating streams like the Au Sable and the Manistee the logs ran quite free once they had reached deep water. On these streams the logs could be floated all the way to the river's mouth. Often a river driver, peavey in hand, came riding into town standing on one of the brown logs that he had cut in the forest during the last winter. Often the end of the drive did not reach the rivers' mouth until late in the summer.

Each logging company was eager to get its logs to the sawmills while the water in the stream was still high enough to float the logs. Therefore, most of the rollways were broken about the same time and the saw logs from several camps were often mixed together in the running water. Sometimes lumber companies got into arguments over driving rights on the streams, and many laws regarding river rights were passed by the state legislature.

In order to do away with the problems that arose when several lumber companies drove the same stream at the same time, "booming and driving companies" were sometimes formed. There were several of these booming and driving companies in Michigan. One of these companies was formed to drive the Tittabawassee River. Another one was formed to drive the Muskegon River. The Menominee River Boom Company was started in 1868, and by 1919 it had handled over ten billion board feet of logs. These booming companies were sometimes formed by the lumbermen whose men were driving the same river. At other times special driving companies were organized by other men. These booming companies drove the logs for the logging companies for a set rate of so much money for every thousand feet of timber brought into the sorting booms at the river's mouth.

Before the time of the spring drive the booming company would get the river ready for the drive. Dams were built to hold back flood water. Stumps and dead trees, called "sweepers," were dragged from the river, and "glance booms" were made so that the logs would have less chance of being stranded. A crew of expert river men would be ready to work for the booming company. It would be the job of these drivers, working for the booming company, to bring all the logs down the river. When spring came, each lumber company rolled its logs into the stream, and the booming company then took up the task of driving the logs from the rollways to the sorting booms at the river's mouth.

These booming companies sometimes also carried on rafting operations. At the mouth of the Tittabawassee River, logs were sorted according to company brands. These logs were then formed into rafts, or held in "bag booms," and then towed down the Saginaw River by tugs to the mill ponds at Bay City and Saginaw. At Muskegon and other places booming and driving companies sorted the

Photo by Ernie Grayson

The last sawmill on the Saginaw River. This sawmill was located on an island in the river. This was the third sawmill to be built on this site. Photo 1949.

logs and rafted them to the various sawmills where they were to be sawed into lumber. As the logs grew scarce, some log rafts were even brought down from the Upper Peninsula and from Canada. Tugs pulled such huge masses of logs, caught in "bag booms," across the Great Lakes.

As the number of lumbering companies increased, it became necessary for each company to mark each of its logs so that its logs could be sorted from the others at the end of the drive. At first the lumber companies marked their logs by cutting their mark into the bark of each log with an ax. This method required great skill on the part of the axman so that there would be no variation in the mark used. Because axmen were not always accurate in cutting the mark and because the bark sometimes fell from the log, newer and better ways of marking logs were soon developed. The "stamp hammer" came into common use during this period. The stamp hammer was a heavy hammer, having raised on the head of it the brand of the lumber company. By hitting the end of a log with the stamp hammer the brand, or "logmark," of the lumber company was dented into the end of the log. Soon hundreds of logmarks were registered by the lumber companies. Sometimes a lumber company used the initials of the company owner. At other times pictures of animals or birds were used. Horseshoes, buildings, etc., were all used to brand the logs that came down Michigan's rivers. Some brands were also used to mark the quality of the logs. Each county kept in its files a record of the logmarks used in the county. Because of this we know that over three thousand five hundred logmarks were used here in Michigan by the lumber companies to mark their logs as they came down the rivers. By thus marking the logs, the "pike-pole men" working on the sorting booms at the river's mouth were able to pick out the logs that belonged to each of the logging companies that were driving the stream.

As the logs entered the sorting booms at the river's mouth, they passed along a narrow waterway where men with long pike-poles pushed the logs into the pockets of the various lumber companies. When a number of these logs had been gathered into a pocket, they were formed into a raft or enclosed in a bag boom. A boom was made by fastening several logs together with short iron chains called "boom dogs." These chains were short and had an iron pin fastened to each end. These pins were driven into the end of two logs and thus the logs were fastened together with the chain. Several of these logs fastened together formed a boom. A "bag boom" was made by bringing the two ends of the boom together and thus enclosing within it the logs that the booming company wished to deliver to the mills.

In driving logs, every lumber company lost many of them. Some logs, known as "dead heads," became filled with water and sank to the bottom of the streams. Sometimes logmarks were very similar, and timber thieves would place their logmark over the old one and thus change the ownership of a log while it was coming down the river. Other timber thieves would sometimes steal logs from the river or booms and saw off a short cut on each end. This would remove the owner's original brand. They would then place their mark on the logs and send them on their way down the river. Such stealing of logs, however, was usually difficult to do because of the many rivermen going up and down the river watching the drive.

Nearly all the cities and villages now located in the upper part of the Lower Peninsula and the eastern half of the Upper Peninsula had their beginning because of the lumber industry. Some of these are known as inland towns while the others are known as port towns. The port towns sprang up first. Among the port towns might be listed Alpena, Tawas City, Oscoda, Cheboygan, Boyne City, East Jordan, Frankfort, Menominee, Escanaba, Manistique, Ontonagon, and Munising. These towns grew up around the sawmills that had been built at a river's mouth where saw logs could be had for the sawmills. The life of these towns depended upon the spring log drive and upon the fact that before them spread one of the Great Lakes over which boats could come to carry the newly cut lumber to market.

The river mouths, where these early sawmill towns were located, made very good harbors if the sand bars were not too high to keep the boats from entering. This was especially true on the west side of the state where the drifting sand dunes often made a large lake at the mouth of each river. These lakes made good harbors for the lumber boats and also provided quiet waters for booming grounds where logs could be sorted and stored until they were needed in the sawmills.

At first these port sawmill towns were rough, rowdy places. But as time passed there grew up around the sawmills large villages with houses, churches, hotels, saloons, and schools all built of the newly cut lumber. Women brought home life to the sawmill towns. Churches were started. Schools were built and children went to school. Side-walks, made from planks, ran along the village streets in front of the houses. Bright, yellow sawdust was sprinkled along the streets to keep the lumber wagons, with their wide, flat, iron tires, from sinking into the sand. In the summertime this sawdust also kept the dust of the street from blowing into the houses. White picket fences were built around many homes and gardens.

As the cutting continued in the pineries upriver, many of the saw-mill towns grew in size and took on a more dignified appearance. As the forest grew smaller, the number of wealthy lumbermen and their fortunes grew in size. These newly rich, many of whom had worn the calked boots of a shanty boy only a few years before, built large frame houses on spacious lots along the city streets of many of the growing sawmill towns. Today these huge old houses, built when good lumber was thirteen or fourteen dollars a thousand board feet, stand with their cupolas, fancy cornices, and spacious porches to remind us of the "Gay Nineties." They tell of an era when pine was king and gentlemen and ladies rode in surreys pulled by prancing bobtailed horses with heads held high by taut check reins.

At these port towns, to which the streams brought their annual spring supply of logs, the logs were cut into lumber. Each morning the whistles of the sawmills announced the beginning of another day's work in the sawmills. Then the shining, buzzing, noisy saws again took up their daily task of cutting logs into bright yellow lumber.

The fresh-cut lumber was carefully stacked in lumber piles along the harbor where it could easily be loaded onto the boats that would carry it to market. During the long, warm summer days the hot sun shone down upon the fresh-cut, drying lumber. The soft warm wind from the forest land carried the pleasing pine smell of the newly sawed timber out over the blue waters of the nearby lake or inland

Courtesy Ralph Price

Barge Three Brothers and two tows docking at Boyne City to load lumber

across the countryside. At night, or on cloudy days, sailboat captains said they could tell by the pleasant pine odor which came to them that they were nearing a lumber port.

At first the sawmills ran only in the summertime, and many of the shanty boys, after they had spent their winter's wages, worked in them during the summer. But by the end of the last century sawmills were running all the year around. When electric lights were developed, some of the mills ran both day and night. A day's work in these early mills was ten to twelve hours. The mills ran six days a week, so a sawmill worker around 1880 worked a sixty-hour week, or more.

With the increase in camps and sawmills Michigan rapidly became a leading lumber-producing state. For a few short years it was the largest lumber producer in the United States. From its many noisy mills came lath, shingles, pickets, lumber, barrel and keg staves, barrel and keg hoops, and barrel and keg heads. Smaller trees, not large enough for lumber, were cut to make thousands of railroad ties to firmly hold the new steel rails that were then spreading across the growing nation, and to make fence posts to enclose the ever-increasing farm lands of the western plains.

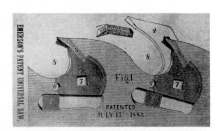

Teeth on a circular saw. From Sawyer's Own Handbook, Emerson Smith and Company, 1883-1884.

At first the lumber came slowly from the little sawmills, but the rate of cutting steadily increased. In an earlier chapter it was shown how the gate saw was replaced by the muley and how the muley gave way to the circular saw. After 1876 the band saw gained first place over other saws then in use because of its thinner "kerf." The band saw not only was able to cut a log up quickly, but because it was thinner, it cut a smaller kerf, or gash in the wood, and thus the sawmill owners were able to get more lumber from each log since the thinner blade of the band saw saved as much as twenty per cent of the log.

To make lumber, a slab not only had to be cut from a log but the two edges of the slab had to be removed so that the board would be the same width for its entire length. This was called "edging." As the slabs fell from the band saws and circular saws, they were taken to smaller saws, called "edgers," which were set to cut the boards their desired width. By pushing the slabs between these edging saws the width of the board was made uniform.

Another type of saw that began to be used in the sawmills during the later part of this period was called the "gang saw" or "hog." The gang saw was really a series of saws, like the one found in the earlier muley. All of the blades stood upright and they cut with an up-and-down stroke. The blades stood parallel with each other and were spaced as wide apart as the lumber was to be cut.

In using this saw the log was first passed by a circular saw, or band saw, four times to make a square timber or "cant." Thus a huge square beam was made. When this square timber, or cant, was pushed through the blades of a gang saw, the boards that came from it were already edged. This saved several operations and reduced the cost of sawing a log into finished lumber.

In the early sawmills the boards coming from the saws were carried

A gang saw or "hog"

away by men known as "offbearers." But as the saws were speeded up, this task became too hard for men, and live rollers were put into the mills to carry the lumber away from the saws. Sometimes endless belts were used. Better saw carriages, with steam "niggers" for holding and turning the logs on the carriage, and other mechanical devices helped to make the sawmills more efficient as well as to increase the rate of cutting. Planers were developed to change the rough lumber into finished boards ready for use.

From the saws, edgers, and planers there now came an ever-increasing amount of scrap material, sawdust, bark, edgings, planer chips, and slabs of all sizes. Smaller saws called "slash saws" cut the larger scrap pieces into lath or pickets and thus part of the waste was saved. However, there was still a large amount of waste. Large piles of bright-yellow, sweet-smelling sawdust grew up beside the saw-mills. At other places the refuse was dumped into a nearby lake. For years many of Michigan's lakes had in them water-soaked logs which had sunk to the bottom and were never raised for the mills, chunks of logs, and sawdust. During the past fifty years many of these old logs have been raised from Michigan's lakes and rivers and sawed into lumber. By now most of the old sawdust that once filled these

Remains of the sawdust pile at Cheboygan. Photo June, 1961.

lakes with decaying material has rotted away. At other mills a series of blowers, belts, and chutes carried the waste material to the boiler room where it was burned to make steam to run the sawmill. Sometimes there was far more of this waste than could be used by the mill, and the excess was then burned in large refuse burners to get rid of it. When salt was discovered at Saginaw and on the west side of the state at Manistee, some of the sawmills used their waste to evaporate the water from the salt brine. Thus the waste from the sawmills became useful in helping to develop Michigan's early salt industry.

Men called "filers" were hired by the sawmill owners to take care of the saws in the mill. These men made their work a secret skill. Usually they worked in a small room all by themselves, and the

Courtesy Morton Salt Company

Old stanchion bears scars from cooper's hatchet used around the turn of the century in heading up barrels of salt at Port Huron. When not in use in shaping or fitting of top on barrel, the hatchet was conveniently buried in a post. This was a time and effort saving proposition.

secrets of their trade they kept carefully guarded. By hammering, filing, and grinding they kept the saws sharp and running true. Later, machines were developed to grind the saws and fit them for cutting.

Nearly all sawmills, by 1880, were driven by steam engines. As the steam engines increased in power and size, so did the size of the sawmills and the speed of the saws. All the power to run a sawmill came over one large belt from the boiler room. This belt turned an overhead shaft, or shafts, and all saws and other machinery took their power by means of smaller belts from the main shaft. Various-sized pulleys gave each machine the desired power or speed. It took many miles of belts to keep Michigan's sawmills running. In the larger sawmills craftsmen known as "belt lacers" kept the belts in running order.

In the Saginaw area there were fourteen sawmills in operation in 1857 and this number grew to thirty-six in 1872. Between 1873 and 1879 there were 105 sawmills in the Saginaw Valley alone. Seventy-nine of these were between Saginaw and the mouth of the river. These mills were then cutting about four million feet of lumber a day. Thus in 1880 Saginaw alone was cutting about one billion feet of lumber a year. At their peak 112 sawmills were spread along the Saginaw River bank for twenty miles. To carry away the newly cut lumber, schooners, called "lumber hookers," sailed into Saginaw Bay and were then towed by tugs up the Saginaw River. So many

Sawmill at Lewiston (1905)

lumber boats came to carry away the lumber from the busy sawmills that the bridges over the Saginaw River at Bay City often had to be opened as many as fifty times in a single day to let the boats pass.

For many years Muskegon was a typical rough, frontier lumber town. By 1859 there were six mills at Muskegon. In 1874 a fire burned seventy business places and some two hundred houses. Yet the brown pine logs still came floating down the Muskegon River every spring and before long a new and bigger Muskegon was built. By 1887 there were forty-seven sawmills lining Muskegon Lake, and a maze of booms, where the logs were sorted for the sawmills, spread out across the water in Muskegon Lake. In that year the sawmills of Muskegon cut 665,450,000 board feet of lumber and made more than 520,000,000 shingles. More lumber is said to have been cut in Muskegon than any other single point in the state. Because of this record, Muskegon was known during the lumbering days as the "Sawdust City" and the "Lumber Queen of the World."

The harbor at Muskegon was filled with schooners and "hookers" loading the fresh-cut lumber for the Chicago market. Some of the lumber stayed there and helped to build the rapidly growing city of Chicago, but most of it was sent on to the West to build villages, cities, farmhouses, and barns in the rapidly growing Midwest where hundreds of settlers were taking up land along the expanding railroads.

Into the busy smaller port harbors spread along the shores of the Great Lakes came hundreds of white-winged schooners, especially designed for the lumber-carrying trade, during the warm weather shipping season. They slipped silently into port to carry the clean, knotless, dry lumber to the busy lumber markets at Tonawanda, New York, in the East, and Chicago, Illinois, in the West. Into their empty holds and upon their decks the light, clean, sweet-smelling pine lumber was piled. Then with sails spread wide to catch the offshore wind the schooners stood out across the lake, until even their top sails disappeared beyond the distant horizon. Another boat load of Michigan's choice pine lumber had gone to market.

As the steadily increasing cutting of the uplands bit farther and farther into the forests, the haul to the river bank became longer and longer. Soon the busy sawmill days of the port cities had passed. Some remained shipping centers where lumber, cut in the inland towns, was tranferred from trains to boats, but to others the lumber boats came no more. Far out on the horizon could be seen their

Courtesy Ralph Price

Loading the barge "Pine Lake" at Charlevoix Lumber Co. dock about 1889.

trailing smoke as they steamed to other lake ports in the Upper Peninsula where the sawmills were following the cutters in the woods. By 1890 Menominee claimed to be the largest lumber port in the world.

During the second half of the last century, railroads pushed into the upper part of the Lower Peninsula and into more of the Upper Peninsula. There were still large tracts of land that could not be lumbered by the older methods but could be cut if the railroads were used to bring the timber from the pineries to the rivers or the sawmills. A railroad was built from Bay City to Mackinaw City by way of Alpena and was called the Detroit and Mackinaw Railroad. Another line was pushed up from Bay City through the central part of the state to Mackinaw City. This line, once called the Jackson, Lansing, and Saginaw Railroad, is now part of the New York Central lines. By about 1876 this line reached as far north as Gaylord. Another line, then called the Grand Rapids and Indiana, was pushed north from Grand Rapids to Mackinaw City. This line is now part of the Pennsylvania system. Branch lines ran from these main railroads to the small inland sawmill towns and to the many lumber camps.

Both the federal government and the state government aided the building of Michigan's railroads by granting timber lands to the rail-

Real horsepower used to build the Boyne City Railroad in the early 1890's.

road companies. When a new railroad was planned, the route was laid out and then the state, or Federal Government, often gave the railroad company land on each side of the track. As the most valuable lands were the pine lands, the early railroads often ran their tracks so that they would get as much of the best pine land as possible. Although this seemed a wise move at the time, it later proved to be very unwise. The areas covered by pine forests did not

Logs decked beside a railroad track. Green River camp about 1917.

make good farm land and thus today Michigan's railroads sometimes run through the poorest farming areas in many places. Sometimes the railroads were granted land in every section touched by the line. This often caused strange wanderings of the railroad so that as many sections of land would be touched as possible.

By 1875, much of the best pine forests that had stood near the banks of the rivers had been cut. The team haul to the river bank became longer and longer. Yet, much good pine was still standing in the vast areas between the rivers. There were also immense stands of hardwoods that could not be floated on the rivers but could now be sawed by the faster, more powerful saws if hardwood logs could be taken to the sawmills. Lumbermen began to wonder if sawlogs could not be taken to the sawmills on flat cars on the newly expanding railroads. The first such railroad haul was just north of Clare in 1876. Before long the new railroads were bringing major changes into the growing lumber industry.

Train near Hillman (about 1910)

These new railroads brought into being the inland lumber towns. By the time that lumbering reached its height, steam-driven machinery made it possible to locate a sawmill at any convenient place. As the timber cutting spread farther and farther away from the rivers, new inland sawmill towns came into being on rivers where railroads crossed, and on lakes where booming could be easily carried on.

Along the railroads the inland lumber towns sprang up. Among these towns might be listed Big Rapids, Cadillac, Kalkaska, Mancelona, Alba, Roscommon, Grayling, Topinabee, Vanderbilt, Wolverine, Atlanta, Seney, and many others. These little towns, of which there were many, came into being quickly and sometimes lasted only a short time. Some were deserted as cutting spread to new areas. Some of these sawmill towns were small. Others grew to be good-sized communities and then with the passing of the lumber days they disappeared altogether. Some few remained as thriving communities because of their ability to turn to other ways of making a living.

The coming of the railroads brought many changes in logging methods. Hundreds of miles of private railroads were built into the timber lands by the logging companies. At loading points, the logs from the forest were loaded onto flat cars by hoisting devices called "jammers." Most jammers were worked by a team of horses, but as the last century came to a close, some of the jammers were worked by steam and were called steam loaders. When an area had been cut, the branch lines of the private companies were extended to new cuttings or they were taken up and laid down in other forest areas belonging to the company.

Sometimes the new railroads carried the logs to the old rollways on the river bank. There the logs were dumped into the river and driven to the mills. But as railroad transportation improved, the river drives grew fewer and fewer. Finally the puffing engines were bringing the logs all the way to even the older sawmill towns.

A David Ward logging crew on the Manistee River in 1902. Notice the big wheels and the horn "Gabriel" that was used to get the men up and to call them to their meals.

By 1900 with the coming of the railroads and other changes in lumbering, lumbering became a year-round industry. In the wintertime the logs were still hauled from the woods to the railroad tracks on sleighs, but in the summertime they were now hauled from the woods on "big wheels." These big wheels were so large that their axles could clear a small pile of logs. When the wheels had been driven over the logs, a chain was passed under one end of the pile. The tongue on the wheels acted as a long lever, and when pulled down by the team it raised one end of the pile of logs from the ground. When the logs had been raised, a chain held them in place. The other end of the logs trailed behind on the ground as the horses pulled the big wheels and the logs to the decking ground beside a railroad track.

The railroads brought many changes in logging methods. Pine was becoming scarce, but the new railroads could haul the hardwoods that could not be driven down the streams. As the pine grew scarce

Courtesy Ralph Price

This picture was taken about 1908 in the eastern part of Charlevoix County during the construction of the Boyne City, Gaylord and Alpena Railroad.

long trains of flatcars, some over one hundred cars in length, brought the hardwoods from the forests to the sawmills until about 1918. Railroads, too, made it possible to cut forest areas that were too far from the streams to be profitably hauled by team to a river bank. Because of the coming of the railroads, many mills in the Saginaw Valley continued to run for some years cutting timber brought to them from the north by rail, but one by one the noisy mills stopped running and the huge piles of lumber, once stacked like canyon walls along the river bank, grew smaller and smaller. Once the river had been filled with schooners loading the fragrant, clean lumber, but now the boats came less and less often. There remains today not one of that noisy, screaming chorus of sawmills that once lined the busy river front.

The area around Cadillac was once covered by mixed stands of hardwood and coniferous forests. Cadillac's real development followed the building of the Grand Rapids and Indiana Railroad. Soon Cadillac became an important inland lumber town. Its location on the easterly shore of Lake Cadillac had the advantage of westerly winds helping to keep the logs in the booms. For many years Cadillac was a busy center of pine sawing, and millions of board feet of pine lumber were shipped away on the flatcars that had brought the logs in from the forest.

Once many miles of logging railroads spread into the adjoining area and reached as far away as Emmet County. Over these lines, trains, loaded with logs to feed the whining saws, came puffing into the city. In 1872 four large sawmills were cutting 4,000,000 board feet of lumber a day. By 1907 the white pine and Norway pine upon which the sawmills of Cadillac had depended were nearly all gone. As the pineries gave out, Cadillac turned to making lumber from hardwood and then to the manufacture of hardwood products. Maple flooring began to be made during the years just before 1900. Cadillac became the first manufacturing center of maple, beech, and birch flooring. Soon its mills were literally "flooring a nation," for it was found that Michigan's hardwoods were well adapted to this use.

From about 1875 on, some of the lumber from Michigan's hardwoods was used in industries manufacturing agricultural implements such as binder and reaper parts, plow handles, and wagons and wagon boxes. Furniture, buggies, interior finishes, and veneer also were made from hardwoods. But even these manufactured products declined as the wood supply became exhausted and industry turned more and more to the use of steel.

During the period from 1860 to 1910 Michigan had several forest fires. Often these occurred in the slashings left behind when the lumberjacks had cut an area. Usually these were local burns that did not cover an extensive area. There were, however, two years that are outstanding for the destruction that was done by forest fires. These years were 1871 and 1881.

The Chicago fire has received much publicity, although it took fewer lives and did less damage than many other fires that started in Michigan and Wisconsin on that same day in 1871.

Sunday, October 8, 1871, was a day of tragedy for many people. All summer long, it had not rained and the ground and slashings were powder dry. In many areas, around the lumbering communities and early settlements, the clearing fires of the settlers had been smoldering off and on all summer and fall. Many times, during that dry summer, people had to fight fires that spread from clearing fires, both from the early settlements and those made by workmen clearing the right-of-way for new railroads.

On that fateful day a warm gust of air came suddenly from the south and soon it was followed by a strong hot wind, which fanned the smoldering fires and turned them quickly into roaring tornadoes that spread burning pieces of wood over vast areas. When they fell they started other fires that were fanned by the strong, warm wind.

The worst disaster of that day took place at Peshtigo, Wisconsin, where some 1,152 people perished in the blaze that swept into Peshtigo and across the farming areas that spread around the village. This fire ran north, before the wind, into Michigan, just west of Menominee, but by that time its fury had been spent and not as much damage was done in Michigan.

On the same day, fire broke out at Holland and destroyed the college and 73 business houses and 243 homes. At Manistee sparks from outlying fires caught the lumber yard on fire and some 206 houses were burned. At Lansing fires also threatened the new community, but students from the new State Agricultural College helped to fight the blaze and little damage was done.

Fires also struck Midland this same day and destroyed some of the lumber yards there. In Gratiot County, the clearing fires also spread into several villages and burned them. Near Saginaw fires burned all the way from St. Charles to Birch Run. Fires also broke out in the area around Kawkawlin. Fires also spread along the Au Sable River, taking vast areas of standing pine. Farther to the north, fires threatened Alpena.

On that same day fires swept through the Thumb district from Lapeer to White Rock, and several small communities were wiped out. The toll of loss from the fires of 1871 can hardly be counted. No one knows the exact number of people that perished nor can one estimate the damage that was done to standing forests, second growth timber, and soil.

In 1881, in a similarly dry summer, fires again swept across much of Michigan. The old burn of "71" from Lapeer County to Port

Huron and into the Thumb area was again swept by huge fires. So many were these fires, and so hot was the heat from them, that many wild animals, cattle, horses, and humans were driven into Lake Huron in their attempt to escape the pursuing flames. This fire was particularly hot because of the dry timber, which was still lying in the area from the earlier fires of 1871. These fires were also brought on by sparks from clearing fires and logging operations.

By 1900 most of Michigan's timber had been cut. After the lumberjacks had passed, they left behind drying branches, rotting bark, and many stumps. Then came huge forest fires whose flaming tongues of red grew bright as they went burning across the "slashings" that had been left behind by the lumbermen. At night the horizon glowed with the yellow-red of the forest fire, and by day the sun was turned to an orange color by the dense clouds of wood smoke and soot that filled the air. Year after year such fires swept across large areas of the state. Behind remained smoking stumps, smoldering logs, and fire-scarred, black ground. These were all that remained to remind one that a stately forest had stood there before it met its greatest enemy, man. Sometimes these fires burned farm buildings, lumber camps, and even some sawmill towns. So large and hot were some of these fires that people could not flee from them and were burned to death. So hot were these forest fires that not only did they burn the wood upon the surface of the ground but also the best soil, called humus. So completely did the forest fires destroy much of the soil that it will be many, many years before some areas again will have good soil deep enough to grow trees of any size.

After the forest fires had passed, another force set to work to further destroy the cut-over lands: erosion. The forests had kept the soil in place and checked the run-off water that fell upon the land. But now that the forests were gone and the soil had been burned to a black-gray powder, much of the soil began to blow away. The rains too helped to destroy the land. The quick heavy rains of summer fell upon the wasted land and carried some of the soil away. Hills gullied. Plains were washed and blown bare. The barren sand beneath the good top soil was swept clean.

But forest fires, if they did not burn standing timber, were of little interest to Michigan's "lumber kings." They thought only of the dollars that could be made from cutting Michigan's trees. To them it was a policy of "cut out and get out." When Michigan's forests were destroyed, they moved farther west into the forests of Wisconsin and Minnesota. They took the large trees and destroyed many of the smaller ones and put nothing in their places. Lumbering one hundred years ago was far different from our modern ideas of tree farming.

In 1870, Michigan cut a little over two billion board feet of lumber. In 1880, the cut was 4,172,572,000 board feet. The highest cut was in 1890 when Michigan produced 4,245,717,000 board feet of lumber. But trees could not last forever, and in 1899 the cut had dropped to 3,012,057,000 board feet. By 1890 most of Michigan's timber had been cut. The frontier came to an end here in Michigan at about the same time that it did in the West.

In what had been busy sawmill towns, the sawmills ran less and less until they stopped running altogether. What once had been bright-yellow piles of sawdust soon turned to gray-black, rotting, wood fiber. In some towns the sawmills burned down and were not rebuilt. In other towns they were wrecked for their lumber and machinery. The machinery was sent away to new sawmills where forests were closer. When the mills stopped running there was no longer any work for the families living in the little sawmill towns. They, too, left and followed the sawmills into new areas. Morning came to the deserted sawmill towns, but no longer did the mill's morning whistle call men to their day's work. The trains of logs came no more. The railroad rails were taken away to make new lines where timber still grew. Weeds and young trees sprang up between the abandoned, rotting ties. Sawdust-covered streets, where once straining horses had hauled wagons loaded with lumber, grew up to fresh grass. Board sidewalks, on which a busy people had once gone to church, to visit a neighbor, or to a day's work, now lay rotting and half hidden in the tall grass and weeds that had sprung up between the boards over which the shanty boys and sawmill people had once trod. Houses stood deserted. Broken windows were not repaired. Doors swung on creaking hinges and the winds from the cut-over and burned-over lands passed unhindered through the buildings which had once been homes where families had lived. Many of the houses were later wrecked for their lumber and the lumber was sent to help build the growing cities of Flint and Detroit. Michigan's "lumber ghost towns" had come into being. The list of such places is a long one. Today many are still small communities, but in other places, like Eldorado, Seney, Deward, and Waters, few, if any, people now live.

Once the lumbermen had cut the trees from the land they had little or no use for the land. Often they let it go back to the state rather than pay the taxes. Sometimes they sold part of it to people who wished to settle on it and make farms. Many people, especially immigrants from Europe that came to work in the camps, bought farm lands in the lumbered areas. In a few spots successful farming on the better land was later developed, but in much of the area the soil was found to be too poor for farming. Much of it was too sandy and lacking in minerals. Other areas had been so badly burned by the forest fires which swept across the cut-over lands that there was no longer soil deep enough for farming. Some areas did not have enough frost-free days to allow most crops to mature.

For a few years men and women sometimes struggled along on these little farms. As long as the men could get work in the camps in the winter to help increase the family income they stayed on the land. However, when they had to depend upon the income from the farm alone, they found that it was not enough and the land then had to be abandoned. Hundreds of these deserted farms can be found in northern Michigan today.

Today, the land of northern Michigan, that once grew the spreading forests that drew the lumberman to Michigan a hundred years ago, is a different place. Although in some places there are farm lands, most of it is not suited to agriculture. Forests, cared for by private owners, the national government, or the State Department of Conservation, are again growing in the badly burned-over and cut-over areas. Trees, once vanquished by the woodsman's ax, are again taking possession of their ancient lands, and the fragrant odor of the pines is again being carried by the northern winds that blew across the forest lands. We have come to learn that trees are a crop and should be harvested just like any other crop when they are ripe. Mature trees should be cut and the others left to grow until they too are ready for harvesting.

Although Michigan's lumber industry destroyed her forests and ended the fur trade, it aided Michigan's growth in many ways. As the lumber was shipped out, supplies were shipped in to care for the men in the mills and in the camps. It brought people to Michigan. In those days of poor transportation, it gave many farmers, especially those living near the lumber camps, a market for their products. Farmers sold to the camps berries, hogs, veal, potatoes, and vegetables and took money or supplies such as flour, sugar, and salt.

Many of Michigan's early farmers found work in the lumber camps in the wintertime and thus they were better able to support their families and to pay for their farms. It laid the ground work for some of Michigan's industries, for the lumbermen needed manufacured products. It brought money into the area in exchange for the timber that was shipped out. The lumber industry brought many of

Lumberman's Memorial on the Au Sable River West of Oscoda

Michigan's towns into being. It helped in the building of the railroads. It aided the beginning of the salt, petroleum, and pulp mill industries. It aided the building of some of Michigan's roads. Many of Michigan's fortunes, later used to develop some of her other industries, were started in the lumber industry, for many were the men who made themselves wealthy by cutting and selling Michigan's forest trees.

CHAPTER FIFTEEN

The Great Lakes Carriers
and Their Cargoes

AFTER the Civil War, the northern part of the United States entered a period of very rapid industrial growth. Steam engines had, by then, been developed in both size and power and were being used to furnish power for ships, railroad engines, and the new factories and sawmills which were springing up across the country. Our vast natural resources of coal, iron ore, copper, and other minerals had hardly been touched. In fact, many mineral deposits had not yet been discovered. High tariffs on foreign goods protected the new and growing industries. Cities were growing rapidly around the increasing number of steam-powered factories. Railroads were pushing west across the Great Plains and through the mountains to the Pacific Ocean. The vast plains west of the Mississippi River were being rapidly turned into farm lands as settlers pushed onto them to take up homesteads along the new and spreading railroads.

Michigan played a leading part in this industrial growth that followed the Civil War, for here in Michigan at that time were located copper mines, iron mines, and spreading forests from which lumber could be made. Here, too, shortly before the Civil War, Mr. Kelly worked on some of his early experiments in making steel. The lumber story, the copper story, or the story of the rise of steel-making in the United States cannot be told without telling about Michigan's mines, forests, ports, boats, and shipping on the Great Lakes.

In 1860, there were 138 sidewheelers, 197 propellers, and 1,122 sailboats carrying the growing commerce of the great Lakes. Although the number of steamboats was growing, the sailboats had not yet reached their largest number.

In those days many things were made of wood. Wood was used to make roads, houses, barns, sidewalks, wagons and buggies, and even machinery parts. Most of the boats then used for Great Lakes shipping, both sailboats and steamboats, were boats whose hulls

327

The USS Wilson, DDG 7. This is a Guided Missile Destroyer that was built at Bay City. It is 437 feet in length. (1961)

were still made of wood. From Michigan's forests, and from the forests of Wisconsin and Minnesota, came the heavy oak timbers which boat builders of that day wanted to fashion into the staunch wooden hulls of the Great Lakes boats.

During the period from 1860 to 1890 the building of lake boats was a major occupation in many of the growing lake port towns. Bay Port, Oscoda, Alpena, Cheboygan, Manistee, and Muskegon were all lake ports in the northern part of the Lower Peninsula where wooden boats were built. At Saugatuck, on the Kalamazoo River, at Bangor, inland from South Haven in the Grand Valley, at South Haven, and at Benton Harbor boats were built in the southern part of the state. Bay City and Saginaw were also important shipbuilding centers during the years between 1860 and 1870, for in the Saginaw River Valley grew both the needed white oak for hulls and pine for masts. At Bay City, shipbuilding has continued past the end of the nineteenth century and into the present era of the modern huge steel freighters and ocean going ships, but Saginaw saw her last boat built in the year 1889.

Tugs, schooners, propellers, and sidewheelers all took their places in the growing lake trade and helped to carry the copper, lumber, iron ore, grain, and passenger commerce of their day. In general, the boats of that day were very small by modern standards. But they could be sailed into and out of the shallow mouths of the rivers, especially those along Lake Michigan where sand bars often blocked the rivers' mouths.

During the early years of this period, most of the boats were still small sailboats. As commerce increased on the Great Lakes, larger sailboats were built. Many of these larger boats found difficulty in getting into the harbors where sand bars blocked the entrance.

If boats were built too shallow, they often slipped sideways while sailing on the lakes. But boats of deeper draft could not get into many of the harbors. For this reason some of these early craft were built with centerboards that sailors could drop down while on the lakes and raise when they entered a harbor. But the centerboard took up valuable cargo space in the very center of the hold.

The period from 1850 to 1900 was a colorful era in the story of Great Lakes shipping. The little boats of that day—sloops, barques, brigs, brigantines, schooners, and barquentines—were usually privately built and owned. Their grayish-white, billowing sails made a pretty contrast against the white-caps on the deep blue color of the water and the lighter blue of the summer sky.

Many of the sailing boats of this period that were engaged in the Great Lakes lumber trade had only two masts. These two-masted schooners became the most popular type of sailboat. Their construction was best for the lumber-carrying trade because there was more room in their hold to pile the lumber. These, as well as all the other sailing craft and steam lumber boats then carrying lumber from the sawmill port towns to the market, were known as "lumber hookers."

By 1870, there were fifteen hundred sailboats sailing the Great Lakes. The largest number of sailboats on the Great Lakes was reached in the year 1873. After that date the number of sailboats grew steadily smaller and smaller as larger and larger steamboats took their places in the carrying trade. By 1880, the number of sailboats had dropped to about fourteen hundred. By 1890, the number had dropped to a little over twelve hundred, and by 1900 there were only about eight hundred sailboats left.

During the early years of shipping on the Great Lakes, following the settlement of Lower Michigan and the area west of Chicago, grain was the major cargo carried. One million five hundred thousand tons of grain was received at Buffalo, New York, in the year 1866. In that same year only 278,796 tons of iron ore were delivered to all the Lake Erie receiving ports. The busy days of carrying iron ore were just beginning.

To meet the new and growing demands for faster shipping and large cargoes, a new type of freight steam barge began to be built in the early 1860's. These barges, which at first had rather strange shapes, were a new challenge to the older staunch schooners because they could move on regular schedules, whereas the older schooners had to depend upon the changing winds. What is more, the new steam barges found no trouble in going up the Detroit and St. Clair rivers or in and out of the narrow channels leading into some of the harbors.

As the lumbermen cut deeper and deeper into the northern forests, the piles of drying lumber grew beside the sawmills at the port towns. It was the new steam barges and the early sailing boats which, during Michigan's lumbering days, carried much of this lumber from the little port towns to the cities of Cleveland, Tonawanda, and Buffalo in the East and to Chicago and Milwaukee in the West. On these old sailing boats and barges went millions of board feet of the finest pine lumber as well as shingles, laths, fence posts, railroad ties, and telephone poles. The lumber-carrying trade was a major part of the carrying trade on the lakes between 1860 and 1890.

But sailing vessels on the Great Lakes, as on high seas, had many disadvantages that in the end resulted in their being replaced by steel steam-driven boats. Sailing boats were always slow and uncertain. Their sailings depended upon the winds and during a limited season of navigation, as on the Great Lakes, shipping time became a valuable factor in transportation. Then, too, narrow channels, such as the Detroit, St. Clair, and St. Mary's rivers and those leading into some harbors, were hard for these little sailboats to master, especially when they had to sail against the current of a river. Sometimes in the early days, the sailboats were towed through such channels by sailors, horses, or oxen. With the coming of steam tugs, they were pulled through by steam power. The decks of the sailboats, too, were partly covered with masts and rigging that made it impossible to easily pile the lumber or to install the newer, faster, and cheaper loading machinery that was then being placed on the steamboats whose decks were clear of rigging.

Another thing that hastened the end of the sailboat era was the change in the type of freight then beginning to be shipped on the Great Lakes. Small bundles of furs, boxes, and barrels were giving way to larger and bulkier cargoes. Huge holds filled with coal, iron ore, wheat, or lumber were to become the main cargoes as the last century came to its close.

To increase their speed, to cut labor costs, and to adapt their sailboats to the changing age of steam power that was coming to the Great Lakes, some owners, as early as 1860, began to have their schooners towed. During the last half of the last century steam barges often towed as many as five or six of the older sailing craft behind them in a long string. Such a string, often called a "sow and her pigs" by the sailors of that day, was a common sight on the Detroit and St. Clair rivers in the 1870's and 1880's.

From Lake Erie, boats coming up the Detroit River had to pass through a narrow channel at the mouth of the Detroit River, then known to sailors as "Hell Gate." Though the Detroit River is broad at its mouth, it is very shallow because the river flows over the rim of the Devonian saucer as it enters Lake Erie. "Hell Gate" was a narrow and slightly deeper channel leading from Lake Erie into the Detroit River. Once through the narrow channel the little steam barges towed their strings of sailboats, with sails furled, up the Detroit River, on across Lake St. Clair, up the St. Clair River, and out into Lake Huron. If the tows still had sails the sailors then spread them and the little sailboats continued on their way up the lakes to a lumber port. The others were towed on to some port where they too were filled with lumber.

As the sailboats became old and rotten, they were discarded or burned. On some of the better ones the masts were taken down. Only a few years before, they had been sailing proudly under their own power with the grace and beauty known only to sailboats. Now they became lifeless hulks to be towed here and there about the Great Lakes in the wake of the sudsy foam of a steamboat. If these former sailboats still had masts and sails, the sails were only used when the wind was blowing in the right direction or when a barge broke its tow line and became separated from its mother tug or steam-propelled barge.

Many of the smaller boats from 1850 to 1870 were known as package freighters. They were given this general name because they carried freight in packages, boxes, crates, barrels, kegs, or hogsheads. None of their cargo was bulk cargo. These package freighters were the railroads and trucks of their day, for they supplied freight service to many small communities along the lake shore that had no other way to receive goods from the outside world. It was these package freighters which kept many little communities of that day alive.

With the spreading of the railroads across the state the package freight, which had been carried by boats to lake ports, was carried by the new railroads that ran in the winter as well as in the summer months. This aided the further decline of many of the port towns. Inland towns became the main distribution centers for this class of freight.

As early as 1859, some people were making plans for building a canal across the Keweenaw Peninsula along the old portage route past Houghton and Hancock. Such a canal would not only shorten the distance from Keweenaw Bay to the west side of the peninsula by some eighty miles but would also do away with the dangers, during a storm on Lake Superior, of sailing around the rocky peninsula.

In 1865, Congress granted 500,000 acres of land to the state of Michigan to aid in paying for the cost of building the Portage Lake Ship Canal. In that same year work on the new canal was begun. Eight years later, in 1873, the new canal, thirteen feet deep and one hundred feet wide, was opened for lake traffic along the old Keweena Portage route. No longer would boats have to take the long and dangerous route around the Keweenaw Peninsula. At first tolls were charged for the use of the canal, but in 1891 the federal government paid the canal owners for their rights in the canal and the waterway then became federal property, free to any boat that wished to use it.

Later the canal was widened and deepened so as to care for the larger boats appearing on the lakes. Today, this waterway is maintained by the federal government. A Coast Guard station now stands at the western entrance to the canal. Each year many ore and grain carriers pass through the Portage Lake Ship Canal on their way to or from the western end of Lake Superior and the lower lake ports. The canal is also a harbor of refuge for ore boats and small pleasure craft when heavy storms sweep across Lake Superior. Ore carriers, by using this canal today, can often make better time than by going in the open lake around the Keweenaw Peninsula.

To aid lake shipping many of the entrance ways leading into harbors were later dredged so that the newer and larger boats could get in and out. As early as 1872, the channel through the St. Clair Flats, where the St. Clair River empties into Lake St. Clair, was deepened so that the larger boats could pass up and down the channel. Some buoys were also set up so that sailors could more easily follow the winding channel in the river.

In 1871, the United States Government and the Canadian Government signed a treaty that gave both countries the use of the entire Great Lakes-St. Lawrence System. That is, boats of either nation could use the waterways of the other. Today, a freighter going

from Lake Erie to Lake Superior passes through waters belonging
to each country at several places during the trip.

By 1870, lake shippers were beginning to see that the future
cargoes of the Great Lakes were not to be package freight, passengers,
or lumber, but iron ore and other bulk cargo. At that time nearly
all the boats built, both sail and steam, were still made of oak hulls
and none of them were really designed for the iron ore trade. Sailboats could only carry three or four hundred tons of the dusty, red
ore and their construction was poor for that trade. Large chunks of
iron ore coming from the chutes in the ore docks sometimes punched
holes in their wooden bottoms. They were difficult also, because of
their masts, to load and trim. Better boats and better waterways
would have to be made so that the iron ore could be carried in
greater volume to meet the ever-growing demands for more and
more of it.

The expanding economic growth of the nation was demanding
more and more steel that could now be easily made by using the
new Bessemer process. In 1856, Henry Bessemer, in England, discovered that if large amounts of air were blown through molten iron
ore the carbon and other impurities would be removed from the ore.
Once removed, the proper amount of carbon, along with various
other minerals, could again be added to the molten iron ore to make
steel of any desired quality. At about the same time that Mr. Bessemer,
in England, was experimenting with this method of making steel,
Mr. William Kelly was making similar experiments in Kentucky and
at Captain Ward's Eureka Iron and Steel Company which then stood
at what is now Wyandotte, Michigan.

By 1880, a few eastern steel plants were using the new Bessemer
process for making steel, and steel was beginning to come from their
blast furnaces in ever-increasing amounts. In 1875, steel production in
the United States was only 375,000 tons. By 1879, it had increased
to 929,000 tons. The Bessemer process was a large step forward for
the steel industry. It meant that larger and larger quantities of cheap
steel could be made for railroad rails, railroad engines, steel plates
for ships, machines, bridges, and a thousand other things now common
in America.

As the years passed, the center of the iron and steel industry
developed along the upper Ohio River Valley and in the East where
extensive soft-coal fields easily supplied abundant coal that could

be made into good coke. During the years between 1850 and 1900, the steel industry chose to take the iron ore to the coal fields rather than the coal to the iron mines. Fortunately for the steel industry the Great Lakes provided a broad, almost natural, highway over which huge bulk shipments of iron ore could easily be carried to the lake ports in northern Ohio or to the southern end of Lake Michigan.

To make a ton of iron today takes about two tons of iron ore, one-half ton of limestone, one ton of coke, and about three and-half tons of air. In some furnaces today pure oxygen is fed into the furnace at jet speed. When the ore is smelted in the Chicago, Ohio, or Pennsylvania areas, it is near the center of population and the commercial market.

For a few years after the discovery of iron ore in Michigan the Marquette range was the only range producing iron ore, and Marquette was the only place from which iron ore was shipped on the Great Lakes. But later a new iron port was opened on the south side of the Upper Peninsula, at Escanaba, and iron ore from the Marquette range was shipped to Escanaba, by train, as early as 1864.

As the steel industry developed so did men's ideas about the boats that were to carry the iron ore on the Great Lakes. The first Great Lakes boat classed as a bulk freighter, designed especially for carrying iron ore on the Great Lakes, is considered to be the wooden steam barge named the "R. J. Hackett," which was built at Cleveland, Ohio, in 1869. The "R. J. Hackett" was 211 feet long, had a single bottom and could carry 1,200 tons of iron ore. Later double bottoms and sides were constructed in ore carriers to increase their floatage.

Fortunately for the steel industry other sources of iron ore, besides the Marquette range, were soon discovered northwest of Escanaba. Iron had been known to exist in that area since 1870. Within a few years deposits worth mining were located. This second range became known as the Menominee range. The Menominee range runs south and west of Marquette County into Iron and Dickinson counties. The iron from this district was first taken to Escanaba on sleighs, but in 1877 a railroad was built from Escanaba into the Menominee range. After that date railroad cars, filled with the "red gold," were carrying iron ore to Escanaba from the mines in the Menominee range as well as from the Marquette range.

Several mining centers developed on the Menominee range. The Vulcan Mine was opened in 1874, the Norway in 1877, the Iron

Mountain district in 1878, and the Iron River and Stambaugh areas in 1882. Escanaba became a busy lake port sending to market fish, lumber, and iron ore. For some years it was known as "The Iron Port of the World."

By 1880 because of the changing nature of Great Lakes' commerce, the era of the sailboats was already passing. Better harbors and deeper channels, built at government expense, brought into being larger and larger steamships and more and more screw propellers. The sailboats slowly passed from the lakes as the lumber-carrying trade declined. But newer and larger steel boats took their places on the lakes to carry the increasing cargoes of iron ore, limestone, coal, and wheat. The age of wood and iron had passed. The nation was entering into the new age of steel.

The years between 1860 and 1916 were busy ones for the copper mines as well as for the iron mines. In 1860, Michigan produced 12,069,120 pounds of copper and each year that followed, with a few exceptions, more and more copper came from the mines until the peak year of production was reached in 1916. In that year 269,794,531 pounds of copper were produced. These were busy days in the copper country and many improvements were made in the area. In 1872, the first bridge was built across Portage Lake between Houghton and Hancock. The Portage Lake Ship Canal was completed in 1873. In 1879, a road was completed between Ontonagon and Copper Harbor. In 1883, a railroad reached Houghton. A canal was dredged between Portage Lake and Torch Lake so that the largest boats of that day could pass into Torch Lake. Between 1847 and 1883 Michigan alone produced over half of all the copper produced in the

Portage Lake Ship Canal between Hancock and Houghton. This canal lets boats cross the Keweenaw Peninsula during periods when storms sweep across Lake Superior. Photo 1957.

United States. Until 1887 Michigan ranked in first place as a copper producer, and once again, in 1891, it ranked first.

Many changes came into both the iron and copper mines during

this period. Air drills began to be used in 1871. Some of Michigan's earliest telephones were first used in the iron and copper mines. In 1879, a telephone was installed between the lower part of the Quincy Mine and the superintendent's office. Steam pumps were used to pump water from the mines. Electric pumps began to be used in

Courtesy Pickands Mather & Company

This is a new experimental drill machine built by Ingersol-Rand & Company and paid for jointly by Ingersol-Rand and Pickands Mather & Company. The idea of the machine is to drill out a pattern of holes from one level in the iron ore to the next level (150' to 250'). The holes would then be loaded from the top level, and a raise could be blasted out between levels without having to send men and machines up into a raise for each segment of advance. Plan on shooting up to 10' of hole per blast. Holes are 4" diameter. Machine drills 6" per minute in granite. Photo taken in the Geneva Mine. (1960)

1892. Acetylene* lamps, that gave a bright white light, replaced the earlier candles on the miners' caps. Mechanical crushers replaced the hand-pounding that had been used to free the copper from the rock and to break up the larger chunks of iron ore.

The growing demand for electricity for light and power created an ever growing demand for more and more copper wire. Miles and miles more of copper wire were needed for the expanding telephone and telegraph systems. By 1905, the Calumet and Hecla Mines alone had produced 95 million pounds of copper ore.** Down, down went the copper miners farther and farther into the earth. From far below the surface of the ground came the ore-bearing rock that was crushed in the larger new crushing plants that had been built. Torch Bay was jokingly called the "Red Sea" because of the red color of the water caused by the red oxides that came from the copper stampings which had been dumped into Torch Bay by the big copper stamping mills on the west shore.

Calumet, Laurium, Houghton, Hancock, Mass, and Rockland were all known for the bright, shiny copper ore that came from the nearby copper mines. In those days when one spoke of copper one thought of the Upper Peninsula of Michigan.

This constant mining for copper honeycombed vast areas under the mining towns with drifts, shafts, rises, and crosscuts. By 1896, the Red Jacket Shaft of Calumet and Hecla Mine was 4,900 foot deep. At Hancock the Quincy Mine was also nearing 5,000 feet in depth.

Unlike iron ore, most of the copper was smelted and made into various sized copper bars near the area where it was mined. To do this much wood was used at first, but later the large ore freighters returning from Lake Erie ports brought shipments of coal to be used in the copper smelters. The bars were then taken to one of the copper ports such as Ontonagon, Eagle River, Eagle Harbor, Copper Harbor, Houghton, or Hancock. There the bars were placed on a boat and sent down the lakes to the growing industrial centers.

By 1880, good oak for making boat hulls was almost gone. A new and better material was needed for building boats, so boat builders soon turned to iron and steel. As early as 1861 a boat made

---

*Calcium Carbide reacts when water is applied to form acetylene gas. These lights are also called carbide lights and are still preferred by many miners because of their light weight and bright light.

**Michigan's total copper production from 1845 through 1960 was 10,708,300,881 pounds.

of iron, called the "Merchant," had been built of iron at Cleveland, Ohio. This boat was the first iron constructed bulk carrier on the lakes. But the new steel that was beginning to come from the blast furnaces in ever larger amounts from the iron ore that the boats were bringing down the lakes provided an even better material for boat construction.

The first bulk carrier built of steel was the Spokane, that was built in 1886. By 1888, iron ore had become the leading commodity carried on the lakes. By this same year, ore carriers were docking at Marquette and Escanaba that were able to carry in their holds between 2,500 and 3,000 tons of the heavy red ore. Ore carriers as long as 400 feet were being built by 1895. Side tanks to further increase floatage were first built into boats beginning about 1904. About 1906, sliding steel hatch covers began to be used.

The third Michigan iron range, known as the Gogebic range, was discovered in 1884. This range, which began to be developed in 1885, runs through the extreme western end of the Upper Peninsula and into Wisconsin. In this area the mining centers of Ironwood, Bessemer, and Wakefield developed. At first the ore from this range was sent to Escanaba, but when the Chicago and Northwestern Railroad extended its lines from Ashland, Wisconsin, the iron ore from this range began to be shipped from that port on Lake Superior.

By 1878, there were fifty-five mines producing ore on the Marquette range. In 1886, there were sixty iron mines in operation in Michigan. During the years between 1886 and 1900, Michigan ranked first as the iron ore producer in the United States. But before many more years had passed Minnesota was to become the leading iron ore producer.

Many of the earlier mines on the Marquette range were soon worked out and abandoned. Champion, Michigamee, and Republic declined when their mines closed down. Up to 1880, most of the iron mining had been open-pit mining in which the ore was dug from huge holes in the ground, but by that year deep shaft mining was well on its way to becoming the usual way to mine iron ore in Michigan. The diamond drill had come into use about 1870 and this drill made it easier for the miners to cut down into the rock. Shaft mining was more expensive, but as the surface deposits gave out miners were forced to dig deeper and deeper to get the iron ore from the pockets where nature had concentrated it long before. The coming of electricity made it possible to light the deep shaft mines better and more safely. Electric power also brought into being better hoisting equipment to lift the iron ore from the mines. Huge steam plants were set up to pump the water from the mines.

The presence of iron ore in northeastern Minnesota had been known as early as 1875. In 1890, a rich deposit of high-grade hematite iron ore was discovered on the Mesabi Range. This was by far the best discovery of iron ore up to that time. But the deposit was located far inland and it would be a long railroad haul to bring it to a dock on Lake Superior. Then, too, it would take more hours sailing time for a carrier. So high was this iron ore in quality that it took fifteen years for steel men to learn how to use the high quality ore found on the Mesabi Range. But once the Minnesota mines got into operation they soon far surpassed the Michigan mines in volume production.

The part of Michigan, Wisconsin, and Minnesota bordering on western Lake Superior was for many years the largest iron ore producing area in the world. About seven-eights of all the iron ore produced in the United States once came from this area. Fortunately these vast mineral deposits of iron ore were close to Lake Superior and Lake Michigan and could therefore be easily shipped on the greatest inland waterway in the world.

As the cargoes of iron ore increased in size and volume, men began building special boats designed only for the iron ore carrying trade. One of the first of these special boats was known as the "whaleback." A whaleback looked like a huge cigar upon which, at one end, was placed a pilot house and, at the other end, a cabin. The prow, or front, usually rose above the water like the pointed end of a cigar except that instead of coming to a point, a whaleback had a round, flat plate for a nose. Her deck, which was curved on the top, let the waves of the lake pass freely over her. The sailors of that time called these boats "pigs" because of the way the whalebacks rooted through the waves.

In 1888, two years after the building of the Spokane, the first whaleback appeared on the Great Lakes. This boat was only 187 feet long, twenty-five feet wide, and eighteen feet three inches deep. Between 1888 and 1898 some forty of these newly designed ore carriers appeared on the Great Lakes.

The whalebacks built at Duluth, Minnesota, and Superior, Wisconsin, were given numbers such as 101 and 102 in place of names. It was the "102" which carried the first cargo of Mesabi iron ore to

Cleveland, Ohio. This first cargo of iron ore from the Mesabi of 2,073 tons was loaded at Superior, Wisconsin, on November 11, 1892.

In 1892, one of these whalebacks was made into a passenger boat named the "Christopher Columbus." It was used during the World's Fair at Chicago, in 1893, to carry people from Chicago to Jackson Park, which was six miles away. Later this whaleback was used on the passenger run from Chicago to Milwaukee. In 1936 the "Christopher Columbus" was dismantled at Manitowoc, Wisconsin.

Courtesy Henry Ford Museum, Dearborn, Michigan

The "Christopher Columbus"

Whaleback "Meteor" at Zug Island, June, 1959. She has just unloaded a cargo of gasoline. This is one of the two American owned whalebacks still in service.

The whalebacks did not prove to be as satisfactory ore carriers as their designers had expected. They carried too small a cargo, and were too difficult to unload. They were good for their day, but as time passed they were replaced by larger and better boats. Some whalebacks were used for a time as tows, but they have almost disappeared from service on the Great Lakes. Four of these old whalebacks are still in service on the lakes, the "Meteor," built in 1896, and the "Comet," built in 1913, are now used as tankers to carry gasoline and fuel oil. Two others are Canadian owned.

As the number and size of the boats increased, the State Locks at the "Soo" became too small. Then too, some people thought that there should be no toll for boats using the locks. Up to 1877, any boat passing through the locks had to pay four cents a ton for every ton of cargo. In 1877 the toll was reduced to three cents a ton for all boats except those belonging to the United States Government or boats that were carrying army supplies or federal troops. In 1881 the State Canal was taken over by the United States Government. Since that time it has been free to any ship of any nation desiring to use it.

In 1876 work on a second lock at the "Soo" was begun. Whereas the State Canal had had two locks, this new one was to have only one lock which would raise and lower a boat in one operation. This new lock, called the Weitzel Lock, was to be 515 feet long, eighty feet wide, and seventeen feet deep. This seemed at the time large enough for any boats that would ever be built on the lakes. This new Weitzel Lock was opened on September 1, 1881. But the Weitzel Lock had hardly been finished before lake men found that new and larger locks were needed at the "Soo."

In 1886 Congress set aside funds for a new lock which was to be called the Poe Lock. This new lock was to be built on the site of the old State Canal that had been completed thirty-one years before. The old State Canal locks were removed and the new lock, built on the site of the former State Canal, was opened in 1896. This new lock was eight hundred feet long and one hundred feet wide.

In 1895, a Canadian lock was opened on the Canadian side of the St. Mary's River. This new lock was nine hundred feet long.

But as shipping increased, more locks and larger ones were needed at the "Soo." In 1908, work was begun on a new lock. This third lock at the "Soo" was called the Davis Lock. It was opened in 1914, the same year that the Panama Canal was opened. This new lock was 1,350 feet long. Just as it was finished, World War 1 began. Steel in ever larger amounts was demanded, and all three locks at the "Soo" were soon busy raising and lowering the ore carriers as they hurried across the lakes with their cargoes.

In 1913, a fourth lock was begun. It was built beside the new Davis Lock and was called the Sabine Lock. This new lock was opened in 1919.

By the close of the last century the shipping of iron ore from northern Minnesota and Michigan had become big business. Men not only began thinking about how larger and better boats could be built but also how they could be better loaded and unloaded. At the Lake Erie ports men were still shoveling the dusty, red ore from the holds of the freighters. Tubs, or barrels, were lowered into the ore carriers. Then when they had been filled by the sweating men, who were shoveling the ore in the carrier's hold, mules or horses pulled on ropes that ran through a crude pulley hoist arrangement that raised the barrels, or tubs, to the deck of the boat. Men using wheelbarrows then wheeled the red ore from the boat to the dock.

In 1899 a new type of steam-powered unloader, invented by George Hulett, was first used at Conneaut, Ohio. It was a huge clam shell that could raise ten tons of iron ore at once from the hold of a carrier. Above the large clam scoop was a cab from which the operator controlled the movement of the scoop. Once a scoop full of ore had been raised from the hold of the carrier it could be rolled sideways along the dock. In eight hours this new machine unloaded as much iron ore as a hundred men could unload in a week, No longer would men have to shovel the red ore from the freighters and, what is more, the ore carriers could be much more quickly unloaded. Because of it, carriers could spend less time unloading and more time on the water bringing down iron ore.

By 1900 the copper mines were running into trouble. In 1887 new shallow surface mines in the West were beginning to produce copper at ten cents a pound. By this time the shallow copper mines in the Upper Peninsula had been abandoned and the workers in the other mines were digging far below their very homes. In these mines sometimes as much as six miles and more of cable was wound on an elevator drum each time a skip was raised from the bottom of a mine. To hoist the rock and crush it to free the copper began to cost the mining companies more than the value of the copper that was mined. To keep the deep mines dry also required huge pumps that worked day and night. Some of these pumps pumped enough water to supply a large city. One by one the mines closed down. The huge pumps were stopped and the mines were allowed to slowly fill with water. The copper ore bars coming down the lakes steadily grew fewer in number. Many miners, now out of work, left the mines to find other employment. Many came south to Detroit and the other growing cities in the southern part of the state and found work in the new automobile factories and other industrial plants.

The bulk movement of iron ore, coal, wheat, and limestone during the past seventy-five years has brought into being huge steel freighters whose holds are large enough to carry thousands of tons of cargo. What is more, the lake boats have developed a type of construction that is all their own. Because of the winding channels and their shallow depth, the canals, and the sudden storms that blow across the lakes during the summer, the lake boats are built differently from ships used on the ocean. Ocean freighters must carry large supplies of fuel for the long distances they travel while on a voyage. They must also carry large supplies of food and fresh water. Therefore they can carry less cargo. The lake boats are never far from some port where fuel and water can be had, and therefore most of their huge hold can be used to carry cargo.

Many of the most modern ore boats are built much alike. Their pattern and speed is one that has been found to be best adapted to the "Soo" locks, the narrow winding channels of the rivers, and the wave action of the Great Lakes. In general they are about 600 to 800 feet in length, seventy feet wide, and thirty-six feet deep. They have a twenty-five-foot draft. That is, they sink into the water not more than twenty-five feet when loaded. Twenty-seven is the greatest depth in many of the channels,

Courtesy M. A. Hanna Co.

Building the George M. Humphrey. Note the air pocket in the bottom and sides that makes an ore carrier float its heavy cargo.

and many of the ore carriers are nearly touching bottom as they pass along them. Some of the newer and larger ore boats have a capacity of 20,000 long tons. Up until a few years ago all the boats burned coal and were hand fired. Today, some of the newer ore boats have oil burners to heat the water to make steam. Some of the most recently built use diesel engines and are called motorships. In a normal shipping season an average carrier travels about 50,000 miles and brings down the lakes around 400,000 tons of iron ore.

If you were to go on board one of the large lake freighters you would find in the back, or stern, of the boat the machinery that makes her move. In the rear of the boat is the engine room. Ahead of it is the boiler where steam is made to turn the propeller shaft. Still farther ahead is the place where coal or oil is carried for fuel. At the back of the boat is a propeller which usually has three blades. When

the propeller is turned the boat is driven forward or pulled backward. A huge rudder in the stern guides the carrier on her way. Above the engine room is the cook's galley and quarters for the cook, his helpers, the engineer, the oiler, and the firemen. In the cook's galley good meals are provided for the crew during the night as well as in the day time. Near the back of the carrier are hung

Courtesy Republic Steel Corp.

Mess cooks at work aboard the Republic Steel Carrier, "Tom M. Girdler." Meals have to be served around the clock to care for the hungry crew.

lifeboats that can be used if the crew has to abandon the carrier.

Ahead of you stretches the long, slim hull of the ore boat in which the bulk cargo is carried. The top of the deck is flat. On it you will see the large flat doors, called hatches, which lie flat with the surface of the deck. These doors are opened when the carrier is loading or unloading. On the "George M. Humphrey" the hatch covers weigh twelve tons each and have to be lifted by a special electrohydraulic crane which rides across them on rails. During the voyage the hatches are fastened down so that the waves of a storm can sweep over them and do no damage to the cargo in the hold. On the older ore carriers sailors had to walk on the open deck in going from one end of the boat to the other but in some of the newer ore carriers a catwalk passes along inside the hold and this allows a sailor to go from one end of the boat to the other without going along the open deck where sailors are sometimes washed into the water during a storm. The huge hull of the ore carrier is built with cargo in mind. The heavy shell must make space for the cargo and at the same time must be able to stand the pounding of the tons of ore dropped down upon its bottom. It must also be rigidly built so that during a storm the boat will not break in two and sink with the loss of the cargo and crew. In the construction of these boats there is a shell within a shell. The air chamber between the outer and inner shells causes the steel boat to float and to carry the heavy cargo.

The pilot house is located high above the deck on the front end, or bow, of the boat. It is on the second or top deck. It is usually a small room with glass windows all around so that the men in charge of the boat can see in all directions. In this room is found the large wheel that steers the boat by turning the huge rudder in the stern. That is how an ore carrier is guided across the lakes and through the channels from one lake port to another. On the ocean the man who steers a ship is called a "helmsman" but on the Great Lakes he is called a "wheelsman." Vessels on the ocean are called ships but the word "ship" is seldom used for the vessels on the lakes. They are called boats. The wheelsman must know the weather signals, the channel markers, and how to bring the boat safely into port in fair

Courtesy Republic Steel Corp.

Left: Looking through a porthole down the deck of the Republic Steel Corporation carrier, "Tom M. Girdler," preparing to take aboard ore at Escanaba, Michigan. Right: Instructions from the bridge are received in the engine room of the "Tom M. Girdler" on the engine room telegraph by the chief engineer.

weather, foggy weather, stormy weather, during the daylight, or during the darkness of the night.

Under the pilot house are the captain's quarters. Here also are found the quarters for the first and second mates and part of the crew. Some ore carriers have rooms here also which can be used by the owners of the line and their guests. Under the officers' quarters, deep in the front of the boat, are rooms in which needed supplies and provisions are stored. On the new freighters the sailors' quarters are fireproof, steam heated, and furnished with private baths.

Some of the newer boats are being equipped with bow-thrusters. These are power driven propellers that are placed in a cavity on each side in the front end, or bow. This makes it easier to turn the the boat. Another new device is the automatic anchor drop for letting the anchor drop more quickly in case of an emergency. Because of the red iron ore dust most ore carriers are painted red. Cement carriers are often painted gray, and most coal boats are painted black.

Some boats are now provided with radiophones. These radiophones permit the sailors on one boat to talk to the sailors on another boat. They can also talk to people on land. By using radiophones, company officials can give orders to, or receive messages from, captains while they are still far from land. Some lake boats also have radio direction finders. Some are also equipped with radar. Radar warns the crew of the presence of nearby boats or land. By using their radar equipment ore carriers can come into the "Soo" locks or any port, even in darkness or foggy weather.

The ore carriers are all loaded at one of the ore docks. The present ore docks are really huge bins into which the iron ore is dumped from ore cars that are pushed along the top of the docks. When an ore carrier comes alongside to load a cargo of iron ore, huge chutes are lowered into the hatches. Then the iron ore is allowed to go rumbling down the chutes into the hold of the ore carrier. Limestone is loaded at one of the limestone ports in the same way. To load 20,000 tons of iron ore into an ore carrier takes about two or three hours, but it has been done in sixteen and one-half minutes. To carry this same load by railroad would take four trains having about one hundred cars each.

When their holds have been filled with wheat or iron ore, the carriers set out across the lakes. The average ore carrier takes six and one-half days to make the round trip from one of the points along Lake Erie to Duluth, Minnesota, and back. Some of the newer ore boats are even faster. Some of the iron ore goes down Lake Michigan to Gary, Indiana, and South Chicago. Some of it goes to ports along the Detroit River, but by far the larger amount goes to the iron ore receiving ports on the south shore of Lake Erie.

In order to keep an ore carrier from losing any time during the busy shipping season, provisions for each boat are usually supplied at Sault Ste. Marie. The Pittsburgh Steamship Division of the United States Steel Corporation has sixty-four ore carriers engaged in bringing down ore from Lake Superior to the receiving ports along the south shore of Lake Erie. This fleet of ore carriers is the largest inland fleet in the world. To provision this fleet the company keeps a supply store at Sault Ste. Marie. Ore carriers and other boats, not belonging to the Pittsburgh fleet, can also purchase supplies from the same supply store. Nearly everything is carried in stock that the men and boats might want or need—groceries, fresh meats, fresh vegetables, shaving supplies, dry goods, radios, and even chains and anchors large enough to hold an ore carrier should it need a new one. If supplies are needed quickly the needs are radioed ahead, but usually a shopping list is left when a boat passes Sault Ste. Marie on its way up the lakes. The supplies that have been ordered are then made ready while the ore carrier goes on to get her load of ore, and are

Coming down the lakes with a load of iron ore

picked up by the freighter as it passes Sault Ste. Marie on its way down the lakes.

Ore carriers do not carry unloading equipment but are unloaded by huge Hulett unloaders that are located at the receiving ports. Today there are over sixty of these Hulett unloaders in the receiving ports on the Great Lakes. At first they were powered by steam but today they are all electrically operated. These unloaders are huge machines having a clam-like jaw that is capable of carrying seventeen to twenty tons of iron ore at one bite. These huge jaws, over which a man rides in a small control room, are lowered through an open hatch into the hold of a carrier. There they bite into the ore piled in the carrier's hold. Then the huge jaws, filled with iron ore,

Coutresy "Steelways," published by American Iron and Steel Inst.
A modern unloader

are lifted out and carried away from the boat on an overhead track. The ore is then dumped into huge stock piles or put into railroad cars to be sent to the smelters. Five Hulett unloaders can unload 14,000 gross tons of iron ore in less than three hours.

Many of the ore carriers return up the lakes with no cargo, but others carry coal to ports on the Upper Lakes. During the past few years some fifty million tons of soft coal have left Lake Erie ports, each year, for ports on the Upper Lakes.

Some of the freighters on the Great Lakes are coal and limestone carriers. Because some of them are smaller boats, they can go into

Courtesy Michigan Limestone Division, United States Steel Corporation

Self-unloader vessels of the Bradley Transportation Line of Michigan Limestone, a division of United States Steel Corporation, take on their cargoes of high quality limestone at the Port of Calcite, Rogers City, Michigan, for delivery to steel, cement or chemical industries around the Great Lakes. (1961)

the smaller ports and leave shipments of coal. These boats carry their own unloading equipment and are called self-unloaders. Ore carriers are not self-unloaders because the lumps of heavy iron ore are often too large and heavy to be handled by a self-unloader. On the decks of the self-unloaders there is a huge crane, or boom device, that swings far out from the side of the boat. Endless belts carry the coal or limestone from the hold out along the boom and dump the cargo in a pile on the shore. There are about fifty self-loaders now sailing the Great Lakes.

During the winter, when the lakes are frozen, the bulk carriers are carefully overhauled and made ready for active service during the coming summer. When spring comes the nine ice-breakers which are run by the U. S. Coast Guard begin opening the channels and harbors so that another busy shipping season can begin.

Official U.S. Coast Guard Photo

The "Mackinaw" breaking ice

The 6,000-ton "Mackinaw" is the largest of the ice-breakers on the Great Lakes and one of the largest in the world. She is 290 feet long. Because of the size of the locks in the Welland Canal she is confined to the upper Great Lakes. She has three propellers. One is in the bow and the other two are in the stern. The bow propeller sucks the water from under the ice just ahead of the boat, thus weakening the ice by its own weight. The huge prow of the ice-breaker is then shoved upon the ice and breaks it by its massive weight. The "Mackinaw" can be heeled from 7 degrees on one side to 7 degrees on the other by pumping water from one set of tanks to another. It takes only 90 seconds to complete the full cycle. During World War II she kept the inland waterways open to navigation longer than usual and thus made it possible to ship extra supplies of wheat, limestone, coal, and iron ore. She is strong enough to force her way through any ice found in the Great Lakes. Each spring the "Mackinaw" opens the St. Mary's Waterway through the "Soo" to Lake Superior and then keeps the channel open so that the boats will not be stopped by new or wind-blown ice.

The other ice-breakers are smaller than the "Mackinaw." They are stationed from Duluth, Minnesota, to Toledo, Ohio. So powerful are these ice-breakers that they can force their way steadily along even through ice twelve to fourteen inches thick.

After the channels have been opened the ice-breakers act as buoy tenders and begin placing the buoys back on their regular stations so that sailors can be guided across the lakes and through the narrow winding channels.

When the shipping season opens, the boats leave their winter harbors to begin another busy shipping season carrying iron ore, oil, grain, coal, pulpwood, cement or limestone. Escanaba, because of its more southerly location on Lake Michigan, is usually the first iron port to load a cargo of iron ore each spring.

During the busy shipping season the bulk carriers run day and night, seven days a week. By changing crews every few hours the strong steel boats are kept steadily on the move. Lake boats do not corrode or rust like ships on salt water do; therefore, many very old boats are still in the active carrying service today. Navigation continues all through the spring, summer, and fall. In the winter the lakes freeze and all boats, except the railroad car ferries, are docked in some port for the winter.

Besides the sailboats and bulk carriers, there have been many other boats on the Great Lakes during the last hundred years. From the Civil War period to 1900, many passenger boats were running on regular schedules between ports on the Great Lakes. The earlier ones, like the freighters of their day, were built of wood. At first these early steamers lacked the graceful lines of the later passenger boats. Almost all of them were boats which had a large paddle wheel on each side. Many of the earlier ones were also rigged with sails. This was then required by the insurance companies of that day, for they did not trust the new steam engines to safely bring the passenger boats back into port.

The names of many of the passenger steamers were well known by the people then acquainted with the lakes. Some of the best known of the passenger boats were the "India," "China," and "Japan." Each summer season thousands of people used these boats for transportation to new areas or took a trip on one of them for a vacation.

The heaviest traffic of these boats was between Buffalo, New York; Cleveland, Ohio; and Detroit, Michigan; but many smaller steamers ran between such ports as Detroit and Alpena, Duluth, Mackinac Island, St. Ignace, Milwaukee, and Chicago. These boats carried not only passengers but mail and package freight as well.

These larger passenger boats were like large floating hotels, for they had not only rooms in which the passengers slept but also

The "Manitou." This passenger boat stopped at Charlevoix on Tuesday, Thursday, Saturday, and Sunday.

The last two of the over-night passenger boats at Detroit. October, 1956. Shortly after this picture was taken these two boats were towed into Lake St. Clair and burned.

large dining rooms in which tastily prepared food was served to the passengers. There were usually one or more large ballrooms for dancing and entertainment.

At the turn of the century much package freight was still being carried on lake boats, especially the passenger boats, and steamship lines had warehouses where the freight was collected and from which it was distributed. Since 1942, there has been no package freight carried on the American side of the Great Lakes. All the cargo is bulk cargo, and the present fleet of lake boats is designed for such cargo.

With the coming of better railroad accommodations, better roads, the automobile, and passenger planes, fewer and fewer people traveled by lake steamer. By 1950, passenger boats on the Great Lakes were nearly a thing of the past. The last two old passenger boats, from the Detroit area, were burned on Lake St. Clair on December 10, 1956. Today, only one passenger boat on the Great Lakes, the "South American," runs on vacation cruises each summer. The "Milwaukee Clipper" runs from Muskegon to Milwaukee, Wisconsin, carrying autos and tourists across Lake Michigan in the summer.

By 1900, a different type of passenger boat was taking people, during the summer season, from Detroit on short one-day trips to points of interest on the nearby lakes and rivers. Sometimes these pleasure boats took people to parks where the people found relief from the crowded cities. In the morning these steamers were waiting at their docks to welcome the eager crowd of people who were arriving, loaded with picnic baskets, ready for a day of pleasure and leisure.

Courtesy Chicago, Duluth & Georgian Bay Transit Company
Passenger vacation cruise ship "South American"

From Detroit these pleasure craft ran up to Port Huron; to Tashmoo Park on Harsens Island; to "Bob-lo" at the mouth of the Detroit River across from old Fort Malden; to Sugar Island at the mouth of the river; to Put-in-Bay in Lake Erie; and to Chatham, Ontario. In the evening they brought the weary pleasure-seekers back. With empty baskets on their arms, and wearing clothing soiled by the picnic activities of the day, the tired passengers crowded across the gangplank to the land and then hurried up Woodward Avenue on their way home.

Today, nearly all of these boats run no more, but to those who rode on them during the period from 1900 to 1935 such names as "Tashmoo," "Put-in-Bay," and "Columbia" are familiar reminders of happy days on the Detroit River. The only pleasure boat left on the Detroit River runs from Detroit to Bob-Lo during the summer.

There are only a few tugs left on the Great Lakes. But if you had visited one of the busy lake ports fifty years ago you would have seen many of these busy little boats. They were built just large enough to carry a powerful steam engine and a small amount of fuel but no cargo. Their job was to push and pull the sailboats, freighters, and passenger boats when they could not operate under their own power. If one of the larger boats got stuck in shallow water the tugs pulled her off and into deeper water. These busy little boats though not large in size, once played an important part in lake commerce just as they do in ocean commerce today. However, with the passing of the sailboats, the improving of the harbors and channels, and the use of only the larger major ports, there is no longer much need for tugs in Great Lakes shipping.

At Detroit a small boat, known as a mail boat, meets the freighters and gives them mail and takes the letters that the sailors have written. You would enjoy watching this busy little craft at work as it hurries up beside each passing freighter. Men on the mail boat take the mail bag that is lowered to them in a bucket. They then place the mail for the boat in the bucket which is then pulled on board the moving freighter. A daily newspaper can also be purchased by any sailor from the mail boat.

In some ports, such as Detroit, you will see fire boats. These boats are used to fight fire just as any fire engine. When a fire breaks out on a boat, or in a building near the water front, these boats hurry to the fire. On the decks of these craft are long nozzles through which large streams of water can be forced to put out a fire.

Courtesy Board of Fire Commissioners, Detroit

The fire boat "John Kendall." The "Kendall" has been in the service of the Detroit Fire Department since 1929.

For many years boats known as ferries carried people and vehicles across the Great Lakes and their connecting waters. Little ferries ran for many years between Detroit and Windsor, Ontario; between Port Huron and Sarnia, Ontario; between Sault Ste. Marie, Michigan, and Sault Ste. Marie, Ontario; between Mackinaw City and St. Ignace; and between Mackinaw City, St. Ignace, and Mackinac Island. Auto ferries no longer run between Detroit and Windsor. Auto traffic now uses the tunnel under the river or the Ambassador Bridge. Railroad-car ferries still cross the Detroit River although there is also a railroad tunnel under the river. Since the building of the Blue Water Bridge at Port Huron, auto ferries no longer run between Port Huron and Sarnia, Ontario. Railroad cars here use the tunnel under the St. Clair River. Three auto ferries still cross the St. Clair River to carry autos and passengers between the United States and Canada. They cross the St. Clair River from St. Clair, Roberts Landing, and Algonac. Passenger ferries still carry people from St. Ignace and Mackinaw City to Mackinac Island during the summer months. Railroad car ferries still run across the Straits of Mackinac, but the automobile ferries stopped running in November, 1957, when the new Mackinac Bridge was opened for auto traffic. This new bridge now provides a four-lane highway between the Lower and Upper Peninsulas. Auto ferry service between Sault Ste. Marie, Michigan, and Sault Ste. Marie, Ontario, ceased on October 31, 1962 when the new International Bridge was opened to auto and truck traffic.

Railroad car ferries still carry railroad cars across the Detroit River, across the Straits of Mackinac, and across Lake Michigan. These ferries have a wide, flat deck so that railroad cars can be pushed onto the railroad rails that are fastened to their decks. All the machinery in these ferries is placed beneath the main deck in the hull of the ferry. These boats tie up at a dock so that the rails on their deck match rails leading from the railroad. Usually the deck carries four tracks upon which cars are pushed onto the ferry by a railroad engine. Other engines pull them off at the other side of the lake or river. The ferries on the Detroit River have no superstructure except the pilot house which is above the railroad cars. Those on Lake Michigan have a second deck above the railroad cars.

To haul railroad cars around the Great Lakes often causes much delay as well as added expense. This is especially true of Lake Michigan which, though not so wide, reaches north and south for some distance and thus blocks east-west railroad and automobile traffic. Because of this, large railroad car ferries cross Lake Michigan every day of the year carrying railroad cars and automobiles. At the present time there are three railroad ferry lines crossing Lake Michigan. One is the Ann Arbor Railroad with ports at Manistique, and Elberta, across the Betsie River from Frankfort. Another is the Chesapeake and Ohio Railway which runs ferries from Ludington. The Grand Trunk railroad runs ferries from Muskegon to Milwaukee.

The railroad car ferries that cross Lake Michigan are deep-hulled boats with high sides. When the railroad cars have been pushed onto the ferry the car wheels are locked into place by clamps that fasten onto the rails to keep the cars from moving, should the boat run into the high waves of a storm. All the railroad car ferries run day and night all year long. Therefore, they are also ice breakers. Because sometimes ice has to be broken for ten or more miles from shore, these boats are equipped with extra power. When the ice breaks up in the spring the strong winds often pile the ice in huge ridges along the shore, especially on the Michigan side. These ice ridges have to be crushed by the ferries as they push forward with their load of railroad cars, automobiles, and passengers.

Above the tops of the railroad cars is the second deck. Here there

Courtesy Chesapeake and Ohio Railway
Chesapeake and Ohio Railway's trainferry, "S.S. Badger" crossing Lake Michigan. (1961)

Courtesy Chesapeake and Ohio Railway
Loading operations aboard the "S.S. Spartan," Chesapeake and Ohio Railway trainferry, at Milwaukee, Wisconsin. (1961)

is a cabin in which passengers can sit in cold or stormy weather, a dining room and several small bedrooms that are used at night by the passengers as the boat sails across the lake. Outside the central cabin, along the sides of the boat are chairs where the passengers can sit when the weather is nice.

On the Great Lakes there are twenty oil tankers that, during the summer shipping season, carry some 200,000 barrels of oil a day. The Standard Oil Company of Indiana has the largest fleet of oil tankers on the Great Lakes. Five of these boats have each a capacity of 60,000 barrels. These boats carry only the finished product. Most of it is brought from the Toledo area to the Detroit area and from Chicago to cities on the west coast of Michigan.

For many years there were several shipyards located at various ports around the lakes where boats were made and kept in repair. At first these shipyards were really large carpenter shops where boats were built of wood. Later, with the coming of steel construction, these shipyards were greatly changed. If you had visited one of them you would have seen men using huge cranes to handle the heavy steel plates with which the boats were built. Then, too, you would have heard the rivet hammers as they riveted the large plates into place before they were welded together. Today, there are only a few shipyards left on the lakes where boats are made and kept in repair.

Shipping on the Great Lakes has had its tragic side as well as pleasant one. Sometimes storms pass across the Great Lakes during the shipping season that are too violent for the boats to withstand. In the early days of sailboats many went down during a gale. Many hulks now lie on the lake bottoms. Today, many of them are being explored by scuba divers. Even the huge steel freighters have found the lake gales too strong to withstand. During the past one hundred years many of them have gone down with all hands. Sometimes some of the sailors have been fortunate enough to be rescued.

The worst storm ever to damage Great Lakes shipping occurred on November 9, 10, 11, and 12 in 1913. During this storm gale winds from 60 to 80 miles an hour raged across the lakes pushing the water into waves thirty-five to forty feet in height. During this storm eleven ships vanished while some eight others were wrecked. Two hundred and fifty-one men and women lost their lives during this four-day storm.

In the early days there were few provisions for the saftey of the passengers or the sailors. During the darkness of a storm, boats

The English ship, "Montrose," on her side in the Detroit River after colliding with a cement barge. August, 1962.

were sometimes driven against rocks or upon the shore. Going through the narrow channels was always a dangerous and trying task. When a vessel had to pass through these places a special pilot, who was familiar with the dangers, was often hired to guide the boat.

All this has greatly changed during the past one hundred years. Today, all boats must be provided with life preservers and lifeboats. The coming of the radio, radio-telephone, and radar has helped to produce greater safety for those who travel on the Great Lakes. When a boat is in distress, a radio message can be sent to ask for help from nearby boats or from a lifesaving station. Warnings of approaching storms can also be sent to boats far out on the lakes.

The United States Government has done much to improve shipping on the Great Lakes. Each spring the channels of the rivers are carefully marked with buoys of various kinds which tell the sailors where the channels are and how deep the water is. There are many kinds of buoys used: nun buoys, can buoys, spar buoys, whistling buoys, bell buoys, and light buoys. Each one has its special meaning to the men sailing the lakes. These signals are so made that a wheelsman can follow his course by them during the daytime, at night, or during the blinding darkness of a storm.

Other safety measures are also provided. Along the coast at dangerous places are lighthouses. Each of these houses has a large light that shines far out across the water of the lake. Not all of them have the same kind of light. Some are red, others are green, but the usual color is white. Some lights burn all the time while others flash their light at regular intervals.

To help guide lake boats little vessels, known as light ships, were sometimes used. The only remaining light ship on the Great Lakes is known as the "Huron" and is stationed at the south end of Lake Huron, near Port Huron, to help guide boats coming south across Lake Huron into the narrow channel of the St. Clair River. Each shipping season this little light ship is manned by men in the United States Coast Guard. Usually light ships have no power of their own and remain anchored in one place during the shipping season. All the machinery is automatic but is constantly checked by the men on duty. A radio beam is flashed constantly. Bells, fog horns, whistles and lights are also used. When night comes, the light is turned on and its beams begin to flash across the lake through the darkness. When a fog comes, the fog horns begin to blow.

The National Government has also spent millions of dollars to make breakwaters and deepen the dangerous and shallow channels so that larger boats can be used and shipping will be safer. The national government also maintains Coast Guard stations at dangerous points along the shore of the lakes. The lifeguards at these stations are provided with all the necessary equipment to rescue people from sinking boats.

In 1942 work was begun on a new and larger lock at the "Soo" to replace the Weitzel Lock. This new lock, named the MacArthur Lock, was completed in 1943 at a cost of fourteen million dollars. This new and larger lock is eight hundred feet long, eighty feet wide, and thirty feet deep. It can be filled with water in ten minutes and emptied in eight.

At the present time there are four American locks at the "Soo." From the American side going out toward the rapids they are the MacArthur Lock, opened in 1943; the Poe Lock, opened in 1896; the Davis Lock, opened in 1914; and the Sabine Lock, opened in 1919. There is one Canadian lock, opened in 1895, on the Canadian side of the St. Mary's River. In 1960, a new lock 1,000 feet long, 100 feet wide and 32 feet deep, with a lift of 27 feet was begun to replace the present Poe Lock. It is to be completed by 1967.

During the last fifteen years many changes, besides those already mentioned, have taken place in the commerce of the lakes. In 1954, the Congress of the United States passed an act that joined the United States and Canada in the construction of a larger and deeper St. Lawrence Waterway so that larger ships from foreign countries could enter the Great Lakes. The channel was to be deepened from 14 feet to 27 feet. This new St. Lawrence Waterway was officially opened on April 25, 1959. During the fall and winter of 1957-58, the Livingstone Channel, at the mouth of the Detroit River, was deepened to twenty-seven feet. A new channel was dug through the flats at the mouth of the St. Clair River to replace the old crooked South Bend Channel by Harsens Island. This new cut is 700 feet wide and 27 feet deep. Much work was done to deepen the West Neebish Cut in the Saint Mary's River. This cut was opened to traffic in July 1961. Other channels have now been deepened to the same depth. Port facilities, capable of receiving or discharging ocean

Lock	Date	Length	Width	Depth
Poe	1887-1896	704 ft.	95 ft.	16.6 ft.
Davis	1908-1914	1,350 ft.	80 ft.	23.1 ft.
Sabine	1913-1919	1,350 ft.	80 ft.	23.1 ft.
MacArthur	1942-1943	800 ft.	80 ft.	31.0 ft.

Courtesy U.S. Army Corps of Engineers

The St. Mary's Falls Canal at Sault Ste. Marie, Michigan. Work has started on the new Poe Lock which is scheduled to be finished in 1967. Photo 1964.

commerce, have been constructed at several places on the Great Lakes or along the St. Lawrence Waterway. Now foreign ships can pass up from the Atlantic over this 2,000 mile waterway to Chicago, or to ports on Lake Superior that lie 602 feet above sea level. Today, eighty per cent of the world's ships can enter this new seaway.

The deepening of the Saint Lawrence Waterway has already brought more changes in lake commerce. In its first year of operation, 18 Canadian ports and 51 United States ports along the Great Lakes and St. Lawrence River engaged in foreign commerce. In that same year, 1959, grain shipments from Chicago alone increased by one-half million tons from the previous year before the waterway was opened. In 1962, grain for foreign ports from the United States and Canadian ports on the Great Lakes totaled 235,000,000 bushels. This was a 42 per cent increase over wheat shipments for 1961. In 1962, some 26 million tons of freight were shipped over the St. Lawrence Waterway. This was a 60 per cent increase over 1961.

This new seaway will do much in the near future to change the routes of much of the nation's commerce. Large bulk freighters can load wheat at Duluth, or Canadian ports on Lake Superior, and can then sail directly to Europe, thus avoiding trans-shipment cost. Other bulk cargoes will be wood pulp, petroleum, coal, coke, and iron ore. Big lake boats can carry grain to Sept Isles below Quebec and return to the lakes loaded with Canadian iron ore from Burnt Creek, Labrador. Because foreign ships can sail directly into the Lake Region it will be easier to bring in the many alloys used in making the various kinds of steel we need today. Foreign manufactured goods, also, can be sent direct to Detroit, Chicago, Duluth or any lake port with facilities for loading and unloading. American exports such as meat from Chicago and autos and trucks from Detroit and Cleveland can now be shipped direct to foreign ports. Some Great Lakes ports are now increasing the depth of their harbors and building new port facilities so that they, too, can take a part in this new world commerce that has come to Great Lakes area. Ocean-going passenger-cargo ships now carry vacationers on summer cruises all the way from Quebec to Chicago, Illinois, and Duluth, Minnesota. This new waterway, together with Michigan's many natural resources, will soon cause many industrial changes to take place here in the Great Lakes Area.

Several other changes have come to the Great Lakes commerce during the last twenty years. World War II greatly depleted our iron ore reserves in the Lake Superior area. There is now only a little high concentrated ore left to be mined. Steel companies, seeing the diminishing iron ore supply in our country, sent geologists all over the world to search for new sources of supply. At the same time, the steel companies put on an intensive research program to find ways of using our vast reserves of low-grade ore found in the Mother Lode. Vast deposits of ore were found in eastern Canada, in Venezuela, Brazil and Africa. These are huge deposits that will last the world for many years, but they are not in our nation and will have to be purchased from foreign sources. This causes our money to leave the country. What is more, the overseas supply lines to these sources are vulnerable in case of war. Foreign countries have less tax on mines, and labor costs are much less. What is more, because ocean ships are deeper they can carry 40,000 tons of iron ore in place of the 20,000 or less carried by lake boats. All these factors cut the cost of the raw material. The decrease in iron ore shipments has greatly lowered the tonnage passing through the "Soo" locks at Sault Ste. Marie. For many years the "Soo" Canal was the busiest canal in the world from the point of freight tonnage passing through it. This vast tonnage was caused by the large quantities of bulk cargo in the form of iron ore, wheat, and coal, which was shipped through it each year. But today the Suez Canal has passed the "Soo" Canal in tonnage. In 1960, 185.3 million long tons passed through the Suez Canal while the "Soo" Canal handled only 91.4 million short tons. The year 1953 was the busiest year at the "Soo." The following figures show the recent tonnage passing through the "Soo" Locks.

1953	128,510,232 Tons	1959	71,060,728 Tons
1955	114,648,927 Tons	1961	80,089,120 Tons
1957	112,803,498 Tons		

In 1960, the United States used 102,200,000 tons of iron ore. 34,600,000 tons, or about one-third of this ore, was imported from foreign sources. This recent change in foreign commerce has brought a great decrease in lake shipping of iron ore. In 1961, even with the increase of foreign ships, there were 2,817 fewer passages of freighters on the Detroit River than there were the year before. Counting the up and down river passages, they totaled only 15,015 for the year. Because of this shift in commerce, some 40 Canadian and 40 United States owned boats were taken out of service on the lakes during the shipping season of 1962. These were the older, smaller, slower boats. The larger ones are still in operation because of their larger carrying capacity and faster speed. They can make a complete trip in four and one-half days; whereas, the slower, older ones require about one week.

During the last few years, many small, privately-owned cruisers and sailboats have been appearing on the Great Lakes. Each year sees an increase in their number. Because sudden storms come over the Great Lakes during the summer season and because these craft are small and not designed for severe storms, the United States Army Corps of Engineers is helping to build a series of harbors, which are not over 30 miles apart along the entire shore line of Michigan. When storm warnings are given these small pleasure craft can find refuge in one of these natural or man-made harbors. Many of these harbors have already been completed. Several others are being planned. In this work the United States Army Corps of Engineers works with the Michigan Waterway Commission. Funds for the building of these harbors comes from the United States government and from the state tax on gasoline that is used in small boats.

CHAPTER SIXTEEN

More Industries Develop In Michigan

Up to the end of the Civil War, Michigan was primarily an agricultural state. The little farms of that time were nearly all in the southern part of the Lower Peninsula. Most of the things needed in the community were made in the nearby village or at home. But this way of life was soon to change as industries developed in Michigan.

One of Michigan's oldest industries was fishing. Commercial fishermen began operating on the Upper Lakes soon after 1800 and by as early as 1830 they had begun to use gill nets. Many fish, especially pickerel, were caught by the settlers each spring as the fish came up the rivers to spawn. A small amount of the commercial catch was sold as fresh fish but most of it was either smoked or salted to prepare it

Fish nets hung to dry on the lower end of the Garden Peninsula. Many nets like these were once used to catch Great Lakes fish. Photo 1956.

Fish boats at the lower end of the Garden Peninsula. Once many boats like these brought in large catches of fish but during the last few years the fishing industry has greatly declined. Photo 1956.

for the market. Much of the fish was salted and put in barrels especially after the salt industry began to develop in Michigan. Commercial fishermen have marketed over twenty kinds of Great Lakes fish. In 1899, the catch of fresh-water fish from the Upper Lakes was about 113 million pounds. Since 1910, however, commercial fishing has been on the decline. In 1928, the commercial catch from all the Great Lakes was only 89,557,000 pounds. Today, few of the better grades of fish are caught in the Great Lakes.

Several reasons have been advanced to explain the decline of the fishing industry on the Great Lakes. One of the major causes has been the coming of the sea lamprey into the upper lakes from Lake Ontario. Just how this predator made its way through the Welland Canal, between Lake Ontario and Lake Erie, is not known but it is known that sea lampreys will cling to boats and go along with them.

The native home of the sea lamprey is the salt water of the Atlantic Ocean. The adult life of the sea lamprey is spent in the ocean waters. When the adult lampreys are ready to spawn, they go up the streams that flow into the Atlantic. After they spawn, they seem always to die. A dwarf form of the sea lamprey has been known to inhabit the fresh waters of Lake Ontario for many years. This enemy of fish life in the Great Lakes was first noticed at Merlin, Ontario, in western Lake Erie in 1921.

Courtesy Michigan Conservation Department
An adult sea lamprey

In 1927, sea lampreys were found in the waters of western Lake Erie. By 1930, they had entered the waters of the St. Clair River. In 1936, they were found in the waters off Milwaukee, Wisconsin, and at Elk Rapids in Michigan. By 1947, they had reached the waters around Isle Royale in Lake Superior.

The adult sea lamprey reaches a length of from fourteen to thirty inches. It has a long snake-like body. It is smooth and scaleless, with fins at the top and tail. It has seven gill openings on each side just back of the head. On the top of the head is a single nostril. The mouth has no jaws but is rather a round sucking disc with sharp needle-like teeth around the circle.

The tongue is like a rasp and is used for puncturing the skin of the fish it has attacked so that it can suck the blood from the fish. This is the only part of the fish that it eats.

The smooth, scaleless lake trout were at first the special prey of the sea lamprey. In 1935, the commercial catch of lake trout in Lake Erie was 1,399,901 pounds. By 1945, it had dropped to a mere 172,937 pounds. When the supply of lake trout had diminished, the sea lampreys then began attacking bass, whitefish, and even the large scaley carp. The attack of the sea lamprey has greatly reduced not only commercial fishing but recreational fishing as well in many areas. Many lakes once visited by fishermen because the lakes provided catches of trout and bass now have only a small percentage of the

Smallmouth bass showing raw sore caused by lamprey attack. Photo August, 1957.

number of fish they once had before the lampreys entered these lakes by way of the streams.

Each spring the sea lampreys move up the stream to spawn. Their largest runs take place during late May and early June, usually during the night. The males go up the streams first and begin to make the nests. Later the females come and help the males. Nests are made in sand, gravel, and small stones in shallow water in the streams where the water runs less fast. The adult lampreys carry the stones in their mouths and put them on the down side of the stream. Thus, a nest twelve to thirty inches across is made. In this nest the eggs are laid. One female lamprey will lay between seventy-five thousand and two hundred fifty thousand eggs. After spawning, the adult lampreys die. The eggs hatch in from one to three weeks. The little lampreys then burrow into the sand bed of the stream and live there for the next three to five years. They live on the little organisms that the stream brings down to them. Then they go through a rapid change and appear as little lampreys that set out downstream to attack fish in the Great

Lakes. Both state and federal conservation departments have tried to find a way to save the fishing industry. Today, a chemical is put into streams. As it goes downstream with the water it kills most of the lampreys in the stream. During the last few years this chemical has been used in the streams flowing into Lake Superior in hopes of reducing the number of lampreys in Lake Superior. Catching lake trout has also been limited in Lake Superior in hopes that the lake trout can again have a chance to multiply.

Lake trout, whitefish, and walleyes were fish that brought a high price per pound and made Great Lakes fishing a profitable industry. When these species declined in numbers the smaller species such as deep water ciscoes (chubs), smelt, alewife, gizzard shad, weather fish, and yellow perch rapidly increased in numbers. The alewife was known to be in Lake Ontario one hundred years ago. It was noticed in Lake Erie in 1931 and by 1954 it had reached Lake Superior. The gizzard shad at the present time is mostly in Lake Erie and southern Lake Huron. The weather fish has been brought from Japan. It was first noticed in the Shiawassee River but it entered outer lakes and streams in 1939. These species of fish are now classed as trash fish and do not bring a high market price.

Because of the disappearance of lake trout and whitefish most fishing companies have ceased operations. The few that have remained have adjusted their fishing methods to volume production such as the use of trawls that sweep the lake to catch the trash fish in large quantity. Most of their catch, such as bull heads, smelt, ciscoes, and alewife, is sold for animal food to fur farmers and pet food manufacturers at a very low cost per pound.

Though the species now caught are the smaller, less wanted species, the volume production remains about the same. In 1960, the Great Lakes catch was 104,651,000 pounds. This figure is close to the 107 million pounds average for the past twenty years. In terms of cash value, however, it is much below what it would have been if the species more in demand could have been caught.

Another of Michigan's earliest industries was the making of barrels, for in the years between 1800 and 1900 many articles such as fish and salt were shipped in barrels. From the abundant wood supply local coopers made kegs and barrels that they sold to commercial shippers. Later special saws and machinery were made for the making of barrel staves and barrel heads, and then barrels were produced in small mills, but with the passing of the hardwoods this industry came to an end in the early part of this century.

Another of Michigan's oldest industries was the making of brick, for in many areas the heavy clays were found suitable for brick making. Bricks for the Detroit Arsenal, located in present-day Dearborn, were made in the Dearborn area as early as 1833. Later the bricks made from local brickyards were used in building some of the large homes that were built in Detroit before 1900. Many of the farmhouses that are still standing from this period, in Wayne County and the adjoining counties, were made from bricks made in local brickyards.

Brickmaking in Michigan has now almost become an industry of the past. In 1900, there were nearly two hundred brick and tile manufacturing plants in the state, but since that time the number has steadily decreased.

Another of Michigan's present industries that had its beginning between 1800 and 1900 was drug manufacturing. During the past one hundred years there have been many important dis-

Brick making was once one of Michigan's major industries. This brick plant still makes brick in Dearborn. Photo 1955.

coveries made in medicines for conquering diseases. Up to about 1850, people did not know what was in the medicine they were taking, or how strong it was. Many medicines that were sold were frauds and did the buyer little, if any, good.

Perhaps the first drug company to be formed in Michigan was the Michigan Drug Company which was started in 1819, at Detroit. In 1843, Eberbach and Sons started a drug manufacturing business at Ann Arbor. Another early company was Farrand, Williams, and Clark, which was founded at Detroit in 1845. Hozentine and Perkins started in the drug business in Grand Rapids in 1852. Another pioneer in the drug field was Frederick Stearns. Mr. Stearns owned a drugstore in Detroit. In 1855, he started a little laboratory in which he prepared his first medical preparations. Another early Detroit firm was that of Parke, Davis and Company. This company was started by Dr. Samuel P. Duffield, who at that time owned a drugstore. In 1862, Dr. Duffield

Courtesy Parke, Davis and Co.

The beginning of Parke, Davis and Company

began to manufacture a few medical supplies such as ether and nitre. Mr. Harvey C. Parke joined Dr. Duffield in 1866. In 1871, Dr. Duffield retired from the company. Mr. Davis joined with Mr. Parke in 1875, and thus formed the present company of Parke, Davis and Company. Today, Parke, Davis and Company have large laboratories in both Detroit and Ann Arbor.

In 1880, Dr. W. E. Upjohn was one of the leading physicians in Kalamazoo. Dr. Upjohn developed a new method of manufacturing pills. The new pills not only were given a coating on the outside but were so made that they would easily dissolve. From this early beginning has grown the large Upjohn Laboratories in Kalamazoo.

In 1899, Nelson, Baker and Company started to manufacture drugs in Detroit. The Du Pree Chemical Company has been a leading drug producer in Holland. The Dow Chemical Company, although a large manufacturer of industrial chemicals, is also a producer of some medicines.

Before 1900, one of the problems of a doctor was to know just how strong medicines were. Drugs were not then prepared with the care that they are today. Sometimes the drugs were too strong and thus injured the patient. At other times medicines were too weak to have the desired results. Modern drug companies have developed medicines of standard quality and strength. Now, when a doctor uses their preparations he knows how much of any drug he is giving his patient.

When doctors found that they could rely upon the carefully prepared preparations that were being put on the market by these new companies, they began to use more and more of them.

These pioneers in the field of medicine have not been content merely to standardize such drugs as were already known. The world has been searched for plants and soils that might yield new preparations that could lessen the suffering of mankind. As a result of this continuing experimentation in the field of medicine, Michigan's drug companies have been able to develop many new preparations that have aided mankind as well as animals.

The crude little laboratories of a century ago have given way to large biological farms and huge laboratories in which hundreds of men and women work to make the many chemical preparations that are used by doctors all over the world. Huge machines make capsules and tablets of many kinds. Each capsule, or tablet, must be made a certain size and strength or else it is discarded by the machine. Each day the drug industry goes on preparing medicines that are already known while scientists and doctors are continually doing more research work in hopes of developing new medicines and serums to aid both animals and mankind.

Although iron mining began in Michigan before the Civil War, Michigan did not take a leading part in the rise of the huge steel industry. Perhaps this was due to the low quality of coal found here. Some iron was smelted by using charcoal but this amount was always limited. Michigan had, however, some early steel companies. In 1853, Captain E. B. Ward, and some other men, organized the Eureka Iron and Steel Company. This new company bought land, near the Detroit River, in Wyandotte and there built a blast furnace and rolling mill. In 1864, this plant installed one of the first Bessemer furnaces in the United States, and it was at this plant that the first Bessemer steel was made in America. Here also the first rolled T railroad rails were made. In 1874, the Eureka Iron and Steel Company was one of the largest industries in the Detroit area but it stopped production in the 1890's. Three years after Captain Ward started his plant in Wyandotte, Mr. G. B. Russell built a blast furnace and iron works in Hamtramck. This furnace and iron works was known as the Hamtramck Iron Works and remained standing until 1905. The chief use made of iron ore in those days, here in Michigan, was in making stoves and supplying the iron needs of blacksmiths for making horseshoes and household articles.

Today, one of the leading industries in Michigan is the making of various kinds of heating units. This large industry developed from the early stove industry which was started here in Michigan in 1864 by James and Jeremiah Dwyer. These two brothers began making stoves of cast iron in a little foundry at the foot of Mt. Elliott Avenue in Detroit. The first of their stoves were also sold by the two brothers.

The Dwyer brothers believed that stoves, besides being able to give heat, should also possess other qualities, such as beauty and

Courtesy of the Detroit-Michigan Stove Co.

A page from an old stove catalog

usefulness. Moreover, they felt that stoves should be built to last a lifetime with only minor replacements, such as grates, lids, and other small parts that might break or burn out.

The Dwyer brothers were joined by other men, and the Detroit Stove Works was founded. Other stove companies that were later formed were the Peninsular Stove Company, the Art Stove Company, and the Detroit Vapor Stove Company. By 1881, the Detroit Stove Works and the Michigan Stove Works were each employing nearly one thousand men. Detroit was then recognized as the leading stove-manufacturing center of the nation. The lumbering and settling of northern Michigan and the rapidly growing West provided a good market for stoves. Then, too, the beauty and serviceability of the new stoves became known in other nations, and soon the companies were exporting their products to foreign lands.

One should remember that half a century before Detroit became known as the automobile center it was known for its stove industry. Since its early beginning many kinds have been made—cook stoves, hard coal heaters, soft coal stoves, wood ranges, gas stoves, and even stoves that burned whale blubber for Eskimos. As the years have passed, the early stoves have given way to newer heating units. Today, many companies scattered over the southern part of Michigan make heating units or parts; such as, oil burners, gas burners, stokers, fans, furnaces, boilers, safety valves, thermostats, and air conditioners.

Another of Michigan's first industries was a Stained Glass Works which was started at Detroit in 1861 by a German immigrant youth. From this glass works came colored glass that was used in the wealthy homes that were then being built in Detroit before 1900. Some of this stained glass was also used in Great Lakes passenger steamers that were built during this same period. Much of it has been used all over the country for making church windows. The beautifully decorated windows of many of Michigan's churches have been made by this glass company which is still in operation.

As the railroads expanded there grew a demand for more and more locomotives and railroad cars. As Detroit in those days was the hub of transportation in this area, it was only natural that the building of railroad cars began in Detroit in 1853. Locomotives, passenger cars, boxcars, and even flatcars for the growing logging industry were all made at Detroit. The Michigan Car Company was organized in 1864. In 1868, the Detroit Car and Manufacturing Company was organized. This company was purchased in 1871 by George M. Pullman, now

known for his Pullman railroad cars, and in 1879 Mr. Pullman trans-
ferred its shops to Chicago. The Peninsular Car Company was formed
in 1885. Later interurban cars were also built. The railroad-car-
building industry used iron, steel, and also the local supplies of wood.
At the turn of the century this industry employed about nine thousand
men. The railroad shops were later moved to Port Huron, Battle Creek,
Marshall, and Jackson.

Today, Michigan is a leading center for the making of paints and
varnishes. This industry began in 1874 when the Berry brothers
began making paints and varnishes at Detroit. Since that early date
other paint and varnish companies have been started.

In 1856, Mr. Dexter M. Ferry started a company that began to
sell seeds. No doubt he got his idea from others who began raising
and selling selected seeds in the East. Up to this time people did not
buy seeds to plant. Each person usually gathered his own seeds each
fall and carefully saved them for the coming spring planting by
wrapping the seeds in brown paper. Sometimes neighbors exchanged
seeds and thus better varieties of flowers and vegetables spread
slowly across the state. Mr. Ferry's plan was to select and raise only
choice plants and from these plants to carefully gather their seeds
and offer them for sale. At first the seeds were sent out in small,
unattractive brown paper envelopes or in little cloth bags tied with
a string. The name and the kind of seed was printed on each package.
After the Civil War a picture of the plants that could be grown from
the seed was placed on each package by means of wood cuts. Later,
pictures, bright with colors, showed the buyer the kind and color of
plant he could expect from the seeds in a package. At first all these
packages of seeds had to be carefully hand packed by girls, but
today packing machines fill and seal the envelopes and packages.
A few years ago the D. M. Ferry Seed Company joined another seed
company to form the Ferry-Morse Seed Company. In 1959, most of
the Detroit plant was moved to Fulton, Kentucky.

The making of tobacco products is another of Michigan's early
industries. At Detroit, cigars, chewing tobacco, and snuff were
manufactured. Clothing factories began to develop after 1880. A
copper smelter was for some time located at a dock in Springwells,
just below Detroit. In 1860, copper smelting was one of Detroit's
main industries, but this industry was moved to Lake Linden, in the
Upper Peninsula, soon after that date so it would be nearer to the
copper mines. A brass foundry was started as early as 1833. Today,

with the coming of the automobile industry, several brass working plants are now located in Detroit. The making of bicycles was one of Michigan's major industries just before the coming of the automobile at the turn of the century. Many bicycles were made at Bay City at this time. In 1888, the Buhl Manufacturing Company, at Detroit, began making tin-dipped dairy milkware such as tin pails, milk cans, milk pans, and milk strainers. Much of this tinware was sold to farm women who preferred it to the earlier wooden and crockery utensils. Bissell carpet sweepers and typewriters were manufactured at Grand Rapids.

An industry of a more general nature that developed in Michigan about the time of the Civil War was the furniture industry. Only a few of the early settlers who came to Michigan brought furniture with them. Many of these early settlers were young people just getting started in married life. Others were so poor that they could not afford to buy furniture. All, rich or poor, knew how hard it was, with the poor roads and small wagons at that time, to bring bulky pieces of furniture with them to the new settlements. Usually, when a family planned to move to Michigan they sold their farm and almost all their belongings in order to get money enough to buy the land for their new farm. Some families had a "choice piece" of furniture, as they called it, that had been made by one of their relatives or had been in the family for several years. These pieces of furniture the settlers sometimes brought with them.

Crude furniture for their little cabins was often made by the settlers themselves. Some of the settlers had been craftsmen in Europe or in New England. These craftsmen were called "cabinetmakers." They were usually carpenters and joiners who owned a kit of tools. The census of 1850 lists 704 men in Michigan who classed themselves as cabinetmakers. From the lumber of that day these men began making articles of furniture such as chairs, tables, kitchen tables, and beds. They also made the coffins that were needed by the community and sometimes also acted as the undertakers. As the settlers prospered and wanted better furniture for their homes, they often traded grain, flour, pigs, chickens, or beef to the cabinetmakers in exchange for such articles of furniture as they desired.

To make strong, lasting furniture required good wood that was well cured. To properly season wood, so that it would be thoroughly dry at the center, took about four years. Few craftsmen could afford to purchase a wood supply four years in advance or provide a place in which to store it. Many of the pieces of furniture that were made by these early craftsmen continued to dry out after they had been made and often fell apart. Sometimes, so we are told, the pieces of a chair would be brought back in a bag to the cabinetmaker who had made it. Later, as the industry grew, better methods of curing lumber in dry kilns were developed.

The really good pieces of furniture at that time were made at other places such as Boston or Cincinnati. If they were to be sent to Michigan, such pieces had to be carefully wrapped, crated, and handled with much care. Only wealthy people could afford such expensive furniture. Most people used the locally made furniture which was then made at many different places in southern Michigan. But as the years passed one Michigan city developed as the leading furniture center and that city was Grand Rapids.

The furniture industry began at Grand Rapids in 1836, when Mr. William Holdane set up a cabinet shop there and began making handmade furniture for sale. Other cabinetmakers also came to Grand Rapids. At first these cabinetmakers worked by hand and made chairs, bedsteads, bureaus, and such other useful pieces of furniture that would sell to the settlers coming into southern Michigan. In 1848, a circular saw was brought to Grand Rapids and soon other power machinery was also used. A small steam engine was used by Mr. Holdane, in 1863, to furnish power for his little furniture shop. From the work of these early craftsmen at Grand Rapids the furniture industry developed until the products of Grand Rapids became known throughout the world for fine workmanship, quality, and design. By 1870, Michigan's furniture ranked with any then being made in the nation and for some time Grand Rapids ranked as the leader in furniture making. In the early furniture industry style and workmanship were the measurements of success. Because of this, mass production of standard models was never a goal of the early furniture makers.

At first, like in colonial times, only single pieces were made but about 1875 the furniture makers began making whole suites of furniture rather than individual pieces. Bedroom suites and dining room suites began to appear on the furniture market. Each of the individual pieces in each set was made of the same design and of the same quality of wood.

For several years lumber produced in Michigan, or the nearby states, furnished the material from which furniture was made. At first the clear, soft, easily worked pine was the wood used for making the frontier furniture for the settlers. Later, as the settlers prospered, the hardwoods were also used. Oak, birch, walnut, and maple were all used to make Michigan's quality furniture. But, as the local supply of timber declined, and as the demand for more costly furniture increased, woods, such as rosewood, walnut, and satinwood were brought from foreign lands.

Because these woods were expensive they were cut into veneer; that is, the wood was cut into large thin sheets. These thin pieces of veneer were then glued onto wood of a cheaper quality. Thus, there was a large saving in the cost. Moreover, the finished furniture did not warp as easily and it looked more beautiful than if it had been made of solid wood.

About 1890, Michigan's furniture factories began making office furniture; such as desks, chairs, filing cabinets, and bookcases. Much church furniture was also made. The factories also began to produce large quantities of school furniture to meet the needs of the increasing numbers of young people who were then going to school. For a few years, after 1900, the furniture factories built wooden iceboxes to meet the needs for refrigeration in homes and stores.

During the past thirty or forty years many of the furniture factories have turned to using metal and plastics for materials rather than to use the more expensive wood. Today, several companies make desks, filing cabinets, chairs, typewriter stands, card tables, lamps, and other pieces of metal furniture for home and office use. Wooden iceboxes are no longer made, but all-metal units, covered with white or colored enamel, are built to encase refrigerating units.

Furniture is now being made, or has been manufactured, at Allegan, Ann Arbor, Big Rapids, Buchanan, Charlotte, Detroit, Grand Ledge, Holland, Manistee, Menominee, Monroe, Muskegon, Newago, Niles, Northville, Owosso, Saginaw, St. Johns, and Sturgis.

Many of the earlier factories in Michigan used wood as a material for much of their products, Several companies made organs. Others made doors, sash, tool handles, blinds, matches, boxes, barrels, barrel heads, and toothpicks. Fanning mills, for separating chaff from grain, were made at Plymouth and near St. Charles. Corn planters were made at Grand Haven. Plows were made at Albion and forks and hoes were made at Jackson. Farm equipment, such as threshing machines and threshing engines, was once made at Birmingham, Battle Creek, and Port Huron. Wagons and carriages were made at Pontiac, Lansing, and Flint. At first, two-wheeled carts were made from the hardwoods found in the nearby forests. This industry later developed into the making of wagons and carriages and gave Flint the name of the "Vehicle City." During the peak years of manufacturing, the early carriage makers at Flint were making nearly one hundred thousand wagons and carriages annually. One of these successful carriage makers at Flint was Mr. William C. Durant. When automobiles began to be made, at the turn of the century, the skills of the carriage makers were used in making automobiles.

The making of paper and paper products is another of Michigan's early industries. At first most paper was made from rags, but as the years passed more and more paper began to be produced from wood pulp. In 1850, there were ten plants in Michigan making paper or paper products. In 1905 there were thirty-one paper mills in the state. At that time Michigan ranked fifth in tonnage produced and seventh in the number of paper mills. Paper is now being produced, or has been produced at some time, in Kalamazoo, Manistee, Monroe, Munising, Ontonagon, Otsego, Parchment, Plainwell, and Port Huron. The leading paper centers in the state today are Kalamazoo and Monroe.

The production of salt is one of Michigan's oldest industries. During the periods of Michigan's geological history, many salt layers and brines were deposited in the Michigan Basin. These salt deposits make Michigan one of the leading salt producers of the United States.

Early settlers coming to Michigan discovered the presence of salt in the water coming from the ground in some areas, but no attempt was made to secure salt in commercial quantities until about 1860. In that year the state offered a bounty of ten cents a bushel to encourage salt production. Perhaps the first company to produce commercial salt was the East Saginaw Salt Company. During the early sawmill days, in the Saginaw River Valley, much of the refuse from the sawmills was burned to heat the brine and evaporate the water. The salt industry thus got its start as a side line of the lumber industry.

Once started, the salt industry grew rapidly. In 1880, 2,485,000 barrels of salt were produced. Since that time Michigan has been one of the leading salt producers of the nation. During the period from 1880 to 1890 Michigan produced nearly half of the total amount of salt produced in the United States. In 1907, Michigan produced over ten million barrels of salt.

There are three salt producing areas in Michigan: first, along the Detroit and St. Clair Rivers; second, in the Ludington and Manistee area; third, in the area around Midland.

Salt is secured in two different ways. One way is to pump water down to the salt layer. The water then dissolves the salt into a brine. The brine is then pumped to the surface and when the water is evaporated from the brine the salt is left. All of our common table salt is made this way. Wells from which brine is pumped are known as "salt wells" or "brine wells." The other way that salt is secured is to actually sink a shaft and blast the salt from the layers in which it lies. Such an operation is called a salt mine. Michigan has only one salt mine.

Courtesy Dow Chemical Company

Part of the Dow Chemical Company's Midland Division Plant at Midland, Michigan, as it appears today. The Midland operation, with more than 500 buildings covering approximately 1,000 acres, is one of the largest chemical plants in the country. (1961)

A salt brine was discovered at Midland in 1878. It was also discovered at Manistee in 1882, and at Wyandotte in 1887. All of these areas have since been large salt brine producers. Two of the areas, Midland and Wyandotte, have since become large industrial areas whose products are based primarily on the salt brine underlying the area.

Courtesy Wyandotte Chemicals Corporation, Wyandotte, Michigan

North Plant of the Wyandotte Chemicals Corporation, Wyandotte, Michigan

Up to 1890, American glass manufacturers had to depend upon foreign sources for soda ash to use in making glass. In 1891, Capt. J. B. Ford, a Pittsburgh plate glass manufacturer, came to Michigan looking for salt deposits in order to supply his factory with American-made soda ash. He became interested in the drilling that had been made at Wyandotte on the property of the old Eureka Iron and Steel Company. Capt. J. B. Ford spent nearly a million dollars learning how to change this salt into soda ash. This early company began the alkali industry now located in the Wyandotte area. The J. B. Ford Company was for many years the world's largest manufacturer of specialized cleaning materials and heavy chemicals. Other companies developed in the area. Some of these earlier companies are now combined into the Wyandotte Chemicals Corporation. The salt of the region, together with limestone shipped from the Alpena area, provides the resources used in the principal industry, which is the changing of salt into its by-products, such as soda ash, chlorine gas, caustic soda, soda bicarbonate, and baking soda. Lye is also produced. In the plants at Wyandotte the salt brine and limestone are processed to form a group of basic alkalies. These alkalies are then carefully blended, under heat and pressure, and other materials are added to make a long list of products.

After the discovery of a salt brine at Midland the early lumber companies in the area produced salt as a side line for about ten years. But, by 1890, the lumber industry had passed on to the north and it seemed that Midland's days of prosperity had passed. But the unusual nature of the salt brine at Midland had been noticed by Dr. Herbert Henry Dow. In 1888, Dr. Dow came to Midland to test the salt found there as he was interested in making bromine, from the brine, to be used as medicine. In 1890, Dr. Dow organized the Midland Chemical Company. Ten years later the Dow Chemical Company was organized and by 1902 the company was making 14 products based on bromine. Today, this company makes 110 products based on bromine. One interesting use of one of these products is to put it in gasoline to help prevent engine knock. To get more bromine one of the Dow Chemical plants, located in Freeport, Texas, uses millions of tons of sea water each day to secure the bromine and other elements.

Photography and medicine, at first, created demands for Dr. Dow's products. World War I brought a need for more and more chemicals. The need for a better gasoline in the 1920's brought other demands. During the last few years the development of sprays to kill insects, bacteria, and weeds, has opened other fields. To meet all of these demands many chemicals, based mostly on salt brine, have been produced. The Dow Chemical Company now makes over 700 products. Some are used only in industry but others like aspirin, camphor, epsom salts, and iodine are common household medicines. One of Dow's main products is chlorine and large cities use vast amounts of this each day to help keep their water supply pure so that people will not become ill from drinking impure water.

The Dow Chemical plant at Midland, in the southwestern part of the city, covers 2,800 acres. It is one of the largest chemical companies in the United States with other plants in other states and countries. It is the largest producer of chlorine. The brine from which Dow's products are manufactured lies in a basin of about three hundred square miles extending from Midland to Mt. Pleasant. For many years the company used the brine found in the Marshall sandstone layer at a depth of about 1,200 feet. At the present time the company is also taking salt brine from a deeper layer, which lies about 5,000 feet deep and is found to be much richer than the upper layer.

At Marysville, St. Clair, Manistee, and Montague, salt is also secured from brine. At St. Clair it is made into table salt by the Diamond Crystal Salt Company. At Manistee and in the Port Huron area, the Morton Salt Company also processes the salt brine into table salt. At Montague, the Hooker Chemical Corporation uses salt to make several industrial chemical products.

Michigan has only one salt mine. The mine is located on the west side of Detroit and extends under part of Melvindale. This mine produces salt from the Silurian formation at a depth of 1,137 feet. At first, beginning in 1895, the salt was used as a brine but, in 1906, the Detroit Rock Salt Company started digging a shaft downward to the salt layers. Workmen soon ran into difficulty, as both gases and an underground stream of water hindered their work. But after much hardship the shaft was completed in 1910 and the company began the production of rock salt. In 1913, this mine became one of the mines of the International Salt Company of Scranton, Pennsylvania.

The salt layer that is being mined is about twenty-six feet in thickness. It is made up of alternate layers of salt and anhydrite. In order to keep the overhead rock from settling, the "room and pillar" system of mining is used. This forms a large checkerboard pattern. Rooms fifty to sixty feet wide are cut away while large pillars of the same size are left to support the overhead rock.

At the working face of the mine miners undercut the room face at the bottom, on the working level, with a large saw like a chain saw. This saw cuts back into the salt layer about ten feet and takes out a six-inch kerf that gives the salt space to settle when it is blasted. Then another large machine, with drills projecting from it, is moved up to the working face. Holes are then drilled into the salt layers. Into these holes the miners place charges of explosive. About midnight, when only a few men are left in the mine, these charges are set off by electricity. One after another, from the bottom upward, the charges are exploded and the salt drops into a pile in the room.

The next day scoop shovels scoop up the shattered salt and drop it into huge trucks that carry from fifteen to twenty tons. These electric trucks then carry the salt and anhydrite to the first crusher. From this first crusher, to the mine shaft, runs an endless belt which is over one and one-fourth miles long. This belt carries the salt along from crusher to crusher, where the salt is crushed and most of the anhydrite is removed, and then to the hoisting shaft.

From the hoisting skips the salt is dumped into the tipple, where the salt is further crushed, cleaned, and classified. This rock salt is used for farmers' stock, for making chemicals, for curing hides, for bleaching and dyeing textiles, for making water softeners, plastics, and synthetic rubber. Much of it is used each winter to keep city streets and state highways free from ice. Salt from this mine is shipped away by rail, by truck, and by boats that dock on the River Rouge near the salt mine. None of it is used for table salt.

A deposit of bituminous coal lies under all the central part of the Lower Peninsula. This deposit of coal was formed during the Pennsylvanian period. Some coal was mined at Jackson as early as 1835. Coal was mined near Grand Ledge in 1838 and 1839. At one time coal was mined near Williamston. But there was little use for coal in a land that provided good firewood from wood lots and sawmills. But as the supply of wood grew smaller, Michigan's industries turned more and more to coal as a fuel.

Around 1900, coal was being mined in Genesee, Tuscola, and Huron counties. At that time there were over thirty mines producing coal in Michigan. Nineteen hundred seven was Michigan's peak year in coal production. In that year a little over two million tons were mined. By 1920 there were only eighteen mines producing coal, and their production had dropped to about one and one-half million tons. By 1931, there were only six major mines still producing coal. Michigan's coal mines ceased operation in 1946. Today only local noncommercial mines are used.

Although Michigan has a large coal basin underlying much of the central part of the Lower Peninsula and although Michigan uses a large amount of coal, all of the coal used in this state today is shipped here from other areas. Michigan's coal basin reaches from Jackson to Saginaw, and it is thought to contain about eight billion tons of coal. In general, the veins are thin except near Saginaw. The coal that was mined here was very soft and easily broken. It also had a high content of acid. It could not be made into coke and was therefore found useless in the iron and steel industries. Then, too, Michigan's coal miners faced many other problems. Unlike the coal veins found in many other places, the coal in Michigan is covered by glacial till instead of sedimentary rock that forms a protective ceiling. The loose sand and gravel of the glacial till slips and slides easily and must be heavily timbered to protect the miners. This is very expensive and coal from the mines cannot compete in price with coal mined in strip mines in other areas and shipped into Michigan by train or boat.

Slate is found near Huron Bay on Lake Superior. During the period from 1870 to 1890 some effort was made to secure and market this resource. The efforts, however, were not very successful for, although the slate was found to be of excellent quality, it was also discovered that nature had badly shattered the slate formations, thus making much of it useless.

Along the south shore of Lake Superior is found a sandstone that is called "brownstone." Several small quarries that produced this stone were once worked along Keweenaw Bay. From an old quarry at Marquette, opened shortly after the Civil War, came "brownstone" that was used in making buildings in Detroit and Chicago. This stone was also used in some of the early buildings at Michigan Technological University at Houghton. This stone is no longer used for building purposes because it turns a yellowish brown color when exposed to the weather. In the southern peninsula one of the underlying saucers is called Marshall sandstone. This sandstone was quarried at Marshall as early as 1840. It was also later quarried at Napoleon, in Jackson County, and at Grindstone City at the top of the Thumb. Sandstone from these early quarries was used for making grindstones. At Grindstone City can now be seen the old quarries from which the Marshall sandstone was once taken to make grindstones. With the coming of carborundum the grindstone industry has ceased to be. Grindstone City was once a busy center of this little industry but little remains there today to be seen of this early industry.

Michigan is fortunate in having vast deposits of marl, clay, shale, gypsum, and limestone that can be used in making cement. These deposits are well scattered over the state so that cement can be made in many places. Cement was first manufactured in Michigan at Kalamazoo in the early seventies. Although the first attempt was a failure, cement plants made rapid progress after 1895. In 1900, there were six cement plants, and the production for that year was four thousand barrels. As cement is a very heavy product, it costs much money to ship it very far. Therefore, there are now ten cement plants scattered over the state. Each plant cares for the needs of its surrounding area. Large plants are located at Alpena, Port Huron, Petoskey, and Dundee. Lake shipping from these plants provides a cheap method of transportation for this heavy commodity. In 1960, cement ranked second in value in Michigan's mineral production.

Of all of the varieties of stone, limestone is the most widely used. Limestone is used for railroad ballast to form a firm bed for the rails, for sweetening agricultural land, for making granulated sugar in sugar beet plants, in the making of cement, and in the manufacturing process of many things such as paper, glass, leather, soaps, and paints.

Along the shores of the Great Lakes, where the underlying limestone saucers outcrop, is often found a high quality of limestone free from other sedimentary impurities. Because of this the quarrying of limestone has been one of Michigan's industries. Industries seeking high quality limestone have developed large limestone quarries along the lake shore where the limestone can be quarried and the crushed limestone easily and cheaply transported by means of Great Lakes boats. Because of the high quality and purity of Michigan's limestone much of it is used for making cement and as a furnace flux in the smelting of iron ore.

An early quarry at Sibley, now part of the city of Trenton, once provided limestone for making iron and steel and for the alkali industries at Wyandotte. This early quarry is no longer worked. Limestone for the Wyandotte Chemicals industry, at Wyandotte, is brought by boat from the large quarries in the Straits of Mackinac—Alpena area.

At Calcite, located just east of Rogers City, a high-grade limestone has been quarried since 1912. Each summer Michigan Limestone, a Division of United States Steel Corporation, ships vast quantities of crushed limestone from this port. The quarry is operated as a strip mine. During the winter the glacial till overlaying the rock is removed. During the summer shipping season the limestone is blasted from its place in the sedimentary layer. The rock is then hauled to a crusher where it is broken into many sizes. Ninety-eight per cent of the limestone quarried here is shipped by boats to smelters and manufacturers. This high-grade calcium limestone is used in blast furnaces in purifying iron ore. About eight hundred to one thousand pounds of limestone are required for each ton of iron ore smelted. This limestone is also used to make steel in open hearth furnaces. A new port from which limestone has been shipped since 1955 is Stoneport on the Presque Isle Peninsula between Alpena and Rogers City. At Alpena are located other quarries of limestone and shale. Most of the limestone and shale quarried here is used to make cement. In 1907, the Huron Portland Cement Company began producing cement at Alpena. Today this company's cement plant located here is the largest cement plant in the United States.

East of Manistique, on the shore of Lake Michigan, is Port Inland from which limestone is also shipped. Port Inland ranks second among the Great Lakes ports in the volume of limestone shipped. It is a privately owned port of the Inland Lime and Stone Company. It was opened in 1930. The limestone is hauled by rail to the port from the company quarry, which is located about seven and one-half miles inland from the port. Most of this limestone goes to Gary, Indiana, and Chicago and is used in the steel industry there.

On Drummond Island is located the world's largest dolomite quarry. Much dolomite was taken from this quarry to be used in making the footings for the Mackinac Bridge. In 1960, a new quarry was opened about five miles east of the older quarry.

A new port to ship high purity dolomite was opened in 1955, by Michigan Limestone just three miles east of Cedarville, at Port Dolomite on McKay Bay. This dolomite is used for fluxing by the iron and steel industry.

Gypsum is a formation similar to salt. In 1827, gypsum deposits were discovered along Plaster Creek in Kent County. A mill there began grinding gypsum as early as 1842. The crushed gypsum was used by the farmers to put on their land. Later, deposits were found at Alabaster and National City. From 1901 to 1907, Michigan led the states in the production of gypsum. The United States Gypsum Company operates quarries at Alabaster and also a port from which the gypsum is shipped by boat. The National Gypsum Company has a quarry at National City and a port at Tawas City. Three other companies have gypsum mines at Grand Rapids. The Grand Rapids Gypsum Company was organized in 1860 and is one of the oldest gypsum companies in the United States. Gypsum is used for making plaster, plasterboard, and insulating materials.

Courtesy Kellogg Company

The present large Kellogg plant in Battle Creek where breakfast foods are made. The Kellogg Company also has plants abroad to provide service in over 100 countries. (1961)

Battle Creek has been known as a health and cereal food center for many years. As early as 1866, the Western Health Reform Institute was formed here. In 1875, Dr. John H. Kellogg started the Battle Creek Sanitarium, and became interested in health foods. In 1895, the Postum Company was organized and began producing "Postum," a cereal coffee, and "Grape Nuts." At one time thirty-two companies in Battle Creek were producing health foods. Today, only four companies produce breakfast cereals.

Just before 1880 a few telephones began to be installed in Michigan. It is difficult to say just where the first phone was installed, but in 1877 one of the first lines was a two-mile line running between the office of the Frederick K. Stearns Drug Company and its laboratory. People were invited to talk over the new phone. Many of them were sure that the new phone was only a trick. A telephone company was organized in Ontonagon in 1877. Public interest in the new telephone grew rapidly. Soon many local telephone companies were organized to serve villages and the surrounding area. The Michigan Bell Telephone Company was started in 1883. Before many years had passed many companies had connecting lines with other companies and people were able to talk to other people in many parts of the state. Today, there are still about eighty independent companies in Michigan. The smallest one has only twenty-seven customers. All the phone companies are now interconnected and one can talk to people all over the United States.

Courtesy Henry Ford Museum

With the coming of telephones many people were soon employed as switchboard operators. This early switchboard is from the period about 1900.

Michigan's water power became an important factor only after electricity began to be developed and larger dams were built across the streams. What is now the Consumers Power Company was started in 1886 by two brothers, W. A. Foote and J. B. Foote. They left their milling business in Adrian and went to Jackson to establish a city lighting system. They were joined by Samuel Jarvis, and the firm of Foote and Jarvis was started. Later these men started lighting systems in Albion, Battle Creek, and Kalamazoo.

In Grand Rapids, William T. Powers and his partners were also helping in developing electricity in Michigan. They installed on the west side of the Grand River the first hydroelectric plant in the United States. Foote's company began to work in the Muskegon River Valley on the problem of transmitting an electric current over long distances. In 1904, the Grand Rapids-Muskegon Power Company was organized and the Croton Dam was soon built by the company. In 1910, several small companies were combined into one single company named the Consumers Power Company. This company became a single system in 1915. At that time it had well over one hundred thousand gas and light customers. Since that time this company has done much to develop Michigan's water power and better transmission of electrical power.

At first poles were used to carry the transmission lines from the dams to the cities, but soon these were replaced by steel tower transmission lines. These steel tower lines were first developed here in Michigan. In 1906, a voltage of 70,000, a new record for the country, was carried over the company's lines. This record was broken in 1907 by increasing the voltage to 110,000, and again it was broken in 1911 by an increase to 140,000 volts.

Gradually this company has been expanded until today Consumers Power Company has dams located on the Au Sable, Kalamazoo, Thornapple, Tobacco, Muskegon, Grand, and Manistee rivers. These dams catch the water of the rivers and store it in huge basins between hills. Each evening as more power is wanted more water is allowed to flow through huge turbines in the powerhouses at the bases of the dams. The turbines turn large generators that produce electricity. From the dams the electricity is carried by high-power transmission lines to many cities and rural homes.

Today, the Consumers Power Company operates 30 hydro-electric plants and 40 coal burning generating plants. It supplies electricity for 61 of the 68, and gas in 32, of the counties of the Lower Peninsula. Power is also supplied to the Edison Sault Electric Company by means of a cable on the floor of the Straits of Mackinac. This company also provides steam heat for downtown Battle Creek, Kalamazoo, Grand

Rapids, and Saginaw. To date, along its river holdings the company has planted over 25,000,000 trees. Each year it sets out about 750,000 seedlings. This reforestation project stops erosion, checks run-off water, and provides soil conservation. In time the company can get home grown utility poles from its own holdings.

In the Detroit area most of the electrical power is supplied by the Detroit Edison Company. Some large industrial companies supply all or part of their own power. Since 1930, several smaller electric

The large Edison power plant at Trenton. Power plants like this one are used to generate the huge amounts of electricity used in the Detroit metropolitan area. Photo 1956.

companies have supplied electric power to rural communities and small villages. Ten of these companies are privately owned, forty-nine are municipally owned plants, and fifteen are cooperatives. Today, there are only a few areas in Michigan where electric power cannot be had.

Michigan's largest industry today is the manufacturing of automobiles and automobile parts. But, although Michigan is the center of the automobile industry, the automobile was not invented in Michigan.

One of the first types of power tried in early automobiles was steam power. As early as 1886-1887 Ransom E. Olds, of Lansing, built one of the first steam-driven cars. Several steam cars, such as the White, Stanley Steamer, and Locomobile, later appeared on the market, but steam power was not to prove successful in supplying automobile transportation. Before the owner of a steam car could drive, he had to wait a few minutes for steam to build up pressure in the boiler. Once the steam had formed, the car moved easily and with no need to shift gears. But at the end of thirty miles or so the driver had to stop, hunt for a water supply, and get up steam again. Then, too, boilers froze on frosty nights, and the owner of a steam car had to be sure that the boiler was drained or kept warm if the car was left to stand for any length of time. One interesting feature of these early steam cars was that they had whistles in place of horns to warn people of their approach.

Courtesy Henry Ford Museum, Dearborn, Michigan

An early steam buggy

Another type of power tried in early cars was electric power. Large batteries, placed under the seat, ran an electric motor. These cars started easily and one did not have to shift gears, but the life of a battery was short, and it had to be taken out and recharged every little while. This meant that one could not drive very far from a place where batteries could be charged again.

From France and Germany, in 1875, came an engine for which engineers had long been searching. The engine used coal gas for fuel which was made to explode inside a cylinder by means of an electric spark. Here was the basic principle. If the little engine could be made to explode time after time, this would give it power—power to really drive a carriage. This engine would not have to depend on water and fire, nor, like the first attempts at an electric carriage, would it have to depend on batteries. It could carry its power wherever it went.

But coal gas was too expensive. A cheaper source of explosive material had to be found before the gas engine could become practical. The search for a better gas was soon on, and it was finally found in gasoline. The petroleum industry had already begun to develop. Refineries were taking petroleum and heating it and making refined kerosene for use in lamps and lanterns. While petroleum was being heated to make kerosene, it gave off a gas that was highly explosive. It was found that this gas, now called gasoline, could be used to run the new combustion engines. What before had been a waste product now began to be sought after as a motor fuel. These gasoline motors that were developed at the turn of the century thus furnished a new kind of power. A tank full of gasoline would carry one much farther than one could go on a boiler full of water. About this time, too, new finds of vast petroleum fields in Texas provided a limitless supply of power fuel.

With the development of the gasoline engine it was only natural that carriage makers would try putting the new engines into wagons and buggies. In fact, the first automobiles were sometimes called auto-buggies and auto-wagons. Several automobile companies, like Studebaker at South Bend, Indiana, grew from the carriage industry.

Only a few gasoline-driven vehicles were built before 1900. In 1894, Mr. R. E. Olds built his first gasoline-driven automobile and began driving it about the streets of Lansing, much to the displeasure of most people who saw in it only a public danger and a death trap for Mr. Olds. In 1895, he began to produce cars for sale. For some years Mr. Olds was the most successful of the early car makers. In 1896, a young man in Detroit, named Henry Ford, built his first gasoline-driven car. This car can be seen today in the Henry Ford Museum at Dearborn. Mr. Ford's gasoline motor was a two-cylinder engine made from pipe that he had bought from the Detroit Edison Company where he was then employed as an engineer. Around his little engine he built his first car. It was five feet in length. For

Courtesy Oldsmobile Division, General Motors Corp.

The ability to climb hills was as important in an automobile back in 1901 as it is today. Bowler-topped Ransom Eli Olds, founder of the company that is now Oldsmobile Division of General Motors Corporation, strains to get the last bit of energy out of his Curved Dash Runabout in an early test run at Detroit. Riding with him (right) is a friend, John Maxwell, who founded Maxwell Motors.

wheels he used four bicycle wheels. At first he planned that the car
would be driven by the front wheels, but he soon found that this
made the little car steer too hard and that the back wheels were of
little use in steering it. The car had just two speeds, one forward and
one backward. In 1898, the chambered spark plug was invented by
a Michigan lumberman named Frank W. Canfield. This was a great
advance in the development of the gasoline engine because one could
now regulate the time when the gasoline would explode.

Several car manufacturers soon began offering automobiles for
sale. By 1899, there were already twenty-five firms manufacturing
automobiles. The early auto manufacturers numbered almost a
hundred. Many of these early auto companies did not last long. A few
like Mr. Olds and Mr. Winton began to make cars by the thousands.
Most of the first cars were very expensive, and there were as yet no
good roads on which to drive them.

After 1900 many other car manufacturers began making cars. In
1902, the oldest car company still making cars in Detroit was formed.
This company is now the Cadillac Motor Car Company. In 1903, the

Courtesy Ford Motor Co.
The home of the first Ford automobile. 1896

Ford Motor Company came into being. To house the Ford Motor Company, a building on Mack Avenue was rented. The Ford car was to be an assembled job. The motors were to be made by the Dodge brothers, who at that time manufactured bicycles and ran a machine shop in Detroit. The wheels were to be bought from one firm and the bodies from another and the tires from still another.

The City of Flint was also a pioneer in the automobile industry. In 1900, David Buick was running the Buick Manufacturing Company located there and making stationary farm engines. Mr. Buick became interested in the new automobile and built a car for himself. In 1904, Mr. Buick joined with the Flint Wagon Works and formed a new company to manufacture the Buick car. Later William Crapo Durant, who was already well known as a member of the Durant-Dort Carriage Works, joined the Buick company.

Many companies were formed between 1900 and 1925. By 1920, many of the early companies had already failed. Today, the names of such automobiles as the Jackson, Maxwell, Cartorcar, Randolph, Rebance, and Earl are unknown to us. For about thirty years one of the leading automobile companies in Detroit was the Packard Motor Car Company. Packard cars were first made at Warren, Ohio. In 1902, Henry B. Joy and some other men from Detroit became interested in the Packard car, which was then selling under the name of the Ohio Auto Company. They added three more cylinders to the little car, named it the Packard, and moved the factory to Detroit in 1903. In that same year Mr. B. T. Fitch drove the "Old Pacific," a Packard car, from San Francisco to New York on the first automobile trip across the continent. Mr. Fitch made this trip in fifty-five days. The Reo car first appeared in 1904. Hupmobile appeared in 1908. Hudson and Chevrolet cars came on the market in 1909. For several years the Hudson Motor Company made a little six-cylinder car called the Essex. Among the other early automobiles appearing before 1930 were Oakland, Winton, Saxon, Maxwell, Huroon, Paige, Rickenbacker, and Willis Sainte Claire. The Huroon car was made at Wayne. The Willis Sainte Claire was made at Marysville. The Paige, Maxwell, and Saxon cars were made at plants located in Detroit and Dearborn.

One of the best known and most popular of the early cars was the Model T Ford. The Ford Motor Company began production of this car in 1908. The car was strong and light. The motor was made of vanadium steel. It had a block of four cylinders which was cast all at one time instead of putting four separate cylinders together. The motor also had a removable head. This was a new development that made it possible to repair a motor with much more ease. Because traffic in America keeps to the right, Mr. Ford changed the steering wheel to the left side of the new car. The Model T created a sensation. It was cheap enough for even the common workman to buy. Thousands of people rushed to see it. Over one thousand were sold the first week. By 1908, the Ford Motor Company was making one hundred cars a day. This was four times as many cars as any other manufacturer was making at that time.

About this time the method of making cars changed in the automobile plants. The old method of taking cars around the plant to the parts was changed for a newer method now known as the "assembly line." The parts were to be brought to the cars as they passed slowly along. As each car passed a man, he did one thing toward making each of the finished cars. Side conveyors brought the parts to each man, and he in turn placed the parts into the cars.

Up to this time each mechanic had found it necessary to fit every part to each motor or car. This had caused much useless delay and extra expense. Car manufacturers now began to make each part exactly alike. These identical parts are now called standard, or interchangeable parts. They will work on each car just as well as on another, and there is no need of fitting each separate part to the machine. To do this the automobile makers had to introduce precision measurements into their parts manufacture. This system of production has now come to be called mass production. It was not developed in the automobile industry but was adopted by the early car makers. Today, it is used in many lines of manufacturing.

Many people saw little use in buying the new cars. There were few roads on which to drive them. In some of the cities there were a few streets that had wooden block pavement, or were coverd with macadam, but country roads were almost impassable for automobiles. Motorists who attempted to drive on these roads often got stuck in the sand or mud. When they did get stuck, they were often greeted by passers-by with the comment, "Better get a horse." The first mile of cement road in Michigan was built in the year 1908. By 1917 there were still only a few miles of paving in the state.

Early cars were a great annoyance to people having horses. Horses in the field would become frightened at the horseless carriages putt-putting down the road. Even cattle were disturbed, and farmers said that they did not give their usual quantity of milk. Farmers did not keep their chickens penned up, and many chickens were killed by the automobiles. People riding in wagons and buggies were especially annoyed when they saw one of the early cars coming down the road. Many times horses became frightened at the noisy, ill-smelling cars and ran away, smashing wagons and buggies and sometimes injuring the people who were riding in them. Often a man would get out of his buggy and put his coat over his horse's head and lead him past the car. But as the years passed and more and more cars appeared on the roads, the horses became more used to them and often disregarded them altogether. This was especially true of the younger horses.

General Motors Company came into being on September 16, 1908. This company was succeded by the General Motors Corporation on October 13, 1916. This corporation was a combination of many early auto manufacturers and various producers of auto parts. Buick was taken in in September, 1908. Olds was added to the corporation in December, 1908. Oakland and Cadillac were taken in in June, 1910. Chevrolet was added in 1918, and in 1919 the Fisher Body Company became a member of the growing corporation. In 1919, General Motors began the building of their general office building in Detroit. This new building was fifteen stories high and was occupied as their general offices in 1921.

In July, 1913, the Dodge brothers decided to build a car of their

Courtesy Henry Ford Museum

This picture, taken about 1915, shows what many of Michigan's roads were like at that time. There were a few miles of pavement and gravel roads but many country roads were like this one.

own, and gave the Ford Motor Company notice that they would not continue to make motors for them after July, 1914. From the time that Mr. Ford had started to make cars to that date the Dodge brothers had built all the motors used in Ford cars. In 1914, Cadillac pioneered in a new field and brought out the first V-eight high-speed motor. In that year Mr. Ford startled the world by increasing the wages of his employees from an average of $2.34 a day to a minimum of $5.00. At the same time, Mr. Ford changed the working day for his men from nine hours to eight hours. By making the working day one of eight hours, he made it possible to work his men three shifts in place of two.

In 1915, ground was broken for a new and larger Ford plant to be located on the River Rouge in Dearborn. As the plant on the River Rouge in Dearborn grew larger and larger, the river was deepened so that boats loaded with coal and iron ore could come up the river and bring their cargoes to the factory. During World War I the Rouge Plant supplied eagle boats, tractors, cars, tanks, as well as liberty motors for airplanes. After the war the Rouge Plant became the center of the Ford industries.

All the auto industries did much to help the United States win World War I. The Dodge Brothers used their plant to manufacture needed war supplies. The Packard Motor Car Company designed and built the first liberty motor. During the war the Packard plant built more of these motors than any other company. Each auto plant in Michigan helped in some way to aid in winning the struggle against Germany.

In January, 1924, the first Chrysler car appeared. This corporation soon purchased the Dodge Plant. The rise of this corporation has been rapid, and today it ranks as one of the "big three" in the production of automobiles.

During World War II the auto plants again aided in making war materials, and the skilled craftsmen together with the available machinery made Michigan really an arsenal of democracy. From their plants poured a steady stream of supplies for the fighting forces.

Following World War II, the Kaiser-Fraser Corporation occupied the Willow Run Bomber Plant, where bombers were made during World War II, and for a few years Kaiser and Fraser cars were made there.

One of the leading manufacturers of automobiles and refrigerators is now the American Motors Corporation. Like General Motors Corporation, it is a combination of several older companies.

One of the oldest companies that was combined into the American Motors Corporation was the Hudson Motor Car Company. This company was located at Detroit and began making automobiles in 1909. The first Hudson car was the first automobile to have a selective sliding gear transmission with three forward speeds. During the twenties the Hudson company also made a very popular, smaller car called the Essex.

Another former company now in American Motors Corporation

was the Kelvinator Corporation, which was one of the early Detroit manufacturers of refrigerators.

In 1916, Mr. Charles W. Nash, who once ran a carriage and wagon factory in Flint and became president of General Motors in 1912, bought a motor car company then making cars in Wisconsin. There he began making a car called the Nash. In January, 1937, the Nash Motors Company merged with the Kelvinator Corporation. In 1950, Nash-Kelvinator introduced the first of the modern compact cars. It was called the Rambler after an earlier Rambler that had been made from 1902 to 1914. In 1952, Nash-Kelvinator purchased the Kalamazoo Stove and Furnace Company and the following year added the company making ABC washers at Peoria, Illinois. In 1954, the

Courtesy Kelvinator Division, American Motors Corporation

Refrigeration compressors are assembled in a special room equipped with an air filtering system to insure dirt-free, trouble-free mechanisms.

company merged with the Hudson Motor Car Company to form the present American Motors Corporation. The Hudson car was no longer made. Today, American Motors Corporation makes the Rambler car at Kenosha and Milwaukee in Wisconsin. For many years the Ford Rouge Plant produced more automobiles than any other single plant in the United States, but today the Kenosha plant produces more automobiles than any other single plant in America. At Grand Rapids, Michigan, the Kelvinator branch of the corporation now produces refrigerators, freezers, laundry equipment, and other products. At Evart, Michigan, plastic parts for automobiles and appliances are made.

During the past fifty years much progress has been made in automobile making. Up to about 1925 nearly all automobile bodies were made of wood and covered with metal. Today, all automobile bodies are made of welded steel parts. Up to 1920 only a few of the most expensive automobiles had a hard top and windows in the sides. People of that time jokingly said they would not care to ride in one of those glass showcases. All other models were open models with a collapsible top and side curtains that could be put up in case of rain. At first there were no garages, and cars were usually kept in horse barns. Repair parts were hard to get, and everyone had to be his own mechanic.

Many standard features that we now take for granted when buying an automobile were not included on those early models. Such features as a gasoline gauge, oil pressure gauge, self starter, accelerator, windshield wipers, automatic choke, heater, and radio all came later. All the early cars were cranked by hand. The first electric lights ran directly from the generator, and the brightness of the light depended on the speed of the motor. When one needed light the most, one had the least of it. Cars today have over ten times the horsepower of the early cars.

Today, automobiles not only are well engineered but are works of beauty and comfort as well. The automobile has become, in just fifty years, a necessary part of our American way of life. Hundreds of them roll off the factory assembly lines each day. Our streets and highways are filled with automobiles carrying people to and from work, on necessary errands, and on pleasure trips. Distance is less of a handicap than it was up to 1900.

Soon after the automobile appeared, the first trucks also appeared. At first these trucks were used mostly as delivery wagons on city streets, but by 1925 large trucks that could be used for hauling coal, gravel, limestone, or sand had appeared. Gradually they took over the work that had been done by horses and wagons up to that time. All kinds of trucks, little ones used by farmers, heavy ones to haul huge loads of soil, and long "haul-away" trucks, are a common sight on our streets and highways.

Automobile manufacturing is Michigan's largest industry. Not only are there large plants in Pontiac, Lansing, Saginaw, Flint, and Detroit devoted to the manufacture of automobiles, but there are hundreds of smaller plants scattered all over the state which make parts that find their way to the assembly lines in the huge automobile plants. These plants give to thousands of men living in Michigan their regular daily employment.

Today, our fastest means of travel is in the air. Since World War I this means of travel has progressed rapidly. Although the Michigan automobile factories made many airplane parts during World War I and World War II, they have not become manufacturers of airplanes. Michigan's transportation industries have centered around wheels, carriage wheels, wagon wheels, bicycle wheels, railroad car wheels, and later automobile wheels, and wheels still play a major part in Michigan's auto industries.

For a few years after World War I, Mr. Ford made a tri-motor airplane, jokingly called the "tin goose," near the present Ford Museum, in Dearborn. Bombers were made by the Ford Motor Company at the Willow Run Plant during World War II and many companies again made airplane engines and other parts. But after the war was over, the automobile companies, still thinking in terms of wheels and mass production, let other companies make the airplanes. These airplane companies are now mostly located in the western part of the United States.

Airports, that care for small planes, are now found near many of Michigan's cities and villages. Larger and better equipped airports are found at Michigan's larger cities, especially in the area south of Bay City and Muskegon. Michigan's largest airports are located just west of Detroit. They are Willow Run and Metropolitan Airport. At these two airports large, fast planes that carry many people, can be seen as they arrive at or leave the airport. Today, huge planes fly across our state carrying passengers, mail, and freight. Each year planes are being made larger, faster, and safer; and more people are using this fast mean of going from one city to another.

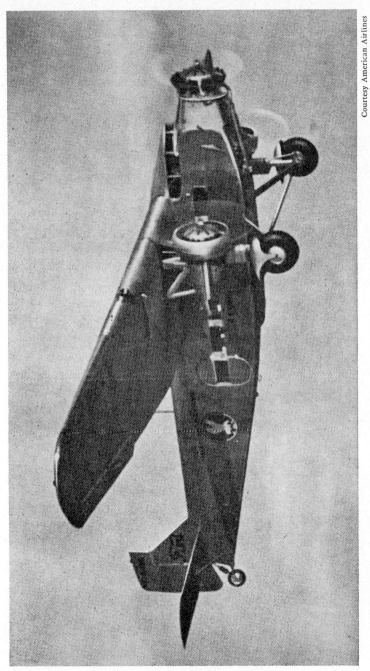

Courtesy American Airlines

The Ford Tri-Motor "Tin Goose," built by Stout Metal Airplane Co., a division of the Ford Motor Co., carried 10 to 14 passengers. The all-metal plane had corrugated skin and a two-man cockpit. Some models of this plane are still in use in various parts of the world.

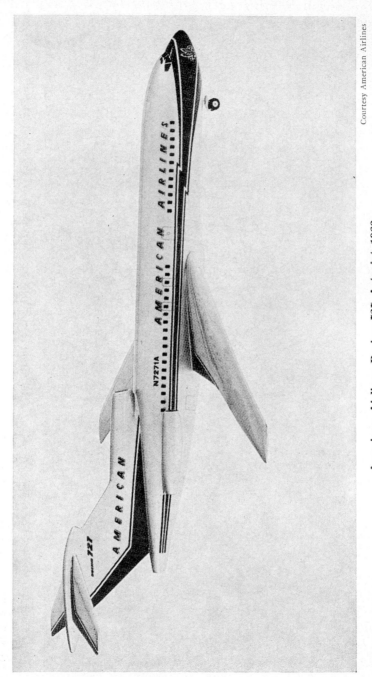

Courtesy American Airlines

American Airlines Boeing 727 Astrojet. 1963

With the coming of the space age, Michigan's factories, with their technological skills, have become important producers in this field. The Chrysler Corporation began making the Jupiter rocket, and it was the Jupiter "C" that launched the free world's first satellite, Explorer I. Control mechanisms are produced by Bendix and the Burroughs Adding Machine Company. The Chrysler Corporation has also been making Redstone Rockets. The power that put our first spaceman, Comm. Alan B. Shepard, into space, on May 5, 1961, was a Redstone Rocket made in the Detroit area.

One other industry in Detroit is closely allied to wheels and the automobile and truck industry and that is the United States Rubber Company. This company first started as the Morgan and Wright firm in Chicago. It began making double-tube bicycle tires. Because this new type of tire proved to be much superior to the solid or cushion type then in use, the company became the largest manufacturer of this commodity in the world.

In 1900, the Morgan and Wright Company was purchased by the United States Rubber Company. About this time, automobiles were beginning to want tires and the company saw in the new automobile a new field for tire making. As the auto industry seemed to be centering in Detroit, the company decided to move their plant to Detroit. A new plant was built at the foot of Bellevue Avenue and, in 1906, the company moved into its new quarters. As the automobile industry expanded so did this company. Today, this plant has grown to be the world's largest tire plant. As some 7,200 people are now employed at this plant, it is probably the largest industry in what used to be old downtown Detroit.

In the early twenties radio first appeared. WWJ, The Detroit News, was one of the first commercial broadcasting stations. Soon hundreds of people had radio sets in their homes. In the following decade television also appeared. Again hundreds of people purchased these sets for their homes. The manufacture of radios and television sets as well as the parts for these sets now employs hundreds of men and women here in Michigan.

With the coming of the gasoline engine and electrical power at the turn of the century, many mechanical appliances such as washers, ironers, sweepers, electric refrigerators, and toasters appeared on the market. Some of these appliances were developed here in Michigan. Today industries making these appliances are scattered over the state.

As the automobile industry and the manufacturing of electrical

Curing, or vulcanizing, is begun when the barrel-like tire is placed in a mold. An inflated "shaping bag" is forced inside the tire. The mold gives the tire its permanent shape and tread design. (1961)

Courtesy United States Rubber Company

Looking like a real tire after its curing, tubeless U.S. Royal is removed from "bagomatic" mold. (1961)

Courtesy United States Rubber Company

appliances developed, there grew a greater and greater demand for more and more steel. About the time Captain Ward's Eureka Iron and Steel Company closed down, mines opened in Minnesota, and great quantities of iron ore began coming down the lakes. Nearly all of it for thirty years sailed past Detroit to the receiving ports on the south shore of Lake Erie. This is no longer true, for Michigan today produces large quantities of iron and steel. Large rolling mills and huge blast furnaces, standing along the Detroit river, have replaced the crude furnaces and mills of seventy-five years ago.

In 1902, a blast furnace was built on Zug Island at the mouth of the River Rouge. A second blast furnace was built on the island in 1909. These furnaces produced what was known as merchant pig iron that was sold to foundry companies. Later Mr. Ford began producing some steel at his Rouge Plant. Today Ford's steel mills annually produce well over half a million tons of steel.

Mr. G. R. Fink, a sales representative for an eastern steel firm, saw the need for steel to be produced here in Michigan and in 1922 organized the Michigan Steel Corporation. Mr. Fink then built a plant on the Ecorse River. At first this company did not smelt iron but bought rough steel from the Pittsburgh area and rolled it into sheets and desired shapes. In 1929, the Michigan Steel Corporation was enlarged, and it became the Great Lakes Steel Corporation. It is now a division of the National Steel Corporation. The site for the new plant was a swamp beside the Detroit River. One hundred thousand piles were driven into the ground to support the new plant. After long months of hard work the new steel mill started production in August, 1931. Other plants including the blast furnaces on Zug Island were brought into the new corporation. A new blast furnace was added in 1938 and another was built on Zug Island in 1953. To these former steel-making facilities were later added 130 coke ovens, a by-product plant and docks and storage space for coal, iron ore, and limestone. Since that time both hot and cold mills have been added to roll steel. Today, Great Lakes Steel is the largest producer of steel in the state. Much of the steel it produces goes into the making of automobiles.

The Detroit Steel Corporation was formed in 1923. In 1944, this corporation was merged with the Reliance Steel Division. In 1953, this company produced 450,000 tons of coke, 504,000 tons of pig iron, and 1,290,000 tons of steel ingots.

In 1934, Donald B. McLouth formed the McLouth Steel Corporation. In 1935, this company rolled its first hot-rolled steel. Cold rolling mills and blast furnaces have since been added. The McLouth Steel Corporation has its plant in Trenton.

That gas and oil exist in Michigan has been known from the earliest days of settlement. Early settlers found oil and gas escaping in Montcalm, Wayne, and Monroe counties. Sometimes films of oil appeared on streams and ponds. This oily film was sometimes so thick that stock refused to drink the water.

The first oil well was struck at Port Huron in 1886. This well produced only two barrels of oil a day. From this oil a small local industry made greases for greasing axles of buggies and wagons. About this time, while drilling for salt, oil and water were struck at Manistee. The oil and water were under such pressure that it shot upward with a strong enough force to wreck the derrick. Between 1889 and 1914 several very shallow wells, going about 600 feet in depth, were drilled. The most important of these were drilled at Port Huron, but even these were soon out of production.

In 1912, several test wells were drilled in a large circle around Saginaw. Unfortunately, all of these wells were drilled around the edge of what later proved to be the Saginaw oil pool. Some of these wells at first produced around eighty barrels of crude oil a day, but soon their flow had dropped to only two or three barrels a day. Very little gas was found in these wells. In 1925, the Saginaw pool was discovered lying within the circle of wells that had been drilled. The first well was only a twenty-five-barrel producer, but soon over one hundred wells had been drilled in the area. Michigan's real oil development had begun. The boom of the Saginaw pool, however, was short-lived for it lasted only until 1928. Too many wells were sunk within a small area. When the pressure on the pool was released, the crude oil ceased to flow.

In 1927, oil was discovered in the Muskegon field near Muskegon. More than five hundred wells were drilled by 1929. Again too many wells were drilled. Much natural gas was lost and thus the pressure was reduced. For a time this area ranked second in oil production in Michigan. Some of these wells are still producing. In 1928, the state passed a law to prevent waste and regulate the number of wells that could be drilled in a given area.

About this time studies were made of the drillings that had been made by the Dow Chemical Company in its search for salt deposits. These drilling cores showed the presence of crude oil in the area.

On March 31, 1928, a well giving thirty barrels a day was struck in Greendale Township in Midland County. That same year oil was struck ten miles east of Mr. Pleasant in Isabella County. The wells in this area in general produced from one hundred to three hundred barrels a day. They have been better spaced than were the earlier drillings. Not much natural gas has been found in this area.

The following year, 1929, oil was struck at the Leaton Pool in Isabella County. The wells in this area range all the way from dry holes to some which produced over five hundred barrels a day. In the same year gas was struck in the Bloomfield Township Pool and in the Vernon Township Pool in Isabella County. In the Vernon Township Pool, oil as well as gas was found. In 1931, oil was struck in the Porter Township field in Midland County. In 1933, some gushers were struck that produced fourteen thousand barrels a day.

In 1933, the Jasper field in Midland County was located. Shallow wells have also been located near Grand Rapids. In 1940, the Reed City field was located. In 1946-1947 new fields were discovered north of Muskegon. Crude oil is produced in forty-one counties.

In 1954, crude oil was struck near Northville and Clinton. In 1958, Michigan's largest strike was hit in the Albion-Pulaski-Scipio field. Oil here is found in the Trenton-Black River formation. In 1959, there were 108 wells in this field and the production for that year was 2,046,600 barrels of crude oil. The oil producing pockets of this area are very irregular because of varying size fractures and openings in the rock pockets. Much natural gas is also found in this field. Locating oil pockets in Michigan is difficult because of the overlaying glacial till and the fractured nature of some of the underlying rock strata.

The following figures show how Michigan's oil production has increased and decreased.

1925	4,000 barrels	1939	23,462,000 barrels
1927	439,000 barrels	1957	10,740,000 barrels
1937	16,628,000 barrels	1963	15,973,000 barrels

Michigan has also produced some natural gas as well as crude oil but the gas consumption is far higher than can be supplied by Michigan fields alone. In 1948, a twenty-four-inch pipeline was completed that connected Detroit with Texas. Since that time much natural gas has come to Michigan from Texas, Kansas, and Oklahoma. During the winter months the gas is usually used as fast as it arrives. Then, too, at this time of the year more gas is often needed than the pipelines can supply. To provide this extra gas, during the summer months much gas is piped to old Michigan gas fields and stored as a reserve for winter use. One of the largest of these natural storage basins lies under the Big Rapids area.

Michigan's second largest industry today is her tourist industry. Because of the fact that Michigan touches four of the five Great Lakes, has many lovely inland lakes, has many pretty streams, and has gently rolling hills, it is visited by hundreds of people who come here each year to spend their vacation. Thousands of cottages, motels, hotels, and clubs are scattered all over the northern country. Each summer the people living in these areas are busy caring for the people who come here to spend their vacations. Winter sports are also becoming more and more popular. Several recreation areas cater to those who like to ski, toboggan, and ice skate. Hundreds of others like to hunt and come to Michigan's hunting areas each fall. As people travel along our highways or stay at motels or cottages, they spend much money. This money helps today to keep many of the smaller northern communities alive.

CHAPTER SEVENTEEN

Agricultural Development
Since 1860

BETWEEN 1860 and 1885, settlers began farming the better land in the upper part of the Lower Peninsula and in the Upper Peninsula. By 1900, almost all the farm land in the state had been taken. Some of this land the settlers bought from lumber companies that had cut the timber from it. Some they bought from railroad companies that had been given land grants to help them build their railroads, some they bought on school sections that had been set aside to build up the Primary Fund, and some was settled under the Homestead Act of 1862. This act made it possible for the head of the family to claim, free of cost, one hundred sixty acres of government land if he would settle on it and live there for five years. Some three million acres of land were thus claimed in Michigan under the Homestead Act.

Many of the people who settled northern Michigan were sons and daughters of the earlier settlers that had settled southern Michigan. Some of the men were veterans of the Civil War who had gone north to find work in the lumber camps during Michigan's prosperous lumbering period. Others were immigrants who came to Michigan to find work in the woods and mines.

In the years that followed the Civil War, many of the little log cabins of the early pioneers were replaced with houses made from the pine lumber that was coming from the many Michigan sawmills. Along the country roads these frame farmhouses, usually two stories high and painted white, gave evidence of the better life that was coming to the children of the early pioneers. These were plastered homes with large rooms and high ceilings. They were shingled with the new cedar shingles that were cut at one of the shingle mills. Later in the period from 1880 to 1900, some farm homes, especially in Wayne County, were faced on the outside with red brick that was then being made in the local brick yards.

New cast iron stoves were used for both cooking and heating the houses. For fuel for these stoves the farmers used wood from their own wood lots. At first all of this wood still had to be cut with an ax; but later, around 1875, crosscut saws were used for felling trees and cutting up the tree trunk into stove-length blocks of wood. For the kitchen range the blocks had to be split into still smaller pieces.

Lumber was not only used for houses but for building barns, granaries, sheep sheds, chicken coops, buildings for pigs, barnyard fences, and tool sheds. Some farmers even built board fences along the road in front of their houses and barns. These were usually painted white. Many large barns, usually painted red, were built to house the horses and cattle and to store their feed during the winter months. High up on each barn usually sat several lightning rods and sometimes an ornate weather vane. These weather vanes were far more important to farmers at this period than they are to us today, for each farmer had to be his own weather prophet and plan his day's work according to what he thought the weather might be, for there were no daily weather reports to tell him what weather could be expected.

Farmers began to use kerosene lamps for lighting their homes and

This is a typical kitchen in the 1890 period. Note the wood range for cooking, the small cistern pump for water, the wooden dishes and coffee grinder on the table, and the kerosene lamps sitting on the shelf. How does this kitchen compare with yours today? Courtesy Henry Ford Museum

kerosene lanterns for use in their barns. Kerosene lamps and lanterns not only gave a better light than candles but lessened the danger of fire. During this period carpeting began to be used on the floors in many farm homes.

From 1860 to 1900, farming was still hard toil. Most of the time of the men was still spent in growing food for their farm animals and for their families. During the summer season they worked in their fields from sun-up to sunset. About the only power on these farms was still muscle power, that of the farmers and their animals.

Almost all of the farmers raised the same general crops to care for their animals and family. What they had extra they sold if they could. This gave them a little money to buy the new machinery then coming on the market, and a few supplies from the village store that they could not raise on their farms such as: sugar and molasses, coffee, tea, salted cod fish and mackerel from the New England fisheries, bologna, and in season such luxury food as oranges and bananas. By selling their extra crops the farmers also got money to pay their taxes.

Each fall when the animals were in prime condition, after the better feed of the summer, some were slaughtered for home use and for marketing. Some farmers not only slaughtered their own stock but also went from farm to farm for a month or two each fall to do the slaughtering for other farmers. Slaughtering time was a busy time on the farms. Water had to be heated in big tubs to scald the slaughtered hogs. The meat had to be salted, brined, or smoked. Sausages were made and the lard "tried out" for use in cooking.

All of the members of the family, even the children, spent long hours working each day. Each day the milk had to be put into tin pans, or crocks, and left so that the cream would rise to the top. The cream was then skimmed off and saved to be churned into butter. The skimmed milk, along with the other garbage from the kitchen, was then fed to the hogs as "swill." Women dried fruits and berries for use during the winter. When home canning in glass one-quart and two-quart jars began to replace the older methods of drying foods, the farm women and their daughters spent long hours by the hot kitchen stove during the late summer and fall to preserve food for their family. Potatoes, carrots, turnips and other root crops, as well as apples, were stored in a hole in the ground, or in the side of a hill, called a "root cellar."

After 1850, horses began replacing oxen on the farms as draft animals. Horses, larger than the earlier French ponies, especially bred for farm work, became more and more common on the farms. Other horses of smaller size, called "drivers" were used for light farm work and for pulling the family buggy. They were faster than the "draft horses" that were used for plowing, cultivating, and general heavy farm work. Because of the number of horses needed on a farm, much of each farmer's land had to be planted to hay and oats to raise feed for the horses.

Better breeds of cattle were also developed. Herds of Herefords, Aberdeen Angus, Holsteins, Jerseys, Guernseys, and Brown Swiss cattle were found on Michigan farms. Many families living in villages also had one or more cows to supply them with their daily dairy needs. As all the milking was done by hand the usual farmer had about four or five cows.

During the period between the Civil War and 1900 many changes took place on Michigan's farms. The agricultural revolution, that had begun before the Cival War, continued to develop new machines that brought about more productive ways of farming and also decreased the need for as many men on the farms.

Courtesy Henry Ford Museum, Dearborn, Michigan
An early reaper

As steel became more abundant, after the development of the Bessemer process, it began to be used in many forms on Michigan farms as in plows, harrows, and cultivators. Galvanized barbed-wire was first used during the 1880's. This wire with its barbs was especially good for fencing in horses and cattle. The earlier stump and split rail fences were gradually replaced by new barbed wire fences made of posts onto which the barbed-wire was fastened. For fence posts the farmers usually used cedar posts that were cut in the cedar swamps in northern Michigan. Woven-wire fencing was also becoming common by 1900. This type of fencing could be used to confine chickens, hogs, and sheep.

Steel watering troughs replaced the earlier ones, that had been made of wood, for holding water for horses and cattle. Steel pipes and steel pumps replaced the old open wells with their water buckets. Windmills, made of steel, were also erected on many farms. These steel windmills, with their wide metal fan blades, mounted so they would turn to face the wind, were one of the first sources of mechanical power that came to the farmer's aid. As the wind blew a windmill slowly raised and lowered a pump that pumped water into the stock watering trough. Sometimes water was also piped into the house so that it would not have to be carried in any more.

Threshing machines, made mostly of wood with a few steel parts,

Courtesy Henry Ford Museum, Dearborn, Michigan

An early threshing engine of about 1880. Notice the teamster's seat on which he could sit as the horses pulled the engine from one farm to another to run the threshing machine.

powered by four or five teams of horses walking around and around in a circle to turn a sweep, were used in the years following the Civil War. This made the threshing and winnowing of grain much easier and faster and saved many man hours of work.

Steam engines had been used for nearly a hundred years to run boats, railroad engines, factories, and sawmills. But steam engines were heavy and not easily adapted to general farm work. Their weight caused them to easily become stuck in soft sand or mud and this made them useless for plowing or cultivating. In the years just before 1900, however, they began to be used for running threshing machines in place of the earlier sweeps that had been powered by teams of horses. These engines were taken from farm to farm, along with a threshing machine, to thresh a farmer's grain. If the roads were hard and there were no steep hills to climb, these huge threshing engines moved slowly under their own steam power, but often the aid of one, two, or three teams of horses was needed to get the engine to the next farm. Better plows, spring-tooth lever harrows, discs, corn planters, seed drills, better harvesting machines such as the twine binder, mowing machines, winnowing machines, corn shellers, horse drawn hay rakes,

A threshing machine of about the period of 1900 when they were run by threshing engines. This one was being used about 1960. It is being driven by power from a tractor. Note the straw stack at the left of the picture and the bag to catch the threshed grain at the left end of the machine.

wooden and rope slings and hay forks to carry the hay up into the hay mow, manure spreaders, hay balers, and better cultivators all began to be used on Michigan's farms to reduce labor and increase production.

As the settlers spread their farms throughout the state they learned that Michigan's soils and climate often changed radically from place to place. Because of this they found that a wide variety of crops could be profitably grown in Michigan.

All of the soil of Michigan is glacial drift that was carried south from Canada by the advancing glaciers. Since that period, the crushed material has been altered by the weathering agents that have been at work upon it. Rivers carried the finer pieces of feldspar to old lake bottoms and outwash plains, where deposits of clay were formed. Some areas were very sandy. Rains soaked into them and the down-seeping water carried the former minerals, in solution, away from the surface of the land. These areas are of little value for farming. In some areas, decaying vegetation has been deposited and muck lands have been formed. Some of these muck lands are of good fertility and grow special crops, while others, looking equally good, are valueless for farming.

Good land to farmers means land having the necessary qualities for healthy plant growth. Michigan's land varies all the way from loose, shifting sand, like the sand dunes along the Great Lakes, or the barren sandy plains of the High Plains Area, to heavy clays that bake hard under the warm summer sun. Some of the sandy areas drain too easily while other clay areas scarcely drain at all. The amount of humus, organic matter that is necessary for normal plant growth, also varies from place to place. Some areas are rich in humus while other areas have very little. What is more, there is no uniformity in the soil in the amount of elements such as minerals, lime, or nitrogen. Because Michigan was a forest land, most of the soils were originally podsol; that is, they were high in acid content.

Often a farm of just a few acres has several kinds of soil, and extensive changes in soil take place within just a few miles. One can notice this as one drives along our highways. At one point one may be passing good farm land with beautiful farm homes and large barns, while a few miles farther along the road the farms are gone and only brush land lines the highway. A few miles farther on and one may again be passing through good farm lands.

Good crops require not only good soils but also a favorable climate. By climate is meant the minimum and maximum temperature, the number of frost-free days, the degree of cloudiness, the amount and length of sunshine, the amount of rainfall and snowfall, and the effect of the prevailing winds. Over an area of land as large as Michigan, with large bodies of water touching so much of its border, one finds many variations in climate. Michigan is a large state bordering on four of the largest lakes in the world. These lakes in many ways affect Michigan's agriculture. So large is Michigan that it reaches across six degrees of latitude. Although most of the state is low gently rolling land, some of it, in the High Plains Area of the Lower Peninsula and in the western part of the Upper Peninsula, reaches a height high enough to affect crops by causing a shorter growing season.

In order for plants to grow they must have the right amount of moisture. Fortunately for Michigan, the heaviest rainfall, in the Lower Peninsula where the farms are the most numerous, comes in May, June, and July when plants are growing. Rains are less frequent in the fall when crops are ready for harvesting. Droughts are not uncommon but they are usually local and do not often affect wide areas. The same area is seldom affected by drought two years in succession. Most of Michigan has an average rainfall of about thirty-one inches a year. This rainfall varies from about twenty-eight inches in the drier parts of the state, such as the Thumb area and the eastern half of Mackinac County, in the Upper Peninsula, to about thirty-six inches

Courtesy Michigan Milk Producers' Association

A good herd of Holstein Cattle

in the areas of heaviest rainfall. Michigan's heaviest rainfall occurs in the area where Michigan touches Indiana.

Crops usually mature in a definite number of days. Therefore, the number of days from the last killing frost in the spring until the first killing frost in the fall often determines what crops can be grown. In Michigan the number of days free from killing frosts varies all the way from one hundred eighty days in the eastern half of Berrien County, in the southwest corner of Michigan, to only ninety days in the area just north of Iron River in the Upper Peninsula and in Crawford County in the Lower Peninsula. In some places in Michigan spring frosts occur as late as June 10. Some areas have warm days and cool nights during the growing season. These cool nights retard growth in some plants.

The length of the growing season in the various parts of Michigan is affected by the altitude, the latitude, and the effect of the Great Lakes upon the land.

Although most farmers were still general farmers, some had, because of the soil and climate in their area, already begun to specialize in special crops by the turn of the century. Farmers in the Thumb area and in Kent County found that beans grew well. Today, these areas are large bean producers. In fact, the area around Saginaw is the largest bean producing area in the United States. Farmers near Kalamazoo and Holland found that celery grew well in the muck lands of that area and for many years this was a leading producer of celery. Onions grew well in other muck lands, especially around St. John's. Around 1900, much chicory was grown near Bay City.

Settlers in the southwestern part of the state found their area well suited for growing fruits and vegetables. Soon they were producing strawberries, grapes, pears, apples, and cherries. These fresh fruits were shipped by boat to Chicago. They also found that mint grew well on the muck lands, and some farmers began growing peppermint and spearmint and extracting peppermint and spearmint oil.

The soils near Kalkaska and Gaylord were found to be good for growing potatoes, and at the turn of the century many potatoes were being grown in the area.

As the railroads spread across the state they provided the farmers with a better means of transporting their produce to market. But long shipment often consumed a major portion of the farmer's profit. What is more, perishable products until recently could not be carried for long distances.

Although many changes came in farming between the Civil War and 1900 even greater changes have come since 1900. These changes have largely been the result of new sources of power that have been made available to the farmers.

The first power to come to the farmer's aid after the steam threshing engine was electric power. Electricity was coming to the cities but as yet it had not come to rural areas. Soon after 1900 small electric power units, driven by gasoline engines, were purchased by many people living in small villages and on farms. These small electrical units made it possible to have electric lights in the house, barn, and animal sheds, to pump water, run milking machines and cream separators, and such household appliances as there were at that time. However, electricity was available only during the time the gasoline engine was running. As time passed, especially during the period from 1930 to 1940, large power companies began extending electric power lines to reach more and more villages and rural areas. As these lines spread across the state the little home power units were abandoned.

The coming of electricity helped the farmer and his wife in many ways, but it still did not aid him in his work in the fields where he and his horses toiled all day. What the farmers needed in their fields was a mobile power that was light in weight, strong, and easily maneuverable. As men began making automobiles, some of them began experimenting with a gasoline driven vehicle that could be used on a farmer's field for power to replace the horses. This new device they called a "tractor." By 1920, these tractors were coming into practical use. Soon they were being made on assembly lines in several factories. With a tractor a farmer could plow faster and also pull more than one plow at a time. It also pulled his wagon faster and this saved time in going to and from a field. It could pull disks, drags, cultivators, and all kinds of farm machinery in larger sizes and at a faster rate than horses could pull them. Also a farmer, by fastening a belt to it, could saw his wood with a circular saw, run a threshing machine, or any other device that was at that time belt driven.

The development of the tractor changed farming and farm production in many ways. Less men were needed to run a farm, for there was less hand work to do. Horses, which had been the main source of power were no longer needed. The number of horses in Michigan reached its peak in 1917 when there were about 680,000. By 1930, after the development of the tractor, truck, and automobile, the number of horses had dropped to 381,357. Today, there are only about 30,000 horses and mules in the state and many of these are racing and riding horses. Before the general use of the tractor about one third of a farmer's acreage was planted to hay and oats to be used for horse feed and to sell to livery stables and city folks who kept driving horses. Now this acreage was freed for the production of other crops to help feed the increasing number of cattle and for crops for human consumption. Thus, as our population has grown, hundreds of acres have been freed to produce food for human consumption either

Courtesy Tractor and Implement Division, Ford Motor Company, Dearborn, Michigan

A Ford 6000 tractor, the largest and most powerful tractor ever built by the Ford Motor Company. It weighs 10,000 pounds when fully loaded and delivers 60 drawbar horsepower. Photo 1961.

directly as wheat and vegetables or indirectly by producing more milk and meat.

Several companies now manufacture machinery to be used by farmers. Some of these machines are used to prepare the ground and in planting crops such as gang plows, disks, and drills or planters. Large cultivators taking four or more rows at a time greatly speeds the work of keeping the fields free from weeds. In harvesting, combines cut, thresh, and winnow the grain as the combine is pulled across the field. Other modern machines used in harvesting are corn pickers, choppers, balers, rakes, elevators that carry the baled hay up into the barn, and also silo fillers. One modern machine can pick, husk, and shell 6,000 bushels of corn in one day. Other machines are used for raising potatoes and sugar beets from the ground. In the barn, dairy men and cattle men now have automatic feeders, and barn cleaners that carry

A corn sheller, such as was used by farmers about 1890 to take the kernels of corn from the cob. This device saved much hand labor and time. Photo 1956.

the manure and used bedding along a trough behind the cattle and dump it into manure spreaders. Many dairy men now milk their cows mechanically in milking parlors. The milk flows directly from the cow through pipes to a bulk milk storage tank where it is kept cool until it is picked up by a bulk tank truck and taken to a pasteurizing plant. Fruit growers have mechanical sprayers. Some fruit pickers, that shake the tree, are being developed. Electrically heated pens help in keeping animals alive and healthy. Mechanical incubators hatch thousands of chickens and turkeys each year. Mechanical clippers are used to shear sheep, power lawn mowers are used to cut the farmer's lawn, and power chain saws have replaced the old cross-cut saws.

A modern farmer has much money invested in land and machinery.

Because of this most farmers are now growing special crops and are no longer general farmers as their fathers and grandfathers were.

Hay, corn for grain, and wheat are Michigan's three leading crops. For many years hay was Michigan's leading crop in terms of value, but since hay is not used very much as a food for dairy cattle and as the number of horses has decreased, less hay is now grown. The spring rains and cool days are favorable for the growing of hay crops. The hot days of early summer permit the farmers to cure it before it is placed in barns for winter use as stock food. Most hay is used near where it is grown but some is baled and shipped to other areas. Hay is grown all over the state, but the southern counties are the largest producers. Sanilac County is the leading hay producing county. Other large hay producing counties are Washtenaw, Huron, Lapeer, Hillsdale, Kent, and Ingham. Alfalfa is grown mostly in the Lower Peninsula and in Dickinson, Menominee, and Delta counties in the Upper Peninsula. In 1963, Michigan ranked sixteenth among the states in the production of hay. In that year Michigan farmers harvested 1,750,000 acres and produced 3,202,000 tons of hay. Today United States farmers grow about 125 different species of forage grasses and legumes. Some

This photo taken in 1910 shows how farmers at that time harvested their hay. Note the sling hanging in the front of the wagon for carrying the hay up into the barn, and also the hay loader drawn along behind the wagon.

of these are native grasses but many have come from foreign lands. Clovers, timothy, orchard grass, and alfalfas were brought by the early settlers to the United States. Other strains have been added by men who visit foreign lands for the United

Bailing straw. Photo July 1961.

States Department of Agriculture. Better means of cutting and curing may make hay a better food for cattle.

Wheat was first brought to the United States by the early colonists. It is one of our oldest known grains. Many kinds, because they were not adapted to the new soils and climates did not do very well. However, through selection new varieties were developed that met local conditions. Wheat because of its keeping qualities was one of Michigan's early cash crops. By 1880, Michigan ranked in fourth place as a wheat producer. During the years between 1880 and 1890 nearly two million acres were planted in wheat each year. During each of those years Michigan harvested about 30,000,000 bushels of wheat. As more and more wheat was produced in the western states,

Courtesy Massey-Ferguson, Inc.

MF 35 S P Combine. (1961)

Michigan's crop for some years declined. During the past few years more wheat is again being grown in Michigan. Most of Michigan's wheat is now grown in the south central and southern part of the state and is what is known as winter wheat. It is sown in the fall, in areas where it is not apt to be killed by the cold winter, and harvested late the following spring. Because of the colder winters, spring wheat is grown in the upper part of the Lower Peninsula. Spring wheat is sown in the spring and harvested in the fall. Huron, Lenawee, Saginaw, Tuscola, and Sanilac Counties are Michigan's leading producers.

About eighty-five per cent of the wheat now grown in Michigan is soft white and the remaining fifteen per cent is soft red. Both of these wheats are used in making pastry, biscuits, crackers, cakes, and ready-to-eat cereals. For pastries a wheat that has less than ten per cent protein in the kernel is preferred. For bread and macaroni a higher content of protein is desired. The hard red western wheat is thus used for baking bread while the Durum wheat, grown in eastern North Dakota is used for making spaghetti and macaroni. In 1963, Michigan ranked in tenth place among the states as a winter wheat producer. In that year 1,060,000 acres were planted and 40,280,000 bushels were produced.

Corn is one of Michigan's three most important crops. The Indians living here raised corn for their own use and also to sell to the French voyageurs. From the early days of the first settlers in Michigan corn has been an important crop. It was used as stock food and also ground into corn meal to make corn bread, or johnnycake, as they called it. It was also used to make mush which was an important food item on the early settlers' tables.

Courtesy Massey-Ferguson, Inc.

The MF 422 four-row combine corn picker. As it passes along the corn rows it picks the ears from the stalks and takes the outer husk from the ears of the corn.

Corn now is grown all over Michigan but does best, except in some local areas, in the area south of Clare County. To grow corn there must be at least 170 frost-free days. Corn does best where the nights are warm and humid. Michigan's southern counties are on the northern edge of what is known as the "Corn Belt." Lenawee, Branch, Hillsdale, St. Joseph, and Monroe counties are Michigan's leading corn producing counties. Some of the crop is harvested as a grain and used mainly as a food for hogs and poultry. Some is ground into corn meal. In the dairy areas most of it is cut before it is completely ripened and ear as well as stalk is cut up into silage and used as cattle feed. If the ears are harvested the stalks are cut into silage or chopped up and plowed under for fertilizer the following spring. Besides field corn Michigan also produces sweet corn and popcorn.

In 1963, Michigan ranked tenth among the states in corn grown for grain and eighth in the growing of popcorn. One of the leading advances in growing corn in the United States during the past twenty years has been the use of the new hybrid varieties that have increased corn production by about twenty per cent more corn on twenty-five per cent fewer acres than was grown in 1930. About ninety-five per cent of the corn now grown is hybrid corn.

Oats grow best on the heavier soils that hold moisture. Most of the Michigan crop is grown south of Bay City and Muskegon. The leading counties in oat production are Lenawee, Sanilac, Huron, and Tuscola. Oats are a good feed for livestock and are very good to use in crop rotation. With the decline in the number of horses there has

Harvesting oats. Photo July, 1961.

also been a decline in the amount of oats produced. In 1963, Michigan ranked in eighth place as an oat producer.

In 1963, Michigan ranked in ninth place in the production of rye when 1,012,000 bushels were grown. In barley production Michigan took twenty-second place with 1,890,000 bushels. In buckwheat Michigan ranked in third place with 170,000 bushels.

Another crop that was grown by the Indians was beans. It is now one of Michigan's leading crops. The fertile soil and temperate climate found in some areas of Michigan make it possible for Michigan to be a leading bean producer. Winter freezing kills the bean weevil. Most of the beans grown are navy beans but other kinds are grown as well. Huron and Tuscola counties are the largest producers of beans. Red kidney beans are grown in large amounts in Newaygo and Oceana counties. Bean acreage varies from year to year, and so does the yield per acre. Beans are very subject to weather changes. Wet springs cause the beans to rot. Rains during the ripening season cause the beans to discolor and thus they lose their market value. Beans are grown throughout the state but mostly in the Thumb and Saginaw area. Saginaw has the largest bean elevator in the world. In 1963, Michigan ranked in first place as a dry bean producer with 8,480,000 hundredweight. Huron, Saginaw, Tuscola, Gratiot, and Bay counties are the largest producers. Michigan also produces many soybeans, lima beans, and both green and yellow snap beans.

Some sugar cane was grown in Michigan up to and for a few years after the Civil War. Like most of the other crops it grew best in the lower part of the Lower Peninsula. From the crushed cane, the early settlers secured a syrup that took the place of sugar and added to the

Courtesy Farmers and Manufacturers Beet Sugar Association

Michigan's sugar beet crop is harvested and delivered to the state's five sugar factories by train and trucks. During the 1964 harvest season Michigan farmers harvested and delivered over one million tons of sugar beets. The bumper crop will produce nearly 300,000,000 pounds of pure sugar.

limited supply of maple syrup. Later developments in transportation and the cultivating of sugar beets have placed cheap sugar on the market, and sugar cane is no longer grown.

In 1881, the state offered a bounty of two cents a pound for all sugar made from beets, or cane, grown within the state. In 1890, the Michigan State Agricultural College bought 1,760 pounds of beet seeds in Europe, where sugar beet growing had already developed on a large scale, and distributed the seeds to farmers who would plant the new crop. More seeds were later distributed. Now Michigan is one of the leading states of the union in the production of sugar beets. In 1963, Michigan ranked in seventh place as a sugar beet producer with a production of 1,175,000 tons.

The soft, sandy soil of Michigan, in some areas, is well adapted to the growing of sugar beets. Because the soil is soft, the growing beets can easily push it aside as they grow larger. In clay soils the earth sometimes bakes quite hard, and the growing beets cannot easily expand in size. Few beets are grown in the Upper Peninsula except in the area near Menominee.

Courtesy Farmers and Manufacturers Beet Sugar Association

This Michigan Sugar Company's Carrollton factory is one of five operating mills in the state. Three other plants located at Caro, Croswell and Sebewaing are owned and operated by the company. The fifth plant, located at Bay City, is owned and operated by the Monitor Sugar Company.

To produce sugar beets requires not only good soil but also much labor. The small plants have to be thinned and weeded with care. To do this work many people used to be brought to Michigan to work in the beet fields. Over the past years many of these people have come from central Europe and Mexico. Many of them were migrant laborers. Some have remained and added new nationalities to our rural population. Many of these people who came to Michigan as laborers, or their children, now own farms within the state. Today much of the hard labor that was done by migrant workers is done by modern machinery.

Most of Michigan's sugar beets are grown in the Saginaw River Valley and the Thumb district. Tuscola, Huron, Saginaw, Bay, and Sanilac counties are the leading producers.

Michigan is not only a producer of sugar beets but also a producer of sugar as well. Michigan's first sugar beet refinery was built at Bay City in 1898. Today, sugar beet refineries are located at several places in the southern and eastern part of the Lower Peninsula. Each of these refineries uses the beets that are raised near it. Beets are usually brought to the refineries by trucks but sometimes they are shipped in by train in large hopper cars. Beets grown in Lenawee and Monroe counties are processed in plants in Ohio. The pulp that remains after the sugar has been taken from the beets is used for stock feed.

Because of the foreign situation sugar beet yields in Michigan have increased about sixty per cent in the past ten years. Better highways and better prices have expanded the areas of production in the state.

The potato plant is a native Indian plant of South America. Michigan's sandy loams, especially in the upper part of the Lower Peninsula and in the Upper Peninsula, are well adapted to potato growing. At one time Michigan produced many more potatoes than are now grown. In 1935, Michigan ranked third among the states as a potato producer. By 1963, Michigan had dropped to eleventh place with a production of 6,738,000 hundredweight. In that year Montcalm, Bay, Presque Isle, Allegan, and Monroe counties were the leading producers.

Potatoes are subject to viruses that often cause them to give dimishing yields. These viruses are transmitted from year to year by potatoes used for seed. Potatoes are also subject to many diseases such as fungus, aphids, leafhoppers, potato beetles, and other insects. Because of this, potato production has shifted to other states where there is less danger from disease. Consumer demands have also affected the varieties of potatoes produced. Whereas a few years ago potatoes were produced for consumption at mealtime, today about one third of the total United States crop is processed into many forms such as chips, dried, frozen or canned before it goes on the market.

Each year thousands of bushels of potatoes are sent from Michigan farms to the cities of the nation. Potatoes do best where the growing season is cool and moist and a soft loamy soil allows the growing potatoes to push the soil aside as they grow. The short growing season of the Upper Peninsula does not keep farmers, in the western part, from being potato producers. In fact, potatoes are an important cash crop there as well as elsewhere in the state.

New disease resistant types of potatoes are being developed and new processes in washing, grading, and packaging potatoes are helping the potato growers meet competition from other areas.

Another of Michigan's special crops is mint. Peppermint was first grown on White Pigeon Prairie in St. Joseph County in 1835. Only small pockets of muck soil are suitable for growing mint. For many years it was one of the state's most valuable muck crops. It was grown in Shiawassee, Clinton, Van Buren and St. Joseph counties. Spearmint and peppermint are grown and harvested in much the same way as hay. The freshly cut plants are taken to a small local distillery where the plants are placed in vats and put through a steaming process which releases the oil. The pulp, when dried, is used as a stock food. The oil is used to flavor medicine, chewing gum, candy, and cake icings. In 1963, Michigan ranked fifth among the states in the production of peppermint and third in spearmint oils. Both of these mint crops have greatly declined in production since 1956 because of a soil-borne disease called verticillium wilt.

Small fruits and vegetables have, from the early days of settlement, always been a part of the crop produced on most farms. Because transportation was poor and these crops spoiled easily unless carefully cared for, each farmer grew these crops for his own family use. During the summer and early fall, fruits and vegetables were taken from the orchard and garden and eaten while still fresh. These were the only fresh fruits and vegetables most people ever got.

But as the years passed and the cities grew, there became more and more of a demand for fresh fruits and vegetables to supply the families that were beginning to live in the cities. Some farmers found that they could, by using the better means of transportation that were developing, turn their fruits and vegetables into cash crops.

Areas where the soil and climate had special qualities soon began to grow selected crops for market. Most of the vegetables for the market are grown south of Bay City and Muskegon on the soils which are a rich sandy loam. Among the special crops are tomatoes, snap beans, cabbage, celery, asparagus, cucumbers, and berries.

Michigan produces about one fourth of all cucumbers used in

making pickles. Muskegon is the center for cucumber production. Although Michigan is not as large a celery producer as she once was much celery is still grown. Ninety per cent of the celery now grown is produced within a seventy-five mile radius from Zeeland. Tomatoes are grown in the largest amounts in Berrien, Bay, Macomb, Wayne, Lenawee, and Monroe counties. Green beans are grown all over the Lower Peninsula. Mecosta, St. Clair, Oceana, and Montcalm counties are the largest producers. Snap beans grown here are canned in local canneries. Many melons are grown near Bay City. Early cabbage is grown by market gardeners in Allegan, St. Clair, Macomb, Wayne, and Monroe counties. Late cabbage is grown in the muck areas throughout the state and sold to sauerkraut factories. About five and a half million pounds of mushrooms are grown in Macomb county each year.

Michigan is one of the leading states in the growing of small fruits such as strawberries, dewberries, blackberires, raspberries, and grapes. Berrien County, with about 180 frost-free days is the leading producer. Good transportation makes it possible to quickly send the fresh fruit to the large Chicago market.

The strip of land along the eastern shore of Lake Michigan is known as the fruit belt. This is one of the major fruit producing areas in the United States. Here the soil is a sandy loam and not very good for most crops. Beneath the loam lies a clay. Fruit trees push their roots through the loam and into the clay. Not only is the soil adapted to fruit growing but so is the climate as well. This climatic condition is produced by Lake Michigan. Lake Michigan is some eighty to one hundred miles wide and extends north and south along the entire western side of the Lower Peninsula. The prevailing westerly winds that blow across the lake onto the Lower Peninsula are affected by the temperature of the water in Lake Michigan.

During the summer, when the sun shines on the Great Lakes, the water absorbs heat and tends to warm. But even in the summer, winds coming from the drier lands farther to the west, are cooled as they pass over Lake Michigan. Moreover, they pick up moisture as they pass over the lake and that increases the humidity in the air blowing onto the land during the growing season. These winds bring a more even, cooler summer climate to the area lying along the western side of the Lower Peninsula. The days are not as warm or the nights as cool as they are farther inland. The western part of the Lower Peninsula, during the summer, has more sunshine than the rest of the state

Courtesy of Traverse City Chamber of Commerce
Cherry orchard in blossom

because the land is warmer than the water and the westerly winds bringing moisture do not condense and form clouds. This extra sunshine is good for the ripening fruit.

When fall comes, the inland area being less affected by Lake Michigan, tends to cool more rapidly. The autumns along Lake Michigan's shore are long and mild. During October and November, Lake Michigan is fifteen or twenty degrees warmer than the cooling land. During this season winds blowing in from Lake Michigan bring warmth from the lake to the land until about the middle of January. This gives the area along the eastern shore line of Lake Michigan some twenty to fifty more frost-free days than are found in the more inland areas. During this period the new summer's growth on the fruit trees has time to harden and this helps to protect the new growth from the winter's cold. During the fall months this area has less sunshine than any other part of the state for when the warm air, coming in from Lake Michigan, strikes the cooling land the moisture which it carries condenses and forms clouds. During the fall these clouds often condense and bring rain to the area bordering the lake. Later in the early winter this humidity falls on the land as snow and thus the snowfall is often heavier here than it is farther inland toward the east.

By midwinter the lake has cooled and is partly covered with ice. There is less evaporation and the air masses moving over the lake are not heated as much and therefore pick up less moisture as they pass over the water. As a result the snowfall along the eastern shore of Lake Michigan in the late winter and early spring is usually less.

During the winter, Lake Michigan slowly gives up the warmth it has stored during the summer. The water of the lake often freezes solid for some ten miles or more out from the shore line where the water is less deep. Because land warms faster than water, when spring comes, the increasing sunshine quickly warms the land farther inland from the lakes; this warming air during the daytime promotes plant growth but at night killing frosts often occur. Such night frosts often do much harm to most varieties of plants and trees. This is especially true of fruit trees, and that is why Michigan's fruit growing area is largely limited to the eastern shore of Lake Michigan from Indiana to Petoskey. The winds, blowing in from the cooler lake, keep the land along the Lake Michigan shore from warming too rapidly. This retards the opening of the buds on the fruit trees until danger of killing frosts is usually past. Some years, however, the fruit trees, even in this area, are frosted and the fruit is destroyed as soon as it begins to form.

Lake Huron, because of its location on the eastern side of Michigan and the prevailing westerly winds, has far less effect on Michigan's agriculture. Lake Superior, also because of its location and the direction of the prevailing winds, has little effect on agriculture.

The amount of sunshine is an important factor in growing crops. Western Michigan has more sunshine during the summer than areas farther east. The Upper Peninsula, being farther north, has more hours of sunlight each day during the growing season. The days there have about forty-five minutes more sunlight in the summer than they have in southern Michigan .

It was discovered, by 1905, that cherries could become a very important crop because of the climate. Large cherry orchards were soon spreading across the rolling countryside of the fruit belt. Refrigerator trains began to run at night during the picking season to speed the fresh-picked cherries to the large cities of the Midwest. In 1912, a cannery began to process the fruit. Other canneries soon were built. In a single year, Traverse City has been known to process nearly thirty-five million pounds of cherries.

The region around Traverse City is now known as the "Nation's Cherry Bowl." Leading cherry producers are Antrim, Benzie, Leelanau, Charlevoix, and Grand Traverse counties. From this area each year comes over fifty million pounds of cherries. Grand Traverse

County has over eight hundred thousand cherry trees and it is the largest producer of the section. Most of the cherries grown are of the Montmorency variety and are red and tart. During the last few years more sweet cherries have been grown than in past years. Over four million cherry trees on the west side of the Lower Peninsula now produce more than sixty per cent of the red tart cherries grown in the United States.

From the Traverse City area comes a third of all the cherries produced in Michigan. Each season, when the cherries are ripe, hundreds of cherry pickers come north to the area to harvest the

bright red fruit. They are paid by the lug, a box containing about twenty-eight pounds. During the busy picking season the canneries run at capacity day and night to keep up with the truck loads of cherries that come rolling in from the cherry orchards. The ripe cherries are carefully washed, sorted, and then pitted by mechanical pitters. They are then placed in cans and steam cooked.

Many canneries like this one at East Jordan prepare Michigan's fruits and vegetables for market. In these canneries asparagus, beans, cherries, tomatoes as well as other crops are prepared for your table. Photo 1957.

Some cherries are brined and thus prepared for the marachino trade.

Little fruit is grown on the High Plains Area. Here the late frosts of spring often damage the buds or blossoms. Some fine fruit is grown in the Upper Peninsula in Delta County, but most of that area is not suited to fruit production. The winters are cold, and killing frosts in the late spring often destroy the crop.

California grows about ninety per cent of all grapes grown in the United States. The varieties grown there were introduced from Europe. The grapes grown in Michigan, New York and Pennsylvania are called Concord grapes and are derived from grapes which the early settlers found growing wild along the Atlantic seaboard. Van Buren, Berrien, Kalamazoo, and Cass counties are large grape producers. Here the summer heat is strong enough to allow for the development of sugar in the fruit, which gives the grapes a good quality. The long mild fall lengthens the growing season and gives the grapes time to mature. Local markets for the fresh grapes, juice factories, and wineries give the farmers of the area a ready market for their crops.

Wild strawberries are a native crop in Michigan and grow in many parts of the state. They grew in such abundance, especially on the oak openings in the southwestern part of the state, that the feet of the settlers' cattle often were stained red from tramping on the bright red berries. About 1860, tame strawberries began to be grown near St. Joseph and Benton Harbor. The berries grew well in the soil of that area. At first the ripe berries were shipped by boat to Chicago. This ready market for the ripe, fresh fruit caused a large increase in the acreage. Today Berrien and Van Buren counties are one of the leading strawberry-producing areas of the nation, but because of modern freezing and shipping methods many berries and vegetables are also shipped into the state from Florida, Georgia, and Texas.

Peaches and pears are grown in the southwestern part of the state along the shore of Lake Michigan, in the area around Ionia, and the east side of the state from Monroe County to Macomb County. In Washtenaw County and Oakland County, fruit does well especially on the south side of slopes where the summer sun can ripen the fruit. The rolling country lets the cool air of late frosts in the spring settle to the bottom of the valleys and thus keeps the blossoms from being killed.

During the period to 1900 most milk was locally used. Because milk spoils quickly and the means of transportation was slow, butter was often made at home or in local creamery. Each family usually made butter in a home churn. This was slow, hard work. As better means of transportation developed, people began to depend more and more upon creameries to supply butter and dairy products.

Many farmers, especially those in the southern part of the state, have developed large herds of dairy cattle to supply fresh milk for city use. The Detroit area alone uses well over one million quarts of fresh milk every day. To supply this large demand for fresh milk requires thousands of cattle and many people to care for them. Dairying in Michigan is therefore a large industry. Farmers living in the more remote districts of the state sometimes send their cream to a nearby creamery where it is made into butter. Some milk is also made into evaporated milk. Due to the cost of transportation, and the competition from areas nearer to the cities, fewer and fewer dairy cattle are raised north of Bay City. Farmers still living in this area are turning to producing beef feeder cattle that can later be sent

Courtesy Michigan Milk Producers' Association

Many dairy cattle are no longer kept in barns. They are protected from wind and storms in loose housing as is shown in this picture.

to the corn growing areas for final fattening before being sent to market. In the dairying area south of Bay City there are fewer cattle than there were ten years ago yet they produce a larger quantity of milk. This is because of better breeding. In 1963, there were 1,752,000 cattle and calves on Michigan farms. Of that number 627,000 were dairy cattle.

Dairy cattle are often no longer turned out to pasture during the day as they used to be, for their feet damage the growing forage. They are usually confined to a small area which contains a loafing shed. They are fed by food that is cut for them by modern machinery and stored as silage in huge silos. On the modern farms this silage is pulled from the bottom of the silo by a rotating screw and pushed into feeding troughs for the cattle to eat. Great care is used to see that the feed is suited to milk or beef production. Records of milk production for each cow are carefully kept and only the best milk producers are kept in the herd.

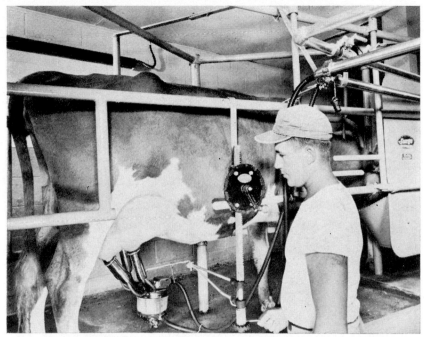

Courtesy Michigan Milk Producers' Association

This cow is being milked mechanically in a milking parlor. Usually four to six cows are thus milked at the same time as they stand on each side of the operator. The operator stands in a pit so as to make it easier for him to fasten and unfasten the milking mechanism. The milk coming from this cow can be seen in the glass container. It passes through pipes to the farmer's bulk tank where it is cooled. Because the milk is kept from the air the bacteria count is reduced.

Dairy farmers, like most other Michigan farmers, have become specialists in producing one product. The average dairy farmer in Michigan has a herd size of from thirty-five to fifty cows. This is as many as he can produce food for and milk. Herds above this size require extra help and this reduces his profit.

Some of Michigan's milk is made into cheese. Once many small cheese factories were scattered over the state. Cheese making has remained a local industry. To develop a large cheese industry means standardization, and this is difficult in cheese making because the various areas produce various stock feeds, and these in turn cause a change in the flavor of the milk and thus of the cheese also. In 1963, Michigan produced 30,220,000 pounds of American cheese, 50,670,000 pounds of creamery butter, and 33,720,000 gallons of ice cream.

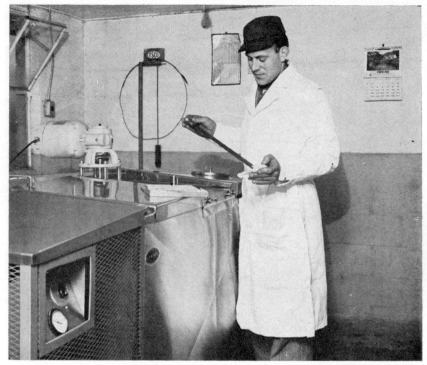

Courtesy Michigan Milk Producers' Association

As the milk comes from the cows it is cooled in a bulk tank such as this one.

Beef cattle are found all over the state, especially in the area south of Bay City and Muskegon where the cost of feed during the shorter winter is less. In the upper half of the Lower Peninsula cattle tend to be in the largest numbers along the shore lines of the Great Lakes. Only a few cattle are found on the High Plains Area and in the Upper Peninsula. Farmers still remaining in these areas are turning to the raising of beef feeder cattle.

Sheep were once more numerous in Michigan than they are today. Wool, besides being used in the home, was one of the leading cash crops one hundred years ago. At one time there were a few small woolen mills in Michigan. Sheep today are found mostly in the central part of the state below Isabella County. Washtenaw and Lenawee counties are leading sheep producers. In 1933 there were 1,035,000 sheep in Michigan, but by 1963 this number had declined to only 342,000 head. In that year there were only 315,000 sheep shorn, and Michigan produced 2,627,000 pounds of wool.

Hogs are not raised in large numbers in Michigan because Michigan is not a large corn-producing state. The largest numbers of hogs are found in Lenawee, Hillsdale, and Monroe counties where corn production is the highest. Most of Michigan's hogs are grown in the two southern rows of counties. In 1963, there were about 792,000 hogs in Michigan.

Bees are important to crop production because of the fact that they help in pollination. Honey bees, as we know them, were not native to Michigan but were brought here by the early settlers. In 1963, Michigan produced 8,755,000 pounds of honey.

Many chickens, ducks, geese, and turkeys are raised in Michigan. City markets create a demand for poultry and eggs. Poultry production is centered in two areas. One is close to Detroit in the Hillsdale, Lenawee, and Monroe county area. The other is in the Allegan, Ottawa, Kent county area. Poultry production is closely liked with the growing of suitable poultry feed. Because of the lack of grains north of Bay City, only a few chickens are raised in the upper part of the Lower Peninsula or in the Upper Peninsula.

Farmers today spend large sums of money to purchase fertilizer and various chemicals. Soils are tested and lacking minerals added to it to get the highest production possible. Chemicals are used to check weeds, kill insects, and retard plant diseases. Today, there are far more insects and plant diseases than there were one hundred years ago. Shipments of grain and other crops from foreign lands, although checked as carefully as possible, have introduced many weeds, plant diseases, and insects not native to Michigan or the United States. An example of this is the cereal leaf beetle that appeared in southwestern Michigan about 1960. Sometimes insecticides are applied by sprays; at other times they are spread over large areas by means of airplanes.

Markets and economic conditions are two factors of major importance to all farmers. A farmer must not only be able to grow crops but also must have a market for his crops after they are grown, or there is little use in producing more than his family needs. If a farmer is to buy the needed items his farm cannot produce, he must have a profitable market for at least part of his crop.

The cost of getting a farmers' produce to market has always been one of his major problems and expenses. Often this cost uses up a large share of his profit. Transportation changes such as roads, railroads, and airplanes have brought about many changes in farming areas in the past twenty years.

Up to 1900, most farmers had local markets. In the southern part of the state they were the growing villages and cities. In the upper part of the state mining and lumbering industries brought hundreds of people into northern Michigan. These people, living in lumber camps, sawmill and mining communities, required large amounts of farm produce. Since 1900, this market has greatly declined in volume.

Today farmers market their produce in several ways. Some produce, such as beans and wheat, is trucked to elevators. Milk is hauled to cities and creameries in cans and bulk trucks. Stock is taken to market, for slaughter, in trucks. Fruits and vegetables are taken to canneries and local city farmers' markets. Michigan's first farmers' market was established at Detroit, in Michigan Territory, in 1802. Other cities also have farmers' markets to which produce is brought and distributed by wholesalers and retailers. Since 1890, Detroit has had two farmers' markets. Each year the cash value of produce passing through these markets is about sixteen million dollars. It would take about 10,000 railroad cars to carry all this produce. Other terminals also distribute agricultural produce that is shipped in from other states. Some produce is also sold at the farm to people who stop to buy fruits, vegetables, eggs, etc., direct from the farm.

Good roads that make it possible for a farmer to get his produce to the market have always been one of the farmers' greatest needs. By 1890, there were only about two hundred miles of stone or macadam roads in all of Michigan and these were largely in or near the urban areas. All the remaining roads were mud and sand. Up to 1893, roads were mostly a township responsibility and very little work was done on them. In 1893, the state legislature passed the County Road Act. This made it possible for a county to create a road system and to purchase some of the better road equipment then being made.

By 1900, there were many bicycles and a few automobiles. Those that owned bicycles and automobiles wanted to ride in the country and this meant that better roads had to be built. But better roads would cost money and that meant that the people of the cities would have to help pay for their cost. Bicycle clubs and automobile clubs began to work along with the farmers to get better roads for Michigan.

In 1905, the Michigan State Highway Department was started. Those who owned automobiles were required to register them. A state-wide system of highways began to be planned. By 1913, some sixty thousand autos were registered. In order to help pay the cost of building better roads, cars were to be taxed on their horsepower and their weight. A three-thousand-mile main trunk-line system was set up. In 1916, the Federal Government passed a Road Aid Act to help states build roads. As late as 1918, even main highways like US 16 and US 10 were still only gravel roads.

In 1925, a tax was placed on gasoline to get more money to build and keep in repair state trunk lines. Since 1934, this tax has been the main support of the state trunk-line system.

The legislature, in 1951, increased the gas tax for the purpose of financing the building of new highways and repairing those already built. The weight tax was also increased.

Today, a system of state trunk lines spreads across the state. Each highway is designed to carry the flow of traffic. Some are four-lane roads and still others are four-lane divided highways. These later

Courtesy Michigan Milk Producers' Association

Much milk is now taken from the farms to the cities in large bulk pick-up trucks. Note the hose that carries the milk from the farmer's bulk tank to the truck. This helps to keep the milk free from bacteria. Photo 1964.

highways carry traffic fastest and safest. Most of the main trunk lines lie south of Bay City and Grand Rapids. During the last ten years wide expressways have also been built across the state. Much of the expense of building these expressways has been paid for by the federal government.

One of the main reasons for the decline of the railroads during the past thirty years has been the rapid advance in highway building. Today, much freight is hauled by trucks. Millions of dollars are now invested in the trucking industry. Modern manufacturers use trucks for shipping their goods to market and for bringing raw materials to their plants. Cement, drugs, salt, paper products, chemicals, automobiles, and furniture are hauled to market in trucks. This type of shipping can be handled by padding and the expenses of crating and repeated handling are eliminated. Trucks can go almost anywhere, even to the consumers' doors. These main highways also serve the farmers living in the state. Perishable products can be hastened to the market.

The farmer, as well as the manufacturer, has found that better all-year hard-surfaced roads have become a part of his way of life. Nearly all farmers own cars and most of them own trucks as well, especially in the fruit and vegetable growing districts where perishable products must reach the markets quickly. More and more of Michigan's livestock is going to market by truck. In this way a farmer can sell his stock quickly and take advantage of fattening and market prices.

Migrant laborers use highways to go from job to job as the seasons pass. Better fire protection is possible because better equipment can be hurried to the fire. All-weather roads have brought better police protection and education as well. Each day, during the school year, nearly seven thousand school buses pass over Michigan's highways, carrying Michigan's rural children to consolidated schools.

Rapid and easy transportation is now a part of our modern way of life. Today, we have come to depend more and more upon our state system of highways. Each day hundreds of gallons of fresh milk are carried by special trucks to cities and creameries. Over our roads go the men in cars and trucks to carry on the work of delivering mail to people scattered all over the state. Today, there are fewer Rural Free Delivery routes than there were in 1920 but their length has more than doubled. Rural Free Deliveries in Michigan alone cover some fifty-five thousand miles each day.

Modern refrigeration, rapid transportation, and canning have brought great changes in modern farming. Fruits and vegetables are now shipped over long distances to market. This brings new areas, some in other states, into competition with the older areas closer to the cities. Meat packing plants and modern laws regarding sanitation of foods make marketing more standardized than it was fifty years ago.

The Industrial Revolution has changed not only the farmer's means of marketing but also his manner of farming as well. Today, a modern farm represents a large investment not only in land but also in machinery. Most of Michigan's farms have electricity provided by the Consumers Power Company or some other electric company. This means that farm homes can have electric lights, radios, television, electric stoves, washing machines, ironers, sweepers. Electric pumps have replaced the windmills that were so common in 1900.

Few horses are now used on Michigan farms. Iron-tired wagons are a transportation means of the past. Farmers plow and cultivate by means of tractor power. Loose hay is seldom put in the barn. Little stock is butchered on farms. Only a few still use wood for fuel in the furnaces that have replaced the earlier stoves. Only a few windmills still pump water. Autos have replaced buggies. Kerosene lamps and lanterns no longer are used. Modern machinery has increased the farmers' output 111 per cent in the past forty years.

One of the many problems facing Michigan farmers today is soil conservation. When the forests were cleared from the land much of it, because it was hilly, began to quickly erode. Erosion was aided by poor farming methods. Fire, wind, and water have also destroyed much of Michigan's crop and forest land. But today farmers are becoming aware of this soil loss problem and are doing much to check it. New methods, such as contour plowing, check dams, cover cropping, strip cropping, reforestation, and setting out wind breaks, have done much to check erosion and to restore the land. Because of a better knowledge of soils and soil usage, farmers today are putting more elements back into the land.

Some land not suited to agriculture has been returned to private forests known as tree farms. Many of these tree farms have been started here in Michigan and are already providing a large percentage of our Christmas trees. The trees help hold moisture in the ground and also provide shelter for birds and other animals that help the farmers in many ways. In the future these tree farms will help supply lumber to our children.

Michigan farmers today have the help of many organizations to aid them in their work. Michigan State University, located in East Lansing, teaches young farmers scientific agriculture, helps to develop better breeds of stock and crop varieties, experiments in soil fertilization, and carries on a large educational extension program throughout the state. Here also is located one of the outstanding schools in veterinary medicine in the United States. The work of this college has done much to help reduce diseases in livestock such as tuberculosis in cattle and cholera in hogs. It has also done extensive work in establishing the need for vitamins and minerals in stock feed and overcoming deficiencies in some of the soils in Michigan. In all of its programs, it works closely with the United States Department of Agriculture.

The State Department of Agriculture was set up in 1921. Several former state agencies were then put under this new department. Since 1945, this department has been run by a five-man commission which is appointed by the governor.

Most counties in Michigan have a county agent who is a member of the extension division of Michigan State University. From him, farmers can get advice as to crops, soil, stock, and such services as the state and nation provide.

In 1875, the state legislature provided for the founding of the Michigan Grange, or as it is called, the Patrons of Husbandry. The Michigan State Grange operates as a part of the national organization. Many counties have a branch of this state organization. The Michigan Farmers' Union and the Michigan Farm Bureau are also other farmers' organizations.

In 1917, the United States Government started the 4-H Club movement among young people living on farms. Today, this movement in Michigan is directed by the extension service of Michigan State University in cooperation with the county governments. The 4-H Clubs do much to educate young people living in Michigan's rural areas.

The Future Farmers of America is another national organization. It is made up of farm boys who are interested in studying agriculture. The Future Farmers of America carries on local, state, and national activities.

Many national farm journals, as well as the *Michigan Farmer*, which was first published in 1843, carry the latest farm news and reports into the farmer's home. Daily quotations on the radio give the farmers the latest prices and warn of the danger of frost.

Farming in Michigan has undergone many changes during the last ten years. These changes have been brought about by several factors: the rising cost of machinery necessary to meet competition, changes of transportation routes within the state, competition from other areas made possible by better and faster transportation, and cheaper labor costs in other areas. Because of these factors many marginal or submarginal farms have been abandoned or placed in the soil bank.

Small farms, or farms with poor soil, no longer provide a livelihood for a farm family. Many of these farms have been forced out of production. In some areas the abandoned land has been put to use as recreational areas for people living in the nearby urban areas where they can hunt, fish, ski, or picnic. Farms are now becoming "farm factories" with heavy investments in land, stock, and machinery. Only a few farmers are still general farmers. Most farmers are dairy men or producers of one or two special crops.

The number of farms in Michigan in 1964 was estimated to be about 105,000. The number of farms has declined every year since 1933 when there were about 200,000. This is a drop of about forty-eight per cent in the past thirty years. With modern machinery farmers can farm more land than they could thirty years ago when many horses were still being used. Many farmers today farm twice as much land as their fathers did. This is shown in the fact that although the number of farms has decreased by forty-eight per cent the total land in farms has declined only about twenty-two per cent from about 18,300,000 acres in 1933 to 14,300,000 acres in 1964. Since 1960 farms have been disappearing at the rate of about 3,000 a year. The average farm size is about 136 acres as compared with 97 acres in 1940.

There are only about 5,000 farms remaining in the Upper Peninsula. There are some 15,000 farms north of Clare in the upper part of the Lower Peninsula. Some of this land has been abandoned for taxes, some has been put in the soil bank, and some has been put into tree farms. Michigan now has about 1,000 tree farms. The remaining farms, about 90,000, are in the area south of Clare. Many farms in this area have been destroyed by the building of our new super-highways that have cut wide strips through them. In building these super-highways it is estimated that for one mile of highway it takes forty acres of land from production.

Michigan's best farming lands in general are in the southern part of the lower Peninsula below the Bay City-Muskegon line. Some five million people live in this area and perhaps twice as many live in the nearby area in Ohio, Indiana, and Illinois. Today, this area is well supplied with both roads and railroads, and farm products can be easily and quickly shipped to market. Because of this easily accessible transportation, many of Michigan's farmers specialize in such products as milk, fruits, vegetables, and poultry.

Another change that has taken place on Michigan farms is the increase in part-time farmers. By part-time farmers is meant a farmer under 65 years old who worked off the farm for 100 or more days each year. Modern transportation has made it possible for many men to add to their farm income by working part-time in some local industry. At the present time there are about 47,000 part-time farmers in Michigan.

In 1910, the urban population of Michigan had grown enough to about equal the rural population. Today, in Michigan the rural population is a little over two million, whereas the urban population has climbed upward to about six million people.

It is less than one hundred and fifty years since Michigan was a vast wilderness. In that time Michigan's farmers have changed much of that wilderness into farm land that gives Michigan one of her three largest occupations. In 1963, the principal crops and livestock grown in Michigan had a total value of $786,066,00. Government payments to Michigan farmers amounted to $36,790,000.

CHAPTER EIGHTEEN
Cultural and Political Growth Since 1875

By 1875, MANY social changes had begun to appear in the way of life of the people living in Michigan. Ten years had passed since the Civil War had ended. People were beginning to forget the war and were becoming more and more interested in the new machines that were then beginning to be made. Most of the good farm land had been taken by this time, and people began leaving the farms and going to the cities where the men in the family could find work in the growing factories, and the wives and children could enjoy some of the new comforts that machines were bringing into people's lives. For many centuries there had been little change in the way people lived and did things. Now the new machines began to change people's lives both on the farms and in the cities. More and more machines were beginning to do much of the hard work that had before been done by men and animals. Steam engines were running boats, trains, sawmills, gristmills, and factories. The new sewing machines began to relieve the women from the long hours they had spent in sewing. Men's clothing began to be machine-made and men began buying their clothing at the stores rather than having it made at home. Machine-made shoes began replacing shoes made by the local cobbler. The Civil War, with its standardized guns, shoes, and uniforms, had helped to bring this change about. Hundreds of patents were applied for at the United States Patent Office as inventive men and women developed new ways of doing things. Among the many inventors of this period was Thomas Alva Edison, who became known as the "Wizard of Menlo Park."

Other inventors, too, were finding out many things in the field of science and making new machines. People liked the new inventions that brought pleasure into their lives or saved them time and labor. The World's Fair which was held in Chicago, in 1893, called people's attention to these new inventions.

Just as these new inventions were beginning to demand more steel, new discoveries of iron ore in Michigan and Minnesota made possible an abundant supply of the metal. Better boats, brought down an increasing supply of iron ore while trains, with their tracks now stretching across the nation, brought raw materials to the new factories and carried the new products to the growing nation.

Larger railroad engines and better coaches began to replace the little trains of the period before the Civil War. The earlier coaches had been made of wood and were heated by a stove that sat in the middle of the car. Those seated near it suffered from the heat while those nearer the doors were chilled by the cold and drafts. The

Courtesy Henry Ford Museum, Dearborn, Michigan

This train is like the one from which Thomas Edison was thrown with his experimental equipment. Note the wooden coaches and the wood in the coal car.

newer coaches were heated with steam coming from the engine's boiler, and they were thus heated more evenly. At first the railroad coaches had been lighted with candles, then with oil lamps, then with gas lamps; but with the coming of electricity they, too, soon had electric lights.

The railroads of this period had fences along their right-of-way. At the road crossings, metal cattle guards kept the cattle and horses from straying onto the tracks. At some of the most dangerous crossings, viaducts began to be built to reduce the number of accidents and to save life. Later, at other crossings, electric signals were installed to warn people of a train's approach.

At first the cars of a train were coupled together with a large chain link that was held in place by an iron pin that stood upright at each end of the car. These large chain links were heavy, and to couple or uncouple a car a brakeman had to step in between the cars. Often while uncoupling or coupling cars brakemen were injured or killed. To provide a better way of fastening cars together, the automatic coupler was invented. Each coupler fits into one on another car like the bent fingers of one hand hooked into the bent fingers of the other. Couplers are now made so that when an engine pushes one car against another the couplers automatically fasten together without someone having to step between the cars. A coupler can be unfastened by means of an iron rod that runs from the coupler to the side of the car. The automatic coupler has thus done much to reduce railroad accidents.

Another improvement in railroading was the coming of the air brake. The first trains had had only hand brakes. When an engineer wanted to stop, he blew his whistle as a signal for brakes. Then a brakeman climbed over the tender and set the brakes on the first three or four cars. While he was doing this, another brakeman set the brakes on the last four or five cars. This was a slow and dangerous way to stop a train. Today, the air brake has become standard railroad equipment. With the air brake, compressed air is carried from car

A Detroit railroad yard about 1910

to car by means of a hose. When the air is let out of the hose, it sets the brakes on every car on the train.

To keep the tracks clear of snow in the wintertime was often a huge task. In places where snow drifted deeply, snow fences, made of boards, were built to keep the snow from drifting onto the tracks. After a blizzard, huge snowplows, called "jumbos," pushed the snow from the tracks so that the trains could get through.

Many changes were also made in railroad engines. The first ones were crude machines having little power. These were followed by

Steam engines ready to be taken out of service. Photograph taken at Battle Creek in September, 1958.

huge engines, weighing many tons, that were able to pull long strings of loaded freight cars at a high rate of speed. Whereas the early engines often had names, the engines of this period were given numbers.

From the simple little cars of a century ago have grown many types of railroad cars to meet the changing needs of transportation. Boxcars, flatcars, gondola cars, drop-bottom gondola cars, hopper cars, stock cars, tank cars, poultry cars, refrigerator cars, sleeping cars, sight-seeing cars, chair cars, and baggage cars are all common on our railroads today.

Ferrying railroad cars across the Detroit River sometimes slowed traffic because of ice or bad weather. To remedy this, the railroads began to look for another way to get trains across the river. The river was too large to build a railroad bridge at that time. The land on both sides was too flat and low to provide height enough for a bridge that would allow the passage of the large lake boats. So, soon after 1870, work was begun on a tunnel that would let trains pass under the river. The workers had not gone far before they ran into

One of the last steam engines. Photo 1958.

sulphur and quicksand. The work of building the tunnel was then stopped. In 1906, New York Central Railroad again tried to build a tunnel under the river. Using newer methods, the work this time was a success and the tunnel was completed on July 1, 1910. Today, many trains running between New York and Detroit pass under the river through the tunnel.

In place of trying to bore a tunnel beneath the river bed, the railroad tunnel was built in a new and different manner. First a huge ditch was dredged across the river bottom from shore to shore. Into this ditch were placed sections of a huge steel tube reaching all the way across the river. The tube was then covered with concrete. Since the building of this railroad tunnel, a tunnel and a suspension bridge, known as the Ambassador Bridge, have been built for auto traffic crossing the Detroit River.

Michigan's longest mileage of railroad tracks was in 1916. This was before our modern highways were built. Since that time automobiles, trucks, buses, barges, and airplanes have cut into the traffic carried by railroads. Many spur lines running to the old lumber towns have been abandoned and the tracks taken up. Today, about fifty-four per cent of Michigan's rural communities are served only by trucks. There were still 32 railroads and terminal companies in Michigan in 1962. At that time Michigan still had 11,124 miles of railroad track. Only two of Michigan's 83 counties do not have some railroad service.

In spite of the increased competition from the other carriers since 1930, the railroads still remain our nation's largest bulk carrier for land transportation. During the last few years the railroads have made many changes to meet the competition from the other carriers. Steam engines have all been replaced by the less attractive but more efficient diesel engines. Lighter cars made of aluminum and having better roller bearings have cut down hauling costs. New cars that are designed for carrying new automobiles have been developed. Some are triple-deckers and will carry 12 to 15 automobiles on one car. The Chesapeake and Ohio Railroad is experimenting with a boxcar, called a "RoadRailer," that has two sets of wheels. One set of wheels

Courtesy Chesapeake and Ohio Railway Company

These cars, fastened to the back of a passenger train running between Grand Rapids and Detroit, are called "RoadRailers." They can run on the railroad tracks or be hauled as trailers on the highway. Photo 1961.

fits the railroad tracks. The other set has tires and can be used on the highway. Each set is retractable. These cars are fastened on the back of a fast passenger train to speed shipment.

Another of the major changes in railroading during the last few years is the hauling of loaded truck-trailers on top of long flatcars. This is called "piggyback." Some railroads own their own truck-trailers, and by using them, every highway becomes a branch line of the railroad. Freight can be picked up and delivered wherever there is a highway. Trains made up of such truck-trailers are called "truck-trains." This not only provides faster service but also reduces cost, as one train crew can haul many trailers.

Courtesy New York Central System

These cars are used to haul truck trailers. Photo 1961.

Courtesy Chesapeake and Ohio Railroad

A tri-level car on Chesapeake and Ohio Railway train. Photo 1961.

Steamboats and trains were good for carrying heavy loads for long distances. However, there grew up a need for better personal transportation to various parts of a city and from city to city. To meet this need, streetcars and interurbans were developed. At first, streetcars were small and were pulled by horses. In 1886, the first streetcar line in Michigan, and the third in the United States, was built in Port Huron. This line was about one mile long.

In 1890, an interurban line was built between Ypsilanti and Ann Arbor. The builders of this line saw the growing need for personal transportation that was developing. They saw, too, that the number of young men attending the University at Ann Arbor was far larger than the number of young women, while at Ypsilanti there were far more young women than there were men attending the Normal College. The promoters of the line said that five hundred persons a day could be carried between the two places. This number was not idle fancy, for soon interurbans were carrying over six hundred people each day between Ann Arbor and Ypsilanti.

The first ride over this line was a gala affair. City officials from Ypsilanti and Ann Arbor boarded the steam car at Ann Arbor and rode to Ypsilanti. The car and passengers arrived safely at Ypsilanti and only one farmer's barn had been set on fire. At first the interurbans were driven by steam but soon electricity was used as the source of power.

In 1895, an interurban line was built from Mt. Clemens to Detroit. In 1899, another was built from Grand Rapids to Muskegon. The line from Ypsilanti to Ann Arbor was later extended until it ran from Detroit to Jackson, Battle Creek, and Kalamazoo. Most of the interurbans in Michigan ran out from Detroit to other cities such as Toledo, Jackson, Lansing, Saginaw, Bay City, and Port Huron. There were, however, lines in other parts of the state. Some were built in the Upper Peninsula. In 1918, there were 1,747 miles of interurban lines in operation in Michigan.

The streetcars and interurbans gave a much needed transportation service to the people. They ran on a regular schedule every hour or two during the day and late into the night. This regular service from city to city made it easy for people to go from one city to another. Many people left the city and went to live in the country. Each morning, the breadwinner of the family would go to the city on the interurban and return to his home on it at the end of his day's work. People who could not otherwise have gone to the cities to trade went by means of this interurban service. This aided the development of business sections of the city.

Streetcars and interurbans thus rendered a service that roads and railroads could not give to the people. There soon came, however, a new means of transportation that was to drive the interurbans out

Streetcars on Woodward Avenue in Detroit just before they stopped running. Photo 1955.

of business and also take much of the passenger traffic from the railroads. This means of transportation was the automobile and bus, made possible by the gasoline motor.

The automobile enabled the people of both city and country to go when they wished, where they wished, and as fast as they wished. The last streetcar in Michigan ran on Woodward Avenue in Detroit on Sunday afternoon, April 8, 1956. Today, the interurban lines and all streetcar lines have been replaced by buses. From our cities stretch miles and miles of paved road over which each day run thousands of automobiles, buses, and trucks carrying people and freight from place to place.

During the years from 1875 to 1900, many changes came in the field of education. As Michigan grew in population and wealth, more colleges were started, more courses were offered, and more and better grammar schools were established. During the years from 1875 to 1915, the University of Michigan grew rapidly and several new colleges were added. The first to be added was the College of Dentistry in 1875. A College of Pharmacy was started in 1876 and a College of Engineering in 1895. In 1894, the University of Michigan offered its first summer school courses. In 1912 it opened its graduate school.

Cars changed the lives of farmers as well as city people. This picture was taken about 1914.

The Jesuit order of the Catholic Church founded a Jesuit college in Detroit in 1877. This college later became the University of Detroit. For many years this university was located on East Jefferson Avenue near Woodward. But, by 1927, the University of Detroit had outgrown its buildings on Jefferson and six new buildings were built on a large new campus on the corner of McNichols Road and Livernois in Detroit. In 1881, the Detroit Normal College was started to prepare teachers for the Detroit Public Schools. In 1921, the name of the college was changed to Detroit Teachers College.

As lumbermen and settlers pushed into the upper part of the Lower Peninsula and the eastern part of the Upper Peninsula, grammar schools were started in the rural areas and the villages. Most villages of any size also had a high school. But, because of the migratory nature of the lumber industry, no colleges developed in the area. At Big Rapids, however, Woodbridge N. Ferris started the Ferris Institute in 1884. For sixty-five years the Ferris Institute was run as a private school. Hundreds of young men and women, mostly from the upper part of the Lower Peninsula and the eastern half of the Upper Peninsula, came to the Ferris Institute to finish their high school education, take commercial courses, or prepare to go on to a college or university. In 1949, the Ferris Institute was offered as a gift to the state if the state would continue running it and did not change its name. This offer was accepted and on July 1, 1950, Ferris College became a state college.

Because of the mining industries that were developing in the Upper Peninsula, the Michigan Mining College was started at Houghton in 1886. This early college is now known as Michigan Technological University. It is located on a campus that covers one hundred and twelve acres. It also has a branch at Sault Ste. Marie.

Alma College, at Alma, was also founded in 1886. Much of Alma College's support comes from the Presbyterian church.

Detroit, during the period before 1900, was known for salt, seeds, oils, and the manufacture of railroad cars, carriages, parlor organs, stoves, drugs, and paints and varnishes. Michigan's largest city then boasted of having four miles of asphalt pavement. Passenger boats were running between Detroit and several lake ports. Day excursions to Walpole Island or Sugar Island were very popular especially among the young people of that time. By paying the ten-cent fare one could ride all day on the Detroit-Windsor Ferry, or the Belle Isle Ferry, if one cared to do so, and many did, especially on warm summer days.

Many large homes were built in Detroit and the other urban centers during this period. Some of these homes were made of bricks, but most of them were built of lumber which could then be easily bought from any one of Michigan's many sawmills. Houses of this period can usually be told by their size, their wide porches, their high ceilings, and their fancy windows and ornate trim. These were homes that were built by men who had made money in farming, lumbering, mining, or in the new growing industries.

Some of these houses had furnaces, but most of them had several stoves here and there about the house. Upper rooms were often heated during the winter by vents in the ceiling that allowed the warm air from below to rise to the upstairs rooms. Most houses had a parlor. The parlor was an extra living room which was used only on very special occasions. Usually the furniture in the parlor was stiff and uncomfortable. Here, on a table, one usually found a fancy-bound family album which was filled with pictures of members of the family. Often under the table on a shelf could be found a basket full of stereopticon views that were supposed to furnish entertainment to guests. There were few pianos during this period, but nearly every parlor had one of the foot pump organs that were common in that day.

The living room, or sitting room as it was called, often had a large fireplace that had a marble front, but a stove was usually set up in the winter to heat the room. Often in these houses there was a large dining room in which one quite often found a large massive dining room furniture suite such as was then being manufactured. The best of the houses had a plate rail running around the dining room. On this ledge, made of wood, the lady of the house placed her choice hand-painted china. The kitchen was the most used room in the house. It usually had a large wood range, but gas cookstoves were beginning to be used in some cities. Here one found such new inventions as egg beaters, gas toasters, and iceboxes.

Courtesy Henry Ford Museum, Dearborn, Michigan

A typical parlor of 1890. This is the parlor in Henry Ford's birthplace now in Greenfield Village.

People had found that iceboxes kept their food from spoiling much longer. The cutting of lake ice in the wintertime became a major occupation in some communities. The ice was cut and then stored in large sheds where it was covered with sawdust. Delivering ice became a daily occupation in many communities. Ice was also used to ice railroad cars, and fresh frozen meats began to be shipped from packing houses to city markets. Later artificial ice was made and used. By 1930, mechanical refrigeration was beginning to replace ice as a better means of preserving food.

Up to 1890, it was very common for men to wear beards. During this period, however, beards became less common. Men's suits were all made of wool and these suits were worn both winter and summer. Black or dark blue was the usual color. Derby hats were then the style. Shirt collars and cuffs were heavily starched and thus were very stiff. Socks were heavy, and shoes were quite pointed. The well-dressed man wore a vest and across the front of it, from one pocket to another, usually hung a heavy gold watch chain. From the chain was often suspended an emblem of some lodge or club to which the wearer belonged.

Young ladies of this period never went out alone or with a gentleman friend. They were chaperoned whenever they appeared at a restaurant, theatre, ball game, party, or at the races. Even in their own living rooms someone had always to be present whenever a gentleman called.

Ladies' dresses were long and often dusty at the bottom, especially during bad weather. Stockings were black and shoes were high. Ladies' dresses had high collars of satin, linen, or lace. Often women wore tightly laced corsets that made them as thin around the waist as possible. Even when swimming, they were fully clothed. But dresses for women began to change with the coming of bicycles. Bicycles soon put an end to bustles and also long full skirts that swished along the ground.

Monday was wash day. A few city folk were getting water from city water systems, but most women were still pumping it from a well. Clothes were often soaked overnight so that they could be washed more easily. Early on Monday morning women got up and began the task of washing. Washing was still done by hand. Up and down the clothes were scrubbed on the hand washboard. A few hand-powered washers were beginning to appear, but as yet they were not very successful, and they had to be worked by hand.

Tuesday was ironing day. Heavy flat irons were heated on the cook stove in the kitchen. As fast as one would cool it was replaced by another. Ironing, especially on warm days in the summertime was a hot, tiring job.

On Wednesday the women usually did their "darning" and mending. Thursday was somewhat of a rest day. Friday was house-cleaning day. With a dust cap on her head and a broom in her hands, mother or daughter swept the house. Most homes had carpets which were stretched tight and tacked on all four sides near the wall. Sweeping brushed off the top dirt but it also pushed some of the dirt through the carpet onto the floor. Once each year the carpet tacks were pulled and the carpet taken up. The floor was then cleaned.

It was in Detroit, in 1909, that the vacuum cleaner industry started. Fred Wardell in that year organized the Eureka Vacuum Cleaner Company. At first women did not like the new machines, but soon they learned that they did not stir up the dust like brooms did and soon many vacuum cleaners were being sold. After sweeping came the dusting. Then, too, there was always the stove to polish.

Saturday in most homes was baking day. Each housewife usually made enough bread to last her family during the following week. Some bread was then beginning to be sold in cities, but usually it was not thought to be as good as home-baked bread. Saturday night was bath night. After supper, as the evening meal was then called, water was heated on the kitchen stove. At bedtime a tub was brought into the kitchen, and into it was poured the heated water. The small children were usually bathed first. Then came the older children in their turn. Mother and dad came last. Bathrooms were beginning to appear in some city homes and new bathtubs with white enamel on the inside were coming onto the market. Inside toilets were beginning to be put in some homes.

Few foods bought at the store were wrapped. Sugar, coffee, and crackers came in barrels and were sold by being weighed out to each customer. Spices also came in bulk and usually had to be ground

Courtesy Henry Ford Museum, Dearborn, Michigan
Visiting the country store about 1875

at home. Cookies came in cookie boxes and were usually handled by the storekeeper as he sold them to the customer. More and more food was beginning to be packed in tin cans.

In the period around 1900 there was a marked difference in the lives of people. Some had grown very wealthy and lived in large homes. They had servants and rode in the finest carriages. Many of them began to travel in Europe and in other ways show that they were people with money. But many of them had little education. Though they had money, they lacked the true culture that comes with education, and often they showed poor taste in style, home furnishings, and in speaking. Operations were becoming more common, and many a person who had had this new experience entertained her friends by going into all the details.

Whereas a few grew rich, most of the people were poor. Many of them were newly arrived immigrants that had just come from Europe. Men worked ten to twelve hours a day and often received little pay for their work. City slums developed in the newly growing industrial areas. In the rural areas many families lived in poorly built homes. There was no social security or workmen's compensation. When men were injured or died, their families got along as best they could.

Bicycles became common during the period from 1890 to 1900. Many of the first bicycles had one large front wheel and one small wheel in back. The rider usually rode on top of the large wheel, which he turned by pedals which were fastened to its center. Only young men rode these bicycles, but about 1895 the low, modern bicycle, known as the safety bicycle, with two wheels the same size, came on the market. Soon these new bicycles were being made for women as well as men. Workers, mail carriers, physicians—all rode bicycles.

Courtesy Henry Ford Museum, Dearborn, Michigan

Two types of early bicycles. Bicycles like these were ridden about 1890. These men are resting their feet on a stone watering trough for horses.

Between the years 1890 and 1910 Michigan was in the bicycle age. Bicycles were then almost as common as autos are today. Men and women rode bicycles to and from their work and on week ends for pleasure. Bicycles were made by the hundreds at that time. Various sizes and shapes could be bought. Some were made for men while others were especially designed for women. Ladies' bicycles had special guards to keep their skirts from catching in the chain or in the rear wheel. Still other bicycles were made for two persons. Then there were yet others that could carry four, five, or six. A few were made that could carry as many as ten people. These bicycles were provided with a pedal arrangement for each person, although there was only one steering bar at the front end. On Sundays and holidays groups of people went cycling together into the country. They did not travel so far as people do today but they had, no doubt, just as much fun. But a bicycle had to be pedaled by the rider and that was hard work. Soon they were replaced by a new means of transportation, the automobile.

Comic strips were beginning to appear in the daily papers. Theatres were beginning to open for Sunday shows. In 1896, the first real movie was shown in the Detroit Opera House. It was a picture of a Mexican bullfight. Basketball also was played for the first time that year. Roller skating and croquet were both popular, and the people were also beginning to show some interest in baseball. Telephones began to be installed in more and more business places and in homes. In 1889 the ten-story Hammond Building, one of the largest buildings of the time, was built of masonry and was the wonder of Detroit. The coming of structural steel meant that larger buildings could be built. In 1897, the Bankers-Equitable Building was built around a steel frame. Inside were fireplaces to heat the rooms.

In the small villages and rural areas, the manner of living did not change as fast as it did in the growing cities. Sometimes a group of theatrical players stopped for a night or two and put on "Uncle Tom's Cabin," or some similar performance, in the town hall. But rural people and village people still found most of their amusement in dances, bobsled parties, ice skating, clambakes, barbecues, and Sunday School picnics.

Life in the rural areas was still hard. The homes did not have the new conveniences that were coming to the cities. Most of the homes were still lighted by kerosene lamps. City stores were far away. But most farmers began to receive the Sears-Roebuck and Montgomery Ward catalogs and from them the farm families selected many of their needs, such as hats and dresses for mother and daughters, work clothes and Sunday clothes for father and sons, harnesses for the horses, and tools for working in the fields. Farmers also started receiving daily mail deliveries with the coming of the Rural Free Delivery that began to spread across the country at this time. Rural telephone lines also brought the farmers and village people closer together.

In 1891, the Detroit College of Law opened and the Y.M.C.A. began offering vocational classes. The Y.M.C.A. now has a college in Detroit that is known as the Detroit Institute of Technology. Michigan's second teachers college was started at Mt. Pleasant, in 1894, as a state normal school. In 1958, the state legislature changed its name to Central Michigan University.

Michigan State University also made many advances. In 1896, a School of Home Economics was started. A School of Veterinary Medicine was begun in 1909. Today, this university has one of the best colleges of veterinary science in the United States. Two other departments, Hotel Management and Police Administration, have also been added.

Today, the campus of this university is one of the most beautiful in the United States. Several experimental farms are scattered over the state so that studies of crops, soils, fertilizers, and insecticides can be made. Each year, besides the regular enrollment, some fifty thousand people attend short courses, or conferences, sponsored by Michigan State University.

In 1896, Suomi College was started in Hancock. This is the only Finnish Lutheran college in the United States. Northern Michigan College of Education was started at Marquette in 1899. Today, this college campus covers some eighty acres and is known as Northern Michigan University. St. Joseph College and Academy, at Adrian, was started in 1900, it is taught by the Sisters of St. Dominic. Western Michigan University was started in Kalamazoo in 1904.

In 1917, the Detroit Junior College was formed when the first two years of college work were added to the high school program at Detroit Central High School. Soon many students were attending the new junior college. In 1923, the Detroit Junior College became the College of the City of Detroit, and in 1925 this new college graduated its first class. Soon many students were coming to this college, especially for afternoon and evening classes.

In 1927, the Detroit City Law College was started and in 1928 the College of Pharmacy began. In 1934, the Detroit Teachers College,

Courtesy Henry Ford Museum, Dearborn, Michigan

Michigan Avenue near Dearborn about 1912. The rails are for the interurban cars.

the Detroit College of Medicine and Surgery, the College of the City of Detroit, the Detroit City Law College, and the College of Pharmacy were all brought together as Wayne University. In 1956, Wayne State University became a regular state supported university.

After 1900 major changes took place in Michigan's system of education. More and more girls continued their education above the eighth grade. School programs began including courses in homemaking and industrial arts. Less attention was paid to the older classical subjects. In 1903, a law was passed allowing school districts to tax so that transportation to a high school could be given to pupils not having a qualified school in their district. In 1909, such districts were required to place this tax. In 1905, a law was passed requiring all children from the ages of seven to sixteen to attend school for nine months each year. In general the city schools were better than the village and rural schools.

Since 1900, higher qualifications for teachers have brought better prepared teachers into Michigan's classrooms. During the years from 1900 to 1950 adult education became a large part of the educational program in many communities. More and more people began to further their education by attending evening classes. Many people attended evening classes so that they might qualify for citizenship. Others have taken industrial or hobby courses. Hundreds of students attend Wayne University and other urban colleges each evening so that they can earn a degree. Extension classes are now conducted by several institutions of higher learning at villages and cities far distant from their campus.

Since 1915, the junior college movement has expanded in Michigan. Junior colleges, spread across the state, make it possible for high school graduates to continue their education for two years before attending a senior college. This movement has made it possible for many people to get two more years of higher education and still live at home. If present trends continue, more junior colleges will be started, and more and more young people will avail themselves of this opportunity to further their education for at least two years after high school.

As Michigan has grown, many changes have come into her government. In 1963, the voters of Michigan adopted the fourth constitution of the state. In 1920, the nineteenth amendment, permitting women to vote, was added to the Federal Constitution. Since that time, women have played an ever-increasing part in local, state, and national government. As Michigan's government grew, the old capitol became too small to house the offices of the state government and another building called the Lewis Cass building was completed in 1928. This building now houses many of the governmental agencies.

The years from 1875 to today have witnessed the rapid exploitation of our natural resources in land, fish, forests, copper, iron, and petroleum. But slowly people have become aware that conservation of our natural resources is becoming more and more necessary. In 1873, the State Board of Fish Commissioners was established. The office of Game and Fish Warden was established in 1887. Our first state park appeared in 1895. By this time our forests were nearly gone and people were beginning to see the need of forests and parks for recreation as well as timber. In 1899, the state established a Forestry Commission and in 1903 the first State Forest was established.

In 1908, President Theodore Roosevelt became interested in conserving the natural resources of the nation. The influence of President Roosevelt was felt in every state and people began to be more conservation-minded. They began to realize that conservation does not mean hoarding our resources, but rather wise planning and use of our natural resources so that we can get the greatest use of them.

A State Park Commission was established in 1919. Our present State Department of Conservation was begun in 1921, when the state legislature combined the various commissions already established into the State Department of Conservation. At the present time the Department of Conservation is divided into several divisions.

The work of the Education Division is to tell the people of Michigan of the need for conservation and what can be done about it. This is done by means of pamphlets, lectures, motion pictures and radio programs. Special units on conservation are taught in the schools. Thus, people are made aware of the need to keep our forests and streams clean for their own benefit and for the benefit of others, and of the danger and the ease of setting forest fires.

The Fish Division checks on fisherman to see if they have their licenses. They also see that fish are not caught out of season or that not more are caught than the law allows. The Conservation Department also operates several fish hatcheries where fingerlings are raised until they are large enough to plant in streams and lakes. Lake and stream improvements are also carried on under this division.

The Forest Division cares for our state forests. Today, there are twenty-two state forest districts in Michigan. There are also four national forests. About forty-five per cent of Michigan is now classed as forest land. Once our forests were badly burned by forest fires, but today, because of public education and better means of fighting forest fires, damage is much less. Two million three hundred acres were burned in the year 1908. In 1954, only 3,384 acres burned. In 1958, nearly twelve thousand acres burned. Such forest fires are a tragic loss of timber resources for the state. Michigan uses the most modern methods to fight forest fires. Fire towers are located throughout the forest areas. At the Forest Fire Experimental Station, at Roscommon, new methods for fighting forest fires are developed. There are 107 state forest camp grounds located in the state and national forests. Hundreds of people use these camp grounds each summer. The Forestry Division runs three tree nurseries where little seedlings are grown and then sold to people who wish to plant them. These nurseries are located at Manistique in the Upper Peninsula and at Higgins Lake near Roscommon, and west of Wolverine in the Lower Peninsula. Each year these nurseries grow some thirty million trees and shrubs. Two nurseries are also operated by the United States Forest Service in Michigan. One is the Chittenden Nursery located at Wellston. The other is the J. W. Toumey Forest Tree Nursery at Watersmeet.

The Game Division makes surveys of the amount of game in the state and recommends laws that will keep the game from being overhunted. Studies are made to see how game can be helped to live so that it can be harvested by trappers and hunters.

The Geological Survey Division is the oldest division in the department. It was set up in 1837. This division keeps a record of test drillings so that we will know more about the rocks underlying the state. It also aids in the use and conservation of our mineral resources.

The Parks and Recreation Division cares for our many state parks. There are more than sixty state parks and recreational areas in Michigan today.

To help in training people for the work of the Conservation Department a training school was set up at Higgins Lake in 1941. The work of the Conservation Department is paid for by money granted it by the state legislature and by fees collected for licenses for fishing, hunting, and trapping.

CHAPTER NINETEEN

The Upper Peninsula Today

SOUTH of Lake Superior and north of Lake Michigan and part of Lake Huron and the State of Wisconsin stretches a vast land known as the Upper Peninsula of Michigan. For many years it was the homeland of the Chippewa Indians. Today, it is occupied by many peoples: Cornish, Scots and Scots-Irish, Finns, Swedes, Poles, and French Canadians. From this area, during the past one hundred years, have come lumber, copper, iron ore, and limestone. Although some of these resources still come from the Upper Peninsula, much of the wealth of the region has already been taken from it. Unfortunately for the Upper Peninsula, only a small part of the profit that was derived from its natural resources remained in the area to aid in its future development.

The Upper Peninsula contains about one third of Michigan's area but has only about six per cent of the state's population. The population of the Upper Peninsula was the highest in 1920, when there were

Courtesy Michigan State Highway Department

Straits of Mackinac auto ferry "Vacationland." This was the largest and newest of the ferry fleet that stopped running in 1957. This ferry now runs between Rimousik and Baie Comeau across the mouth of the St. Lawrence River. Photo 1952.

464

332,556 people living in the area. In 1960, this number had decreased to only 305,622 people. During the past twenty years many people, especially young people, have been forced to leave the Upper Peninsula because of low farm income, decreased production, and automation that has greatly decreased the man hours of labor needed.

Much of the land from which excellent timber was once taken has reverted back to the state for taxes. Nearly nine tenths of the Upper Peninsula is now classed as forest land. Today, the state and federal government own some thirty-five per cent of this land while other vast tracts of land are owned by large corporations.

In the state as a whole nearly twenty million acres are classed as forest land. This is about fifty-four per cent of the state's total area.

Although the forests were wantonly destroyed, between 1860 and 1910, forests are a renewable resource. Due to the reforestation work that has been carried on by the state, federal government, and private individuals, the Upper Peninsula is again becoming a forest area. About forty thousand acres of idle land are being planted to forests each year in the state as a whole. These new forests are one of the Upper Peninsula's best present and future sources of employment and wealth. Timber growth in Michigan each year exceeds the amount that is harvested and lost by natural causes. These growing forests also provide recreation areas for canoeing, camping, fishing, and hunting. They also conserve water by stopping run-off water and this helps to prevent erosion.

Wood pulp is now an item of great demand, for the per capita consumption of paper is about 450 pounds a year. Until recently the demand has been for the long fiber species of trees, such as the spruces and hemlocks, as they were the best for pulping. During the last few years chemical research has made it possible to use the wood found in the short fiber trees for making both paper and the new laminated wood products. Because of this, many trees formerly of little value, such as the poplar, or aspen, have become usable to the expanding paper industry. The poplar is now the leading pulpwood species in the lake states. Each year several hundred thousand cords of these trees are harvested for pulpwood in the northern part of the Lower Peninsula and in the Upper Peninsula. Three paper making plants are located in the Upper Peninsula, while at L'Anse is located the plant of the Celotex Corporation. At the present time about 5,000 people are engaged in the paper and wood products industries. Christmas trees are also providing another cash crop for many growers

Courtesy Mackinac Bridge Authority

Mackinac Bridge, built across the Straits of Mackinac

in the upper part of the Lower Peninsula and in the Upper Peninsula. Christmas trees are shipped to many states such as, Ohio, Florida, Georgia, and Texas.

Modern mechanization and automation has made it possible, by selective logging, to harvest the mature trees for lumber. Four sawmills that once cut lumber during the lumber period, are still in operation. Some hardwood flooring mills still remain. Many small mills are again cutting lumber in local areas. Two new, large sawmills will soon be built; one at Munising and the other at Newberry. There are also many sawmills operating in the upper part of the Lower Peninsula. At present there are more than five hundred sawmills operating in the state. Like in the earlier lumbering period, most of the lumber cut today in the Upper Peninsula is now shipped to the Milwaukee and Chicago area. These growing forest industries will soon supply employment for many men, especially during the winter months.

Because much of the land is forest area, local income from property taxes is often very small. This lack of tax support hampers local development, in many areas, just as it does in much of the upper part of the Lower Peninsula. Because of this, both the state and national governments have made provisions to supply some funds for local areas. On state owned land the state now taxes itself fifteen cents an acre each year and pays this money to the local school district and township. In the national forest areas, one fourth of the money received from the sale of timber in the area is returned to the local school district and township. As the selective cutting increases, this will become a much larger sum. It already has become a worthwhile figure as can be seen in the following statistics. In the Ottawa National Forest alone, in 1960, 115,000 cords of pulpwood and 4,000,000 board feet of lumber were cut. Today, the forest areas of the upper part of the Lower Peninsula and the Upper Penninsula bring to the people of Michigan some three hundred ten million dollars a year in payrolls and provide full time employment for about one hundred twenty-seven thousand people in the forests, pulp mills, and wood industries.

Closely related to the forest situation is the present status of farming in the Upper Peninsula. During the years between 1950 and 1960 the Upper Peninsula saw the abandonment of about half of its farms. As was explained in the chapter on agriculture, soil, transportation, climate, and the high cost of mechanization are all adverse factors against farming in the Upper Peninsula. Some farmers have turned to raising feeder cattle. Some have supplemented their income by working in the forest industries in the winter time, by boarding summer vacationers, fishermen, hunters, and those that like to come to the area for winter sports. Some farms have just been deserted, some have been placed in the soil bank, and others have been converted to tree farms.

By 1916, Michigan's mineral resources began to show the effects of extensive mining and outside competition, but Michigan's iron ore production did not decline as rapidly as did her copper production. In 1860, Michigan produced 114,401 tons of iron ore. Gradually production rose to 7,221,252 tons in 1890 when Michigan began to compete with Minnesota as an iron ore producer. In 1916, the Marquette range reached its peak production with 4,792,987 tons of iron ore. Michigan's peak year for iron ore production was in 1920 when 18,992,931 tons of ore were produced. In 1961, iron ore ship-

Courtesy Pickands Mather & Company, Ironwood, Michigan

This is a picture of a new type of conveyor. Instead of a heavy rubber belt, this conveyor consists of a pan with side plates over which two chains (one on each side) pull small cross bars along on top of the pan. When this belt is loaded, the cross bars move the dirt along. This picture shows the drive motors on the discharge end of the conveyor of iron ore. Photo 1961.

ments from Michigan were 9,285,000 long tons and about twenty-one per cent of this was in the form of concentrate pellets.

During the last few years, many changes have taken place in Michigan's iron mining industry. These changes have been brought about by several causes; such as, the depletion of the natural, high concentrated pockets of good iron ore, the rising cost of labor at the mines, the rising cost due to the depth from which the ore has to be brought to the surface, the fact that five men are required in a shaft mine for only one in an open pit mine, the increased cost in railroad and lake transportation, local taxes charged against the mines, the recent opening of the St. Lawrence Waterway which allows foreign ores to enter Lake Erie, the fact that ocean freighters because of their depth can carry about twice as large a cargo as most lake carriers, and the competition from foreign ore fields like those in the Ungava area of Quebec and the vast deposits of Venezuela and other parts of the world that have been discovered during the past few years. Whereas, Michigan ores run only about fifty-one per cent, imported ores grade as high as sixty to sixty-eight per cent. This means lower furnace output for Michigan ore as will be shown later on.

Because of these factors the United States has imported from foreign sources about thirty-five per cent, or more, of the iron ore it used during the last few years. What is more, the competition of foreign steel makers has also become very strong. During the three years, 1959 to 1961, the United States imported 10.8 million tons of manufactured steel and exported only 6.6 million tons. In 1961, steel imports were 3.2 million tons while steel exports were 2 million tons. This means the United States imported 1.2 million more tons of steel than it exported. Along with iron ore, steel making today requires many other minerals to make our modern alloys. Many of these minerals came from foreign lands. Thus our steel industry is becoming more and more dependent on ocean shipping and thus becoming much more vulnerable in time of war.

All of these factors have helped to bring many changes in the Lake Superior iron mining areas. Nearly all of Michigan's iron mines are now closed, while those still in operation are forced to put out a high quality product and to watch costs very closely if they are to remain in operation. At the Geneva mine, at Ironwood, a new $150,000 drying plant has been installed to reduce the water content of the ore and thus reduce its shipping cost. Because diesel engines are now used in place of the earlier railroad steam engines, the Chicago

Courtesy Marquette County Historical Society

A group of iron ore miners around an air drill. Notice the boxes of Aetna dynamite. The men are wearing carbide lamps. This picture was taken about 1927 at the Barnes-Hecker mine in Marquette County. (1961)

and Northwestern Railroad has completed a new $250,000 infra-red iron ore thawing plant near its ore dock at Escanaba. This new plant is 24 feet wide and 276 feet lang. During the freezing weather, in late fall and early spring, some 1,700 quartz lamps can be used to thaw out the iron ore in ten, seventy-ton railroad ore cars at one time. New machinery to cut labor costs has also been installed in most of the mines that are still in operation.

All of these changes in the iron mining areas has resulted in hundreds of men becoming unemployed. Some have found work in the woods during the winter, and work on the new highways during the summer. Others have left the area to try and find employment elsewhere.

The vast mineral wealth that has been taken from the Upper Peninsula during the past one hundred years can never be replaced. Most of Michigan and Minnesota's high-grade iron ore has now been mined and unless new pockets of iron ore are discovered most of the few remaining shaft mines will soon cease production.

Until recently, prospecting for iron ore deposits has been discour-

Courtesy Gogebic Industrial Bureau

Miners drilling long holes prior to blasting in a Michigan underground iron ore mine.

aged because mine owners were taxed on known reserves even though the reserves were not being mined. In 1947, the state legislature passed the Lindquist Bill which now exempts owners of mineral deposits from such taxation for ten years after its discovery or until the mine is in operation. This has encouraged diamond drilling, and no doubt some new deposits of iron ore that do not come to the surface will be discovered in this manner.

Unless new pockets of iron ore are discovered in the future our domestic iron ore production must come from the lower grades of iron ore bearing rock. There still remains in the Lake Superior area vast quantities of low grade ore which is called "taconite" in Minnesota and "jasper" in Michigan. This is the mother lode that was deposited during the Huronian Period. It is in this sedimentary layer by a leaching, or depositing, process that the high grade deposits of iron ore were formed.

This mother lode extends over hundreds of square miles around the western end of Lake Superior where the Killarney Mountains once stood. The lode varies in richness but most of it is about twenty-five per cent iron and lies in a layer 175 to 300 feet in thickness. Processes of taking lower grades of ore and processing from them higher concentrates are known in general as beneficiation. Beneficiation includes many present processes; such as, washing ores, sizing ores, and the making of high-grade ore concentrates from the low grade deposits. Today, all iron ores are graded and tested. Each railroad ore car is tested as to the quality of the ore before it leaves the mine. Then the cars are carefully selected and dumped into the proper bins at the ore dock so that only ore of the proper quality will be shipped.

As early as the 1880's Thomas Edison, seeing the limits of the Marquette Range, conducted experiments in changing low-grade deposits into a higher concentrate. The discovery of the vast deposits in Minnesota brought a temporary end to such experiments. But as early as 1916 mine owners began to realize the limits of what was then still a vast ore supply and again began experimenting to beneficiate low-grade deposits. Their early experiments were costly and not very successful and so about 1924 experimentation was stopped. World War II cut deeply into our already limited reserves and so in 1942 further experimentation in upgrading iron ore again began. In 1943, the first pellets of iron ore were made from taconite. In 1954, the Cleveland Cliffs made the first shipment of iron concentrate, produced by the flotation process in Michigan, from the Humboldt Mine. Experimentation in developing a process to make it possible to use low-grade deposits has already cost the steel industry millions of dollars. While these costly experiments were being carried on vast deposits of iron ore were also being discovered in foreign lands as was explained in chapter fifteen.

The mother lode is near diamond hardness, and ordinary drills cut into it very slowly. Today, however, a new drill called the 'jet piercer" has been developed. The jet piercer burns a mixture of oxygen and kerosene and throws a hot jet flame at the rate of 6,000 feet per second. In an hour this flame can burn a nine-inch hole twenty to thirty feet deep into the hard rock of the mother lode. The principle used is the same as the Indians used in heating and cooling the rock and thus causing it to chip off or flake. The hot flame from the jet piercer causes the heated rock to chip, and as it does, hot steam, forced into the hole with the flame, flushes away the flakes of rock as they break from the mother lode.

After holes have been drilled into the low grade iron-bearing rock, the rock is shattered by blasting. The shattered rock is then taken to a rod and ball mill where it is ground into a very fine powder so that the iron ore and silica particles are separate grains. This releases the iron ore from the original sedimentary rock layers.

If the iron ore is magnetic, as it is in Minnesota, it can be gathered by magnets from the crushed rock. However, most of Michigan's iron ore is of a nonmagnetic type called "jasper." The iron particles are secured from the crushed rock by a flotation process in which air bubbled through oil picks out the little pieces of iron ore and leaves the unwanted rock behind. The captured ore is then mixed with a clay binder and then made into pellets about one-half inch in diameter. These pellets are then heated to 2,450 degrees in a long rotary kiln and thus dried and hardened.

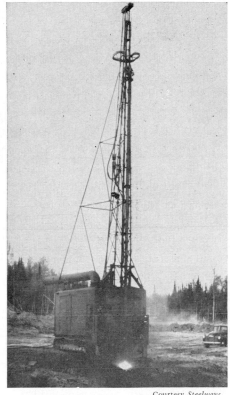

Courtesy *Steelways*

This is a picture of the jet piercer that is now used to make blasting holes in the hard low grade ore beds. It cuts much faster than a diamond drill.

High concentrate ore, about 60 per cent, is thus secured and formed into small balls, called pellets, about the size of pecan nuts that can be charged into a furnace. The pellets are then shipped to the ore dock and loaded into one of the ore carriers. In 1948, the first pig iron was made by using only these man-made concentrated pellets.

In Minnesota large sums of money have already been spent in developing taconite processing plants. Here in Michigan this new process is being developed at the Humboldt mine, the Republic mine, and the Empire mine, all of which are in Marquette County where the ore lends itself best to beneficiation. The Humboldt mine

This is an aerial view of the Humboldt Mine near Champion, which was the first beneficiation operation in the Lake Superior District. The first two buildings on the left contain crushing facilities which are used to reduce the physical size of the ore. The central building contains equipment which further pulverizes the ore and then separates the iron mineral from the worthless material. The building at the right is the pelletizing plant where the beneficiated ore or concentrate is agglomerated into hard, durable balls of one-half-inch size for shipment and use in the blast furnaces.

and the Republic mine use a flotation process whereas the Empire mine uses magnetic separation. One other plant is located on the Menominee range. Michigan's plants will have a combined capacity of producing about three and a half million tons of high-grade concentrate each year.

As yet no beneficiation plant has been built on the Gogebic range. Here the steep dip in the iron formation, some 68 degrees, the many faults in the earth's structure, and the fact that the ore is fine grained, creates peculiar characteristics that will have to be overcome if ore from this district is used.

To secure the low-grade iron ore bearing rock open pit mines can be utilized and the expense of deep shaft mining is not necessary. Labor costs are reduced because only one man is needed in an open pit mine to five in a shaft mine. This reduces labor costs. What is more, large power shovels and huge trucks can be used in open pit mines and the expense of hoisting and hoisting machinery are not necessary. Once the pellets have been produced this type of high concentrated iron ore, about sixty per cent, is free from water and other unwanted silicates. This reduces bulk and thus lessens shipping costs. When the pellets reach the blast furnaces they are more usable than the raw ore.

Courtesy *Steelways*, published by American Iron and Steel Inst.
Rod mills at Ishpeming

The steel companies have not only opened new mines in Canada but they are also spending millions on new plants for processing the ore there. By 1970, if present plans are carried out, the Lake Superior area will be producing about thirty-four million tons of concentrate while Canada will be supplying about forty-seven million tons of concentrated iron ore. Pellets are not only being produced in Michigan and Minnesota but in a number of other areas, including New York and Pennsylvania. Plants are now being constructed in Missouri, Wyoming, and California.

Just how the use of low-grade beneficiated ores will affect the mining areas of Michigan and Minnesota remains to be seen. Most of the answer to this problem lies in the cost of production compared to that of foreign ores. It is now an expensive process to produce taconite pellets. Vast new deposits of iron ore have been located in the Ungava district of Labrador. Railroads, some three hundred and fifty miles long, have been built across the hard old Canadian Shield from ports on the St. Lawrence River to the new mines that have been developing in the area. High-grade Canadian iron ore is now

**A large freighter, down bound, about to leave the MacArthur Lock.
Photo August, 1963.**

coming south in ore cars to the St. Lawrence River. Some of it is
being shipped to Atlantic seacoast ports. The new St. Lawrence
Waterway now makes it possible for ore carriers to bring this rich
Canadian iron ore from Canada to the furnaces south of Lake Erie.
Another vast deposit of high-grade iron ore has been discovered in
Venezuela, in South America. Ore from Venezuela, as well as Africa,
is being shipped to the United States.

Although taconite pellets are expensive to produce they do possess
some advantages over the natural ores. Less waste material has to be
shipped to the blast furnaces. Pellets of desired minerals can be
prepared before they are smelted. By using taconite pellets some
steel companies have been able to raise their furnace output almost
100 per cent above production when using the older natural ores.
This is a great saving when new furnaces to increase production cost
several million dollars. Furnaces using pellets also require less coke
to melt the ore and slag.

It now requires about 420 pounds less iron ore in a blast furnace
and about 520 pounds less of coke, as well as less limestone, to
produce a net ton of pig iron than it did in 1947. This use of less
materials results in less tonnage having to be carried in lake commerce.

Vast as were the copper deposits the bright mineral could not
be mined forever. By 1913, Michigan had fallen to third place
among the states as a copper producer. From its peak year, in 1916,

Michigan's copper production has gradually declined as one mine after the other ceased operating. In 1954, only 44,786,803 pounds of copper were produced. The known copper deposits are far from being exhausted but the cost of mining copper has now caused nearly all of the older copper mines to cease operating. Abandoned shaft houses, water-filled mines, rusting machinery, deserted homes, and villages declining in population mark the sites of former, once prosperous copper mining communities just as they do in the areas where iron ore was once produced.

Copper production in Michigan, although only three companies are now producing, has shown a slight increase during the last few years. In 1961, Michigan produced 115,438,537 pounds of copper. Of this, 75,142,046 pounds came from the new White Pine Mine, which is located just north of Bergland at the southern end of the copper range. This mine is now Michigan's largest producer of copper. The ore taken from this mine, however, is not the native copper taken from the older copper mines. Here the copper occurs as small grains of native copper or as a copper sulphide (chalcocite) found in the siltstone and nonesuch shale beds. To extract this copper takes new techniques and different equipment than earlier copper mining. To extract the copper the rock has to be very finely ground. Then by means of a floatation process, and other refining techniques, the copper is collected and the sulphur removed. The finished product is 99.98 per cent pure with about twentyfive to thirty-eight ounces of silver per ton of copper.

The present White Pine Mine is a near-surface mine. It produces about 16,000 tons of 1.1 per cent copper ore a day and is now

Courtesy White Pine Copper Company

Aerial view of the White Pine mine site looking northwest. This mine is now Michigan's largest copper producer. Photo 1963.

the largest copper mine east of the Rocky Mountains. Its annual production is between 75 and 100 million pounds. New drillings on

Courtesy White Pine Copper Company

Molten White Pine copper being poured, in ingot form, into molds mounted on the casting wheel. When the ingots have cooled they are ready for shipment.

the southwest ore body, about two miles west of the present mine, show a new copper deposit some 2,000 feet below the surface. This layer, eight to fifteen feet thick, is much richer than the one now being worked, and will yield twenty-five pounds of copper per ton. This bed seems to run from the top of the Keweenaw Peninsula to Mellen, Wisconsin. If this ore body is later developed it will have to be mined through a vertical shaft and this will increase the cost of production. At the present time a nineteen-foot circular shaft has been sunk down to the ore body.

During the past twenty years, many test borings with diamond drills have proven that much copper still remains in the Copper Range, but what the future of the copper towns will be is still uncertain. Copper at present can be more cheaply produced from the low-grade ores dug in the open-pit mines of the West than it can be from Michigan's deep shaft mines. Copper is also being imported from Chile and Africa where it can be more cheaply secured than by being mined here in the state. At present a few of the older mining companies are still reworking the tailings that were thrown out many years ago when it was more difficult to crush the rock. New processes of crushing the rock now make it possible to reclaim copper from rock once discarded as useless. Much of this discarded tailings is being raised from the bottom of Torch Lake near Calumet.

A new deposit of conglomerate copper, known as the Kingston lode, has been opened between the old Allouez and Kearsarge mines. It is being worked by the Calumet and Hecla Company. When this mine gets into operation it will boost Michigan's copper production above the present figures.

There are several small industrial plants in the Upper Peninsula. Axes, gun sights, compasses, furniture, lift trucks, excavators, deck machinery for ocean liners, gym flooring, and paper products are all manufactured.

With our greatly expanding population there is a growing need for outdoor recreation areas. With our improved modern highways the entire Upper Peninsula can become an all-year-around recreation area for the thousands of people that live in the southern part of the state and in the Chicago area.

One of the greatest remaining resources of the Upper Peninsula is its vacation and recreational potential. Here are vast state and national forests that provide multiple uses; such as, space for timber growth, wood products, serving as wild life habitat by providing food for ducks and geese, rabbits, partridges, deer, and other animals, for hunting and fishing areas, for camping and canoeing, as well as income from their forest products. Besides the state and national forests, there are several state parks, some 4,300 inland lakes, 150 pretty waterfalls, many of which have not as yet been made available to tourists and vacationers, 1,723 miles of Great Lakes shoreline, the rocky remains of the old Killarney Mountains which can be seen in the Huron Mountains, the Keweenaw Peninsula, and the Porcupine Mountains. There are also abandoned mines and sites of once prosperous mining communities. The "Soo" canal, the Pictured Rocks, and the big spring near Manistique, and Lake Superior, are also tourist attractions. Then, too, there are many

Courtesy Modern Portrait Studio, Ironwood

Presque Isle Falls on the Big Presque Isle River north of Wakefield. Many pretty waterfalls like this one are found in the western part of the Upper Peninsula.

pretty streams that wind their way through forest lands and often tumble over the rocky formations as pretty waterfalls as they approach Lake Superior. The heavier snows and more constant cold of winter

The beginning of Yondota Falls north of Marenisco. Photo 1962.

also makes this peninsula a good winter sports recreation area for many people who come north each winter from Wisconsin and the Chicago area.

Because of its location there has been little commerce between the two peninsulas. Most of the tourists, especially those that come to the western part, come from the Chicago area. Until recently the Upper Peninsula has carried all the east and west auto traffic of Canada. But with the recent opening of two highways north of Lake Superior, Canadian cross-continent traffic can now pass across the Canadian Shield north of Lake Superior. Some Canadian east-west railroad traffic still passes across the Upper Peninsula.

People coming to the Upper Peninsula usually enter it by way of one of four cities: Ironwood, Menominee, Sault Ste. Marie, or St. Ignace. Many people visiting the Upper Peninsula cross over to St. Ignace from Mackinaw City. From 1921 to 1957, the State Highway Department ran auto ferries across the Straits of Mackinac and all auto and truck traffic used these ferries. In November, 1957, the new Mackinac Bridge, one of the largest bridges in the world, was opened to auto traffic and the auto ferries ceased to run. Today, auto and truck traffic quickly passes from one peninsula to the other.

The Eastern Part of the Upper Peninsula

The eastern part of the Upper Peninsula is flat or gently rolling land. Like the upper half of the Lower Peninsula, it is a land of mixed soils and suited to agriculture in only local areas. Most of it is sandy plains, swamps, or marshlands. On much of the sandy soils there once grew spreading stands of pines that drew timber cruisers to the Upper Peninsula. For a few years this area was a busy lumber center, but when the forests were gone the people moved on to other areas. Just a few years ago this area was a cut-over, burned-over wasteland with scattered farms and declining villages. Today, much of this area is state or national forest land, and new green timber stands are spreading across much of the land. Some of it is still farm land. In the area south of Sault Ste. Marie much hay is grown. Because of the climate few fruit trees are found in the eastern part of the Upper Peninsula.

Between Big Bay de Noc and Munising spreads part of the Hiawatha National Forest. West of Whitefish Bay is the Lake Superior State Forest. South of it is the Mackinac State Forest that touches Lake Michigan from Brevort to Naubinway. South of Whitefish Bay and reaching down to St. Ignace is the other part of the Hiawatha National Forest. For several years this part of the Hiawatha National Forest was called the Marquette National Forest.

Along the south shore of Lake Superior, the Cambrian sandstone, that underlies most of Michigan, comes to the surface. Rivers spilling over this rocky shelf make several waterfalls such as the Tahquamenon Falls. Flowing eastward and northward into Whitefish Bay is the Tahqua-

Miner's Castle northeast of Munising. This is a Cambrian rock formation on the south shore of Lake Superior.

menon River. This river is known as Hiawatha's River. In the Indian language Tahquamenon means "black waters." Before reaching Whitefish Bay the Tahquamenon River, which drains extensive swamps and wooded lands, falls over a Cambrian rock ledge and gives to

Michigan her largest waterfall. There are two falls, the Upper Falls and the Lower Falls. They are about three miles apart. The Upper Falls is a single waterfall and has a drop of some fifty-two feet and a width of two hundred feet.

ST. IGNACE is today one of the major points of entry into the Upper Peninsula. When one visits St. Ignace one sets foot on ground that has been trod by many Indians and famous Frenchmen, for to this place came Marquette, Cadillac, Tonty, Allouez, Joliet, DuLhut and many others when this area was a part of New France. Father Marquette founded his mission at St. Ignace in 1671. St. Ignace, therefore, is the second oldest settlement in Michigan. After Marquette had established his mission, the French became aware of the important location of St. Ignace and soon built a small fort which they named Fort De Buade in honor of Governor Frontenac. Fort De Buade was for a few years the major French outpost in the Great Lakes Area. To this area, called Michilimackinac, came the French voyageurs with their Indian friends in large, bark trading-canoes from across the blue waters of the Straits of Mackinac.

During the lumbering days St. Ignace was a port city for the lumber trade. At one time iron smelters were located here, but they closed down in 1900. Some of the people now living in St. Ignace are descendants of Indians or the early French settlers. For many years some of the people living here were engaged in commercial fishing. Just east of St. Ignace lies Mackinac Island, while farther to the northeast are the pretty Les Cheneaux Islands.

MACKINAC ISLAND is one of Michigan's most beautiful islands. People crossing the straits on the new Mackinac Bridge can get a good view of the island. Mackinac Island, sometimes called "The Fairy Isle," is now a state park and is well known as a summer resort. Because of its historic interest, its beauty, and the fact that it is surrounded by miles of pure water, many people visit the island during the summer and early fall. People wishing to go to the island usually go by ferry from either Mackinac City or St. Ignace.

Automobiles are not allowed on the island. Horse-drawn vehicles are the only means of transportation. Everything is kept just as it was in the days before automobiles. Horse-drawn sight-seeing wagons carry hundreds of tourists to the points of interest on the island each day during the busy summer tourist season. Several hotels care for summer visitors. Only a few people live on the island all year around.

Perhaps the most important tourist attraction on Mackinac Island is old Fort Mackinac which was built by the English at the time of the Revolutionary War. In 1781, the English moved their garrison from the old fort, at what is now Mackinaw City, to their new fort on Mackinac Island. It was this fort that the Americans occupied in 1796 when the island became American. It was here that the English surprised the Americans and captured the fort during the War of 1812.

There are many other points of interest on the island. The Grand Hotel, one of the best-known summer hotels in the country, is located here. For many years Mackinac Island was a fur-trading center, and today the old Astor fur warehouse, with its unusual large wheel for raising and lowering bundles of furs from the first to the second story, stands as a silent reminder of the days when furs were Michigan's major export. The restored Beaumont house keeps fresh in the minds of tourists the work that Dr. Beaumont did in studying the action of the human stomach. Dr. Beaumont was one day called to the fur warehouse to attend a trader who had accidentally been shot in the stomach at close range. When the trader's stomach wound healed a strange flap that never closed made it possible for Dr. Beaumont, for the first time in history, to look into a human stomach and observe the manner in which it functioned. Other points of interest on the island are Arch Rock, Natural Bridge, Sugar Loaf, Skull Cave, Fort Homes, and the oldest Protestant mission still standing in the old Northwest.

NEWBERRY, the largest community in the Tahquamenon Valley, owes its beginning to the iron smelting industry. Because of the immense stands of hardwood in the area iron ore, for smelting, was brought to Newberry by railroad after 1884. Hardwood in the area was burned in the old-type beehive kilns to make charcoal for the Vulcan Furnace Company, that manufactured charcoal pig iron. Limestone from the nearby quarries was used as a flux. The making of charcoal pig iron ceased in 1945 when the hardwood supply in the area gave out. Because of the nature of the forests surrounding Newberry, this community never figured prominently in the white pine lumber area in the Upper Peninsula.

Some logging still continues in the area and is increasing as the new forests mature. There are some farms near the village. At one time this area was known for the production of celery. Today, the Newberry State Hospital, which was started here in 1895, is the largest employer in the community.

From Newberry a hard-surfaced road leads to the Upper and Lower Tahquamenon Falls and from there on to Paradise on White-fish Bay. East of Newberry is Soo Junction. From Soo Junction the "Toonerville Trolley" carries tourists, during the summer and early fall, over an old narrow-gauge railroad through forest lands to the Tahquamenon River. Boats then carry tourists down the Tahquamenon River to the falls. From Hulbert, just east of Soo Junction, the river trip can also be taken. The boats follow the winding river through the forest land of Hiawatha.

Northwest of Newberry on M-77 is Grand Marais. About one mile west of Grand Marais can be found the eastern end of sand dunes that run westward along the southern shore of Lake Superior for about seven miles. A United States Coast Guard station is located here.

West of Newberry, on M-28, is the little village of Seney. During the lumbering days Seney was a busy sawmill town. South and west of Seney is the "Seney Federal Migratory Waterfowl Project." South of Seney, on M-77, is Blaney Park, a well-known summer resort.

Courtesy International Bridge Authority

Sault Ste. Marie International Bridge looking from Canada as it spans the St. Mary's River at the "Soo" Locks. Photo 1962.

SAULT STE. MARIE is located on the St. Mary's River not far from Lake Superior. Before the white man came, this spot was a well-known meeting place for Indians who came here to fish, in the rapids, for whitefish and trout. This area was visited by Frenchmen in 1641, although Etienné Brulé or other fur traders may have been here before that date. In 1668, the Jesuits founded a mission here, and thus Sault Ste. Marie is not only the oldest settlement in Michigan but perhaps the oldest in the northern part of the United States west of the Allegheny Mountains. It was here that Simon Francois Daumont took possssion of the entire Lake Region in the name of the king of France in May, 1671.

In 1823, the Americans built a fort here named Fort Brady. The settlement, however, remained small until the St. Mary's Falls Ship Canal was opened in 1855. Since that time it has grown to be one of the largest communities in the Upper Peninsula. Across the river, in Canada, is Sault Ste. Marie's sister city, Sault Ste. Marie, Ontario. For many years a little ferry ran across the river between the two cities, but on October 31, 1962 a new bridge called the Sault Ste. Marie International Bridge was opened to auto and passenger traffic. A new railroad bridge has also been constructed across the Lake Superior end of the Mac-

For many years little ferries like this one carried all the auto and truck traffic between Sault Ste. Marie, Michigan, and Sault Ste. Marie, Ontario.

Arthur and Poe Locks. It is similar to the new one connecting Houghton and Hancock.

Each year during the shipping season, hundreds of tourists visit the "Soo" locks to see the freighters as they pass through the busy locks. In the daytime one can see the huge lake freighters and ocean ships as they steam slowly along the St. Mary's River. At night their twinkling lights and the deep-pitched blasts from their noisy whistles give a new charm to the river so filled with memories of the days of the French missionaries and fur traders.

Because of the "Soo" locks, the Saint Mary's River area is one of Michigan's most visited places. Many cottages line the nearby shore of Lake Superior and the St. Mary's River, others are located on the large islands in the river. For many years there were small industries located here, but now none of them are left. The hydroelectric power plant formerly operated by the Union Carbide Company, is now municipally owned. It supplies electrical power for the local area and also for the operation of the "Soo" locks. Nearby is Kincheloe air force base. A branch of Michigan Technological University is located in the city.

Sault Ste. Marie, Ontario, across the river, is a larger community with some industries. Here is located a large pulp mill to which comes pulpwood that has been cut on the Canadian Shield. A steel plant is also located here.

DETOUR is a small village located at the far eastern end of the Upper Peninsula on Detour Passage. Detour has been for many years a bunkering port at which passing freighters have refueled. On Drummond Island to the east, across Detour Passage, are dolomite quarries.

MUNISING is located on the south shore of Lake Superior about half way between Sault Ste. Marie and Hancock and Houghton. A completely land-locked harbor provides a good port. Just north of Munising lies Grand Island in Lake Superior.

The Pictured Rocks begin on the south shore of Lake Superior about five miles east of Munising. They extend along the lake in a northeasterly direction for more than twenty-seven miles. These rocks are composed of Cambrian sandstone, and their present formations are the result of the ice action and wave action of Lake Superior. Oxide deposits have stained the rocks many hues that give them their beautiful yellow reddish-brown colors. Each summer hundreds of people take the boat trip from Munising to see these pretty rock formations. Perhaps some day a state park, or national forest, can be made here so that more tourists can enjoy the unusual beauty of the Pictured Rocks.

Near Munising can be found nine waterfalls which are formed by streams spilling over the ancient rocks as they near Lake Superior. Unfortunately, better roads will have to be built nearer to them and better viewing conditions developed before most of the falls will be the tourist attraction to the Munising area that they should be.

Munising produces stationery paper, plastic-coated board, waxpaper, and box and crate material.

MANISTIQUE began in 1860 as a lumber sawmill town and port. From the large spreading forests nearby, pine logs were floated down the Manistique River to the busy sawmills. At one time sawmills, docks, and booms extended several miles along the stream, but by 1900 even the hardwoods had been cut and the sawmills had nearly closed down.

The Seul Choix lighthouse stands at the top of Lake Michigan, near Manistique in the Upper Peninsula, to warn boats coming north on Lake Michigan. Photo 1957.

Northwest of Manistique lies Indian Lake and the big spring, Kitchiti-ki-pi. The Ojibway Indians called this spring "The Mirror of Heaven," "The Evening Star," and "The Boiling Cauldron." Each year many people visit the big spring. A large raft with two open wells in the deck, carries people out onto the surface of the spring. Once over the moving water, one can see through the crystal-clear, cold water to the bottom of the spring and watch the icy water as it comes bubbling up from the sandy bottom.

State forests and the Hiawatha National Forest spread north across the peninsula to the shore of Lake Superior. Today, the remaining timber and the nearby stone deposits form the main basis of local industry.

East of Manistique on the shore of Lake Michigan is Port Inland from which limestone is shipped. There is no community at the port. Most of the workers live in Manistique or Gulliver. Just south of Port Inland is Seul Choix Point, on which stands Seul Choix Lighthouse at the top of Lake Michigan. Southwest of Manistique lies the Garden Peninsula with its pretty Silurian limestone rock formations along the shore of Bay de Noc. Here at Fayette is located one of Michigan's latest and most attractive state parks. At one time the old charcoal furnace located here was used to smelt iron ore.

The Western Part of the Upper Peninsula

The western part of the Upper Peninsula is higher and rockier than the eastern part. Most of the land is covered by glacial till, but underneath, near the surface of the land, are the remains of the old Killarney Mountains from which have come vast quantities of iron ore and copper. The highest point in the state is in the Huron Mountains northeast of L'Anse where the elevation reaches up to a height of 1,978 feet above sea level. West of the Keweenaw Peninsula lie other highlands known as the Porcupine Mountains.

Much of the land is still covered by hardwood forests and some coniferous trees. Some sections, especially in the south from Iron Mountain and Gladstone south to Menominee, have developed into dairy regions, but the major industries of this part of the Upper Peninsula are still mining and lumbering. From Iron River north to Lake Superior spreads the huge Ottawa National Forest, the largest national forest in Michigan. Many pretty lakes, the largest of which is Lake Gogebic, the largest lake in the Upper Peninsula, are scattered throughout this area.

MENOMINEE is on Green Bay at the mouth of the Menominee River. When the French first came to the area they found the Pottawattomie Indians living in the area. About 1650 they moved to southwestern Michigan. When they left, the Menominees moved into the area. The Menominees left the area in 1854 and are now living near the Wolf River in Wisconsin. What few Indians there are in the area are again mostly Pottawattomies. The Indian word Menominee means "wild rice." During the Indian days this area was well known for its wild rice and good fishing.

The Green Bay area was important in the fur trade for many years as it lay along the Fox-Wisconsin River route to the Mississippi and the West. In 1832, the first sawmill was built and not long afterwards the Menominee River was used for driving logs to the mills. For some time Menominee was a leading sawmill town. In 1871, Menominee was partly damaged by the tragic Peshtigo fire that did so much damage in Wisconsin. The last log drive in Michigan was on the Menominee River in 1910. The Menominee River for some distance forms the boundary between Michigan and Wisconsin. Menominee lies just a little above the 45° parallel. Across the River is Menominee's twin city, Marinette, Wisconsin. Menominee is the most southerly city in the Upper Peninsula. Because of its location it is a meeting place of roads, railroads, and lake shipping. It is one of the western terminals for the Ann Arbor Railroad car ferries. Menominee is the natural distribution center for much of the Upper Peninsula.

One of the first industries located here was the making of charcoal for the iron furnaces. As the forest declined Menominee turned to making furniture, paper, boxes, containers, boats, paper board, and wood products. The adjoining farm land produces a large yield of high-grade potatoes. Menominee also produces sawmill machinery, maple flooring, and dairy products.

ESCANABA takes its name from an Indian word which means "The land of the Red Buck." Escanaba is favored by a splendid location on Little Bay de Noc. Not only is it located on one of the best natural deep-water harbors on the Great Lakes, but it is also at the intersection of two highways, US-2 and US-41.

Lumbermen, looking for pine, came to Escanaba as early as 1830. For many years it was a lumber center, but in 1864 it became an iron port when iron ore from the mines of the Marquette range began coming to the port. Escanaba and Marquette are the two iron ports of Michigan.

For some time Escanaba was called the "Bird's-Eye Maple Veneer Capital of the World." This industry was made possible by the fact that nearly all the world's supply of bird's-eye maple was located within one hundred miles of this city. Escanaba is also the home of the Upper Peninsula State Fair. This fair was started in 1928. It is held near the last of August each year. The usual agricultural displays, livestock exhibits, horse-pulling contests, 4-H Club contests, together with birling contests, and other forms of entertainment make the Upper Peninsula State Fair an outstanding attraction for Escanaba.

Escanaba manufactures truck cranes, paper, paper boxes, bird's-eye veneer, and fencing. Dairying is the chief source of agricultural income. On the farms nearby potatoes are grown for the Milwaukee and Chicago market. Many peas and snap beans are also grown.

GLADSTONE is just north of Escanaba. It was founded in 1887. Once it was a lumber town. It is now a woodworking center making hardwood flooring, veneer, and plywood. Hunting and sports equipment are also manufactured.

IRON MOUNTAIN was an iron mining and sawmill town. With the discovery of iron ore on the Menominee range, the Chapin Mine made Iron Mountain a booming town after 1879. Today, most of the nearby timber is gone and so is the high-grade iron ore. The deep underground mines have nearly all closed. Today, Iron Mountain is an industrial town making engineering equipment, gray iron castings, equipment for ocean going and lake steamers, such as the "Siporter" which is used to load and unload ships through their side, mine transport units, and sportswear. Nearby are the scenic attractions of

Fumee Falls, Shultz's Rapids, and Piers Gorge in the Menominee River.

Here at Iron Mountain, on Pine Mountain, is located the highest all-artificial ski scaffold in the world. The tower is 156 feet high. Iron Mountain is a winter sports center. Every winter a ski tournament is held. The present distance record is 316 feet—made by Jim Brennan in 1960.

KINGSFORD is a very close neighbor of Iron Mountain. In 1921, Mr. Henry Ford began buying forest lands near Iron Mountain to get timber to make station-wagon bodies. For some time the Ford Motor Company operated a sawmill and chemical plant at Kingsford. The Ford Motor Company sold its holdings at Kingsford in 1951. The plant is now used to make charcoal briquettes. East of Iron Mountain and Kingsford lie the former mining towns of Norway, Vulcan, Loretto, and Quinnesec. Quinnesec is the oldest village on the Menominee range.

IRON RIVER developed after the discovery of iron ore in the nearby region in 1851. Because of the low quality of the iron ore, lumbering for several years remained the major industry. Northwest of Iron River on US-2, on the west side of Golden Lake, is Camp Filibert Roth, the University of Michigan School of Forestry and Conservation. Near Iron River are located the mining centers of Mineral Falls, Stambaugh, Caspian, Gaastra, and Crystal Falls. Farther west of Iron River on US-2, in a heavily forested area, is Watersmeet. From this point the run-off water drains into Lake Michigan, Lake Superior, or the Mississippi River.

IRONWOOD is located farther to the west on the far western edge of Michigan where US-2 crosses over into Wisconsin. It is the largest of several mining towns located on the Gogebic range. Mining was begun here in 1885. Because of the deep shafts in the steeply tilted mines, very expensive machinery was necessary and much underground tunneling was required. The first iron ore from this region went to Erie, Pennsylvania, by way of railroad to Milwaukee, Wisconsin. In 1885, the Milwaukee Lake Shore and Western extended its line to Ashland, Wisconsin, and completed an ore dock at Ashland. After that date all ore from the area moved to Ashland, Wisconsin. By 1965, all the mines on the Gogebic Range had ceased production except the Peterson Mine.

Ironwood is a wholesale center for the area. Some lumber is still produced. Many pretty waterfalls, that are attracting more and more tourists each year, are found along the Black and Presque Isle Rivers as they flow over the rocky area toward Lake Superior. West across the Montreal River is Hurley, Wisconsin.

East of Ironwood are the old mining centers of Bessemer, Ramsey, and Wakefield on the Gogebic Range. At Bessemer, woodworking plants make varied products. At Wakefield one can see the large open pit Plymouth Mine, that is now abandoned and partly filled with water.

Iron ore dock at Marquette. Notice the ore cars on top of the dock and the ore carrier being loaded. Photo 1947.

MARQUETTE, one of the largest cities in the Upper Peninsula, is located on a good harbor on Lake Superior. It became a village in 1859 and was named after the French missionary Father Marquette who had visited the region nearly two centuries before.

Marquette's location on Lake Superior makes it a natural shipping center. For over a hundred years the red iron ore from the nearby mines at Ishpeming and Negaunee has come to its ore docks. When the opening of the St. Mary's Falls Ship Canal made it possible to ship iron ore direct to the lower port cities, the little trickle of ore that had found its way to the port at Marquette on wagons and sleighs greatly increased in volume. Railroad cars were soon bringing the ore to the dock by the trainload. Each shipping season, some iron ore still goes rumbling down the huge chutes of the ore docks into the empty holds of waiting freighters. There are two huge ore docks at Marquette. The dock of the South Shore Railroad is in the lower harbor while the dock of the Lake Superior and Ishpeming Railroad is in the Upper Harbor. Today, these huge docks can load about 20,000 tons of iron ore into one of the huge ore boats in a few hours. To this port also come each year a half million tons of coal from the coal fields south of Lake Erie. During the winter season a heavy snowfall covers the area and Lake Superior freezes, but with the coming of spring another shipping season begins.

Marquette is also a college town. Here is located Northern Michigan University. Some of the older buildings are made of Brownstone that was quarried at L'Anse in 1914. Presque Isle public park is a local tourist attraction. Here at Marquette is also located the Upper Peninsula branch of the Michigan State Prison. This prison cares for about eight hundred prisoners. The Cliffs Dow Chemical Company, a branch of the Dow Chemical Company of Midland, is the world's largest producer of charcoal products. Each year over 100,000 cords of wood are used here to make charcoal. Local industries also produce foundry machinery, women's clothing, dairy products, core and diamond drills, and mining machinery.

ISHPEMING and NEGAUNEE are the two oldest mining towns in Michigan. It was here that Mr. Burt's surveyors first discovered iron ore in 1844. Here on the Marquette range has been mined some of the most valuable high-grade iron ore in the world. Both shaft mines and open-pit mines have been operated in this area. The Mather A shaft at Ishpeming is the largest underground iron mine in the United States. Two miles away in Negaunee is the Mather B shaft.

The nearby forests are still being lumbered. The snowfall here is very heavy, and this community has become a winter sports center. Ishpeming's ski jump, "suicide hill," is the scene of an annual ski meet held by the National Ski Association.

Just west of Ishpeming and Negaunee is Humboldt, where a plant has been built to make taconite pellets. Farther west are Champion, Lake Michigamme, and the old mining center of Michigamme. To the north are the Huron Mountains that so far have not been crossed by a state highway.

L'ANSE is located at the southern end of Keweenaw Bay. The Celotex Corporation has a large automated and mechanized plant here to make fiberboard. This plant uses large quantities of pulp-wood that is cut in the nearby area. Just south of L'Anse, at Alberta, is located the Ford Forestry Center that is run by Michigan Technological University. South of Alberta, where M-41 crosses the Sturgeon River, is Bacco Falls and Gorge where the Sturgeon River cuts into quartzite rock formed during the Huronian Period.

Courtesy Celotex Corporation

L'Anse Plant of the Celotex Corporation. Note the piles of pulpwood on the right side of the picture and the forest area on the upper part. It is from the vast forest areas of the Upper Peninsula that the supply of pulpwood comes. Photo 1962.

BARAGA is named after Bishop Baraga who did parish work among the whites and missionary work among the Indians about a hundred years ago. Baraga County once produced slate and brownstone. It was formerly a lumbering area with mills at L'Anse, Baraga, Skanee, and Pequaming.

THE KEWEENAW PENINSULA, known as the "Copper County" because of the many copper mines that were once worked in this area, juts northward some seventy-five miles into the largest freshwater body in the world. Because it was once part of the Killarney Mountains it is one of Michigan's most scenic areas. Much of the coast line is rocky and pounded by the waves of Lake Superior.

Good highways run through the forests that still cover most of the rocky land. At the top of the peninsula is the restored Fort Wilkins. Brockway Mountain Drive runs along the crest of a hard old mountain ridge. From the turn-out near Copper Harbor one can look far out across the deep-blue water of Lake Superior and often see in the distance a smudgy plume of smoke from a freighter as it pushes slowly across the lake with a cargo of wheat or iron ore.

To this land once came Indians to mine the copper ore from

the hard old rocks. Some of their mining pits can still be found. Later others came to mine the bright shiny metal. Between 1850 and 1900, many copper mines could be found along the Copper Range of the Keweenaw Peninsula where copper was being brought from deep under the ground. Today, only three or four of these old copper mines are still in operation. As one drives throughout the peninsula one now passes many old abandoned mines and mining villages now marked only by signboards to point out to the traveler the sites of the once busy copper mining days when Michigan supplied the nation with much of its copper.

HOUGHTON and HANCOCK are twin cities, each one standing on one of the steep hillsides along Portage Lake. These are two old copper mining centers. Today, one can still see some of the old shaft houses where copper ore was taken from the now abandoned copper mines that spread deep down under the two cities.

Courtesy Michigan State Highway Department

The new Houghton-Hancock Bridge. The ore carrier "Norman W. Fay" is shown passing under the bridge as she passes along the Portage Lake Ship Canal. The bridge is in its highest position. Photo 1961.

Before it was abandoned the Quincy Mine, at Hancock, had a shaft 9,400 feet deep. This was the equivalent of a 6,400-foot vertical shaft and at that time it was one of the deepest mines in the world. The Mesnard shaft went down to the fifty-three level. The Quincy, Pontiac, and Mesnard Mines, like many of the shaft iron and copper mines, opened into one another at one or more points. The combined passageways in the Mesnard, Pontiac, and Quincy Mines total almost 200 miles. Today, these mines are used as a source of water for the Hancock area.

Between the two cities runs the Portage Lake Ship Canal. Crossing the Portage Lake Ship Canal, between the cities of Houghton and Hancock, is the new Portage Lake Bridge that was built in 1958-1959 to replace the older bridge across Portage Lake. It is the world's widest and heaviest lift span and replaces the old swing bridge that for fifty-four years carried all traffic going to and from the Keweenaw Peninsula. The new bridge carries all railroad, automobile, and pedestrian traffic between Houghton to Hancock. Some 7,000 tons of steel and 35,000 tons of concrete went into its construction. The lower level carries railroad traffic and the upper level carries pedestrian and automobile traffic. It has three positions. When completely lowered, the bridge provides for both rail and auto traffic. When raised to its second position, a rise of thirty-two feet so that small water craft can pass, auto traffic uses the lower part of the span on which are the railroad rails. When large freighters pass, the bridge must be raised to its highest position and all auto and rail traffic must stop.

From Houghton one can now take the new, fast motor ship, Ranger III, to Isle Royale. This new, fast motor ship leaves Houghton each morning, during the tourist season, and returns from the island each evening. Each year more and more vacationers are crossing over to Isle Royale to visit our nation's only island park to enjoy its rugged rocky shore line, its herd of moose, its many pretty bays and lakes, and its natural forests which, except for forest fires, have been untouched by man. Many people visit Isle Royale each summer to see the ancient copper pits from which the early Indians once took copper. In some of these ancient pits one can still find the old stone hammers with which the prehistoric miners pounded the pieces of rock to free the copper.

At Houghton is located Michigan Technological University. Near Hancock, at Ripley, tourists can now visit an old copper mine. South of Houghton are the copper mining towns of South Range and Painesdale.

CALUMET and LAURIUM were once important copper mining cities. Here one of the richest strikes on the copper range was made. Farther north are the little villages of Eagle Harbor, Eagle River, and Copper Harbor. Greenland, Mass, and Rockland are now small villages standing on the south end of the Copper Range. In this area were located the Mass and Minesota Mines. Some Indian pits and stone hammers can still be found in the area. Between 1850 and 1860 most of the copper mined in this area was shipped from Ontonagon.

ONTONAGON is on the south shore of Lake Superior at the mouth of the Ontonagon River. It was from this river that the Ontonagon Boulder was raised. Here also the first copper mine in the Upper Peninsula was started by Alexander Henry. Much copper from the mines to the southeast once passed through Ontonagon. West of Ontonagon is Silver City at the mouth of the Big Iron River. This village was the center of the silver mining activity of the early 1870's. South of it today is the White Pine Mine, which is now Michigan's largest copper producer, and Lake Gogebic, the largest lake in the Upper Peninsula. From Silver City the highway, running along the pretty shore of Lake Superior, leads west to the Porcupine Mountains. Much of this area is still covered with virgin forests.

Today, the Upper Peninsula is a changing land. Its future economic development lies in its increasing forest products, its jasper, its vast areas of copper bearing shales, and in its ability to develop its many scenic, historic, and recreational possibilities to attract tourists and vacationers. Automation in the forest and mining industries will not require as large a labor force as in the past but the income to those that work in the Upper Peninsula should become as high as those employed in other areas of the state.

CHAPTER TWENTY

The Northern Part of the Lower Peninsula

THE NORTHERN part of the Lower Peninsula in many ways is similar to the eastern part of the Upper Peninsula. Both are areas of sandy glacial till, of extensive swamp lands, and areas of cooler climates.

Sixty years ago the upper part of the Lower Peninsula was a land of dying lumber towns and burned over waste lands. The hundreds of lakes and many miles of streams were seldom visited because it was not easy for people to get to them. Today, this area is covered by new second growth trees that have taken their stand in the old cut-over areas. These forest stands now cover about 70 per cent of the land in the upper part of the Lower Peninsula and are similar to those found in the Upper Peninsula, but a larger percentage of pine trees are found in this area.

Because much of this area is occupied by the High Plains Area little farming is done. The soil in much of the area is a porous glacial till lacking in proper mineral content. Because of the altitude there are less frost-free days and this also limits crop production.

Since 1900, this area has developed into a resort area and today the tourist industry is the largest general industry in this part of the state and in the Upper Peninsula. Each year hundreds of people come to the area between the three cities of Bay City, Muskegon, and Mackinaw City for their vacations. The short distance to this area, together with our improved highways, from the southern part of the state and in northern Ohio, Indiana, and Illinois, where millions of people live, makes it possible for many of these people to spend a week end here or to come for all the summer.

Seventy years ago only wealthy people took vacations and visited the newly developed resorts in northern Michigan. In those days their personal things were carefully packed into a large trunk or two. Then the trunks were taken by a horse-drawn dray to the village depot. The vacationers then took a train to a northern resort hotel that was usually a large wooden building with wide porches on which sat many easy chairs. The hotel stood near one of the larger lakes and not far from the railroad tracks. Once there, there was little for the vacationers to do and hardly any place for them to go, for as yet there were no automobiles or good roads. Many sat on the cool front porch and rocked and visited with the other guests. Some played croquet or tennis. Others walked through the village or along the beach. Some went swimming, or bathing as they called it—that is, if they were properly clothed in a long heavy bathing suit. Only a few of the hardy ventured closer to nature and went camping overnight or for a few days.

Today, all this has changed. Only a few of these old resort hotels remain. Some burned and others were wrecked. Trains carry few

Courtesy Michigan State Highway Department

US-10 Freeway between Midland and Clare. Bridge carries freeway over Sanford Lake.

passengers in northern Michigan. In fact there are only a few passenger trains that run in this area. The recent changes in transportation and hours of work have had much effect on the northern part of the Lower Peninsula and on the Upper Peninsula. Men do not work as many hours a day as they did sixty years ago. Many workers are now given one, two, or three weeks vacation each year. Because of our modern roads and automobiles many people spend their free time in traveling or at a summer vacation area. Trunks, to the modern tourist, are as out of date as the old one-horse dray that pulled them to the village station sixty years ago.

Automobiles make it possible for many people to get away from the cities, even on week ends. All year long, especially on week ends, hundreds of automobiles speed along good highways carrying people to Michigan's vacation lands. In the spring they visit the area to pick mushrooms, see the spring flowers, and new growth on the trees. During the summer they swim, water ski, canoe, fish and enjoy the cooler weather. In the fall they come to hunt and see the pretty colors of the autumn leaves. In the winter they come to ski and toboggan. Many new motels, cottages, ski lodges, and resorts care for the vacationers.

Along the shore of the many lakes and along the banks of the many clear, cold streams that run down from the High Plains Area to the Great Lakes now stand hundreds of cottages and cabins where people spend their vacations. These cottages, cabins, motels, and ski lodges have greatly increased the taxable property of the area and replaced the economic loss that followed the passing of the forests. Vacationers also spend much money in the area. This money passes from person to person and helps bring better economic conditions to communities that were declining after the timber was cut. In this area there are many state parks and camping grounds. There are also many summer camps for boys and girls. Some of these camps are privately owned. Others are run by church groups, Boy or Girl Scout organizations, the Y.W.C.A. or the Y.M.C.A.

The Saginaw-Bay City Area

This area for many years was the homeland of the Sauk Indians. When settlers moved into the area, the Saginaw River Valley became one of Michigan's leading lumber and salt producing areas. After the forests had been cleared from the land, many of the lumbermen who had saved money from the lumber industry invested it in the fertile farm land they found in the Saginaw River Valley.

The Saginaw River Valley, and the adjoining Thumb area, forms a low lying plain. Much of it is sandy soil or sandy loam free from stones. This valley is today one of Michigan's best farming areas. It is often spoken of as "The Garden Spot of Michigan." Navy beans, of which Michigan produces about ninety per cent of all that are grown in the United States, wheat, corn, sugar beets, oats, hay, and vegetables are the major crops raised in this area.

The many small streams that flow into the Saginaw River drain the east central part of the Lower Peninsula. Nearby is Saginaw Bay. The new 24-foot-deep channel in the Saginaw River now makes it possible for larger lake freighters and some ocean ships to reach Bay City and Saginaw, thus making them port cities.

For many years Bay City and Saginaw were busy shipping centers sending out huge quantities of fresh cut lumber and salt to market. Today, these two cities still act as receiving and shipping ports for the area. This is especially true of Bay City. To it come shipments of steel, coal, limestone, gasoline, and fuel oil that are used in the nearby area.

Near Freeland is a large airport which serves the three cities of Bay City, Midland, and Saginaw. Delta College, a two-year college, makes it possible for college students living in the Bay City, Saginaw, Midland area to get the first two years of their college education.

BAY CITY lies near the mouth of the Saginaw River. For many years it was a busy sawmill center. When the local supply of timber had been cut, hardwood for many years was shipped into the city to keep the sawmills running; but, as the timber slowly disappeared, Bay City took on a more general industrial character. One of its earliest and best known industries was the manufacturing of bicycles. Bay City now produces railroad equipment, steel cranes, magnesium castings, electric furnaces, welding machines, power shovels, wood products, and cement. From its earliest days, Bay City had been a ship-building center. Today, the Defoe Shipyards produce guided missile carriers for the United States Navy. One hundred fifty-four ships were made here for the navy during World War II. The local sugar beet refinery is the largest east of the Mississippi River. Meat packing plants process meat that has been produced in the Saginaw Valley and on the farms lying farther to the north. The Dow Chemical Company has a large plant located here that manufactures a variety of products, one of which is Handi-Wrap. Crude oil is the main raw material. Some of this crude oil comes from Michigan, but Canadian Oil is also obtained from the Canadian pipe line that comes down from Edmonton to Sarnia. Bay City is also a large retail and whole-sale trading center for people living farther north in the state. A large electrical power plant supplies electricity for the local area.

The nearby, sandy shore of Saginaw Bay provides an excellent setting for cottages, and camping grounds. Many people from the southern part of the state come to this area each summer season.

SAGINAW means the "Land of the Sauks" and thus derives its name from the Sauk Indians that once lived in the Saginaw River Valley. It lies up the Saginaw River about ten miles inland from Saginaw Bay.

In 1816, Louis Campeau built a fur trading post here. It was Mr. Campeau's friendship with the Indians that helped Governor Cass make the Treaty of Saginaw with the Indians at Saginaw, in 1819. In 1822, the United States Government built a small fort on the west side of the river. In 1834, a Mr. Todd built an inn and began running a ferry across the Saginaw River. In that same year, Mr. Harvey Williams built the first sawmill in the Saginaw Valley.

At first there were two communities, Saginaw City on the west side of the river and East Saginaw on the east side of the river. For about twenty years, there was much rivalry between the two communities. Finally, in 1889, the two cities united to form the present city of Saginaw.

Because of the vast pine forests that stood along the banks of the Saginaw River, and its many smaller tributaries, Saginaw, like Bay City, was a leading lumber producer from 1840 to 1885. But, by 1885 the pine in the river valley was almost gone, and Saginaw turned to cutting hardwood and manufacturing articles made from it. This hardwood was brought to the Saginaw-Bay City area from the northern part of the state on the new railroads that were beginning to play their part in log transportation.

During the lumbering era, Saginaw was also a producer of salt. Today, this brine is used to produce magnesium and other items. For some years, coal mining in the nearby area was a major occupation, but today all of the coal mines have ceased operation. No commercial coal has been mined since 1946. Now only local non-commercial mines are used. Oil and natural gas are produced in the Birch Run area.

Today, Saginaw is a city of many industries that produce many different products. General Motors Corporation has plants here that produce parts for General Motors cars. The Lufkin Rule Company is well known for its manufacture of rulers and other measuring devices. Because of the large crop of beans that is grown in the Saginaw Valley and the Thumb area, the largest bean elevator in the world is located here. This consists of 36 silos for storing grain and edible beans. The combined silo capacity is two and one half million

A train load of gypsum at Alabaster. Photo 1957.

bushels. Ships can be loaded at the rate of 40,000 bushels an hour. About one-third of the nation's bean crop is handled at Saginaw. Saginaw also has one of the largest county fairs to be found in the state. Saginaw's water supply now comes from Lake Huron. To get this pure water, a huge pipe, sixty-two miles long, was constructed.

The Eastern Side of the Upper Part of the Lower Peninsula

Just north of Bay City the good soil of the Saginaw River Valley changes to sand and swampland. Most of the upper half of the Lower Peninsula is a land of light soils. Farms are scattered throughout the

At Alabaster gypsum is carried off shore to the loading dock in these buckets. From the dock it is carried in freighters to plants where it is made into plaster and plasterboard. Photo 1957.

area on the better soils, but most of the land is forest land. In the area along the shore of Lake Huron from Bay City to Cheboygan are many old sawmill towns. Today, limestone and gypsum form the basis of the major industries. Gypsum is shipped by boat from Alabaster and East Tawas. At both Alabaster and National City gypsum is quarried. One railroad, the Detroit and Mackinaw, passes through this area. It runs along the shore of Lake Huron.

TAWAS CITY, EAST TAWAS, AU SABLE, and OSCODA were once sawmill towns. Au Sable and Oscoda, at the mouth of the Au Sable River, cut and shipped more than a million board feet of lumber. But when the logs stopped coming down the river, the twin towns declined. In 1911, a forest fire swept in upon the towns. It took several lives and burned most of the buildings.

West of Oscoda on a high bluff on the Au Sable River, at an old rollway where pine logs once went splashing into the river, now stands the Lumberman's Memorial which is dedicated to the memory of the lumbermen who once made Michigan a leading lumber producer. It is composed of three figures: a riverman holding a peavey in his hand, a woodsman holding an ax and a crosscut saw, and a land looker, or timber cruiser, studying his map.

Today, dams on the Au Sable River, owned by the Consumers Power Company, produce electric power for the nearby area and for cities farther to the south.

ALPENA is the largest community in the northeastern part of the Lower Peninsula. Like the other Michigan port cities it owes its location to a natural, partly land-locked harbor at the mouth of a river. In its early days Alpena was a sawmill town where logs were brought to its sawmills on the Thunder Bay River. In 1887, the Detroit and Mackinaw Railroad reached Alpena. Over this railroad, and later spur lines in the area, hardwoods were brought to the Alpena sawmills.

As the timber supply declined, new occupations based on the local resources were developed. Farmers found the local clay and loam productive and some farms developed. Alpena County now has more farms than any of the other adjoining counties in this part of the state. Hay, potatoes, raspberries, strawberries, and beef cattle are the major products produced on the local farms.

As early as 1886, a pulp mill was built here. During the last few years, with the increase of pulpwood in the upper part of the Lower Peninsula, the plant's capacity for making paper has been greatly increased.

Where once the local forests supplied the main raw material for industry, today the high quality limestone found in the area is the basic raw material for the major local industry, which is the making of cement. Alpena has today the largest cement plant in Michigan and one of the largest in the United States.

Courtesy Huron Portland Cement Company

This picture shows the Huron Portland Cement Company plant at Alpena. This is the largest cement plant in the world. Notice the large quarry back of the plant where the limestone for making the cement is taken from the Devonian limestone layer. Because this layer comes near the surface at this point it is possible to make cement here where it can be shipped by boats operating on the Great Lakes. Photo 1961.

Shipments of limestone from Alpena began as early as 1903. In 1907, the Huron Portland Cement Company began producing cement at Alpena. By 1917, the amount of limestone and cement shipped had reached as high as one million tons a year.

Limestone, for the making of cement, is secured from the Devonian layer that outcrops along the northeastern shore of the Lower Peninsula. The shale that is mixed with the limestone, to make cement, comes from a shale pit about eleven miles away at Paxton. The limestone, shale, and other materials are then fused into cement clinker. This burned clinker is then ground into cement.

At first the cement was bagged and shipped on passenger boats and package freighters. Today, both cement and cement clinker are shipped as bulk cargo. The bulk cement flows into the carrier through round hatches into the cargo hold of the vessel. Cement clinker is shipped to several lake ports; such as, Duluth, Milwaukee, Cleveland, Toledo, Green Bay, and St. Joseph where it is ground into cement at plants located in these places.

During the last few years the Huron Portland Cement Company has deepened and enlarged the shipping channel at its plant so that boats as long as 600 feet and 26 feet deep can load at the new storage silos. These large silos will store as much as 250,000 barrels of cement and the cement can be directly loaded from the silos onto the cement-carrying boats.

The Wyandotte Chemicals Corporation, at Wyandotte, secures much of its limestone from this area. Much limestone is also shipped away to be used in refining iron ore and to make chemical products. North and west of Alpena are some large holes in the ground, called sink holes, that have been leached into the limestone layer.

Alpena is also a recreation center. Nearby are several large lakes: Black Lake, Hubbard Lake, Long Lake, Grand Lake, and Fletcher's Pond. These lakes and many smaller ones, together with the rivers, the shoreline of Lake Huron, and the Alpena State Forest of nearly 24,000 acres, make the Alpena area a busy resort and recreation center. In this entire area, the winter hunting of snowshoe rabbits, fox, and bobcats, has become a major sport.

Alpena manufactures cement block manufacturing machinery, air brakes, hydraulic cylinders, sheet metal, and iron and steel castings. The pine and harwood forests supply material for paper products, insulation, and hardboard. A National Guard Air Force Base is located here and each summer members of this force spend two weeks in training in the area. A community college to care for students in the area is located at Alpena.

To the west are located the former lumber towns of Atlanta and Lewiston. To the northwest lie Millersburg, Onaway, Posen, Metz, and Hawks. All of these towns helped to make Michigan's lumber story. In 1908, when huge forest fires swept this northeastern area, Hawks, Metz, and Posen were completely destroyed. North of Millersburg is the Ocqueoc Falls in the Ocqueoc River. There are two falls a short distance apart. East of Onaway is found Rainy River Falls.

Just northwest of Alpena on the shore of Lake Huron is Rogers City. At Rogers City is a large limestone port known as Calcite. It is one of the largest limestone quarries in the world. Here a high grade limestone is being quarried by Michigan Limestone, a Division of United States Steel Corporation. Limestone quarried here is used in blast furnaces for the smelting of iron ore, and also in chemical industries. Each year several million tons of limestone are shipped from Calcite. This quarry alone supplied about one fourth of the 25 million tons of limestone used by the steel industry in 1961. Limestone is also used in the manufacturing process of many things, such as steel, paper, glass, leather goods, soaps, paints, and in the process

Courtesy Michigan Limestone Division, United States Steel Corporation

Aerial photograph of the Michigan Limestone operations at Rogers City shows a section of the quarry, the largest limestone quarry in the world, the screening plant, storage piles and the loading docks. Viewing stations are provided where visitors can see the quarry operations at one point and the harbor activities at another.

of making beets into sugar. Crushed limestone also acts as a soil sweetener and is used by farmers to improve their land. Some of the limestone quarried in this place is also used in the manufacture of cement at other places along the Great Lakes.

The Northern and Northwestern Cities of the Area

With the passing of the lumber industry, this region turned as early as 1900 into a resort area. Besides the waters of Lake Michigan there were also Grand Traverse Bay, Little Traverse Bay, and many beautiful inland lakes such as Mullett, Burt, Crooked, Walloon, Charlevoix, Torch, and Elk. Railroads, then feeling the decline of the logging era, were pleased to get the new tourist traffic and often ran special trains to resort centers. Three resort centers developed in the northern and northwestern part of the Lower Peninsula. The first one was the area of Mackinaw City and Mackinac Island. The second one was found around Petoskey and the Little Traverse Bay area. The third one that developed in this section was in the Grand Traverse region around Traverse City. The many lakes of this area, the cool breezes from Lake Michigan, the rolling hills with their hardwood forests, and the pretty sunsets all helped to develop this area into one of Michigan's major resort areas.

CHEBOYGAN began in 1845, when Mr. Jacob Sammons brought his family to the area and began making barrels. Before long, it became a busy sawmill town. During its early days, Cheboygan, like all the other sawmill and fishing communities along the shore of the lake, had to be completely supplied by boats carrying freight during the summertime. Where the lakes froze, all of these early communities were cut off from the area "down below."

In 1881, the Michigan Central Railroad, now the New York Central, reached Cheboygan. In 1890, as many as twenty boats at one time were here loading lumber from its nine sawmills. In 1904, the Detroit and Mackinaw Railroad ran its line into Cheboygan.

When the local supply of timber had been cut some timber was rafted to Cheboygan from the Upper Peninsula and from Canada. But, as the supply of timber declined so did the city.

Today, Cheboygan is a resort center. Close by are Black Lake, Mullet Lake, and Burt Lake, as well as several smaller lakes and attractive streams. Hundreds of cottages and summer homes line their banks.

North of Cheboygan lies Bois Blanc Island, which is about five miles wide and twelve miles long. Within the city limits still lies the remains of what was once said to be the world's largest sawdust pile. Southeast of Cheboygan is a large fruit farm of some 600 acres of apple trees and 100 acres of cherry trees. Cherries are also raised in the nearby area.

What is known as the "Inland Water Route" begins here at Cheboygan. Running up the Black River the route passes into Mullett Lake, Burt Lake, and Crooked Lake. Around 1900, an excursion steamboat took vacationers along this pretty winding waterway. Today small pleasure cruisers follow the inland water route from Cheboygan almost to Lake Michigan, near Petoskey. Although not included in the Inland Water Route, a special lift makes it possible for small cruisers to go from Cheboygan to Black Lake.

Cheboygan is the home port for the ice-breaker, "Mackinaw."

MACKINAW CITY lies at the northern tip of the Lower Peninsula. Its history dates back to the early French period, for it was
here that the French, after Cadillac left Detroit, built a new fort
to replace Fort Du Buade that had once stood in St. Ignace. In
1761, the fort, at what is now Mackinaw City, was occupied by
the English and it was here two years later, in 1763, that the Indians,
during Pontiac's Conspiracy, captured the fort and killed most of
the English garrison.

With the coming of the lumber industry, Mackinaw City became
a typical lumber town. For many years, Mackinaw City was the
southern terminus for auto as well as railroad car ferries that crossed
to St. Ignace in the Upper Peninsula. During the summer tourist
and fall hunting seasons, thousands of autos left Mackinaw City
on the auto ferries for the Upper Peninsula. In May, 1954, work
was begun on the new Mackinac Bridge. In November, 1957 the
new bridge was opened to auto and truck traffic and the ferries
stopped running.

During the 1930's a reconstructed fort was built on the old site
just west of the bridge. In 1959, a careful archeological, historical
investigation, and reconstruction of this historic site was begun under
the Mackinac Island State Park Commission. Since that time much
has been learned about the old fort and a more accurate reproduction
has been made to make it look as much like it was in 1760 as possible.
This commission is also preserving and restoring the old fort and
many buildings on Mackinac Island and in the straits area.

Ferries from Mackinaw City take hundreds of people to Mackinac
Island each summer. Mackinaw City is the northern point of three
railroads: the New York Central, the Detroit and Mackinaw, and
the Pennsylvania. Railroad car ferries still carry railroad cars across
the straits to St. Ignace. West of Mackinaw City, on Waugoshance
Point, is Wilderness State Park.

PETOSKEY is located on the south shore of Little Traverse Bay.
The bay received its name from the French voyageurs and means
"the little crossing." Petoskey is the distributing center for Charlevoix, Cheboygan, and Emmet counties. It is surrounded by beautiful
rolling hills and forested areas. On Little Traverse Bay, and on many
of the lakes nearby, are hundreds of summer homes and cottages.
During the summer months the population of this area more than
doubles. Besides being a resort city, Petoskey is also a manufacturing
center. The cement plant here produces about six million sacks of

cement every year. Auto parts, furniture, wooden novelties, butcher blocks, maple tables, radio cases, paper twine, and stampings are also made by local industries.

On Little Traverse Bay, one mile from Petoskey, is Bay View, a well-known summer resort. As early as 1876, Bay View was the site of religious meetings. In 1886, these gatherings became known as the Michigan Chautauqua Assembly. Each summer programs under the direction of the Bay View Assembly are held here. On the programs appear many of the nationally known musicians and speakers. Albion College offers several classes here each summer.

On the north shore of Little Traverse Bay is located Harbor Springs, one of Michigan's most fashionable summer resorts. From this point a scenic road follows the Lake Michigan shore line of Emmet County through the old homeland of the Ottawa Indians. At some points the road, overlooking Lake Michigan, runs along the top of a two-hundred-foot sandy bluff. The entire area from Little Traverse Bay to Sturgeon Bay is known as L'Arbre Croche from the French, meaning "the crooked tree." It is so called from the fact that at one time voyageurs going north from the south shore of the bay headed their canoes in the direction of a large crooked tree that then stuck out along the northern shore.

Good Hart and Cross Village are old Indian settlements. A large white cross now stands on the lake shore at Cross Village at the place where French Jesuits once came to work among the Indians. It is said that a cross has stood on this site for two hundred years.

Northeast of Petoskey is Conway, on Crooked Lake. North of Conway are the old lumber towns of Alanson, Brutus, and Pellston. Pellston often records the lowest temperature in the Lower Peninsula during the winter. The local airport serves the Mackinaw City, Gaylord, and Petoskey area. South of Petoskey is Walloon Lake, a well-known summer resort since 1900.

CHARLEVOIX was first called Pine River, but its name was later changed to Charlevoix in honor of a French priest by that name. In the early days, the location of Charlevoix between Lake Michigan and Lake Charlevoix made it an important lumber port. Today, a dredged canal leads from Lake Michigan to Lake Charlevoix and allows medium-sized boats to enter Lake Charlevoix. Each year boats bring to Lake Charlevoix enough coal to fill more than 1,000 railroad cars. This coal is used to generate electricity for the area and to supply other local needs. Each year about 500 pleasure

Charlevoix. Lake Michigan in the foreground. Round Lake in the center of the picture. Lake Charlevoix in the background. The connecting channels allow cruisers and small self-unloading boats to enter Lake Charlevoix. Photo 1961.

cruisers dock at the harbor at Charlevoix on Round Lake. North of Charlevoix, at Big Rock Point, the Consumers Power Company has built a 50,000 kilowatt electric atomic generating plant, which will be used to help supply electricity for the area. This new plant can supply enough electricity for 50,000 homes. Charlevoix is now an important resort and recreation center. The waters of Lake Michigan and nearby large lakes bring many people to this area each summer.

Just north of Charlevoix lies Beaver Island, the largest in a group of islands lying in the northern part of Lake Michigan. A ferry runs from Charlevoix to Beaver Island each day during the summer. On this island a group of people who belonged to the Church of Jesus Christ of Latter Day Saints once made their homes. These people are often spoken of as Mormons.

About 1850, there were about a thousand Mormons, together with other fishermen and woodcutters, living on Beaver Island. James Jesse Strang was their spiritual leader. Strang was an educated leader and for some time the Mormon settlement prospered under his guidance. Little cabins were built and in these the Mormon people

Courtesy Consumers Power Company

The Big Rock Nuclear Plant on Lake Michigan between Charlevoix and Petoskey. This new plant will produce 50,000 kilowatts of electric power. (Photo 1961)

lived. A log house served as a meeting place for worship and recreation. The people called their settlement St. James. Although the Mormons were industrious, they were disliked by many people then living in Michigan. After Strang's death the little colony disbanded.

The little town of St. James, on the northern end of Beaver Island, is at present a small village. Fishing was for many years the major industry, but with the coming of the sea lamprey this industry has stopped. Two other things remain to remind us of the earlier Mormon settlement on the island: a road called the King's Highway and a lake known as the Sea of Galilee.

EAST JORDAN is located at the mouth of the Jordan River on the south arm of Lake Charlevoix. It was a lumber sawmill town and shipping center during the years the Detroit and Charlevoix Railroad was running here from Frederic. Dairy farms are located nearby. Many cherries are grown in the area and canned at the

Main Street in East Jordan about 1900

local cannery. Iron products, such as storm sewer gratings and pipe valves, are manufactured here.

BOYNE CITY also was a lumber center in the days when lumber schooners entered Lake Charlevoix to load lumber for the Chicago market. A tannery here makes shoe sole leather. Boyne City also serves as a coal distributing center for the area as large boats can

Ski lift at Boyne Mountain

dock on Lake Charlevoix easier than at Petoskey on Little Traverse Bay. A local electric power station supplies electricity for much of northern Michigan. Seven miles east of Boyne City is Boyne Falls. The Boyne Mountain Lodge located here is one of the most popular summer and winter recreation spots in Northern Michigan.

TRAVERSE CITY is located at the southern end of Grand Traverse Bay. The words Grand Traverse, meaning "great crossing," come to us from the French voyageurs and no doubt refer to the necessity of paddling canoes from the Leelanau Peninsula to the mainland.

In 1839, two years after Michigan had become a state, a Protestant missionary sent by Henry R. Schoolcraft, the Indian agent at Sault Ste. Marie, founded a mission on what is now known as Old Mission Peninsula.

About 1846, white settlers began to arrive in the area and a little village, later called Traverse City, began to develop at the southern end of West Bay near Lake Boardman. In 1847, the first sawmill in the region was built by Horace Boardman on what is now known as Asylum Creek. Not many years later newer and larger mills were built, and the timber harvest of the locality began.

This area is now Michigan's largest cherry growing area. In 1924, the first cherry celebration was held. In July, 1928, the first real "cherry festival" took place. Since that time a cherry festival has been held each year and is now known as the "National Cherry Festival."

Traverse City is also an important distributing center for the area. Because of the many miles of shore line on Grand Traverse Bay and because of the many lakes near it, Traverse City is also a busy summer resort center. Old Mission Peninsula is a tourist attraction as well as a cherry-producing area. The 45th parallel crosses just north of the peninsula.

Northwest of Traverse City is the Leelanau Peninsula which stretches north between Lake Michigan and Grand Traverse Bay. In this area one finds several small lakes as well as Glen Lake and Lake Leelanau. Here, in the Leelanau Peninsula, at Glen Arbor, is found Sleeping Bear sand dune. Each summer many people visit Sleeping Bear sand dune and take a ride in one of the dunemobiles. These are automobiles that have extra large tires that keep them from sinking into the dry, soft sand.

Traverse City has some industries. Tools and dies, gears, fire hydrants and fittings, cherry products, such as jams and jellies, dairy products, frozen and fresh meats are its main products. Here is located Traverse City State Hospital. Traverse City also has a junior college called Northwestern Michigan College.

Southwest of Traverse City is Interlochen. Each summer nearly one thousand high school and college musicians come here to enjoy the northland and to study under well-known music instructors. Musical concerts are given on Sunday afternoons and on many evenings.

The West Coast Cities of the Upper Part of the Lower Peninsula

Because of the prevailing westerly winds, sand dunes reach from the southern tip of Lake Michigan along its eastern shore to Mackinaw City. Some dunes are found along the west shore of Lake Huron from Mackinaw City to Tawas City.

Beach sand is the remains of fragments of rock that contained quartz. Quartz is about the most durable of the minerals from which rocks are made. After the other minerals have been reduced to dust or dissolved and carried away by the water the quartz remains as sand which the waves deposit along the beach. More sand (quartz) is also constantly brought into the lakes as the rivers deposit the glacial materials they have been carrying. Wave action tends to thrust this material up onto the beach. There it is slowly ground into smaller particles by the churning action of the waves. On warm

Courtesy Department of Conservation

What is left of the Sleeping Bear Sand Dune. This dune sat on the top of a terminal moraine. It was a landmark even in the French and Indian days.

summer days this dry, finely-ground beach sand is picked up by the wind and carried onto the land along the shore of the lake. There it accumulates in hills and ridges known as sand dunes.

The dunes along the eastern shore of Lake Michigan often reach a height of between two and three hundred feet. These huge sand deposits are slowly growing larger as the winds carry the dry sand inland from the beach. Nature is ever trying to conquer them and cover them with grass and trees. Sometimes they are conquered, but often they slowly creep inland killing grass and trees as they cover them with the ever-shifting sand. Some of these dunes have been made into parks so that tourists may see these huge sand ridges that have been made by the waves and winds.

The west coast port cities were well located for the lumber trade. The rivers that flow into Lake Michigan usually have a large lake located near their mouths just before they enter Lake Michigan. The lakes are large in size and are separated from Lake Michigan by large sand dunes. Once the sand bars were removed from the river mouths, these sheltered lakes made good harbors for the lumber boats as well as booming places to store the logs coming down the rivers. The high dunes also protected the cities from the winds of winter that blew from Lake Michigan. From these good harbors the boats had an open road to the busy lumber ports of Chicago and Milwaukee.

When the lumber had been cut from this area, much of the area, because of its nearness to Lake Michigan, became a fruit-growing region.

FRANKFORT, which was founded in 1850, lies just south of the Leelanau Peninsula. Nearby are Crystal Lake, Platte Lake, and the Fife Lake State Forest. Frankfort is an important summer resort city and fruit market. It is located in the heart of the cherry-producing region of Michigan. Canneries for preserving the fruit are located in or near the city. In its early days Frankfort was an important lumber center.

Frankfort has the northernmost ice-free harbor along the west shore of the state. The Ann Arbor Railroad was the first railroad to operate car ferries across Lake Michigan, and it began this ferry service from Frankfort in 1892. Today Frankfort is the home port for the Ann Arbor Railroad car ferry fleet.* From this port railroad car ferries, carrying railroad cars, automobiles, and tourists, run to

---

* The dock is at Elberta across the Betsie River from Frankfort.

Manitowoc, and Kewaunee in Wisconsin, and to Menominee and Manistique in the Upper Peninsula of Michigan.

MANISTEE, is located on the eastern shore of Lake Michigan at the mouth of the Manistee River. The city lies between Lake Michigan on the west and Lake Manistee on the east. Nearby are Portage Lake and Bear Lake. The Manistee River is now known as one of the best trout streams in the state, but during the last half of the past century it was known for the pine logs it brought to the sawmills at Manistee. This fine saw timber, together with the booming possibilities of Manistee Lake, made Manistee one of Michigan's well-known sawmill centers. The first sawmill at Manistee was built in 1841. On October 8, 1871, the year of the big fires, a fire from an old chopping, fanned by a strong wind, set the town on fire. The town was soon destroyed but a new one sprang up on the old site.

As Manistee's lumber industry declined, Manistee was fortunate in being able to turn to other industries. Salt was discovered at Manistee in 1882. Today, Manistee is a large salt-producing center. Salt wells reach down into the ground some two thousand feet to vast deposits of salt. Water is pumped down pipes into the salt bed. There the water dissolves the salt and forms a brine, which is pumped to the surface. Then the water is evaporated from the brine. This is done in huge vacuum pans that are as large as a three-story house and hold as much as twenty-two thousand gallons of salt brine. When the water is evaporated, cubic salt crystals are formed. About four hundred thousand tons of salt are produced in this manner each year. Much of this salt is made for cooking and table use. Salt for industrial uses and for animal feeding is also made.

Later drillings have revealed a salt brine heavier in chemical content than that to be found in any other salt deposit in the state. Because of this, new chemical plants have developed in the area that now produce many chemical products. Manistee has two salt plants and three chemical firms, all of which use the brine found underground in the area.

Other industries have also developed in Manistee. Manistee's industries now produce drop forgings, chemicals, clothing, shoes, maple furniture, iron castings, speedboats, paper boxes, paper board, rotary pumps, and oil burners.

Besides being a resort center, Manistee is located in the heart of the western fruit belt. Manistee County is a large producer of fruit. Both apples and cherries are grown.

Extending to the south and eastward lies the large Manistee National Forest, which covers thousands of acres and extends through several counties. At Wellston, east of Manistee on M-55, is the Tippy Dam on the Manistee River and the Chittenden Nursery, where young trees are grown for replanting in forest areas.

LUDINGTON is located at the mouth of the Pere Marquette River, on the shore of Lake Michigan and Pere Marquette Lake. Originally the city was called Marquette, but the name was later changed to Ludington after James Ludington, an early lumberman. Between Pere Marquette Lake and Lake Michigan, on a narrow strip of duneland, stands a cross marking the spot where Father Jacques Marquette died on May 18, 1675.

In 1849, a small sawmill was built at the north end of Pere Marquette Lake. The splendid harbor, together with the logs that could be floated down the Pere Marquette River, soon made Ludington a busy, growing lumber town. Where once the lumber hookers came into port, to this Lake Michigan harbor, now come the Chesapeake and Ohio Railroad car ferries. Among the car ferries running from Ludington are the "Spartan" and the "Badger," which are two of the finest car ferries of their type. The latest type of tourist accommodations are provided on them. Each year many tourists cross Lake Michigan on these car ferries and thus save time and many miles of driving. These ferries run to Kewaunee, Manitowoc, and Milwaukee, Wisconsin. About two thirds of the freight moving across Lake Michigan from the three car-ferry ports is incoming freight from the west. It consists of lumber and grain and other bulk commodities.

Along the shore of Lake Michigan and the smaller nearby lakes, hundreds of cottages have been built. East of Ludington is the Manistee National Forest. North of Ludington along Lake Michigan is Ludington State Park in which stands Big Sable Lighthouse. In this park is found the site of Hamlin Village, a lumber town founded in the middle of the nineteenth century. Hamlin is remembered for a tragic flood which occurred in 1888 when a dam burst and released nine miles of backed-up water down upon the village.

Besides being a port and resort center, Ludington is also an industrial community having some thirty-nine diversified industries. Here are made cement products, chemicals, castings, boats, fruit crates, brooms, wood products, watch cases, canvas goods, clothing, printers' equipment, and auto parts.

HART, located south of Ludington, is in the center of a large fruit and vegetable growing area. Two large canneries here run from early June to late October to prepare choice canned products. Rides up and down the huge sand dunes along Lake Michigan in specially built dunemobiles can be taken from Silver Lake.

MUSKEGON was for many years one of Michigan's leading lumber producers. Its location at the mouth of the far-reaching Muskegon River, whose headwaters reached into large pineries, and the presence of Muskegon Lake made Muskegon an ideal sawmill center.

Today, Muskegon is the largest city in western Michigan. Busy industries have replaced the forty-seven noisy sawmills that once stood along the shores of Muskegon Lake. Among Muskegon's many products can be listed tools and dies, motor blocks, combustion engines, auto parts, foundry products, office equipment, refrigerators, paper, wire, coil springs, electric cranes and hoists, bowling and billiard equipment, sanding machines, metal awnings, and buses. Two refineries process about ten thousand barrels of petroleum a day.

Courtesy Hooker Chemical Corporation

Eastern Chemical Division Plant. Hooker Chemical Corporation at Montague, Michigan.

Railroad car ferries run across Lake Michigan from Muskegon to Milwaukee, Wisconsin. The car ferry tonnage from this port is about forty per cent of the total tonnage carried across Lake Michigan. The tonnage that passes through this port is about one million tons annually. The "Milwaukee Clipper," a passenger boat, also runs between Muskegon and Milwaukee, Wisconsin, during the summer months. It carries passengers and automobiles. Muskegon is the one port of western Michigan that has lake freight traffic. Being in the industrial area of the state helps in these freight shipments. Oil, coal, cement, and pulpwood account for most of the incoming tonnage, while molding sand taken from Muskegon Lake accounts for much of the outgoing shipments.

Besides being a port and an industrial center, Muskegon is also a resort and agricultural community. Northeast lies the Manistee National Forest. Much fruit is grown nearby. The area is a large producer of apples, celery, and small fruits.

MONTAGUE. Extensive deposits of a rich salt brine are found in this area. Since 1954, chemical plants have been built to process this brine into many chemical products. Synthetic rubber is also produced here in the area.

FREEMONT lies northeast of Muskegon. The Gerber plant here was the first to pioneer in the manufacture of baby foods. Today, the Gerber plant makes a large percentage of the total baby foods now being produced each year.

The Inland Towns in the Upper Part of the Lower Peninsula

Most of the inland towns in this area are located on the sandy High Plains Area. All of them had their beginning, and many their end, in the lumber industry. For many years after the timber was gone these towns declined, but with the building of better roads in the area and the rise of the tourist traffic, many of these towns have again grown in size. Some farming in scattered areas is carried on, but most of the area is now covered by second-growth timber stands. The clear, swift, shallow streams of the area and the many pretty tree-lined lakes with their sandy beaches make this area a popular place for people to spend their summer vacations. Many of the older buildings in the little villages that were built during the lumbering days are still standing, while others have been torn down. Newer, more modern stores, churches, and homes are replacing the older buildings. Along the busy highways many new attractive motels have been built to care for the hundreds of people that come to, or pass through, the area each year.

CADILLAC, the highest city in the Lower Peninsula, is located just east of two beautiful lakes, Lake Mitchell and Lake Cadillac. Cadillac began as the village of Clam Lake, but in 1877, during the lumber era, it was incorporated as the city of Cadillac in honor of Antoine de la Mothe Cadillac, the French commandant who founded Detroit in 1701.

At one time, many miles of logging railroads spread into the adjoining area. Over these railroads logs were brought to the mills at Cadillac. In 1872, four large mills were cutting about 4,000,000 board feet of lumber each day. But, by 1907, the white and Norway pine were nearly gone. As the pineries gave out, Cadillac turned to making lumber from hardwood. Maple flooring began to be made here during the years just before 1900. Cadillac became the first manufacturing center for maple, beech, and birch flooring.

Unfortunately for Cadillac, most of the land surrounding the City is a sandy loam unsuited to agriculture. On the better strips of soil, where once the hardwoods grew, some farming is carried on. Many of the farms are dairy farms. Farmers in this area have turned to raising Christmas trees as a crop. Many Christmas trees are sent from the area each year. On the abandoned forest lands, saw timber is again growing, as well as much pulp wood. These reforested areas will soon become an economic asset to the Cadillac area.

Today, Cadillac is an industrial community producing cheese, concrete blocks and pipe, furniture, truck heaters, malleable iron castings, brass and aluminum castings, grey iron castings, paper boxes, extruded and molded rubber goods, and fiber glass and aluminum boats. Two railroads and four main highways make Cadillac a natural traffic center.

Cadillac is the center of a summer and winter recreation area. It is well known for its painted forests in the fall of the year when the first frosts have turned the hardwoods into brilliant displays of gaudy colors. Nearby is the Manistee River, well known for canoeing and fishing. Between Cadillac and Traverse City is located the Fife Lake State Forest. Because Cadillac is located in a hollow saucer on top of the highest land in the Lower Peninsula, it often is the coldest spot in the state.

Sixteen miles west of Cadillac is Caberfae, a well-known winter sports area which is operated under a permit from the Forest Service of the United States Department of Agriculture. The heavy snowfall of the high area makes this a good winter sports area. As many as fifteen hundred skiers come here on some week ends during the wintertime. Caberfae has rope ski tows, several cross-country trails, two ski jumps, and seventeen ski runs. Northwest of Cadillac at Mesick is the Briar Hill ski area. Here is located one of the longest ski jumps in the Lower Peninsula.

MANTON lies north of Cadillac. It was settled in 1871 and was for some years a lumber center.

REED CITY and BIG RAPIDS lie south of Cadillac. Reed City was settled by German immigrants after 1848. Big Rapids, located on the upper Muskegon River in what used to be a pine forest area, was settled shortly after 1850. During the lumbering days it prospered. Much of the nearby land is unsuited to agriculture, but oil has been discovered. In 1884 Mr. Woodbridge N. Ferris, later governor of Michigan and also senator from Michigan, started a private school

Courtesy Dow Chemical Company

This view shows one of the early steps in production of Saran Wrap in the Dow Chemical Company's plastics department plant at Midland, Michigan. After molten saran polymer is extruded from circular dies, it is cooled quickly and transformed by special equipment into large "bubbles," as shown. Thus enlarged, the film passes through a series of rollers which deflate the "bubbles" and prepare the film for eventual winding on household and commercial rolls. Saran Wrap is made from vinyl-vinylidene chloride, a Dow basic plastic. (1961)

here known as the Ferris Institute. For many years this institute was the leading educational center in northern Michigan. Today, the Ferris Institute has been taken over by the state and is now run as a state college.

MIDLAND, the county seat of Midland County, is located on the Tittabawassee River. One hundred years ago this area was an important lumber region. At Averill, the lumberjacks piled logs along the river bank each winter. In springtime the river was filled with large pine logs drifting downstream to Bay City and Saginaw.

Today, Midland, the home of the Dow Chemical Company, is a busy industrial town. The Dow Chemical Company located there is one of the largest chemical companies to be found in the country.

Courtesy Dow Chemical Company

Brine is one of the Dow Chemical Company's basic raw materials. Here is shown a typical brine well providing brine for the company's manufacturing operations at its Midland Division, Midland, Michigan.

Nearby are oil wells which have been some of the best producing wells in Michigan.

ALMA and ST. LOUIS. At Alma is located Alma College which is supported by the Presbyterian Church. Here also is located the Masonic Old People's Home. The Leonard Refineries use the local petroleum supplies and also petroleum received by pipeline for making gasoline. St. Louis claims to be located at the geographical center of the Lower Peninsula. A chemical company, using the salt brine of the area, produces chemical products. Some tile is also made here.

MOUNT PLEASANT, like the other communities in the area, began as a lumber producing center. It is pleasantly situated amid the farm lands of Isabella County where general farming is carried on. The principal crop is sugar beets. In 1892, the United States government started an Indian industrial school here. The old buildings of this school are now used as state hospital units. Today, some Indians still live on about 450 acres of restricted land located just east of Mt. Pleasant. Some industries, such as refining gasoline, making auto parts, milling flour, and condensing milk, are carried on in the area. Mt. Pleasant is also an educational center for here is located Central Michigan University that was founded as a normal college in 1895.

GRAYLING was named after the grayling fish that once lived in large numbers in Michigan's rivers but have now become extinct. Their place has been taken by brook trout, which were first planted in Michigan in the Au Sable River at Frederic in 1884. At one time Grayling was a busy sawmill town, but the passing of the lumbering era left Grayling without an important industry. Nearly all the nearby land, which has little agricultural value, has been taken over by the state and is now in state forests. North and northwest of Grayling is the Au Sable State Forest. South of it lies the Higgins Lake State Forest. In this area oil has been discovered. East of Grayling lies the Huron National Forest. The entire area, with its clear, fast-flowing rivers, clear lakes, and sandy soil, is an ideal summer playground. Hundreds of people come to the nearby forested

Courtesy Adjutant General

Camp Grayling. Each year the National Guard trains at this camp for two weeks in August. Photo 1963.

areas each year to spend their vacations. Grayling is the starting point for people who take canoe trips down the Au Sable River. Grayling is also a winter sports area.

Seven miles northeast of Grayling is Hartwick Pines State Park. Each year many people visit this park to see the few remaining pine trees that are still left standing from Michigan's original pine forests in the Lower Peninsula.

Four and one-half miles from Grayling is the Hanson Military

Reservation comprising some eighteen thousand acres of land. In this reservation on the shore of Lake Margrethe is located the camp site for the Michigan National Guard. Each August the Michigan National Guard spends about two weeks in training in this area. During this period the National Guardsmen go through various military maneuvers necessary to preserve order and defend the state.

The Michigan National Guard, though called by other names, had its beginning even before Michigan became a state. As early as 1812 a militia of two hundred men was enrolled to help defend the territory. In 1835, it helped in the so-called "Toledo War." In 1838, it became known as the State Guards, and in 1848, it sent several companies to the Mexican War. In 1861, at President Lincoln's call the Guards were some of the first to respond. In every major conflict of the Civil War, Michigan men took part. About thirteen thousand five hundred men from Michigan were killed in that war. The total number of men from Michigan who took part in the Civil War was nearly ninety-one thousand.

In 1870, the name was changed to the Michigan State Troops. In 1891, the name was again changed to the Michigan National Guard. With the coming of the Spanish-American War five regiments were sent and three left the States for Cuba. The National Guard was made a part of the Army of the United States in 1916.

During World War I, Michigan Guardsmen joined those of Wisconsin to form the 32nd Infantry Division which arrived in France in February, 1918. Michigan soldiers were among the first of the United States soldiers to go into active service as part of the "Red Arrow Division" and they continued in active service until the close of the war. Some of Michigan's soldiers were sent to Russia and were known as the "Polar Bears."

During World War II, Michigan sent over eight thousand National Guardsmen into the federal service, and they served in the Middle East, Africa, Europe, the Aleutians, and the South Pacific. Again the 32nd Infantry wrote heroic pages in our nation's history.

The tradition and glory of the old 32nd Division is now carried on under the post-war reorganization by the present 46th Division. Today, as in the past, the National Guard stands ready to be called to serve the state or to defend the nation.

ROSCOMMON is the center for some of the work being carried on by the State Department of Conservation. Nearby, on the north shore of Higgins Lake, is located one of the state nurseries where thousands of white pine seedlings are grown each year for replanting on private lands or in the state forest areas. Near the nursery is located a camp where meetings having to do with conservation are held. On the southeast shore of Higgins Lake is Higgins Lake State Park.

In Roscommon are experimental shops where work is done on producing new and better fire-fighting equipment. During the past fifty years the fighting of forest fires in Michigan has been largely concerned with low fires and ground fires. However, during this time

Courtesy State Department of Conservation

Model III Michigan Sand Caster. This machine has been developed at Roscommon to retard and suppress forest fires.

Michigan's forests have been growing upward and a new threat now faces Michigan's forest areas—the crown fire. Today, new machinery, like the "sandcaster" which works like a rotary snowplow and throws a steady stream of sand upward as high as the tree tops, is being developed to protect Michigan's present and future forests.

OTHER INLAND TOWNS in the area are Wolverine, Vanderbilt, Gaylord, West Branch, Indian River, and Clare. Between Wolverine and Boyne Falls is a state forest nursery where thousands of seedlings are grown for replanting in state and private forests. Vanderbilt, once a lumbering center, was named after the Vanderbilts of the East.

INDIAN RIVER lies at the south end of Burt Lake and is on

the "Inland Water Route." Caring for tourists and vacationers is the community's major occupation. Here is located a Roman Catholic

Shrine. In 1943, a large cross 55 feet high, made of California redwood, was erected. In 1959, a 31 foot figure of Christ was attached to the cross.

GAYLORD. It was one of Michigan's early lumber towns. Some of the finest cork pine that ever grew in Michigan was cut just south of Gaylord in the Otsego Lake-Manistee River area. Some hardwoods also grew nearby. When the timber was cut, a few farms developed in the area. Potatoes were once an important crop. Some grain is grown and some cattle, especially beef cattle, are raised

The cross at the shrine at Indian River. Photo 1960.

in the area. Much of the old farm land has now been abandoned, reforested, or turned into tree farms. Because of the hills, lakes, and cold weather, Gaylord is becoming a winter sports area as well as a summer recreation area. Like Cadillac, it has a heavy snowfall and is often, during the winter, the coldest place in the state. Several ski slopes are located in the nearby areas. Northeast of Gaylord, by Wolverine, the state introduced some elk a few years ago. These elk have now developed into a herd of some size. In 1964 hunting permits, to kill elk, were issued. This was done to reduce the size of the herd.

Some small industries are located in Gaylord. Nearby are several small communities, such as Alba, Elmira, Johannesburg, Waters, and Otsego Lake, that were small sawmill towns during the time the area was being lumbered.

WEST BRANCH derives its name from being on the west branch of the Rifle River. Once a lumber town, it is now a recreation center. Some farming is carried on in the area. Oil is produced in the region and a small refinery is located here.

CLARE lies at the intersection of US-27 and US-10. It lies in the center of a resort and farming area, but some industry is carried on.

CHAPTER TWENTY-ONE

The Southern Part of the Lower Peninsula

Most of michigan's population, and nearly all of her major industries, are found in the area south of Bay City and Muskegon. Much of this population and industry lies in the little industrial triangle bounded by the Clinton, Huron and Detroit rivers. This important area will be discussed by itself in the next chapter.

Like the rest of the state this area is covered by a layer of glacial till. The highest elevations are found in the Irish Hills and in Oakland County. Much of the Thumb area is low, flat land, but most of the area is gently rolling land now covered with farms and wooded areas of second-growth hardwood. Only seventeen per cent of this area is forest covered. A large percentage of the trees are hardwoods, such as maple, ash, elm, and oak. Only a few of the softwoods are found. Most of the timber is in farmers' woodlots which now supply a large amount of saw timber for lumber.

Though greatly varied, the soils found in this part of the state are, in general, better than those found farther to the north. The growing season is longer and the summers warmer. The winters are not as cold. Because of these factors agriculture is a major occupation. In some of the poorer areas, where the soil is lighter and less fertile, the farms have been abandoned and the areas have been made into state parks or recreation areas. Because of the variations in the soil and the differences in climate, many different crops are grown. The nearby large centers of population provide a large, close market for much of the farm produce. Part of the crop is marketed at the farms to city folks who drive into the country with their cars. Because there is a big demand for milk and milk products in the nearby urban centers, dairying is one of the major types of farming in this area, for milk, which is a very perishable product, can be quickly taken by large bulk trucks from the farms to the cities.

Many of the villages and cities in the area began as little agricultural communities some one hundred and fifty years ago. Some

527

have remained small; others have grown larger; a few have become large cities and are now industrial communities from which comes a variety of industrial products.

Many highways and trunk lines run across this area. Over them pass not only passenger cars but much freight that is hauled in large trucks. This spreading network of highways not only provides rapid transportation from city to city, but also provides access to ready markets for the farmers in the area. Along these highways, as along those farther north, picnic tables are placed in wooded spots or in pretty wayside parks. During the summer these picnic tables are much used by people who stop to eat and rest as they drive from city to city or stop on their way to, or from, a vacation area.

PORT HURON is located at the source of the St. Clair River where Lake Huron spills its overflow water into the channel that carries the run-off water to Lake Erie. This is the most easterly point in the state of Michigan and is some fifty miles nearer Buffalo, New York, than is the city of Detroit.

At the center of Port Huron, the Black River empties into the St. Clair River. This was once the meeting place of Indian trails that led from Michigan into Canada. When the French became interested in this area, Daniel DuLhut, in 1686, built Fort St. Joseph just north

Courtesy East Michigan Tourist Association

Blue Water Bridge crossing the St. Clair River from Port Huron to Sarnia, Canada

of where the Blue Water Bridge now crosses into Canada. As early as 1782, French fishermen and trappers began to live in this locality, but it was about 1790 before real settlement began. This area was further opened to settlement when the Fort Gratiot Turnpike was built from Detroit in 1826. The Americans built Fort Gratiot on the site of the old French Fort St. Joseph to protect the American settlers from the English and the Indians. The fort was abandoned in 1879 and dismantled in 1882. The region along the St. Clair River was for many years an important boat-building center. From 1840 to 1870 lumbering was the major industry of the district.

Many farms are located in the nearby area. Tuscola and Huron counties are well known for their bean production. Sanilac County is noted for its dairy cattle. Lapeer, St. Clair, and Macomb counties produce much beet sugar as well as fruits and vegetables. In this vicinity are located the agricultural communities of Imlay City, Lapeer, Marlette, Vassar, Sebewaing, Bad Axe, and Sandusky. At Lapeer is located the Lapeer State Home and Training School.

Port Huron is one of the three Michigan cities to have sister cities in Canada. Across the St. Clair River from Port Huron is the Canadian city of Sarnia which, because of the salt underlying it and the oil that is now being piped to it from western Canada through Michigan, is destined to become one of the major industrial cities of Canada. Auto ferries for many years carried traffic across the St. Clair River, but now the auto and truck traffic uses the Blue Water Bridge. The Blue Water Bridge was paid for by the United States Government and the Canadian Government. Its total cost of construction was over four million dollars. It is 8,021 feet long. It rises one hundred fifty feet above the St. Clair River so that the large freighters on the Great Lakes can pass under it. It was opened for traffic on October 10, 1939. The Grand Trunk Western Railroad Tunnel carries railroad traffic between the United States and Canada under the St. Clair River.

At Port Huron, and in the nearby area, are located some seventy-two diversified industries, some of which produce salt, copper wire, autombile parts, pulp products, farm and road machinery, cement, speedboats, hardware, brass products, paper, and paints. The salt plants turn out many carloads of salt each day. At Port Huron shops are maintained by the Grand Trunk Western Railroad for rebuilding and repairing railroad cars. Port Huron is the Thumb's largest city and trading center. A junior college provides the first two years of college work for people living in the area.

North of Port Huron spreads the clear blue water of Lake Huron. The entire Thumb shoreline all the way from Lake St. Clair to Bay City is a summer playground. Hundreds of cottages have been built along the St. Clair River, on the islands in the river, and on the shore of Lake Huron and Saginaw Bay. South of Port Huron are the communities of Marysville, St. Clair, Marine City, and Algonac. These communities are small industrial centers but primarily resort communities. North of Port Huron, along the shore of Lake Huron, are also several resort communities: Lakeport, Lexington, Port Sanilac, and Harbor Beach. Near the tip of the Thumb are the remains of Grindstone City and the old quarries from which the Marshall sandstone was taken to make grindstones. Farther to the west lie Point Aux Barques, a summer resort, and Port Austin.

Courtesy Diamond Crystal Salt Company

Brine wells from which salt brine is secured to make table salt

CARO lies almost in the center of the Thumb area. It is surrounded by good farmland on which large crops of sugar beets are grown. Many cattle are also raised in the surrounding area. Nearby at Wahjamega, is located the Caro State Hospital for the mentally ill.

FRANKENMUTH. The site of Frankenmuth was selected, in 1845, by German Lutheran missionaries who were interested in working with the Indians and also locating good land for the German settlers that were then coming to Michigan. Many of the early settlers in the area came from Bavaria. Today, many of the people living in the area still speak Bavarian although many Americanisms have been added to their native language. "Bavarian Week," which is held each year, keeps alive some of the German culture and traditions.

Grindstones on the beach at Grindstone City at the top of the Thumb. These were discarded because of the imperfections found in the Marshall sandstone. Photo Fall, 1958.

FLINT is Michigan's second largest city in population. It also ranks second in the value of manufactured products.

In 1819, a fur trader built a trading post at the place where the Detroit-Saginaw trail crossed the Flint River. The first family to settle at what is now the city of Flint was that of Mr. John Todd, who came from Pontiac in 1830. Mr. Todd ran a tavern and also a ferry across the river. Three years later the new road from Detroit to Saginaw reached Flint and soon many settlers from the Genesee Valley in New York state came to settle in the area. That is why the county in which Flint is located is called Genesee County.

The settlement was called Grand Traverse but in 1855 it was incorporated as the city of Flint. At first, lumbering was the major

Courtesy Buick Motor Division
A 1965 Buick automobile. Buick cars are manufactured at Flint.

industry but as the forests were cleared away farmers took over the land. Besides the sawmills there soon developed woolen mills and shops to manufacture articles that were needed by the increasing number of people in the area. One early industry that developed was the making of wagons and other vehicles from the excellent hardwood found in the area. An early two-wheeled cart, known as a "road cart" became very popular in the area. From this early wagon and carriage industry developed the larger carriage factories that have made Flint widely known as "The Vehicle City." At one time the annual output of these carriage factories was more than 110,000 vehicles. In one year Flint produced some 300,000 sets of wagon wheels. From these early carriage industries there later developed the automobile industry for which Flint has been so well known for the last sixty years.

In the Flint area there are over one hundred manufacturing plants. Here are found many General Motors plants, such as Buick, Chevrolet, Fisher Body, and A. C. Sparkplug. Flint has no raw materials in its vicinity to give it any commercial advantages, nor has it any special location favorable for transportation. Yet, in spite of these two handicaps the leadership and vision of the men in Flint's industries have made the city of Flint a leader in the automobile field. From its busy factories come automobiles, trucks, automobile finish, upholstering for cars, carburetors, motors, spark plugs, pressed metal parts, speedometers, trailer coaches, automobile accessories, paper, cotton products, and many other special items needed by a population as large as that of Flint.

Flint is also a cultural and educational center, as well as an industrial community. A new civic center occupies six square blocks near the main business district. Here can be found the new city hall, a court building, and a health center. Flint also has an Institute of Art and a large public library. Here also are located Flint Junior College, which provides the first two years of college work; a branch of the University of Michigan, which offers the last two years; the General Motors Institute, and the Michigan School for the Deaf.

OWOSSO was named after a Chippewa Indian chief named Wasso who lived with his tribe in the area. Owosso is located in one of the state's best farming and grazing areas. Once the forests were cleared from the area, settlers occupied the farm lands. Some turned to furniture making. Owosso was the home of the late James Oliver Curwood who wrote many interesting novels. Some of them were written at his castle on an island in the river. Owosso is also the former home of Thomas E. Dewey, the Republican candidate for President of the United States in 1944 and 1948.

The Harris Milling Company is the largest buckwheat milling company in the Midwest. Among the items manufactured here are dairy products, stampings, furniture, electric goods, concrete products, abrasives, castings, tanks and boilers.

LANSING is located where the old Grand River trail crossed the Grand River. It was settled in 1837 when the site was chosen for a dam across the Grand River to develop water power. Settlers moving into the area from New York state named it after their former home, Lansing, New York. When the state capital was moved from Detroit in 1847, Lansing was chosen because of its central location.

In January of each year the state legislature begins a new session in the capitol building. Here the laws that govern our state are made. Among the points of interest in Lansing are the Michigan State Library, the Michigan Historical Museum, the Michigan School for the Blind, the Michigan Vocational School for Boys and the Capitol Building.

Lansing soon became an industrial center as well as the state capital. Ransom E. Olds was the city's first leading industrialist. At first he made the Oldsmobile and later the Reo cars. Today, many industries are located in Lansing. Among the plants are Oldsmobile, Motor Wheel Corporation, Reo Motors, Duplex Truck Company, and Fisher Body Corporation. Among the many other things made at Lansing can be named aircraft instruments, dairy equipment, concrete products, chemicals, mattresses, tools and dies, refrigerator units, conveyor belts, rubber stamps, tents, and boilers.

EAST LANSING is a residential community. It has no industries. It is the home of Michigan State University. This university, founded in 1855, is one of the oldest land grant colleges in the United States.

ALMA. Here is located Alma College, which was founded in 1886 by the Presbyterian Church. At Alma are also located an oil refinery and the Masonic Old People's Home.

SAINT LOUIS is said to be located in the geographical center of the Lower Peninsula. Much of the area around Alma and St. Louis is good farm land. Corn, beans, and oats are major crops of the area. Here is located the Michigan Chemical Company, which uses the salt brine found in the area as the basis of many of its chemical products, such as salt, magnesium oxide, calcium chloride and bromine.

IONIA, located on the Grand River, is in a good farming and fruit-growing area. One of Michigan's prisons, known as the Michigan Reformatory, is located here. Ionia also has a state hospital. Just west of Ionia is Lowell, which is well known for its "Show Boat" that hundreds of people come to see each July.

GRAND RAPIDS is Michigan's third largest city in population. It is well known throughout the nation as "The Furniture City." Grand Rapids was first settled in 1827 when Louis Campeau founded a fur trading post here. After 1854 Grand Rapids became a lumber center, and for several years the whining saws ripped into lumber the logs that came floating down the Grand River. It was from this supply of lumber from Michigan's forests that the first furniture makers at Grand Rapids chose their materials. Later trains brought in the fine hardwoods from the Grand River Valley.

Some years ago the furniture manufacturers at Grand Rapids started the Grand Rapids Furniture Exposition so that customers could come to Grand Rapids and see the furniture they were producing. Shown at these expositions is not only fine furniture made in Grand Rapids but also quality furniture made by other furniture manufacturers. Twice each year, in January and July, buyers of furniture visit this leading market for furniture and buy for the nation's markets.

Not only does Grand Rapids make furniture for home use, but it is also the world's largest producer of school, church, and theater seats. Many of the factories have acres of floor space devoted to displays where one can, at any time, see the furniture they are making.

The Grand Rapids furniture museum is located in what had once been the home of Mr. T. Stewart White, a wealthy Michigan lumberman. Mr. White's son, Stewart Edgar White, was one of Michigan's early authors. Two of his books were written on lumbering in Michigan. *The Riverman* tells about the problems of driving logs on one of Michigan's larger rivers. *The Blazed Trail* tells about life in a Michigan lumber camp. The Michigan room in the Ryerson Library has over sixteen thousand volumes on Michigan and the Great Lakes area.

Other places of interest in Grand Rapids are: Michigan Veterans Hospital, Calvin College and Seminary, the Grand Rapids Public Museum, the Grand Rapids Art Gallery, the Kendall School of Design, and the large Civic Auditorium. Outside Grand Rapids one can see gypsum plants where gypsum is mined and made into plaster and plaster board.

Although furniture making is Grand Rapids' major industry, many other products are also made. Among the products made here can be named radio and electrical equipment, chemicals, textiles, paints and varnishes, carpet sweepers, business machines, refrigerator cabinets, auto bodies, and auto parts. Grand Rapids is also a center for printing and photoengraving.

Grand Rapids is the leading trading center in western Michigan. Nearby are several smaller cities and good farm land from which come potatoes, vegetables, fruits, and dairy products.

GRAND HAVEN is located west of Grand Rapids at the mouth of the Grand River. The Grand Haven, Ferrysburg, Spring Lake area is a summer resort and vacation area for people living in southwestern Michigan and the Chicago area. The mineral waters also make it a health center. The area, like that of all western Michigan along the Lake Michigan shore, has pretty sand beaches, sand dunes, and air purified by having passed over one hundred miles of water.

Much celery and many grapes are grown on the farm lands near Grand Haven. Each year about two million dollars' worth of celery and grapes pass through Grand Haven on their way to the Chicago market. Many of the people living in this area are descendants of the early settlers who came from Holland about one hundred years ago.

Grand Haven is an industrial center producing boilers, tools, dies, presses, cutters, hardware specialties, wooden articles, plastic products, aluminum and brass products, and dairy products. A Coast Guard Training School is located here.

HOLLAND was settled in 1847 by immigrants who came here from Holland. The city is located at the mouth of the Black River, on Lake Macatawa, some six miles from Lake Michigan. At first the Hollanders bought one thousand acres of land on which to build their settlement. They found that the rich soil of the region made good farm land. During the years that have passed, since the first settlers came, their children have spread over the surrounding area and established other communities. Today the people living in the cities of Holland, Zeeland, and Vriesland, and the Hollanders living in the rural sections of the area form the largest group of Hollanders to be found in the United States.

During the early days of the settlement, lumbering formed the major industry, but with its passing the thrifty Hollanders turned

Tulips at Holland at "Tulip Time."

the cut-over lands into one of Michigan's best agricultural sections. Many of the Hollanders turned to truck gardening. On the lowlands of former glacial lakes, celery and onions are now grown. Flower bulbs are also grown. The poultry industry also forms a major occupation of this area. Each year some fourteen million baby chicks are hatched.

The skilled craftsmen of the community turned to making furniture. A large furniture industry developed in the community, and the products of these early craftsmen helped to make Michigan widely known as a furniture center. Other industries followed. At present Holland makes furniture, drugs, auto parts, cosmetics, beet sugar, leather goods, dyes, auto parts, dairy products, and heating units. One of the largest heating unit factories in Michigan is located here at Holland. One of Parke, Davis and Company's new plants is located here.

In 1886 Hope College was founded by the Dutch Reformed Church. Here is also located Western Theological Seminary, where ministers are trained for the Dutch Reformed Church.

At Holland is located the Netherlands Museum. Here are preserved such articles as have local historical importance to the people of Holland. The Netherlands government has also supplied it with much rare and valuable material.

Lake Macatawa is one of the large sand-dune-locked lakes on the shore of western Michigan. After the sand bars at the mouth of the river had been removed, Lake Macatawa made an excellent harbor. Today, the steamship "South American" uses Lake Macatawa as its winter port.

Many Dutch customs have been kept by these people from Holland. Their Dutch novelty shops are an interesting attraction to tourists. Tulips and wooden shoes (klompen) mark their spring festival, and people come to Holland by the thousands each spring at "Tulip Time."

Tulip Time was started in 1930. It is now held each spring at the time thousands of tulips are in bloom. It is a gala occasion that lasts for nine days. On the first day of Tulip Time, many men and women of Holland dress in their colorful Dutch costumes and scrub the streets with large scrubbing brushes. If you visit Holland at Tulip Time, you will see the miles of tulip lanes, and perhaps you will see some of the old men smoking their long pipes in one of the many coffee shops.

ANN ARBOR is located on the Huron River in Washtenaw County. It is the home of the University of Michigan. Early settlers coming into the state found this region not only pleasant but also one of good farm land as well. Settlement began in 1824. Other settlers soon arrived, and by 1829 the little village had a newspaper, the *Western Immigrant*. At first the Huron River provided the only highway to other communities, but before long a road and a railroad were cut through the forest to Detroit.

Courtesy Parke, Davis and Company
Parke, Davis and Company's new Ann Arbor Research Laboratories

One of the first acts of the new state legislature, in 1837, was to reorganize the state university. Many cities desired that the university be located in them, but it was decided to locate it at Ann Arbor. Buildings were soon under construction, and in 1841 the university was opened. In 1870 coeducation, a very progressive step for the time, was adopted.

Today, the assets of the university exceed one hundred million dollars. Its libraries have more than one million volumes. The William L. Clements Library possesses many rare books, first editions, maps, and manuscripts on American history up to 1800. Among the places of interest in Ann Arbor can be listed: the University Hospital, the Law Quadrangle, the William L. Clements Library, the Burton Memorial Tower, the Baird Carillon, the Michigan League Building, the Michigan Union Building, the University Museums, the Hill Auditorium, the Botanical Gardens, and the University of Michigan Stadium at Ferry Field which seats over ninety-seven thousand people.

Ann Arbor is well known as a medical center. A new Parke, Davis and Company research center has been built here and the research scientists employed by the company work with the medical faculty of the university and the University Hospital. Several other companies have established research laboratories here so that they can also work in conjunction with the university faculty in other fields.

In general, the main occupation of Ann Arbor is caring for the students attending the university. Yet, while primarily a leading educational center, Ann Arbor is an industrial community as well.

At one time watches were manufactured here. Pianos and organs were made here for many years. These early industries have given way to others. Today skilled labor in over seventy industrial plants produces castings, automobile instruments, scientific instruments, piston rings, machine parts, duplicating machines, wood products, and books.

JACKSON was settled about 1830 at a point where an Indian trail crossed the Grand River. The good farm land near the city soon attracted settlers. In 1838, the Michigan State Prison was established and located here. In 1841, the Michigan Central Railroad reached the city. Today, Jackson is one of the most important railroad centers in the state. Since 1873, when the railroad moved its shops from Marshall to Jackson, the New York Central has maintained a large roundhouse and repair shop in the city.

Courtesy of the Warden

State Prison of southern Michigan at Jackson. Photo 1962.

Jackson was once a carriage-making center. When automobiles first appeared, several early cars, such as the Jackson, Imperial, Briscoe, and the Earl, were made in the city. Though these early cars are no longer made, Jackson is still an important industrial center having about 150 manufacturing plants. Among the products produced in Jackson may be named cushion springs and other parts for automobiles, tires and tubes, automobile accessories, furniture, sleeping garments and clothing, lawn mowers electric dishwashers, candy, and grinding wheels.

Courtesy Jackson Chamber of Commerce

The Illuminated Cascades at Jackson. During the summer many people come in the evenings to see these illuminated water falls.

Jackson is the birthplace of the Republican party, which was founded here on July 6, 1854.

Until 1930, or for almost a century, the Michigan State Prison was located just north of the main business section in downtown Jackson. In that year it was moved to new buildings and grounds on the north side of the city. Fifty-seven and one-half acres are enclosed inside the prison wall. At the present time the prison houses almost six thousand prisoners. In many ways the prison is self-supporting. It operates a number of farms where food for the prisoners is grown. The prisoners make their own shoes and other clothing as well as uniforms for the guards. They also operate their own cannery. Besides these activities they also make automobile license plates and road signs for the state. Prisoners are paid a small wage for their labor. They have religious, recreational, and educational opportunities. Both Parke, Davis and Company and Upjohn maintain laboratories within the walls of the prison. Many prisoners volunteer for drug tests so that others may live healthier and longer lives.

HILLSDALE is the home of Hillsdale College. This college has the distinction of being the first college in Michigan to grant degrees to women. Near Hillsdale College is Slayton's Arboretum. East of Hillsdale on M-34 is the birthplace of Will Carleton, Michigan's best known early poet.

ADRIAN, first called Logan, was founded in 1826 and is one of the oldest settlements in Michigan. It is located in beautiful rolling country where farming is the major occupation. Corn, sugar beets, cattle, sheep, hogs, and truck crops are the major farm products. At Adrian are located two canneries and five milk processing plants which care for the crops and milk produced in the area.

The fact that Adrian is an agricultural community has not hindered its industrial development. Today, some fifty products such as castings, farm gates, auto parts, leather goods, and paper products are made here. Adrian is also an educational community. Adrian College, St. Joseph's Academy, Siena Heights College, and the Girls' Training School are located here.

MONROE is located in the southeast corner of Michigan between Detroit and Toledo. It was settled, in 1784, by Frenchmen who began a settlement on the River Raisin not far from Lake Erie. For some years the little community was known as Frenchtown. It was here, during the War of 1812, that the massacre at the River Raisin took place. Here also the first American flag to be raised in the area now making up the state of Michigan, was flown in 1796.

Monroe is very favorably located for transportation. Several railroad lines and two trunk highways pass through the city. Moreover, it is Michigan's only port on Lake Erie. A canal leads from Lake Erie into the Raisin River where a turning basin for boats, of twenty-two

Freighters docked at Monroe for the winter. Photo 1955.

acres, is located some two miles up the Raisin River. Several lake freighters are docked here each winter.

Several industries are located at Monroe. It is also surrounded by a rich farming area. Large nurseries here produce trees and shrubs for landscaping. For many years Monroe has been one of Michigan's leading paper-producing centers. Paper board, shipping cases, and cartons are manufactured. Among Monroe's many other products can be listed tools, machinery, stokers, automobile parts, office supplies and furniture, crushed stone, aluminum products, and foundry steel. St. Mary's Academy, a school for girls, is located here at Monroe. Sterling State Park is located north of Monroe on the shore of Lake Erie. Near Monroe is located the Enrico Fermi Atomic Energy Plant.

Near Monroe, at Dundee, a new cement plant owned by the Dundee Cement Company was opened in December, 1959. At this place a high quality limestone lies near the surface of the land. Clay, needed in cement making, lies above the limestone layer. The new quarry, started in a 1,600 acre area, will supply material for this new plant for more than one hundred years. The location of this plant was also chosen because it is only 50 miles from Detroit and 27 from Toledo. Both of these communities are large markets for cement. What is more, the plant is only 14 miles from Monroe where cement can be shipped by boat to ports around the Great Lakes and by way of the St. Lawrence Seaway to other ports as well.

COLDWATER lies west of Hillsdale at the junction of the old Indian Sauk Trail that ran between Detroit and Chicago, which is now U.S. 112 and U.S. 27, which runs north to Mackinaw City. At Coldwater is located the Coldwater Home and Training School. Many good farms are found in the area around Coldwater. West of Coldwater, on M-86, is Colon, which is known as "The Magic Capital of the World." Here magician's equipment is manufactured.

STURGIS is located on U.S. 112, southwest of Coldwater. It is located in a good farming area. Several small industries are located here, which manufacture a variety of products. An industrial fair is held annually. Sturgis also produces prepared baby foods. North of Sturgis is Centreville which is noted for its manufacture of children's sleeping garments.

ALBION is in the center of a good agricultural community. It is also a college town. Here is located Albion College that was founded in 1835 by the Methodists. Several oil wells have been developed in this area in the last few years. This is now Michigan's largest producing oil field.

MARSHALL, on the old Territorial Road, was settled in 1831. It was named Marshall after John Marshall, Chief Justice of the United States Supreme Court. It was at Marshall that Rev. John D. Pierce, a missionary of the Congregational Church, and Isaac E. Crary, a Marshall attorney, in 1834, made plans for the Michigan Public School System. The plan set up by Pierce and Crary was adopted by the Constitutional Convention in 1835. The oak tree under which Rev. Pierce and Mr. Crary sat while discussing Michigan's new school system is still standing in Marshall. It is often spoken of as Michigan's "Educational Oak." Marshall was the scene of the Crosswhite Case. Marshall is also the birthplace of America's oldest continuous labor organization, the Brotherhood of Locomotive Engineers, which was founded here in 1863.

Marshall has some local industries, but it is primarily the center of an agricultural community. Here is located a large pickle salting station.

BATTLE CREEK derived its name from a dispute between a party of surveyors and some Indians. It stands at the meeting place of the Battle Creek and Kalamazoo Rivers. It is one of the larger cities in Michigan and one of the best known. About 75 years ago, the community began what we would call today the breakfast food industry. The idea of these early manufacturers was to produce a healthful breakfast food that would not have to be cooked. The name of Battle Creek has been carried to every state in the union and to every country in the world on the packages of various cereals and health foods which are, or have been, produced at Battle Creek. Battle Creek can

Courtesy Michigan State Highway Department

A typical cloverleaf interchange on Michigan's freeway system is this one on I-94 and M-78 south of Battle Creek. Cloverleaf interchanges eliminate left-turn and cross-traffic conflict for all movements. 1964.

easily claim the distinction of being not only the largest producer of breakfast foods in the United States but also the first producer in this field. Today, the leading producers of breakfast foods at Battle Creek are W. K. Kellogg, Post Division of General Foods, Battle Creek Foods, and the Ralston Purena Company.

Battle Creek was also known for many years as a leading health center. People came from all over the world to the Battle Creek Sanitarium, which was run by Dr. John Kellogg, to take advantage of the expert medical service offered at the sanitarium. The former Battle Creek Sanitarium later became the Percy Jones Hospital and was used by the United States Government as an army hospital during World War II and also the Korean conflict. For some time this large building was used by the Federal government as the headquarters of the United States Civil Defense. Today the building is used as the United States Defense Logistics Services Center.

Sojourner Truth, one of the early leaders in the Civil Rights Movement, lived here for some years and is now buried in a local cemetery.

Northwest of Battle Creek, on Gull Lake, is located the Kellogg Bird Sanctuary. Hundreds of people stop here each year to see the birds, especially the Canadian Geese, as they migrate each spring and fall. Such sanctuaries for birds during their migration, and also

A Werner Wolff Photo, Courtesy Post Division, General Foods

Packing line workers at the Post Division of General Foods Corporation, Battle Creek, Michigan, placing packages of Corn Flakes into corrugated shipping cases. The filled cases then proceed down a conveyor to the shipping warehouse for placement in box cars for shipping to General Foods distribution warehouses located throughout the country.

the studies that are carried on at these places, let us learn more about birds and their movements.

While well known for its work in the field of health and the manufacture of breakfast foods, Battle Creek is also an important manufacturing center. Many industries are located here. Among the products made at Battle Creek can be listed breakfast foods, auto parts, boxboard, cartons, printing presses, and bread-wrapping machines. For several years, Battle Creek was a leading stove manufacturing center but heating units are no longer made in the area. The Grand Trunk Western Railroad has shops here for the repair of its railroad equipment It also has a large switching yard in the northeastern part of the city.

KALAMAZOO is located on the Kalamazoo River about thirty miles from Lake Michigan. It lies midway between Detroit and Chicago. The area for many years was the homeland of the Pottawattomie Indians. At first the area was called Ke Kalamazoo from the Indian language and means "boiling pot."

In 1823, a trading post was located at the meeting place of the Indian trail and the river. The first settler was Titus Bronson, who came to Kalamazoo in 1829. Until 1836, the little settlement was called

The Burdick Street Mall in Kalamazoo. This is the first permanent pedestrian installation of its type in the United States. The three block span was once one of the busiest north-south streets in the downtown section. Now it is filled with grassy plots, fountains, flower beds, and a children's play area. (Photo—Kalamazoo Gazette 1961)

Bronson, but in that year the shortened Indian name of Kalamazoo was given to the settlement.

In 1847, and in the years that followed, many Dutch settlers came to the city and county. In 1870, these thrifty farmers began to grow celery. Large areas of swampland and marshland were drained and the rich, black soil was found well suited to the new crop. For many years Kalamazoo was a leading center of celery production and the city was known as the "celery city." The growing of celery is no longer of major importance. Several farmers now use their greenhouses and muck lands to grow flower bulbs. Today, the variety of soils in the area makes it one in which diversified agriculture is carried on.

Kalamazoo is also an industrial center. For years the Kalamazoo Stove Company, with its slogan "Kalamazoo Direct to You," was an important producer of stoves. But stoves are no longer made in Kalamazoo. Several paper-making plants are located here. All grades of paper, from cardboard for boxes to the finest grades of writing paper, are produced. The Upjohn Company is a large manufacturer of pharmaceuticals. Heating units, auto parts, school furniture, hydraulic pumps, motors and valves, and plastic products are also produced at Kalamazoo.

Kalamazoo is also a college community. Here are located Kalamazoo College, the oldest college in Michigan, Nazareth College, a Catholic girls' school, and Western Michigan University. In keeping with the cultural environment of Kalamazoo the city has a large public library and museum. A new art center was opened in September, 1961.

Lawton, Decatur, and Paw Paw are nearby communities. In this area the making of grape juice is a major occupation. Dowagiac manufactures heating equipment and fishing tackle.

BENTON HARBOR AND ST. JOSEPH are twin cities located on opposite sides of the St. Joseph River at the place where it empties into Lake Michigan. In 1679, La Salle visited the area and built a small fort. Mound builders once occupied this vicinity, but the Pottawattomie Indians were living here when the settlers arrived.

The early settlers in the area found the land of southwestern Michigan good for farming and especially well adapted to fruit growing. Today, because of the fertile soil, the effect of Lake Michigan on the climate, and the nearby location of large markets—especially Chicago, which is only sixty miles away—the entire area of Berrien,

Van Buren, and Allegan counties has become a leading fruit and vegetable producing center.

Because of the longer growing season, southwestern Michigan produces most of Michigan's peach crop. Apples are produced in such volume that the area is considered to be one of the more important apple-producing localities of the country. Plums, pears, grapes, cherries, strawberries, and tomatoes are also important crops. In the spring when the "Blossom Festival" is held, the countryside is fragrant and colorful.

Much of this fruit, destined for the Chicago market, passes through St. Joseph and Benton Harbor, which act as distributing centers. The local open-air fruit market at Benton Harbor is the largest non-citrus fruit market in the country. It was first started about 1870 when the fruit was shipped to Chicago by boat. Later, railroads and the more recent truck transportation changed the method of distribution. The market opens early in June and stays open until about November the first. Each year sales in this market total about nine million dollars.

These cities and the nearby shore line of Lake Michigan furnish a recreational area for people from Chicago and northern Indiana and Illinois. The cities are also known for their sulphur baths. The twin cities are also industrial communities producing auto and aircraft parts, washing machines, pumps, dies, rubber goods, hosiery, canned fruits, jams and jellies.

NILES, on the St. Joseph River, is located on a site where Indian trails once crossed. At one time it was the homeland of mound builders. Later it was the homeland of the Miamis and then the Pottawattomie Indians. During the latter part of Allouez's life this early French Jesuit missionary carried on his missionary work among the Indians in the St. Joseph valley of southwestern Michigan. After spending almost a quarter of a century as a missionary among the Indians of Wisconsin, Illinois, and Michigan, he died and was buried somewhere near Niles in August, 1689. A large granite marker near Niles marks the scene of Allouez's last missionary activity.

Another large boulder marks the site of a French fort first built in 1697. After the fall of New France, the English occupied the fort. During Pontiac's Conspiracy, on May 25, 1763, the Pottawattomies attacked and killed most of the English garrison. Later, during the Revolutionary War, on January 2, 1781, a Spanish raiding expedition from St. Louis made its way overland across Illinois and captured the fort. Because of this Spanish raid, Niles is the only city in Michigan to have been under four flags: French, English, Spanish and American. From 1822 to 1832 the McCoy Mission was located here.

Niles is located in an area of fertile farm land. Besides producing general crops, it is known for its apple orchards and its mint and mushroom production. The industries of Niles produce dress patterns, architectural metal work used in front entrances of stores, shops and theaters, auto parts, electrical appliances, telephone parts, tools and dies, spring steel, tanks, furniture, wire, paper, toys and ventilator equipment.

Courtesy Twin Cities Area Chamber of Commerce

One section of the Benton Harbor Fruit Market. Because of the large amount of fruits and vegetables grown in the area around Benton Harbor and St. Joseph, Benton Harbor has one of the largest, non-citrus, fruit and vegetable markets in the world. About seven million packages of fruits and vegetables are sold here each year. Peaches, pears, plums, apples, cherries, grapes, strawberries, raspberries, tomatoes, cantalopes, snap beans, and cucumbers make up a large part of the produce handled.

CHAPTER TWENTY-TWO

Michigan's Southeastern Industrial Triangle

ALTHOUGH some of Michigan's industries are scattered over much of the state, the major portion of her industries are located in the southeastern part of the state near the Detroit River. The area bounded by the Clinton, Huron, and Detroit Rivers forms an area that is sometimes referred to as Michigan's Southeastern Industrial Triangle. In this area more than half of Michigan's people now live. The area for several miles on the west side of the Detroit River was once old lake bottom when Lake Erie was larger than it is today. This flat, gradually sloping land, which forms a large half saucer in Macomb, Wayne, and Monroe counties, makes an ideal location for Detroit and its spreading suburbs. By this area flows the Detroit River as it carries the run-off waters from Lake Superior, Lake Michigan, and Lake Huron. Although not as much traffic passes along it as did a few years ago, it is still one of the busiest rivers in the world. On its waters boats carry iron ore, cement, limestone, pulpwood, wheat from the north and west, and manufactured products. From the south by way of Lake Erie come shipments of coal and petroleum products. Foreign vessels bring in products from overseas.

Several railroads and truck lines running into this area also bring in a variety of raw materials needed in manufacturing. The railroads and trucks also bring in the vast quantities of food and personal items needed in this densely populated area. From this area goes out each day a large volume of manufactured products. So large are the industries in this part of Michigan that they use about ten per cent of all the steel used in the nation. Much of this steel is used in making automobiles and auto parts.

Here in the southeastern part of Michigan are found the industrial or residential cities of Allen Park, Berkley, Birmingham, Bloomfield Hills, Brighton, Center Line, Dearborn, Dearborn Heights, Detroit, East Detroit, Ecorse, Farmington, Ferndale, Flat Rock, Garden City, Grosse Pointe, Grosse Pointe Farms, Grosse Pointe Shores, Grosse

Pointe Woods, Hamtramck, Hazel Park, Highland Park, Huntington Woods, Inkster, Lincoln Park, Livonia, Melvindale, Mount Clemens, Northville, Oak Park, Pleasant Ridge, Plymouth, Pontiac, River Rouge, Riverview, Rochester, Rockwood, Romulus, Roseville, Royal Oak, Southgate, St. Clair Shores, Trenton, Utica, Warren, Wayne, Wyandotte, and Ypsilanti.

Some of these centers are residential areas only and do not permit manufacturing to be carried on within their city limits. Other communities are made up of both residential areas and industrial areas. Nearly all these communities have grown rapidly during the past few years. Automobile transportation has made it possible for people to live in nearby suburban residential areas and to drive each day to the factories and offices in the industrial areas to work. The entire area is covered with villages, cities, farms, parks, and recreation areas. During the past few years, many homes, sitting on wide, deep lots, have been built along the rural highways. Large parks and bathing beaches have been provided for the recreational needs of the people.

DETROIT is the oldest city in Michigan's industrial triangle. It was settled in 1701 by the French. For over a century after its founding, Detroit remained a small wilderness fort and trading center. Today, there is little left to remind one that this area was a part of New France from 1701 to 1760.

The strategic location of Detroit was known at the time of its founding, but the real importance of its location became more evident after the opening of the Erie Canal in 1825. Detroit soon became one of the leading ports for traffic going east or west across the canal.

The Americans began settling the area around Detroit soon after the opening of the Erie Canal. Every census since that time has shown an increase in Detroit's population except the last one which was taken in 1960.

In 1850, Detroit's population was only about twenty-one thousand people. But each year after that saw new buildings, such as houses, hotels, stores, churches, and warehouses, being built. After 1850, many industries were started in Detroit as many workmen came from both Canada and the East. The Civil War also brought about the need for many manufactured articles and this stimulated industry. As men grew wealthy from these new industries many of them built

---

Courtesy Detroit and Convention Bureau. A Detroit Free Press Photo

Detroit skyline with Cobo Hall in foreground. (1960)

large brick homes along some of the city streets. These large brick homes with their spacious lawns easily let it be known that rich men as well as laborers lived in the rapidly growing city.

Although Detroit had a normal growth during the years between 1850 and 1900 most of the people that came to the area just passed through it on their way to other places farther north and west. Up to 1900, all of the area around Detroit, where heavily populated suburbs are today, was still used as farmland. On market days the nearby farmers drove their teams of horses to town and sold their produce at the open city market. The entire city, in 1900, lay within what is now the well-known street called Grand Boulevard. At that time Grand Boulevard formed a half circle around the city of Detroit.

Detroit's rapid growth, as well as that of many other cities in the area, can be traced back to about 1900 when Detroit began to be a center for the making of automobiles. Today, Detroit is known

Courtesy Ford Motor Company

SEAT INSERTION. Near the end of the final assembly line a new Mustang gets its bucket seats. The Mustang is built at Ford Motor Company's Dearborn (Mich.) Assembly Plant. 1965.

throughout the world as the "automobile city." Although many auto parts are still made in Detroit only a small percentage of the total automobiles produced in the area are made in Detroit. Today, Detroit has become a city of many diversified industries. Only about 15 per cent of Detroit's workers are now employed in the automobile industries.

About 1900, when automobiles began to be manufactured here, Detroit's population was only a little over one quarter of a million people. It had reached nearly one half million by 1910. By 1920 it had grown to nearly a million. By 1930, it had a little over one and one-half million people. By 1950 it had reached nearly to the two million mark. In 1850, Detroit was ranked thirty-third among American cities in size but today it holds fifth place among the cities of the nation. Between 1950 and 1960 Detroit's population declined by nearly 180,000 people but the surrounding suburbs showed large population gains.

From the time of the first settlement at Jamestown in 1607 up to 1880 most of the immigrants coming to the United States were Protestants from the countries of northern Europe. It was these people, or the children of such people, who came to Michigan from the South or from New England and New York to settle here.

After 1880, a major change came in the nationality of immigrants coming to live in the United States. More and more people began coming to the United States from southern and eastern Europe such as the Polish and Italians. These new immigrants were largely Roman Catholic or Greek Catholic. As most of the land had already been settled by the earlier Protestant groups these later immigrants settled in America's rapidly growing cities where work could be found in the new and expanding industries. Most of this new immigration settled in the cities north of the Ohio River and east of the Mississippi River where the new industries were developing. After 1900, many of these new immigrants came to live in Detroit, and the other cities of Michigan, where they found work in the rapidly expanding automobile factories.

Since 1900, many other people have come to Michigan's urban areas from the Southern states. Many of them were Southern whites whose ancestry dates back to the early settlement of the United States. Many negroes have also come to Michigan to find work in the expanding industries and to get better living conditions. Today, this negro group in Detroit, and the other larger Michigan cities, forms a large segment of the urban population. Only a few negroes are found in the rural areas. This shift in people during the last fifty or sixty years has brought about a marked contrast in the nationality groups and religious beliefs between those living in the urban centers and those living in the rural areas which have always been dominantly Protestant.

Courtesy Detroit Marine Terminals, Inc.

Today, large ships from all over the world are docking at several Great Lakes ports. Shown here are four vessels docked at Detroit and being unloaded at Detroit Marine Terminals, Inc. Starting at the left of the picture, the first vessel is Norwegian, the second German, the third Canadian, and the fourth is a United States lake boat. Notice the difference in the construction, and unloading equipment, in the seagoing ships from that of the lake boat on the right and the other lake boats shown in this chapter. Photo 1961.

During the past twenty years a new and different Detroit has been in the making. Hundreds of old houses and warehouses have been torn down to make way for a newer and more beautiful city. Along the Detroit River waterfront, where passenger steamers docked for over a century, a new Civic Center is now being developed. Visitors now coming to Detroit find new city buildings and a green parkway along some of the river's waterfront. New expressways, cut through old residential areas where once stood hundreds of old homes, have been and are now being built. These new highways have done much to speed up auto and truck traffic moving from one part of the city to another.

On the south side of the Detroit River, across from Detroit, stands Detroit's sister city, Windsor, Ontario. For over a hundred years little steam ferries carried wagons, buggies, automobiles, and people across the Detroit River from one country to the other. These little white ferry boats, hurrying back and forth across the river, were always of interest to local people as well as visitors that came to the area. But today these picturesque little ferries no longer run. Automobile, truck, and bus traffic moving between the two cities now goes through the Detroit and Windsor Tunnel or over the Ambassador Bridge. One railroad tunnel runs under the river. Much railroad traffic to and from the eastern part of the United States thus moves under the Detroit River. But some railroad car ferries still carry railroad cars across the river. Fast trains run across Canada from Windsor to Buffalo, New York, and from there to Albany on the Hudson River.

Today, Detroit is an educational center as well as a manufacturing center. Here are located Wayne State University, the University of Detroit, the Detroit Institute of Technology, Marygrove College, and Mercy College, and also several private schools and colleges. These institutions of higher learning, along with Michigan's other specialized schools and universities, supply the area with the needed technological training.

Among the buildings and places of interest in Detroit the following can easily be listed: Cobo Hall, the Ford Auditorium, the new City-County Building, the Detroit Public Library, which also contains the Burton Historical Collections, the finest collection of historical material on the Old Northwest to be found in Michigan; the Detroit Institute of Arts, the Detroit Historical Museum, the Detroit Zoological Park, the site of Old Fort Pontchartrain, on West Jefferson Avenue, in front of the new Veterans' Memorial Building, Mariners Church, the Detroit and Windsor Tunnel, which runs between Detroit and Windsor; the Ambassador Bridge, Fort Wayne, the site of old Fort Shelby, the site of Michigan's first capital, where Stevens T. Mason lies buried; Belle Isle, a city park lying in the Detroit River; and the Michigan State Fair Grounds where the Michigan State Fair is held each fall. The salt mine is not open to visitors, but many manufacturing plants take visitors on guided tours through their plants. Each year hundreds of people visit Detroit's industries. During the summer months people like to watch the foreign ships and the huge lake freighters as they push steadily along on the Detroit River past Detroit.

At the present time there are several hundred manufacturing concerns in the Detroit area. Most of them are producers of automobiles or are allied in some way to the automobile industry. However, many other articles are produced in Detroit besides automobiles. Here are located drug, varnish and paint, button, rubber, hardware, machine tool accessories, and inorganic chemical manufacturing plants. Detroit is also a salt producing center.

Among many important products manufactured may be listed: oil burning furnaces, business machines, chemicals, vacuum cleaners, electric refrigerators, electrical equipment, buttons, fertilizer, gelatine, overalls, brass and copper products, books, bolts, nuts, screws, soft drinks, tires, tools, and steel. Detroit also has meat packing plants.

During the past few years Detroit's suburban areas have built more new factories and created jobs faster than has Detroit. No doubt this is due to several factors: many early factory buildings are now old and were not designed to hold the heavy, new automated machinery that is now being installed; land is cheaper in the suburbs, there is more land to be had, and old expensive buildings do not have to be wrecked to make room for new factories. Many older companies that were once in Detroit have moved to new buildings in outlying areas, especially north of the Eight Mile Road in Oakland and Macomb counties.

DEARBORN is one of Detroit's oldest suburbs. Not including the early little French forts which were built in Michigan, Dearborn's history is as old as any community in the state. As the land along the Detroit River became occupied by farms the early French, as they expanded in numbers, began to lay out ribbon farms along the banks of the Rouge River. The location of some of these early French ribbon farms can still be seen on a map of Dearborn at the present time. The oldest continuing Protestant church, and the second one built in Michigan, was built near the bank of the Rouge River, in what is now Dearborn, in 1818.

Settlers began clearing farm lands in this area soon after the land was put on sale by the government in 1818. This was before the Chicago Road was built. The earliest settlers in the Dearborn and Northville area found their way into the Michigan wilderness along the Ann Arbor Trail that before had been the old Sauk Trail, that followed along the north bank of the Rouge River. Today, what remains of this old road is known as the Ann Arbor Trail. Later, after the Chicago Road had been cut westward through the forest, hundreds of settlers, with their horse drawn wagons, passed through Dearborn during the years between 1830 and 1950 as they went westward to start new homes in Michigan's wilderness.

For many years what is now the western part of Dearborn was a small rural village on the old Chicago Road. All of the land around it was still farm land as late as 1915. After Mr. Henry Ford began building his large plant on the Rouge River, in 1915, to build Eagle boats for use in World War I, people began building homes on the farm land near the factory. The area near the plant became known as the city of Springwells. Later its name was changed to Fordson. The present city of Dearborn is made up of two former cities, Dearborn and Fordson, that were joined together into the city of Dearborn in 1929.

Because of the clay in the area, brick making was Dearborn's first industry. Up until about 1925, brick making was a major industry but today only one company still manufactures bricks. Most of the old clay pits have been filled in and today they are covered with homes. Since 1915, Dearborn has been known as the center of the Ford industries. The Ford Rouge Plant is Dearborn's largest manu-

Courtesy Ford Motor Company

Ore carriers docked at the Ford Rouge Plant in Dearborn, Michigan. (1961)

facturing plant. To it come railroad cars, trucks, and large lake boats that bring in materials to be used in the plant. Here too are located the large general office buildings of the Ford Motor Company. Ventilating equipment is also manufactured in Dearborn. Here at Dearborn are located Greenfield Village and the Henry Ford Museum.

Greenfield Village was started as an educational and cultural project by Mr. Ford in 1929. Greenfield Village covers about two hundred acres and includes nearly one hundred buildings. It is built around a village green similar to that of many early American villages. Most of the buildings were brought to the village from other places in the United States. Some of them are as old as 1650

Courtesy Henry Ford Museum

Eagle Boat made for World War I at the Ford Rouge Plant in Dearborn.

but most of them represent the period from 1800 to 1900 and are closely associated with the Industrial Revolution.

Beside Greenfield Village stands the Henry Ford Museum. This large museum is devoted to the story of the economic freedom of man. The front central section is a replica of Independence Hall in Philadelphia. The entire building covers nearly eleven acres. In it are exhibits showing man's progress in agriculture, industry, transportation, and illumination. Here also is found one of the nation's best furniture exhibits with displays of the various styles of furniture from colonial times to the present. There are also displays of silverware, porcelain, pressed glass, and ceramics.

At Dearborn is located the Henry Ford Community College. This college offers the first two years of college work as well as many other classes that are helpful for people working in the local industries. Adjoining the Henry Ford Community College campus, on what was once Mr. Henry Ford's Fairlane Estate, is the Dearborn branch of the University of Michigan that offers the junior and senior years of college work.

HIGHLAND PARK for many years was a northern suburb of Detroit, but now Highland Park is surrounded by Detroit and Hamtramck. After 1910, when the Ford Motor Company moved its factory from Detriot to the newly built Highland Park Plant, the city grew rapidly. For a few years this plant was the main plant of the Ford Motor Company, but with the building of the Ford Rouge plant in Dearborn, the Ford Motor Company moved its main offices to Dearborn. The old Ford Highland Park plant is now used to make Ford tractors and upholstery. During the past few years Highland Park has declined in population. Here at Highland Park are located the Highland Park Junior College and the main business offices of the Chrysler Corporation.

HAMTRAMCK was named after Colonel John F. Hamtramck, who was one of the men that fought along with General Anthony Wayne in the Indian Wars in the Northwest. Colonel Hamtramck came from a German, French-Canadian background. He was the first American military commander at Detroit. Hamtramck township was created in 1798 and was largely settled by German settlers coming to Michigan. By 1925, the township had lost much of its land to Detroit, Highland Park, and Grosse Pointe. The village of Hamtramck was organized in 1901. It was here that John and Horace Dodge set up their factory to make engines for Mr. Ford's Model T Cars. Many immigrants came to Hamtramck to work in the Dodge plant. Seventy per cent of this immigrant group were Polish. Other outstanding groups were Ukrainian, and Russian. During the past few years, Hamtramck has declined in population as more industries have moved into the area. The best known plant in Hamtramck is the main Dodge plant of the Chrysler Corporation.

MT. CLEMENS is located on Lake St. Clair at the mouth of the Clinton River. French settlers from the Detroit area began settling along the Clinton River about 1775. The Moravian Indians built the first Protestant Church in Michigan at what is now Mt. Clemens when they settled there during the Revolutionary War. American settlers began coming into this area soon after 1880. In 1818, Mt. Clemens became the county seat of Macomb County. In its earlier days Mt. Clemens was a center for the manufacture of barrels and boats for the growing lake trade. In 1862, drillers looking for oil in the area found salt water instead. This salt water was found to be good for health baths. In 1873, a bath-house and hotel was built at Mt. Clemens. Since that time, Mt. Clemens has been nationally known as a health center. Each year many people come here and stay at one of the large bath-houses in order to avail themselves of the healing value of the water. For many years caring for these people furnished the major occupation for people living in Mt. Clemens, but today Mt. Clemens is feeling the press of the expanding Detroit industrial area and several large factories have developed that produce a variety of products. Among the products manufactured here are electric ironers, electric ranges, freezers, air conditioners, and television sets. Mt. Clemens also has several machine shops and die shops.

One of Mt. Clemens' major industries is the manufacture of light-weight dinnerware. Hundreds of dishes are made each day at the Mt. Clemens Pottery. These dishes are sold throughout the nation by one of the leading chain stores. Mt. Clemens is also known as the "Rose City." Some fifteen million roses, as well as other flowers, are produced here each year. These flowers, which are grown in large greenhouses totaling sixty-five acres covered with glass, are shipped all over the United States.

Three miles north of Mt. Clemens, on the shore of Lake St. Clair, is located Selfridge Field, one of the nation's many air bases. Planes of many kinds including jet-propelled fighter planes are stationed here. This air base is one of the air bases that help to protect the locks at the "Soo." Mt. Clemens and the nearby area is also a recreational and resort center for many people living in the industrial area. Close to Mt. Clemens on the shore of Lake St. Clair are located St. Clair, Metropolitan, and Jones Beaches.

YPSILANTI is located where the old Sauk Trail, later the Chicago Road, crossed the Huron River. It was first a trading post on the Huron River and did not get its first settlers until 1823. Ypsilanti was named after a young Greek military hero, Demetrius Ypsilanti, who led the fighting for the freedom of Greece from Turkey. After the

Courtesy Kaiser-Frazer Corporation

Bombers were made in this plant during World War II. Then it was used by the Kaiser-Frazer Company to make automobiles. Today, the plant is used by the General Motors Corporation. Willow Run Airport in the background.

coming of the Chicago Road and the Michigan Central Railroad, the area around Ypsilanti settled rapidly. With the increased development of the industrial area, many industries have developed in Ypsilanti. Today, Ypsilanti has several manufacturing plants that make auto parts, hardware, soaps, paper, and plastic products. Ypsilanti is also known as the home of Eastern Michigan University, the oldest normal college in Michigan. Here also is located the Ypsilanti State Hospital.

Just east of Ypsilanti is the Willow Run Bomber Plant where bombers were made during World War II. Following World War II this plant was used by the Kaiser-Fraser Corporation to make automobiles. The plant is now used as the General Motors Detroit Transmission Division. Here is also located the Willow Run Airport, one of the largest airports in Michigan. This port is run by the University of Michigan. Much of the air traffic into and out of the industrial area uses Willow Run Airport. A little farther to the east is Detroit Metropolitan Airport which has expanded rapidly during the last few years because of its closer location to Detroit. Both airports are on the expressway between Ann Arbor and Detroit.

South of Ypsilanti, at Milan, is located a federal penitentiary where federal prisoners from this area are kept.

PONTIAC is another of Michigan's rapidly growing industrial centers. It lies twenty-five miles north of Detroit. Its first settlers were a group of men from Detroit. These men purchased land in the area and came up the Clinton River to settle in the year 1818. Their little village was named Pontiac after the Ottawa chieftain who had attacked the little fort at Detroit. Pontiac early turned to the making of wagons from the good hardwood found in the area. One of the best-known wagon companies was the Pontiac Spring Wagon Works. For several years Pontiac was known as a carriage center. Later, when the automobile industry developed, the city's carriage industries began making automobiles. Today, the Pontiac automobile is made near the spot where Pontiac buggies were once made. For many years the village grew slowly, but after World War I it began a rapid growth and expanded along with the other cities in the industrial triangle.

Pontiac's industries now produce automobiles, General Motors trucks, buses, taxicabs, auto bodies, paints and varnishes, grey iron castings, and auto parts.

Pontiac is located in the center of a good farming area. Nearby, in the rolling farm lands, are the old towns of Orion, Rochester, Ortonville, Holly, Oxford, and Highland. These communities are still agricultural centers. The farming area around Pontiac is largely devoted to dairying, the raising of fruits, and truck garden crops. This area is the best fruit-growing area in southeastern Michigan. Pontiac is also a recreational center. The nearby area is some of the most beautiful rolling land in southern Michigan. Some four hundred lakes are located near Pontiac. Thousands of people from the busy cities find rest and relaxation in this area.

At Pontiac is located the Pontiac State Hospital. South of the city near Birmingham is located the Cranbrook Foundation, which is a leading center of art and culture.

"THE DOWN RIVER COMMUNITIES" are several rapidly growing communities that lie along the west side of the Detroit River south of Detroit. In this group are Ecorse, Grosse Ile, River Rouge, Riverview, Southgate, Trenton, and Wyandotte. The future looks bright for the further growth and development of industries in this area. Because of the salt beds under the area and because of the limestone that can be easily shipped in by boat this area is the center of alkali industries. Fourteen large chemical companies are located in this down river area. Heavy industry has also been developing in this area during the last thirty years.

Located as they are along the Detroit River these communities can easily receive bulk shipments from Great Lakes boats. Now that the Livingstone Channel, leading into Lake Erie, has been deepened to twenty-seven feet, these communities can use ocean transportation as well as lake transportation to receive needed raw materials such as coal, limestone, gypsum, and iron ore. These same ships can carry away the finished products. Railroad transportation is also good to the nearby large centers of population in northern Ohio, Indiana, and Illinois. Detroit's many diversified industries also provide a large market for the steel and chemicals produced in this area.

RIVER ROUGE was just a small village in 1899 but after the Great Lakes Engineering Works began to build boats here in 1902 the community grew rapidly. Over 250 Great Lakes boats have been built here by this boat building company. Among the boats built here were the "William Clay Ford" and the ice breaker "Straits of Mackinaw." The Great Lakes Engineering Works, when in operation, also built boats for use on the New York State Barge Canal and several for ocean service. But due to the changing conditions in lake commerce this company closed down in the spring of 1961.

At the mouth of the River Rouge, where it empties into the Detroit

River, for many years there once was a marshy island. Today, this island is a busy industrial area. On it now stand large blast furnaces operated by the Great Lakes Steel Corporation. On the island are also units of oil and chemical companies.

River Rouge has a little over twenty manufacturing plants. One of the plants is the United States Gypsum Company's plant where gypsum shipped from Alabaster is processed into plaster and plaster board.

ECORSE is known today as the home of the Great Lakes Steel Corporation. Its early history dates back to the time of Pontiac when, in 1764, the Labadie family settled here on the west bank of the Detroit River. For some time Ecorse was called Grand Port. With the coming of the Great Lakes Steel Corporation and other industries the area grew rapidly. Today, there is little area left in Ecorse for residential expansion. At present Ecorse has twenty industries. Among the products made here can be listed parts for screw machines, stamping machines, folding tables, and chairs, electric welded steel tubing, chassis frames for automobiles, rolled and stamped moldings, and toys. The Nicholson Terminal and Dock Company is located here. Large quantities of steel shipments from Chicago, Youngstown, Pittsburgh, Cleveland, and Buffalo are unloaded here as well as other bulk commodities used in industry. Repairs on lake boats and small lake craft are also made here.

Courtesy The Great Lakes Steel Corporation

Great Lakes Steel Corporation, Ecorse, Michigan

South Plant of the Wyandotte Chemicals Corporation. 1961.

WYANDOTTE is named after the Wyandotte Indians who once lived in the area. After the founding of Detroit, the remaining Hurons, sometimes called Wyandottes, came here to live so they would be near the protection of the French at Fort Pontchartrain. The first white settler at Wyandotte was George Clark, who moved into the area in 1817. During the early years of the settlement there was much speculation in land. It was here that Captain Eber Ward built his Eureka Iron and Steel Works, just before the Civil War. When these works were destroyed by fire, the town declined until the coming of the alkali industries at the turn of the century.

Today, Wyandotte is the largest of the "down river communities." It is the nation's largest producer of cleaning compounds. The largest bleach plant in the United States is located here. This plant makes bleaching powder or chloride of lime. Among the many chemicals made in this city can be named sodium chloride, soda ash, sodium carbonate, atabrine, caustic soda, and baking soda. These products are made from the salt brine found under the area and from limestone. For many years limestone was quarried at nearby Sibley, but today large lake carriers bring limestone from the Alpena area to be used in manufacturing the products produced at Wyandotte. Wyandotte also produces some half million gallons of paint each year. This paint is used for automobile, industrial, and household finishes.

RIVERVIEW is a newly developing community. Here is located

Sharples Chemicals, Inc., which produces more than sixty products. One of its products is a gas odorant which is put into natural gas to give it an odor so that one can tell when it is leaking from a pipe. Its other products are used in such things as paints, and the average person never sees them although he uses them. The Firestone Steel Products Company produces steel rims, stampings, and steel cabinets.

Courtesy McLouth Steel Corporation

Electric blast furnace—Trenton Plant (1954)

TRENTON is another of the "down river communities" lying along the Detroit River. Just below Trenton a railroad bridge, now a county road bridge, once crossed to Grosse Ile. Another bridge connected the railroad to Stony Island. From Stony Island, trains were for many years ferried across the Detroit River to Canada. At one time the building of a railroad tunnel under the Detroit River at this point was planned, but the rocky nature of the river bottom caused the work to be dropped. For many years Trenton was a boat-building center.

Within the present city limits of Trenton is located one of the largest units of the Detroit Edison Company. It has capacity to produce three quarters of a million kilowatts an hour. Each summer, during the shipping season, many boats filled with coal from the mines of Pennsylvania dock at the plant and unload their cargoes of coal. In this day of electrical power one is apt to forget that the source of most of our electrical power is still coal. Coal is turned into steam power at these huge electric plants. The steam power is then turned into electrical power. It is this electrical power, derived from coal, that is used in the homes and industries of the industrial area.

Nearby is Sibley Quarry. From this quarry limestone was once taken to supply the chemical industries of the area. Sibley was annexed to Trenton in 1929. Several large chemical companies are now located in Trenton. These companies use as their basic materials, salt, limestone, sulphur, coal, and petroleum. A gasoline refinery is located here. Trenton is also the home of the McLouth Steel Corporation. Their plant located here has some of the most modern steel-producing equipment in America, such as a modern electrical blast furnace, hot and cold rolled strip mills, and pickling and finishing facilities. The Chrysler Corporation manufactures marine engines, truck engines, and industrial engines here at Trenton. South of Trenton near Rockwood is a large quarry where high quality silica sand, formed during the Silurian Period, is quarried by the Michigan Silica Company for making glass.

GROSSE ILE is a residential community on Grosse Ile in the Detroit River. The island is about nine miles long and two miles wide. Two bridges, one toll and one free, cross from the mainland to the island. At the southern end of Grosse Ile is located a United States Naval Air Station where for many years reserve Air Force squadrons practiced flying.

INDEX

Acetylene Lamps—337
Admission of state—229-230
Adrian—177, 185, 387, 459, 540
Adrian College—235, 540
Agriculture (see Farming)
Ague (see Fever and Ague)
Ahmeek Mine—286
Airplanes—398-400, 560
Airports—509, 561
Alabaster—29, 385, 502
Alanson—509
Alba—318, 526
Alberta—492
Albion—22, 188, 236, 376, 387, 405, 542
Albion College—233, 509, 542
Alfalfa—419
Algae—5, 7, 9
Algonac—355, 530
Algonkin Era—5
Algonquin Indians—64, 78
Alkali Industries—379, 384
Allegan—376
Allegan County—51, 192, 425, 427, 435, 546
Allen, Col.—156
Allen Park—549
Allouez, Fr. Claude—84, 86, 88, 482, 547
Allouez Mine—286, 478
Alma—453, 522, 533
Alma College—453, 522, 533
Alpena—27, 34, 308, 316, 322, 328, 351, 383, 384, 503
Alpena State Forest—505
Ambassador Bridge—355, 447, 554
American Fur Co.—163, 483
American Motors Corp.—395
Amhurstburg (Ont.)—140, 143, 146, 151
Amygdaloid—10, 14, 283
Andaste Indians—83
Anhydrite—24, 381
Animals—55
Ann Arbor—174, 175, 176, 177, 188, 225, 230, 234, 236, 255, 368, 369, 376, 450, 537
Ann Arbor Railroad—356, 488, 515
Anti-slavery Movement—239-240
Antrim County—429
Apostle Islands—85, 101
Appalachia—2
Apples—110, 415, 507, 516, 546, 548
Archeozoic Era—1
Arrow Heads—56, 60, 65, 66
Articles of Confederation—132
Art Stove Company—372

Ashland, Wisconsin—338, 490
Asparagus—426
Astor Fur Company—146, 150, 163
Astor Fur Warehouse—163, 483
Astor, John Jacob (Boat)—247
Atlanta—318, 505
Atlantic Mine—286
Atomic Plants—510, 511, 541
Au Sable—503
Au Sable River—52, 291, 306, 322, 387, 503
Au Sable State Forest—523
Auto-ferries—355, 480, 529
Automobiles—388-398, 539, 552
Averill—522
Axes—60, 207, 252

Baby Foods—519, 542
Bad Axe—529
Bad River—52, 190
Bad River Canal—190
Baltic Mine—286
Band Saw—259, 311
Bangor—328
Banks—225-226, 243
Baraga—493
Baraga, Bishop—493
Baraga County—46, 47, 48, 75
Barclay, Capt.—159
Barley—423
Barns—206
Barrel Heads—248
Barrels—367, 559
Barrel Staves—248
Basalt—1, 3, 9, 14
Baseball—458
Base Line—134
Basketball—458
Baskets—68
Battle Creek—177, 181, 182, 188, 225, 236, 373, 376, 385, 386, 450, 542-544
Bay City—53, 307, 315, 316, 328, 374, 415, 424, 425, 427, 450, 499, 500
Bay County—423, 425, 427
Bay de Noc (or Noquet)—481
Bay Mills—75
Bay Port—328
Bay View—509
Beans—70, 415, 423, 499, 501-52
Beans, Snap—426, 427
Bears—65, 206
Beaujieu—115, 117
Beaumont House—483
Beaver—50, 55, 65, 70, 105, 106, 164
Beaver Island—46, 510
Bees—435

Beets, Sugar—418, 423-425, 500, 522, 529
Belle Isle—45, 114, 118, 122
Bendix Corp.—401
Beneficiation—472, 473
Benton Harbor—328, 431, 546
Benzie County—429
Bergland—286, 477
Berkley—549
Berrien County, 55, 182, 415, 427, 431, 546
Berries—211, 426
Bessemer—338, 491
Bicycles—374, 392, 436, 455, 457-458, 500
Big Rapids—318, 406, 452, 521
Big Spring (see Kitch-it-ki-pi)
Big Wheels—319-320
Bill of Rights—138
Biological Desert—55
Birch Run—322
Bird's Eye Maple—489
Birmingham—187, 376, 549, 562
Blab Schools—233
Blackberries, 427
Black Lake
    Near Cheboygan—49, 507
    Near Holland (see Lake Macatawa
Black River
    Near Bessemer—52
    Near Cheboygan—52, 291
    Near Holland—192, 535
    Near Port Huron—52, 254, 258, 527
Black Swamp—151, 166, 174
Blainsville, Sieur de—114
Blaney Park—484
Blasting Powder—284, 287
Blind, Michigan State School for the—238, 533
Block Houses—252
Bloody Run—124
Bloomfield Hills—549
Blue Water Bridge—355, 528
Boardman River—291
Boat Building—245, 327-329, 562
    (see Shipyards)
Boats—190, 195-196, 244-251, 289, 310, 315, 327-363, 504, 540, 549
Bobsleighs—294, 295
Bois Blanc Island—45, 114, 140, 146, 151
Bois Brulés—105
Booming and Driving Companies—306-307
Boone, Daniel—126, 128, 130
Boundary Dispute—133, 148, 229, 230
    (see Toledo War)
Bows and Arrows—65

Boy Governor
    (see Mason, Stevens T.)
Boyne City—308, 512
Boyne Falls—512, 513
Boys Vocational School (see Vocational School for Boys)
Brachiopods—20, 21, 22
Braddock, Gen.—114, 115
Branch County—422
Brands, Log—307
Brandy Trade—94
Brass—373
Braves, Indian—65, 69
Brébeuf, Father—80, 82
Brevort—481
Brick making—40, 557
Bricks—31, 368, 407
Brighton—549
Brine, Salt—30, 32
British Landing—153
Broad Ax—245, 252
Brock, General—153, 154-155
Brockway Mountain Drive—493
Bromine—380
Brownstone—383, 492, 493
Brownstown, Battle of—153
Brulé, Etienné—79, 485
Brush, Capt. Henry—153
Brutus—509
Buchanan—376
Buckskin—68, 213
Buckwheat—423, 533
Buffalo (Animal)—65, 72, 106
Buggies—390 (see Wagons)
Buhl Manufacturing Co.—374, 394
Buick, David—392
Buick Manufacturing Co.—392
Bulk Cargo—220
Buoys—167, 195, 247, 332, 351, 359
Burgoyne, Gen.—129
Burroughs Adding Machine Co.—401
Burr Stones—218
Burt Lake—49, 507, 525
Burt, William—271, 272, 492
Buses—438, 451
Butter—431

Cabbage—426, 427
Caberfae—520
Cabinetmakers—374
Cabins—200, 204-206, 215, 252-253, 407
Cadillac, Antoine de la Mothe—108-111, 127, 147, 482
Cadillac, City of—48, 318, 321, 520
Cadillac, Madam—110
Cadillac Motor Car Co.—391, 394
Cahokia—99, 112, 128, 130
Calcite (see Rogers City)

Calhoun County—51
Calumet—283, 286, 337, 495
Calumet and Hecla Mine—283, 286, 337
Calvin College—534
Cambrian Period—17
Cambrian Sandstone—11, 279, 481, 486
Campau, Louis, 170, 501
Camp Filibert Roth—490
Canadian Constitutional Act—141
Canadian Shield—1, 42, 480, 486
Canals—163, 164, 171-172, 188-190, 229, 279-281
Candle Making—215
Candles—287, 337
Canfield, Frank W.—391
Canoes—71, 102, 103, 110, 167
Canots du Nord—104
Capital (Detroit)—230
Capital, Michigan State—236, 533 (see Lansing)
Capital Park—230
Capitol Building—179, 237, 243, 461, 533
Carbide Lights—287
Carey Mission—181
Carleton, Will.—540
Caro—424, 530
Carp River—273
Carriages (see Buggies and Wagons)
Carrollton—424
Carrying Strap (see Tump Line)
Cash Crops—220
Caspian—490
Cass, Capt. C. L.—170
Cass County—55, 182, 183, 430
Cass, Gen. Lewis—101, 165, 169, 170, 181, 287, 501
Cass River—52
Catholics (see Roman Catholics and Greek Catholics)
Cattle—212, 214, 410, 414, 417, 431, 434, 503
Cedarville—26, 385
Celeron, Pierre—114
Celery—415, 426, 427, 535, 546
Cement—27, 383, 503, 508, 541
Cenozoic Era—33
Centennial Copper Mine—14
Center Line—549
Central Michigan University—459, 523
Centreville—542
Cephalopods—21, 22, 27
Cereals, Breakfast—542
Chalcocite—15

Champion, Village of—288, 338, 474, 492
Champlain, Samuel—43, 76-78, 81
Chapin Mine—(Copper) 286, (Iron) 489
Charcoal—274, 278, 286, 370, 483, 488, 490, 492
Charlevoix—352, 509
Charlevoix County—429
Charlevoix, Fr.—111
Charlotte—236, 376
Cheboygan—73, 308, 328, 507
Cheese—433
Chemicals—378, 379, 380, 381, 516, 522, 533, 562, 563, 564, 566
Cheneaux, Les (see Les Cheneaux Islands)
Cherries—415, 429-430, 511, 513, 515, 516, 546
Chesapeake and Ohio Railroad—356, 357, 517
Chevrolet Motor Car Co.—392, 394, 532
Chicago and Northwestern Railway —338, 470
Chicago, Ill.—89, 155, 190, 249, 315, 340, 385, 415
Chicago Road—175, 176, 181, 182, 199
Chicago, Treaty of—170, 181
Chickens (see Poultry)
Chicory—415
Chinkers—206
Chippewa Indians—47, 64, 74, 109, 150, 464
Chittenden Nursery—517
Chlorine—380
Cholera Infantum—177, 216
Christmas Trees—439, 465, 520
Chrysler Motor Car Corp.—395, 401, 559, 566
Churches—140, 224-225
Churning Butter—214
Circular Saw—260, 375
Citizenship—145
Civil War—238, 241, 281, 282, 524, 551
Clare—318, 525, 526
Clarke, George Rogers—121, 129, 130
Clay—40, 368, 383, 413
Cleveland Mine—288
Cliff Mine—272, 274, 275, 282, 286
Climate—413, 427, 527
Clinton—175, 181, 405
Clinton County—426
Clinton-Kalamazoo Canal—189-190
Clinton River—52, 133, 167, 190, 255, 559
Clothing—443, 542

Clothing Factories—373
Clover—419
Club, 4-H—440
Coal—31, 32, 337, 348, 349, 370, 382, 492, 501, 509, 512, 566
Coast Guard—332, 349, 359, 360, 484, 535
Coldwater—175, 177, 181, 541
Coldwater Home and Training School—541
Colleges (Refer to name of college) (see Junior Colleges)
Colon—542
Comforters—214
Commons—107
Company of Canada—111
Comstock—181
Conestoga Wagon—173
Congé—95
Conglomerate Copper—15, 283, 478
Conglomerate Rock—40
Congressional Twp. (see Townships)
Conservation (see State Department of Conservation)
Constitutions—229, 237, 461
Consumers Power Co.—386-387, 439, 503, 510
Continental Congress—132, 134, 138
Conventions—229, 230
Conway—509
Cooking—211
Copper—10, 11, 14-15, 32, 35, 40, 56, 59, 79, 85, 266-290, 335-337, 342-343, 464, 476-478
Copper Country—335, 493-496
Copper Harbor—15, 270, 271, 275, 286, 335, 337, 493, 495
Copper Smelting—373
Coral—20, 21, 22, 23, 24, 28
Cord Wood—195, 210, 249
Corn—65, 70, 166, 218, 219, 248, 419, 421-422
Cornishmen—286, 464
Corn Shocks—208
Counties (see County Names)
County Agent—440
County Road Act—436
Coureur de bois—83, 95, 117
Cranbrook Foundation—562
Crary, Isaac Edwin—230, 542
Crawford County—48, 415
Crogan, Lieut.—162
Crooks, Ramsey—163, 164
Crop Rotation—221
Cross-cut Saws—294, 408
Cross Village—75, 509
Crosswhite Case—240, 542
Croswell—424
Cruisers (see Timber Cruisers)

Cruisers (Boats)—363
Crystal Falls—490
Crystal Lake—49, 515
Cucumbers—426
Cultivators—223
Cummins, Benjamin, 260
Curwood, James Oliver, 532
Cuyahoga (Schooner)—151

Dablon, Fr. Claude—86
Dairy Products and Dairies—431, 488, 489, 492, 511, 527
Dalyell, Capt.—123
Dams—52, 387
Dances—216
Danes—286
Daniel, Fr.—82
Daumont, Simon Francois—88, 485
Davis Lock—341, 360
Deaf, Michigan School for the—238, 532
Dearborn—176, 188, 199, 224, 228, 368, 392, 395, 398, 549, 556-558
Dearborn Heights—549
Decatur—546
Deer—55
Deere, John—222
Delaware Indians (see Moravian Indians)
Delta College—500
Delta County—419, 430
Depression of 1873—243
Detour—486
Detroit (Boat)—244
Detroit, City of
    French Period—73, 99, 108-111, 112
    English Period—115, 120, 122-125, 127-131, 134, 136, 140
    Early American—142, 143, 146, 148, 149, 154, 157, 166, 169, 173, 174, 175, 176, 177, 179, 181, 187, 188, 190, 192, 196, 220, 225, 226, 229, 230, 234, 235, 236, 238, 244, 245, 249, 253, 258, 268, 275, 324
    Since 1900—351, 354, 355, 357, 362, 368, 369, 371, 373, 376, 381, 383, 388, 392, 398, 405, 431, 436, 450, 453, 549, 551-556
Detroit and Charlevoix Railroad—511
Detroit and Mackinaw Railroad—316, 502, 503, 507, 508
Detroit and Pontiac Railroad—184, 187
Detroit and St. Joseph Railroad—187
Detroit Arsenal—199, 228, 238, 368
Detroit Car and Mfg. Co.—372

Detroit College of Law—459
Detroit College of Medicine and Surgery, 242
Detroit Edison Company—388
Detroit Institute of Technology—459, 555
Detroit Metropolitan Airport—561
Detroit River—24, 27, 41, 52, 85, 92, 109, 123, 124, 140, 143, 151, 160, 166, 167, 168, 174, 178, 196, 238, 245, 249, 330, 331, 347, 354, 355, 360, 363, 378, 403, 549, 562
Detroit Steel Corporation—403
Detroit Stove Works—372
Detroit Teachers College—452, 459
Detroit, Treaty of—150, 166, 182
Detroit Vapor Stove Company—372
Dewey, Thomas E.—533
Dexter—236
Diamond Crystal Salt Co.—380
Dickinson County—334, 419
Dishes—560
District of Hesse—141
Dodge Brothers—392, 394, 395, 559
Dodge Motor Car Co.—559
Doeskin—68
Dog Sled—102
Dolomite—9, 24, 27, 32, 385
Dow Chemical Co.—30, 369, 380, 404, 492, 500, 521, 522
Dow, Dr. Herbert H.—380
Drenthe—193
Drug Companies (see Pharmaceutical Mfg.)
Drummond Island—26, 46, 152, 280, 385, 486
Ducks—65
Duffield, Samuel P.—368
Du Lhut—92, 109, 482, 528
Dundee—28, 383, 541
Dunes (see Sand Dunes)
Durant-Dort Carriage Works—392
Durant, William C.—377, 392
Dutch on the Hudson—78, 82
Dutch Settlers (see Holland)
Dwyer Brothers—371
Dysentery—193, 216

Eagle Boats—395, 556, 558
Eagle Harbor—270, 272, 275, 286, 337, 495
Eagle River—272, 275, 286, 337, 495
East Detroit—549
Eastern Michigan University—238, 561
East Jordan—308, 511
East Lansing—239, 440, 533
East Tawas—502, 503
Eaton Rapids—236

Ecorse—549, 562, 563
Ecorse River—118
Edison, Thomas A.—186, 443, 472
Education—138, 140, 226-227, 230-236, 238-239, 242-243, 451, 460
Educational Oak—230, 542
Elberta—356
Eldred, James—268
Electric Automobiles—389
Electricity—339, 386-388, 416, 450
Electric Lights—310
Elephant, Hairy, 41
Elevation—46-48, 488, 497
Elk—55, 65, 526
Elliott, Capt.—140
Elmira—526
Elmwood Cemetery—124
Emmett County—75, 321
Empire Mine—473, 474
Enrico Fermi Atomic Energy Plant—541
Erie Canal—37, 163, 167, 171-172, 188, 194
Erie and Kalamazoo R.R.—184-185
Erie Indians—83
Erosion—323, 439
Escanaba—11, 48, 73, 259, 282, 288, 289, 308, 334, 335, 338, 345, 351, 489
Essex Motor Car—392, 395
Etherington, Capt.—118, 120
Eureka Iron and Steel Co.—333, 370, 379, 564
Eureka Vacuum Cleaner Co.—456
Evart—397
Everett, Philo M., 272

Fanning Mills—376
Farming
    Indian Period—69
    French Period—107, 112, 174, 556
    American period—216-220, 221, 407-442, 467, 499, 502, 503, 526, 527, 529, 536, 546
Farmington—225, 549
Feather Ticks—214
Fences—210, 410
Ferndale—549
Ferries—177, 250, 351, 355-357, 453, 480, 485, 508, 510, 554 (see Autoferries, Railroad Ferries)
Ferris State College—452, 522
Ferris, Woodbridge N., 452, 521
Ferry, Morse Seed Co.—373
Ferrysbury—525
Fertilizer—221
Fever and Ague—184, 216
Fife Lake State Forest—515, 520
Filers—313

Fink, G. R.—403
Finns—286, 291, 464
Fire Boat—354-355
Fireplace—205, 211, 232
Fish and Game—76, 364-367
Fisher Body Co.—394
Fisher Body Corporation—532, 533
Fishing—66, 166, 192
Fishing (Commercial)—364-367, 511
Fitch, B. T.—392
Flail—218, 223
Flat Rock—549
Flint and Pere Marquette R.R.—186
Flint, City of—221, 236, 238, 324,
    376, 392, 398, 531
Flint Stone—65, 66
Flint River—52
Float Copper—15, 35, 266
Flooring—321, 520
Flour—248
Foote, W. A. and J. B.—387
Ford, Capt. J. B.—379
Ford Forestry Center—492
Ford, Henry—390-391, 556
Ford Motor Company—392, 394, 395,
    403, 557, 558
Ford Museum, Henry—557, 558
Forest Fires—321-324, 462, 503, 505,
    525
Forests—53, 198, 206, 325, 439, 462,
    464, 479, 497
Fort Brady—256, 485
Fort Crevecoeur—92
Fort Dearborn—155, 182
Fort de Buade—108, 111, 482, 508
Fort de Chartres—112, 115, 125, 127
Fort Duquesne—115
Fort Gratiot—175, 529
Fort Holmes—483
Fort Lernoult—130-131, 143, 147
Fort Mackinac—131, 132, 266, 483
    (see Mackinac Island)
Fort Malden—143, 150, 151, 153, 154,
    156, 159, 160, 167, 182
Fort Miami—92
Fort Michilimackinac (see Michili-
    mackinac)
Fort Niagara—123, 125, 154
Fort Pontchartrain—109, 127
Fort St. Joseph (Niles)—111, 120,
    127, 131, 547
Fort St. Joseph (Port Huron)—93,
    528
Fort Shelby—160, 179
Forts, Indian—62
Fort Wayne—238, 241
Fort Wilkins—271, 282, 493
Fort William—145, 147, 267
Fossils—7, 21, 22, 27

Fox Indians—74, 111
Fox Islands—46
Fox River (Wis.)—88, 146
Frankenmuth—530
Frankfort—308, 356, 515
Frederic—511, 523
Freeland—500
Fremont—519
French and Indian War—114
French Canadians—141, 278, 286,
    304, 464
French River—38, 80, 97, 98
Frenchtown—143, 156, 157, 165, 540
    (see Monroe)
Frontenac, Governor—88
Frost Bitten Convention—230
Frost Free Days—325, 414, 415, 422,
    427, 428, 497
Fruits—415, 426, 427, 518, 519, 529,
    546, 562
Furniture—206, 262, 454, 534, 541,
    563
Furniture Industry—321, 374-376,
    488, 534, 536
Fur Trade—39, 50, 65, 76, 80, 81-82,
    83, 93, 95-106, 112, 116, 117, 126,
    134, 140, 145-147, 162-164, 248,
    267
Future Farmers of America—440

Gaastra—490
Gang Saw—311-312
Garden City—549
Garden Peninsula—23, 487
Gas, Natural—29, 30, 31, 32, 404,
    405, 501
Gasoline Engine—389, 391
Gasoline Tax—363, 437
Gastropods—20
Gate Saw—255
Gaylord—73, 316, 415, 526
Geese—65, 543
General Motors Corporation—394,
    501, 532, 560
General Motors Institute—532
Genesee County—382
Genesee Road—171, 194
Geographical Twp. (see Township)
Geological Survey—173, 268, 271
Georgian Bay—36, 64, 79, 81, 98, 141
German Settlers—191, 521, 530, 559
Ghent, Treaty of—244
Girdled Trees—69, 200, 207
Girls Training School—540
Girty, Simon—128
Glacial Age—33
Glacial Till or Drift—40, 46, 48, 50,
    382, 413, 527
Glaciers—33-37

Gladstone—488, 489
Gladwin, Major—120, 121, 122, 123
Glass Sand—566
Glass Works, Stained— 372
Glen Arbor—513
Gogebic County—46
Gogebic Lake—49
Gogebic Range—338, 474, 490
Good Hart—75, 509
Gouvernail—105
Grand Blanc—256
Grand Haven—52, 188, 376, 535
Grand Hotel—483
Grand Island—11, 19, 46, 486
Grand Ledge—376, 382
Grand Marais—19, 99, 484
Grand Portage—101, 102, 104, 145, 147, 267
Grand Rapids—28, 52, 73, 177, 181, 233, 258, 259, 316, 368, 374, 375, 385, 387, 397, 405, 450, 534
Grand Rapids and Indiana Railroad —316, 321
Grand Rapids Gypsum Co.—385
Grand River—52, 175, 190, 387
Grand Traverse Bay—26, 75
Grand Traverse County—429
Grand Trunk Western R.R.—356, 529, 544
Grange (see Patrons of Husbandry)
Granite—1, 49
Grapes—415, 427, 430, 535, 546
Grass Lake—181
Gratiot County—322, 423
Gravel—40, 48
Graves, Major—156
Grayling—73, 318, 523
Grayling (Fish)—55
Grayson Land Ordinance—134, 137
Great Lakes—36, 43
Great Lakes Shipping—43
Great Lakes Steel Corporation—403, 563
Greek Catholics—553
Green Bay (Wisconsin)—22, 23, 36, 81, 86, 88, 89, 92, 94
Greenfield Village—557
Greenland—275, 495
Griffin—90-91, 244
Grindstone City—30, 50, 383, 530
Grindstones—30, 383, 530, 531
Grist Mills—166, 167, 218, 219
Grosse Ile—45, 105, 114, 562, 566
Grosseilliers—83, 84, 87
Grosse Pointe—114, 549
Grosse Pointe Farms—549
Grosse Pointe Shores—549
Grosse Pointe Woods—549
Growing Season—48, 414

Gulliver—487
Gypsum—18, 24, 27, 29, 383, 385, 502, 535, 563

Habitants—95
Half-Breed—15
Hamilton, Col. Henry—127, 130
Hamtramck, City of—370, 551, 559
Hamtramck, Col. John Francis—143, 559
Hancock, City of—275, 283, 286, 332, 335, 337, 459, 494
Hanks, Lieut. Porter—153
Hannahville—75
Hanson Military Reservation—524
Harbor Beach—530
Harbors—247, 259, 309, 328, 332
Harbor Springs—509
Hardwoods—41, 53, 209, 264, 278
Harmar, Gen.—141, 182
Harrison, Gen. Wm. H.—151, 156, 158, 160
Harrisville—27
Hart—518
Hartwick Pines State Park—523
Harvey, Charles T.—280
Harvey, John—149
Hastings—182
Hats—106
Hawkes—505
Hay—219, 279, 410, 417, 419, 481, 503
Hazel Park—551
Heald, Capt.—155
Heating Units—372, 536, 546
Hecla Mines (see Calumet)
Hell Gate—331
Hemitite—8
Henry, Alexander, 266, 496
Hiawatha National Forest—481, 487
Higgins Lake—49, 52, 524
Higgins Lake State Forest—523
Highland—561
Highland Park—551, 558
High Plains Area—40, 48, 52, 413, 414, 430, 434, 497, 499, 519
Highway Department (see State Highway Department)
Hills (see Moraines)
Hillsdale—190, 235, 540
Hillsdale College—236, 540
Hillsdale County—48, 51, 419, 422, 435
Hogs (see Swine)
Holdane, William—375
Holland—191-193, 238, 258, 259, 322, 369, 376, 415, 535
Holly—561
Homestead Act—242, 407
Honey—70, 211, 213

Hooker Chemical Corporation—381, 518
Hope College—238, 536
Horses—208, 219, 222, 224, 293, 409, 410, 422
Houghton, City of—275, 283, 286, 332, 335, 337, 383, 494
Houghton, Dr. Douglass—268, 272
Houghton Lake—49
Houses—204-206, 309, 407-408, 416
Houses, Long—64
Howell—221
Hudson Bay—33, 87, 111, 125
Hudson, Henry—78, 87
Hudson Motor Car Company—392
Hudson River—37, 43, 173
Hudson's Bay Company—87, 141, 163
Hulbert—484
Hulbert, Edwin J.—283
Hulett Unloader—342, 347
Hull, Gen. William—149, 150-156, 174
Humbolt Mine—472, 473, 492
Hunting and Fishing—65, 66
Huntington Woods—551
Hupmobile—392
Huron (schooner)—123, 125, 244
Huron Bay—100, 382
Huron County—30, 382, 419, 420, 422, 423, 425
Huronia—74, 80
Huronian Period—5, 8, 471
Huron Indians (see Wyandottes)
Huron Mine—275, 286
Huron Mountain—17, 46, 479, 488, 492
Huron National Forest—523
Huron River—52, 166, 168, 537
Huroon Motor Car Co.—392, 395
Hussey, Obid—223

Ice Boxes—454
Ice Breakers—349-351, 356
Igneous Rock—1, 10, 14
Illinois and Michigan Canal—38
Illinois Indians—89, 92
Illinois River—89, 112
Imlay City—529
Indiana Territory—148
Indian Department, English—127
Indian Reservations—75, 522
Indian River—525
Indians (see Tribal Names)—56-75, 106, 127, 128, 140, 141, 142, 143, 181
Industries—39, 364-406, 549
Ingham County—419
Inkster—551
Inland Water Route—507, 526
Inns—176, 179, 180, 196, 199, 200

Interlochen—514
Internal Improvements—241
International Bridge—356, 484
International Salt Co.—381
Interurbans—373, 449-450
Ionia—431, 534
Irish—191
Irish Hills—40, 527
Iron and Steel Industry—333, 403
Iron County—46, 48, 334
Iron Mountain—335, 488, 489
Iron Mountain Railroad Co.—281
Iron Ore and Mining—7, 11, 13, 32, 35, 40, 268, 271, 333, 334-346, 362, 384, 468, 472
Iron River—335, 415, 488, 490
Ironwood—338, 469, 480, 490
Iroquois Indians—43, 64, 78, 79, 82-83
Isabella County—75, 405, 522
Ishpeming—279, 288, 491, 492
Islands—45
Isle Royale—14, 15, 35, 46, 56, 57, 58, 60, 266, 365, 495
Isle Royale Mine—275, 286
Italians—553

Jack Pine—53-54, 263
Jackson—30, 177, 181, 241, 373, 376, 382, 387, 450, 538-540
Jackson County—51
Jackson Mine—272-273
Jasper—8, 471, 473
Jay's Treaty—143
Jerked Meat—68, 248
Jesuit Relations—80
Jesuits—80, 94, 108, 485, 509 (see Names of Jesuits)
Jet Piercer—472, 473
Jogues, Fr.—81
Johannesburg—526
Johnny Cake—219
Joliet, Adrian—85
Joliet, Louis—88-89
Jonesville—22, 175, 180, 181, 258
Jordan River—291, 511
Joy, Henry B.—392
Junior Colleges—461

Kaiser-Fraser Corporation—395, 560
Kalamazoo—73, 170, 177, 181, 188, 190, 192, 193, 225, 234, 241, 369, 377, 383, 387, 415, 450, 544-546
Kalamazoo Case—242
Kalamazoo College—233, 546
Kalamazoo County—51, 430
Kalamazoo River—51, 190, 387
Kalkaska—318, 415
Kaskaskia—99, 112, 128, 129

Kellogg Bird Sanctuary—543
Kellogg Company, W. K.—385, 386, 543
Kelly, William—327, 333
Kelvinator Corporation—396, 397
Kent County—385, 415, 419, 435
Kenton, Simon, 130
Keweena Portage—100, 101, 267, 332
Keweenawan Period—5, 9, 11
Keweenaw Bay—19, 100, 383
Keweenaw Peninsula—10, 14, 15, 17, 19, 35, 56, 58, 60, 100, 266, 269, 270, 283, 332, 478, 479, 493-496
Key River—98
Killarney Mountains—9, 20, 21, 32, 35, 40, 46, 51, 275, 285, 471, 487, 493
Kincheloe Air Force Base—486
King George's War—112
Kingsford—490
Kitch-it-ki-pi—479, 487
Knapp, Samuel—274

Lachine Rapids—45, 89
La Crosse—118, 120
Lake Agassiz—39
Lake Champlain—42, 43, 78, 129
Lake Charlevoix—49, 509
Lake Erie—36, 37, 45, 85, 90, 115, 123, 125, 142, 158, 159, 166, 168, 177, 195, 196, 198, 245, 247, 347, 348, 540
Lake Gogebic—488
Lake Huron—26, 36, 45, 52, 79, 85, 189, 429
Lake Linden—373
Lake Macatawa—192, 258, 535, 537
Lake Michigamme—492
Lake Michigan—27, 36, 38, 45, 192, 259, 356, 427, 428
Lake Nipigon—93
Lake Nipissing—38, 79, 98
Lake of the Woods—93, 104, 133
Lake Ontario—36, 38, 43, 140, 141
Lakeport—530
Lake Saint Clair—52, 85, 123, 141, 142, 559
Lake Simcoe (Ont.)—140
Lakes, Inland—36, 39, 49, 50
Lake Superior—2, 4, 10, 38, 43, 81, 84, 99, 189, 244, 247, 250, 268, 270, 332, 338, 339, 361, 383, 429, 471, 484
Lake Superior and Ishpeming Railroad—147, 491
Lake Superior State Forest—481
Lake Talon (Ont.)—97
Lake Tracy—84
Lalement, Fr.—82

Lamprey (see Sea Lamprey)
Lamps—293, 299, 337, 389, 408, 409, 416, 444, 458
Land Grant College Act (see Morrill Act)
Land Grants—332
Land Offices—173, 181, 203, 262
Land Survey—134-138, 166, 168, 173, 262, 271
Land Types—46
Langlade, Charles—115
L'Anse—75, 465, 492
Lansing—237, 322, 376, 390, 398, 450, 533
Lapeer—322, 529
Lapeer County—419, 529
La Pointe (Wisconsin) 84, 86
L'Arbre Croche—509
La Salle—90-92, 546
Latter Day Saints—225, 510
Laurentian Mountains—3, 5, 9, 35
Laurentian Upland—1
Laurium 286, 337, 495
Lava—3, 10, 14
Lawrence (Perry's Flagship)—159
Lawton—546
Le Caron, Father—80
Leelanau County—429
Leelanau Peninsula—26, 513
Lenawee County—420, 422, 425 427, 434, 435
Lernault, Capt.—130
Les Cheneaux Islands—114, 482
Lewis Cass Building—461
Lewis, Colonel—156
Lewiston—170, 314, 505
Lexington—530
Lighthouses—167, 195, 247, 359, 487, 517
Lightship—359
Lima—181
Lime—18, 21
Limestone—9, 24, 26, 27, 32, 334, 346, 348, 379, 383-385, 502, 503, 505, 541, 562, 564
Lincoln, Abraham—241
Lincoln Park—551
Lindquist Bill—471
Lingstone Channel—24, 360
Little Turtle—141
Livingston County—52
Livonia—551
Locks (see St. Mary's Ship Canal)
Log Drives—259
Logging Bees—208
Log Marks—307
Long Knives—129, 133
Loretto—490
Lowell—534

Loyalists—140
Ludington—90, 356, 378, 517
Lufkin Rule Co.—501
Lumber and Lumbering—180, 250, 253, 291-326, 467, 488, 515, 520
Lumber Camps—264-265, 292-295
Lumber Hookers—314, 329
Lumberman's Memorial—326, 503
Lumber Statistics—324
Lutheran Church—225, 530
Lye—214, 379

MacArthur Lock—360, 476
Mackinac Bridge—355, 385, 466, 480, 508
Mackinac County—414
Mackinac Island—45, 121, 131, 142, 146, 147, 150, 153, 162, 163, 164, 351, 355, 482, 508
Mackinac Island State Park Commission—508
Mackinac State Forest—481
Mackinaw (Icebreaker)—350, 507, 562
Mackinaw City—73, 111, 115, 119, 120, 131, 316, 355, 482, 508 (see Michilimackinac)
Macomb County—37, 427, 527, 549, 556, 559
Madison, Major—156
Magnetite—13
Mail Boat—354
Malaria (see Fever and Ague)
Mancelona—318
Mangeurs de lard—104
Manistee—30, 313, 322, 328, 376, 377, 378, 380, 404
Manistee National Forest—517, 519
Manistee River 52, 306, 387, 516, 520
Manistique—26, 52, 308, 356, 384, 462, 479, 486, 516
Manistique Lake—49
Manistique River—52, 291
Manitou Islands—46
Manitoulin Islands—23, 86, 99
Manton—521
Maple River—190
Maple Syrup and Sugar—70, 213
Marenisco—480
Marine City—180, 245, 530
Marji Gesick—273
Markets, Farmers—436, 552
Marl—383
Marlette—529
Marquette, City of—9, 273, 277, 279, 281, 288, 289, 334, 338, 383, 459, 491
Marquette County—46, 334, 473

Marquette, Fr. James, 86, 88, 482, 517
Marquette National Forest—481
Marquette Range—13, 288, 334, 338, 472, 492
Marquis de Tracy—84
Marshall—30, 181, 188, 230, 233, 235, 236, 240, 373, 383, 542
Marshall College—233
Marshall Sandstone—30, 50, 380, 383, 530
Martins—55, 106
Marygrove College—236, 555 (see St. Mary's Academy)
Marysville—380, 392, 530
Masonic Old People's Home—522, 533
Mason, John T.—228
Mason, Stevens T.—228-229, 555
Massacre at the River Raisin—157, 182, 540
Mass Mine—285, 495
Mass, Village of—286, 337, 495
Mastodons—41
Mather Mine—492
Mattawa River—38, 80, 97
Maumee River—37, 99, 114, 130, 151
Maybee—227
May's Creek—149
Maxwell Motor Car—392
McCormick Reaper—223
McCoy, Rev. Isaac—181, 184
McKee, Capt.—140
McLouth Steel Corporation—403, 404, 566
Mears, Charles—427
Meets and Bounds—137
Melons—70, 427
Melvindale—381, 551
Menominee—70, 74, 258, 259, 308, 316, 322, 376, 424, 480, 488
Menominee County—75, 419
Menominee Indians—64, 74, 488
Menominee Range—334, 474, 489
Menominee River—52, 291, 306
Mesic—521
Mesnard, Fr.—83-84
Mesnard Mine—494
Metamorphic Rocks—6
Methodist Church—224, 234, 235, 542
Metz—505
Mexican War—524
Miami Indians—74, 109, 547
Miami River—74, 114
Michigamme—288, 338, 492
Michigan, City of—237
Michigan (Schooner)—123, 125, 244
Michigan Basin—7
Michigan Bell Telephone Co.—386

Michigan Car Company—372
Michigan Central College
    Spring Arbor—235
    Mt. Pleasant (see Central Michigan University)
Michigan Central Railroad—188, 190, 191, 250, 507, 538
Michigan Farm Bureau—440
Michigan Farmer—440
Michigan Farmers' Union—440
Michigan Northern Railroad—188, 190
Michigan Reformatory—534
Michigan Southern Railroad—188, 190
Michigan State College of Agriculture and Applied Science (see Michigan State University)
Michigan State Normal College (see Eastern Michigan University)
Michigan State Prison—538
Michigan State Teachers Association —239
Michigan State University—239, 242, 440, 459, 533
Michigan Steel Corporation—403
Michigan Technological University —383, 453, 486, 492, 495
Michigan Territory—148, 165
Michigan Waterway Commission— 363
Michilimackinac—86, 92, 93, 94, 99, 108, 111, 115, 118, 119, 120, 127, 128, 131, 134, 140, 141, 147, 153, 154, 244, 482, 508
Midland—30, 322, 378, 379-380, 521, 522
Midland County—405
Migrant Labor—424, 438
Milan—561
Military Highway—(Ont.) 140-141, (Mich.) 282
Milk—409, 431, 433
Milking—418
Millersburg—505
Milwaukee Clipper—353, 519
Milwaukee Lake Shore and Western R.R.—490
Mineral Falls—490
Miner's Falls—19
Miners, Prehistoric—56
Mines (see Copper, Iron, Coal, Salt)
Minesota Mine—275, 282, 283, 285, 495
Mining—266-290, 333-344
Mink—55, 106
Mint—415, 426, 548
Miquelon—125

Missions—80, 82, 86, 110, 181, 483, 513, 530, 542
Mississippian Period—29
Mississippi River—72, 85, 88, 99, 128, 146
Moccasins—70, 95
Mohawk Indians—64, 84
Monroe—143, 156, 165, 173, 188, 190, 225, 234, 236, 376, 377, 540-541, 551 (see Frenchtown)
Monroe County—27, 37, 404, 422, 425, 427, 435, 549
Montague—380, 381, 518, 519
Montcalm County—404, 425, 427
Montcalm, Gen.—114
Monteith, Rev. John, 226
Montreal—39, 43, 88, 93, 114, 115, 117, 145, 146
Montreal Canoes 104
Moose—65, 106, 495
Moraines—36, 40, 48
Moravian Indians—132-133, 559
Moraviantown—161
Mormons (see Latter Day Saints)
Morrill Act—242
Morton Salt Co.—30, 380
Mother Lode—8, 471, 472
Mound Builders—62
Mounds, Indian—62
Mount Clemens—52, 133, 167, 190, 450, 551, 559
Mount Pleasant—75, 380, 459, 522
Mowing Machines—223
Muley Saw—255
Mullet Lake—49, 507
Munising—11, 48, 308, 377, 481, 486
Mush—219
Mushrooms—427, 499
Muskegon—25, 52, 53, 259, 307, 315, 328, 353, 356, 376, 404, 405, 427, 450, 518
Muskegon River—52, 292, 306, 315, 387
Musk Ox—41
Muskrats—50, 55, 65, 106, 164

Napoleon—30, 383
Nash, Charles W.—396
National City—385, 502
National Guard—505, 524
National Gypsum Co.—385
National Steel Corp.—403
Naubinway—481
Nazareth College—546
Neebish Cut—360
Negaunee—271, 273, 279, 288, 491, 492
Negroes—240, 553
Neutral Indians—83

Newago—376
Newago County—423
Newberry—483
New Buffalo—188, 190
New France—76-114
Newspapers—227-228, 537
New York Central Railroad—251, 316, 508
New York, City of—170, 172
Niagara (Boat)—159
Niagara Falls—23, 38, 45
Niagara River—23, 38, 85, 90, 168
Nickel—15
Nicolet, Jean—81
Niles—111, 120, 131, 177, 181, 234, 376, 547 (see Fort St. Joseph)
Noonday, Chief—184
Normal Colleges—238 (see Eastern Michigan University, Central Michigan University, Northern Michigan University, Western Michigan University)
Northern Michigan University—459, 492
Northville—376, 405, 551, 556
Northwestern Michigan College—514
North West Fur Company—141, 145, 146, 163, 279
Northwest Territory—134, 140, 143, 145, 148
Norway Mine—334, 490
Norway Pine (see Red Pine)
Norwegians—286, 291
Noyon, Jacques de—93
Nuclear Power (see Atomic Plants)
Nurseries—462, 517, 524, 525, 541

Oakland County—40, 48, 52, 55, 198, 431, 527, 555
Oakland Motor Car—392, 394
Oak Openings—53, 55, 69, 73, 111, 181
Oak Park—551
Oats—410, 417, 422
Oceana County—423, 427
Ocqueoc Falls—29, 505
Ohio Company—113
Ohio Fur—248
Oil (see Petroleum)
Ojibway Indians (see Chippewa)
Ojibway Mine—286
Old Mission Peninsula—26, 228, 513
Olds Motor Vehicle Company—394, 533
Olds, Ransom E.—388, 390, 391, 533
Olivet College—236
Onaway—51, 505
Onions—415

Ontario (Canada)—140, 141
Ontonagon—15, 259, 270, 275, 285, 286, 308, 335, 337, 377, 386, 496
Ontonagon Boulder—266, 268-269, 496
Ontonagon County—47
Ontonagon River—53, 266
Ordinance of 1787—138, 226, 229
Ordovician Limestone—36
Ordovician Period—21
Ore Boats—289, 334, 343-348
Ore Dock—289, 346, 472, 491
Organs—376, 453, 538
Orion—561
Ortonville—561
Oscoda—308, 326, 328, 503
Otsego—377
Ottawa County—435
Ottawa Indians—64, 65, 74, 77, 86, 150, 182, 509
Ottawa National Forest—467, 488
Ottawa River—38, 43, 79, 95, 141
Otter—55, 106
Owosso—41, 236, 376, 532
Oxen—219, 293
Oxford—561

Package Freighters—331, 351
Packard Motor Car Co.—392
Packet Lines—195
Paige Motor Car Co.—392, 395
Painsdale—495
Paint and Varnish Companies—373, 555, 564
Paleozoic Era—17
Panic of 1837—188, 190, 225, 236
Paper and Paper Products—377, 541, 546
Parchment—377
Parent's Creek—124
Paresseux Falls—98
Parke, Davis and Company—368, 369, 536, 537, 540
Parks, State—461, 463
Parliament of Upper Canada—141
Passenger Boats—351
Passenger Pigeon—55
Pasty—287
Patriot's War—237
Patrons of Husbandry—440
Paw Paw—546
Peaches—110, 431, 546
Pears—415, 431, 546
Peat—39
Peche Islands—118
Pellston—509
Peninsular Car Company—373
Peninsular Stove Company—372
Pennsylvanian Period—31, 382

Pennsylvania Railroad—316, 508
Peppermint (see Mint)
Pequaming—493
Percy Jones Hospital—543
Pere, Jean—85
Pere Marquette River—517
Permian Period—32
Perry, Commodore Oliver Hazard—
  158-160, 244
Perry's Victory—159
Peshwabestown—75
Petoskey—28, 29, 383, 429, 508-509
Petoskey Stones—29
Petroleum—22, 27, 29, 32, 404-406,
  501, 518, 521, 522, 526, 542
Pewabic Mine—275, 282
Pharmaceutical Mfg.—368-370, 555
  see Parke, Davis and Co. and
  Upjohn Co.)
Phoenix Mine—286
Pictured Rocks—19, 99, 479, 486
Pierce, Rev. John Davis—230, 231,
  542
Pigeon River (Minn.)—101-102, 103
Pigs (see Swine)
Pine (see White Pine, Red Pine,
  Jack Pine)
Pine Mountain—490
Pioneer Life—194-223
Pioneer School—238
Pipes, Indian—66
Pit Sawing—253
Plains (see Oak Openings)
Plains of Abraham—114
Plainwell—377
Plank Roads (see Roads)
Planters—223
Plaster Creek—385
Pleasant Ridge—551
Pleasure Boats—353-354
Pleistocene Era—33
Plows—209, 221-222, 376
Plums—546
Plymouth—175, 376, 551
Poe Lock—341, 360
Pokagon—182, 183, 184
Pointe Aux Barques—530
Polar Bears (Soldiers)—524
Polish—291, 464, 553, 559
Ponies—110
Pontiac, Chief—118, 120, 124, 125,
  182
Pontiac, City of—167, 176, 187, 220,
  225, 234, 376, 398, 551, 561-562
Pontiac Mine—494
Pontiac's Conspiracy—117, 244, 508,
  547
Popcorn—422
Population—464

Porcupine Mountains—17, 47, 479,
  488, 496
Portage Lake—100, 282, 335
Portage Lake Ship Canal 332, 335,
  494
Portage River—100
Portages—72, 97, 99, 101, 279
Port Arthur (Ont.)—147
Port Austin—530
Port Dolomite—385
Porter, Capt. Moses—143
Port Huron—29, 52, 93, 109, 175, 180,
  188, 190, 220, 245, 254, 258, 313,
  354, 355, 359, 373, 376, 377, 380,
  383, 404, 450, 527
Port Huron and Owosso Railroad—
  187
Port Inland—26, 384, 486
Port Sanilac—530
Posen—505
Poses—103
Postum Company—386, 543, 544
Potatoes—415, 418, 425-426, 489, 503
Pot Holes—63
Pottawattomie Indians—64, 70, 74,
  86, 111, 120, 155, 170, 181, 182-
  184, 488, 544, 546, 547
Pottawattomie Trail—175
Poultry—212, 418, 435, 536
Powers, William T.—387
Prairies (see Oak Openings)—181,
  183, 187, 209
Presbyterian Church—225
Presque Isle—114
Presque Isle County—425
Presque Isle Falls—47
Presque Isle River—52
Primary Districts—227
Primary Interest Fund—231
Primary School Fund—230-231, 238
Prime Meridian—135
Prince Rupert's Land—87
Prisons—492, 534, 538, 539, 561
Proclamation of 1763—126
Proctor, Col. Henry—155, 156, 158,
  160, 161, 162
Propeller Wood—195, 249
Prophetstown—151, 155
Proterozoic Era—5
Protestants—80, 133, 224, 288, 483,
  553, 556, 559
Pulp Wood—465, 492, 503
Pumpkins—65, 70
Put-in-Bay—158, 354

Quakers—225, 239
Quarries—26, 27
Quartzite—8
Quebec—43, 76, 88, 114, 140

Quebec Act—126, 127, 133
Quebec, Province of—126, 127, 141
Queen Anne's War—111
Quilts—214
Quincy—175
Quincy Mine—275, 282, 286, 336, 337, 494
Quinnesec—490

Radar—359
Radio—359, 401, 440
Radisson—83, 84, 87, 101
Rafting Logs—307
Railroad Ferries—250, 355, 356, 446, 488, 508, 515, 517, 519, 554
Railroad Land Grants—316-317
Railroads — 184-191, 282, 316-321, 331, 372-373, 415, 438, 444-450, 490, 498, 502, 503, 506, 507, 508, 511, 517, 529, 538, 549, 555, 566
Rainfall—48, 414
Rainy River Falls—29, 505
Raisin River—52, 151, 153, 165, 541
Raisin River, Massacre at—157
Rakes—223
Rambler Automobile—396
Ramsey 491
Rangers—128
Raspberries—427
Rate Bills—227, 239
Raymbault, Fr.—81
Reapers—410
Recollects—80
Recreation—441, 479, 480, 506, 519, 551, 562
Red Arrow Division—524
Red Pine—53, 263
Reed City—405, 521
Remember the Raisin—158
Reo Motor Car Co. 393, 533
Republican Party—241, 539
Republic Mine—473, 474
Republic, Village of—288, 338
Revolutionary War—126, 127-133
Rice, Wild—70
Richard, Fr. Gabriel—149, 175, 226
Richelieu River—42, 77
Rifle River—52, 291
Ripley—495
River Aux Canards—153
River Drives—52, 291-292, 302-308, 488
River Road—123, 153
River Rouge, City of—551, 562
Rivers—50-52
Riverview—551, 564
Roads—151, 174-176, 198, 201, 220-221, 275, 281, 296, 374, 391, 393, 436-438, 498, 528, 529, 531, 543

Roberts, Captain Charles—153
Rochester—167, 190, 551, 561
Rockets—401
Rockland—274, 286, 337, 495
Rockwood—27, 551
Rogers City—27, 349, 384, 505
Rogers, Major Robert—115
Roman Catholics—288, 526, 553
Romeo—176
Romulus—551
Root Cellar—219, 409
Roscommon—318, 482, 524
Roscommon County—49
Roses, Growing of—560
Roseville—551
Rouge River—165, 168, 199, 256, 382, 395, 403
Royal Oak—175, 187, 551
Rules—501
Rum—94, 117
Rural Free Delivery—438, 459
Rush-Bagot Agreement—244
Russell, G. B.—370
Russians—559
Rye—423

Sabine Lock—360
Sac and Fox Indians (see Sauk Indians)
Saginaw—169, 170, 221, 258, 282, 307, 313, 314, 322, 328, 376, 382, 388, 398, 404, 415, 423, 499, 501
Saginaw and Northern Canal—190
Saginaw County—420, 423, 425
Saginaw River—52, 190, 245, 258, 292, 307, 314, 315, 500
Saginaw Trail—73
Saginaw, Treaty of—169
Saguenay River—42
Sailboats—195, 244-249, 327, 329, 330, 363
Saint Anne's Church—149
Saint Charles—322, 376
Saint Clair County—427, 529
Saint Clair, Gen. Arthur—141, 182
Saint Clair River—52, 85, 93, 166, 241, 245, 249, 253, 330, 331, 332, 355, 359, 360, 365, 378, 527, 530
Saint Clair Shores, Village of—551
Saint Clair, Village of—166, 192, 355, 380, 530
Saint Ignace (Mich.)—25, 73, 86, 88, 93, 108, 111, 142, 351, 355, 480, 481, 482
Saint Ignace (Ont.)—81, 83
Saint James, Village of—511
Saint Johns—376, 415
Saint Joseph (Ont.)—82

Saint Joseph, City of—181, 188, 225, 431, 546
Saint Joseph (Niles) (see Fort Saint Joseph)
Saint Joseph College and Academy —459, 540
Saint Joseph County—183, 422, 426
Saint Joseph Island—147, 153
Saint Joseph River—51, 92, 94, 181
Saint Lawrence River—38, 42, 45, 72, 76, 140, 174, 467
Saint Lawrence Waterway—38, 43, 44, 360, 469, 467
Saint Louis (Mich.)—533
Saint Louis (Mo.)—128
Saint Louis (Ont.)—81, 82
Saint Marie (Ont.)—81, 82
Saint Mark's College—233
Saint Mary's Academy—236, 541
Saint Mary's Falls Canal—20, 45, 162, 279-281, 341, 350, 360-361, 362-363, 476, 479, 484, 560
Saint Mary's River—19, 41, 45, 53, 81, 84, 99, 147, 189, 247, 250, 279, 360, 484
Saint Philip's College—233
Saint Pierre—125
Saline—175, 181
Salt—22, 24, 30, 313, 377-382, 501, 516, 519, 522, 529, 533, 555, 562, 564
Salt Mine—25, 378, 381-382
Sandcaster—525
Sand Dunes—27, 309, 484, 513, 514-515, 518
Sandstone—15, 27, 29, 31, 32, 383
Sandusky—529
Sandwich (Ont.)—146, 154
Sanilac County—419, 420, 422, 425
Saugatuck—328
Sauk Indians—74, 111, 499
Saulk Trail—73, 175, 556
Sault Ste. Marie—14, 19, 41, 56, 73, 75, 79, 81, 86, 88, 94, 99, 114, 127, 161, 162, 188, 234, 256, 279, 347, 355, 356, 453, 480, 481, 484, 485
Savoyard River—109, 197
Sawmills—167, 252-266, 306, 308-317, 327
Saxon Motor Car—392
Schlosser, Ensign—120
Schoolcraft, Henry R.—101, 267
Schools (see Education)
School Section—226
Scoria—14
Screw Propeller—250, 335
Scythes—217, 222
Sea Lamprey—365-367, 511
Sebewaing—424, 529

Section—135
Sedimentary Rock—6, 8
Seeders—223
Seed Ferns—27
Seiche—43
Seigneurs—110
Selfridge Field—560
Self-Unloaders—349
Seneca Indians—64
Seneca Mine—286
Seney—318, 324, 484
Seventh-day Adventist—225
Seven Years War—117
Shakes—205
Shale—9, 15, 24, 27, 29, 32, 384, 477, 504
Sharron Hollow—255
Shavehead—155, 182
Sheaves—222
Sheep—198, 212, 434
Shelby, Gov. Isaac, 160
Shiawassee County—426
Shiawassee River—52
Shingles—205, 407
Ships—363 (see Boats)
Shipyards—192, 358, 500, 562 (see Boat Building)
Shocked Grain—217, 222
Shoreline—43
Sibley Quarry—28, 384
Sibley, Solomon—170, 181
Sickles—217, 222
Sickness—216
Siena Heights College—540
Silica—7, 13
Siltstone—15, 477
Silurian Period—22, 36, 487
Silver—15, 283
Silver City—493
Silver Lake—518
Sinclair, Patrick—127, 131
Sink Holes—505
Skanee—493
Skiing—490, 492, 499, 512, 521, 526
Slash Saws—312
Slate—9, 382-383, 493
Slavery—138, 239-241
Slawson, John—275
Slayton's Arboretum—540
Sleeping Bear Sand Dune—513, 514
Sleeping Garments—542
Smokes—105
Snake Heads—186
Snowfall—428
Snowshoes—72, 102
Soap Making—214
Soda Ash—379
Soil—413, 424, 426, 427, 517
Soil Bank—441

Soil Conservation—388, 439
Soo (see Saint Mary's Falls Canal)
Soo Junction—484
South American (Boat)—353, 537
Southgate—551, 562
South Haven—328
South Range—495
South Shore Railroad—491
South West Fur Company—146, 162
Spain—131
Spanish-American War—524
Spanish in Michigan—131, 547
Spark Plug—391
Spearmint (see Mint)
Spelling Bees—233
Spider—211
Spinning Yarn—213
Spits—211
Sponges—20
Spring Arbor—235
Spring Lake—535
Square Timber—245, 252, 311
Squash—65, 70
Squaws—68, 70, 105
Squids—22
Squirrels—65
Stagecoaches—173, 176, 190
Stambaugh—335, 490
Stamp Hammer—307
Standard Gauge—187
State, Becoming a—229-230
State Department of Agriculture—440
State Department of Conservation—325, 461-463, 524
State Fair—555 (see Upper Peninsula State Fair)
State Highway Department — 436, 480
Steamboats—168-169, 177, 195-196, 247-251, 327, 329
Steam Automobiles—388-389
Stearns, Frederick K., 368, 386
Steel Industry—333-334
Stearns, Frederick, 368
Stick Chimney—205
Stone Age—65, 106
Stoneport—384
Stony Creek—156
Storms on Great Lakes—358
Stoves and the Stove Industry—232, 293, 370-372, 407, 453, 544, 546
Straits of Mackinac—45, 81, 355, 387, 480
Strang, James Jessie—510
Strawberries—73, 181, 415, 427, 431, 503, 546
Strata—5, 7, 8
Street Cars—242, 449

Stuart, Robert—163
Sturgeon River—52
  In Upper Peninsula—53
Sturgis—175, 181, 376, 542
Sudbury (Ont.)—15
Sugar Beets (see Beets, Sugar)
Sugar Cane—423
Sugar Island—46
Sunshine—429
Suomi College—459
Superintendent of Public Instruction—231
Superior (Boat)—169
Superior (Mine)—286
Superior (Village)—258
Surface—48
Survey (see Land Survey)
Swedes—286, 291, 464
Sweepers—374
Swine—198, 212, 220, 435

Taconite—8, 469, 471, 473, 475, 492
Tadoussac—42
Tahquamenon Falls—19, 481, 484
Tahquamenon River—53, 481
Tankers, Oil—357
Tanneries—258, 512
Tanning—68
Tawas City—308, 385, 503
Tecumseh, Chief—150, 151, 153, 155, 159, 160, 162, 182
Tecumseh, Village of—234, 254
Telephones—336, 337, 386, 459
Television—401
Temperature—48
Territorial Road—175, 181, 197
Thames, Battle of the—161, 182
Thames River—133, 141
Theatres—458
Thornapple River—387
Three Rivers (Quebec)—88
Threshing—412, 418
Threshing Engines—411, 412
Threshing Machines—223, 376, 411, 412
Thumb Area—30, 322, 415, 423, 425, 527
Thunder Bay River—52
Tiffin, Edward—166
Timber Cruisers—261, 481
Timothy—419
Tin Ware—374
Tippecanoe, Battle of—151, 155, 182
Tires, Auto—401
Tittabawassee River—52, 306, 522
Tobacco—65, 70, 373
Tobacco Indians—83
Toledo War—229-230, 267, 524

Tomatoes— 426, 427, 546
Tonty—92
Tonty, Madam de—110
Toppinabee, Chief—182
Topinabe, Village of—318
Torch Lake—49, 335
Toronto (Ont.)—140, 141
Tourist Industry—39, 50, 406, 497
    (see Recreation)
Townsend, Charles (Boat)—169
Townships—135
Tractors—416, 417
Trails—72
Trans-Canadian Highway—3-4
Traps—65
Traverse City—73, 429, 430, 513
Treaties, Indian—75, 142, 150, 165,
    166, 169, 184, 268
Treaty of Chicago—170, 181, 183
Treaty of Detroit—150, 166, 182
Treaty of Greenville—142, 182
Treaty of Saginaw—169, 501
Tree Farms—439, 441, 468, 526
Trenton—153, 384, 388, 404, 551, 562,
    566
Trilobites—20, 21, 22, 27
Trout Lake—92, 366
Trucks—397-398, 438, 447
Truth, Sojourner—543
Tugs—354
"Tulip Time"—537
Tump-line—70, 102
Tunnels—355, 446, 529, 554
Turkeys—211
Turnpikes—198
Tuscola County—382, 420, 422, 423,
    425
Twine Binder—412
Typewriters—374

Ukrainians—559
Underground Railroad—239-240
United States Gypsum Co.—385, 563
United States Rubber Company—401
University of Detroit—452, 555
University of Michigamia—226
University of Michigan — 41, 234,
    451, 490, 532, 537, 558, 561
Upjohn Company—369, 540, 546
Upper Peninsula—9, 19, 22, 23, 32,
    48, 53, 73, 74, 230, 266-290, 308,
    337, 338, 407, 426, 429, 430, 434,
    435, 441, 450, 452, 464-496
Upper Peninsula State Fair—489
Uruslines, Convent of—80
Utica—190, 551

Vacuum Cleaners—456

Van Buren County—55, 182, 426,
    430, 431, 546
Vanderbilt—318, 525
Vander Mulen, Rev.—191, 193
Van Horne, Col. Thomas—153
Van Raalte, Rev. 191-192
Varles Portage—98
Vassar—529
Vegetables—415, 426
Victoria Mine—285
Ville de Troit—109
Vincennes, Ill.—99, 112, 128, 130, 148
Vocational School for Boys—533
Volcanoes—3
Voyageurs—93, 95, 102, 104, 153,
    163, 269, 421
Voyageurs' Highway—99
Vriesland—193, 535
Vulcan—490
Vulcan Mine—334

Wabash and Erie Canal—37
Wabash River—37, 99, 112, 128, 130
Wagons—173, 176, 195, 197, 219, 262,
    374, 376, 377, 390, 392, 396, 532,
    539, 561
Wakefield—338, 479, 491
Walk-in-the-Water—168-169, 258
Walloon Lake—509
War of 1812—121
Ward, Capt. Samuel—173, 245, 333,
    370, 564
Ward, E. B.—245
Wardell, Fred—456
Warren—551
Washington, George—141
Washtenaw County—52, 419, 431,
    434, 537
Water Falls—51, 53, 479, 486, 490,
    491, 492
Waterford—256
Water Power—386
Watersmeet—462, 490
Water Wheels—254, 258
Wayne, City of—175, 200, 392, 551
Wayne County—37, 40, 52, 136, 147,
    176, 368, 404, 407, 427, 549
Wayne, Gen. Anthony—141, 143
Wayne State University — 459-460,
    555
Weasel—106
Weathering—5
Weitzel Lock—341
Welland Canal—45
Wellston—462, 517
Wendat Indians (see Wyandottes)
West Branch—48, 525, 526
Western Michigan University—459,
    546

Western Theological Seminary—536
Whalebacks—339-340
Wheat—172, 218, 220, 248, 329, 361, 419, 420-421
Whetstones—30, 217
Whip-saw—253
Whitefish—37, 367
White Oak—246
White Pigeon—175, 181, 234, 426
White Pine—53-54, 261, 263
White Pine Mine—15, 285, 477
White Rock—150, 322
White, Stewart Edgar—534
Wigwam—66
Wildcat Banks—225
Wild Rice—488
Williams, Harvey—258, 501
Williamston—382
Willis Sainte Claire Motor Car—392
Willow Run Airport—398, 561
Willow Run Bomber Plant — 395, 398, 561
Winchester, General—156
Windmills—167, 196, 411
Windsor (Ont.)—177
Winnow—218, 223
Wisconsin River—88

Wolfe, Gen.—114
Wolverine—48, 318, 462, 525
Wolves—55, 202, 206, 210
Wooding Stations—249
Wood, Jethro—222
Woodward, Augustus B.—149
Wool—213
World War I—342, 382, 395, 398, 524, 556
World War II—350, 362, 395, 398, 472, 500, 524, 543, 560
Worship, Freedom of—138
Wyandotte, City of—28, 168, 333, 370, 378, 379, 384, 551, 556, 564
Wyandotte Chemicals Corporation— 379, 505, 564
Wyandotte Indians—64, 74, 77, 78, 79, 80, 82-83, 85, 86, 108, 109, 150, 564

Ypsilanti—166, 175, 176, 187, 188, 238, 239, 255, 450, 551, 560
Ypsilanti Normal College—238

Zeeland—193, 427, 535
Zug Island—403